D0979143

ALSO BY ROBERT GELLATELY

Backing Hitler: Consent and Coercion in Nazi Germany, 1933–1945

The Nuremberg Interviews: An American Psychiatrist's Conversations with the Defendants and Witnesses at the Nuremberg Trials (edited by Robert Gellately)

The Specter of Genocide: Mass Murder and Other Mass Crimes in Historical Perspective (edited with Ben Kiernan)

Social Outsiders in Nazi Germany (edited with Nathan Stoltzfus)

Accusatory Practices: Denunciation in Modern European History, 1789–1989 (edited with Sheila Fitzpatrick)

The Gestapo and German Society: Enforcing Racial Policy, 1933–1945

The Politics of Economic Despair: Shopkeepers and German Politics, 1890–1914

LENIN, STALIN, AND HITLER

LENIN, STALIN, AND HITLER:
THE AGE OF SOCIAL CATASTROPHE

ROBERT GELLATELY

ALFRED A. KNOPF NEW YORK 2007

THIS IS A BORZOI BOOK
PUBLISHED BY ALFRED A. KNOPF

Copyright © 2007 by Robert Gellately

*All rights reserved. Published in the United States by Alfred A. Knopf,
a division of Random House, Inc., New York, and in Canada by
Random House of Canada Limited, Toronto.*

www.aaknopf.com

*Knopf, Borzoi Books, and the colophon are registered trademarks
of Random House, Inc.*

Library of Congress Cataloging-in-Publication Data

Gellately, Robert [date]
Lenin, Stalin, and Hitler : the age of social catastrophe / by Robert Gellately.
p.   cm.
Includes bibliographical references and index.
ISBN-13: 978-1-4000-4005-6
1. Dictatorship—History—21st century.   2. Dictatorship—Case studies.
3. Lenin, Vladimir Il'ich, 1870–1924.   4. Stalin, Joseph, 1879–1953.
5. Hitler, Adolf, 1889–1945.   6. Soviet Union—Politics and government—
1917–1936.   7. Soviet Union—Politics and government—1936–1953.
8. Germany—Politics and government—1933–1945.   I. Title.
JC495.G45 2007
947.084—dc22   2007005272

Manufactured in the United States of America

First Edition

TO MARIE

CONTENTS

Abbreviations and Glossary *xi*
Note on Russian Spelling and Dates *xv*
Maps *xvi*
Introduction *3*

PART ONE: LENIN'S COMMUNIST DICTATORSHIP

 1 The First World War and the Russian Revolution *21*
 2 On the Way to Communist Dictatorship *41*
 3 Civil Wars in the Soviet Union *62*

PART TWO: THE RISE OF GERMAN NATIONAL SOCIALISM

 4 Nazism and the Threat of Bolshevism *81*
 5 First Nazi Attempt to Seize Power *102*
 6 Hitler Starts Over *117*

PART THREE: STALIN TRIUMPHS OVER POLITICAL RIVALS

 7 Battle for Communist Utopia *131*
 8 Lenin's Passing, Stalin's Victory *141*
 9 Stalin's New Initiatives *160*
10 Stalin Solidifies His Grip *173*

PART FOUR: GERMANS MAKE A PACT WITH HITLER

11 Nazi Party as Social Movement *185*
12 Nazism Exploits Economic Distress *198*
13 "All Power" for Hitler *211*

PART FIVE: STALIN'S REIGN OF TERROR

14 Fight Against the Countryside *227*
15 Terror as Political Practice *240*
16 "Mass Operations" *253*
17 "Cleansing" the Soviet Elite *267*

PART SIX: HITLER'S WAR AGAINST DEMOCRACY

18 Winning Over the Nation *285*
19 Dictatorship by Consent *298*
20 Persecution of the Jews in the Prewar Years *315*
21 "Cleansing" the German Body Politic *331*

PART SEVEN: STALIN AND HITLER: INTO THE SOCIAL CATASTROPHE

22 Rival Visions of World Conquest *345*
23 German Racial Persecution Begins in Poland *360*
24 Hitler and Western Europe *375*
25 The Soviet Response *384*
26 The War Spreads *397*

PART EIGHT: HITLER'S WAR ON "JEWISH BOLSHEVISM"

27 War of Extermination as Nazi Crusade *413*
28 War Against the Communists: Operation Barbarossa *429*

29 War Against the Jews: Death Squads in the East *441*
30 The "Final Solution" and Death Camps *452*

PART NINE: HITLER'S DEFEAT AND STALIN'S AGENDA

31 Greatest Crisis in Stalin's Career *471*
32 Between Surrender and Defiance *482*
33 Soviets Hold On, Hitler Grows Vicious *498*
34 Ethnic Cleansing in Wartime Soviet Union *511*

PART TEN: FINAL STRUGGLE

35 From Stalingrad to Berlin *525*
36 Stalin Takes the Upper Hand *543*
37 End of the Third Reich *560*

Epilogue *579*

Notes *595*

Acknowledgments *671*

Index *673*

Photographic Credits *697*

ABBREVIATIONS AND GLOSSARY

Bolsheviks	Majority faction of the RSDLP, founded in 1903
Central Committee	Soviet Communist Party supreme body, elected at Party congresses
Cheka (or Vecheka)	Chrezvychainaia Kommissiia (All-Russian Extraordinary Commission for Combatting Counterevolution and Sabotage); the original Soviet secret police, 1917–22, whose members were called Chekists even after many name changes
Comintern	Communist International organization
Gestapo	Geheime Staatspolizei (secret state police, also called Staatspolizei or Stapo)
GPU-OGPU	Gosudarstvennoe Politicheskoe Upravlenie (State Political Administration)–Obedinennoe Gosudarstvennoe Politicheskoe Upravlenie (Joint State Political Administration); the Soviet secret police, 1922–34
Gulag	Glavnoe Upravlenie Lagerei (main camp administration); eventually in charge of Soviet concentration camps
ITK	corrective labor colony (USSR)
ITL	corrective labor camp (USSR)

Kadets	Russian Constitutional Democratic Party (liberals)
kolkhoz	(pl. kolkhozy) collective farm
KPD	Communist Party of Germany
Kripo	Criminal Police
kulaks	"rich" peasants
lishentsy	Soviet people "without rights"
Mensheviks	Minority faction of the RSDLP, founded in 1903
NEP	New Economic Policy (1921–29) introduced by Lenin
NKVD	Narodnyi Komissariat Vnutrennikh Del (People's Commissariat for Internal Affairs), but widely used initials for the secret police when, from 1934, the GPU-OGPU was reorganized into the NKVD and named GUGB NKVD
NSDAP	National Socialist German Workers' Party (Nazi Party)
OKH	High Command of the German Army
Okhrana	tsarist secret police
OKW	High Command of the German Armed Forces
Politburo	main committee of the Central Committee of the Soviet Communist Party
Pravda	main newspaper of the Bolsheviks, and later the semiofficial paper of the Communist Party
RSDLP	Russian Social Democratic Labor Party, the main Marxist party
SA	Sturmabteilung (the Nazi Brownshirts)
SD	Sicherheitsdienst (Security Service of the Nazi Party)
Sipo	Sicherheitspolizei (security police); founded in 1936 as the umbrella organization for the Gestapo and Kripo
Sopade	Executive of the Exile SPD, with headquar-

	ters in Prague (1933–38), Paris (1938–40), and London (1940)
soviet	Russian for "council"; in German, *Rat*
Sovnarkom/SNK	Council of People's Commissars; the government body established by the Russian Revolution
SPD	Social Democratic Party of Germany, briefly fractured into the MSPD (Majority wing) and the USPD (Independent wing)
SS	Schutzstaffel; Himmler's Black Corps
Stavka	High Command of the Soviet Armed Forces
vozhd'	leader
Wehrmacht	German Armed Forces
zek	slang for *zaklyuchennyi,* Gulag prisoner

NOTE ON RUSSIAN SPELLING AND DATES

I have generally used the most common translations of Russian names, such as Leon Trotsky; Maxim Gorky, rather than Gorki; Georgy, rather than Georgii. I have omitted diacritical marks and other such features of the Russian language in the endnotes. Dates in the Russian section of the book prior to February 1918 are given according to the Julian calendar (or "Old Style"), which was twelve days behind the Western calendar in the nineteenth century and thirteen days behind it in the twentieth. January 31, 1918, was the last day of Julian calendar in Russia, with the next day becoming February 14.

Europe under German Domination in 1942

Arckangel'sk

FINLAND

German Reich
Powers cooperating with the Axis
Areas under German occupation
Italy and areas under its occupation

Ielsinki · Leningrad

Magnitogorsk

Tallinn

Kazan

Pskov

Moscow

Kuybyshev

Riga

HSKOMMISSARIAT
OSTLAND

Vitebsk

unas)
vno)

Minsk

U   S   S   R

aw

Don R.

Kiev

Stalingrad

NERAL
RNMENT
LAND

REICHSKOMMISSARIAT
UKRAINE

Caspian Sea

AKIA

Rostov

Odessa

ROMANIA

Sevastopol

Baku

Bucharest

R.

Tiflis
(Tbilisi)

Danube

Black   Sea

e

Sofia

BULGARIA

Istanbul

IRAN

Salonika

Ankara

ECE

TURKEY

Smyrna

IRAQ

Athens

SYRIA

CRETE

CYPRUS

Baghdad

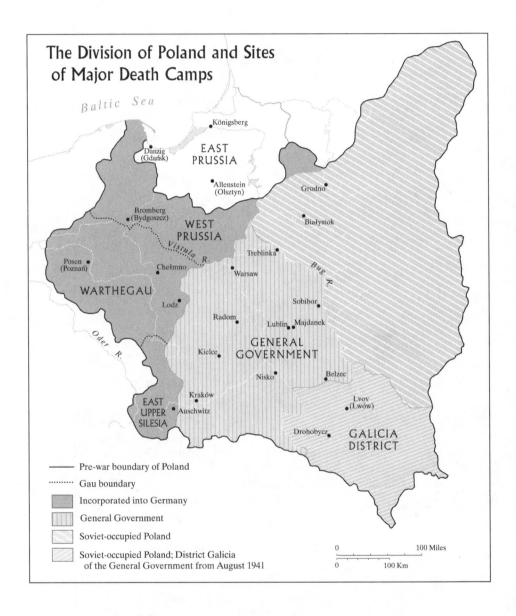

The Division of Poland and Sites of Major Death Camps

Baltic Sea

Königsberg

Danzig (Gdańsk)

EAST PRUSSIA

Allenstein (Olsztyn)

Grodno

Bromberg (Bydgoszcz)

WEST PRUSSIA

Białystok

Posen (Poznań)

Chełmno

Vistula R.

Treblinka

Warsaw

Bug R.

WARTHEGAU

Lodz

Sobibor

Radom

Lublin Majdanek

Oder R.

GENERAL GOVERNMENT

Kielce

Nisko

Belzec

Kraków

EAST UPPER SILESIA

Auschwitz

Lvov (Lwów)

Drohobycz

GALICIA DISTRICT

—— Pre-war boundary of Poland

·········· Gau boundary

Incorporated into Germany

General Government

Soviet-occupied Poland

Soviet-occupied Poland; District Galicia of the General Government from August 1941

0   100 Miles

0   100 Km

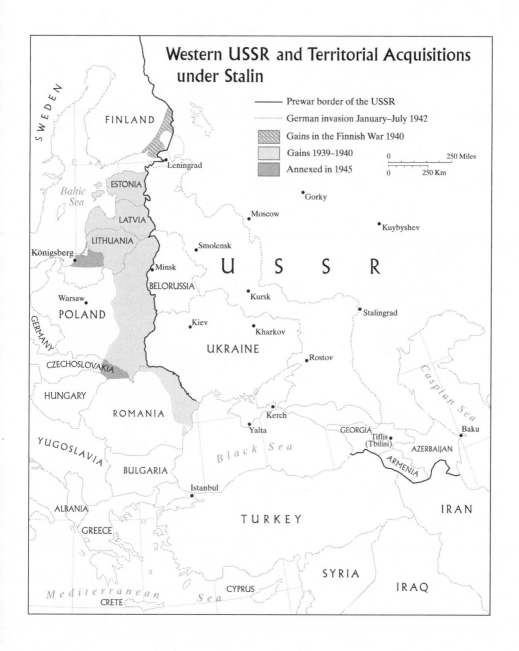

Western USSR and Territorial Acquisitions under Stalin

— Prewar border of the USSR

······· German invasion January–July 1942

Gains in the Finnish War 1940

Gains 1939–1940

Annexed in 1945

0 ———————— 250 Miles
0 ———————— 250 Km

SWEDEN

FINLAND

Leningrad

Baltic Sea

ESTONIA

Gorky

Moscow

LATVIA

Kuybyshev

LITHUANIA

Smolensk

Königsberg

Minsk

U S S R

BELORUSSIA

Warsaw

Kursk

POLAND

Stalingrad

GERMANY

Kiev

Kharkov

CZECHOSLOVAKIA

UKRAINE

Rostov

HUNGARY

ROMANIA

Kerch

Caspian Sea

YUGOSLAVIA

Yalta

GEORGIA

Baku

Tiflis (Tbilisi)

AZERBAIJAN

BULGARIA

Black Sea

ARMENIA

Istanbul

IRAN

ALBANIA

GREECE

TURKEY

Mediterranean Sea

CYPRUS

SYRIA

IRAQ

CRETE

LENIN, STALIN, AND HITLER

INTRODUCTION

The names of Lenin, Stalin, and Hitler will forever be linked to the tragic course of European history in the first half of the twentieth century. Only weeks after the Russian Revolution the Bolsheviks created secret police forces far more brutal than any that had existed under the tsar. The Nazis followed suit and were no sooner in power than they instituted the dreaded Gestapo. Under both regimes millions of people were incarcerated in concentration camps where they were tortured and frequently worked to death. The Nazis invented camps equipped for the industrial killing of millions of Jewish women, men, and children on the basis of supposed racial criteria.

The Soviet and Nazi dictators were themselves products of the structural changes generated by the Great War. Before 1914 they were marginal figures and would not have had the slightest hope of entering political life. Only in their dreams could they have imagined themselves as powerful rulers and leaders of mass movements. But once the "war monster" was released in 1914, the social and political crisis that swept across Europe opened up wholly new opportunities for the radicals and the utopians.[1]

Every corner of Europe was affected by catastrophe that enveloped the continent for the next three decades. There were two world wars, the Russian Revolution and civil war, the Fascist takeover in Italy, the Nazi tea Part

seizure of power, and the Holocaust. As well, there were numerous other uprisings and coups. The dark energies released by the hatreds, anxieties, and ambitions can be gleaned in part from the enormous scale of the killing. Far more men in uniform and still more civilians were struck down than in any comparable period in history. This book focuses on the dominant powers of the time, the Soviet Union and Nazi Germany, but analyzes the catastrophe itself in global terms, in an effort to lay bare its large-scale political and ideological nature. From this perspective, we can see that the tragedies endured by Europe were much more than discrete events. They were inextricably linked and an integral part of the bitter rivalry waged by the Communists and the Nazis for world domination.

In the First World War something on the order of eight million men were killed in action, seven million permanently disabled, and another fifteen million seriously wounded. An estimated five million civilians lost their lives through "war-induced causes," such as disease and malnutrition. These civilian casualties do not include those of Russia, where the situation was worst of all, magnified ultimately by (two) revolutions in 1917, followed by a civil war and famine.[2] All this happened in what was to be only the first phase of the great social and political catastrophe. The next round was to be deadlier still.

The First World War's social effects cannot be underestimated. "All inhabitants of Europe were exposed to the militarization of life and language, the erosion of individual freedom and social differences, the disruption of economic life, the drain of wealth, the hardships caused by food shortages, the growth of collectivization and bureaucracies, the collapse of the international system, and the release of huge reservoirs of aggressivity and violence."[3]

There would be no returning to the old ways. In tsarist Russia the regime had been tottering before 1914, and after more than three years of sacrifice the national will to carry on was all but dissipated. By early 1917 despair and resentment had led directly to the overthrow of Tsar Nicholas II. A new provisional government disastrously tried to carry on the war, but the army's morale and will to continue went from bad to worse. By October, Lenin and the Bolsheviks, seizing the moment to their own political advantage, had succeeded in taking power almost without firing a shot; there was no one left to defend the government. The war had opened the door to revolution and Communism. Thereafter, Lenin and the Bolsheviks combined terror and missionary zeal at home with a fervent belief that it was their destiny to bring the blessings of Communism to the West.

Russia was not alone in losing its monarchs. In 1918 and 1919 in Central Europe, Socialist and Communist revolutions followed the lost war and drove out the old leaders. There were also unsuccessful attempts to establish Communist regimes in Berlin, Munich, Vienna, Budapest, and elsewhere. In the early 1920s there were several renewed efforts, with Soviet encouragement and assistance, to bring about a Russian-style revolution in Germany.

The postwar "normality" in Europe was marked by political violence, attempted (and successful) coups, assassinations, bands of uniformed thugs in the streets, and general instability. This climate was conducive to the rise of new parties, and above all to the emergence of radicals and dictators of the right and the left who, backed by the enraged, the zealots, and notably also by young "idealists," tried to turn the general crisis to their own advantage. After 1918, when the war ended, there was a persistent feeling of living merely in an interregnum between wars.

The war monster was prepared for the next round that began in September 1939. The Second World War was, however, anything but a rerun of the old conflicts that had been in abeyance since 1918. From the mid-1930s, the ideological and political conflict between Nazism and Communism that had raged for more than a decade was reflected in growing international tensions. The new conflict erupted over Poland, and it escalated across Western Europe until ultimately the world descended into a maelstrom of destruction and horror that was far deadlier than even the Great War.

In Europe the ideological clash between Nazism and Communism added an entirely new dimension to the conflict that had engulfed the same nations during the Great War. There was a new viciousness, as the armed forces threw aside the conventions of war and national and ethnic hatreds roared out of control. Ethnic cleansing, "population transfers," deliberate targeting of civilians, and mass crimes became the order of the day. One way or another every country on the continent became entangled in the Holocaust.

The systematic mass murder of the Jews at the hands of German

forces during the Second World War was at the heart of the great catastrophe I deal with in this book. The Jewish people in Europe became
caught up in the hatreds and emotions following the First World War.
They were killed in the hundreds of thousands in the Russian civil war
(1918–21). Those crimes, committed mainly by "White" forces against
the "Reds," were the worst pogroms in Russian history, far deadlier than
anything that had been seen in the days of the tsars.

The sheer scale of the calamity that befell Europe in the Second
World War defies the imagination. A sense of being immersed in the
great catastrophe was conveyed in numerous ways by many people, few
more strikingly than a Russian artist during the siege of Leningrad. She
wrote in her diary:

> In all this worldwide phantasmagoria, I feel some kind of satanic roman-
> ticism, and in addition, grandeur, a head-long irrepressible rush to death
> and destruction.
>
> Some horrible and violent whirlwind has landed on earth, and every-
> thing has gotten mixed up and has started to spin in black smoke, fire,
> and snowstorm.
>
> And we, we Leningraders, choking in the siege, are microscopic
> grains of sand in this whole, immense cyclone.[4]

A monster like the one unleashed in 1941 could not be chained up so
easily, and the war did not end abruptly with V-E day, on May 8, 1945,
when the Allies celebrated their victory. Social strife in the form of brutal acts of retribution, ethnic cleansing, and civil wars raged on until 1953
and the death of Stalin.[5]

This book began as a study of the conflicting ideologies of Communism and Nazism and the murderous rivalries of Stalin and Hitler. I
did not initially include Lenin as a major figure. However, as I conducted
my research and tried to reconstruct the events leading up to the Second
World War, I began to see that much of what I wanted to say was leading
me back, over and over, to Lenin and the beginnings of the Soviet dictatorship.

The two best studies dealing with Soviet Communism and German
National Socialism focus on Stalin and Hitler and hardly mention Lenin

at all. Their point of departure is to compare the two regimes through a methodology that takes Hitler as the principal figure and then examines the parallels with Stalin. But it is never explained why Hitler is placed before Stalin. After all, long before anyone had ever heard of Hitler, Stalin was politically active, and he was a powerful Soviet dictator many years before the Nazi leader became chancellor of Germany.[6]

My book deviates from the standard approach by giving significant attention to Lenin and by putting the story in proper chronological sequence. It also corrects for the tendency of most studies of Stalinism to ignore Lenin or relegate him to a background role. Too often Lenin comes across as a prudent and wise, or at least well-intentioned, founding father whose vision was polluted by the murderous Stalin. Yet Lenin is central not just to the foundation of Soviet Communism but also to its subsequent development. It was precisely his will to power that drove on the doubters among fellow Bolsheviks in 1917. Without a hint of moral scruple or sense of national loyalty, Lenin desperately hoped for Russia's defeat in the First World War and ridiculed fellow Bolsheviks who thought they should defend their country.

In March 1917 the world of the tsars came crashing down, and for a short while, under the new provisional government, Russia became one of the freest countries in the world. At the time Lenin was nowhere near Petrograd, the capital; he was living in Switzerland. Emboldened by events, he now returned to his homeland. He was determined to destroy what remained of the old social and political order in Russia and intent on killing any chance that the new Russia would become a liberal democracy.

Lenin, the man born Vladimir Ilych Ulyanov on April 10, 1870, "Old Style," grew up in a family of comfortable means. He had been an early convert to revolutionary activism and was perhaps the most intransigent practitioner of Russian Marxism in the prerevolutionary period. As the founder of Soviet Communism, he was the key advocate of establishing the one-party state, the concentration camps, and the terror. He insisted, within days of the October Revolution, that civil and legal rights had to be curtailed. Only weeks later he pushed for a new secret police (the Cheka). He set the intolerant tone of the new regime and relentlessly pursued a widening circle of enemies. Nor were terror and dictatorship simply reactions to the exigencies of governing, for Lenin embraced both more than a decade before the Russian Revolution. When the tsarist regime came under pressure in 1905, for example, Lenin was not satisfied with the idea of reforming it into a constitutional monarchy or even liberal democracy.[7]

When they met for the first time in mid-December 1905, Stalin was already in tune with Lenin but disagreed with Lenin's change of tactics to participate in elections made possible by the October reforms. Nevertheless, Stalin learned to take his cues from the "great man," for the two agreed that the ends justified any means and that the ultimate aim was dictatorship of the proletariat—with the emphasis on the former.[8]

Lenin had remarkably little empathy for the hopes and aspirations of the common people, whether they were peasant farmers or members of the industrial working class. He believed that the workers were the only "revolutionary class" but, if left to their own devices, they would want "merely" better wages and social improvements—in other words, trade-union demands that, in his eyes, betrayed their limited imagination. The Russian writer Maxim Gorky accurately summed up Lenin's attitude in November 1917, at the very start of the new regime, when its character was barely defined. "The working class is for Lenin what ore is for the metalworker. Is it possible, under all present conditions, to mold a socialist state from this ore? Apparently it is impossible; however—why not try? What does Lenin risk if the experiment should fail?"[9]

Leninism was based on the idea that professional revolutionaries would form an avant-garde or vanguard party and rule in the name of the proletariat. They would not waste time on the "sham" of liberal democracy, which they regarded as nothing more than the government of the hated bourgeoisie. Getting rid of the absolute monarchy and replacing it with a constitutional system was merely a prelude to a more authentic revolution. None of this was going to happen without bloodshed, and Lenin took it as self-evident that the class struggle meant civil war. He was convinced that Communism had to be forced through violently. His followers were elitist to the core and assured of their own superiority. They took it upon themselves to create a new world from top to bottom.

Joseph Vissarionovich Dzhughashvili, or Joseph Stalin, was born December 21, 1879, according to the official biography published during his lifetime, but historians now agree that the real date was December 6, 1878. We have no idea why he lied about the date of his birth. The man himself had undeniable gifts, but originality was not one of them. He proudly and intentionally built on Lenin's foundations. To put it another way: Stalin initiated very little that Lenin had not already introduced or previewed. Stalin was Lenin's logical successor, priding himself on being a true disciple, though he was to transform the Soviet Union in ways his idol could only dream about.

The myth of the "good Lenin"—the savior—was built into the political culture of the Soviet Union from the start, and Stalin shrewdly played it to his own political advantage. Lenin was actually merciless and cruel. Even the inner circle of the Bolsheviks shuddered at his ferocity and the executions he ordered without any compunction. We should understand the figure of the "good Lenin" as a political instrument, meant to inspire followers at home and abroad.

The "good Lenin" existed before there was a "bad Stalin." Stalin came from a peasant family in Georgia and was a seminary student prior to taking the path of a professional revolutionary. But his career in the distant Caucasus had little direction until he adopted Lenin as his leader. When Stalin fought for supremacy among Soviet Communists in the early 1920s, he did so not by laying out his own aims but by proclaiming himself Lenin's most loyal follower and interpreter.

There has been some talk that Lenin, who was growing more seriously ill by the day, wanted to get rid of Stalin in December 1922–January 1923. In his so-called political testament Lenin complained that Stalin was "too rude" and wrote of "removing" him as general secretary of the Party. Lenin's annoyance with Stalin can be traced to a private event: Stalin had had a personal confrontation with Lenin's wife, Nadezhda Krupskaya. However, as much as he demanded an apology and muttered about Stalin's manners, he said nothing about removing him from the most important committees in the country (the Politburo and Central Committee), and there is no documentary evidence to suggest he was looking to another possible successor. His main concern was about a split in the Party around the two powerful personalities of Stalin and Leon Trotsky. But he appreciated Stalin deeply. He had fostered him in important ways and ultimately favored him above all the other rivals at the top of the Party.[10]

The first dictator of the Soviet Union and his future successor had no major theoretical or political differences in the area of Communist doctrine, least of all on the wholesale and ruthless use of terror. Stalin stayed on as general secretary of the Party. In the struggle for power after Lenin died, he easily pushed aside Trotsky, his main rival. From the mid-1920s, when he asserted his dominant position, Stalin justified every zigzag in policy, every twist of the screws, every dose of terror, by tracing it to some statement or other that Lenin had made. I show in this book that far from perverting or undermining Lenin's legacy, as is sometimes assumed, Stalin was Lenin's logical heir.

After Stalin's death in 1953, the "good Lenin" was resurrected to chase out the "bad Stalin" and his personality cult. Something had clearly gone wrong with Communism: there were obvious abuses and a gigantic concentration camp system with more than two million prisoners, and the rights of citizens meant nothing. The question was how all that had come to pass. Nikita Khrushchev's famous speech in 1956, which signaled a "thaw" in the Soviet Union, claimed that Stalin had corrupted Leninism. Khrushchev trotted out the myth of Lenin the noble and good to save the "inner truths" of Communism from association with what were belatedly recognized as "Stalinist evils." Everything that had gone wrong in the country was now placed squarely on Stalin's shoulders. Khrushchev brought up Lenin's "testament" and his charges about Stalin's rudeness to "prove" that the brilliant Lenin had been right all along. Khrushchev asked rhetorically: "Were our Party's holy Leninist principles observed after the death of Vladimir Ilich?" That they were not was Stalin's fault, because there was supposedly nothing wrong with Leninism.[11]

This fable about Lenin no longer convinces, as is made abundantly clear from the content and character of the documents coming out of the newly opened Russian archives.[12] They reveal Lenin to be the most extreme of the radicals, and the leader who pressed for terror as much as, and probably more than, anyone.

The image of Lenin that emerges from the pages of this book, even the mere mention of him in the title alongside Stalin and Hitler, will disturb some people. A good friend at my American publishers said the very thought of putting Lenin next to Stalin and Hitler in the book's title would be enough to make her Russian grandmother turn in her grave.

Communism has not suffered the same obloquy as Nazism, notwithstanding all we have come to learn about persecution and mass murder in the Soviet Union, China, and elsewhere. That may be because Communism was meant to have a universal liberating purpose. It was to bring the end of inequalities and establish real social justice. To many of its adherents, it did not seem to matter much that the Soviet regime produced the exact opposite on almost all counts.[13]

Like Stalin, Adolf Hitler (born April 20, 1889) was a man of modest origins. For the first three decades of his life, he gave no thought to a career in politics and was instinctively a loner who dabbled in art. He was not even a German citizen, but an Austrian with an odd southern accent who set out in his twenties for Germany, where he continued to peddle his artwork. His personal qualities were not the stuff of the born leader. He was painfully shy, spoke little in public, and wrote less. He served as a volunteer in the German army during the entire First World War but rose no higher than the rank of corporal. He was an outsider even in the trenches at the front.

At the close of the war, Hitler became uncannily attuned to the wave of resentment and bitterness that swept over the defeated country. He spewed hatred for the "November criminals," those who were allegedly responsible for Germany's loss, and like many others he wanted to tear up the Treaty of Versailles, which shackled his adopted country with the guilt for the Great War. Unlike the Marxists, Hitler had no grand theory that posited an end point "beyond" history. For Hitler, history was all there was, a constant striving in which German survival and supremacy could only be ensured through the creation of a racially pure "community of the people," cleansed of Communists, Jews, criminals, social outsiders, and those classified as racially unfit.

We do not know much about Hitler's views before 1919. What is certain is that as he grew up in Austria, he held a highly romanticized understanding of all things German, developed contempt for Austro-Hungarian governmental officials, and had an unmistakable, if vaguely defined, yearning to have his people find a home in a Greater Germany. On the eve of the Great War he was living in Munich and overjoyed in his belief that Germany was at last going to establish itself as the world power he felt to be its birthright. The war eventually threatened to put an end to his nationalist aspirations. At that point the corporal who had heretofore led an uneventful life became politically awake to the meaning of defeat and humiliation and joined the chorus that laid the blame on the Jews.

It should not surprise that Hitler fell into league with nationalist groups, given his long-standing emotional attachment to Germany. But his passionate commitment to a "rebirth" of the nation was fundamentally tied to the view that the Jews were responsible for its betrayal. He had no difficulty adopting a biological racist outlook, though his social Darwinism was in all probability little more than a convenient rationale for his increasingly bitter anti-Semitic views. Growing up in Austria, Hitler likely did not differ from many of his generation in tending toward anti-Jewish attitudes, though it was not until after the Great War that he became the type of rabid anti-Semite we associate with the Nazi movement.

Hitler stood out among the disaffected after the war not just because of his rhetorical skills but, more important, because of the radical nature of his politics, the all-or-nothing attitude he was to demonstrate the rest of his life. By September 1919, it was already on his agenda to "remove" the Jews from Germany "altogether." It is extremely doubtful that even he, at that time, could have imagined how that impulse would play out in the Second World War, but those who thronged to hear him speak in the 1920s could sense that fanatical right-wing politics—a crackdown on "law and order," the Communists, and above all the Jews—would be at the heart of a Hitler leadership.

Hitler's anti-Semitic phobia soon became entangled with a feverish anti-Bolshevism. He followed the pattern of other anti-Semites in grossly exaggerating the number of Jews involved in Communism in Germany and the Soviet Union, but his hatred of the Jews could not be reduced to their supposed sympathy for Communism. More significantly, he portrayed them as the natural enemies of the nation.

On August 13, 1920, in Munich, Hitler gave what amounted to his "programmatic" statement on anti-Semitism. He invited his audience to envision what great heights of culture and art Germany might reach if the nation came together. He claimed that the Jews could never be part of this effort because, unlike Germans (more generally "Aryans"), they did not see work as a social and moral obligation. He maintained that the Jews would always live as outsiders in another state, as agents, businessmen, and dealers.[14] He continued to hone this theme. For example, on November 2, 1922, he described the Jews as a people who were by nature international. They were able to thrive throughout history in so many diverse environments, speaking different languages, always having a sense of themselves as a people, he said. His greatest fear was that this "race," which he regarded as "lower," might well be capable of undermining German culture and thus its national identity. He believed the Jews had been "destroyers of culture" from the earliest times, in Egypt, Palestine, Greece, and ancient Rome.[15]

Whereas many observers might perceive capitalism and Communism as deadly enemies, with little in common, Hitler saw both as infused with the spirit of internationalism and thus as sharing a common ground of natural enmity against the nation. From this perspective, one simply could not be both for internationalism and for Germany. Hitler held stubbornly to the view that the Jews, as a people with no homeland of their own, had no stake in belonging to the nation because their real interests lay elsewhere, with capitalism or Communism.

It was with this inflexible belief in the Jews as the natural enemies of Germany that Hitler became the most resolute opponent of Lenin and Stalin and what he disparagingly called "Jewish Bolshevism." He fought for more than a decade to get into power, and thereafter set out to reshape Germany and then Europe according to an ideology to which he had committed himself early and held on to until the end. He was intent on war almost from the day of his appointment as chancellor on January 30, 1933, and in 1939 he got it. The clash of Nazi and Communist ideologies reached critical proportions in June 1941 and became the *Vernichtungskrieg*—or war of annihilation against Jews and Communists— for which he lusted.

This book, then, holds that Hitler's anti-Semitism was rooted in his radical and racially tinged German nationalism and that his war against Communism was an extension of his war against the Jews. My position is strictly opposed to that of Ernst Nolte, who believes that Nazi anti-Semitism was a reaction to Soviet Communism and that the crimes of the Nazis, including the annihilation of the Jews, were "copies" of crimes committed by the Soviets. Nolte goes so far as to maintain that there was a "rational core" to Hitler's persecution of the Jews in that as a group they were active in the Communist movement. He suggests that the Jews could be taken as having declared war on Germany, with the implication that Nazi Germany was put in the position of defender of the homeland. Nolte's statements are an astonishing and reprehensible replication of Nazi rhetoric, notwithstanding his unsuccessful maneuverings to distance himself from the racist ideology of the Third Reich. Suffice it to say he has been roundly and rightly condemned not only for advancing the untenable and shocking position that the Jews were somehow to blame for their own destruction but also for denying against all the evidence that Nazi anti-Semitism was rooted in German nationalism.[16]

For Hitler, anti-Semitism was a fundamental plank of Nazi ideology. It drew for its sustenance on nationalist aspirations in place before the Great War and was heightened to a maddening degree by the country's defeat. With Hitler's idea of Soviet Communism as yet another Jewish plot to destroy the nation, Nazi ideology soon overreached the national dimensions of a country fretting over the lost war and despised Versailles Treaty. As he created the Nazi movement and built the Third Reich, with continuing scrutiny of the Soviet Union, his determination to "remove" the Jews from Germany assumed a mission of worldwide scope.[17] It is only by examining Hitler's venomous attitudes toward the Jews and how these were connected to his anti-Bolshevism that we can get a sense of the viciously obsessive nature of his anti-Semitism and its primacy in Nazi ideology and politics, nationally and internationally.

In the 1930s the struggle between Communism and Nazism became a deadly rivalry for world domination. It was above all this clash that led to the darkest chapters of the great social and political catastrophe of the century. The democratic European countries were no match for these two power-hungry upstarts, and it was only the entrance of the Americans into the Second World War, albeit on the side of the Soviet Union, that managed to overcome the might of Germany. In return, the United States would have its hands full with the Communists in the ensuing Cold War, which was to last half a century.

This book provides a social-historical account of the Soviet and Nazi dictatorships and documents their similarities and differences. I agree with Charles Maier that it is crucial to preserve the distinctions and contrasts.[18]

Russia in 1914 was arguably the most politically repressive state on the continent. It was still an agricultural and undeveloped society, with more than one hundred languages spoken by its multiethnic population. Seventy-nine percent of them were illiterate according to the census of 1897. Germany by contrast was modern, highly cultured, ethnically homogeneous, and economically advanced. It had long since attained nearly universal literacy and was on the way to liberal democracy. Good citizens in Germany, as in most parts of Austria, prided themselves on the rule of law. "Social peace and good order" was a well-known German proverb, and in that respect it was quite unlike the far more violent and unruly Russian society. The uproar and chaos in the streets of Germany after the war—much of it caused by the Nazis—made people ready to embrace Hitler, who promised to bring an end to such unquiet times. The older contrasts with Russia did not disappear, but colored the Communist and Nazi dictatorships that emerged.

Stalin and Hitler have been viewed as "populist politicians."[19] My research does not support that perspective. In fact, the two dictators were very different. Hitler was a model example of a charismatic leader, a man with the gift of instant communication with the masses. Stalin was utterly lacking in charisma, at least until the end of the Second World War. He was a workaholic, the ultimate bureaucratic pencil pusher. In his concern for administrative details he was the exact opposite of Hitler, who wanted others to make most of the decisions "in his place" while he reserved the important ones—perhaps only 5 percent—for himself.[20]

Far from being "populists," Stalin and Lenin before him were self-proclaimed leaders of the vanguard. They did not appeal to public opinion nor try to build on the popular mood. Even in their own minds they derived their legitimacy and authority not from the people but from Marxism and the laws of history, of which they supposedly had superior knowledge. Hitler, on the other hand, believed passionately that political authority had to be based on popularity and that no regime could be a true nation if not backed by the people belonging to it.

Hitler had nothing but contempt for the Soviet-style dictators and the terror they used on their own people, and in stark contrast he set out to win over the hearts and minds of all non-Jewish Germans in a communal bonding based on the "exclusion" of the Jews and others deemed racially unfit. What he wanted was dictatorship by the consent of the initiated.[21] Hitler's hybrid form of government can be called a consensus dictatorship.[22] I agree with Ian Kershaw that Hitler's popularity and authority "formed the central vehicle for consolidating and integrating society in a massive consensus for the regime."[23]

Unlike his Soviet counterparts, Hitler proceeded relatively cautiously. For example, he tried to prepare popular opinion in advance of new initiatives, and when these ran up against objections, he frequently backed off. That point held true for the campaign against the churches and for the persecution of the Jews inside Germany. This tendency was in marked contrast to Lenin and Stalin, who never retreated in the face of opposition and often resorted to immediate and ruthless terror. The Orthodox Church, beloved by so many traditionalist Russians, was all but wiped out. The Communists burned down many ancient houses of worship and enslaved the priests, whereas the Nazis recoiled when a few people objected to some local radical's decision to remove crucifixes from the schools.

In the USSR, Party purges and the rituals of public self-criticism and self-flagellation formed an integral part of Communist practice under both Lenin and Stalin. There was nothing of the kind in Nazi Germany. Hitler operated by heaping praise on the German spirit and cheering on good citizens as they responded in kind to him. He reserved his venom for the Jews, political opponents like Communists, and outsider groups like homosexuals and Gypsies. There was one (relatively small) purge in 1934, horrible, to be sure, but not to be overestimated. Hitler was loath to dismiss even corrupt Party officials, as if he did not want to admit his misplaced faith in them. To keep up morale during the war and also to avoid having Germans question his authority, Hitler merely asked generals to resign or take sick leave when he found them wanting, whereas Stalin had many such people shot. The popular field marshal Erwin Rommel was allowed to take poison in October 1944 because of his suspected involvement in the attempt to assassinate Hitler in July.

Above all, Hitler despised the universal claims of Communism. His movement, like his regime, saw itself as anchored in "blood and soil," in the here and now, even as it preached a future utopia for racially fit Germans only. The Nazi message was exclusivist or particularist. It opened its doors, but barely a crack, for a relatively few Nordic Europeans. Otherwise the Greater Germania of the future or the New Order—or whatever it would be called—would be sealed off, and the only contact with other "races" would be of the kind between masters and slaves. There would be no "brotherhood of man," but what Hitler imagined as an inevitable and endless Darwinian struggle of the "superior" to fend off the "inferior." (Needless to say, like many others before and since, he possessed only a crude understanding of Darwin.) The Nazi "final solution" took the lives of millions of innocent people before Hitler was finally stopped, in 1945, amid the rubble of a bombed and burning Germany.

Soviet and Nazi regimes both gained followers from among the idealists, the young, and the better educated. Such people virtually worshipped their leaders, and even the ice-cold rationalists among them could recall the ground seeming to tremble beneath their feet when they came into the presence of these men. One young Russian Communist, who was found guilty at war's end of "showing pity for the Germans, for bourgeois humanism, and for harmful statements on questions of current policy," was not only expelled from the Party but imprisoned. Actually the word "prison" could not be tolerated in the Soviet "utopia," so he was sent to what was called Kharkov's House of Corrective Labor. Remarkably enough, inside this "house" he said he "became even more consistent a Stalinist. What I was afraid of, more than anything else, was that my sense of personal injury would impair my view of what remained most important to the life of my country and of the world. That vision was essential to me as a source of my spiritual strength, of my conception of myself as part of a great whole." Even if the judges and secret police were wrong, he "believed that no amount of mistakes or miscalculations or injustices could alter the aggregate or halt the coming triumph of Socialism."[24]

The promise of material gain and improvement in their way of life won converts to Communism and Nazism. Both regimes had to provide a minimum of life's necessities to win and maintain support. Moreover, many Soviet Communists and Nazis were fixated on making life comfortable for themselves and practiced every form of immorality, perversity, cruelty, and criminality imaginable. In the Third Reich the extent of profiteering and corruption knew no limits, above and beyond how Party leaders, members, and ordinary citizens gained at the expense of the Jews.[25] In the Soviet Union the *nomenklatura,* or those whose names were entered on "lists," had every possible privilege, from special apartments and stores to schools and dachas.[26] They embodied the cruel commandment issued by the pigs in George Orwell's satirical *Animal Farm* (1945): "All animals are equal but some animals are more equal than others."

But materialist explanations for Communist or Nazi supporters are inadequate. Millions committed to the cause, not simply for personal gain but in spite of suffering and loss. Indeed, the spirit of self-sacrifice among committed Communists and Nazis was one of the features that make this era in Europe so striking. What is transmitted in diaries, letters, and autobiographies from the period was the faith and conviction of the "true believers."

Contrary to some recent works, I believe the Nazi persecution of the Jews was not aimed primarily at acquiring their property in order to finance the Third Reich. In conversations with Goebbels, as elsewhere, Hitler comes across as someone who was fanatically focused on what he regarded as the anti-Semitic mission in defense of the fatherland. Killing all the Jews was a war aim in his mind and extended to the murder even of those Jews working for the armaments industry, where there was a short supply of labor by 1943. All were killed not for economic gain but in spite of economic losses. Materialist explanations for killing working-age Jewish males in 1943 and 1944, at a time when the regime needed their labor, are not plausible, and the claims do not hold up under scientific scrutiny.[27]

My previous work and research interests have been in social history, and this book is no exception. Once again I have placed special emphasis on the victims and their stories, but my account of what happened to them is by no means exhaustive. It is a harrowing tale, even if whole volumes of suffering and death could not be included within the constraints of one book. I have dwelled longer on what seem to me to be the representative mass crimes and tried to explain these as best I could.

The Soviet side of the story could not have been told before the collapse of Communism and the opening of the Russian archives. I gathered so much material on the period as a whole that I could not possibly include it all and had to cut much that was already written. I regret not dealing in depth with Soviet and German public opinion, and the cultural side of these dictatorships, but these matters must await another book. In addition, I have planned a sequel study that focuses in greater detail on the last part of the war and the first years of the peace that followed.

PART ONE

LENIN'S COMMUNIST DICTATORSHIP

1

THE FIRST WORLD WAR AND
THE RUSSIAN REVOLUTION

The First World War strained the regime of Tsar Nicholas II to the breaking point. Initially, in August 1914, the nation rallied around the flag. Politicians and the urban middle classes welcomed the war, and the army went off to defend their "Slavic brothers" in Yugoslavia against German and Austrian aggression. The Duma, Russia's national assembly, dissolved itself to symbolize the country's support of the government. But no one in Europe, let alone in Russia, visualized the war to come, the devastation it would cause, and how long hostilities would last.

The tsarist empire had the largest army in Europe but lacked the resources to fight a prolonged struggle. Before the first year of the fighting was over, there were shortages of all kinds. Replacement troops were being trained without rifles and sent onto the battlefield, where they were to go among the dead and wounded to pick up the weapons they needed.

By the beginning of 1917, widespread discontent over the ghastly sacrifices of the war, food shortages, and high prices led to bitter strikes and hostile demonstrations. A police report for January 1917 from Petrograd, the newly renamed capital, spelled out the darkening situation:

"These mothers, exhausted from standing endlessly in lines and having suffered so much watching their half-starving and sick children, are perhaps much closer to a revolution than Messrs. Miliukov, Rodichev, and Co. [leaders of the liberal Kadet Party], and of course much more dangerous."[1]

The pent-up resentments and grievances were ignited by a demonstration in the capital on February 23, when a peaceful march for women's rights was joined by striking workers. Cries rang out for bread, and people exclaimed, "Down with the tsar!" By February 26, under orders from the tsar, troops fired on demonstrators. Some of the soldiers were sickened by what they did, and then the next day the revolution began as mutinous troops rampaged through the streets killing or disarming police. Crowds shouting "Give us bread," "Down with the war," "Down with the Romanovs," and "Down with the government" attacked police headquarters.

Instead of charging the crowds, tens of thousands of peasant soldiers, their mentality shaped by decades of grievances against the system, went over to the people. Together they exploded in a mixture of rage and revenge that rumbled on for days. The police put machine guns atop buildings, but even these were ineffective against the angry tumult.[2]

Tsar Nicholas II was informed, and on March 2, in a meeting at the front, Aleksandr Guchkov and Vasily Shulgin, deputies of the State Duma, laid out the stark options. Guchkov pronounced the home front and military out of control. The situation, he said, was not "the result of some conspiracy," but represented "a movement that sprang from the very ground and instantly took on an anarchical cast and left the authorities fading into the background."

The upheaval had spread to the army, Guchkov continued, "for there isn't a single military unit that isn't immediately infected by the atmosphere of the movement." He believed that it might be possible to prevent the inevitable if a radical step was taken. He explained:

> The people profoundly believe that the situation was caused by the mistakes of those in authority, in particular the highest authority, and this is why some sort of act is needed that would work upon the popular consciousness. The only path is to transfer the burden of supreme rulership to other hands. Russia can be saved, the monarchical principle can be saved, the dynasty can be saved. If you, Your Majesty, announce that you

are transferring your power to your little son, if you assign the regency to Grand Duke Mikhail Alexandrovich, and if in your name or in the name of the regent instructions are issued for a new government to be formed, then perhaps Russia will be saved. I say perhaps because events are unfolding so quickly.[3]

Dismayed at this turn of events, Nicholas II accepted the inevitable, and on March 3, 1917, he abdicated, also in the name of his gravely ill son. The tsar stepped down in favor of his brother Grand Duke Mikhail, who tried to get assurances of support in the capital. He asked leading figures from the Duma, including Prince Georgii Lvov, Mikhail Rodzianko, and Alexander Kerensky, whether they could vouch for his safety if he accepted the crown. None thought they could, so Mikhail was left with little choice but to refuse the crown.[4] In fact a third of the members of the State Duma formed a "provisional committee" on the afternoon of February 27, and by March 2, with the tsar's abdication, that became the new provisional government.[5]

The American ambassador in Petrograd witnessed what he regarded as "the most amazing revolution." He reported that a nation of 200 million living under an absolute monarchy for a thousand years had forced out their emperor with a minimal amount of violence. The three-hundred-year rule of the Romanov dynasty was over.[6] In fact the revolution was not "bloodless," for in Petrograd alone estimates of the new government put the killed or wounded at 1,443. Even the higher figures mentioned were small in comparison with what was to follow.[7]

LENIN AND THE BOLSHEVIKS

The main Marxist party, the Russian Social Democratic Labor Party (RSDLP), including the Bolshevik and Menshevik factions, had nothing to do with this liberal revolution that swept away the Romanovs. Lenin was in Switzerland. Stalin was isolated in western Siberia, in exile since 1913. Most other top Bolshevik and Menshevik leaders were far removed from the action as well, with Leon Trotsky and Nikolai Bukharin five thousand miles away in North America.

But just over seven months after the February liberal revolution, the world learned of the October Communist revolution, headed by Lenin and the Bolsheviks. It was to change the course of world history, and the twentieth century was to be the bloodiest ever.

Lenin was born into a well-to-do family in Simbirsk. His parents named him Vladimir Ilych Ulyanov. Later, following the practice of Russian revolutionaries, he took Lenin as his pseudonym. His grandfather on his mother's side, Dr. Alexander Blank, was Jewish, about which a great deal was made later on, but Lenin had no memory of him at all, and there was no connection with Judaism in his life. Lenin's father was a higher civil servant, and the family lived in the style of provincial dignitaries. His father died from a sudden illness in early 1886.

Lenin's older brother Alexander was at university in St. Petersburg at the time. He was involved with one of the many revolutionary groups and identified with Russia's intelligentsia, who were raised on Western education and saw their own society as culturally and politically backward.

For decades the intelligentsia had striven to bring Russia up to Western standards. Each generation experimented with different revolutionary tactics. Sometimes the mood gave rise to nihilists who rejected everything, and at other times revolutionaries were inspired by the idea of going to the people to "instruct" them.[8]

The intelligentsia from the 1870s onward grew more radical. On March 1, 1881, one of many splinter groups assassinated Tsar Alexander II, in hopes of stirring up massive social and political unrest and sparking revolution. Lenin's brother joined another group intent on killing the successor to the throne, Alexander III. However, the ever-vigilant Okhrana, the secret police, got wind of the conspiracy. The plan had been to attack the tsar on March 1, 1887, the anniversary of the last tsar's death. Arrests followed, and, shockingly for his family, Lenin's older brother was hanged along with four others in May.

The young Lenin reacted quietly to these dramatic events. He had always been diligent in school, and he went back to his books and continued his studies. He registered as a student in the law faculty at Kazan University in the fall of 1887.

Little is known about Lenin's extracurricular activities in this period, but as one might expect, he had some contact with student radicals and probably participated in protests against the government. As the brother of the conspirator and would-be assassin Alexander, he likely came under particular scrutiny from the tsarist authorities. While he was certainly not the student radical that subsequent Soviet lore made him out to be, he was duly rounded up by the police for the part he allegedly played in demonstrations. He was expelled from the university in December 1887 and exiled to Kokushkino, but by mid-1890 he was allowed to begin the process of registering as an external student at St. Petersburg University, from which he was awarded a law degree in November 1891. In the meantime, he had become a voracious reader of left-wing literature.

Lenin gravitated toward the fledgling Russian Marxist movement rather than the Russian populists, who emphasized agrarian Socialism. According to Karl Marx, the Socialist revolution was to be expected in the most advanced countries when the contradictions of mature capitalism reached a crisis that could not be resolved within the prevailing economic conditions. Even for committed Russian Marxists, it was certainly debatable whether Marx's theories really fitted Russia, but Lenin took a doctrinaire approach and tried to "prove" that capitalism already existed there. He did not waver from this position and later, in 1899, published a large tome on the topic. Although it was filled with statistics and analysis of the driest kind, it surprisingly got the attention of young radicals in distant parts of the Russian Empire. Anastas I. Mikoyan, slightly younger (born 1895) than Lenin, but later to become a long-serving member of the Soviet government under Stalin, was given the book. His circle in the Caucasus first became acquainted and impressed with Lenin's thought in that highly technical volume.[9]

No matter what the statistics were supposed to prove, the plain fact was that capitalism in Russia was still in its infancy. (Lenin admitted as much many times later in life.) For Russian Marxists, the dilemma was what to do in the here and now. They lived in a society that was more feudal than capitalist, and thus—according to Marx himself—was not yet "ready" for a Socialist revolution.

Lenin's revolutionary activities got him arrested in December 1895 and held in a St. Petersburg prison. He was allowed to have books and was anything but mistreated. It was not until early 1897 that he was sent to "administrative exile" in Siberia. Nadezhda Konstantinovna Krupskaya (herself an exiled radical), one of Lenin's staunchest supporters, called herself his fiancée and in 1898 asked the authorities if she could join him in Shushenskoe. They soon married. He was permitted considerable freedom to study and write, so exile for Lenin was more of an opportunity than a deprivation. Just after the turn of the century, when they left Siberia, Lenin's self-image as a fighter for the cause had been strengthened, his Marxist convictions had taken a yet more radical turn, and he had written *What Is to Be Done?* That small pamphlet would make him widely known to the underground Russian Marxist movement just getting off the ground.[10]

The largest Marxist Party of the day was the German Social Democratic Party. It had hundreds of thousands of members, Party newspapers, and a substantial delegation of elected Socialist politicians. The Russian Social Democratic Labor Party (RSDLP) was founded at a congress held in Minsk in March 1898. The meeting hardly merited the title of congress, with a total of nine activists present, the low number indicating how marginal the Russian Marxists were at the time.

Lenin was in exile when the RSDLP was founded, but he won considerable attention when, in 1902, he published *What Is to Be Done?*[11] He advocated a party of professional revolutionaries dedicated to the cause. In this model, revolution would be brought about not by elections and democracy but by small cells of dedicated revolutionaries who would use violence and any means necessary. Many young people like Stalin were attracted by Lenin's "heroic idea" and by the optimism he and others found in Marxism.[12] The full implications for political violence of this theory became clear only later. But Lenin was convinced early that revolution without terror and dictatorship, on the model of the French Jacobins, was all but impossible. In the meantime, his work struck a chord among radicals by fusing the European and Russian tradition of revolutionary terrorism with Marx's idea of "dictatorship of the proletariat."[13]

By the time of the second congress of the RSDLP, which was of necessity held outside Russia (first in Brussels, then in London), in July 1903, Lenin had attracted attention and gained followers. It was at this gathering that the fateful split took place between the Bolsheviks (majority) and the Mensheviks (minority). Lenin stood out, and while some of his more radical demands were defeated, he won a tactical political advantage when he cleverly named the group gathering around him the "Bolshevik" faction at the right moment during the meetings.

The Russian revolution of 1905 broke out on January 9, "Bloody Sunday," when troops shot at peaceful marchers. The events that followed

offered fresh hope to émigré radicals like Lenin who called on Russian
Marxists to hold a unifying congress, even if in his heart his disdain for
the Mensheviks was unchanged. The delegates met in London in April,
albeit with few of the major Russian figures in attendance.

Lenin's admiration of the previous generation of Russian terrorists
led him to craft slogans that suggested Leninism was already taking
shape. He advocated "armed insurrection" and "mass terror" and disdained any form of liberal democracy.[14] In a pamphlet on tactics in July,
he ridiculed those who did not want "a revolutionary-democratic dictatorship of the proletariat and the peasantry."[15]

The tsarist regime held on to power by granting a constitution in
October, and Lenin assumed it was safe enough to return. The Romanov
dynasty and its advisers merely bent before the storm, however, and as
the unrest subsided, the regime clawed back many of the reforms. Lenin
was always aware of historical precedents, particularly the French Revolution. He also drew lessons from the failed Paris Commune that had
been defeated in 1871 (supposedly) because of reservations about using
mass repression. He knew he might well fail in all his efforts, just like the
Communards of Paris, and he wanted to leave behind a heritage that
would inspire the next revolution.[16] The lesson for him was that the only
answer to the utter bankruptcy of the tsarist regime was to use every
means available, including terrorism.

At the Fourth Party "Unity Congress," held in Sweden in April 1906,
Lenin managed (briefly) to bring the Bolsheviks and the Mensheviks
together again. Although he favored participation in the system provided by the new constitution in Russia, he was unequivocal in calling
for nationalization of the land, an armed uprising, and guerrilla operations.[17] Increasingly, he advocated a "revolutionary-democratic dictatorship of the proletariat and peasantry" and dropped the caveat that it
would only be "provisional."[18]

After the 1905–6 revolution Lenin went into exile again in the West.
Not everything on the revolutionary front lived up to his expectations.
He bemoaned having to deal with so many compromisers and "legalists"
whose will to power was not nearly steadfast and ruthless enough for
him. He despised all opponents, including even left-wingers who merely
disagreed with him. He wanted an elite party committed to him and the
cause as he saw it. He had no time for vacillating Socialists, much less
"philistine" liberals and democrats.

War in 1914 represented for Lenin the ultimate betrayal of Marxian internationalism. As he saw it, the war was waged in the interests of capitalism, but wrongly supported by Socialists and cheered by the masses. This turn of events was a vindication of his view that it was an illusion to attempt a democratic approach to Socialism. On the other hand, he was delighted with the coming of war, because he rightly saw that it would likely hasten the revolution he yearned for. That millions would die in the conflagration did not matter to him in the least.

However, against his expectations, the war dragged on interminably, and by early 1917 he had all but given up on seeing revolution in his lifetime. Thus he was taken completely unawares when the Russian monarchy suddenly collapsed, so little did he understand his native land and the government's crisis.[19] When the Romanov dynasty was deposed in February and a provisional government took over, he recognized that Russia had become "the freest of all the belligerent countries in the world." The new regime was all the more hateful to him, because it might seem to represent progress to those who could not see the underlying social basis. To Lenin the new system functioned to reduce revolutionary energies and was a step backward. The provisional government carried on the war as before, and the people grew quiet again.

In a famous article published in *Pravda* on April 9, 1917, he remarked that "the basic question of every revolution is that of state power." At the earliest possible moment that was what he wanted. He cared less about the fine words of the constitution makers or the advocates of civil rights. He preferred to say there was a "dual power," embodied by the provisional government and the Soviets. The latter had emerged everywhere on the model of those in 1905. In the short run he bet on the Soviets, even though the Bolsheviks had little support among them. However, that was a tactic to make it appear he and his tiny group stood for the people, particularly the workers and peasants, while the provisional government represented the bourgeoisie. The Soviets, he insisted, had the power of the people behind them, in the tradition of the Paris Commune of 1871.[20]

The German government, in the meantime driven to desperation, came to Lenin in Switzerland and offered to send him back to Russia. The provisional government allowed even outlawed revolutionaries to return home. And so Lenin and the Bolsheviks made the trip to Petrograd. He and thirty-one others left Zurich on March 27 in a sealed train and, traveling via Sweden and Finland, arrived in Petrograd on April 3. There was a hullabaloo in Russia that the Bolsheviks would even travel through enemy territory, but a month later some Mensheviks and others took the same route.[21]

Recent revelations from Russian archives show that before and after the Bolshevik Revolution of October 1917, Lenin received millions of marks from the German government to make antiwar propaganda in Russia.[22] He had disdain for patriotic Russians, including those in the revolutionary movement, for their "defensism." In his view, they were wrongheaded and failed to see that only Russia's defeat would lead to revolution.

The militants who gathered round him on his return to Petrograd were shocked by his demand that Russia leave the war at all costs, even if it meant giving away large tracts of territory to the Germans.

During the trip to Petrograd, Lenin composed what became known as his "April Theses," which formed his platform for what needed to be done. He said it was mistaken to support the new democratic government and nonsensical to aim merely for a bourgeois revolution—stage three of Marx's grand historical schema. According to Marx, history progresses through five stages closely tied to economic conditions: early forms of human community, feudalism, capitalism, Socialism, and international Communism. Lenin had been trying to prove for some time that capitalism already existed in Russia. He now urged his fellow revolutionaries to be bold and proceed immediately to stage four, that is, make the transition to Socialism. This conclusion had major ramifications not only for the coming revolution but for the development of Russia thereafter. What he really wanted was power, which he considered the crucial target in all revolutions.

Lenin's program was summed up in the phrase "All power to the Soviets," which was a cry to overthrow the provisional government. He expressly rejected a parliamentary republic and democracy as a "retrograde step." He wanted a republic of workers, peasants, and other kinds of Soviets. To mobilize that support, he was prepared to confiscate all landed estates and to nationalize all land—to be handed over to the peasant Soviets. He said it would be no simple matter to "introduce Socialism" and that it would have to be fought for with violence. A hint of his growing confidence and radicalism was that he wanted a name change, from the Russian Social Democratic Labor Party to the Communist Party.[23]

Throughout 1917 Lenin used another slogan—"Peace, land, and bread"—to highlight the Bolsheviks' social agenda. But he would not compromise with the Mensheviks, whom he saw as moderate and committed to issues like civil rights and mere reforms. Other leaders of the RSDLP (including Stalin) wanted the factions to merge.

The Bolsheviks thought Lenin mistaken to conclude that "bourgeois democracy," or stage three of Marx's historical schema, had already been attained when the provisional government took over from the tsar. They knew Russia as a vast, underdeveloped country, burdened with mass illiteracy and, despite what Lenin said, closer to a feudal than to a capitalist society. What they failed to understand was that Lenin's schematic thinking provided a rationalization for attempting to take power immediately. Once back in Russia, however, Lenin won over most of the Bolsheviks and wanted to expel anyone who disagreed with him.[24]

Stalin was elected to the new Central Committee, despite differences with Lenin. While he soon became one of Lenin's closest collaborators, he did not assume an important role in the events leading up to the revolution in October.

FAILURE OF THE PROVISIONAL GOVERNMENT

The pursuit of the utopian goals espoused by Lenin would never have had a chance if the provisional government had been able to make peace with Germany, but the new government put patriotism first, even as its armies were ground to dust.

The Petrograd soviet added to the crisis atmosphere when it immediately allowed soldiers to elect committees to run the army. They exceeded these instructions, abolished military codes of discipline, and even elected officers. Saluting became a thing of the past. Social hierarchies crumbled everywhere, including in factories, where bosses and owners were humiliated and assaulted. Peasants began seizing land and engaged in arson and murder. The old order was falling apart but still had surprisingly more support than is often assumed.[25]

The Bolsheviks tried to capitalize on demonstrations in Petrograd with slogans such as "All power to the Soviets" and "Down with the provisional government." There was rebellion in Petrograd and Moscow on April 20–21, which some have likened to the first attempt at a Bolshevik coup. Either way, the provisional government barely managed to survive this first major crisis.[26]

Alexander Kerensky was named minister of war on May 5 as part of a shake-up to cope with the situation. Much was expected of him because of his charismatic personality and fiery temperament. He was the product of the revolutionary times, but he symbolized patriotism, not an end to war, which would in fact destroy the provisional government no matter what else he might try. Kerensky and the new commander in chief, Aleksei Brusilov, thought victory over Germany was possible and wanted to fulfill commitments made to the Allies for an early offensive. They believed success would win popular support for the new democracy and give the government a strong hand to deal with rebellion. They suffered from illusions (shared by many Russians) similar to those that had led the tsarist regime in July 1914 to risk what elites and the patriots supposed would be a "short little war."[27] Russian estimates put the total losses in the war at 900,000 dead and 400,000 wounded by 1917. These casualties, the apparent senselessness of the war, and shortages on the home front led to a crisis across the great land.

Kerensky's gamble in June–July 1917 was that if Russia could win, all sins would be forgiven. The attack aimed at the Austro-Hungarian lines fell apart with the appearance of German troops. Again there were unacceptably high casualties, which came on the back of years of suffering. Kerensky reported from the front on June 24 that "after the first days, sometimes even after the first hours of battle," the mood of a breakthrough "changed and spirits fell." Desertions spread and mutinies threatened.[28]

These setbacks brought greater tensions than ever to Petrograd, and on July 4 as many as fifty thousand soldiers and workers prepared to storm the soviet and the provisional government. It is not possible to establish whether the Bolsheviks had planned a coup at that point or tried to take advantage of the chaotic situation. Lenin addressed a mass demonstration but, overwhelmed by the moment, failed to inspire the unruly crowd. He spoke only a few lines, issuing neither a call to arms nor a demand for the overthrow of the government.[29]

The crowds melted away, and loyalist troops restored order. The next day the press published a bombshell about Lenin's collaboration with the Germans and blamed the Bolsheviks for reverses in the war. Lenin went into hiding, aided by Stalin, who became a kind of special assistant.[30] They both branded the government the embodiment of counterrevolution but were sure Kerensky would continue the war, which would inevitably end in defeat.[31]

Indeed, on July 6, Kerensky returned from the front and just days later became the new prime minister after Prince Lvov resigned in disgrace. Kerensky named General Lavr Kornilov the new army commander in chief but kept the portfolios of minister of war and navy. His resolve to carry on the war was unbroken, but power went to his head, and he adopted scandalous habits for a Socialist leader. He lived in the luxurious Winter Palace and even slept in the tsar's bed.[32]

On July 18 the more radical Petrograd soviet was expelled by the government from the Tauride Palace and moved into the Smolny Institute, a former school for daughters of the nobility on the outskirts of the city. Whatever Kerensky's intentions, the new quarters created a distance between "the people" and what many considered their "real" representatives and the provisional government. The soviet was incensed not only by this move but by harsh measures that were reintroduced to restore order and discipline in the army and on the streets.[33]

Lenin drew rigorous lessons from the failure in July. The slogan he advocated until then—"All power to the Soviets"—had not worked. Henceforward he demanded simply "the dictatorship of the proletariat established through the medium of the Bolshevik Party." In a pamphlet he wrote in August–September 1917, he tried to disabuse his followers of the idea that there could ever be a peaceful "withering away of the state," as some assumed to be the meaning of Marx and Engels's famous phrase. The dictatorship of the proletariat, he told wavering comrades, could not be created without a "violent revolution." The old state machine and the resistance of capitalist exploiters had to be smashed. An impressive-sounding dictatorship—"the organization of the vanguard of the oppressed"—would take over and go beyond "democracy for a minority" and strive for a Communist society.[34]

Lenin brushed aside the criticism of the doubters, even among his closest collaborators, and heaped scorn on longtime Marxists among the Mensheviks. His anger knew no bounds when it came to enemies beyond these ranks. He hated compromise and was impervious to argument. He insisted on aiming for the mythical Communist society as if it were a realistic option and damned anyone who questioned an assumption. He had the rigid mentality of an extremist convinced, despite all evidence to the contrary, that he is on the verge of victory.

In the summer of 1917 Lenin believed the government would have the Bolsheviks hunted down and shot—which is precisely what he would have done had the situation been reversed.[35] But Kerensky faced a more immediate challenge than the handful of fanatical Bolsheviks, since the Germans, in a new offensive, had shattered what remained of the morale of the ten-million-strong Russian army. Between June and October as many as two million soldiers deserted, some even murdering their officers. The peasant army, fed up with war, wanted to go home and claim their share of the land redistribution. The Germans pressed their advantage until the Russian lines broke on August 22 and the way to Petrograd was open.

General Kornilov, now commander in chief of the army, was disgusted at the new government and on August 27 started toward the capital in mutiny. He did not want Russia to lose the war and at the same time was determined to stem the left-wing tide. He may or may not have hoped to depose the provisional government, but in any case ended up being branded as the embodiment of the counterrevolution. Kerensky sacked him and took over the post of commander in chief himself.[36]

If Kornilov had succeeded, he would have had the propertied classes on his side and driven out Kerensky. But social crisis was spreading by the minute, and it would have been impossible for such a right-wing government to keep the peasant army in harness and repress popular rebellion in the cities. Kornilov's advance on the capital was stopped on August 30 when his troops were met by the Committee for the Struggle Against the Counterrevolution, which comprised Bolsheviks, Mensheviks, and Social Revolutionaries. They told the troops of their general's treacherous plans. Kornilov was arrested the next day, and though the affair ended, it deepened the distrust of many soldiers, and tens of thousands began deserting each day.[37]

For months, and even years later, Lenin and the Bolsheviks used the phantom of the Kornilov affair as the right-wing conspiracy waiting in the wings to take back the gains made by the people. This supposed threat became one of the great excuses for introducing terror and putting off democratic reform.[38]

THE OCTOBER COUP

Kerensky's dilemma was that if he withdrew from the war, no matter how disastrous the situation, he would be attacked by all sides, including the Bolsheviks. But to keep up the fight would fritter away his credibility. His only real hope was that the Western Allies would destroy Germany, and soon.

On April 6, when it looked as if Germany might win and Russia might be forced out, America finally entered the war. The United States did not want Germany dominating the continent, but to save the fledgling Russian democracy, America would have to defeat the kaiser's army quickly. Yet Germany's own greed for Russian territory precluded making anything but sizable annexations there. The war had taken on a momentum of its own, not stopping until it devoured hundreds of thousands of more lives.

Kerensky called for new elections to a Constituent Assembly, to be held on November 12. That was the democratic thing to have done. Lenin was hiding in Finland, but he was insistent that Bolsheviks reject such an approach. He knew they would do poorly in free elections because the peasants would vote for "their" Social Revolutionary Party.

In mid-September, in two letters, Lenin tried (in vain) to browbeat the Central Committee into attempting another coup. Some comrades worried about preempting the forthcoming elections. But Lenin said, in a statement that represented his views perfectly, that "it would be naive to wait for a 'formal' majority." He added that "no revolution ever waits for that. Kerensky and Co. are also not waiting and are preparing to surrender Petrograd. . . . History will not forgive us if we do not take power now." He cursed comrades who wanted the democratic process to take its course as "miserable traitors" suffering "constitutional illusions."[39]

The Bolshevik coup was precipitated by a German offensive in September. A month later the Germans were preparing to land troops and move on Petrograd. Faced with this crisis, Russian military leaders met with the government and drew up plans for the evacuation of key offices and industries from the capital to Moscow.

On October 6, when these plans were published, there was an immediate outcry on the left that they amounted to a "bourgeois" trick to defeat "Red Petrograd." Three days later, in response, the Petrograd soviet—one of the few institutions where the Bolsheviks had real support—proposed the creation of the Military Defense Committee, subsequently renamed the Military Revolutionary Committee (MRC), to defend the capital. The Bolsheviks said the committee would carry the day against both German "imperialists" and the ever-present "counterrevolutionaries."[40]

Lenin was frustrated that other Bolsheviks would not agree to a coup. He was determined to get his way, however, and on October 10 returned to Petrograd for a meeting of the Central Committee. In an all-night session he won comrades over to the principle of making an attempt. He was too impatient to wait on the democratic process, which he knew he could never win. Thus he concluded, "It is senseless to wait for the Constituent Assembly which will obviously not be on our side, for this will only make our task more complicated."[41]

At this meeting, on Felix Dzerzhinsky's suggestion, a special politburo (political bureau) of seven was established. It included Lenin, Trotsky, Grigory Zinoviev, Lev Kamenev, Stalin, Grigory Sokolnikov, and Andrei Bubnov. Though Trotsky later said that nothing came of the committee and it never met, its creation showed that Stalin was already part of the inner circle.[42]

Another meeting of the Central Committee was held on October 16. Again Lenin argued they could not afford to dither about and put the alternatives simply: "either Kornilov's dictatorship or the dictatorship of the proletariat and the poorer sectors of the peasantry." The majority in the country might not be behind the Bolsheviks, but for Lenin that was no reason to wait. He ridiculed members of the Central Committee like Kamenev and Zinoviev, who disagreed, and, in a foretaste of the later Party purges, soon demanded their expulsion.[43] That was too much even for Stalin, who offered to resign from the editorial board of the Party newspaper. (The offer was not accepted.)[44]

While the precise timing of the coup remained open, the general strategy was to avoid the kinds of mistakes made in July 1917, and not encourage large demonstrations, which were hard to control. The Bolsheviks also decided to act not in their own name but through the MRC, and thus in defense of the Petrograd soviet. The first meeting of the MRC was held on October 20. By then the inner circle of the Bolsheviks had decided to develop plans for a coup and to use the MRC to carry it out. Lenin himself was kept at arm's length by the planners perhaps because they "thought he lacked the close knowledge and temperamental stability required." At any rate, he was not in the driver's seat during the last crucial days leading up to the revolution, but fuming away in isolation and writing frantic notes. He was not even invited to the three vital planning meetings held by the Central Committee between October 20 and 24.[45]

The key to success was keeping the provisional government and General Staff from calling out the garrison, as had happened in July. On October 20 the Bolsheviks sent two hundred commissars to speak with the garrison troops, and on October 21 the MRC arranged a meeting of regimental committees at the Smolny Institute, home of the soviet, to discuss the imminent danger of counterrevolution. Trotsky addressed the meeting. He was resolute in saying the country was "on the brink of doom. The army demands peace, the peasants demand land, the workers demand employment and bread." The only option remaining was for the All-Russian Congress of Soviets, due to meet on October 25, "to take power into its hands and secure peace, land, and bread for the people."[46]

The Bolsheviks promised troops the one thing they really wanted, which was peace with the Germans. Minister of War Alexander Verkhovsky spoke about demoralization in the army at a cabinet meeting on October 20, a message the government did not want to hear, and he was sent off on sick leave for daring to propose immediate peace. The General Staff began to lose its grip on most (not all) of the Petrograd garrison, which had 160,000 troops billeted in the city and another 85,000 stationed nearby.[47]

Some commentators have suggested that only a small percentage of these troops supported the Bolshevik agenda, but surely many were pleased with the slogan of the moment, "Peace, land, and bread." It is true that most remained passive during the events that followed.[48]

Beginning on October 21, the Bolsheviks (through the MRC) quickly found ways to loosen the hold of the central authorities over the Petrograd garrison. Troops were unnerved by rumors that they would shortly be sent to the front. At the same time, the Bolsheviks used the MRC—in fact little more than a front for a similarly named Bolshevik committee—to claim authority over the garrison in the name of the Petrograd soviet. The MRC asserted through agents it sent to meetings with the troops that the provisional government and General Staff were weapons of the counterrevolution. The MRC supposedly would have no choice but to assume control.

By October 23 the MRC had devised a plan to send small armed detachments to occupy the strategic points in the capital. All that was needed was an act by Kerensky that could be taken as a sign that the counterrevolution had begun. Almost on cue the provisional government closed several newspapers, two of them Bolshevik. The next day Stalin published a short article demanding revolution to bring "peace, bread, land, and liberty." He wanted a new government to "ensure the timely convocation of the Constituent Assembly."[49] It sounded democratic, but the revolutionaries would soon repudiate every word. The government responded by sending a small number of loyal troops to protect the Winter Palace and other vital buildings. The Bolsheviks portrayed these moves as the beginning of the long-forecast counterrevolution.[50]

Units of the army might still have been mobilized to stop the coup in Petrograd, had they been sent into action. There were loyal officers who rejected unauthorized orders from the MRC, and some members of the General Staff showed a willingness to resist. The MRC managed to blunt such opposition by keeping up a semblance of negotiations with the General Staff. On October 24, Kerensky vowed to prosecute the MRC and arrest Bolshevik leaders and mutinous sailors from Kronstadt. By that time, however, such threats were no longer realistic. He also put in desperate calls to frontline commanders but failed to get their help. He and many cabinet colleagues were still sitting in the Winter Palace but were defenseless against the coup already under way.[51]

In the early evening of October 24 and into the morning hours, the MRC used small bands of troops loyal to their cause or Red Guards (the latter created six months earlier) to take control of the railway station, telephone exchange, electricity plants, post offices, the state bank, and key bridges. The total number of insurgents was small, estimated at twenty-five to thirty thousand, or roughly 5 percent of the workers and soldiers in Petrograd. More were not needed, because the government was almost without defenders. Sometimes the revolutionaries merely posted someone with a picket in front of a government building or told the guards to go home.[52]

Late on October 24, Lenin finally came out of hiding and set off for the Smolny Institute, incongruously taking a streetcar to the world revolution. In disguise and with beard shaved, he was hardly recognized. Everything went like clockwork mainly because there was next to no resistance. His own belated role was important, but it was mainly to harangue, cajole, persuade, and plead with the Bolsheviks to go all the way.[53]

During lulls in the action and in anticipation of success, they began drawing up a new government. Trotsky suggested ministers be called "people's commissars," and Lenin chimed in to add that the cabinet be termed the "Council of People's Commissars." The labels stuck.[54]

By early morning on October 25, the coup was all but over. The only building of note still under the control of the provisional government in Petrograd was the Winter Palace. Kerensky slipped away in disguise at 9:00 a.m. An hour later, Lenin issued a press release, in the name of the MRC, which stated that the government had been deposed. As he quite misleadingly put it, "The cause for which the people have fought—namely, the immediate offer of a democratic peace, the abolition of landed proprietorship, workers' control over production, and the establishment of Soviet power—this cause has been secured."[55] In fact, none of these issues was settled.

There was no mythical storming of the Winter Palace as vividly portrayed in Sergei Eisenstein's movie *October*, scenes from which have been repeated in numerous documentaries. Instead, ministers and troops inside the palace kept waiting for word that Kerensky was returning with support from the front.

A few halfhearted attempts by the insurgents to get inside the palace were easily rebuffed. At 6:50 p.m. the MRC gave the remnants of the government an ultimatum, but that had no effect at all. They ordered shots from the battleship *Aurora* at 9:00 p.m., but the ship used only blanks to shake the nerves of troops guarding the palace. The defenders gradually melted away, with three hundred or so remaining until midnight. Some offered to fight to the last, but ministers decided to avoid bloodshed and told the would-be martyrs (among them a battalion of women) to surrender. The capture of the Winter Palace involved little shooting and few casualties—estimated at the time by one observer to be about ten.[56]

Sporadic violence and plundering followed, as opportunists took advantage to loot. There were in addition an unknown number of crimes against people, including murder. For the most part, though, the city remained calm. Scheduled social events generally went ahead, and people carried on as if little had changed.

Back at the Tauride Palace, a ready-made national forum was due to meet in the afternoon of October 25 and provided the Bolsheviks an opportunity to proclaim the revolution. The Second Congress of Soviets was supposed to convene then, but there was a delay because the Bolsheviks wanted to be able to announce the fall of the Winter Palace. Of the 650 or so representatives (the figures vary) who finally assembled, the Bolsheviks had around 300. As it was, they ended up with more than their fair share of delegates, because many of their staunchest opponents among the peasants and the army had refused to participate in the elections, so their representatives were not there to speak for them.[57]

A new presidium was elected from the floor. If the Bolsheviks were to follow democratic procedures, they would not be able to govern on their own. They had the most seats (fourteen) in the Presidium but would have to share government with seven Social Revolutionaries, three Mensheviks, and one Internationalist.

Such a result was just what Lenin dreaded. He was relieved when, late in the night on October 25, the Mensheviks and Social Revolutionaries walked out of the congress to protest the Bolsheviks' "military conspiracy."[58]

Yuli Martov, one of the leaders of the Social Revolutionaries, tried to prevent the rupture but was interrupted by Trotsky, whose words were recorded by the American eyewitness John Reed. Trotsky wanted no more compromisers and told the congress to let them go. "They are so much refuse which will be swept away into the garbage-heap of history."[59]

The politicians who marched out of the congress rejected the coup as a blatant attempt to preempt democracy. Three weeks later the voice of the people was even stronger in the elections to the Constituent Assembly. The Bolshevik Party managed only 24 percent of the vote and 175 seats out of 715.

The victors, with 40 percent of the ballots, were the Social Revolutionaries, who stood for giving land to the peasants. The Bolsheviks' electoral defeat was just what Lenin expected, and for that reason—no matter what he had said earlier—he had no intention of letting the Constituent Assembly meet.[60]

"Revolutions," Lenin once said, "were festivals of the oppressed and the exploited" when the masses could be "creators of a new social order." During such times the leaders of the revolutionary party had to act more boldly, "always be in advance" of the people, and provide slogans as beacons to show them "the shortest and most direct route to complete, absolute, and decisive victory." What he claimed to want was "real freedom" as brought about by the "revolutionary-democratic dictatorship of the proletariat and peasantry." He denounced all compromise, which he believed was based on fear of revolution and of taking the most direct path to the future.[61]

In December 1917, Lenin made the case for forcing through a vanguard dictatorship, in full defiance of the will of the people:

> We [Marxists] have always known, said, and emphasized that Socialism cannot be "introduced," that it emerges out of the most intense, the most acute class struggle—which reaches heights of frenzy and desperation— and civil war; we have always said that a long period of "birth-pangs" lies between capitalism and Socialism; that violence is always the midwife of the old society; that a special state (that is, a special system of organized coercion of a specific class) comes into existence between the bourgeois and the Socialist society, namely, the dictatorship of the proletariat. Dictatorship implies and means a state of simmering war, a state of military measures of struggle against the enemies of the proletarian power.[62]

Lenin's desire to pursue "real freedom" by dictatorial means undermined the project of democracy before it got off the drawing board. His millennial dreams for the peoples of the Russian Empire were to lead down a road of greater suffering and misery than anything in their worst nightmares.

2

ON THE WAY TO COMMUNIST DICTATORSHIP

The immediate task was to consolidate the coup. Lenin left the Smolny Institute late on October 25 while the Congress of Soviets continued until it adjourned its first session at 6:00 the following morning. It reconvened at 10:40 p.m. the same day. Lenin was not a charismatic orator during the historic meeting on the night of October 25–26. He was safely out of sight during most of the action. His contribution was not so much as a general than as a political strategist behind the scenes. While away from Smolny on October 26 he wrote three important decrees, on land, the workplace, and one-party rule. Together these were meant to have broad appeal and to radicalize the revolution. The first item on the new government's agenda, however, was the war with Germany.

It was widely recognized that without peace, Lenin and his comrades would not hold power for long. Certainly, the troops milling about Petrograd were tired of the fighting, and it was the pledge to end the war, more than anything else, that brought them over to the side of the new government. Lenin called on "all the belligerent peoples to negotiate a just, democratic peace" without annexations. He proposed an immediate armistice. More controversially, he announced the abolition of secret diplomacy and his intention to publish Russia's treaties with Western Allies to show the dirty dealing that went on behind the backs of the people.[1]

The "land question" was directly related to the war for the army of peasant-soldiers. Since July, Lenin had promised to give them land "without any payment."[2] That news won many rural folk to the Bolshevik cause. Landed estates were expropriated, as was the land of the Crown and the Church. This property and everything on it were to be turned over to the localities until the Constituent Assembly decided what should happen. The government said it would be guided by the peasants, as these had formulated and published their demands. Some "instructions" from the countryside sought the outright abolition of private property. Others said "the land has to belong to those who work it," while still others listed thirty-three separate claims.[3] The decree opened the door to violence and plundering but won support in that it gave official blessing to what the peasants were already doing.[4]

In another decree Lenin formulated regulations for workers' and office clerks' control of their workplaces. Its practical effect was to make it next to impossible for capitalism to exist in Russia. As one Red Guard later put it, the revolution was about not just material gain but also redressing wrongs. He thought it was bringing peace to the poor and war on the rich.[5]

The new regime aimed at a more radical revolution than anything seen in European history before. Perhaps only in such a poor country, where so many possessed so little, could such sweeping changes be seriously contemplated. The population of richer countries, like those in Western Europe, would feel threatened by such radical claims and thus came to fear the "Reds."

In a third major decree proclaiming one-party rule, Lenin followed his own plan to establish a dictatorship. The Council of People's Commissars, henceforth known by the acronym Sovnarkom, with Lenin as the chairman, was packed with Bolsheviks. Some left-wing Social Revolutionaries were invited to join, but they had left by October 27, unable to agree with what they called Bolshevik "political terrorism." Thus Sovnarkom (SNK), despite its populist-sounding name, heralded the beginning of what would become the dictatorship of the Bolshevik Party.

Stalin was named chairman for nationality affairs, an important position that gave him oversight over more than a hundred nationalities, many of whom (Poles, Ukrainians, and others) wanted to break away from Russia. Keeping the country in one piece was a challenge, all the more because of Lenin's well-known advocacy of national self-determination. The other major historical figure appointed to Sovnarkom was Leon Trotsky, chosen as commissar of foreign affairs.

Sovnarkom was supposedly responsible to the Congress of Soviets but styled itself as a provisional government "until the Constituent Assembly" could convene. Lenin was passionately determined, however, that the assembly would never meet.[6]

STAMPING OUT CIVIL LIBERTIES

Lenin's understanding of "real freedom" was soon clarified. The first civil liberty to be excised like a diseased limb was freedom of expression. Not forty-eight hours into the revolution a "decree on the press" was issued under Lenin's signature. This was on October 27, and it already marked the end of any hope that the new regime would be tolerant, much less that it would establish democracy. He boldly declared that he was keeping his promise to close the press of the middle class or bourgeoisie.[7] Any opposing opinions identified with their interests were anathematized. Henceforth, any newspaper that incited (broadly defined) resistance to Sovnarkom could be shut down. John Reed, the American who chronicled the revolution, noted but did not criticize Lenin's rationale during a debate in the Congress of Soviets: "We Bolsheviki have always said that when we reached a position of power we would close the bourgeois press. To tolerate bourgeois newspapers would mean to cease being a Socialist. When one makes a Revolution, one cannot mark time; one must always go forward—or go back. He who now talks about the 'freedom of the press' goes backward, and halts our headlong course towards Socialism."[8]

Leon Trotsky also spoke at length in favor of the resolution. He said that "during civil war the right to use violence"—this less than forty-eight hours into what was still a bloodless revolution—"belongs only to the oppressed." There were catcalls at the meeting: "Who's the oppressed now? Cannibal!" Trotsky pressed on to say, "If we are going to nationalize the banks, can we then tolerate the finance journals? The old regime must die: that must be understood once and for all."

The press clampdown did not sit well with all Bolsheviks, and Kamenev, Zinoviev, and others resigned from the Central Committee. (They would never be forgiven.) The new censorship appalled supporters of the revolution, who correctly saw it as a portent of worse to come. Lenin's excuse to Sovnarkom was that "the civil war is not yet finished; the enemy is still with us; consequently it is impossible to abolish the measures of repression against the press."[9]

His vision was decisive at almost every turn, but Trotsky, who later blamed Stalin for everything that went wrong, supported the same course. The few who resigned from the Central Committee or Sovnarkom over the suppression of the press and other antidemocratic measures quickly made peace with Lenin and begged their way back into his good graces before the year was out, even as he was establishing full-fledged dictatorship based on terror.[10] They put "the cause" before civil and legal rights.

SIGNS OF RESISTANCE

Despite Lenin's best efforts, the Bolsheviks' hold on power remained tenuous, and resistance began to form. On October 29 the railway union (Vikzhel) threatened to strike. Many workers wanted democracy, not a dictatorship. Lenin and other leaders tried to keep this threat at bay by promising to include other parties in the government and even allowed some left Social Revolutionaries back on Sovnarkom.

The peasants had their reservations, but they were a vast body with numerous and conflicting interests who could hardly vote as one. In their way they saw to it that the Bolsheviks did not gain a majority in the Congress of Peasants' Deputies that began in Petrograd on November 26. At the meeting Lenin and his Party adopted disruptive tactics that eventually led to a walkout of the majority (mostly members of the Social Revolutionary Party), whereupon the Bolsheviks and some left Social Revolutionaries dissolved the congress. Much more trouble would flare up in the countryside once the peasants began to learn what was in store for them.[11]

There was also significant armed resistance to the seizure of power in Moscow beginning on October 28 with pitched battles for control of the city. The Bolsheviks mustered fifteen thousand armed men, opposed on the other side by an equal number of troops and guards still loyal to the Kerensky government. The Committee of Public Safety in Moscow, led by Mayor V. V. Rudnev and the military commander K. I. Riabtsev, was determined to resist but did not relish being seen as part of the counter-revolution. They refused to hand over the Kremlin fortress in the heart of the city, and armed clashes dragged on until November 2.[12]

Another source of resistance was the civil service. During the week following the coup, when newly minted commissars showed up at government offices, white-collar employees refused to let them in. Various ministries joined to create their own strike. They had built a national coordinating committee by October 29 and called on all government employees to stop work. The response was positive and spilled over into the private sector. Banks would not open despite demands from Sovnarkom, which eventually dealt with them by nationalizing the lot. The new commissar of finance, Vyacheslav Menzhinsky, who was desperate for funds to carry on government business, was left with little choice but to authorize armed robberies of the state bank and other financial institutions until December.

The will of other white-collar workers was broken over several weeks, but in some cases the strikes stretched into 1918. The Bolsheviks eventually came to dominate the upper reaches of the civil service but in the short run had to rely on carryovers from the old regime. Initially the new commissars, barred from their own offices, often had to force their way into their ministry buildings.[13]

The opposition put its dwindling hopes on the elections to the Constituent Assembly called in August and due to take place on November 12. There was no choice but to let them go ahead. Given the vast expanse of the country and its backward infrastructure, the elections took two weeks. The Bolsheviks got 24 percent of the vote, well below the 38 percent gained by the Social Revolutionary Party.

Lenin minimized the results and claimed they were unrepresentative of the "people's will." Sovnarkom came up with one reason after another to delay opening the assembly and soon postponed it again. In protest the Union for the Defense of the Constituent Assembly was organized by a variety of people, including some from the Petrograd soviet, trade unions, and all other Socialist parties. On November 28 a large crowd of ten to twenty thousand that included white-collar workers on strike, students, and some workers demonstrated in Petrograd about these delays. They made their way through guards ringing the Tauride Palace and, once inside, tried to convene the assembly. The next day the building was surrounded by armed troops, and no one was permitted to enter.[14]

After this incident, and in the context of continuing white-collar resistance, Lenin opted for harsher measures. The liberals (Kadets, or Constitutional Democrats) were a convenient target, for they were considered the bourgeois enemy. Pursuing them distracted from the fact that the opposition was broad and growing. On December 1 the Kadet Party was outlawed and all its leaders arrested, a sure sign the terror was starting. To judge from a memorandum issued on December 12 and published in *Pravda* just over two weeks later, Lenin was leaning toward either abolishing the Constituent Assembly before it met or calling new elections. Most of his comrades shared those views. His statement was replete with code words about the "transition" under way from a bourgeois to a Socialist system. Their "dictatorship of the proletariat," he claimed, represented a "higher" form of democratic institution than a mere republic with a Constituent Assembly. He had a way with words, heaping abuse on anyone who opposed him. The struggle was pictured as pitting the virtuous workers and peasants against the "ruthless military suppression" of the nefarious "slave owners."[15]

REPRESSION

To stamp out resistance, the regime established three new institutions: the Cheka, or secret police; concentration camps; and the Red Army. Outbreaks of violence and looting made it necessary to establish the People's Commissariat for Internal Affairs (NKVD) on October 26. The NKVD had to secure their headquarters, and Felix Dzerzhinsky, one of the top Bolsheviks on the MRC, suggested on November 21 that they set up a special commission; by December 5, the MRC had been dissolved to make way for this body, which was in fact a full-time secret police. It would deal with the counterrevolution and with strikes and unrest.

Lenin's note to Dzerzhinsky prior to the Sovnarkom meeting on December 7 shows that he thought about "enemies" in social rather than only in political terms. The crackdown would be in the name of the "exploited" masses. Lenin's note—which basically formulated the rationalization for creating the secret police—said the decree on "fighting counterrevolutionaries and saboteurs" might run along the following lines:

The bourgeoisie, the landowners, and all the rich classes are making desperate efforts to undermine the revolution, the aim of which is to safeguard the interests of the workers, the working and exploited masses. The bourgeoisie are prepared to commit the most heinous crimes. They are bribing the scum of society and giving them drink to use them in riots. The supporters of the bourgeoisie, especially among higher clerical and bank officials and so on, . . . are organizing strikes in order to undermine government measures for bringing about social reforms. They have even sabotaged food supplies, thus threatening millions with hunger. Urgent measures are needed to fight the counterrevolutionaries and saboteurs. Consequently the Council of People's Commissars [Sovnarkom] decrees: . . .[16]

Following this colorful prelude, Lenin set forth a series of measures that were to be enforced by the NKVD. Sovnarkom agreed not to disperse until Dzerzhinsky presented specific steps to take. The result was the creation of the All-Russian Extraordinary Commission for Combatting Counterrevolution and Sabotage, or Cheka. Although Lenin's immediate worry was the general strike of state employees, it is obvious that he wanted to use radical measures against the "wealthy classes" and the "bourgeoisie"—that is, his opponents on the right—as well as anyone who disrupted the economy and a host of other people.

The minutes of the December 7 Sovnarkom meeting that discussed establishing the Cheka already reveal a striking propensity for extreme violence. The tasks of the new police were as follows:

1. To suppress and liquidate all attempts and acts of counterrevolution and sabotage throughout Russia, from whatever quarter.
2. To hand over for trial by revolutionary tribunal all saboteurs and counter-revolutionaries, and to work out means of combating them.

3. The Commission [that is, the Cheka] solely carries out preliminary investigation, in so far as this is necessary for suppression.[17]

It is one of the ironies of the Russian Revolution that the Bolsheviks, who had suffered most at the hands of the tsarist secret police (the Okhrana), should now invent an infinitely more horrific successor. Some have argued that neither Lenin nor his comrades envisioned that setting up the Cheka would lead to full-scale terror. However, that outcome was very likely, given how they also stripped away citizens' legal and civil rights. The results can hardly have surprised the Bolsheviks.

One of the best studies of the Cheka places the main responsibility for its creation on Dzerzhinsky's shoulders.[18] But Lenin was the driving force behind Dzerzhinsky. He never had a second thought about giving the secret police the upper hand over the rights of citizens. On the contrary, he invariably wanted more rather than less terror.

On January 5, 1918, the gathering of the elected representatives from across Russia in the Constituent Assembly could not be put off any longer. The Union for the Defense of the Constituent Assembly had taken up the challenge and campaigned to ensure the process went ahead. It planned a march to the Tauride Palace on the day the assembly was to meet.

Lenin and the Bolsheviks called in loyal troops. The demonstration, estimated at fifty thousand, was made up of striking civil servants, students, and others from the educated classes. There were not as many workers or soldiers as organizers had hoped. As the marchers approached, troops opened fire, and about twenty people were killed.

Here was another first. The Leninists were shooting at unarmed civilians, and even some supporters were quick to point to the uncanny resemblance to the tsarist atrocities on the infamous Bloody Sunday of 1905. The burials took place on January 9, the anniversary of Blood Sunday, and the dead were laid to rest alongside those killed by the tsarist forces.

Maxim Gorky, one of Russia's leading intellectuals, wrote a scathing newspaper account and wondered whether the new people's commissars—"among whom there must be decent and sensible people"—knew what they were doing. "Do they understand," he asked rhetorically, that they would "inevitably strangle the entire Russian democracy and ruin all the conquests of the revolution?"[19]

Lenin awaited events, and once he heard that the marchers were dispersed, he called the Constituent Assembly into session in hopes of ramming through his agenda. Only one resolution was put to the gathering—a Bolshevik proposal titled the "Declaration of the Rights of the Toiling and Exploited Masses"—which was soundly defeated by a vote of 237 to 136. In fact, every member of the house not in Lenin's Party voted against. Never one to take such complete lack of support seriously, Lenin used the result as an excuse to stage a walkout, after he declared the assembly part of the omnipresent counterrevolution. When the other delegates finally left early the next day, none was allowed back, the assembly was dissolved, and the building was sealed. The road that might have led to democracy was now irrevocably closed off.

On January 6, in an article published in both *Pravda* and *Izvestia,* Lenin announced that he was prepared to use terror in "the interests of workers, soldiers, and peasants" and to do what was necessary "for the good of the revolution." As he saw it, "the enemies of Socialism" were to be "denied for a time not only inviolability of the person, and not only freedom of the press, but universal suffrage as well. A bad parliament should be 'dismissed' in two weeks. The good of the revolution, the good of the working class, is the highest law."[20]

His explanation for abolishing the assembly was that the elections had been held "on the basis of electoral lists drawn up prior to the October Revolution," and allegedly reflected the outdated power of the "compromisers" and the Kadets. According to Lenin, the "bourgeois parliamentary republic" that would have resulted would inevitably have become an "obstacle in the path of the October Revolution and Soviet power."[21] On January 8, a new assembly met, the so-called Third Congress of Soviets, in which the Bolsheviks reserved a majority of seats for themselves. It passed every measure put to it, including rubber-stamping a law that made Sovnarkom the government of a newly created state, the Russian Soviet Federated Socialist Republic.[22]

A new constitution, quickly drafted by a committee dominated by the Bolsheviks, gave powers to central over local authorities. It restricted voting rights on the basis of social origins and political attitudes. The vote in the future would carry almost no weight, but even so it was to be withheld from a wide range of people—the so-called *lishentsy,* or disenfranchised. The *lishentsy* was not a firm category, but could include anyone who employed hired labor, lived from investments, or had been a trader. Also deprived of their rights were monks and clerics, former members of the police, the royal family, and anyone "convicted of crimes of greed and depravity."[23]

DEALING WITH GERMANY

Russia was still at war, and the terms demanded by Germany for peace were harsh. The Bolsheviks wanted to extend the armistice of mid-November 1917 and dragged out negotiations. With the exception of Stalin and others close to Lenin, they balked at surrendering Russian territory. On February 17 the Germans gave notice they were resuming the war, soon swept past demoralized Russian troops, and advanced on the capital. Lenin convinced the Central Committee to return to negotiations, but now got no response from the other side.

It was at this point on February 21 that Lenin signed the notorious decree—written by Trotsky—titled "The Socialist Fatherland in Danger." It mobilized the entire country, called for a scorched-earth policy in case of retreat before the Germans, and threatened dire consequences to anyone who might take advantage of the invasion. It demanded the immediate execution of "enemy agents, profiteers, marauders, hooligans, counterrevolutionary agitators, and German spies."[24] When the commissar of justice, Isaac Steinberg, questioned these measures, Lenin asked rhetorically: "Do you really believe that we can be victorious without applying the cruelest revolutionary terror?"[25]

Steinberg later wrote how exasperated he was. After all, they were discussing a decree with the potential to be misused, and Lenin was putting him off by claiming it was needed in the name of vaguely defined "revolutionary terror." In frustration Steinberg called out: "Then why do we bother with a Commissariat of Justice? Let's call it frankly the *Commissariat for Social Extermination* and be done with it!" Lenin perked up and replied: "Well put . . . that's exactly what it should be . . . but we can't say that." According to Steinberg, the "soil of revolutionary Russia was poisoned in that period; it was inevitable that in the future it should bear poisonous fruit."[26]

The Cheka announced it would show no more mercy to the long list of enemies. In fact, the new secret police refrained from wholesale bloodletting and focused on ending lawlessness in the streets. We do not know how many people were executed in the first half of 1918, but estimates put the number in the tens or hundreds, and not yet in the thousands.[27] Disorder continued in the capital following its bombing by German planes on March 2. The unrest spread after March 10, when the new government ignominiously left Petrograd for Moscow.

Lenin was convinced the German invasion would continue even though Russia had finally signed the Treaty of Brest Litovsk on March 3. This turn of events brought little joy to Russian patriots, because the once-great empire was forced to cede the western part of the country. The Germans took about one-quarter of the population, more than one-quarter of the industry, and even heavier percentages of the most productive agricultural lands and ore deposits. By signing this treaty, the Bolsheviks mobilized not just those who hated the new dictatorship but perhaps even more who despised the national humiliation.[28]

"SUPREME MEASURE"

In the spring and early summer of 1918, more opposition newspapers were closed and political parties outlawed. Lenin demanded that revolutionary tribunals (which existed from the start of the revolution) now be "mercilessly harsh in dealing with counterrevolutionaries, hooligans, idlers, and anarchists."[29]

The death penalty was reinstated in mid-June. Within a week one of the new tribunals used it against Admiral A. M. Shchastny, who thereby became the first counterrevolutionary shot "legally." Lenin advocated the death penalty not merely because it was "expedient," as some have suggested, but because he saw it as belonging to heroic deeds and radical change. As he put it at the meeting of Sovnarkom on July 5, "There has not been a single revolution, or era of civil war, without executions." So any revolutionary "who does not want to be a hypocrite cannot object to capital punishment."[30]

The regime showed a passion for renaming everything, and the new label attached to the death penalty was the "supreme measure." It was officially permitted for "social defense" and used against those defined under the new criminal code as counterrevolutionaries. In a "radiant" workers' state, where the death penalty could not exist, the only "logical" explanation for its use was that it applied to traitors. By 1936, after years of temporizing, even as it carried out hundreds of thousands of executions, the regime admitted that the "supreme measure" was not only a social defense but also a punishment.[31]

Lenin had long advocated terror and itched to get started. By mid-1918 he was ranting at comrades he deemed unwilling to shed blood. Commissar Moisei Volodarsky-Goldstein was assassinated, and Lenin upbraided Zinoviev in a stern letter on June 26, because he understood the workers had wanted to use "mass terror" in response but the Party in Petrograd had restrained them. Lenin roared: "This is im-poss-ible! The terrorists will take us to be spineless." That could not be allowed to stand. "It is necessary to applaud the energy and mass character of the terror against counterrevolutionaries, and especially in Petrograd, whose example *is decisive.*"[32]

Zinoviev responded belatedly to Lenin's criticism and favored more bloodletting than ever, stating as follows: "To overcome our enemies we must have our own socialist militarism. *We must carry along with us ninety million out of the one hundred million of Soviet Russia's population. As for the rest, we have nothing to say to them. They must be annihilated.*"[33]

Here was a "moderate" calmly contemplating the murder of millions of his own people whose "crime" was not sharing the dream of Communist utopia. Bloodcurdling statements such as this were rife in those days.

The Cheka purged and arrested the personnel of the old tsarist secret police and made up in brutality and enthusiasm what it lacked in experience. Bolshevik proponents of letting the Cheka run amok included Yakov Sverdlov, Stalin, Trotsky, and particularly Lenin. They defended the Cheka's ruthless methods. By mid-1918, it was organized in every district and armed with extensive powers to stop counterrevolution and fight class enemies.

Felix Dzerzhinsky said in a June 1918 interview that the Cheka's mission was "to fight the enemies of Soviet authority and of the new way of life." These enemies, he continued, were "both our political opponents and all bandits, thieves, speculators, and other criminals who undermine the foundations of the socialist order."[34]

In early 1919, just over a year after it was established, Cheka person-nel counted around 37,000, and that number grew to a high in mid-1921 of 137,106, with an additional 94,288 in the frontier troops. Its new title (and broad mission) in mid-1920 was summed up in its long name: the "All-Russian Extraordinary Commission for Combatting Counterrevo-lution, Speculation, Sabotage, and Misconduct in Office."[35]

Lenin's style of rule was to take a hands-on approach, especially when it came to the terror. He sent notes and telegrams by the hundreds to leaders in the provinces to apply the most draconian measures. He did not act alone, but was supported by Trotsky, Stalin, and others. In early August 1918, for example, he told officials to take hostages from among the bourgeoisie and to make these people "answer with their lives" if requisitioned grain was not delivered. He ordered the Nizhni Novgorod soviet on August 9 to create a dictatorial troika and "*instantly* com-mence mass terror, *shoot and transport* hundreds of prostitutes who get the soldiers drunk, ex-officers, and so forth. Do not delay." Anyone found in possession of weapons was to be executed, and unreliable ele-ments were to be deported.[36] The same day he instructed the soviet in Penza to put "kulaks, priests, White Guards, and other doubtful elements in a concentration camp."

He instructed comrades to be hard and heartless, as, for example, in Penza on August 11 when he told them to crush rebellion as follows:

The uprising of the five kulak districts should be *mercilessly* suppressed. The interests of the *entire* revolution require this, because "the last deci-sive battle" with the kulaks is underway *everywhere*. One must give an example.

1. Hang (hang without fail, so *the people see*) *no fewer than one hundred* known kulaks, rich men, bloodsuckers.
2. Publish their names.
3. Take from them *all* the grain.
4. Designate hostages—as per yesterday's telegram.

Do it in such a way that for hundreds of versts [one verst is about one kilometer] around, the people will see, tremble, know, shout: *they are strangling* and will strangle to death the bloodsucker kulaks.

Telegraph receipt and implementation.

P.S. Find from truly hard people.[37]

Seizing "all the grain" meant that the relatives of those not killed might well starve to death, and that was the point in taking it.

This state-sponsored terror came before the serious attempt on Lenin's life on August 30, which is usually suggested as the rationalization for the terror. In January 1918 there had been an attempt on Lenin's life, but he was not wounded. The commands for stifling the kulak uprising, rattled off by Lenin in early August, are worth mentioning as they give the flavor of his language and convey his rage.

His right-hand man during the revolution, Leon Trotsky, shared his views on the need for terror. According to Trotsky, terrorists were an integral part of modern history, and their methods inevitably grew out of intense political conflicts. In a pamphlet published in 1920, he claimed that the Bolsheviks were following the pattern established by the English and American civil wars.[38]

NEW CRIMINAL CODE

Karl Marx had postulated that ordinary criminals could be corrected through productive labor. Russia's new leaders adopted that principle, but then extended it to include political criminals. The theory was that the "humane" thing was not to shut criminals in a cell but to rehabilitate them through labor. As early as January 24, 1918, the Commissariat of Justice decreed that "all able-bodied prisoners should work."[39]

The underlying principle of the criminal justice system and the prison camps was that criminality was rooted in adverse social conditions. Once capitalism was replaced with the perfectly harmonious Socialist system, crime would disappear and there would be no need for prisons or police. In the meantime, however, something had to be done about criminals, and a new criminal code had been drawn up by 1922. "Compulsory work" was to be used to "rehabilitate" offenders.[40]

The new code dropped the word "punishment." Slogans in places of detention read: "We are not being punished: we are being corrected." The Party had declared in 1919 that "labor is the principal method of correction and re-education" of criminals, so the concept of "prison" was now dropped in favor of "places of detention." They told themselves that within five years all delinquents would be "converted."[41]

But criminality increased, partly because of social breakdown, also because the new regime criminalized completely new aspects of social life. Even though Lenin was nearing exhaustion and growing ill, he wanted to be sure that the "substance of terror" was in the new law code. He wrote to Commissar of Justice Dimitri Kursky on May 17, 1922: "The courts must not ban terror—to promise that would be deception or self-deception—but must work out the motives underlying it, legalize it as principle, in straightforward language, without any make-believe or embellishment." He said the death penalty should be used freely, including against those who only belonged to organizations whose (widely defined) aims were deemed to be the overthrow of the Communist system.[42]

FIRST CONCENTRATION CAMPS

Concentration camps were not invented by the Communists. Rather, they were established prior to the First World War and in areas involved in colonial wars. The Spanish general Valeriano Weyler y Nicolau, the new governor who landed in Cuba on February 10, 1896, had already decided he would introduce *"campos de reconcentración"* and use other harsh measures to repress the rebellion there. In a continuation of the Spanish-American War in the Philippines, Americans built similar camps in 1900 to hold rebels opposed to the new "masters." These "model" camps were copied by the British in South Africa against the Boers from mid-1900 onward. Unlike the relatively modest numbers who died in these hellholes during the Spanish-American War, the camps in Africa held over a hundred thousand women, children, and old people and resulted in more than twenty thousand deaths. The century of the concentration camp was born.[43]

In the Soviet Union the terms "concentration camps" and "forced-labor camps" (*kontsentratsionnye lageri* and *lageri prinuditel'nykh rabot*) were mentioned for the first time in the spring of 1918. Whereas those in Cuba, the Philippines, and South Africa were used against local insurgents, the Soviet camps were designed for their own citizens.

In May 1918, Trotsky said that rebellious Czechs (prisoners of war behind the lines in the east who escaped captivity) who would not lay down their arms would be sent to a camp. On June 4 he ordered camps for them, but on June 26 he went further and suggested to Sovnarkom that concentration camps be introduced for what he called "parasitic elements." At that time he was trying to create the Red Army and needed the expertise of former tsarist officers. They were reluctant, and to get them to serve, he resorted to threatening them with internment. In some cases he proposed holding their wives and children in camps as hostages. On August 9, as we have seen, Lenin mentioned sending rebels in Penza to concentration camps. Two days later Trotsky spoke of such camps for various categories of people, including counterrevolutionary officers.[44]

Several assassination attempts on leading Bolsheviks removed the last reservations about unleashing full-blown terror. Fanny Kaplan, the woman who shot but did not kill Lenin, had acted on her own in the name of saving Socialism from such leaders. A front-page newspaper story the next day proclaimed: "We call on all comrades to maintain complete calm and to intensify their work in combating counter-revolutionary elements. The working class will respond to attempts against its leaders with even greater consolidation of its forces, with merciless mass terror against the enemies of the Revolution."[45]

"RED TERROR"

Lenin had recovered from his wounds by September 3 and instructed Sovnarkom to form a commission. "It is necessary secretly—and *urgently*," he wrote, "to prepare the terror." This note was the key impulse behind what became the "Red terror."[46]

In an article in a Party newspaper on September 3, the deputy head of the Cheka, I. K. Peters, threatened "instant execution" to those found without proper papers, and "anyone who dares to agitate against the Soviet authority will be arrested immediately and confined in a concentration camp. The representatives of the bourgeoisie must come to feel the heavy hand of the working class. All representatives of plundering capital, all marauders and speculators will be set to forced labor and their properties will be confiscated; persons involved in counter-revolutionary plots will be destroyed and crushed by the heavy hammer of the revolutionary proletariat."[47]

In the same issue of the paper Stalin called for "open, mass, systematic terror against the bourgeoisie and its agents." The press also reported that the Cheka had executed over 500 hostages in Petrograd, but the rumor was that the number was 1,300 or more.[48] Lenin was involved in mass killings elsewhere at this time. For example, in September 1918, 25 former tsarist ministers and high civil servants were shot out of hand in Moscow. Another 765 so-called White Guards were also killed. Lenin personally signed the execution lists, thereby inventing another tradition that was carried on under Stalin.[49] Terror in the form of summary judgment and execution of political enemies or suspects rolled across the country. Dozens were murdered without trial in one place, more somewhere else.

On September 4, the press reprinted a telegram from Commissar of Internal Affairs G. I. Petrovsky. He complained that the terror was still insufficient. Assassination attempts on Bolshevik leaders continued, and there were revolts in Ukraine and among the Don Cossacks. He advocated "mass shootings" of suspects on the slightest provocation and wanted no wavering or indecision "in the application of mass terror."

On September 5, Petrovsky and Commissar of Justice Kursky signed a Sovnarkom decree that was regarded by the Cheka as the "official" beginning of the Red terror. It stated that the area behind the lines in the civil war had to be protected "by means of terror." Specifically, "all persons" involved in White (counterrevolutionary) "organizations, plots and insurrections are to be shot." The names of those executed were to be published. It was "essential to protect the Soviet Republic against its class enemies by isolating these in concentration camps." So the decree gave the secret police the right to execute suspects on the spot and marked the official birth date of state-sanctioned concentration camps.[50]

The day after the declaration of the Red terror, the *Krasnaja gaseta* (Red Journal) reported that the first camp for (five thousand) "class enemies" was to be set up at a former women's convent in Nizhni Novgorod.[51]

Relatively few camps were built in 1918, but there were more in the following spring. The political explanation on February 17, 1919, of the need for the camps was provided by a report written by Dzerzhinsky and co-authored by Kamenev and Stalin:

> Along with sentencing by courts it is necessary to retain administrative sentencing—namely, the concentration camp. Even today the labor of those under arrest is far from being utilized in public works, and so I recommend that we retain these concentration camps for the exploitation of labor of persons under arrest: gentlemen who live without any occupation [and] those who are incapable of doing work without some compulsion; or, in regard to Soviet institutions, such a measure of punishment ought to be applied for unconscientious attitude toward work, for negligence, for lateness, etc. With this measure we should be able to pull up even our very own workers.[52]

The camps retained their mixed aims as "schools of work" and labor pools for decades. They were supposed to have an economic role, teach certain social classes that the free ride was over, instruct the lazy, and provide a demonstration effect to society outside the camp.

The first type of camp was administered by the Cheka. They were called concentration camps and based on the demand for Red terror. A second type was under the Commissariat for Internal Affairs, or the NKVD (at a later point the initials for the secret police). In fact, the Cheka's facilities proved inadequate, and they sent thousands to the facilities of the NKVD or the justice system. At the end of 1919 there were 21 camps, and a year later there were 107.[53] We have only fragments of the statistics of men and women held in these places. In September 1921 there were 117 camps and just over sixty thousand prisoners in NKVD camps and around fifty thousand in perhaps as many controlled by the Cheka.[54]

Already by mid-1919 the Cheka had prisons or camps of one kind or another in all regions and major cities of Russia. During 1920 at the Kholmogory camp the Cheka adopted the practice of drowning prisoners in the nearby Dvina River. A "great number" were bound hand and foot and, weighted down with stones around their necks, were thrown overboard from a barge.[55]

In 1922 the term "concentration camps" was replaced by "forced-labor camps." But they went by other labels as well. Conditions in Cheka camps led to high mortality rates, and there were "repeated massacres," so estimations of the total number of prisoners may bear little relation to the reality. Isolated figures suggest that the scale of the killings was enormous. At certain points, prisons were emptied by shooting all the inmates.

PERMANENT CONCENTRATION CAMPS

Lenin firmly supported the idea of camps in the north, and on April 20, 1921, the Politburo under his chairmanship approved the foundation of camps in the region of Ukhta that could hold up to twenty thousand. Ukhta is in the northern taiga area, almost fifteen hundred kilometers by railway from Moscow. Other camps were soon created on Lenin's watch. Some thought was given to dissolving the camps in 1923. In that year a survey located twenty-three of them even though the civil war had ended.[56]

Instead of being set free, prisoners were transferred to the north, where the Cheka began setting up more camps. Dzerzhinsky used the Solovetski Islands—Solovki for short—to establish what later became known as the "northern camps of special significance." Boris Sapir, a political prisoner sent to Solovki in 1923, said that when he left in 1925, there were around seven thousand in the camp. By 1929–30 the Solovki system had been extended to the mainland, and the number of prisoners had increased to over a hundred thousand.[57]

The Russian organization Memorial estimates that for the Russian Republic alone in the years 1924 to 1927, the number of prisoners in the camps grew from 78,000 to 111,000.[58] If we extrapolate from the Russian Republic to all republics of the USSR, we might conclude that perhaps 200,000 people were then in the camps. An amnesty to celebrate the tenth anniversary of the Russian Revolution led to the release of half of them, but in 1929 the NKVD counted 118,000 prisoners in their camps and a year later 179,000.[59]

According to one survivor of the northern camps, until the mid-1920s prisoners met the needs of the camp itself but soon had to provide goods or services for the national economy. The contradiction at the heart of this system was that prisoners were treated so poorly that productivity wasted away to nothing.[60]

RED ARMY

The Bolsheviks created the Red Army as their other arm to defend the revolution. What was left of the tsarist armies dwindled away with the October Revolution, and the new regime had to find a way to mobilize a new force. In early 1918, Leon Trotsky took over the task, and by summer, as the situation on all fronts deteriorated, he had recruited former officers of the tsarist army. From the first days of the revolution under Kerensky, special political commissars had been appointed, and Trotsky continued this procedure. The commissars were there to maintain vigilance on the morale and "political reliability" of the troops and discourage desertions—which were and remained endemic.[61]

Trotsky pushed for universal conscription because there were not enough volunteers for the Red Army. The ruling Party disdained and distrusted the peasants, and the first call-ups in the summer of 1918 were directed at the cities and working classes. By November the Communist Party itself "volunteered" forty thousand of its own members, many of whom were lost in the war almost immediately. Inevitably, the draft had to be extended into the countryside, a move much resented by peasants.[62]

The number of deserters ran up to one million in 1918, and the next year went higher. Nevertheless, by the fall of 1920 the strength of the Red Army had reached an astounding five million. It prevailed against the Whites and all other forms of opposition. Thereafter the army was reduced in size but played a key role in socializing the population by schooling millions in reading and writing, thus winning many over.[63]

Although the Communists did not kill off all their opponents in 1917 or during the civil war, sooner or later they tracked down many. In wave after wave of terror they gradually destroyed all or most of the groups and individuals who opposed them during the revolutionary upheaval. The stain of opposition was indelible. It might amount to no more than the accident of being born a member of the bourgeoisie—the son or daughter of a shopkeeper, for example—but the mark could never be erased.

Such thinking was inherent in Lenin's project from the start. In a tract written two months after the October coup, he laid out what he wanted.

The old elites were supposedly waiting for the revolution to fail and thought the economy could not survive without them and without competition. Lenin said the workers and peasants still did not realize that as the new ruling class, they had to learn about accounting and control, particularly as concerned "the rich, the rogues, the idlers, and the rowdies." The people had to figure out what to do with such hangers-on. His language oozed with venom, and his imperative was

> to clean Russia of all vermin, fleas, bugs—the rich, and so on. In one place a handful of rich, a dozen rogues, or a half-dozen lazy workers will be put in prison. In another place they will have to clean toilets. In a third place they will be given "yellow tickets" after serving their time, so that everyone can keep an eye on them, as harmful persons, until they reform. In a fourth place one out of every ten idlers will be shot on the spot. In a fifth place a mixture of methods may be adopted.[64]

The Communists meant to abolish private property, collectivize farms, nationalize industry and banking, and eliminate religion. To introduce such changes against the will of so many was bound to foster resistance. Lenin counted on this turn of events to lead to violent clashes, but coldly and falsely calculated that the misery, suffering, and death would be offset in the long run by the establishment of the Socialist "new way of life."

3

CIVIL WARS IN THE SOVIET UNION

L enin, and Karl Marx before him, said that the ruling class would
never give in without a fight. Not only did the prospect of such
an upheaval not give Lenin cause for concern, but he took civil
war—with all the horror that would entail—as a sign the revolutionaries were on track. He had often said that such a conflict was the
logical and inevitable extension of class war and thus a vital phase of
the revolution.[1]

Marx was quoted by revolutionaries like Stalin as saying it might be
necessary to go through fifteen or twenty years of "civil war and international conflicts" in order to gain and exercise political power.[2] Lenin was
driven to distraction when other Bolsheviks did not grasp or agree that
Communism could be realized only by paying a heavy price in human
lives.[3]

The continuing war with Germany disrupted food production, and
soon there was a specter of famine. Lenin's reflexive response, as indicated in a January 14, 1918, Sovnarkom decree, was to use force against
private trade, speculation, and profiteering. He favored requisitioning
food from better-off peasants—the so-called kulaks. These people were
not an ethnic group, but negative attitudes toward them went back for

decades. Anyone could be labeled a kulak, from the person who lent neighbors money to one who kept a tidy garden.

The demands made by the new interventionist state rose as food stocks fell, and in the spring the Food Supply Commissariat began using force to get supplies from the peasants. After Lenin spoke of a "crusade for bread" on May 24, local branches of the commissariat, along with the Cheka and volunteers, created a veritable "food dictatorship." The system of setting grain quotas and extracting grain from peasants became known as *prodrazverstka* and was nothing less than outright confiscation. The authorities incited poorer peasants to a "merciless war on the kulaks," the latter termed the "village bourgeoisie." Anyone so stigmatized was in trouble if suspected of hoarding. In early June, Committees of the Poor (Komitety Bednoty, or *kombedy*) were set up to find hidden grain. The recruits from the urban unemployed were promised a share of anything they gathered. Special detachments set out to get food for the cities; by July there were nearly twelve thousand in this "food army," and by 1920 it may have been forty-five thousand strong.[4]

In the heady days of late 1917 and early 1918, peasants had been enthusiastic about Bolshevism, which promised them land without payment and encouraged them to pillage the bourgeoisie and nobility. By mid-1918 much of that support had faded. Over the next two years there were thousands of riots and revolts as the peasants fought back. What most of them wanted, as they had for generations, was free title to their own land. All such attitudes, however, as well as protests, were now labeled "kulak rebellions" and savagely repressed.[5]

ARMED OPPOSITION TO THE BOLSHEVIKS

The greatest internal threats to the revolution were in the Don region to the southeast, where in the spring and summer of 1918 several well-known generals assembled troops, particularly Cossacks, who were famous for their independent ways and fighting traditions. The White generals in that area included Lavr Kornilov, Mikhail Alekseyev—former army chief of staff under Nicholas II—and Anton Denikin, who was briefly succeeded by General Peter Wrangel.

A second front threatened from Ukraine in the west, where the

Germans continued to menace until the war ended in November 1918. Another point of attack was from the east, where in July 1918 a small Czechoslovak legion of former prisoners of war (about forty thousand) caused havoc along the Trans-Siberian Railway. There were centers of opposition in the vast area from the Volga to the Pacific, including one controlled by the Committee for the Constituent Assembly in Samara and the so-called Provisional All-Russian Government in Omsk. There Admiral A. V. Kolchak took over after a coup in November 1918, with vague intentions about getting rid of the Bolsheviks and saving Russia. In early autumn 1919 there was still another threat by the former tsarist general N. N. Yudenich from the Baltic.

Stalin's first role of note in the revolution, apart from his scrupulous support of Lenin, came on May 29, 1918, when Sovnarkom put him in charge of procuring food in the south. In June, Stalin went off to Tsaritsyn (renamed Stalingrad in 1925). The city on the Volga stood at the gateway to the North Caucasus grain-growing region. When Stalin arrived, it was defended by the Red Army under Kliment Voroshilov, later one of his allies, who recalled that Stalin took immediate control and demanded "open and systematic mass terror." He told Voroshilov to hold the Red banners high and "mercilessly root out the counterrevolution of landlords, generals, and kulaks and prove to the world that Socialist Russia is invincible."[6]

Stalin complained to Lenin that military leaders had devised a "bungler's" plan to defend Tsaritsyn. He organized a local Cheka to execute "traitors," and new plots were discovered daily. Stalin's orders were simple: "Shoot!"[7]

He craved military command and appointed himself head of the armed forces after arresting those who stood in his way. He devised a plan to defend the city, which failed and caused many casualties. New leaders were sent out, and they eventually drove the White Cossack forces back across the Don. Lenin would always forgive the sins of the overzealous, especially those of someone like Stalin, who declared his personal loyalty so often.

Stalin claimed to want to work with Trotsky, who had enormous prestige. Trotsky was the brains behind the Red Army and distrustful of Stalin, and by early October he wrote Lenin to have Stalin recalled to Moscow. Trotsky said Stalin was responsible for the "total anarchy at the top" in Tsaritsyn. Lenin went along but as compensation gave Stalin something of a promotion by appointing him to the Revolutionary War Council of the Republic.[8]

In his brief stint on the front lines, Stalin showed self-confidence, determination, and brutality. He never forgot those who stood by him, like Voroshilov or the cavalry leader and later marshal Semyon Budenny. Their personal loyalty mattered more than their competence.

WIPING OUT THE TSARIST DYNASTY

Lenin was uncertain about the fate of the Romanov dynasty, which was exiled to Yekaterinburg. Amid growing concern that the family might be liberated by armies from the east, Lenin opted for execution. The decision was meant to rob White counterrevolutionaries of a figurehead and to put an end to the question of a restoration in Russia. He ordered the executions, which were carried out on July 18 with the utmost savagery.[9]

Once the Red terror was declared in September 1918, the radicalization process quickly accelerated. Peasants were killed if suspected of holding back grain, and workers were shot if they protested. In the first two months of the terror some ten to fifteen thousand summary executions were carried out. In the Crimea, when the White Army withdrew in the early summer of 1920, an estimated fifty thousand people who remained were slaughtered by the Reds. Far from trying to cover up the crimes, the Bolsheviks lauded them as heroic deeds, sung praises in the press, and promoted the officers in charge.[10]

The Cheka killed and abused their victims without mercy. They robbed and plundered and in drunken orgies raped and killed their way through one village after the next. Completely innocent family men were arrested so that Cheka officers could take their wives as mistresses. Daughters were blackmailed into trying to save their families by offering themselves for the pleasures of some drunken official.

Suspected enemies could expect cruel torture, flogging, maiming, or execution. Some were shot, others drowned, some frozen or buried alive, and still others were hacked to death by swords. Just who all these "enemies" were depended on the whim of someone in the Cheka, the Red Guard, or the Red Army. The killers honed the practice of having those about to be executed dig their own graves.

The Cheka and Red Army faced a wide spectrum of revolt. In the coal-mining and metallurgical Donbass, or Donets Basin, an area that straddled Ukraine and Russia in the south, the Reds fought not only the Whites but also the Blacks (or anarchists) and the Greens (peasant armies). More than twenty different regimes were set up one after another in this area, and in the first months of 1919 alone some cities changed hands dozens of times. The victors carried out reprisals, tortures, mutilations, and massacres.[11]

The Bolsheviks also had to deal with Allied intervention. Troops came in the autumn of 1918 mainly from Britain, France, Japan, and the United States, but Germany continued to represent a threat even after the Treaty of Brest Litovsk. In early 1918 the Allies had sent small numbers of troops to Murmansk at Russia's invitation. The Western powers had hoped Russia could still be brought back into war against Germany, with or without the Bolsheviks in power.

When Germany was defeated in November 1918, the rationale for sending Allied troops to Russia changed, and they turned against the Bolshevik regime. Some Western soldiers assisted the Whites, but after the long struggle of the First World War there was little enthusiasm for a prolonged effort, particularly in the face of staunch resistance.[12]

The White armies kept up the pressure on the Reds until the end of 1919, by which time the major armed threats had been defeated and the Allies had withdrawn. The Whites who were mostly on the outside fringes of Russia, while the Reds held the vast center, were unable to gain and hold a real base of support but came to stand for restoring the old system, including returning lands to their "rightful owners."

The majority regarded the civil war, no matter who was winning, "as a plague that brought only death and destruction."[13] The Reds represented "no return to the past," and enough peasants took consolation in that. It meant they could hold on to personal gains made in the revolutions, but of course the Communists wanted more.

The first issue of the Cheka newspaper in Kiev from mid-August 1919 printed an article on the universal mission of the revolution:

> For us there do not, and can not exist the old systems of morality and "humanity" invented by the bourgeoisie for the purpose of oppressing and exploiting the "lower classes." Our morality is new, our humanity is absolute for it rests on the bright ideal of destroying all oppression and

coercion. To us all is permitted, for we are the first in the world to raise the sword not in the name of enslaving and oppressing anyone, but in the name of freeing them from all bondage. . . . Blood? Let there be blood, if it alone can turn the grey-white-and-black banner of the old pirate's world to a scarlet hue, for only the complete and final death of that world will save us from the return of the flag of the old jackals![14]

"JEWISH-BOLSHEVIK PLOTS" AND POGROMS

A major problem faced by the Bolsheviks in their multiethnic country was the nationality question. Stalin was the main theorist of Bolshevik nationality policies and in a 1913 book established the fundamentals of what would later become official doctrine. Socialists felt that anti-Semitism would disappear, like all other prejudices, with the great revolution. What was to happen in the meantime?

Following Stalin's theory, the Bolsheviks opted for giving the nationalities and ethnic groups in Russia regional self-determination or autonomy, but within a unified national context. The dilemma was how to avoid separatism. Stalin later tried to get around the problem with the 1925 slogan "Socialist in content and national in form." Boiled down to essentials, the idea was to allow all nationalities their language and culture, but not at the expense of the disintegration of the country or the communal effort to introduce Socialism.[15]

Stalin proposed granting cultural rights to Jews and treating them as a nationality like all the others. The Jewish minority in Russia came under pressure during the revolution and especially during the civil war. At the turn of the century there were 5.2 million Jews in the Russian Empire, roughly 4 percent of the population. Since 1791 and the reign of Catherine the Great, Jews were forced to live in what was called the Pale of Settlement and generally not allowed to reside in Petrograd or Moscow. Persecution led many to emigrate—over one million in the period 1897–1915. The provisional government in 1917 put an end to what remained of restrictions, and Jews began to move from the countryside to urban areas.[16]

Some Jews were drawn to the revolutionary movement. Their participation in the Bolshevik Revolution in absolute terms was not great, but five of the twelve members at the Bolshevik Central Committee meeting on October 23, 1917, were Jews. The Politburo that led the revolution had seven members, three of whom were Jews. During the stormy years 1918–21, Jews generally made up one-quarter of the Central Committee and were active in other institutions as well, including the Cheka.[17]

It was not that all the Jews were Bolsheviks but that many leading Bolsheviks were—or at least had been raised as—Jews. Inside Russia, and not only among the Whites, they became identified with the Reds and the terror. Indeed, the propaganda of the Whites in the civil war against the Reds "portrayed the Bolshevik regime as a Jewish conspiracy and spread the myth that all its major leaders were Jews." Many among the White armies came to accept it as axiomatic that the Jews deserved to pay with their lives.[18]

During the civil war, pogroms were carried out by the Red Army. The White armies, however, were the greatest killers of Jews. The White terror was not centrally directed and was sometimes more horrific when renegade troops ran wild. Major population centers like Kiev changed hands more than a dozen times, and thus gave the Whites the opportunity to find victims. Captured Bolsheviks were often brutally butchered, as indeed was anyone suspected of sympathizing with the "Judeo-Bolshevik" cause.

The accusation that the Jews were behind the Russian Revolution, which was part of a larger conspiracy to win control of the world, was common currency among White armies. Although the notorious forgery *The Protocols of the Elders of Zion* appeared well before 1914, it was popularized in Russia during the civil war. White officers carried abbreviated copies of the book and read it to their troops. The theory was that the Jews were behind the Russian Revolution, and it was considered "proven" by Trotsky's prominent role as head of the Red Army. Posters put out by the Whites showed Trotsky as a Jewish monster.

The murder of the royal family helped to turn *The Protocols of the Elders of Zion* into a publishing success especially among Whites and exiles. New forgeries updated the conspiracy charges. These "revealing documents" had aftereffects, and not just in Russia. They were widely published in Germany and found a ready audience on the right-wing fringes where conspiracy theories linked Jews to the disastrous end of the war and the rise of Communism.[19]

For many in the White armies, the nefarious role of the Jews was beyond dispute.[20] The catchwords circulating in the Donbass ran as follows: "Beat the Jews and Save Russia," or "Death to the Jews and Communists," and "Jews and Russians, Get out of Ukraine."[21]

Pogroms swept the area occupied by the Whites in the south. The scale of the murder was unprecedented. Estimates suggest that the number killed (in western Russia, Byelorussia, and Ukraine) was between 100,000 and 200,000. Sometimes the killing started with a rumor that Jews had "welcomed the Bolsheviks with joy." Their houses were then plundered and the women ravished.

The pogroms were worst in Ukraine and escalated over the course of 1919, growing with each setback suffered by the Whites, until the year culminated in both their defeat and mass murder of Jews, who were humiliated and tortured before being killed.

White officers claimed they "filtered" their prisoners for Jews and killed them because they were thought of as "microbes" or a "social disease" to be eliminated. What usually followed was the slaughter of defenseless women and children and men.[22]

For example, the Cossacks attacked Fastov, a small village near Kiev, on September 23–26, 1919. The prosperous village was home to some ten thousand Jews. The Cossacks went from house to house in search of money and tried to extort it with violence. Women of all ages were raped and sometimes ordered to shout, "Beat Yids, save Russia." By the time the Cossacks finished, they left behind between thirteen hundred and fifteen hundred dead.[23] Cossack troops also raped among their own people and shocked young Red idealists who came upon what happened.[24]

General Denikin, head of the southern White army, was disgusted by the pogroms but too weak to stop them. He did not want to appear "pro-Jewish" at a time when these passions ran high. Anti-Semitism filtered down to the troops, who tried to ascertain whether any of their prisoners were "Yids" and shot them out of hand.[25] The Red Army and other Soviet forces also raped and pillaged the Jews, though far less frequently. Lenin issued the mildest rebuke but said surprisingly little about the anti-Semitic rampages of the Whites. He felt no need to deal with the popularity of the allegations spread by "ultra-right-wing bodies claiming that the Bolshevik revolution was a Jewish revolution and that the commissars were all Jews."[26]

DE-COSSACKIZATION

The Cossacks had enjoyed special social and political status under the tsarist regime. After 1917 their regions in the south of Russia were identified as bastions of the old order and part of the hard-core counterrevolution. The Don Cossack government had even gone so far as to offer refuge to Kerensky's provisional government after it was overthrown. Some ordinary peasants wanted to see the status of the proud Cossacks reduced and the red stripes removed from the trousers of their distinctive dress. The approach of the Soviet government was far more radical.

On January 24, 1919, as the Red Army moved into the Don territory, the Communist Party's Central Committee issued detailed instructions on how to proceed: "Recent events on various fronts in the Cossack regions—our advance to the heart of Cossack settlements and demoralization among Cossack forces—compel us to give directions to Party officials on the nature of their work in establishing and consolidating Soviet power in the specified regions. Considering the experience of a year of civil war against the Cossackry, we must recognize the only proper means to be a merciless struggle with the entire Cossack elite by means of their total extermination." The document concluded: "No compromises, no halfway measures are permissible."[27]

This "de-Cossackization" visualized indiscriminate terror to eliminate these people as a recognizable ethnic group. The area's poor were to be resettled on former Cossack lands.

The Bolshevik president of the Revolutionary Committee of the Don set out to conduct what he called "an indiscriminate policy of massive extermination." In the month from mid-February to mid-March 1919, the Bolsheviks executed more than eight thousand Cossacks. Some tried to fight back, but it was hopeless.[28]

By 1920 the Bolsheviks had returned, more murderous than ever. By the end of the year the tide had turned against the Whites, and there were massacres on an unheard-of scale. The Cheka under Karl Lander went to the North Caucasus and the Don and, behind the fig leaf of using "tribunals," set out with a vengeance to "de-Cossackize." In October alone they executed more than six thousand people. In Pyatigorsk the Cheka decided in advance to kill three hundred in one day and took quotas from each part of town. Some locals capitalized on the misfortune of the Cossacks and used denunciations to gain personal advantages. Lander reported that the Cheka in Kislovodsk, "for lack of a better idea," killed all the patients in the hospital. Scores of hostages of supposed counterrevolutionaries were sent to concentration camps, where many died. An integral part of these operations involved the wholesale sexual exploitation of the women.

On October 23, the president of the Revolutionary Committee of the North Caucasus, Sergo Ordzhonikidze, one of Stalin's close allies, ordered the Cossacks to be killed or forced out. Their towns were razed. The most reliable estimates indicate that between 300,000 and 500,000 were killed or deported in 1919–20. These losses were suffered by a population totaling around three million at the time.[29]

Communist leaders expressed few reservations about these events. They were more concerned about whether or not they were on target to eliminate the "appropriate" groups among the Cossacks. They turned to "normalizing" those who remained under the heading of "eliminating the Cossacks as a socioeconomic class."[30] They thereby shamelessly sought to justify their ethnic-based massacres by incorporating them into the rubric of the "class struggle."

MORE TERROR

The Communists were unrelenting in their pursuit of "class enemies." Membership in a class was not defined "subjectively," that is, by one's values and social aims, but rather by "objective" socioeconomic conditions. It did not matter if members of the middle class, for example, were willing to change their attitude and even to embrace the Soviet system.

For the Cheka, the concept of "class origins" was almost the same thing as that of "racial origins." In November 1918, Martyn Latsis, one of the Cheka leaders, put it this way: "We are not waging war on individual persons. We are exterminating the bourgeoisie as a class. During the investigation, we do not look for evidence that the accused acted in deed or word against the Soviet power. The first questions you ought to put are: to what class does he belong? What is his origin? What is his education or profession? And it is these questions that ought to determine the fate of the accused." In May 1920, Felix Dzerzhinsky summed up the operating procedures of the Cheka as calling for "the terrorization, arrest, and extermination of enemies of the revolution on the basis of their class affiliation or of their pre-revolutionary roles."[31]

The classic account of the terror at the local level was published in the 1920s by the Russian émigré S. P. Melgounov. He had been a Social Revolutionary, but he had no need to exaggerate the horrors, and much of the evidence he used had been published in the Bolshevik press. His detailed and shocking account has been confirmed by recent revelations from the Russian archives and by historians.[32]

As the Cheka retook a village or town, they raped, murdered, and pillaged. Hostages taken to extort food or gold were often shot anyway. In a matter of months, thousands were executed. Historians only hazard guesses about the total, but in the Crimea, after General Wrangel (who had succeeded Denikin) was put down at the end of 1920, somewhere between 50,000 and 150,000 were shot or hanged. The witch hunt continued afterward, stoked by Lenin, who talked about how up to 300,000 more "spies and secret agents" in the Crimea should be tracked down and "punished."[33]

Large numbers of White troops and their supposed sympathizers were taken prisoner and sent to concentration camps, where an unknown number perished. A hundred thousand prisoners and an additional number of Cossacks were expelled from their lands and held near Yekaterinburg. In November 1920 a note from the Cheka there reported on the "incredible conditions" in the camps. At the same time thirty-seven thousand prisoners of Wrangel's army were held in Kharkov, and their situation was so bad that even the Cheka asked Lenin what could be done to improve things. He gave no answer, but his terse response was the same one he gave whenever he decided to do nothing. He scribbled on the note that it be shelved and sent "to the archive."[34]

FAMINE AND FAILURE TO EXPORT REVOLUTION

Lenin and his comrades believed that by its very nature, Socialist revolution could not, and should not, be restricted to Russia. It is true that Stalin was more skeptical about revolution in the West and for that reason wanted peace with the Germans in January 1918.[35] He was at least in this judgment out of step with the Leninist viewpoint, according to which the Bolsheviks would lead the workers of the world in a grand and final assault on international capitalism. Thus, for the Russian Revolution to finish what it started, similar upheavals had to occur in the West and eventually throughout the world. The Soviets were encouraged by some rebellions in Germany, Austria, and elsewhere, but these were easily put down. When people in Europe were given a choice, most wanted nothing to do with Communism.

By the end of 1919, Lenin and the Bolsheviks grew bolder in their ambitions to spread Communism to the West. The new Polish government under Marshal Józef Pilsudski, deeply anti-Communist and anti-Russian, became increasingly aggressive. By January 1920, Trotsky was already anticipating an attack and wrote Lenin of the need to mobilize Polish Communists for the front. Both sides threatened war.[36]

Pilsudski struck first, sending his armies into action on April 26. By early May they had captured Kiev, but by June 13 not only had the Polish advance been stopped, it had begun to be reversed. Russian patriots, even military men who despised the Reds, responded to the threat, and a vigorous campaign soon pushed the Poles back. Lenin was not alone in thinking they could turn the fury into a "revolutionary war" through which he would bring Communist revolution to the West.[37]

The scale of Lenin's illusions was monumental. His view was that he would liberate the Polish working class and bring Socialism there, as well as to other countries, such as Hungary, Romania, Czechoslovakia, Austria, and Germany. Convinced that the working classes in all these countries would greet the Red Army as liberators, he ordered it to pursue the retreating Polish forces. On July 19, 1920, the Second Congress of the Communist International (Comintern) met with all the signs pointing to victory. The congress sent its greetings to the Red Army and said it was fighting "not only in the interest of Soviet Russia, but also in the interest of all laboring mankind, for the Communist International." Delegates, like Lenin, fully anticipated that revolution would sweep Poland and the rest of Europe. But the Communists completely miscalculated the reaction of the Poles, who, far from greeting the Red Army, rallied to the flag as the Reds approached Warsaw on August 12. Four days later Pilsudski led a successful counteroffensive, and the war closed to the disadvantage of the Soviet Union.[38]

Lenin never admitted his colossal error in judgment, and he was not alone. Even "moderates" like Nikolai Bukharin, though surprised by the war, soon favored carrying the campaign beyond Warsaw, "right up to London and Paris."[39]

While the Red Army was on Russia's western front, still more peasant uprisings broke out in disparate parts of the country. The Communists, forever concerned to identify conspiracies, labeled these "kulak revolts," but the hundreds of isolated events actually represented last-ditch efforts to resist the Soviet system.

The requisitioning brigades sent out to the countryside to collect foodstuffs used methods that brought torment and affliction. The amount of food demanded far exceeded what peasants could deliver, but the brigades tried to extort "hidden food" by using torture, public humiliation, rape, and pillage.

The food supply problem continued to worsen because the civil war disrupted the rural economy. Nevertheless, the Communists who turned up in villages demanded more, not less, to the point that the peasants were driven to starvation. Secret reports of the Cheka on public opinion (*svodki*) in the countryside reveal a swell of feeling against the Communist system. Armed with what they could find, the peasants banded together and in 1920 killed an estimated eight thousand members of the "requisition" teams. Word spread, and peasant armies numbering into the tens of thousands came together.[40]

The leaders of these rebellions were men like Alexander Antonov, who had previously fought for the Reds against the Whites. He had almost the entire Tambov Province behind him. In other parts of rural Russia, peasant armies rolled back Moscow's control. By early 1921, Antonov himself had gathered a force estimated between twenty and fifty thousand.[41]

The Communist regime was also faced with workers who could take no more of the harsh measures and went on strike. There was a protest of ten thousand in Moscow on February 23, 1921, and the example was followed in Petrograd. Workers called for liberation from oppression and the return of freedom of speech, press, and assembly. These were alarming developments for Communist leaders, who were doubly shocked when mutinies broke out at the Kronstadt naval base.

The sailors there were renowned for their support of the Bolsheviks during the coup in 1917, and their mutiny was symbolic of the backlash across the country. The sailors held out until March 17, when the rebellion was savagely put down. Red Army troops back from Poland, led by the hard-nosed general Mikhail Tukhachevsky, captured thousands, who were deported to the camps. There they suffered a lingering death or were executed.

The Tenth Party Congress of the Communist Party met at this very time (beginning on March 8, 1921) in Moscow. Lenin admitted that the peasant uprisings against Communist taxation policy were worrisome and realized that he would have to back off somewhat. His proposal was that the peasants pay tax in kind, instead of having to submit to "requisitions," that they be allowed to sell some of what they produced once the tax was paid, and that the tax itself be reduced. There was concern among some in the Party that Lenin might be advocating a return to capitalism.

But his proposals were reluctantly accepted as the New Economic Policy, or NEP—on which more below. No doubt the events in Kronstadt helped to convince doctrinaire members of the Party of the necessity of supporting the changed approach, but they bent to the uncomfortable facts ever so grudgingly.

Tukhachevsky was given a month to pacify the Tambov Province and began operations in late May. By June he had deployed a force of over a hundred thousand, but that number was insufficient, because the guerrillas relied on the sympathies of the population. To break the back of that support, the Red Army engaged in systematic terror. Thousands of hostages, including members of families of known guerrillas, were thrown into hastily constructed concentration camps in order to force peasant soldiers to give themselves up. Lenin supported the cruelest measures.[42]

By mid-June, Antonov's army had been surrounded and destroyed, and he himself was eventually tracked down and killed. Although the full casualties suffered in Tambov Province will never be known, estimates suggest that around a hundred thousand were imprisoned or deported and as many as fifteen thousand executed.[43]

The violence and destruction of the revolution and the civil war left the country's economy in a shambles, with production in large-scale industry in 1921 reduced to one-fifth of what it had been in 1913.[44] It was as bad or worse in the countryside. In 1920, the harvest was around half its pre-1914 levels, and the next year it was down still more.[45] The countryside also suffered from drought in 1920 and 1921 that affected the Volga Basin, the Asiatic frontier, and southern Ukraine and produced widespread famine. It was a normal practice in areas like the Volga for peasants to prepare for periodic droughts by setting aside enough grain to tide them over. However, such "surpluses" were now requisitioned, even when the area was hit by famine. The new Soviet government, refusing to acknowledge the serious situation, continued to export grain. Moreover, even though the NEP, which was supposed to alleviate the burden on peasants, was officially under way, requisitions continued with devastating effects.

A group of leading figures in Russia, including authors and well-known scientists, turned to Lenin and got his reluctant approval to appeal for support abroad. On July 13, 1921, Maxim Gorky asked for help from the international community.

Herbert Hoover, secretary of commerce and later president of the United States and usually identified with the Great Depression, responded positively, and the American Relief Administration (ARA), created to help postwar Europe, began supplying tons of food and other essentials to Russia. By the summer of 1922 the ARA was feeding nearly eleven million people a day.[46] It also supplied seed grain, which made it possible for the Soviets to grow their own grain and eventually overcome the famine.

Soviet Communists never understood American philanthropy, did not trust the ARA, and had its operations carefully watched. In fact, many of the Russian notables who mobilized the help were arrested. Lenin saw to it that Gorky, once a supporter, was driven out of the country "for health reasons." Nothing could be allowed to tarnish the glitter of the new Soviet system.[47]

The Americans were appalled to discover that even at the height of the famine the Soviet government was still exporting large quantities of its own grain, supposedly to finance industrialization. A Russian historian who says that the American aid saved millions of lives was shocked to learn that Lenin robbed his own people's taxes, supposedly to purchase grain abroad "but in reality to finance revolution throughout the world and to force the creation of more and more new Communist parties." Considerable sums were sent to agents in 1921, including those in Czechoslovakia, Germany, Italy, America, England, the Balkans, Sweden, and Switzerland. It would be impossible to take seriously the suggestion that Lenin had given up on world revolution and all this was just a bluff.[48]

Lenin's health began to suffer, and from mid-1921 onward his activities were restricted. He was incapable of sustained work and by the end of the year had taken seriously ill again. The misery dragged on for just over another year, punctuated by collapses that left him incapacitated.

Stalin was not merely an aberration or corruption of Leninism. He was also an exploiter, building on the Leninism he inherited and promoted to his own political advantage. Although he eventually introduced many changes, these were variations on policies and practices already established or well rehearsed under Lenin. Thus it is a distortion of history to compare the Soviet Union under Stalin with other dictatorships if we do not take into account the first years of the new regime and Lenin's crucial role.

PART TWO

THE RISE OF GERMAN
NATIONAL SOCIALISM

4

NAZISM AND THE THREAT OF BOLSHEVISM

Adolf Hitler was born in Braunau am Inn, Austria-Hungary, and grew up in Linz. He flirted with art and architecture, lived for a while in Vienna, but led an aimless existence. Throughout these years he held warm feelings about Germany but gave little or no indication of the fanatical nationalist, rabid anti-Semite, and heartless warmonger he was to become. He moved to Munich on May 25, 1913, a little more than a year before the First World War. Although at one point in his autobiography he called the time he spent in Linz the happiest of his life, he said much the same about prewar Munich. In fact he lived an isolated existence in that city as well. Later, when trying to establish a National Socialist identity for himself, he claimed he had talked about politics with like-minded people. They were all convinced "that the question of the future of the German nation was the question of destroying Marxism."[1]

Although there has been a great deal of speculation about when Hitler became anti-Semitic, before 1919 there is no reliable evidence of the hatred and hostility toward Jews of his later years. The First World War and particularly its immediate aftermath in Munich were the catalysts that turned Hitler into the most radical anti-Semitic politician in German history.[2]

On June 28, 1914, Franz Ferdinand, archduke of Austria, was assassinated in Sarajevo, and a diplomatic crisis brewed throughout July. In Munich, from July 26 onward, there were signs of popular support for Austria, and on August 1 the German government finally declared war on Russia and began mobilization. The next day, a Sunday, Hitler was among the thousands gathered at the Feldherrnhalle in downtown Munich to show their support.

Just over two weeks later he volunteered to serve and was accepted. After brief training he was assigned to the Bavarian Reserve Infantry Regiment 16. The volunteers who served in it included students from Munich, as well as members of the educated middle class, but most came from rural areas. Training was complete by late October, and the regiment was sent to Flanders, where it was thrown into what was already a hopeless situation and suffered staggering losses, estimated at around 70 percent. Hitler wrote to friends in early November that of the original 3,600 men in the regiment, only 611 remained. He also told them he had been promoted to corporal (retroactive to November 1). Although he was generally liked by his comrades, he remained a loner and somewhat of an eccentric.[3]

Hitler went on leave to Berlin on September 10, 1918, but by that time the situation had deteriorated, and he was disgusted at the lack of commitment to the war. He was hardly back in Flanders when he was injured in a gas attack on the night of October 13–14. Temporarily blinded, he was sent to a field hospital to recover. Almost exactly a week later he was admitted to the hospital in Pasewalk, near Stettin, where he was treated until November 19 and released. While he was in Pasewalk, not only did Germany suffer defeat, but on November 9 a revolution broke out, a turn of events that left an emotional scar he carried the rest of his life.[4]

SOCIAL REVOLUTION

German casualties in the First World War were staggering, with 2.4 million dead, or 18.5 percent of the 13 million who wore the uniform. Another 4.8 million had been wounded, and, of these, 2.7 million died prematurely. Practically no family was unaffected by death or long-term disability.[5]

In Berlin, on the evening of November 7, the MSPD (Majority Socialists) issued an ultimatum demanding among other things the abdication of Kaiser Wilhelm II. Chancellor Prince Max of Baden asked Friedrich Ebert, the Socialist leader, whether he was prepared to join him in a fight against upheaval, but was told that if the kaiser did not abdicate, the situation would get out of hand. Ebert said he did not want revolution; "in fact, I hate it like the sin."[6]

By 11:00 a.m. on November 9, Prince Max had informed the press of the kaiser's imminent abdication and of his own decision to resign. By early afternoon Philipp Scheidemann of the MSPD had declared a "German Republic" before the crowds from a balcony of the Reichstag. Two hours later Karl Liebknecht of the more radical Independent Social Democratic Party (USPD) proclaimed a "Free Socialist Republic of Germany." This was the long-awaited revolution, but it brought little satisfaction to anyone.

There was initially outer calm with the nonviolent transition from monarchy to republic. The great majority accepted that the days of the kaiser were over. For all that, November 9 marked what became in retrospect one of the most emotionally laden days in German history. Hitler and the nationalist right promptly regarded it as a "stab in the back" of the troops. The home front supposedly let down the battlefront. This myth was constructed by the military, but to Hitler and millions more it became an article of faith. They called Socialists like Ebert, Scheidemann, Liebknecht, and their comrades the "November criminals," a code word for everything the right hated—particularly Marxists and Jews.

An armistice began to be negotiated on November 6 and was finally signed on November 11. The guns fell silent on the western front, but in the east the situation was more complex. Soviet Russia posed a threat to Europe, and in Germany there was fear of an invasion. There soon developed a "basic consensus" between the new Socialists in power and the "old elites" that the attempt by the Bolsheviks to take over the Baltic area had to be stopped. The Allies shared this view, and notwithstanding their demands to disarm, they agreed that German troops could fight on for the Baltic. The "great fear" in 1918—which was Lenin's great hope—was that Bolshevism would spread to the West and particularly Germany and Austria.[7]

When Hitler left the Pasewalk hospital on November 19, the country was still in the throes of revolution. He arrived in Munich two days later to find the Bavarian monarchy gone. Even more improbably, given that region's traditionalist and religious culture, the monarchy had been replaced by a radical Council Republic led by Kurt Eisner, a Socialist and not even a Bavarian.

On a personal level, Hitler felt fortunate to be allowed to remain in the army, given the shortage of jobs and general upheaval. But he hardly jumped at the opportunity to get involved in the revolution, perhaps because, with his world turned into chaos, he did not know what to do. For many such people, what was outrageous about Eisner was not just his radicalism but that he was a Jew. For right-leaning people, Marxism and Socialism became synonymous with Bolshevism and entangled with anti-Semitism.

The fear of Bolshevism was also evident among delegates to the First General Congress of the Workers' and Soldiers' Councils held in Berlin, December 16 to 21. This congress determined the shape of the new republic. The 514 representatives were divided as follows: the MSPD (Majority Socialists) had around 300, the USPD (Independent Social-ists) about 100, with the remainder either left-liberal or without party affiliation. Reflecting their lack of support, Rosa Luxemburg and Karl Liebknecht—the leaders of the ultra-left Socialists in the Spartacus group—were not even elected. The Russian Bolshevik leader Karl Radek, Lenin's representative, and illegally in Germany since Decem-ber 19, supported the radicals. His presence alone confirmed the worst right-wing fears.

The First General Congress firmly rejected (344 to 98) the motion to base the new republic on a council system along the lines of the Soviet Union. Several speakers pointed to the Russian example as one they did not want to follow. The congress decided by an even larger majority (400 to 50) to hold early national elections for January 19, 1919.[8]

Germany was a land of property owners, where millions had invest-ments in stocks, bonds, and savings. The country also had a pension and welfare system that helped integrate state and society. Most workers were opposed to Communism, and even radical left-wingers were not anxious to emulate the Bolsheviks. According to Arthur Rosenberg, eventually a loyal member of the Communist Party, if they had run candidates in what were the first elections in the new republic (January 1919), they would likely have received a "maximum" of 1 percent of the vote. Workers tended to be trade-union oriented, wanting gradual improvements in benefits, an approach despised by Lenin because it meant making the system work rather than destroying it.[9]

Despite the desperate situation at war's end, Germans were not quite ready to embrace even moderate Socialism. Of the first six regional elections held from November 1918 to January 1919, the MSPD won majorities in only two. These public attitudes were confirmed by the national elections in January. There the MSPD gained 37.9 percent of the vote and the USPD 7.6 percent. Even if they could bury their differences, they did not have an absolute majority. Liberal parties did surprisingly well with 18.5 percent; and the Catholic Center Party gained 19.7 percent. Conservative and more right-wing parties mustered between them only 14.7 percent of the vote, a sign that they were discredited for identifying so heavily with the war.[10]

Worries about a "Red scare" did not go away in Germany, and even if popular support for far-left radicals was minimal, that did not mean there was no basis for concern. After all, the Bolsheviks had little backing in Russia and never intended to wait for a majority to claim all power.

Lenin wanted the world. His idea of a vanguard party, which was to "enlighten" and direct the workers, was not meant to be restricted to the Soviet Union. In March 1919 he created the Communist International (Comintern). He said that the Russian Revolution could not stand on its own and pleaded for the world proletariat to support it. This was the rationale for spreading Russian-style Communism, including by force of arms. At the second annual meeting of the Comintern in July–August 1920, he stipulated that Communist parties everywhere had to agree to twenty-one conditions, accepting "iron proletarian centralism," that is, subordinating themselves completely to Moscow. Lenin's top-down approach inside the USSR logically extended to Communist parties everywhere. The Soviets wanted Western counterparts to create "cells" in key social institutions, recognizing the "impossibility of gaining majorities in favor of Communism, even in the working class, until after the revolution." Lenin and Trotsky hoped there would ultimately be Bolshevik-style coups in the West with Moscow leading the way and standing at the head of the world revolution.[11]

The continuing efforts of the Soviet Union to export revolution heightened anxiety about the Reds and helped fuel the rise of radical right-wing parties, such as the obscure one that Hitler discovered in Munich when he returned there at war's end.

COMMUNISTS IN MUNICH

Kurt Eisner, leader of the USPD, persisted as head of government in Bavaria, even though what he stood for was completely out of place there. That point was shown by the first state (Landtag) elections held on January 12, 1919. Eisner was defeated, and the USPD finished last, winning less than 2 percent of the vote and only 3 seats out of 180. The Catholic Party in Bavaria (BVP) did best (66 seats), followed by the MSPD (61) and the Democrats (25). Eisner dithered for more than a month, but on his way to tender his resignation on February 21, he was assassinated by a right-wing extremist, Count Anton Arco-Valley. Scarcely an hour later, perhaps in retaliation, a member of the Revolutionary Workers' Council entered the Landtag and shot (among others) the leader of the Bavarian SPD, Erhard Auer, who survived the assassination attempt.[12]

The German Communist Party (KPD) was founded in meetings held December 30, 1918, to January 1, 1919. The USSR tried to send a delegation, but the German military stopped them at the border. One of the first things Karl Radek discussed with Rosa Luxemburg, a key figure of the Spartacus group, was the use of terror. She had reservations, but her colleague Karl Liebknecht "warmly supported" Radek. His only quibble was to ask why the Cheka was "so cruel." Radek's argument was simple: "We plan for world revolution [and] we need a few years' grace. How can you deny the need for terror under those circumstances?" Leninists like Radek believed a "real" Socialist revolution was just around the corner.[13]

An ill-considered mass demonstration in Berlin took place on January 5. It was sparked by the attempted dismissal the day before of the Berlin police chief and member of the USPD. The KPD had agreed to go along with a protest march, but did not want to try taking power, because it thought a coup was bound to fail. KPD leaders and other radicals were taken aback by the size of the demonstration on January 5 and the amount of unrest in the days that followed. There was no calming these waters. This misnamed "Spartacus uprising" was a confused affair that involved the USPD and KPD, as well as the Spartacus group. Armed bands of followers took over Berlin's leading newspapers, and concluding from false news that the military was on their side, Liebknecht and others who were prepared to use violence as needed called for a general strike to bring down the government.[14]

Radical Socialists like Liebknecht and Luxemburg wanted to dispense with parliamentary elections. They might have had reservations about Lenin and Bolshevism, but they agreed with much that Lenin stood for, including the nationalization of industry and collectivization of agriculture. The economic program of the Spartacus group could have been written by Lenin. Luxemburg criticized the MSPD for not destroying the capitalist class and for insisting on "the inviolability of private property."[15]

These were the leaders of Spartacus, which in total counted perhaps one thousand members at the start of the revolution. Their demands made them sound like German Bolsheviks.[16] Though Luxemburg had crossed swords with Lenin, in Germany she echoed one of his favorite points: Socialism could not just be "introduced." She claimed that there would be a need for violence and civil war because "when the bourgeoisie is hit in its heart—and its heart beats in the cash register—it will put up a life and death struggle." Hence, "the idea that socialism can be introduced without a class struggle and through parliamentary majority decisions is a ridiculous petit-bourgeois illusion."[17]

On January 7, Gustav Noske, a member of the MSPD and of the cabinet, decided it was time to use force. His dictum was: "Fine, let it be me! Somebody has to become the bloodhound, and I do not shy away from the responsibility."[18] Besides regular troops he called for volunteers, who came from right-wing groups like the Volunteer Regiment Reinhard. Noske also used Free Corps troops under General Walther von Lüttwitz, whose men were committed anti-Bolsheviks. These groups later had links to Nazism. By January 11, they had cleared out the occupied buildings in Berlin, and on January 15 the coup was over. Luxemburg and Liebknecht were brutally murdered. The seriousness of the occasion cannot be exaggerated. As one writer put it, "If their immediate aim—the overthrow of the Ebert-Scheidemann government—had been achieved, then that would have led to a bloody civil war in all of Germany and a military intervention of the Allies."[19]

Eisner's assassination on February 21, which was intended to put an end to what remained of the revolution in Bavaria, actually rekindled the determination of some radicals. There was a wave of revolutions in Munich more chaotic and Communistic than Eisner's. Between late February and early May the city threatened to become a smaller and less bloody version of the Russian Revolution. All kinds of experiments were tried, including the declaration of the Bavarian Soviet Republic.

It was precisely at this time that Béla Kun (another Communist with a Jewish background) seized power in Hungary, and there was talk that Austria and Bavaria might be next.[20]

In Munich throughout March and into April various institutions competed for power. Immediately after Eisner's assassination, a radical central council had been created on February 22, with representatives from the MSPD, USPD, and KPD. Uncertain about what to do, they recognized the duly elected Landtag (state parliament). This action created friction within the council and led to the resignation of Max Levien, the head of the Communist Party. On March 17, the Landtag selected Johannes Hoffmann as Bavaria's prime minister. As a moderate member of the MSPD, he built a cabinet with representatives of the MSPD and USPD, as well as some from the Bavarian Peasant Party.

"JEWISH BOLSHEVISM"

The political crisis in Munich was not over, and some radicals tried to create a councils republic (*Räterepublik*) along the lines of the Soviet Union and Hungary. Leaders of the Bavarian Communist Party wanted a second revolution but rejected the idea of a Soviet republic. In the chaos, such a republic was declared anyway. On April 7, in the name of the new Bavarian Soviet Republic, Ernst Niekisch, chairman of the Central Council, asserted after all that the elections to the Landtag (due to meet the next day) were null and void.

The decisive push for the Soviet republic came not from the Communists, who participated in the short-lived regime, but from the USPD and some anarchists. Gustav Landauer, a radical Socialist and Jew, was named commissar of education and enlightenment, and thus put in control of the mostly Christian school system, an appointment that was received as an affront to the mainly Catholic population. Promises to collectivize agriculture were met with disbelief.

Even Communist leaders in Munich were relieved with the collapse of what they called the "Fake Councils Republic" on April 13. From temporary headquarters in Bamberg, Prime Minister Hoffmann laid siege to the city and finally decided on a surprise attack. Violence erupted, but the Soviet republic briefly survived.

Improbably enough, at that moment Eugen Leviné asserted control over the republic and soon issued a proclamation: "The sun of the world revolution has risen! Long live the world revolution! . . . Long live Communism!"[21] Leviné was born in St. Petersburg in 1883 into the family of a wealthy Jewish businessman. He was educated in Germany and a naturalized German citizen. He arrived in Munich on March 5, at the behest of Paul Levi, the new head of Germany's Communist Party, and insisted the Communists have nothing to do with the first Bavarian Soviet Republic, which he called phony.

On April 13, Leviné decided, not on express orders but in keeping with Lenin's hopes, that the moment was right to take power in Munich. The motto of the new regime was "Today finally Bavaria has established the Dictatorship of the Proletariat." However, the sun of Communist revolutions was setting, not rising. To the east, Romanian troops invaded and crushed the Communists in Hungary on April 10, and on April 18 the Austrian Communists were routed in Vienna.[22]

Lenin telegraphed his best wishes to Leviné on April 27 and advised him to broaden support by canceling mortgages and rents of small peasants. Terror was never far from Lenin's mind, and he suggested taking hostages from among the bourgeoisie. But the days of the Leviné regime in Bavaria were numbered.[23]

Munich was under siege, and conditions in the city grew grim. In Bamberg, Johannes Hoffmann was still rightful head of government and issued calls for volunteers to crush the Communist regime. One of his ministers put it this way: "Russian terror rules in Munich. Led by alien insurgents, Communists have seized power. . . . If we do not want to experience the fate of Russia, we must protect our threatened Bavarian land to the last man."[24] "Alien" here was a code word for Jews, Russians, and non-Bavarian Germans.

A hastily assembled Red Army of the Munich Soviet Republic was no match for the forces that "liberated" the city at the end of April. The Reds killed innocent hostages, while the White troops, some Bavarian but reinforced by Free Corps troops sent by Noske, carried out indiscriminate revenge. A total of 606 people were killed, 38 of them government troops. Leviné was tried for high treason and executed. Still others were given prison terms, but many escaped.[25]

Leaders of several other key German states (Prussia and Saxony) in this period were, like Kurt Eisner, also Jewish. In Bavaria the Jews had led the Soviet republic; they included Ernst Toller, Erich Mühsam, Gustav Landauer, Towia Axelrod, Eugen Leviné, and Max Levien. The latter three men were born in Russia, thereby linking them in German minds to Bolshevism in some way, even if they were not specifically Lenin's representatives. Other Communist (and Socialist) leaders in Germany were Jewish, most notably Rosa Luxemburg, whose Polish-Jewish ancestry was well known. Her Jewish colleagues among the German Communists included Leo Jogiches and Paul Levi. Béla Kun's Communist government included a majority of Jewish commissars, and many leading Marxists in Austria were Jewish.[26]

For contemporaries with a penchant for conspiracy theories, it was easy to connect these events to Jewish leaders in Russia, of whom the most prominent were Trotsky, Zinoviev, and Kamenev. It did not matter that they had long since renounced their religious faith. They were taken anyway as the embodiment of international "Jewish Bolshevism," a condemnatory term brought to the West by émigrés who fled Russia.

Hitler was in Munich during these "Bolshevik revolutions," where fear of Moscow's tampering was not merely a theoretical possibility but part of daily experience.

Most people in Bavaria were delighted to see the end of the upheaval. The great novelist Thomas Mann remarked on his "feeling of liberation and cheerfulness" that the "Munich Communist episode is over."[27] Ruth Fischer, one of the leaders of the KPD, recognized after the fact that the revolutions in Munich, which she likened to a civil war, "increased the horror" of the Bavarian middle classes for revolution. Without these events, she concluded, "Munich would never have become the birthplace of the Hitler movement."[28]

Anti-Semitic organizations proliferated in this period and drew hundreds of thousands of members. They emphasized the role of the Jews in the defeat of Germany and in the revolutions from Petrograd to Berlin to Munich and beyond, with the Jews portrayed as the "wire-pullers of the revolution." A common claim was that Germany had become a "Jews' republic."[29]

HITLER'S RIGHT-WING POLITICS

The Bavarian army was revamped, and on May 11 the Bavarian Reichswehr Gruppenkommando 4 (or Gruko 4) was formed under Major General Arnold von Möhl with jurisdiction over regular troops in Bavaria and civilian affairs in Munich. A "news" department of Gruko 4 covered the press, information, and propaganda and also collected information to "school" the troops and influence political developments.

On May 28, General Möhl issued instructions for anti-Bolshevik propaganda to be undertaken immediately by speakers drawn from all ranks after they were given some anti-Bolshevik "schooling." Adopting an anti-Bolshevik perspective, the courses would deal with eight topics, including German history, the theory and practice of Socialism, and Russia and its past.[30]

On May 30, a General Staff officer, Captain Karl Mayr, took over the news department. A radical nationalist and anti-Semite, he got to know Hitler, who was considered reliable and one of the more mature men, at thirty years old. Hitler's education as an anti-Bolshevik speaker began on June 5, 1919, with lectures at Munich's university. For Hitler, the school dropout with pretensions to being better educated than his mates, this was a great chance to hear what professors and experts had to say. Instructors included the historian Karl Alexander von Müller and the economics specialist Gottfried Feder.

Hermann Esser, another participant in the course, said Feder blamed certain "circles"—namely "international Jewry"—for the "cancer" besetting the German economy. Hitler picked up on these themes and became a devotee of Feder's ideas, impressed with his understanding of "the speculative and economic character of stock exchange and loan capital." Breaking "the slavery of interest" became code for ending the economic power of the Jews. Hitler said Feder criticized aspects of capitalism, including its internationalism, but did not question capitalism as such.[31]

Hitler was elected to the minor position of deputy battalion representative by his fellow soldiers during the heady days of the Bavarian Soviet Republic in April 1919. Far from concluding that he might have had Communist or even Socialist sympathies at that time, we should assume he just went along and was at best "neutral." There is no evidence he was ever attracted by Marxists' rejection of capitalism and their enthusiasm for "international brotherhood." To the extent he held "Socialist" opinions, these were critical of "stock exchange" capitalism and speculators. It was no doubt embarrassing for Hitler later that he had anything, however briefly, to do with the left-wingers. He lied about the episode in his autobiography.[32]

Hitler took far more seriously his involvement with right-wingers as a member of a military propaganda detachment. On August 19 he spent five days at a camp in Lechfeld dealing with troops whose sentiments favored left-wing politics and Bolshevism. The task was to knock such ideas out of their heads before they were demobilized.

Anti-Bolshevism was one of the themes on which Hitler was a successful speaker. He would begin by referring to the activities of the Jews to "explain" key developments in German history and problems of capitalism. Thus setting the matter in "context," he became practiced in a story line that combined anti-Bolshevism and anti-Semitism along with nationalism. He presented the message with such passion that he won the enthusiastic approval of the troops.

The first documented anti-Semitic statement we have from Hitler was in Lechfeld during a talk about capitalism. He later responded to questions by Adolf Gemlich, a fellow propagandist, who wanted more information about what to say about the Jews. Hitler's letter of September 16, 1919, shows that he had thought about the topic before, and he considered the Jews to be a racial, not merely a religious, community. He was convinced that something radical had to be done to rid Germany of the Jews. But what? Ordinary citizens would be aghast at pogroms, he said. They had become soft as a nation and made themselves vulnerable to the machinations of the Jews, who allegedly had played on the "higher" values of the Germans—religion, Socialism, democracy—to get what they really wanted, money and power. As a nation Germans were suffering from "racial tuberculosis," and it would be his task to cure them. Hitler drew momentous consequences from this analysis.

Given his line of thinking, it was a matter of what strategy to take in the combat against the Jews. The German people were sick, unable to stomach pogroms, and too democratic for their own good. Thus the only way to get them to see the light was to work through democracy and the legal system. It was a matter of fighting fire with fire. The "anti-Semitism of reason," he said, must systematically and legally eliminate the rights of the Jews. The most important objective was the "removal of the Jews altogether" (*Entfernung der Juden überhaupt*).[33]

Hitler started looking into right-wing politics, and there were at least fifty parties and groups available in Munich to choose from. He learned about these when sent to investigate them by Captain Mayr, and he also gave talks to the military and other groups in and around the city, where he made an impression.

On September 12, 1919, Captain Mayr ordered Hitler to attend a meeting of the German Workers' Party (DAP) and report on it. The DAP was led by Karl Harrer and Anton Drexler, and the evening's speakers happened to include Gottfried Feder, whose theme was "How and by what means does one destroy capitalism?" In the discussions that followed, Hitler showed he was knowledgeable and quick. Drexler was impressed and asked him to join the fledgling party.

Like so much else, Hitler lied in his autobiography about when he joined the DAP and even his membership number—which was not 7 but 555. From September 1919 onward he was in the Party and combined his army job with speaking at political gatherings until he was discharged on March 31, 1920.[34]

FOUNDATION OF THE NAZI PARTY

Hitler began to think of politics as a vocation. It gave him a goal in life, and he dared to imagine himself as someone who might influence Germany's destiny. He never worked out a formal theory or ideology, nor embraced anyone else's, but he was emotionally and temperamentally drawn to right-wing politics.

As a member of the DAP, but by far its best drawing card, he was ambitious enough to want to expand his reach. On January 7, 1920, he spoke to the largest anti-Semitic and *völkisch* (nationalist) groups in Munich and attracted a crowd of seven thousand. He was starting to make a living as a political speaker. Invoking the activity of the Jews to explain the country's misfortunes won immediate applause.

Another favorite theme was the "war guilt question." The Versailles Treaty was worked out without Germany's participation in the discussions, despite President Woodrow Wilson's Fourteen Points and his promise of open diplomacy. Under article 231 of the treaty, Germany was held responsible for the war, and to make matters worse, the country was required to pay all the costs incurred by the Allies, who were asked to compile bills, including veterans' pensions and widows' allowances.

Although people today continue to dispute whether Germany could have paid the final sums demanded, the Versailles Treaty was a political disaster, and every German politician felt duty-bound to oppose it because it signified national humiliation. The country was presented with the finished treaty and threatened with invasion if it did not sign. The moderate Social Democratic chancellor, Philipp Scheidemann, resigned rather than put his signature to it. By June 23, 1919, the government was left with no choice but to accept the peace without any conditions. A delegation was sent to Paris for the distasteful ceremony at the Versailles Palace on June 28.[35]

The territory and possessions lost in the treaty, when combined with the reparations payments, made Germans across the political spectrum regard Versailles as the epitome of unfairness. They called it the *Diktat,* or dictated peace. Right-wing politicians exploited the national outrage, and it became a mainstay in Hitler's repertoire. If we compare what happened after 1945, when Germany was helped in its recovery and democracy took root, the vengeful Treaty of Versailles looks particularly faulty.

Inflation began in the war years, but it soon escalated alarmingly, eventually becoming worse than anything ever seen in an advanced industrial nation. The death of money turned German society from bitterness to chaos. Here was the context in which Hitler's Party came into existence, blossomed, and attempted to seize power.

PARTY PLATFORM

The German Workers' Party (DAP) was changed into the National Socialist German Workers' Party (NSDAP) as of February 1, 1920. Its leader was Anton Drexler, but Hitler was the decisive figure and suggested the new name. The two worked out a twenty-five-point program, celebrated after the fact as having been presented to a public meeting on February 24, 1920.

Compared with the writings of Marxists like Lenin and Stalin, the program was thin fare. There was no pretense at eloquent philosophical rationalization, no grand historical theory. A key contrast to Communism was that there was no effort at making a universal appeal; rather, the target audience of the NSDAP could be read as "Germans only."

The first plank in the platform was for unification into a Greater Germany. Only people of "German blood" could be citizens, and no Jew was to be allowed to be a member of the nation. Noncitizens could live in the country only as guests but not serve in the government or civil service, and their activities were limited even with respect to newspaper writing. All non-German immigration was to cease. It was the duty of the state to feed and care for citizens, and foreign nationals (non-citizens) who could not be fed should be deported.

Another major demand was to tear up the peace settlements of 1919. That was combined with others that sought "land and territory" for the population.

The Party's anti-Semitic character was repeated several different ways and was impossible to overlook. The legal emancipation of the Jews, the pride of their community, was to be reversed, and any who remained in the country would be second-class citizens. In fact, most parts of the platform had an anti-Semitic twist.

The Party did not aim to recruit a specific social class, but tried to offer something for everyone. It echoed Feder's demand to break "the slavery of interest" and contained several points with a moderate Socialist tone. The Party favored some social welfare, state involvement in fostering health, protecting mothers and infants, and extending old-age pensions. As well, the program mentioned educational plans, with emphasis on helping gifted children of the poor.

While critical of capitalism, the Party was hardly anticapitalist. It demanded profit sharing in large industrial enterprises but did not follow through on this point. The Party eventually came out strongly in favor of protecting private property, particularly farm ownership, but here it spoke about prohibiting land speculation. This and the economic demands, such as the abolition of department stores, which in Germany were identified mainly with Jewish firms, were standard anti-Semitic fare.

There was also a strong law-and-order element in the Party program, which threatened death to those such as "common criminals, usurers, profiteers" if their activities "were injurious to the nation."

A fundamental aspect of this kind of "Socialism" was the rejection of what was called "the Jewish-materialist spirit" in favor of the principle "common interest before self-interest." There was no mention of the threat of Communism or Marxian-based Socialism, but nor did it say anything about other political rivals, or even about cultural affairs. The idea was to keep the message simple.

One note about the NSDAP that set it apart was the commitment it made to supporters: "The leaders of the Party promise to work ruthlessly—if need be to sacrifice their very lives—to translate this program into action."[36]

The name National Socialist German Workers' Party underlined both the nationalist and the Socialist themes. That is, it tried to get across the point that this was a Party in competition with the Marxist ones for the support of German workers.

Anti-Semitism was symbolically inscribed in the new flag, put together by Hitler himself. He said that the red background of the flag stood for "the social idea" of the movement. This was an attempt to snatch the attractive red color from the Russians, for whom red held a traditional religious significance. The white on the flag of the NSDAP referred to the "nationalistic idea," and the swastika—which Hitler first saw in prewar Austria—symbolized the mission and struggle of "Aryan man." He claimed that the swastika also stood for "creative work, which has been and always will be anti-Semitic." The swastika, therefore, certainly in Hitler's mind, was a visualization of the Party's anti-Semitism.[37]

Anyone who lived through those times had to be aware that the NSDAP was the most radical anti-Semitic political party in German history. No doubt, on the model of most political parties, it would modify its appeals to fit local circumstances. But anti-Semitism was the central plank, so obvious to the Nazis that it did not warrant debate. Hitler had not always been anti-Semitic. But in postwar Munich his obsessive concern about German national pride developed in such a way that it could not be disconnected from an unholy and abiding hatred of the Jews.

Many people in Germany did not know what the swastika stood for in 1920, but they began to figure it out. The lawyer and newspaperman Sebastian Haffner remembered that as a boy he saw a schoolmate scribbling the symbol in his notebook and asked in a whisper what it meant. "Anti-Semitic sign," he was told, and it meant "Out with the Jews. You have to know."[38]

During 1920 Hitler began to collect large speaking fees, not only in Bavaria but in other German states. The fees ran from two hundred to one thousand Reichsmarks, considerable sums for the time. He also accepted funds from right-wing circles in Munich, people with money or connections like Captain Mayr, Dietrich Eckart, Heinrich Class, and Ernst Röhm, the latter to become one of Hitler's closest friends and allies.[39]

By 1920 Hitler's name had become synonymous with the NSDAP, but he was not its leader. Certainly he did not have to fight for leadership, because Drexler offered him that on several occasions in 1921. Hitler declined, partly because he sensed his gift was for speaking and appealing to the public, not in dealing with the mundane issues of managing a political party.[40]

He claimed leadership of the Party, so he said in his autobiography, when in the summer of 1921 his hand was forced to stop "a group of *völkisch* lunatics" who wanted to take over.[41] The matter came up while Hitler was away in Berlin, and soon after his return, on July 11, he resigned from the Party. In a six-page letter sent to the executive several days later, he complained that they had broken the spirit of the Party and that under the circumstances he was left with no choice but to leave it. Yet Hitler was well aware of his importance to the Party and, ever playing politics, despite his pretensions to be somehow above the political fray, set six conditions under which he would change his mind, the most important of which was that he be made "First Chairman with dictatorial powers." Drexler and the others capitulated, and on July 29 Hitler got what he wanted.[42]

He offered himself as a man of principle who so far as leadership was concerned could take it or leave it. But this self-presentation masked a deep yearning for supreme power that he did not want to share with anyone. He was immensely patient, and now, as he would later, in 1933, he waited until the moment was right to assert his dominance. His wish was to be acknowledged as the only alternative to chaos and disintegration.

He liked to regard himself as the great "theoretician and program maker," not an organizer and certainly not one suited to the drudgery of routine administrative chores. Being a leader to Hitler's way of thinking was "being able to move millions," to "attract supporters."[43] He needed everyone at his feet, loyal colleagues and adoring masses.

For Hitler, the leader had to be the first propagandist with the aim of working "on the general public from the standpoint of an idea" and making them "ripe for the victory of this idea." The organization had a different role to play. Its job was to bring supporters together through persistent work, and Hitler sought out talented organizers. He installed Max Amann, one of his wartime sergeants, as the Party's new business manager. Amann showed skill, and he also worked on Hitler's personal matters. As of January 3, 1921, the *Völkischer Beobachter* (Nationalist Observer) became the Party's official organ, and in August 1921 Hitler named Dietrich Eckart the editor in chief.

Eckart was a Hitler loyalist, a poet and writer with anti-Semitic inclinations. He contributed some of his own money to obtaining the newspaper and the publishing firm Eher Verlag, and he also helped obtain funds from the army and wealthy donors. The publishing company, eventually run by Amann, brought out pamphlets and books, including Hitler's *Mein Kampf.*

Another important touch was added on October 5, when the Party's protection squad—hitherto called the Gymnastic and Sport Department—was renamed the Sturmabteilung (literally "Storming Department"), or brown-shirted SA.

ANTI-SEMITISM AND ANTI-BOLSHEVISM

Hitler's anti-Semitism and anti-Bolshevism took shape at about the same time, following the Bolshevik Revolution, and particularly in the context of the postwar Councils Republic in Bavaria.

Those in Hitler's circle propounded similar views, particularly Eckart and two men from the Baltic area, Alfred Rosenberg and Max Erwin von Scheubner-Richter. Hitler read their publications avidly and exchanged ideas, particularly about Russia. They knew White refugees who had fled from the East and brought with them the forgery *The Protocols of the Elders of Zion*. This book, about an alleged Jewish plot to take over the world, predated the First World War, and both Kaiser Wilhelm II of Germany and Nicholas II of Russia were firm believers in it.[44] The Russian Revolution and murder of the tsarist family helped make the book better known in the West. Eckart, Rosenberg, and Scheubner-Richter accepted the veracity of *The Protocols of the Elders of Zion,* and one of them likely passed this myth on to Hitler in 1920. On August 12, 1921, Hitler first referred to the "Wise men of Zion" in a speech and did so again a week later. He internalized the theory completely and took it as fact.[45]

Reception for *The Protocols of the Elders of Zion* was prepared by news flooding out of Russia about the revolution and the terror. Newspapers covered the story widely. The *Völkischer Beobachter,* even before Hitler's Party took it over, was laden with tales linking the Jews to Bolshevism and its terror. The swastika, so it was claimed in one story from mid-November 1920, was the symbol of anti-Bolshevism.[46]

Hitler's first speech to deal with this general theme was on February 9, 1920. In the talk on the "approach of the Bolsheviks" he spoke about Marx and Engels and the councils system.[47] Later that month he implied that conditions were so bad in Russia that the eastern Jews were leaving. In a speech to a Party meeting on April 27, officially billed as "Politics and the Jews," he went into detail about Russia, from the civil war to the "mass murder" of the intelligentsia, destruction of the economy, and introduction of the twelve-hour workday. He warned that if Germans did not do something, the same thing would happen in their country. "Who managed all this?" he asked rhetorically. He said he and his Party were prepared to carry on the struggle "until the last Jew is removed from the German Reich."[48]

He played on the theme that Russia suffered "hunger and misery" and that "the guilt for this development" was attributable to "none other than the Jews." He warned that the leaders of the Bavarian Soviet Republic wanted the same for Germany.[49] On July 27 he asked, once more rhetorically: "What had Bolshevism promised after the revolution?" It would end class domination and bureaucracy, abolish private property, and shorten the working day. What did Bolshevism do? It delivered workers to state enterprises and forced a piecework system, created a new (and illiterate) bureaucracy, permitted foreign companies to exploit the country, and brought about the great famine.[50]

He painted Lenin as a failure who had surrendered the Russian people to the dictatorship of the Jews. Exaggerating the extent of Jewish influence, he said that they constituted 430 out of 478 people's commissars.[51] In a speech reported in the Nazi newspaper at the end of the year, the numbers he gave were 466 Jews out of 674 commissars.[52] He dwelled on the point that the victory of Marxism in Russia was the triumph of the Jews.[53] It was not enough merely to study Bolshevism to stop Germany from becoming bolshevized, just as it was insufficient to recognize the dangers of the Jews "in order to render them harmless" (*um den Juden unschädlich zu machen*). It was crucial to do something about it.[54]

To be a "Socialist" for Hitler was to oppose materialism and to fight the Jews. The Russians had attacked only industrial capitalism, he claimed. They had not touched Jewish capitalism, by which he presumably meant finance capital. In a January 1, 1921, newspaper article Hitler began referring to the Soviet Union as "the Jewish blood dictatorship" in which allegedly 150 million suffered "bloody terror" at the hands of 600,000.[55]

As for the Soviets, they firmly intended to export Communism, if necessary by force of arms. Lenin ordered the invasion of southern and Western Europe in mid-summer 1920. In early July, with victories against the Poles already behind him, he fantasized about bringing Communism to Italy, Hungary, Romania, Czechoslovakia, and Germany. He said that even failure in Poland (which soon came) should not stop them, because he so firmly believed in world revolution.[56] He never renounced it.

The German Communist Party in early 1921, encouraged by Moscow, tried an uprising in Prussian Saxony, specifically Halle-Merseburg. The so-called March action was launched with the backing of the Comintern and well-known figures in Moscow as well as Communists like the Hungarian Béla Kun. The Prussian police got wind of the plans and moved into the area on March 19. Ten days later, backed by military forces, they struck. The March action was put down at the cost of 145 killed and around 34,700 arrested. Prisoners were treated terribly in what became almost a white terror. The uprising was widely blamed on "Communist Bolshevik" agitators and "Russian Jews."[57]

Hitler saw his movement as a reaction to these kinds of threats. On January 27, 1921, he had said that the Communist Party of Germany wanted to undermine the nation from within and create a dictatorship on the Russian model. Who was going to stand against this "international, Jewish, proletarian mass energy"? Only at the grass roots, he believed, could a counter-energy be found. Trying to get more people elected was not enough. What was needed was a new national and anti-Semitic movement. Mere "electoral anti-Semitism was immoral."[58]

Hitler's anti-Semitic interpretation of events grew more sweeping as the German economy deteriorated. In mid-February 1921 he charged that London and Paris were under the domination of stock-exchange capitalism. This rule worked as follows: first there was the attempt to get reparations from Germany, but when that became impossible, there was a switch to a policy of "exterminating" the country. France was blamed for making outlandish demands and for wanting to bring the German people "to a Jewish dictatorship, to Bolshevism. For that is and remains the final goal of the Jewish stock-exchange leadership."[59]

The Nazi message was taking shape. The big question was how Hitler and his tiny Party could get themselves into a position to act on their beliefs.

5

FIRST NAZI ATTEMPT TO SEIZE POWER

The violent heritage of the First World War, coupled with the outbreak of the Russian Revolution, had dramatic effects across Europe. With the rise of Fascism in Italy, Mussolini opened another radical option on the European political landscape.

MUSSOLINI AS MODEL

On October 28, 1922, Benito Mussolini carried out a "march on Rome." He was a charismatic leader of a relatively small party, and in the last elections his Partito Nazionale Fascista (Fascist Party) managed to win only 35 of the 535 seats. What set Mussolini apart were the Blackshirts, or Squadre d'Azioni. As of April 1922, they numbered probably between 73,000 and 110,000. Many were military desperadoes, disenchanted veterans of the First World War who had little to look forward to by returning to their villages. Mussolini channeled their personal and social discontent into the right-wing politics of action. Together they worked out tactics of intimidation, assault, arson, and other forms of terror, which occasionally led to murder.[1]

Mussolini stoked the myth that Italy was on the verge of a Communist revolution. The Fascists won over landowners and members of the elite who worried that Italy might follow the Soviet example. Fascism promised law and order. Winston Churchill privately called Mussolini a "swine" for his cruelties, but in public praised him for bringing order and for being a bulwark against Red revolution.[2]

The march on Rome in 1922 was the culmination of months of Blackshirt violence. Now they occupied public buildings, kicked out the Socialists, and sacked the offices of newspapers, and on October 28 four leaders led an estimated nine thousand *squadristi* to the gates of Rome. It was a ragtag group that could have been routed by the army with ease and nowhere near the 100,000 men King Victor Emmanuel later mentioned to justify his reluctance to call out the troops. Mussolini was uncertain and waited in Milan, before traveling to Rome by train on October 30.[3] He created the myth that 300,000 had marched, but hardly one-tenth as many were involved. The king dithered, and then appointed the inexperienced Fascist leader (aged thirty-nine) the new prime minister. There was joy in the streets of Rome; people were filled with hope that the years of misgovernment were finally over.[4]

Mussolini's success demonstrated to Hitler that a charismatic leader, backed with the force of popular appeal, could find his way to power. Mussolini was the first politician in twentieth-century Europe to show that the fragile new democracies could be toppled without fighting never-ending elections.

Hitler had "the profoundest admiration" for Mussolini's "resolve not to share Italy with the Marxists, but to destroy internationalism and save the fatherland from it."[5] The Italian left-wing parties did not call a general strike (as Mussolini feared) to stop his takeover. Nationalism was running high in the country, fueled by outrage at the meager territorial gains given Italy at the Paris Peace Conference. For many Italians, the Allies did not show enough respect for the 460,000 soldiers who had died in the war and the nearly one million wounded.

In early November 1922, Hitler was asked about the similarities between his movement and the Italian one. He acknowledged that some called his Party the "German Fascists." He was not sure about that, but agreed that both parties had "in common the unconditional love of fatherland, the will to tear the working class from the claws of the [Communist] International, and the fresh and comradely spirit of the front."[6]

The two left-wing parties in Germany, now under the banners of the KPD (Communist Party) and SPD (Social Democratic Party), thought Hitler wanted to turn himself into a German Mussolini.[7] Jews in Germany were alarmed by the easy Fascist victory and pointed to the implications for the Nazis.[8]

At a meeting of the NSDAP on November 3, one of the first since the march on Rome, Hermann Esser, propaganda chief and one of Hitler's most enthusiastic supporters, called to a large crowd in one of Munich's beer halls: "We also have Mussolini of Italy in Bavaria. His name is Adolf Hitler." This was the first time the leaders of the NSDAP publicly indicated their aims. Their revolution would be according to the Italian, not the Soviet, model.[9]

ECONOMIC CHAOS AND POLITICAL EXTREMISM

The context of Hitler's attempt to take power in November 1923 was provided by the structural collapse of the German economy. The fledgling republic was saddled with large reparation debts, and every government felt more or less obliged to drag its feet when payments were due. They let economic problems go unsolved in part to show that the debt was impossibly high. In the latter part of 1922 the French threatened to invade if payment was not forthcoming. Chancellor Wilhelm Cuno, who took office on November 22, repeated the phrase of his predecessor "First bread, then reparations."

On December 26, 1922, the Reparations Commission concluded that because Germany failed to deliver the required coal and timber, it was in default on its reparations payments. The British suggested a four-year moratorium, but the French used the pretext to invade. On January 11, 1923, French and Belgian troops marched into the Ruhr, western Germany's industrial heartland. The aim of the French premier, Raymond Poincaré, was not just to collect reparations but to push the frontier back to the Rhine.[10]

The uproar in Germany was universal, and all political parties drew together to consider what to do. The notable exception was the NSDAP. Hitler wanted to distinguish his own response from the general outcry, and on January 11 he addressed a mass meeting in Munich. His motto was "Not down with France, but down with the November criminals."[11] The "November criminals" was an instantly recognized code word for those who stabbed the army in the back and signed the hateful Versailles Treaty.

The KPD's call for a general strike was rejected by the "free" trade unions, allies of the SPD, who wanted to use "passive resistance." On January 13 an overwhelming majority in the Reichstag applauded Chancellor Cuno and passed a bill to that effect.[12] The government instructed railway workers and civil servants to follow only the orders of German authorities. The French responded with martial law, leaving the German government to support workers and employers financially. The effort put an enormous strain on the already shaky budget. The economy was imperiled because the Ruhr region—Germany's main source of energy and raw materials—was effectively cut off from the rest of the country. The French and Belgians eventually stationed 100,000 troops to wrest their reparations from the Ruhr. These economic aims failed, and they created a political disaster.

Inflation now flared completely out of control. It had been under way since 1914, when one American dollar could be exchanged for a modest 4.21 marks. By January 1922 one dollar fetched 191.81 marks, but by the end of the year the number had jumped to 7,589.27 marks, and then the French invasion all but killed the currency. The January 1923 average rate was 17,972.00 marks to the dollar, in August the figure was an astounding 4,620,455.00 to 1, and at the beginning of December a dollar could buy 4.2 trillion marks.[13]

The humiliation of invasion and occupation was thus capped by the worst inflation ever to hit an advanced industrial country. A kilo of bread that cost 274,000 marks on September 3, 1923, went for a cool 3 million on September 24. In the same period the cost of a kilo of potatoes skyrocketed from 92,000 to 1.24 million marks. The biggest losers were the solid members of the middle class, holders of monetary assets like bonds and pensions.

The "winners" included those who had been in debt. Some learned the rules of the game and played the market each day as if it were a lottery. There were industrialists who created vast empires. New nightclubs sprang up, sex without love became the new fashion, and the world of middle-class values went down the drain. Some had the time of their life, drank nothing but vintage wines, and ate only gourmet food. Others died of starvation, and the homeless were everywhere.[14]

The psychological and political effects were reflected in the growth of extremist politics on the left and right. The first to act was the KPD, now firmly under Moscow's control. The Communists had badly miscalculated the so-called March action of 1921, but Moscow kept trying to foment revolution. As the economic situation in Germany deteriorated in late 1922 and into 1923, the leaders of the KPD like Heinrich Brandler felt a revolutionary situation was developing. Brandler returned home in the winter of 1922–23 from Moscow, where he had been imbued with the spirit of making bold moves by the Soviet leaders. They generally agreed that German workers would be roused to unrest by the massive inflation.[15]

By August 23, Trotsky, Zinoviev, and most members of the Politburo had become convinced that revolution had a chance. Stalin was far less sure but, like Radek, was inclined to think "the Germans should be restrained." The issue of who was boss inside the Politburo was not fully settled, and a collective decision was reached. In an effort to make history repeat itself, the date for the revolution was to be as close as possible to the anniversary of the Bolsheviks' coup in 1917: it was to be "the German October."

Brandler said he was not so sure he could act the part of "a German Lenin." Ultimately he asked Trotsky himself to take the lead, but that was not to be. The KPD was certainly growing more powerful. Its membership reached 295,000, with over thirty-three hundred local groups in September 1923. Top Soviet Communists felt the situation was comparable to the one in Russia in 1917 and wanted to strike "now or never."[16]

Moscow's plan was to begin in Saxony (as if to repeat the attempt at revolution in 1921) and from there move on to Berlin, Hamburg, the Ruhr, and the rest of the country. Troops sent by Berlin quickly snuffed out the poorly organized effort. Brandler, supported by the Russian experts, then canceled the Communist insurrection. There was miscommunication between Berlin and Hamburg, where the event went ahead on October 21.[17] Over the next several days, much to the chagrin of the Hamburg Communists who went into military-style action, there was no general strike in the city. The uprising was crushed by police, who still suffered seventeen dead and twenty-six wounded. The insurgents had greater casualties. The abortive effort showed good citizens that Communists, under direct orders from Moscow, were attempting yet another revolution.[18]

Stalin had warned the Politburo that it would be premature to attempt such a coup. All his rivals lost face in that to a greater or lesser extent they had supported this fiasco.[19] Germany and Western Europe were not ripe for Communism, but palpable fear of it was fueled by these quixotic efforts.

SOVIET STAR OR SWASTIKA

The Nazi Party became better known in Bavaria during 1923, primarily through Hitler's speeches. His most frequent theme was anti-Semitism. A typical speech was one he gave on January 18, 1923, in Munich. It was advertised under the heading "Two Fronts in Germany" and dealt with the struggle against the Jews and Marxism. The Jews were in charge in the "Soviet Paradise." The same was in store for Germany, Hitler warned. People had to realize that the struggle was not really between the bourgeoisie and the proletariat—one class led by the Jews and the other seduced by them. There were "two fronts" in the war in Germany, one against Bolshevism and one against the Jews. But this one and the same enemy could be beaten, he thundered, by launching a "racial struggle" of Germans against Jews.[20]

As appalled as he was by the invasion of the Ruhr, he maintained in late January that this event was less important than many thought. The real fight was against not so much the outside world as internal enemies, above all the Jews and the Marxists.[21] There were many other such speeches. He furiously charged that the "increasing Sovietization" of Europe was under way and in a single breath said there was a pressing danger that Jewish money in Paris would subject Germany to Jewish "world domination."[22]

Hitler was aware of the growth of the KPD in states such as Saxony, Thuringia, and the Ruhr. Sooner or later, he said, citizens would have to choose between the Soviet star and the swastika. In late March he fired up his storm troopers (the SA): when the French army and the Red

Army march, "we will not sleep."[23] As for the Weimar Republic, he called it a "Marxist-Jewish-International pigsty."[24]

As the currency began its free fall, Hitler pointed to Jewish speculators and asserted that from the ruined culture the Jews would raise the flag of "hammer, sickle, and star." Gradually he used the shorthand version of the "Soviet star" as the symbol of both anti-Semitism and anti-Bolshevism.[25] According to press reports, these speeches were greeted "as always" with stormy applause.[26]

Every misfortune was laid at the door of the Jews. It is impossible to overlook how open and radical Hitler was in his anti-Semitic charges. He said endlessly and proudly that he was a racist and that Jews could never "convert" and be German citizens. Occasionally police reports said he worked up the crowd almost to a "pogrom mood."[27] His usual call was to "throw out the Jews" and remove them from the arts and sciences, the press, theater, and the arts. He said nothing about their mass murder.[28]

Hitler blamed them for the deterioration of the economy and the rise of Communism. In mid-May 1923 he said in a speech in Erlangen that Germany's policies brought gain only to the banks and the stock exchange. "The goal is the Bolshevization of Germany. The unemployed, whose number greatly increased with the occupation of the Ruhr, will make up the Red Army." This was a curious argument in which capitalists supposedly prepared the ground for Communism, with only the NSDAP blocking the way. His remarks were greeted by "long-lasting applause."[29]

Every speech from May until the November putsch played on the same themes. Germany was threatened by the French and the inflation, but those dangers were part of a larger one, namely of the Jews and Bolshevism. Although the Jews were sometimes called stock-exchange capitalists, this allegation was not as common as the charge that they stood behind the Soviet regime. The Jews and Bolshevism were mentioned so often that the two were sometimes elided and made into one.

In August, Hitler delivered a speech titled "Inflation, Republic, and the Fascist Danger" at a large gathering of the Party in Munich. He pointed out how inflation produced dissatisfaction, out of which emerged political extremism, which he summed up as "Soviet star and swastika." "What is the Soviet star? It is the emblem of a race preparing itself for domination from Vladivostok to Western Europe. The sickle is the symbol of cruelty, the hammer the symbol of Freemasonry. The domination of the Soviet star will be a paradise for Jews but a slave colony for everyone else. Not the rescue but the decline of Germany is the aim of the Communists." Elsewhere in the speech he said hunger was preparing the masses for a "second revolution under the golden Star of David." He conflated in other speeches the star symbol on the Soviet Communist flag and the Star of David of the Jews as an "explanation" for inflation and Germany's misfortunes.[30]

American and British reporters were sometimes granted interviews with Hitler. One was particularly revealing, published in New York in October 1923 by George Sylvester Viereck. He asked Hitler what he meant by Socialism and was told Marxism—"a Jewish invention"—had tried to steal the term "Socialism," but in reality Socialism referred to practices in the Aryan, Germanic tradition. He said his Socialism did not "repudiate private property," nor was it international, by which he meant it was not part of the Communist International. He told Viereck that the "greatest menace" of the moment was Bolshevism, a view that many Americans and Europeans might have shared.

Hitler's solution was simple: "Kill Bolshevism in Germany and you restore seventy million people to power." He said France owed "her strength not to her armies, but to the forces of Bolshevism" in Germany. The Treaty of Versailles and Bolshevism were allegedly "two heads of one monster," and he would "decapitate both." German workers had "two souls," one nationalist and the other Marxist. The former had to be fostered and the latter rooted out.

Viereck asked what Hitler would do with the Jews. His answer was that they would be disenfranchised. But what if they had citizenship? Hitler said he looked upon Jews as Americans looked upon Japanese in the United States. The difference was that the Jews supposedly had ruined Germany and were the "carriers of Bolshevism." No violence had been done to them, nor was any planned. Nevertheless, the Nazi slogan was "Germany for the Germans," and that meant all foreigners, whether Jews or not, "will be permitted to live in Germany only on sufferance."

Hitler's foreign policy aims included regaining colonies lost under the Treaty of Versailles. In addition, he said: "We must expand eastward. There was a time when we could have shared the world with England. Now, we can stretch our cramped limbs only towards the East." But there would be no imperialism until Germans came to grips with their situation at home. He went on: "We are in the position of a man whose house has burned down. He must have a roof over his head before he can indulge in more ambitious plans."

He ended the interview by pointing to the future: "In my scheme of the German state, there will be no room for the alien, no use for the criminal, no use for the diseased, no use for the wastrel, for the usurer or speculator, or anyone incapable of productive work."[31]

He told London's *Daily Mail* in early October 1923 that if a "German Mussolini" were given Germany, "people would fall down on their knees and worship him more than Mussolini has ever been worshipped."[32]

HITLER'S FAILED ATTEMPT TO SEIZE POWER

Parties in this period, still influenced by the combative mood of the First World War, used paramilitary groups to protect their meetings. The Communists and Socialists had such organizations of their own. By October 1921 the Nazi brand under Emil Maurice had begun to be referred to as the SA, or Sturmabteilung, with a membership of around three hundred. In the second half of 1922, it gained a reputation for violence, and its image was enhanced because of the role played by the Blackshirts in Mussolini's march on Rome.

On the heels of the Ruhr invasion Hitler called a meeting of the Party for January 27–28, 1923, and in what was to become a ritual, he "blessed" the flags of various SA groups who swore their loyalty to him. The SA's initial task was to protect Hitler and others when they spoke, but it came to embody the militancy of the movement itself.

In February 1923, Captain Ernst Röhm put together an umbrella organization for various right-wing groups in Bavaria, including the NSDAP. The first major event of this new Working Community of Fatherland Fighting Groups (Arbeitsgemeinschaft der Vaterländischen Kampfverbände) was held on May 1, typically the day working-class organizations held their annual parades. The Fighting Groups issued an ultimatum to the Bavarian government to stop the May 1 demonstration of the Reds, and when that was refused, they armed themselves. The police and Reichswehr, backed by reinforcements from outside Munich, would not tolerate street violence. Somewhat sheepishly, the Fighting Groups returned the arms they had stolen and went home quietly.[33]

Throughout the nation political violence rose as the currency fell, but in Bavaria right-wing extremism benefited most. On September 1–2 in Nuremberg a large rally named the German Day was held by nationalist paramilitary groups. There was a celebration of the victory over France in 1870, and for the speeches on September 2 at least twenty-five thousand showed up. The attraction was not Hitler but General Erich Ludendorff, still the "undefeated" hero of the First World War and a man trying to make a political comeback. Hitler was the main speaker, and according to the *New York Times* he gave a "firebrand oration." He concluded as follows: "We must have a new dictatorship. We need no Parliament, no Government like the present. We cannot expect Germany's salvation from the present condition, but only through a dictatorship brought through the sword."[34]

A Nazi flyer provided a long list of demands. The priority was to get rid of the Treaty of Versailles. Redemption would come only through struggle against "the Marxist movement, the [Communist] International in every form, the Jews as putrefactive agents in the life of the people, and pacifism." Germany had to find a new "community of the people."[35]

The creation of the German Combat League (Deutscher Kampfbund) was one result of the event in Nuremberg. Hitler's right-hand man, Max Erwin von Scheubner-Richter, was made business manager and on September 24 drew up an "action program" for taking power in Bavaria. The "basic mission" was "the crushing of Marxism," which would be successful only if the Combat League controlled power in Bavaria, but at the very least they had to aim for the Ministry of the Interior and get command of police power. Scheubner-Richter thought it possible to achieve these aims "in an at least apparently legal manner."[36]

The hope was not so much to follow the Bolshevik model and attempt a violent coup, but to learn from Mussolini's example. However, Munich was not Rome, where in 1922 the Italian police and army sympathized with the Fascists. The people around Hitler could not be sure the police and army in Bavaria would be on their side.

Ernst Röhm saw to it on September 25 that Hitler was given the "political leadership" of the new Combat League. A repeat performance of the German Day was held in Hof (September 16), and one followed in Bayreuth (September 30), the home of the Wagner cult and thus sacred turf for Hitler. In an interview with the United Press at Bayreuth, Hitler almost invited a "Communist Revolution" and said "the Reds would cease to exist in the North, in Saxony and Thuringia, if they were not allowed to work away at their leisure." He felt the Bavarian masses would rally round him: "Our program is that of a national dictatorship. If at a certain point Munich does not march on Berlin, Berlin will march on Munich."[37]

Chancellor Gustav Stresemann decided to end "passive resistance" to the French on September 26. Stresemann, perhaps the most gifted of all the Weimar Republic's politicians, hoped the French and British would agree to negotiate a settlement, but the occupation continued.[38]

In Bavaria, Minister-President Eugen von Knilling was warned that the Nazis were preparing a revolution and took preemptive action on September 26 by appointing Gustav von Kahr as special general state commissar. Hitler regarded Kahr's appointment as a declaration of war.[39]

Kahr's pressure on the Combat League enforced quiet for weeks. Hitler and his advisers were concerned lest followers drift away, all the more as continuing economic distress sapped morale. In the meantime, Communists, egged on by Moscow, tried again to take power in several places. One of the main leaders of the KPD, Heinrich Brandler was proven correct and Moscow wrong. The Communists did no preparatory work, perhaps believing that Germany was ripe for the taking, but it was not, as was made clear in Saxony and Hamburg on October 23 to 26. Yet again the conceit of the Russians was that they could make the revolution happen on or about the anniversary of the Russian Revolution.

The real danger of a successful revolution came from the other end of the political spectrum. Fearful of a Hitler takeover—but wistfully inspired by Mussolini's success—Kahr conspired with Bavarian State Police Colonel Hans Ritter von Seisser and Bavarian Reichswehr commander General Otto Hermann von Lossow to plan their own march on Berlin. In October and early November, they negotiated with influential persons in Berlin, especially General Hans von Seeckt, chief of the Reichswehr. However, Seeckt told them frankly on November 3 that he would not go along and would support the rightful government in Berlin. The Bavarian trio thereupon agreed among themselves that any attempted putsch in Munich would be put down.[40]

Hitler tried to meet with Kahr but failed. He pressed on without thinking through how the police and army might react, and on November 6 he and his close advisers decided on a putsch. The next morning there was another meeting involving Scheubner-Richter, Hermann Göring, and Hermann Kriebel, the Combat League's military leader, likely also Rudolf Hess and Ernst Röhm. They affirmed the decision.[41]

Their strategy was closer to the one Trotsky used in Petrograd in 1917 than the one Mussolini used in Rome. They aimed to take over six key cities in Bavaria—Munich, Augsburg, Nuremberg, Regensburg, Ingolstadt, and Würzburg. In each they would seize railroad stations, communications offices, radio stations, town halls, and police headquarters.[42] The aim was a dictatorship that would keep all Hitler's promises. The economy was to be cleansed of "parasitic elements," but private property left untouched with an emphasis on a strong and independent peasantry. Citizenship was to be "for Germans only," there was to be a crackdown on crime, all opposition parties were to be eliminated, and Communist and Socialist politicians arrested.

Some mention of concentration camps (*Sammellager*) was later found among the papers of one of the conspirators, but it is unlikely that they had really worked out a full-fledged terror system, as is sometimes suggested. The idea of using concentration camps for political enemies was very much in the air, however, and associated mainly with the Soviet Union. There were many stories about them in newspapers, including in the Socialist press, so copying even the hated Soviets was tempting for anyone looking to carry out a revolution.[43]

The timing of the coup fell on the evening of November 8, when Kahr was to address a large audience in the Bürgerbräukeller. This was the fifth anniversary of the revolution of November 1918, and there was bound to be a raucous crowd of anti-Berlin and anti-Socialist activists.

Kahr was speaking to the packed hall when Hitler showed up just after 8:00 p.m. and went to an adjoining room to wait for his armed troop. Upon the arrival of the entourage, which included his bodyguard Ulrich Graf, Max Amann, Putzi Hanfstaengl, Rudolf Hess, and Hermann Göring, he stormed the podium. By the time Hitler, his loaded pistol waving wildly about, reached Kahr, people in the room were in an uproar. He got their attention by firing a shot into the ceiling.[44]

Hitler announced the overthrow of the government and warned that the building was surrounded by six hundred armed men. He then led Kahr, Lossow, and Seisser to a side chamber for discussions. Time passed and the crowd grew restless, so Hitler had to quiet them. The historian

Karl Alexander von Müller wrote down the brief speech Hitler gave when he returned to the main room. The crowd grew calmer when they heard him say, falsely, that the army supported him, but he roused enthusiasm when he told them that Kahr, Lossow, and Seisser would be working for a free Bavaria. He put this question to them: " 'Outside are Kahr, Lossow and Seisser. They are struggling to reach a decision. May I say to them that you will stand behind them?' 'Yes! Yes!' swelled out the roaring answer from all sides. 'In a free Germany,' he shouted passionately out over the crowd, 'there is also room for an autonomous Bavaria! I can say this to you: Either the German Revolution begins tonight or we will all be dead by dawn!' "[45]

Kahr, Lossow, and Seisser caved in. General Ludendorff turned up to offer his support, after assuring himself the outcome was going to be favorable. Hitler then led the four back into the main hall, where they were greeted wildly. This was Hitler's evening. He pressed each of the main players to say a few words, and his three captives grudgingly agreed to stand behind "the new government." Their speeches were received with howls of approval.[46]

But the curtain was about to come down on this political theater. When the lightly armed SA and Combat League tried to secure various strategic places in the city, they realized they were too few. Unlike the situation in Petrograd in 1917, the troops and police were not dispirited. Sometimes they simply locked the front gate of their barracks and left the would-be revolutionaries wondering what to do.

Hitler was still feverishly trying to keep the crowd behind him in the Bürgerbräukeller when he got word that everything was not going as planned. He made the mistake of leaving headquarters to see what he could do, and in his absence Ludendorff, whom he had left in charge, released Kahr, Lossow, and Seisser. The naive Ludendorff accepted their assurances that they would keep their promises, but no sooner were they in safety than they repudiated everything.

There was little or no shooting during the night, and Kahr ordered Lossow to put an end to the putsch as quickly as possible, to avoid bloodshed. The Combat League was not in a position to offer resistance, because large numbers of troops and police were mobilized.[47]

By 5:00 a.m. if not earlier, Hitler had resigned himself to failure. Ludendorff assured him that the army would certainly never fire: "The heavens will fall before the Bavarian Reichswehr turns against me!"[48]

Two thousand or so men from the Combat League, most of them Nazis, with Hitler and his close comrades in the lead, set off at around noon for downtown. The column pushed past the first light police resistance but soon ran into serious opposition. Just who fired the first shot was long disputed, but three or four policemen were killed and fourteen putschists. The most prominent Nazi fatality was Scheubner-Richter, struck by a bullet as he marched arm in arm next to Hitler.[49]

AFTERMATH OF THE HITLER PUTSCH

Following the abortive coup, the ringleaders of the putsch, Hitler among them, were tracked down, arrested, and put on trial between February 26 and March 27, 1924.

The court treated Hitler and the others like celebrities. They were indicted on high treason, but Hitler was allowed to turn the trial into a political grandstand. In his final address he said he never wanted to be just another politician but had "resolved to be the destroyer of Marxism. That is my task, and I know if I achieve that goal, then I would find the title of 'minister' a joke."[50]

Because he was found guilty of treason, it would have been possible for the judges to order his deportation, for he was still an Austrian citizen. Instead, they sentenced him to five years, including time already served, plus a small fine. Three of his co-conspirators received similar light sentences, and Ludendorff was found not guilty. The court's justification for the leniency in sentencing was that the accused had been led "in their deeds by pure nationalistic spirit and noblest, selfless will." The judges were impressed by the aim of the Nazis: "the rescue of the fatherland."[51]

Hitler was released just before Christmas 1924. Like other extremist politicians, he thrived when the socioeconomic situation went from bad to worse. Mixed news began filtering into his cell in late 1923 and early 1924 indicating the economic crisis might be over. One obvious sign was the new currency issued on November 15, when Germans began exchanging their old money for new at the rate of one rentenmark for one billion of the old paper marks.[52]

Chancellor Stresemann managed to create the basis for stability, but he was not rewarded by parliament, which passed a vote of non-confidence against him on November 23. Nevertheless, his accomplishments stood, the inflation ended, and the French went home. The Americans signaled the return of stability by promising to deal with the underlying reparations problem. A commission under Charles Dawes began studying the problem in mid-January 1924.

During the five years that followed, a "precarious normality" returned. The radicals neither went away nor came to accept the republic. In 1924 or 1925 no one had any idea of the great dramas that lay ahead, much less how they would turn out.

6

HITLER STARTS OVER

Hitler wrote an essay in April 1924, just before he was to begin serving his prison sentence in Landsberg. In the unpublished piece he claimed that Marxism had undermined the country since 1914 and that it was foolish of some German leaders to suggest they could simply "forbid" such a movement. He asserted that Marxism was the "deadly enemy of all present-day humanity." With vehemence he insisted that "*Marxist internationalism will only be broken through a fanatical, extreme nationalism of the highest social ethics and morality.* One cannot take away the false idol of Marxism from the people without giving them a better God." He called on the example of Benito Mussolini, whose "greatest merit" was to recognize that point. "In place of destructive, international Marxism, [Mussolini] established national, fanatical Fascism, which resulted in the almost complete dissolution of all the Marxist organizations of Italy."

The task of the National Socialist movement was similar and would be complete only "when Germany appears to be rescued." The battle would not be over until the last Marxist was "either converted or exterminated."[1]

Hitler had never been a friend of parliamentary democracy and elections. Even as a youth in Vienna, he had been decidedly unimpressed with squabbling politicians. The Weimar Republic confirmed his worst fears, and his distrust turned to hatred. Nonetheless, as early as 1919, he calculated that given the present state of German culture, which he regarded as soft and excessively law-abiding, the most effective and lasting way to deal with the Jews was to roll back their civil and legal rights through lawful measures.[2]

For a while, in the midst of the economic and political chaos, he was carried along with the enthusiasm for a Mussolini-style takeover. With that failure, he soon returned to a position that advocated working through parliament to get the revolution he wanted. He told a Party member who visited him in Landsberg, "Instead of working to achieve power by armed conspiracy, we shall have to hold our noses and enter the Reichstag," which is to say, participate in elections "against the Catholic and Marxist deputies. If outvoting them takes longer than outshooting them, at least the results will be guaranteed by their own Constitution!" Moreover, it seemed to him that it was indeed possible for the Nazis to win power through elections. They had thirty-two Reichstag deputies (thanks to the national system of proportional representation) and were the second-largest party in the Bavarian Landtag diet. "Conditions in the country," he mused, "changed so radically."[3]

MEIN KAMPF

Everyone knows about Hitler's notorious autobiography. It has the advantage of being propaganda and so reveals what Hitler wished people to know about him and his ideas. It presents him not so much as he really existed as how he wanted to be regarded and where he thought his appeal lay. What he said was meant to attract followers and win people over. The book was unusually frank about a number of key themes, above all anti-Semitism and anti-Marxism.

Hitler was persuaded to write his book in prison. He dictated it, first to his bodyguard Emil Maurice and later to the ever-faithful Rudolf Hess. Eventually called *Mein Kampf* (My Struggle), the book was brought out by the Party's own publishing house (Eher Verlag) in two large volumes, which together had sold around thirty-six thousand copies by 1929. The first volume was written in 1924 and published the next year. Hitler was released from prison on December 20 that year and wrote the second volume in 1925, publishing it late in 1926. They were expensive, but when Hitler's popularity grew, sales of his book did as well, and eventually it sold ten million copies in the Third Reich.[4]

Mein Kampf was edited by several people and put into shape for publication, but Hitler admitted it was not a great read. The writings of Lenin and Stalin were not exactly page-turners, either, but at least Communism could point to key Marxist and Leninist texts. Stalin won out over his rivals to become Lenin's heir by virtue of his command over these texts and his skill in making his own interpretations appear as scriptural extensions of Leninism and thus beyond dispute.

Hitler's movement, on the other hand, was based on his charismatic leadership, his words and deeds. The Nazi "text" was the schematic one-page program formulated in 1920, and it remained unchanged. Nazism was what Hitler said it was. Unlike Communism, there were no factions offering competing interpretations. Nevertheless, while a Nazi program was not systematically developed, *Mein Kampf* laid out many of Hitler's ideas, if in a disjointed and disorganized way.

The book was written as a political tract and was full of lies and self-deception. Lenin's and Stalin's texts were stitched together with falsehoods and exaggerations as well, but it would be foolish to ignore any of these works if we want to understand and explain how their brutal regimes operated.[5]

Hitler's tome runs to nearly seven hundred pages. Although he did not write much about Bolshevism in it, he continued, as in 1923, to combine anti-Semitism and anti-Marxism and emphasized that his mission was to save the country. His ultimate charge was brutally frank: "In Russian Bolshevism what we see is the attempt by the Jews in the twentieth century to achieve world domination."[6]

The underlying racial theory was culled from a host of authors who had popularized racism. The general synthesis ran as follows: there was a never-ending racial struggle for survival in which the stronger races defeated the weaker. This racial struggle was every bit as foundational for Hitler as class struggle was for Lenin and Stalin.

According to Hitler, in order to preserve the species, the victors in struggle and war created communities, some more valuable than others. Humans were divided into three groups: "the founders of culture, the bearers of culture, and the destroyers of culture." He viewed the "Aryans" as the primary "founders of culture," the Japanese as an example of a "culture bearing" people, and the Jews as the ultimate "destroyers of culture."[7] He endowed Aryans, present in European fantasies from the late eighteenth and early nineteenth centuries, with all the virtues and gave the Jews, or Semites, the worst vices.[8]

He explained his anti-Semitism in terms of striving for racial purity. But the struggle against the Jews had become special and urgent to him, allegedly because they had begun their "great last revolution" via Marxism. The Russian Revolution was held up as "the most frightful example" of what was in store unless Germans fought back. The alternative was National Socialism, which he saw as a "new philosophy of life," *völkisch* or racist in orientation and opposed to Marxism. This new philosophy "finds the essence of mankind in its racial elements. The state it sees in principle as only a means to an end and construes its end as the preservation of the racial existence of man." Hitler proclaimed his belief in the inequality of the races. Not only were the races different, but National Socialism insisted on "their higher or lesser value." This was a kind of knowledge that carried obligations. Those in the know had "to work for the victory of the better and stronger, and insist on the subordination of the inferior and weaker in accordance with the eternal will that dominates this universe."[9]

This racial theory was a deliberate and calculated attempt to make anti-Semitism the centerpiece of a political strategy that would appeal. Hitler's intention was to win over the people by explaining anti-Semitism in terms of science and reason. Similarly, he called on what went for science in other areas of his racial thought. For example, he favored keeping the race pure by sterilizing the incurably ill and forbidding marriage to those deemed unfit. He accepted uncritically the body of teachings on eugenics as if it were revealed gospel. Eugenics was popular at the time not only in Germany but also in the United States. Its simple principle was to foster "racially fit" people and to stop all others (the "dysgenic") from having children. Eugenics and compulsory sterilization were a perfect fit with the rest of Hitler's racial philosophy.[10]

He despised parliamentary democracy, but the dictatorship he wanted had to be backed by the people. In *Mein Kampf* he wrote there were two foundations of political authority: popularity and power. Popularity combined with a firm grasp of power would result in a system we might call a consensus dictatorship, in which by common consent the people agree to be ruled by a strongman. Hitler pointed to the failed German revolution of 1918–19, when the "Marxist gangsters" tried being popular and succeeded for a time but did not know how to rule.[11]

In Germany, he said, "the *real* organizer of the revolution [of 1918–19] and its actual wirepuller was the international Jew," but the German people were "not yet ripe for being forced into the bloody Bolshevistic morass, as had happened in Russia." In Hitler's view, a major factor in the German response to revolution was the "greater racial unity that existed between the German intelligentsia and the German manual worker." In Russia, by contrast, the intelligentsia was "in large part not of Russian nationality or at least was of non-Slavic racial character." There was only a "thin intellectual upper stratum," and it was easily stripped away. Once the illiterate masses turned on this intelligentsia, the "fate of the country was decided, the revolution had succeeded." But far from winning through revolution, "the Russian illiterate had become the defenseless slave of his Jewish dictators who, it must be admitted, were clever enough to let this dictatorship ride on the phrase 'people's dictatorship.' "[12]

In *Mein Kampf,* Hitler established in broad outline what he wanted to do. After reviewing the options, he said, "We National Socialists must not flinch from our aim in foreign policy, namely, to secure for the German people the land and soil to which they are entitled." The "soil" was in the east, specifically in Russia, and it was going to be the "duty" of the National Socialists to get it or else Germany was "doomed to destruction." In a remarkable statement about the alternatives, Hitler said that "Germany will either be a world power or there will be no Germany."[13]

To Hitler's way of thinking, when Russia became a victim to "Jewish Bolshevism," it was a sign given by fate. The empire had been ruled, he claimed, by a "Germanic element" that had provided the intelligentsia and organized the once mighty state. That class was "almost totally exterminated and extinguished. It has been replaced by the Jew. Impossible as it is for the Russian to shake off the yoke of the Jew by his own resources, it is just as impossible for the Jew to maintain the mighty empire forever. . . . And the end of Jewish rule in Russia will also be the end of Russia as a state."[14]

Having said that the "Germanic element" in Russia had been extinguished, Hitler now called on Germans outside Russia to take up the challenge of the racial struggle. "We have been chosen by Fate to witness a catastrophe which will be the strongest confirmation of the soundness of the *völkisch* theory. Our task, the mission of the National Socialist movement, is to bring our own people to such political awareness that they will not see their goal for the future in the breath-taking terms of a new Alexander's conquest, but in the industrious work of the German plow, to which the sword need only give soil."[15]

The war with Russia was presented as a war of self-defense. "Germany is today the next great war aim of Bolshevism. It requires all the force of a nascent missionary idea to lift our people up again, to free them from the snares of this international serpent." The fight was to be "against Jewish world Bolshevization."[16] In a follow-up book, completed only in 1928 and never published in his lifetime, he fleshed out these foreign policy outlines and their unique combination of race and space. The key points, however, were already there in his autobiography.[17]

The views espoused in *Mein Kampf* provided Hitler's followers with insight into his thought. One of the trained speakers of the movement later said, "The book must be the Bible of all National Socialists. The more I became absorbed in it, the more was I gripped by the greatness of the thoughts expounded therein. I felt that I was eternally bound to this man." Not surprisingly, the writer (born in 1890 in Lower Silesia) displayed a high degree of anti-Semitism. His lengthy remarks were made in an essay in 1934 for a contest sponsored by an American professor.[18]

No doubt many did not bother to read Hitler's book, but that was not necessary, because he repeated the same themes often in his speeches. The book was wrong in details about Hitler's life, full of factual errors, and confused about the scientific and linguistic origins of key concepts—most important, terms like "Aryan" and "Semites." But what Hitler offered his followers was a brutal philosophy of life, backed up by "science," radically opposed to Marxism in all its forms, unashamedly racist, and irreversibly committed to anti-Semitism.

Hitler said exactly what he would like to do, and in his hundreds of speeches from 1926 to 1933 there was consistency. That does not mean he had a blueprint from the start. Much of what happened was based on reactions of the moment to opportunities and possibilities that arose. His "theories," however, indicate how the madness of his thoughts and actions held together. What he said and wrote before he got into power revealed an agenda of sorts. Anyone with the slightest interest in politics at the time, including foreigners like Stalin, could have picked up clues just by reading the published record.

FÜHRER CULT AND LEGAL REVOLUTION

Ernst Hanfstaengl, one of Hitler's close friends and connected to the better-off social classes, visited him in prison and helped smuggle out some of *Mein Kampf.* He and Hitler had marched together on the fateful day of November 9, 1923, but Putzi, as he was nicknamed, managed to escape. He happily agreed to read the proofs of Hitler's book, but he was appalled at errors in style and the poor grammar and thought some of it utter rubbish. Nevertheless, he remarked of the book, "If you cut your way through the verbiage it reveals the essential Hitler, with all his blind spots, combined with fantastic energy and single-mindedness with which he adhered to this rigmarole."[19]

Hanfstaengl put his finger on the moment when the führer cult began to form. His impression was that until the putsch in 1923, it was always simply "Herr Hitler." Rudolf Hess seems to have started the cult in the Landsberg prison, where he began using the term *"der Chef"* (the boss), but soon adopted *"der Führer"* in imitation of how the Italians were using *"il Duce"* to refer to Mussolini. In addition, the *"Heil"* greeting, which was (and still is) common in Austria, gradually became something more. "Heil Hitler," at least according to Hanfstaengl, was a password and gradually endowed Hitler with special qualities, and for that reason the snobbish Hanfstaengl refused to use it. He insisted on the old and formal "Herr Hitler" and later "Herr Reichskanzler." Hitler never asked or ordered anyone to call him the führer, much as Stalin played down being called the *vozhd'*, but both took pleasure in the honor.[20]

The leader cult and Heil Hitler greeting fitted together and personalized the Nazi movement around the much-hoped-for strongman. Dictators appeared all across Europe in the interwar period, most notably Stalin, Hitler, and Mussolini. They invariably dressed in full military regalia and often used a salute. Their uniformed followers organized along the lines of the army, as if they were still engaged in war, as, in their own terms, they were.

By mid-February 1925, only months out of prison, Hitler was laying the groundwork for a new approach to gaining political power. He got permission from the Bavarian government to remove the ban on the outlawed NSDAP and the *Völkischer Beobachter*. He called for a new founding meeting, as the Party had all but ceased to exist in his absence. Straightaway he demanded recognition as the leader. Anyone who could not accept his dominance had no place in the Party. The Sturmabteilung (SA) was also refounded, and what both stood for was simple: "The entire force of the movement is directed at the most terrible enemy of the German people: Jews and Marxism."[21]

At a meeting held on February 27 in the Bürgerbräukeller, the scene of his attempted putsch on November 8, 1923, Hitler refounded the Party. The hall was packed with up to three thousand, and the police had to turn away at least two thousand more. As always nothing was for free, and the price of admission — one mark — though small, asked for at least a token commitment from participants. Inspiring the crowd, Hitler called for unity around his leadership and for the main contenders in the Nazi movement to join him.

He revived the Party's flag, reminding the audience of its significance, with the swastika as the symbol for work, the white as a sign of nationalist predisposition, and the red as a sign of the social sentiment. Their aim was summed up: "Struggle against the devilish power that drove Germany into misery, fighting Marxism as well as the spiritual carriers of this world plague and pestilence, the *Jews*."[22]

The speech was reported under headlines such as "Hitler Fever," "A Provocation of the State's Authority," "The Dictator Hitler," and other less colorful terms to signal that he was back, unrepentant, and popular. His challenge was answered on March 9 by the Bavarian police, who banned him from public speaking on the grounds that he incited violence. The gag order was upheld for two years, until March 5, 1927, but he was still able to address "private" meetings.[23]

The Party consensus was that it would have to pursue its aims legally and work through elections.[24] One of the first occasions to see what the Party would do arose with the election of a new president of the republic. Friedrich Ebert of the SPD, the first president, died on February 28, 1925.

Hitler and the right wing despised that man for embodying the betrayal of November 9, 1918. But Ebert's vacant position was too important to be ignored. The president's role as defined under the constitution gave him even greater powers than the American president. He was head of state, elected directly by the people for seven years, and commanded the armed forces. He appointed the chancellor, the head of the government, who had to have the confidence (or toleration) of the Reichstag but who could stay on if the president supported him. Under article 48 of the constitution, the president could declare an emergency and, if he saw fit, pass laws — even the budget — by special decree. In theory, the Reichstag could terminate these emergency powers, but the president could stop such action by dissolving the Reichstag and calling new elections. Ebert had issued 134 emergency decrees to uphold democracy and the republic and demonstrated that the office of the president was the dominant one in the country.

The Nazis could not capitalize on Ebert's death, but Hitler manipulated General Ludendorff into becoming the Party's candidate, one of seven who stood for election. None of them won a clear majority, so a second ballot was needed. Ludendorff's showing was so bad (1.1 percent of the vote) on the first ballot that he dropped out. This result, as Hitler no doubt foresaw, eliminated Ludendorff as a possible right-wing rival. In the second round the right wing came up with a new candidate, the seventy-eight-year-old field marshal Paul von Hindenburg, the hero of Tannenberg. The SPD and Catholic Center agreed to support the former chancellor Wilhelm Marx (of the Center Party). The Communists insisted that the head of their Party (Ernst Thälmann) stay in the race.

Hindenburg did not win an absolute majority, but obtained 14,655,641 votes (48.3 percent) over Marx, who got 13,751,605 (45.3 percent). Thälmann was a distant third, but a spoiler with 1,931,151 votes (6.4 percent), which would have been enough to elect Marx.[25] The Socialists bitterly pointed to the Communists and blamed them for Hindenburg's victory. The old field marshal made practically no personal appearances during the election but rallied large sections of the country in resentment against the SPD and the KPD. His election was a defeat for the republic.

Hindenburg was an antirepublican with strong antidemocratic tendencies, and he now occupied the most powerful position in Germany. The worry was not so much Hindenburg himself as the "General Staff clique" (*Generalstabskamarilla*) surrounding him. In fact, he turned out to be more loyal to the constitution than some hoped and others feared, but for all that it would be Hindenburg, acting on the advice of those around him in January 1933, who would appoint Hitler as chancellor.

New people began to join the NSDAP inside and beyond Bavaria. Some of these men, like Joseph Goebbels from Rheydt in the Ruhr, brought their own ideas, not all of which were a good fit with Hitler's. Goebbels was well educated and articulate and along with some new joiners more "socialistic" than Hitler. He went so far (early in his career) as to empathize with Bolshevism and to suggest an alliance between Germany and Soviet Russia. Gregor Strasser, another highly educated man from Bavaria, carried the Nazi message to the north on Hitler's instructions. Strasser was moderate on anti-Semitism and inclined to socioeconomic positions similar to those taken by Goebbels. Other shadings of opinion could be found in the expanding Party, but there was nothing like the factionalism among the Marxists either before or after the Russian Revolution. The Nazis agreed on one key point, and that was Hitler's indispensability.

Hitler called a "leader meeting" in Bamberg for February 14, 1926, and according to the police report, between sixty and sixty-five Party leaders attended. He firmly rejected any alliance with the Soviet Union. Any "going with" (*Zusammengehen*) Russia would lead to "the immediate Bolshevization of Germany" and thus would be "national suicide." On the question of land, Hitler was concerned about the health of the race and believed the German people needed space in Eastern Europe, not in distant colonies. As for whether to expropriate the lands of the German princes, Hitler came out against people like Goebbels.

Hitler would not hear of nationalizing land. He was not going to have Nazis confused with Communists. "For us there are no princes, but only Germans." He also took the opportunity to link up the more socialistically minded among them to the Jews. "We stand on the basis of the law and will not give a Jewish system of exploitation a legal pretext for the complete plundering of our people." Hitler did, however, want to see the "expropriation of the non-German 'princes' of money, of the stock exchange, trade, and commerce."[26]

Goebbels confided in his diary how shocked he was by Hitler's stand on these questions. He wondered whether the man was some kind of "reactionary," with poor judgment at that: "Russian question: completely misses the point. Italy and England, natural allies. Terrible! Our task is the destruction of Bolshevism. Bolshevism is Jewish work. We must become the heir to Russia! 180 million!" Goebbels wrote that Hitler's speech was "probably one of the greatest disappointments of my life."[27]

It took time to bring him and the northern group around. What helped heal the potential split was the personal impression Hitler was able to make. He invited Goebbels to Munich and explained his speech in person. As he put it, "Russia wants to gobble us up," and with such statements and the personal touch Hitler won over the feisty Goebbels. The latter wrote in his diary on April 13: "I bend to the greater one, to the political genius."[28] Like Gregor Strasser, he understood that without Hitler they had no chance of getting anywhere.

Hitler was clever enough to balance this kind of dressing-down, delivered when necessary in private, by holding out his hand, a gesture soon followed up by a promotion in the Party. In September 1926, Strasser was made propaganda leader, and by year's end Goebbels had become gauleiter (district leader) in Berlin. These were two of Hitler's best appointments, both of them zealous, intelligent, and imaginative, as well as good organizers and gifted speakers in their own right.[29]

PART THREE

STALIN TRIUMPHS OVER POLITICAL RIVALS

7

BATTLE FOR COMMUNIST UTOPIA

By the time Lenin died at age fifty-three on January 21, 1924, the Communist regime was established and its key features in place. The one-party and one-ideology state had a marked tendency to use terror, and power was in the hands of a half dozen men in the Politburo, an executive committee of the Communist Party's Central Committee. Lenin's highly centralized system of rule was in the name of the "dictatorship of the proletariat," but behind all the institutions, the fanfare of the congresses, meetings, and the constitution, the Soviet leader was more powerful and autocratic than the mightiest of the tsars. Lenin annihilated enemies and ignored the will of the people as he saw fit.

Stalin was the most poorly educated of all the Communist leaders, but he had a psychological advantage over his rivals because he was from humble origins in far-off Georgia, an economically backward, non-Russian-speaking province in the unruly Caucasus. He learned Russian as a second language and always spoke with a Georgian accent.[1]

He was born on December 6, 1878—but the date has been questioned. His father, Vissarion Dzhughashvili, was a shoemaker, known for having been a harsh man and excessive drinker who deserted the family altogether. His mother, Ekaterina, like other poor women in the small town of Gori, took work where she could find it, including as a seamstress and housekeeper. She did everything she could to foster Joseph's religious upbringing and education. When he was nine years old, she got him into the Eastern Orthodox elementary school in their little town.

In 1894, at fifteen, Joseph traveled to the provincial capital city at Tiflis (Tbilisi), where he entered the seminary. It was the most important high school in the Caucasus, but grim and regimented. Students were among the brightest in the area and interested in politics. The "hot" topics of the day included Marxism and other advanced Western ideas, but also the grievances of the Georgian people. Even by Russian standards Georgia was behind. Serfdom persisted after it was abolished in Russia in 1861, and when the serfs were finally emancipated in Georgia, they got less favorable terms than those in Russia. The man who was to become the tyrannical Stalin was an impressionable youth, no doubt affected by the oppressive atmosphere and the discontent around him. He ceased being a model seminary student and became rebellious.

The young Stalin committed quickly to the "cause." By eighteen or nineteen he had renounced existing society and given up thoughts of a "normal" future. By 1899 he had left the seminary, not even bothering to write his exams. He was attracted to Marxist circles and involved in discussions of the outlawed texts. His official biography, published half a century later, added a heroic note by claiming he was expelled because of his Marxist propaganda work. Once out of school, he briefly found a regular job, but soon opted for life on the run and committed to being a full-time revolutionary.

The Russian movement comprised a loose collection of socially marginal individuals drawn to Marx's ideas, which already had many adherents in Western Europe. Populist or agricultural Socialism was more widely accepted in Russia, but even that had a marginal following. Marx's ideas were considered the most progressive of the day by the handful of devotees. A few showed up at the founding congress of the Russian Social Democratic Labor Party (RSDLP) in 1898. A more serious effort was undertaken in 1903 with the second congress, but (as indicated earlier) it split at once into two factions, with Lenin and the Bolsheviks (majority) on one side and the Mensheviks, or minority, on the other.

Lenin made his name among young Russian radicals as one of the founding members of *Iskra* (Spark) in 1900. The émigré newspaper was published in Germany and favored underground activity that would "spark" the fires of revolution. Lenin became far better known for the pamphlet *What Is to Be Done?* (1902). It won over people like Stalin, who were excited by the idea that a small band of revolutionaries could bring fundamental change. They accepted Lenin's sneering about the workers' disappointing inclination to work within the system: "The history of all countries shows that the working class, by itself, is not able to get beyond trade-union consciousness, that is, the belief that workers need to join together in unions, fight the employers, and try to force the government to pass necessary labor legislation, and so on." Lenin readily adopted the catchall Marxist dictum that workers who did not agree suffered from "false consciousness" and did not really know their own best interests. Unlike other Marxists, he did not take the paternalistic route to "enlighten" workers, but he determined that revolution would have to be brought to them from outside their ranks.[2]

Stalin was attracted and became a Leninist long before he met the source of the inspiration. He staunchly defended Lenin's *What Is to Be Done?* in the Georgian revolutionary underground. Like Lenin he favored a tightly knit group of highly committed individuals who were prepared to use whatever methods were necessary to bring about the kind of world they wanted. They both felt they knew what was best for those whom they would "save."[3]

STALIN'S EARLY POLITICAL VENTURES

Stalin was the type of extremist who was, in Lenin's terms, "boundlessly devoted to the revolution."[4] Given the vigilance of the tsarist secret police and their spies, however, he no sooner appeared in the radical circles in Georgia than he was hounded and driven underground. He adopted "Koba" as the first of many noms de guerre he would use. It was from a well-known Georgian novel of the day by Alexander Kazbegi in which the heroic character Koba leads a mountain people to freedom and independence. Joseph Dzhughashvili evidently felt comfortable picturing himself as Koba, and his new vocation became that of the full-time revolutionary.

He entered the strange and at times slightly mad underground of writers, dreamers, idealists, fanatics, anarchists, conspirators, and assassins. He became a prime example of a new political breed, men and women who devoted themselves selflessly to some higher cause and who were prepared to deny themselves all the worldly comforts to attain their ends. They wanted the people to have complete happiness and earthly salvation, if necessary through violence and terrorism. Most were ascetics, almost like medieval monks. Koba was arrested at least eight times and exiled, often to distant parts of Siberia. His ardor could not be crushed, and he repeatedly escaped, somehow made his way back to Russia, and threw himself into the struggle again.

He saw poverty and social misery for himself and experienced what happened when large industries replaced handicraftsmen, for his shoemaker father was put out of business by the competition of a new factory. For true believers like Stalin, Marxism offered "scientifically" grounded certainty that the way to happiness was by going forward, not back, and that the "good" would inherit the earth.

Hundreds of men and women took up this message and the vocation of the professional revolutionary at the same time as Stalin. In Russian Marxism, which blended the teachings of Marx with revolutionary terrorism, there was no room for the half measures of democrats or liberals. The desire for root-and-branch change went beyond the Russian Marxists, to include other revolutionary sects. The emotions ran so deep that all those who wanted change were affected, so that mere moderates were considered as bad as the tsarist regime itself.

The number of victims of terrorist attacks, including innocent bystanders, increased steadily. There were approximately one hundred casualties in such incidents between the 1860s and around 1900, but after 1905 terrorist murder reached epidemic proportions. Newspapers stopped carrying full stories, and some only added a short section naming various revolutionary groups thought responsible for the assassinations, bank robberies, and other such crimes. Across the empire in the first seventeen years of the twentieth century, terrorists killed or wounded an estimated seventeen thousand people.[5]

There is little information on Stalin's early career, and even less on his private life. Although he was a rebel against existing society, he was traditionalist enough to get married in 1902 or 1903. His wife, Ekaterina, was the sister of Alexander Svanidze, a revolutionary Stalin met in one of the safe houses in Tiflis. What he liked about Ekaterina was that she was not really one of the fashionable "new women" in the movement, whom he considered amoral because of their belief in sexual freedom. Stalin's wife made a home for him, and he, a terrorist on the run, visited her when he could. Exactly where they lived and how they paid the bills remains a mystery, as does the exact birth date (likely 1908, sometimes given as 1907) of their only son, Yakov. Stalin was deeply saddened when Ekaterina died in November 1907. He continued the life of the hard-bitten revolutionary and moved around to keep one step ahead of the police.[6]

Lenin spelled out more about Party organization through the newspaper *Iskra* after the turn of the century. He was not living in Russia and was out of touch with ordinary people in the vast tsarist empire. He was keen to take the fight into the public arena, but knew so little he did not predict how society would react to the calamities of 1904 and 1905 — brought about in the wake of the disastrous Russo-Japanese War. He did not initially appreciate the significance of Bloody Sunday in January 1905, along with the series of strikes, mutinies, and assorted social protests that would culminate in revolution. The young Stalin was more involved in events as part of the Tiflis Committee of the RSDLP but played no leadership role in distant Georgia, where the repression during the year was severe.[7]

Lenin returned to Russia after the October Manifesto of 1905 was issued. He was psychologically remote from the crowds, however, and unlike Leon Trotsky, the fiery Menshevik and leader of the radical St. Petersburg soviet, he was no rabble-rousing orator. He stood out by his readiness to advocate terrorism of all kinds, including assassinations and "confiscations." He made outlandish and strangely amateurish suggestions, for example, that the political activists keep acid with them at all times, to throw at the police who might pursue them. He was prepared, though, to take advantage of the new elections. Unlike most leaders of the Party, he thought it might be useful to run candidates for the State Duma.

Once the uprising of December 1905 was repressed and the tide of what was still a moderate revolution turned, Lenin went for his own safety to Finland. The lesson of December, he wrote during the following summer, "proved" that the general strike was not the answer. Instead, the "immediate task" was to organize the masses and prepare them to overthrow the regime. He wanted power, not to play at elections. Military tactics would be needed in the coming "great mass strug-gle," or so he predicted with the usual certainty. The time would come, he said, for the attack of the organized masses, who would be led into what he called a "ruthless war of extermination."[8] Toward the end of 1907 he went to Western Europe and did not return to Russia until a decade later, after the collapse of the tsarist regime.

Stalin ventured out of Georgia for the first time when sent as an elected delegate to a Bolshevik conference in Tampere, Finland, in December 1905. He remembered well how he looked forward at last to seeing Lenin, "the mountain eagle of our party, the great man," but he promptly opposed Lenin's suggestion that the Party engage in electoral politics now that the tsar, under the pressure of events in 1905, had granted democratic concessions.[9] Lenin's aim was certainly not a parlia-mentary democracy, but he thought there might be gains to be made by burrowing away at the system from within. Stalin disagreed because he believed that such political participation would sap the strength of the revolutionary movement. He wanted no compromises, but a "demo-cratic dictatorship of the proletariat and peasantry."[10]

Lenin ran into more opposition when he pushed for reuniting with the Mensheviks. That proposal was taken up again in April 1906 and passed at the All-Russian Conference of RSDLP in Stockholm. Although on the surface the Party was reunited, the underlying split did not go away. The Mensheviks (led by people like Trotsky) stood for a revolution, but, in keeping with their version of Marxism—certainly not Lenin's—the revolution would be led by the middle classes and result in civil rights and democracy.

Stalin attended the Stockholm meetings, and though he continued to hold Lenin in awe, he was no sycophant. The two disagreed about impor-tant issues. Lenin believed the land should be taken over by the state and nationalized, whereas Stalin thought Communists should seize the opportunity to win over the poor peasants by giving them the land they longed for. Lenin won the debate, but at the time of the October Revo-lution of 1917, when he had to give land to the peasants to keep them on the side of the revolution, he realized Stalin had been right.[11]

In the prewar era Stalin was generally conciliatory toward opponents within the Party and disliked how Lenin baited and abused them. Never-theless, he went along with the unsavory tactics and in the Caucasus worked on Lenin's behalf with another revolutionary with the nom de guerre "Kamo" (real name Simon Ter-Petrosyan), an Armenian friend from his youth in Gori. They were part of the shady Combat Technical Group, but today we would term it the Party's armed wing in charge of "fund-raising," which is to say, robbing banks. These kinds of activities appalled the Mensheviks and separated them from the Bolsheviks. Lenin and his comrades favored such "expropriations," but Trotsky and others said what they were doing made them little better than common criminals.[12]

Lenin was delighted about an armed and violent robbery of a stage-coach in Tiflis in June 1907 that was organized by Stalin and carried out by Kamo. Bolshevik lawlessness was condemned again by the 1907 London conference of the RSDLP, but under Lenin's aegis terrorism and "expropriations" continued to help finance the lives of the revolutionaries. Some of these "exes" (thefts) in Georgia took large sums of money, and later in life Stalin boasted that some netted as much as a quarter-million rubles. Lenin and the Bolsheviks continued these practices despite what the Mensheviks or anyone else said. Thus, well before the Bolsheviks came to power, they worried little about conventional morality and legality.[13]

Lenin took a great liking to Stalin for his commitment, ruthlessness, and intellectual abilities. He wanted Stalin at his side as a natural ally, but under close watch by the tsarist secret police their holding meetings was no easy matter. Stalin got recognition for his exploits and for some of his publications back in Georgia, but the real turning point in his career came in January 1912. Lenin demanded at meetings of the Bolshevik faction in Prague, though Stalin was not there, that he be brought into the new Central Committee. Lenin convened the meeting in such a way that only eighteen delegates showed up, sixteen of them Bolsheviks, but they went ahead and put together the committee.[14]

Lenin's favoring of Stalin was not surprising given the latter's attitudes, loyalties, and "fund-raising" activities. Stalin was a Leninist to the core and a staunch opponent of the Mensheviks in the Caucasus. By 1912 Lenin was more appreciative than he had been earlier when he had disagreed with Stalin and other *praktiki,* or "practical workers," about giving the peasants land. He was beginning to see something special in Stalin, the "man of steel," as he was calling himself at this time. Stalin had used a variety of aliases until around 1910, when "Koba" began adding the new surname "Stalin." He continued to use Koba as his first name and only started using his real first name, Joseph, during the October Revolution.

STALIN AS A NON-RUSSIAN

Stalin had other qualities that made him a good choice for Lenin. He knew the political situation on the ground in Russia, above all in the Caucasus region, and also had the advantage of being closer in social background to the working class than most other leading lights in the Party. He had organized strikes and was directly involved with workers.

As well, Stalin was a non-Russian and well acquainted with the complex nationality question, an aspect of his background that would have had a natural appeal for Lenin, with his ambitions to carry out a revolution in what was after all a multinational empire. At a Central Committee meeting with Party activists in Cracow in late 1912, the two spoke at length about the nationality question, a topic that was gaining ground everywhere in Europe and a hot issue for Socialists. Lenin suggested Stalin write an article on the topic for *Prosveshchenie* (Enlightenment), the Party's main theoretical journal.

Stalin went from Cracow to Vienna in January–February to do more research. When Lenin received the finished article, he was delighted and, in an oft-cited letter to Maxim Gorky in February, simply referred to Koba as the "wonderful Georgian" who was writing an essay for him. In it Stalin showed that he was at home with the issue of nationalities and the ethnic groups in the Caucasus and that he saw through the sophisticated debates on nationalism among the Socialists in Western Europe. His essay became a classic and paved the way for him to be named commissar of nationalities in Lenin's government five years later.

Contrary to what one might expect, Stalin did not favor merely assimilating the minorities into one great Russian melting pot. He also did not accept the view of some Western Socialists that the answer for minorities was to be granted more autonomy and have their own elected bodies no matter where they happened to live inside a multinational empire. He thought that strategy would lead to fragmentation, and he called instead for national self-determination, whereby the government would foster the language, culture, and schools of minority groups. However, workers of all nationalities would not join their own separate institutions; instead, they would form "integral collective bodies, which would come together as one party" and work for what he called the "complete democratization of the country."[15]

Stalin's approach would stop the splintering of the revolutionary movement into hundreds of national variants. In the long run in a multilingual state, particularly one with as many ethnic groups as the new Soviet Union, there were no easy solutions to nationality problems.[16]

In late February 1913, Stalin ended his stay abroad after about six weeks—the longest period he was ever outside Russia—and returned to St. Petersburg. He was promptly arrested and exiled yet again, this time for four years in Siberia. He did not return until after the collapse of the tsarist regime in February 1917.

STALIN IN 1917

Stalin's role in the revolutionary events of 1917 was small. He missed several important meetings on the eve of the October coup, and his reputation suffered for not being included on an assignment list of those leading it on October 25.[17] He was, however, on the Military Revolutionary Committee (MRC) and the Bolshevik Central Committee, and appears to have been more involved in the events than is often supposed. At the stormy meeting of the Second All-Russian Congress of Soviets on the evening of October 25, Stalin made no speeches and did not make his presence felt. Nevertheless, it seems an exaggeration to suggest he was the man who missed the revolution.[18]

Soon enough he was appointed a member of Sovnarkom, the new government, as the commissar of nationalities. He was the obvious choice because of his ties to Lenin and because as a Georgian he was one of the few non-Russians among Bolshevik leaders. His presence helped convey the appearance that the takeover represented the country as a whole.

However, Stalin could point to no heroic feats, great speeches, or monumental decisions of his own during the revolution itself, a fact that embarrassed him for the rest of his life. It was held against him by opponents like Trotsky, the inspiring speaker, "genius" behind the coup, creator of the Red Army, and renowned military leader during the civil war. Stalin did not seem to have any obvious gifts that marked him for greatness.

A potential Communist leader had to demonstrate expertise in Marxist theory. On that score Stalin was no match for Trotsky or for the younger and brilliant Nikolai Bukharin. Therefore, in 1917 or 1918 it was anything but clear that Stalin would become Lenin's successor.

Stalin would, however, learn better than anyone how to build on the foundations established by Lenin. It might be tempting to think that if Lenin had only gotten rid of Stalin at some point, then all the abuses associated with the subsequent history of the Soviet Union might have been avoided. That assumption would be mistaken. It was Lenin who established the new regime, complete with secret police, concentration camps, and suppression of civil liberties. None of those who competed with Stalin to be Lenin's heir would have changed these fundamentals. However, Stalin was the logical successor to Lenin in the sense that he fully internalized Lenin's thought and built on it faithfully.

8

LENIN'S PASSING, STALIN'S VICTORY

The new Communist leaders were bedeviled by major economic, cultural, and political problems. Russia was a backward society compared with its great Western rivals in 1914, and the Great War, the revolution, and the civil war made things worse. Russia's gross industrial output in 1921 was 69 percent lower than in 1913. Agricultural production was down as much or more, and the country faced famine. The utopian dreamers were professional revolutionaries but were almost completely devoid of any relevant practical experience in governing. Where was the expertise to come from to run the country?

The civil service strike that began at the start of the regime soon ended. The Bolsheviks dominated the higher ranks of the administrative pyramid, but they had to allow the lower levels to be run as of old by tsarist officials they inherited. Lenin admitted to the Eleventh Party Congress in March 1922 that the Communists were incapable of directing the giant bureaucratic machine, which fell off drastically in the countryside. It was difficult enough to control the Cheka in Moscow, for example, but it became almost a law unto itself in the distant parts of the new republic.[1]

Lenin and the Bolsheviks despised the "bourgeois" specialists in the civil service and elsewhere in the economy but had to rely on them. In April 1918, Lenin vented his fury at "the high price" of letting these people stay on. He called the excessive salaries of these specialists a "tribute" that had to be paid for the backwardness of the country. The hope was to educate the masses quickly and thus relieve the Communist state from its regrettable reliance on the bourgeoisie.

A second major problem, arguably even more perplexing than Russia's economic backwardness, was the fact that most people in the country did not want a Communist-style revolution. How was it possible to build a Socialist society when so many rejected its fundamental tenets?

Most Russian Marxists believed that the country was not ready for a Socialist revolution in 1917, and Lenin had been almost alone in pushing for the coup. He famously admitted that Russia was an "inadequately cultured country" and that it was "semi-Asiatic," but he plunged ahead with single-minded fanaticism. However, it was not so easy to solve the two central problems facing the new regime even after the organized opposition was beaten: Russia's underdevelopment and the unpopularity of Communism.

Lenin advocated thoroughgoing violence and even civil war in the name of the higher cause of Communism. Terror was employed on a scale unprecedented in Russian or European history, and Stalin, who was Lenin's keenest disciple, learned his lessons well.

They had awakened enough support to beat the White armies and the forces of the counterrevolution by appealing to the poorest peasants, who worried the Whites would restore the old system and they would lose their lands.

The Communists also aroused a messianic zeal within the minds of some people, who yearned for the universal cause. They won over young idealists, for whom achieving utopia justified any means. The Party grew from 115,000 in January 1918 to 576,000 in January 1921. Despite purges and resignations, membership hit 1 million in 1926 and never fell below that number again. It was and remained mainly a workers' party, with less than 30 percent of its members peasants during Lenin's era and even later. As best we can judge, the new joiners were the "bold and committed," but their motives ran from idealism all the way to a desire for vengeance against the exploiters. The diaries and autobiographies of

Communists who lived through those times reveal that many heartily agreed with the methods and the aims of their leaders.

Lenin's role was crucial in the creation of the regime, but he did not act alone. The disciples in his entourage grew in number and, whatever their earlier beliefs, came round to his view that the revolution justified the use of violence. They saw no contradiction in the fact that utopian Communism could be kept in power only by using untrammeled terror.

By the end of the civil war Lenin had become in practice a dictator. His colleagues usually rushed to agree with him and competed in their radicalism and advocacy of violence. It was a fleeting moment when they dared suggest that the terror might be getting out of hand. If they hinted at some disagreement, he wanted them purged or worse.

"SEEING LIKE A GENERAL"

The inescapable economic problems could not be overcome by applying terror. Holding on to radical Communism was making the situation worse, and the only realistic alternative was to backpedal somewhat, to get the economy going again before trying to steam full speed toward Communism. Lenin decided, in the face of much opposition in the Party, to introduce the New Economic Policy (NEP). As he put it in several speeches at the Tenth Party Congress in March 1921, they had made mistakes. On the second to last day of the meetings he admitted that as "long as there is no revolution in other countries, the only thing that can save the Socialist revolution in Russia is agreement with the peasantry." Given the vast country, some freedom of exchange at the local level was inevitable, and in trying to stamp that out, they went too far. "We must recognize the fact," he continued, "that the masses are utterly worn out and exhausted. What can you expect after seven years of war in this country, if the more advanced countries still feel the effects of four years of war? In this backward country, the workers, who have made unprecedented sacrifices, and the mass of the peasants are in a state of utter exhaustion. What is needed now is an economic breathing space."[2]

This was bitter medicine, and Lenin had to face down the militants who did not want a whisper about appearing to return to the past. He was a more flexible tactician than the doctrinaire Communists. The revolution had started in a country that was backward and disadvantaged. That was why, as he told his comrades frankly at the Ninth All-Russian Congress of Soviets in December 1921, "we have to retreat to state capitalism, retreat to concessions, retreat to trade. Without this, it will not be possible to have good relations with the peasants in the terrible conditions in which we now find ourselves. Without this, the revolution's vanguard might quickly move so far ahead that it would lose touch with the peasants. There would be no contact between the vanguard and the peasants, and that would mean the collapse of the revolution."[3]

Nevertheless, he remained committed to the principle of one-party rule. He introduced the NEP as a necessary evil. He made his undiminished militancy clear at the meeting of the Communist International in early July 1922: "Dictatorship is a state of intense war. That happens to be the state we are in. There is no military invasion at present; but we are still isolated. . . . Until the struggle is decided, this awful state of war will continue. . . . And we say: we do not promise any freedom, or any democracy. We say to the peasants quite openly that they must choose between the rule of the bourgeoisie and the rule of the Bolsheviks."[4]

Vyacheslav M. Molotov, one of the most influential of the Soviet Communist leaders, recalled Lenin's seeing like a general: "Now we are retreating to retrench, but then we will launch an even greater offensive!"[5] Many of the committed, believing the answer was more Communism, not less, were disgusted and turned in their membership cards.

Lenin wanted to relax the terror as well, if only temporarily, and suggested at the Ninth All-Russian Congress of Soviets that the Cheka had done good work but that it had to be reformed:

> The task now facing us is the development of trade, which is required by the New Economic Policy, and this demands greater revolutionary legality. Of course, had we made this the priority when we were attacked and Soviet power was seriously threatened, we would have been pedants, playing at revolution, but not making the revolution. The closer we come to conditions of unshakable and lasting power and the more trade develops, the more important it is to promote greater revolutionary legality, and the less need there is to have the state match the plotters blow for blow.[6]

On January 23, 1922, the Politburo renamed the secret police the State Political Administration—Gosudarstvennoe Politicheskoe Upravlenie, or GPU. The strength of the secret police was reduced from 143,000 in December 1921 to 105,000 in May 1922. But the police had a network of agents and contacts, and perhaps as many as one in four city dwellers was some kind of secret informant.[7]

Lenin still favored isolating or eliminating "class enemies" but wanted to give terror better cover and in that sense advocated a slight retreat. Nonetheless, only a fortnight after dissolving the Cheka and replacing it with the GPU, he wrote to Commissar of Justice Kursky on February 20 that he wanted the courts to fill the vacuum.

He expected Kursky to stage show trials or what he called "a series of model trials (exemplifying swift and forceful repression, and serving to educate the masses through the courts and the press) in Moscow, Petrograd, Kharkov, and several other major centers; see to it, through the Party, that the people's judges and members of the revolutionary tribunals take steps to improve the courts' performance and intensify the repression." Lenin told Kursky to ensure that the new criminal code (then being drawn up) contain a paragraph on terror, with the concept "formulated as widely as possible."[8]

The strain of economic and political problems may have contributed to Lenin's deteriorating health, the deeper causes of which baffled his doctors. Some thought he suffered from syphilis. In any event, the effects of the illness led to sudden collapses that left him partially paralyzed, and by early June 1921 members of the Politburo, the half dozen men at the top of the political pyramid, were quite concerned and insisted he take time to rest.[9]

FROM LENIN TO STALIN

Though Lenin was infirm by the time of the Eleventh Party Congress in March 1922, he attended and certainly influenced the outcome. Leon Trotsky and some of his allies had reservations about the NEP and wanted it offset by creating a state plan (in the State Planning Commission, or Gosplan) for the economy as a whole. In response, Lenin admitted that any retreat for revolutionaries was a difficult matter. However, he tried to put the best face on it by once again using the telling analogy of an army at war:

> During a victorious advance, even if discipline is not so strict, everybody moves forward on his own accord. During a retreat, however, discipline must be more deliberate and is a hundred times more necessary, because, when the entire army is in retreat, it does not know or see where it should stop. It sees only retreat; under such circumstances a few panic-stricken voices are sometimes enough to cause a stampede. The danger here is huge. When a real army is in retreat, machine guns are ready, and if an orderly retreat degenerates into a disorderly one, a command to fire is given, and quite rightly, too.[10]

Lenin saw the Party as the "General Staff," run by an elite of not more than a "dozen tried and talented leaders." Stalin built on this point in his famous exposition of Lenin's teachings in 1924, when he compared the political struggle to an army fighting a war:

> Who can clearly see in these conditions, who can give guidance to the proletarian millions? No army at war can do without an experienced General Staff if it is not to be doomed to defeat. Is it not true that the proletariat is all the more in need of such a General Staff if it is not to be devoured by its mortal enemies? But where is this General Staff? Only the revolutionary party of the proletariat can act as this General Staff. The working class without a revolutionary party is an army without a General Staff. The Party is the General Staff of the proletariat.[11]

Lenin used Stalin and his allies to undermine Trotsky's opposition to the NEP and forced the policy through. Trotsky made a fatal mistake by opposing Lenin at what would be his last Party congress. The NEP became the new official line. In thanks, Lenin spoke out for Stalin and saw to his reelection to the two top committees of the Party—the Politburo and the Orgburo (Organization Bureau).

The first postrevolutionary Politburo elected by the Central Committee (at the time with twenty-one members) was instructed by the Eighth Party Congress on March 25, 1919, to establish three institutions to carry on the growing work of the Communist Party. Lenin felt the Central Committee was too large, and he agreed to the creation of the Political Bureau, or Politburo, initially with five members. The Politburo became the key inner circle of the most influential leaders in the new regime. In addition to Lenin, Stalin, and Trotsky, it included Lev Kamenev and Nikolai Krestinskii, with candidate members Nikolai Bukharin, Mikhail Kalinin, and Grigory Zinoviev. At the same Central Committee meeting, they also created the Orgburo, also with five members, one of whom was Stalin. It was responsible for lower-level Party and governmental organizations and dealt with personnel. A new secretariat was to have five technical secretaries to deal with routine matters, but eventually it became a key institution in charge of central administration.[12]

Yakov Sverdlov was the real creator of the Party apparatus, as he was a kind of one-man secretariat. He died on March 16, 1919, just prior to the Party congress. The Central Committee had to draw up the new Party institutions, partly in response to Sverdlov's death. Until then, if there was a single creator of the Party machine, it was he and not Stalin. The latter was not particularly interested in technical matters and not the perfect "organization man." He wanted to be like Lenin, his model, and "lead the party in great new revolutionary deeds at home and abroad."[13] Nevertheless, Stalin eventually turned out to be a hands-on leader. He spent long hours poring over administrative details and micromanaged the vast Soviet political and administrative system.

Once the Politburo started meeting regularly, as it did under Lenin, it became a kind of "super-government" whose decisions "were supreme, higher than the law or the Constitution, which for this body were mere auxiliary instruments. For the citizens of the great state, the Politburo itself embodied the law. It also acquired from Lenin the rule of total secrecy."[14]

Lenin pursued his goals vigorously, especially during the first months of the revolution. He was the key figure on the Politburo and in the Central Committee during the period of greatest upheaval, sent off notes to comrades in the field urging them on, and additionally wrote endless articles for the press. As chairman of Sovnarkom, the Council of People's Commissars, he was head of government, even though he rejected "bourgois" titles like premier or president. A sense of his devotion to the cause can be gathered from the fact that up until July 27, 1918, he missed only 7 of SNK's first 173 sessions. Meetings were held in the mornings.

Often, a second gathering would take place in the evening and last late into the night. Inevitably the heavy workload and strain of the Revolution and Civil War adversely affected Lenin's shaky health, which declined further as he recuperated after the assassination attempt in August 1918. He tried to conceal his symptoms from those around him, but by mid-1921 his comrades in the Kremlin already knew he could not keep up the pace and pressed him to take an extensive leave. Nevertheless, his radical determination persisted, and, even from his country dacha, he made every effort to keep his hand in politics.[15]

On April 3, 1922, Lenin organized Stalin's appointment to what would become an important position in the Party as the new general secretary of the secretariat. Stalin was thus not just on the two main committees of the Central Committee—the Politburo and Orgburo—but headed the secretariat. These roles raised some eyebrows in the top reaches of the Party, where they worried about the concentration of so much power in one person's hands. His three roles put him in an advantageous position to succeed Lenin. They might not have been enough by themselves, but with his political instincts Stalin proved far too much for any potential rival.[16]

As Lenin's health deteriorated, he grew frustrated with Stalin, but still had more confidence in him than in anyone else and swore him to the most important task of all: he made Stalin promise to provide poison if and when he asked for it. Lenin did not want to become totally infirm and preferred not to drag out his life. He had a massive stroke on May 25, 1922, and a few days later again called Stalin to his side in Gorky, where he had been recovering. He now asked for the poison, but the request was too much for Stalin, who talked it over with Lenin's wife and Nikolai Bukharin, who was also there. They prevailed on Lenin to hold on.[17]

Stalin was still close to Lenin, as is shown by the log of visitors to Gorky for May 25 to October 2, 1922. He was at Lenin's side no fewer than twelve times and was the most frequent visitor. They exchanged notes on all kinds of issues.[18]

One of the concerns that came to separate the two had to do with the touchy nationality question in the new republic. In the summer of 1922 the country consisted of the Russian Federal Republic (which had its own "autonomous" republics), and Russia was linked in turn through bilateral treaties to Ukraine, Byelorussia, and the Transcaucasian Federation. Moscow wanted to put this arrangement on a more formal-rational basis and in August 1922 set up a commission, chaired by Stalin as commissar of nationalities. He concluded it would be best if all the republics were governed from Moscow in the same way that Moscow governed its own "autonomous" republics. The already existing central Russian institutions would simply be extended to rule all the republics.

Lenin called Stalin in on September 26 because he did not like this proposal. The next day he wrote that he wanted the new state to be run along less centralized lines and preferred a separate federal executive committee. Merely extending the existing commissariats of the Russian Federation to the rest of the Soviet Union as a whole, as Stalin wanted, would give the impression that Russia had subjugated the country, including independent Soviet republics like Ukraine and Georgia.

Lenin sought a more open-ended federation that might soon include the Soviet republics of Germany, Poland, Hungary, and Finland. He did not wish the internal and those external (future) Communist republics to feel conquered by Russia. He proposed what became the USSR, in which the Russian Federal Republic would be one among many other "independent" republics. Lenin wanted to create a new level of federation and to appeal to the sense that nations wanted self-determination and should be able to have it inside an ever-expanding USSR. In theory it could expand to govern every country in Europe as each embraced Communism. Stalin believed in this missionary goal as well, but he did not think it was in the cards for the time being. He was realistic enough to see that revolutions were not imminent across Europe as Lenin hoped they were and muttered that the great man was wrong and "hasty" in his judgments.[19]

The differences between the two should not be exaggerated, because they were based mainly on tactical considerations. Lenin and Stalin were as one on the most important principles, namely "their commitment to the one-party, one-ideology, multinational state."[20] Such autonomy as was granted to the individual republics in the USSR was in any case a mere fig leaf behind which the Politburo of the Party in Moscow made all the main decisions.

Hence members of the ruling inner circle were surprised at some of Lenin's heated language and his attacks on them as well, and tended to see his reaction as a symptom of his illness. Stalin disagreed with Lenin but in deference reworked the proposal, and adjustments were incorporated into a charter of the USSR proclaimed on December 30, 1922, and later enshrined in the constitution.[21]

Even when he was seriously ill, Lenin revealed a bloody-minded attitude. In November 1922, for example, he wrote Stalin about the need to use the GPU for more "cleansing" operations against the intelligentsia. He worried that in his absence, the Politburo was not being repressive enough. The letter shows Lenin's persistent determination to use terror against any sign of "opposition." His penciled note to Stalin went through a whole list of political opponents by name. He wanted to know whether this individual or that had been "uprooted," which is to say deported or exiled. He wanted to expel the lot.

Lenin liked creating "lists" of people in and out of favor and felt buoyed up by "cleansings" or purges. He asked for a list of all political "enemies" who should be "expelled abroad without mercy. *We will cleanse Russia for a long time to come.* This has to be done at once." He ended by ordering the "arrest of several hundred" writers and publishers, who would not be told the charges against them. Stalin immediately penciled in his own instructions for action and passed the note to Dzerzhinsky of the GPU.[22]

On December 13, 1922, Lenin called Stalin to his home for what would be their last meeting. He may have had second thoughts about Stalin at the end but never really trusted any of the other leaders, either. On December 16 he had another stroke, and three days later the Central Committee put Stalin in charge of supervising his medical care.

As Lenin's health took a turn for the worse, Stalin, together with Bukharin, Kamenev, and his doctors, decided he should not be allowed even to dictate notes for more than a few minutes a day. An enfeebled Lenin lived on for thirteen long months and during that time refused to meet with any of the Party leaders.

LENIN'S LAST TESTAMENT

Lenin was already a troubled man by the end of 1921. He stayed at meetings only a short time, and as he would find out later, the real decisions were taken after he left. But he wanted to determine the fate of Soviet Communism following his death and on December 23, 1922, began dictating guidelines for the future to his secretary, Lydia Fotieva. These cryptic notes are usually called his "testament."

Lenin was concerned about a possible "split" (*raskola*) in the Party around Stalin and Trotsky—and he used the term four times in the short letter of December 25, 1922. He worried also about the growth of the "apparatus" but proposed, nonetheless, that the Central Committee be expanded to fifty or even a hundred members. He thought a larger body would be more difficult for a strong personality to dominate. He also wanted belatedly to include worker-members in hopes the Party would become or remain in tune with the people.

In his note he mentioned six men who might be possible heirs and had quite mixed comments on each. The two that really concerned him were Stalin and Trotsky. He said that Stalin, as general secretary, had "unlimited authority concentrated in his hands." Lenin was "not sure" he would "always be capable of using that authority with sufficient caution." On the other hand, Trotsky, who was likely "the most capable man" on the Central Committee, showed "excessive self-confidence" and "excessive preoccupation with the purely administrative side of the work." These characteristics of the "two outstanding leaders of the present Central Committee could lead to a split. If our Party does not take measures to prevent this happening, a split may occur unexpectedly."

Lenin mentioned four other leaders in this "testament" but did not consider them material for leadership on the same par with Stalin and Trotsky. He could never forgive Zinoviev and Kamenev for their vacillations at the time of the coup in 1917. Of the two youngest candidates, Bukharin and Georgy Pyatakov, Lenin said they had strengths and weaknesses. He said Bukharin was "the favorite" of the Party and its most valuable theorist, whose views, however, were not entirely Marxist and were somewhat removed from the real world. He said Pyatakov was more concerned with administrative matters than with serious political issues.

On January 4, 1923, Lenin dictated a brief postscript, but this time he came down heavily on Stalin, who was now said to be too "rude" to remain general secretary. He added: "I suggest that the comrades consider a way of transferring [*peremesyeniya*] Stalin from the post [of general secretary] and appointing in his place another man who differs from Comrade Stalin in having one advantage, namely that of being more patient, more loyal, more polite, and more helpful to comrades, less unpredictable, and so on."[23] Lenin said this was no trifling matter because of the growing conflict between Stalin and Trotsky.

It is difficult to interpret Lenin's intentions. Was he really going to get rid of Stalin? To answer the question, we need to focus on Lenin's use of one word, *peremesyeniya*. This is commonly translated as "remove" or even "dismiss," and many have seen in that term Lenin's desire to save Communism from Stalin at the last moment. More likely, Lenin was deeply concerned to stave off a coming split in the Party. He was already facing the problem of succession in the Soviet dictatorship, one that plagued it to the end. He did not want a split, could not really opt for Trotsky, but wanted someone else to take over as general secretary of the Party who was more conciliatory. He made no suggestions about who that might be.

Even if Stalin had been removed as general secretary, however, it would be wishful thinking to assume his career would have been over. He would have remained on the Central Committee of the Party, and, given his ties to many Communist leaders, he likely would have been reelected to the Politburo. His position in the Party was secure, and it would have been hard even for Lenin to replace him as commissar of nationalities on Sovnarkom. Moreover, the split in the Party, which Lenin feared, was already under way, and some of the heavyweights (such as Zinoviev, Kamenev, and Bukharin) had lined up on Stalin's side. Molotov remembered long afterward that next to Lenin, "Stalin was the strongest politician. Lenin viewed him as the most reliable, the one you could count upon. But he criticized him, too."[24]

Stalin had upset Lenin because of a run-in he had had with Krupskaya, Lenin's wife, back in December 1922. Finding that she was, against doctors' orders, taking dictation from her weakened husband, Stalin made an "insulting" phone call to her, and when Lenin heard about it, he sent off a letter complaining about his "rudeness." For all that, Lenin did not issue an ultimatum to Stalin, who in any case promptly apologized.[25]

Lenin's "testament" was embarrassing for Stalin, however, and when Krupskaya turned it over to the Central Committee on May 18, 1924, she may well have hoped for Stalin's dismissal or at least to have him reined in. She said Lenin had wanted Stalin's behavior discussed by the Party and the Central Committee (at that time with forty members and seventeen candidate members), and they did so with Stalin present. His offer to resign was declined. He had enough support, and the matter was shelved. Krupskaya herself soon said she did not appreciate how certain "enemies" inside and outside the USSR tried to use the "testament" to discredit the current leaders of the Party.[26]

In October 1927, Trotsky again tried to break Stalin's power by using the "testament." Stalin turned the tables by saying that Lenin had only charged him with being rude, a charge to which he happily pleaded guilty. He said he intended to stay that way "towards those who rudely and treacherously destroy and split the Party." As usual, he avoided the impression he was pleading for himself and attacked Trotsky in the name of defending Lenin, the fallen hero. At the moment Stalin did this, Trotsky, or so he later recalled, vividly imagined a guillotine dangling over his head.[27]

Some commentators continue to point to the "testament" as one of the great ifs in history. The reasoning is that Lenin was leaning toward getting rid of Stalin, and if he had done so, then the "unblemished" Leninist heritage would have been preserved, and the history of the Soviet Union and Communism would have been different. The unwarranted assumption underlying this line of thought is that Stalin "perverted" Lenin's teachings.

Molotov, who worked closely with both Soviet titans, was asked after 1945 whom he considered more severe. He answered without hesitation: "Lenin, of course." Molotov remembered how Lenin reproached Stalin for his softness. "What kind of a dictatorship do we have? We have a milk-and-honey government, and not a dictatorship!"[28]

DISUNITY IN THE PARTY

The division in the Communist Party after Lenin crystallized around two issues, namely the rapid growth of the Party apparatus and the economy. Matters came to a head in the autumn of 1923, when Leon Trotsky became the focal point of opposition. On October 8 he wrote to the Central Committee to complain that Party leaders had abandoned democratic procedures, and a week later there was a letter by a group of forty-six prominent members of the Party who said leaders were "handpicking" candidates for positions in the apparatus.[29]

The Central Committee noted caustically how Trotsky had, in April 1922, turned down the opportunity to become one of Lenin's deputies, a grave sin in its own right.[30] He was also criticized for not attending meetings of Sovnarkom for years; and instead of trying to work within existing structures, he was accused of wanting to go his own way. Trotsky was charged with leading a "faction" and trying to acquire "dictatorial powers in the economic and military spheres."

These Party factions had been banned on Lenin's insistence at the Tenth Party Congress in March 1921, the same one at which he introduced the New Economic Policy. He said that the Communist Party had so many enemies it could no longer afford the "luxury" of disputes and discord. The "task of the dictatorship of the proletariat in a peasant country is so enormous and difficult," he added, that their efforts had to be "more united and harmonious than ever." They could not show the "slightest trace of factionalism." The conference decided that the Central Committee could, by a two-thirds vote, exclude anyone it considered part of a faction in the Party. Members of the Party's top organs found guilty would be demoted to the status of deputy members. It was precisely this resolution that brought Trotsky down.[31]

A special meeting of the Central Committee on October 23, 1923, voted 102 to 2 (with 10 abstentions) in favor of reprimanding Trotsky on the factionalism charge. Kamenev and Zinoviev recommended expulsion from the Party, and suggestions were floated to have him arrested. Stalin, however, who relished this victory, appeared the moderate now by suggesting that Trotsky be allowed to stay on. Stalin not only was the defender of Lenin but, contrary to mythology, often appeared as the calm voice of reason.[32]

Trotsky made matters worse by brushing aside the Central Committee's condemnation and going public with his complaints. He claimed to be the true Leninist who knew where the country should be headed, and for the Thirteenth Party Congress in January 1924 he mustered some support. However, he was too ill to attend, but perhaps he sensed the outcome was a foregone conclusion.

The congress overwhelmingly condemned "Trotskyism" as a "petit bourgeois" deviation from Communism, and his days as a force in the USSR were as good as over. Trotsky's background was always a factor, because he used to be a prominent Menshevik, the group that broke with the Bolsheviks prior to 1914, and he had said and written a lot that defamed the godlike Lenin. Ultimately his "anti-Leninism" counted more than the fact that as commissar of war he had put together the Red Army and saved the revolution.[33]

By coincidence, Lenin fell into a coma not long afterward and passed away on January 21, 1924. Trotsky, still convalescing in the south, made the additional mistake of not returning for Lenin's funeral on January 27. He later said that Stalin had deceived him about the date. Be that as it may, it was a disastrous error to miss the funeral.

Hanging over Trotsky was the additional factor of his Jewish heritage. Anti-Semitism was a big problem in parts of the country. Though Trotsky had dissociated himself from Judaism, he feared that his background would always be held against him. He had tried to avoid taking on the leadership of the Red Army because he believed—rightly, as it turned out—that opponents would point to his Jewish roots and anti-Semitism would spread.

Zinoviev and Kamenev, two other potential successors to Lenin, also had Jewish backgrounds. To the anti-Semites it was irrelevant that these men no longer saw themselves as practicing members of the Jewish faith. It is very doubtful that the USSR would have accepted Jewish leaders.

At Lenin's death a form of "collective leadership" was in place in the Politburo, so the mantle of power did not fall immediately on Stalin's shoulders. Nevertheless, by that time he had built up a basis of support and was well regarded in the Party.

He used the position of general secretary to foster the careers of those who agreed with him and to deny advancements to those who did not. Candidates for appointments could expect perks—such as having permission to shop in special stores—and Stalin built up networks. He was able to control the central apparatus and thus had an enormous advantage over all other potential challengers.[34]

LENINISM AFTER LENIN

A Lenin cult emerged even before he died. "Lenin corners," which would have a picture of the hero and quotations, became a standard feature of many official buildings, from schools to prisons, and was consistent with the tradition of the religious icon and ritual.

For Lenin's funeral on January 27, 1924, millions stood in the freezing cold across the great land. The turnout was orchestrated by the Party, but by all accounts the wish to venerate Lenin hit a responsive chord. The cult grew, with memorial sites, museums, and a mausoleum for his body at the Kremlin wall in Moscow. It projected an uncritical narrative of the man's life, struggles, and successes and was designed to evoke in the Party as in the country "a mood of loyalty toward the system and its values."[35]

A public signal for the beginning of the cult was sounded by a special commemorative meeting on January 26, 1924. Petrograd was renamed Leningrad. The idea came from local Party officials, and though Stalin got some credit for it, he was not the primary maker of the cult.[36]

Even before he had passed away, there was a national call for a "Lenin enrollment" to join the recently "purged" Communist Party. The Party had expanded from around 25,000 in 1917 to 250,000 by 1919, but membership had been purged of 100,000 "unworthy" people by year's end. In 1921 Lenin advocated another purge to unmask the dishonest and insincere.

In January 1924 an estimated 350,000 members remained. The Lenin enrollment added 240,000 new members in two years. More important, the recruitment was conducted to favor candidates loyal to Stalin, who began to construct the Party in his own image.[37]

In order to inherit Lenin's place, Stalin had to become more than the most important official in the Party. He associated himself with the cult by identifying with the "infallible" doctrine of Leninism, a term heard before the leader's death but one that came into greater use from 1923 onward.

Stalin strove for recognition as the interpreter of the word of Lenin in a series of lectures he gave to the Party university in Moscow just two months after Lenin's death. These were published in *Pravda* and later issued as a short book, *The Foundations of Leninism*. Seminars on Leninism and chairs devoted to the topic were soon introduced at other universities. Stalin's little book, revised and updated, eventually sold in excess of seventeen million copies and was considered a basic text that one had to read.[38]

The Foundations of Leninism offers an easy "textbook" presentation of what Stalin considered the master's central teachings. The text is sprinkled with numerous quotations and aphorisms from Lenin's writings. Unlike the major intellectuals in the Party, Stalin did not consider himself Lenin's equal, but for that very reason the cult worked to his favor. What he learned was how to get the upper hand in any debate by a timely production of supporting quotations from the great man.[39]

Although *The Foundations of Leninism* does not go into details on every future policy, Stalin established a kind of "general line" by using Lenin's texts. The book has some of the qualities of Mao's *Little Red Book* (1964), which became so prominent during the Chinese Cultural Revolution that began in 1966.

Stalin showed dexterity during the Party debates that raged from 1923 to 1928. He spoke in the name of the Party, in the Leninist tradition, and found ways of labeling others as "deviationists." He became a master at putting every line uttered by his opponents through a kind of linguistic strainer.[40]

A good example of his skills was how he fared in the theoretical debates at the time of Lenin's illness and death. Stalin's speech on November 24, 1924, to a Communist group was published as *Trotskyism or Leninism?*[41] He claimed to draw his strategy for the future from the great man and in the course of 1924 worked out his own position as advocating "socialism in one country." He differed with Trotsky on a number of key points, particularly on the latter's theory of "permanent revolution," which stated that a Communist revolution could not survive in the Soviet Union unless matched by revolutions in the West. Lenin and most Bolsheviks, including Stalin, had once accepted this point of view, but Lenin himself had suggested, in 1915, that it might be possible to achieve the victory of Socialism in one country. Trotsky was now accused of being a "permanentist," a new crime; he apparently showed too little faith in the Soviet peoples.

Stalin, Zinoviev, and Kamenev, acting as a troika that dominated the Politburo, dragged up Trotsky's own statements to discredit him. Given the dearth of "spontaneous" revolutions in the West, Socialism in one country seemed a more attractive alternative to "permanent revolution." For those who hoped terror was over, there was some comfort in the fact that Stalin condemned Trotsky for using it.[42]

Another feud, this one pitting Stalin against Zinoviev and Kamenev, came to a head at the Fourteenth Party Congress in December 1925, which supported Stalin's point that "in general the victory of socialism (not in the sense of final victory) is definitely possible in one country."

Zinoviev and Kamenev were goaded into presenting a minority report that seemed to oppose the will of the Party and to be shaky on Leninism. When Kamenev said Stalin was "not a figure who can unite the old Bolshevik staff," commotion broke out on the floor. He added, "We are against the doctrine of the one-man rule, we are against the creation of a Leader." The stenographic record of the meeting notes how delegates reacted: " 'Untrue.' 'Nonsense.' 'So that's what they're up to!' 'Now they've showed their hand.' 'We won't surrender the command posts to you.' 'Stalin! Stalin!' The delegates rise and salute Comrade Stalin. Stormy applause. Cries of 'Here's where the party's united' and 'The Bolshevik general staff must be united.' 'Long live Comrade Stalin!' Prolonged stormy applause. Shouts of 'Hurrah.' General Commotion."[43]

Stalin's resolution on Socialism in one country passed by a resounding 559 votes to 65. The interregnum, the period of collective leadership, was over, and Stalin had become the dominant figure and the Party's most popular leader.[44] Even in Leningrad, which was regarded as Zinoviev's home turf, the overwhelming majority of workers in meetings voted against him, and he was unseated in favor of Sergei Kirov, a Stalin supporter.[45]

An effort to stop the inevitable was made in the spring and summer of 1926 when Trotsky, Zinoviev, and Kamenev joined with others in a united opposition. They attacked the economic policies put forth by Stalin and the Politburo member Nikolai Bukharin and charged Stalin with unduly favoring the kulaks and so-called Nepmen (members of a resurging capitalist bourgeoisie) at the expense of the proletariat.

But with the economy improving, famine mostly beaten, and modest signs of prosperity, there was no real support for an attack on the NEP. This situation favored Stalin, because, in keeping with the Party at that point in time, he stood for cautious optimism rather than adventurous gambling on a world revolution.[46]

Bukharin thought it might be enough if the united opposition admitted it was wrong. They were told to "come before the Party with head bowed and say: Forgive us for we have sinned against the spirit and against the letter and against the very essence of Leninism." They were told to "say it, say it honestly: Trotsky was wrong."[47] This gesture was more than other leaders of the opposition were willing to make, and by the end of 1926 Trotsky, Zinoviev, and Kamenev had been dropped from the Politburo and their places taken by men loyal to Stalin.

A final showdown between Stalin and Trotsky occurred on October 23, 1927, at a meeting to prepare the next Party congress. Stalin launched a fierce attack on the already-routed opposition and again came out in defense of Lenin, whom Trotsky unwisely (if accurately) had called "Maximilien Lenin," a term implying Lenin was a dictator along the lines of Robespierre. There was another exchange about Lenin's "testament," which Trotsky was trying to use against Stalin. Once more Stalin pleaded guilty to the charge of rudeness, which he said was aimed at those (like Trotsky) who would split the Party. He recalled Trotsky's great sins, twisting each one for the most damaging effect. It was a masterful performance, and all in the name of holding high the sacred body of Leninism.[48]

The united opposition persisted in 1927 with a foolish plan to hold street demonstrations in Moscow and Leningrad on November 7, the tenth "official" anniversary of the Bolshevik Revolution. The demonstration was crushed, and within a week Trotsky and Zinoviev were expelled from the Party. The Fifteenth Party Congress, which met in December, followed up by expelling seventy-five other "oppositionists," including prominent figures such as Kamenev, Pyatakov, and Radek. Thirty of those expelled were, along with Trotsky, sent to distant parts of the country early in the New Year. In society at large, there was a purge of sympathizers.[49]

Stalin did not take the attacks on him to be serious threats. However, they provided him an opportunity to show his political authority. By the Fifteenth Party Congress in December 1927, he was the only speaker to receive "stormy and prolonged applause." The Communist Party enthusiastically embraced their now unchallenged leader.[50]

9

STALIN'S NEW INITIATIVES

On December 3, 1927, Stalin gave a lengthy address to the Party congress about the future of the New Economic Policy (NEP). He began by reviewing the errors of the opposition, whom he accused of having too little faith in Leninism. He said Trotsky was incorrectly advocating the forced transformation of light industry to make up for what was called a "goods famine." What was needed was a revolution in heavy industry (manufacturing and military goods).

Bukharin was now faulted for encouraging the kulaks to "enrich themselves." Stalin claimed that the NEP had reached its limits, and more had to be done to cut the kulaks down to size. Agricultural production was falling behind countries like the United States and Canada. The way out was "to transform the small and scattered peasant farms into large farms based on cultivation of the land in common, to adopt collective cultivation guided by a new and higher technique."[1]

Applause greeted Stalin's speech, which concluded: "We are in the process of moving from the restoration of industry and agriculture to the reconstruction of the entire national economy on a new technical foundation, at a time when the building of Socialism is no longer simply a prospect but a living, practical matter, which calls for the overcoming of massive internal and external difficulties."[2]

FIVE-YEAR PLAN

Stalin wanted to end the NEP without causing panic among peasants afraid of a return to the cruel days when government squads simply requisitioned surpluses. He thus had to make the argument that it was crucial to the health and security of the country that the Party take this change of course. An opportunity that came his way was a "war scare" in 1927, one he deliberately exaggerated to drive home the point that the USSR was vulnerable to the hostile West.

In May, Britain broke off diplomatic relations because the Soviets abetted British strikers and looked like they wanted to foment revolution. There was friction with France, but when Foreign Minister Georgy Chicherin returned home in the summer, he was surprised to learn that war was in the air. Stalin played it up as it gave credence to his demand to industrialize the country as rapidly as possible, to focus on heavy industry, and to drop the NEP in favor of a far more Communistic five-year plan.[3]

He also took advantage of political developments at home. For example, local officials in Ukraine during the 1920s blamed the failures of the NEP on what they called bourgeois "specialists" (*spetsy*). Show trials of these "wreckers" (*vrediteli*) proved to be popular because they shifted the blame for shortfalls away from workers and onto the shoulders of management and trade-union leadership.[4] In late 1927 a secret police official and old comrade of Stalin's from the North Caucasus informed him about a "wrecking conspiracy" involving fifty-three engineers from the town of Shakhty and the nearby Donbass in Ukraine. On March 10, 1928, the secret police announced they had uncovered the plot.[5]

Stalin used the opportunity to stage a mass trial in Moscow in May–June. Like Lenin he believed in the educative value of such rituals, which, to be successful, had to reveal a credible threat by providing a story line plausible to ordinary people. Such trials unmasked the double-dealers and demonstrated treason, and to that end, the event had to be stage-managed carefully.[6] Stalin became directly involved and appointed Andrei Vyshinsky judge of a "special judicial presence," not a regular court. The wreckers were charged with sabotaging their factories on behalf of foreign governments. The object of the show trial, which was held in the former Moscow Club of the Nobility, was to attract publicity and teach. Most of the accused were given prison terms; the foreigners (Germans) were released; and of the eleven sentenced to death, five were eventually shot.[7]

The Shakhty trial was supposed to mobilize the country behind the government by demonstrating the imminent threat of war. The message was that enemies within "wore masks"; that is, they were not who they appeared to be, and everyone had to be on the lookout. The miners in the Donbass were evidently convinced about the "conspiracy" and, when the details came out, covered trolleys with the slogan "Long live the GPU!"[8] The latter was the latest name (used since 1922) for the Cheka.

Stalin sounded distinctly warlike at the July meetings of the Central Committee in 1928. Everywhere there were "fronts" to be taken—the "grain front," the "planning front," even the "philosophy front." The refrain was that enemies of the revolution were not going to give up, and the closer they came to defeat, the more desperate they would grow.[9]

"Foreign threats" justified the need to fight on the "industrial front." Whereas imperial Russia's industry was located mainly in the western, European parts of the empire—with the notable exception of Baku in the Caucasus to the south—Stalin now opted, for defense reasons, to situate new industry east of the Ural mountain range. This decision proved important when the Nazi invasion later overran the western parts of the country.

Recent findings in Soviet archives show that in 1929–30, Stalin did indeed take these "threats" seriously, even if they seem far-fetched today. His letters dealing with the show trials indicate that he believed the conspiracies. He was insistent that the trials and punishments be published in the press.[10]

Stalin's policies called on the peasants to provide plentiful grain at cheap prices. The peasants would have to pay a "tribute," that is, offer surpluses to be sold abroad so the government could pay for new technology.[11] Stalin wrote to Molotov on August 29, 1929, "If we can beat this grain thing, then we'll prevail in everything, in both domestic and foreign policies."[12]

The Soviet blueprint for constructing socialism was incorporated in the first Five-Year Plan (*piatiletka*) that began in October 1928 but was only adopted by the Sixteenth Party Conference in April 1929. This plan was discussed as far back as 1925. In its final version, it visualized a kind of second Russian Revolution that would overcome all the enduring problems plaguing the country since Peter the Great.

The Five-Year Plan represented the first attempt by a major power to transform all aspects of society and economy. The only other example mentioned in the literature was Germany's "war Socialism" during the First World War to organize industry and reconcile the interests of labor and management. The new Soviet strategy was much more far-reaching and based on the principle of militant anticapitalism and radical social revolution.[13]

THE PLANNED SOCIETY

In November 1928, Stalin asserted that the Soviet Union had "overtaken and outstripped the advanced capitalist countries by establishing a new political system. That is good. But it is not enough. To secure the final victory of Socialism in our country, we must also overtake and outstrip these countries technically and economically. If we do not do this, we shall find ourselves forced to the wall."[14]

The plan touched all aspects of social and cultural life and enunciated specific goals for industrialization "to catch and overtake" the West. The aim was to surpass capitalism's per capita output; to make greater technological advances; to give priority to heavy industry, rather than consumer goods; to raise the standard of living, including providing people access to better education, health care, and welfare; and to secure the country against foreign invaders by locating much of the new development in areas less vulnerable to attack.

Sergo Ordzhonikidze, the commissar of heavy industry, admitted the challenges were daunting for a "country of the wooden plough." The bitter pill to swallow was that the Soviets, like Peter the Great, would have to import experts and borrow technology from the West.

Large American firms, among them the Austin Company, which had just finished an enormous plant for General Motors, signed contracts to build even bigger facilities in the Soviet Union. On August 23, 1929, Austin agreed to construct a gigantic factory complex and new industrial city at Nizhni Novgorod on the Volga. It was a mammoth undertaking by any standard. The plant was designed to produce over 100,000 vehicles per year. Austin created an entire system so they could be made in one place from blueprint to finished product. To provide for every need of the sixty thousand and more workers, a new city was created. The *New York Times Magazine* published a feature story on the project called "Communism Builds Its City of Utopia."[15]

The Ford Motor Company signed a contract on May 31, 1929, to produce Model A cars and Model AA pickup trucks, with a goal to turn out thirty thousand cars and seventy thousand trucks per year. Initially, Soviet workers would assemble American-made parts until Ford technicians trained Soviets to manufacture parts, as in Nizhni Novgorod. Other American companies were involved in building tractor factories in Stalingrad and Kharkov.[16]

Henry Ford was criticized at home for helping Communists. He responded that getting people to work was the main thing. "The adoption of high wages, low prices, and mass production in all countries is only a matter of time," he declared. "Instead of reducing our foreign markets, it will serve to define them."[17]

One of the spectacular projects put together with the help of the West was the new steel complex at Magnitogorsk, a brand-new city built from the ground up. Everything, from blast furnaces, sources of energy, transportation, and so on, was fashioned as a set piece, but on a grand scale and constructed as quickly as possible. The contract went to Arthur McKee & Co. of Cleveland, Ohio, which was shocked to learn it had to deliver the plan in two months. The engineers were doubly dismayed when they finally got to the construction site: two-thirds of the workers had no previous industrial experience and no skills to speak of, and a good 30 percent were illiterate. Nonetheless, the project, situated on the eastern side of the Ural Mountains in Siberia, was completed in record time and opened on February 1, 1932, to great fanfare by Mikhail Kalinin.

A sense of the difficulties faced by Soviet industry may be gathered from the fact that the first freight shipments arrived in Magnitogorsk from Moscow after a seventy-day trip. But the new "Socialist city" pointed the way to the future and was the kind of project perfectly suited to Stalin's gargantuan visions. It was a prime example of the sixty or more towns created out of nothing during the first Five-Year Plan. The new metropolis was to demonstrate all the Communist virtues, that is, planned and modern. Making these communities really work—like the tractor factory city of Chelyabinsk, the "Chicago of Siberia"—was easier said than done. Who really knew how to plan a complete city? The ambition to create them was part of the utopian quest but driven also by fears of being overrun by the capitalists, as well as by dreams of showing them up.[18]

Under the heading "Year of the Great Breakthrough" (*perlom*), Stalin gave a first review of the Five-Year Plan for *Pravda* on November 3, 1929. The occasion was to celebrate victories on various fronts on the anniversary of the Russian Revolution. The justification for the intense industrialization drive was couched in typically military language:

> The past year was a year of great *change* on all the fronts of Socialist construction. The key to this change has been, and continues to be, an unrelenting *offensive* of Socialism against the capitalist elements in town and country. This offensive has already brought us a number of decisive *successes* in the Socialist reconstruction of our national economy. We may, therefore, conclude that our Party made good use of our retreat during the first stages of the New Economic Policy and that we are thus able, in the subsequent stages, to organize the *change* and to launch a *successful offensive* against the capitalist elements.

After outlining the growth of industry and the strides taken to collectivize agriculture, he asserted that the Soviet Union was finally making progress:

> We are advancing rapidly along the path of industrialization to Socialism, leaving behind the old "Russian" backwardness. We are becoming a country of metal, automobiles, tractors. And when we have put the USSR on an automobile, and the muzhik [common peasant] on a tractor, let the worthy capitalists, who brag so much about their "civilization," try to overtake us! We shall see which countries may then be called backward and which ones advanced.[19]

Stalin was by no means alone in his drive to transform the country. Quite apart from those in the upper echelons of the Party apparatus, he won the support of many educators, engineers, and administrators well down the line.

The first Five-Year Plan was accompanied by its own "cultural revolution," which was above and beyond the kind of sweeping transformation originally envisaged by the Bolsheviks. Taking their cue from the Shakhty case, the changes in 1928–31 called for purges of government offices and institutions of higher learning to root out ubiquitous wreckers. Shakhty and other show trials in 1930 were designed to shake up "bourgeois" specialists and get the technical intelligentsia behind the industrialization drive. The show trials and purges cleared out those sympathetic to the right and made room for those better disposed toward Stalin. These trials were the first "offensives" on the "cultural front," the aims of which included transforming every worker and backward peasant into the proud "new man."

At the end of the 1920s the Soviet Union, with a total population of around 150 million, was still overwhelmingly rural, with only one-fifth classified as urban. A mere 57 percent of the population (aged nine to forty-nine) were counted as literate in the 1926 census, but even that figure probably was overly optimistic.[20]

The cultural revolution sought to create a new intelligentsia, one drawn from the working class, whose entrance into higher education was encouraged. The numbers enrolled jumped from 160,000 in 1927–28 to 470,000 in 1932–33, but as always, care has to be taken with the (often inflated) statistics. The drive opened doors for a new generation of intellectuals and political leaders, people like Leonid Brezhnev—future leader of the post-Stalinist Soviet Union—who rose to prominence during the 1930s. While the offspring of poor families were given a chance to move upward, the other side of the coin was that countless individuals were destined to become superfluous because their parents happened to be "former people," such as members of the bourgeoisie, nobility, or clergy.[21]

ASSAULT ON THE COUNTRYSIDE

In the autumn of 1927 a foreign Communist in Moscow remarked that something had changed from an earlier visit. There was "no meat, no cheese, no milk" in the stores, and the sale of bread was irregular.[22] At the turn of the year 1927–28, the secret police reported numerous "anti-Soviet manifestations" across the country that could be traced to grain procurement problems and a "goods famine"—or shortages of supplies. People in some areas like Ukraine were led to believe the Jews—that is, "the Yids and the government"—had hidden various items "in order to cheat the peasants later." Kulaks and others were supposedly trying to utilize the discontent to get rid of cooperatives and other Socialist institutions.[23] Nearly everywhere in the summer of 1928 there were bread-lines and rationing.

Early in 1928, Stalin sent close associates to key areas to assess the situation and speed up food deliveries. Lazar Kaganovich went to Ukraine, Anastas Mikoyan to the North Caucasus, and Molotov to the Urals. In mid-January, Stalin spent three weeks in Siberia and the Urals, where he browbeat local officials at every stop. He cajoled and threatened, demanding that they use whatever means necessary, including violence, to get food needed for workers and the cities. He was behind the unanimous decision of the Politburo that "extraordinary measures" had to be used.

This ruthless approach became known as the "Ural-Siberian method" of obtaining the grain. Stalin demanded officials use articles 105 (on trade violations) and 107 (on withholding grain) of the criminal code to prosecute "kulak speculators" and others. The campaign employed radical Communists and workers from the city and doled out rewards to poor peasants who informed on the better-off kulaks and then shared in the spoils.[24]

One historian describes the ripple effects of these campaigns as follows:

> Rumors of the most alarming kind began to spread among the population; it was said that there would be famine, that war and the fall of the Soviet regime were imminent. Violence or the threat of violence against Party activists became an everyday occurrence. From Kherson, Melitopol, Semipalatinsk and other regions, came reports of fires, the looting of food from shops and warehouses, civil disorder and attempts to prevent the authorities from taking grain from the agricultural regions. Public discontent in the towns and villages found its expression in riots and demonstrations against the authorities.[25]

Repression was deployed against the slightest signs of resistance or what was called "kulak terror." Over one thousand such "crimes" were reported for 1929, involving everything from murder to "wrecking." For the same period "economic" and "counterrevolutionary" crimes resulted in close to thirty thousand arrests.[26] Repressing the kulaks was meant to beat them into submission and have a demonstrative effect on the entire countryside.

From early 1928, there was a sharp crackdown on small traders, those who found ways to take advantage of the NEP. Thousands of "people with sacks" (*meshochniki*) would search the countryside for food they willingly paid for at higher prices than the state offered. They would then resell these goods for tiny profits in the cities. There were also traders who hired unemployed people to queue for scarce goods, which they later resold for a profit.[27] Some of these Nepmen, so called because they took advantage of small freedoms permitted under the policy, came to be despised by the regime, which, like Stalin, regarded them as wreckers. Stalin wanted them stamped out.[28]

On his trip to Siberia, he concluded that the main cause of the grain crisis was the peasants' cultivation of small plots of land. The problem, he said, was that the practice was economically inefficient and as long as it persisted the crisis would recur. As he saw it, to cure the structural problems, farms had to be collectivized so they could afford and use modern machinery. That was Lenin's plan, he stated, and it would be "decisive for the victory of Socialism in the countryside."[29]

Collectivization of agriculture was not yet government policy, and in 1928 some in the Politburo still believed in the NEP. Bukharin, for example, wanted only to change pricing and taxation and argued that peasants would produce and sell more to the state if they could expect some gain. In the shadow of mounting grain shortages, Stalin came out against Bukharin and labeled his stance a "right opposition" that deviated from the "central line" and favored kulaks and other independent-minded peasants.

Stalin's clash with this opposition was bitter but short-lived. By April 1928, Bukharin had been defeated, and in November he was expelled from the Politburo. His fall resulted mainly from his identification with the NEP, a more liberal approach loved by many people but denounced by Party radicals. Those who favored it were now blamed for the shortages and the petty abuses of the system.

Moscow, Leningrad, and other big cities had to introduce bread rationing in the winter of 1928–29, and on February 15, 1929, the Politburo extended it to the whole country. Procurement of grain was less successful that winter than the year before, and in October 1929 rationing was established for the most important foods (such as bread, meat, butter, tea, and eggs) in some major cities and industrial areas. It was not until the beginning of 1931 that these norms were extended nationwide, but by then famine had already become a real threat.[30]

The Five-Year Plan called for a modest changeover from private to collective farming, but the transformation took on a dynamic of its own. As early as the summer of 1929, local authorities were competing with each other to see who could collectivize most. Peasants were cajoled into joining or given false promises of the advantages of belonging to a collective farm. Even so, by the time of Stalin's speech in November 1929, most of those who were collectivized came from the 30 percent or so of the peasants classified as either poor or farm laborers. The better-off were not persuaded by the propaganda.[31]

The nearly 70 percent of the remaining peasants were "middling" or better off, such as the kulaks. Like Lenin before him, Stalin resorted to terror, but this time on a greater scale than ever.

"ELIMINATING THE KULAKS AS A CLASS"

Stalin explained to Marxist students on December 27, 1929, that it was time to begin "eliminating the kulaks as a class." He claimed that a "new Socialist offensive" was necessary as all other methods of dealing with these capitalist elements had failed. It was a declaration of war on the countryside:

> During the past year we, as a Party, as the Soviet power (*a*) developed an offensive along the whole front against the capitalist elements in the countryside; (*b*) this offensive, as you know, has yielded significant, positive results. What does this mean? In a word, we have passed from the policy of *restricting* the exploiting tendencies of the kulaks to the policy of *eliminating* the kulaks as a class. We have acted on, and continue to act on, one of the decisive planks in our whole program. . . .

An offensive against the kulaks is a serious matter and is not to be confused with declamations against the kulaks.... An offensive requires that we smash the kulaks, eliminate them as a class. Less than that would amount to mere declamation, pinpricks, phrase-mongering, certainly not a real Bolshevik offensive. To launch an offensive against the kulaks, we must make preparations and then strike, strike so hard as to prevent them from ever again rising to their feet. That is what we Bolsheviks call a real offensive. Could we have undertaken such an action, say five years or even three years ago, with any hope of success? No, we could not.[32]

The drift of the argument was that since the regime had made progress in the countryside, by creating farms and (allegedly) producing enough, the country could now afford to "eliminate the kulaks" and build Socialism. The kulaks were not identified with a specific ethnic group, but could be almost anyone.

Should kulaks be allowed to join the new kolkhozy? After all, they were known to be industrious and had skills and initiative. For Stalin the answer was a resounding no. He wanted them uprooted and did not care how. As far as he was concerned, the (alleged) production successes of the collective farms meant the Soviet Union could go beyond tinkering with restrictive measures against the kulaks to wiping them out as a class. In his view it was foolish to spend more time talking about kulaks: "When the head is cut off, you do not mourn for the hair."[33]

Fired up by Stalin, a commission led by Molotov produced a far-reaching decree, with implementation instructions, on January 30, 1930. First-category kulaks, guilty of "counterrevolutionary activities," were to be executed out of hand or sent to concentration camps and their families deported to distant parts and stripped of all property. The second category, "arch-exploiters with an innate tendency to destabilize the regime," were to be dispossessed and deported far away with their families. Finally, third-category kulaks were thought to be loyal to the regime, but in any case had to be moved out of their homes and away from "collectivized zones" and onto poor land.[34]

In keeping with the quota thinking of this era, the commission estimated that "on average" kulaks owned between 3 and 5 percent of all farms and had to be eliminated within six months, and so it set quotas for how many were to be sent to the concentration camps, exiled, and so on.

Everything was laid out, including the disposition of confiscated property, like a military campaign.[35]

The chief of the secret police, Genrikh G. Yagoda, instructed his paladins to mobilize the Chekist ranks, "which once again have a tremendous, difficult job ahead of them. . . . We are engaging in a new battle, we must wage it with minimal losses on our side. This requires a sudden, devastating strike, the force of which depends solely on our preparation and organization, and discipline."[36]

Politburo members such as Kaganovich, Mikoyan, and Molotov went into the countryside, complete with units of the secret police, on armed trains. Their scribbled notes back to the Kremlin told of resistance and, with some relish, of the need to obliterate it. But it was Stalin himself who urged on the whole process, as he pressed regional and local bosses to keep going. His commissars, embracing the murderous activity, told themselves they embodied "Party-mindedness, morality, exactingness, attentiveness, good health, knowing their business well and bull nerves." These self-aggrandizing images covered over self-indulgence, ruthlessness, and amorality.[37]

There developed an atmosphere akin to the days of the civil war. Maxim Gorky, once a voice of conscience, now hailed the cruel campaign against the peasants. He had returned to the Soviet Union in 1928 after a period of exile in the West and apparently wanted to show how Red he was. In leading newspapers and on the radio he stated the matter with brutal simplicity: "We are opposed by everything that has outlived the time set for it by history, and this gives us the right to consider ourselves again in a state of civil war. The conclusion naturally follows that if the enemy does not surrender, he must be destroyed."[38]

Each district slated for collectivization was visited by a troika of officials, which usually included the Communist Party's first secretary, a member of the secret police, and the president of the local Soviet executive committee. The troikas sometimes showed up with "lists" or relied on denunciations.

Regional authorities saw they could benefit from the large pool of "dekulakized" peasants forced off the land and into the burgeoning labor camp system. The free labor would help them fulfill quotas, and so they used these peasants, now turned into serfs, on various grand projects.[39]

Just how savage it became for the victims would take a sorrowful book to tell. "Dekulakization brigades," sent to the countryside and in collaboration with locals, engaged in excesses every bit as dreadful as anything seen during the civil war. City radicals joined up in brigades known as the "25,000ers"—with individual representatives called "Comrade Thousander" by the peasants.

These activists were workers and young members of the Komsomol, or Communist Youth, and included many with disdain for the peasants and hatred for anyone deemed a kulak. The brigades, numbering up to 180,000 in 1930 and assisted by assorted others from trade unions, the Red Army, and the secret police, convinced themselves they had "History" on their side in the war against the kulaks, whose identity was as vague as could be. Stalin himself scribbled on a note at one point during all this: "What does kulak mean?"[40]

By 1929–30, when most peasants were already impoverished, "rich" kulaks could hardly be found, so it became enough for a family to own two samovars, or have a "status symbol," to be condemned. These goods served as "signs" of a kulak, and any peasants so identified were robbed of their every possession down to their underclothes and turned out in the streets. Local priests, resented for their religion, connections with the people, or reservations about Communism—whether expressed or not—were attacked and driven from their homes in the dead of winter.[41]

The "dekulakers" were supposed to confiscate everything and pass it along to the kolkhoz, the new collective farm, but in fact, the confiscations were little more than state-sanctioned looting. The brigades consumed much of the food and drink they found, and their campaigns involved widespread rape and all kinds of other abuses.[42]

Locals took advantage of these brigades to get rid of troublemakers, social outsiders, habitual drunks, or people who did not fit in. Rumor or hearsay that someone was a "harmful element" was sometimes enough to have the peasant deported. The attitude of some spiteful people was: "You've had a good coat on your back. Now it's our turn to wear it!"[43]

In some districts there were too few kulaks for the brigades to meet their quotas, so their wrath fell on "middle-income" peasants, who were barely removed from dire poverty. Their "crime" might be that they made "excessive visits to the church."[44]

This was man-made hell and embittered millions, who lost whatever trust they might have had in the Communist regime.

10

STALIN SOLIDIFIES HIS GRIP

The scope of the upheaval in the countryside can be estimated by looking at the numbers affected. In 1930 alone 337,563 families were dekulakized, or well in excess of a half million people. It is not clear whether these figures include those subjected to sentencing by troikas of the OGPU. A separate document for 1930 lists 179,620 individuals who were sentenced by these "courts." Of these, 10.6 percent (18,966 people) were executed; 55.3 percent (99,319) sent to a concentration camp; and the rest "exiled" (21.3 percent, or 38,179) or "banished" (4.3 percent, or 8,869). Exactly 7.9 percent (14,287) were sentenced "conditionally" and handed over to the Commissariat of Justice or "freed."[1] The data are incomplete, as some areas had not sent in reports.

In 1930 the dekulakization campaign turned the countryside upside down. Some regions—for example, the North Caucasus—went from less than 10 percent of their farms collectivized in 1929 to over 50 percent by mid-1930. Similar if not quite such dramatic changes affected the other major farming areas.[2] Even then, the pursuit of the kulaks and collectivization continued.

"DIZZY WITH SUCCESS"

Stalin signaled a temporary halt by publishing a notorious article, "Dizzy with Success," carried in all newspapers on March 2, 1930. According to this account, the government's efforts had been unexpectedly easy, with no less than 50 percent of the farms collectivized by February 20. The country had "overfulfilled" the goals of the Five-Year Plan by more than 100 percent. The conclusion was that the "radical turn of the countryside toward Socialism may be considered as already achieved."

Stalin admitted in a backhanded way that some Party activists had become "dizzy with success" and foolishly thought they could accomplish anything in the wink of an eye. Acknowledging that some collective farms existed only on paper, he explained that the local officials, all too eager to boast, had apparently been exaggerating their accomplishments. Moreover, some of the overzealous went so far as "to register all the poultry of every household." That was nonsense, he said, and disrupted collectivization. Just as it was important not to lag behind the Communist movement, no one should run too far ahead.[3] Far from accepting responsibility for the dystopia in the countryside, Stalin was proud that the collective-farm movement was supposedly working out so well and that it was "voluntary."

The message was to slow down the collectivization drive—at least for the time being. The peasants had seen enough of the kolkhoz and did not relish being robbed of every possession and forced to join one. They had protested what was happening all along. Stalin now said frankly that some places were not yet ready for collective farms.

After March 1930, the volume of protests fell off, but for all of that year an estimated 2.5 million peasants participated in approximately fourteen thousand protests, revolts, riots, or demonstrations. There was resistance on all kinds of grounds, especially based on hatred of collectivization and the rejection of dekulakization. These protests were linked to others, like those against church closings, taxes, and food problems. The massive opposition, often overlooked by historians, reached a scale not seen since the civil war.[4]

Most affected were the better-off areas such as the Black Earth region, the North Caucasus, and western Ukraine. Some of the borderlands temporarily eluded the control of the central Soviet authorities. "Primitive rebels," often led by women, used traditional weapons to attack and kill officials and to demand the return of their property and the dissolution of the kolkhoz. Against them the authorities used the harshest forms of terror. The protests never solidified into a united mass movement, but fell prey to the concerted actions of secret police. Beaten but not broken, the peasantry persisted in trying to preserve the little autonomy that remained as Stalinism encroached ever more on their lives.[5]

GULAG

Forced-labor and concentration camps were an established part of the Soviet system under Lenin. The camps did not fade away once the civil war ended and a tenuous peace returned.

In the context of the Five-Year Plan, great new building projects, and collectivization, the camps took on a new function. Once primarily a prison system, they now also became a provider of slave labor. The almighty plan and the ambitious projects drawn up without regard to human suffering created an insatiable need for workers. Whereas earlier the Soviets had preached the idea of rehabilitation of criminals by way of forced labor, under the new schemes prisoners were driven until they dropped dead.

Resistance to collectivization produced an enormous number of prisoners, and the Politburo set up commissions, beginning in 1928, to study what should be done.

The OGPU—the newest name given the secret police—was formally adopted in the context of the new constitution of the USSR on July 6, 1923. What was important was that the OGPU was linked directly to Sovnarkom and given all-union status. Felix Dzerzhinsky was named first chairman on September 18, 1923, with Vyacheslav Menzhinsky and Genrikh Yagoda as first and second deputy chairmen.[6]

In early 1929, at one of the meetings of a commission on the future of labor and the camps, Yagoda said larger ones would take advantage of the windfall of new workers and that camps would be used as developmental tools in the north. He said it was difficult to attract workers to those areas, and putting camps there would make it possible to exploit the region's natural resources. Using administrative and other techniques, he thought it would be possible to "force the freed prisoners to stay in the North, thereby populating our outer regions."[7]

The creation and control of the camp system emerged over several months in a haphazard fashion, and there were some turf wars within the commission over which commissariat should control the camps. On April 13, 1929, the recommendation was to create a system in which the old distinction between "ordinary" and "special" camps no longer held. The Politburo adopted a resolution titled "On the Utilization of the Labor of Criminal Prisoners." It called for a network of camps to supplement the already-established Solovki camps. Accordingly, on June 27, 1929, the Politburo decided to transfer all "criminal prisoners" serving three years or more to the OGPU, whose concentration camps were to be expanded. The secret police already ruled the lives of untold thousands who were swept up in the collectivization of agriculture, so that it became one of the largest employers in the country—not to mention the cruelest.

On July 11, 1929, Sovnarkom gave its blessing to these changes, renaming the concentration camps corrective labor camps (*ispravitel' no-trudovye lagerya*). New ones were to be situated in northern, remote regions "for the purpose of colonizing these regions and tapping their natural resources through the exploitation of prisoner man power." The initial plan was for the new camps to hold up to fifty thousand, but that turned out to be far too modest. Some prisoners were to remain in the camps of the NKVD (People's Commissariat for Internal Affairs), but the matter was far from settled.[8]

Soviet leaders had not worked out precisely what part the camps were to play in the economy beyond the vague notion of developing the north. The OGPU began using prisoners on projects like the construction of railway lines and in forestry and fishing. Initial successes "whetted the appetite" of the regime for larger projects to capitalize on the growing pool of cheap labor. From January 1930, Yagoda issued orders for concerted action to pick up the three categories of kulaks, beginning with those of the first category and working down. An unknown but large number of other "socially dangerous elements" were also apprehended.[9]

This second wave of dekulakization in 1930–31 was less dramatic than the first but affected even larger numbers and by the end of 1931 had reached a grand total of 1.8 million. This slave labor was now put at the disposal of the expanding concentration camp system.

Sovnarkom decided on April 7, 1930, to establish the Main Administration of Corrective Labor Camps and Labor Settlements, a title shortened to Glavnoe Upravlenie Lagerei, or Gulag. Sovnarkom attempted to justify setting it up, brazenly publishing a statement to the effect that the camps were designed to "isolate especially dangerous lawbreakers and to make them conform to the conditions of the society of toiling people." All prisoners began by serving hard time. As they proved themselves to be useful, their conditions were to be improved, but everyone had to work to eat. There was mention also of how prisoners' labor would contribute to their "struggle for Communist morals."[10]

Stalin intervened in how the camps would fit into the larger scheme of things. At his urging the Politburo decided on May 5, 1930, to construct the White Sea–Baltic Canal (Belomorkanal or Belomor). It would be 141 miles long, with dams and locks traversing extremely difficult terrain. Stalin was keen on using concentration camp labor to build it cheaply and in the impossibly short time of two years. There was a conflict, however, between the OGPU and the Russian Federation NKVD. Both were developing plans and were competing over the supply of slaves. They appealed to higher authority. In the first instance, on August 31, Sovnarkom decided to permit the NKVD to keep prisoners sentenced to three years or longer—as the NKVD wished. The OGPU chairman, Menzhinsky, wanted more and on September 3 complained to the Politburo, and the matter came to Stalin's attention.

Leaders of the OGPU got word to Stalin that if the NKVD kept "their" prisoners, then construction of his pet project of the moment— the White Sea–Baltic Canal—would fall still further behind schedule. In the event, Stalin was distinctly not pleased. On September 7 he wrote Molotov, urging him to set matters straight by giving the OGPU all the prisoners and removing those of the NKVD. By October 5 the Politburo had decided that was indeed the proper course and overruled itself as Stalin wished.[11]

This turn of events was significant in that it increased the power and influence of the OGPU, which was then firmly put in charge of the Gulag. There were also political ramifications within the elite. Up to this point Stalin was still facing some "right opposition" in the Politburo and Sovnarkom but demonstrated he was able to get his way with ease.[12]

The camps now expanded rapidly. The number of prisoners increased from around 30,000 in 1930 to 179,000 the next year. On January 1, 1933, there were 334,300 prisoners, and the next year there were 510,307. By January 1, 1936, the number had grown to 839,406. This massive increase came even though life expectancy in the camps and on the building sites was low — as little as one year, according to some estimates. The severe treatment and impossibly harsh working conditions on various pet projects left even those who were released in a debilitated condition and shortened many people's lives.[13] By the mid-1930s prisoners were scattered across the entire USSR, with some of the largest clusters in and around major cities like Moscow and Leningrad.[14]

To combat atrocity stories about the camps circulating inside and outside the Soviet Union, the regime opened "model facilities" for the inspection of the curious, including foreigners. Stalin wanted the public to believe that the kulaks were not convicts and worked freely. Supposedly, they had "all the rights of voluntary labor."[15]

Some regional bosses were driven by the plan and their own ambitions to brush such paper distinctions aside. They were desperately short of labor and not at all unhappy with Stalin's decision to "eliminate the kulaks as a class." In the Urals region, for example, there was no way to meet the quota demands for forestry products without more labor. Regional officials ignored all concerns about the fate of the kulaks and "insistently requested" far more prisoners than they could possibly care for. Many were soon worked to death.[16]

As per the blueprint outlining the three categories of kulaks and what should happen to each, some were sent on journeys into the farthest reaches of unoccupied northern and eastern parts of the country, where they would have to work on "poor land." In fact, many were put on trains and then deserted in uninhabited places in what was called, with exaggerated understatement, "abandonment in deportation." Just what was meant by this concept was hinted at in a later report, from May 1933, sent to Stalin. This account pertained not to kulaks but to yet another stigmatized group — "outdated elements" — but it showed well enough what "abandonment in deportation" really meant.

The report concerned two trainloads of these unfortunates, presumably members of the bourgeoisie, nobility, or clergy — more than six thousand in all — who originated in Moscow and Leningrad. In late April 1933 they were sent to the distant and uninhabited island of Nazino. The trip alone caused the deaths of many. The emaciated survivors were weakened by hunger and mistreatment. They were then left on an island in the middle of nowhere, with no tools, no grain, no food. They could not even light a fire. It began to snow, and hundreds died of exposure or malnutrition the first day. Only on the fourth or fifth day did a convoy arrive and dole out a minimal amount of flour to each person. Driven by delirium from exhaustion and hunger, many tried to mix the flour with water in their hats; most tried to eat it straightaway, with the result that they choked to death on the foul mixture. Once their last resources were gone, survivors resorted to cannibalism.

The authorities returned and resettled the unfortunates in one failed "colony" after the next before concluding that the region was uninhabitable. By July these "outdated elements" were finally sent to a more settled area, but were desperate enough to eat "moss, grass, leaves, etc.," and reports of cannibalism persisted. By August 20 more than two-thirds of the original six thousand or so had already died. Thus, the meaning of "abandonment in deportation" was for some four thousand the equivalent of a death sentence dragged out through months of useless suffering.[17]

An official census, on January 1, 1932, of the 1.8 million kulaks deported in 1930–31 counted only 1,317,022. Even supposing the figures were accurate, they indicated nearly a half million missing people. Some had escaped, but many were dead.[18]

Far from solving recurrent grain crises, forced collectivization, with all its attendant heavy-handedness, made the situation even worse. Stalin determined there was no turning back, and the pace was accelerated. Every move was justified by relating it to one statement or another from Lenin. Stalin's address of February 4, 1931, to industrial executives again sounded the drums of war:

> To slacken the tempo is to fall behind. And those who fall behind get beaten. But we do not want to be beaten. No, we refuse to be beaten! Old Russia suffered continual beatings because of its backwardness. It was beaten by the Mongol khans, by the Turkish beys, by the Swedish feudal lords, by the Polish and Lithuanian gentry, by the British and French capitalists, by the Japanese barons. All beat Russia—because of its backwardness, its military backwardness, cultural backwardness, political backwardness, industrial backwardness, agricultural backward-

ness. They beat it because doing so was profitable and could be done with impunity.

He urged the industrial executives to put an end to the economic backwardness of the "Socialist fatherland" in the shortest possible time. He expected them to employ a "genuine Bolshevik tempo in developing its Socialist economy. There is no other way. That is why Lenin said on the eve of the October Revolution: 'Either perish, or overtake and outstrip the advanced capitalist countries.' "[19]

He ended the speech by saying: "There are no fortresses that Bolsheviks cannot capture. We have solved some very difficult problems. We have overthrown capitalism, taken power, and built up a huge Socialist industry. We have put the middle peasants onto the path of Socialism. Already we have met the most important requirements for construction."[20]

THE LEADER

Stalin had emerged as the victor for Lenin's succession and defeated all rivals by 1929. He was still not the dictator he was to become. He exercised power by arguing his point of view and maneuvering policies through the upper echelons of the Soviet system of Party and state. By 1929–30 he had gained powerful positions in the Politburo and was secretary general of the secretariat and the decisive figure on Sovnarkom, the Council of People's Commissars. He wanted more.

Lenin's death left a political-psychological void within the Party and to some extent in the country, a yearning for a strong hero figure, a charismatic leader around whom all could rally. Charisma—"the gift"—conferred authority on the leader by virtue of who he was, not because of the positions he held. Thus, even though Stalin controlled significant leadership positions, the magic of charismatic authority escaped him. The task of assuming Lenin's mantle was made more difficult because the great man had never taken a prominent office, such as supreme leader of the Party or head of state. There was no alluring title to be passed on.

The first major opportunity to establish a Stalin cult along the lines of the one created for Lenin came on Stalin's "official" fiftieth birthday on December 21, 1929. This was by coincidence the year of the "great breakthrough," or turning point of the Five-Year Plan.

For most of 1929, *Pravda* had carried few articles about or by Stalin, or pictures of him. Some people, though, most likely inside the upper echelons of the Party, thought it was about time to bring public attention to the leader. In the course of 1929, and in line with the tradition in the country of celebrating important anniversaries, birthdays, and such occasions, they decided that some tribute would be paid to Stalin.

A wide array of people, numbering in the thousands, were mobilized from all walks of life, major organizations, factories, and military units to show their fealty and devotion by writing letters to *Pravda*. Such a "spontaneous" expression of joy had to have an international dimension. Leaders of Communist parties abroad were encouraged to write about Stalin's accomplishments.

Many of these birthday greetings were published in Soviet newspapers. *Pravda* alone printed 200 messages of congratulations, 117 of them between December 21 and 28. The letters were culled from hundreds more. Some were similar enough to suggest they were tampered with. Thus they cannot be taken as a "scientific" sample of public support for Stalin, but nor can they be dismissed as meaningless.

James Heizer's analysis of the 117 *Pravda* letters shows that there were 483 different terms used to designate Stalin's preeminence, with 201 (42 percent) referring to various leadership roles. Russian has two main words for leader. The first, *rukovoditel'*, was used 76 times. The root of the word refers to guidance or direction, and in this case mostly related to tasks Stalin performed in his capacity as head of the Party, leader of the Central Committee, and so on.

The second word for leader in Russian is *vozhd'* and was commonly used for Lenin. This was the title Stalin coveted, even as he piously disclaimed all interest in a cult of leadership. The *vozhd'* was the undisputed charismatic hero-leader and near-religious prophet of the movement. The word was used in forty-nine greetings on Stalin's birthday, eight of which were translations of messages from well-wishers abroad. Only twenty-eight Soviet letters used *vozhd'* to refer to Stalin. Moreover, to the extent they did, the word applied to his role as leader of the Communist Party. In late 1929, then, he was far from being viewed as the vaunted leader on par with Lenin.[21]

Henceforth the Stalinist cult would be developed with more care. The framework was already sketched out, and no doubt some people sincerely began to look to Stalin as the blessed leader. There were social expectations of many kinds, and there were hints at least that many welcomed the return of the strong leader who would set things right. Stalin himself took a hand in filling in the details during the stormy decade to come.

Lenin had been chairman of Sovnarkom from 1917 to 1924 and was a kind of unofficial premier of the government. He ended up working through the Politburo, as did Stalin, who turned down the chairmanship of Sovnarkom and preferred to have one of his yes-men assume that role. He craved the adoration showered on Lenin, and as the years passed, he dared hope for that kind of glory for himself.

In the course of the 1930s the tradition of collective leadership faded, and Stalin emerged still more as an autocrat and dictator, in fact if not in name. He took a hands-on approach to the minute details of government and administration in many spheres. He became, as was to be expected in such a complex party-state system, not the person who made every single decision, but the one who acted as the "supreme arbitrator" within the hierarchy of power.[22]

Stalin did not openly proclaim his dictatorship, but even as he veiled it carefully, the aura around him deepened. He frightened his inner circle and those who were close to the center of power. The balled fist was covered with a silk glove for the public, who were shown pictures and statues of him in state buildings. He was held up as a great father figure who always knew best, a man who wanted nothing for himself, everything for his people. He remained distant, mysterious, and fearful. When he visited his aging mother (as he rarely did) in the early 1930s, she asked him humbly: "Joseph, what exactly are you now?" He answered, perhaps more honestly than he intended, "Well, remember the Tsar? I'm something like a Tsar."[23]

PART FOUR

GERMANS MAKE A PACT
WITH HITLER

11

NAZI PARTY AS SOCIAL MOVEMENT

Weimar democracy was able to shut out the extremist parties like the Nazis and the Communists for a while, but at the end of the 1920s, when the economy collapsed, Germans gradually deserted more moderate parties and, in desperation and doubt, threw their support behind political extremism. In the midst of the turmoil, many yearned for a strong leader along the lines of a Frederick the Great or a Bismarck who could set things right. The Nazi Party would have had no chance in "good times," but at the end of the 1920s the country was in complete disarray. Voters began to see the Nazis as a plausible alternative, all the more as they were steadfast opponents of the Communist Party, whose support grew with every election.

Nazism was also a social movement that demanded commitment and sacrifice. Even in hard times when money was short, people were charged a fee to listen to what Nazi speakers had to say. The money to finance the Party did not come, as is often supposed, from industrialists and bankers, but mostly from ordinary people who were willing to pay out of their own pockets.[1]

SELF-FINANCING AS A STEERING DEVICE

Headquarters in Munich covered most expenses for national offices but was not in a position to subsidize local branches, which had to come up with their own funds, such as by charging admission for speeches and rallies. Making locals pay the bills meant the Nazis had to tailor appeals to fit circumstances, and the Party out in the provinces was given a fair amount of autonomy to identify the issues and figure out how to exploit them.

Hitler approved the Party's taking on "a somewhat local coloration" and presenting itself slightly differently depending on the area. He told a membership meeting in Munich not to worry about variations in the message as "in principle we are all marching toward the same goal."[2]

From his army days Hitler had learned what it took to be effective as a public speaker and wanted only specifically trained individuals to address Party meetings. They would be recruited and schooled as he had been and given instructions on how to talk about particular issues and attract audiences. Experienced speakers generally had to be brought in from the outside. If these persons were members of the Reichstag, they traveled on a free railway pass. Otherwise district or local branches had to pay those expenses as well.[3]

Self-financing of this kind operated as a mechanism by which the Party homed in on popular issues and avoided others that got little or no support. Nazi officials at the grass roots did not wait on orders from above but exploited the situation they knew far better than Hitler or the propagandists in distant Munich. The larger and more successful the mass meetings these groups could hold, the more they could afford, so there was an incentive to bring in speakers on topics that attracted the largest crowds.[4]

The Nazis found revivalists who became tireless campaigners. Even when the Party was barely getting off the ground, Hitler reported holding no fewer than 2,370 "mass meetings" in the year ending in May 1926. At that time there were only about forty Party speakers, led by Joseph Goebbels, Julius Streicher, and Wilhelm Frick. Hitler himself spoke all over Germany and was invariably a big draw.[5]

He also went with cap in hand to sympathetic industrialists and wealthy people, but with only mixed results. The Party was off-putting for the more affluent classes as it was tinged with the stigma of being "socialistic." That might mean Marxism or Soviet-style policies. Nonetheless, occasional gifts and loans came in during the mid-1920s, like some from Edwin Bechstein and Hugo Bruckmann, and particularly their wives. Winifred Wagner, of the famous Richard Wagner family, was an early convert and, though she had no money of her own to speak of, "worked tirelessly" for the Party and asked artists and singers at Bayreuth to contribute to the cause. Hitler's association with the Wagner cult and these well-connected people provided him with some funding, as well as an air of social respectability.[6] In 1927 the elderly Ruhr industrialist Emil Kirdorf gave the Party 100,000 marks. Hitler later told Goebbels he was on the point of despair when Kirdorf helped the Party get through a financial crisis.[7]

The obvious way to increase income was to carry out recruitment drives, for new members had to pay dues and buy the Party newspaper and literature. Even the unemployed who wanted to join up had to pay, if necessary by finding a friend to help out. The aim was to grow to 100,000, but in May 1926 the Party treasurer, Franz Xaver Schwarz, reported a mere 36,300 members, a number that might have been on the high side. Far better results were needed.[8]

Hitler forever pointed to the growing danger of the German Communist Party (KPD), supposedly with up to 700,000 sympathizers in Berlin alone. The Socialist Party (SPD), with its millions of members and even greater number of allies in the trade-union movement, was still further ahead.[9]

The Nazi Party was moving slowly along. At the July 1926 rally in Weimar, it put on display the Schutzstaffel (SS), or Protection Squad (founded in November 1925), an elite corps of around two hundred who were in effect Hitler's personal bodyguard. Reichsführer SS Josef Berchtold was presented with the "blood flag" carried by the Nazis on the day of the abortive putsch in 1923. Such rituals became part of the religious-like ceremonies that grew with each Party rally. Although the SS technically remained under the SA until July 20, 1934, it went its own way. Whereas the SA (Brownshirts) was subject to local influence, the SS was free from such interference. The SA was also at the 1926 Party rally in Weimar, but no longer under the leadership of Ernst Röhm, who, feeling out of place trying to win elections, left the movement and emigrated. The SA had a modest membership of seven to eight thousand in 1926, obviously paling in comparison with those on the left.[10]

ORGANIZATION AND PROPAGANDA: PREPARING FOR THE FUTURE

On paper the Nazi Party looked like a neat chain of command linking Munich to the *Gauleiter* (district leaders), to the *Ortsgruppenleiter* (group leaders), and on down to the *Blockleiter* (block leaders). Occasionally there were even *Bezirksleiter* (subregional bosses), who interjected themselves between the *Gauleiter* and the *Ortsgruppenleiter.* What happened was that certain individuals in some districts decided to fill links in the chain of command. This rigid hierarchy looked as if it was carved in stone, but the structure was flexible and able not only to adjust to local variations but to encourage initiative "from below."[11]

The classic case of the Darwinian principles Hitler let run wild inside the Party was shown by Gustav Seifert, a Party member from Hanover who had founded a branch there in 1921. He wrote to Munich in 1925 and asked to be reappointed as *Ortsgruppenleiter.* Max Amann, one of Hitler's right-hand men, wrote a telling response on October 27:

> You know from your earlier activity as a branch leader of the NSDAP that Herr Hitler takes the view on principle that it is not the job of the Party headquarters to "appoint" Party leaders. Herr Hitler is today more than ever convinced that the most effective fighter in the National Socialist movement is the man who wins respect for himself as leader through his own achievements. You yourself say in your letter that almost all the members follow you. Then why don't you take over the leadership of the branch?[12]

If there was a method to this madness, it was that the political struggle would weed out the weak, and the committed would come out on top.

The self-selecting mechanism that determined so much of what the Nazi Party became helped to influence a change in orientation away from the city toward the countryside. Hitler's initial aim was to challenge the Marxists for the soul of the German working class. In the first years after the Party was refounded, however, it became clear that during good times, workers were almost immune to Nazism. They voted for the SPD or the KPD.

By late 1927 the Nazi Party was looking to the countryside, particularly Protestant areas where there were pockets of discontent over issues like taxes and foreign imports and where its speakers were far better received than in the cities.[13] Gregor Strasser as head of Party propaganda persisted in focusing on the cities and the workers, but the strategy was not paying off. Hitler kept enjoining members at Party rallies to be prepared "to make sacrifices" for the movement.[14]

Hitler himself took over from Strasser on January 2, 1928, with a young deputy named Heinrich Himmler, the man he made leader of the SS in 1929. Himmler had participated in the abortive putsch of November 8–9, 1923, and joined the SS in 1925. He had served as adjutant with Strasser and now continued in the same role with Hitler, whom he impressed with his propaganda work and organizational ability.[15]

Hitler, convinced of the need for the Party to orient itself to the countryside, proceeded immediately to modify its program of 1920. Point 17 made demands that sounded far too "socialistic," above all to farmers. As stated, it called for "a land reform suitable to our national requirements, the passing of a law for the expropriation of land for communal purposes without compensation, the abolition of ground rent, and the prohibition of speculation in land." Conservative opponents of Nazism had referred to point 17 to brand the Party as radical and Socialist, and on April 13, 1928, Hitler issued a "clarification" to set the record straight. It went as follows: "Since the NSDAP stands on the basis of private property, it goes without saying that the phrase 'expropriation without compensation' refers simply to the creation of possible legal means for confiscation, when necessary, of land acquired illegally or not managed in the public good. It is, therefore, aimed primarily against Jewish companies that speculate in land."[16]

The socialistic-sounding plank was thus changed to appease conservatives but also to promote the anti-Semitic agenda. As expected, membership began to pick up almost immediately.[17]

The elections of 1928, as usual fought fervently by the Nazis, produced meager results. With only 2.6 percent of the vote and nothing close to a majority in any district, they still elected 12 members because of proportional representation. Even though the 12 represented a small percentage of the 491 members in the Reichstag, they were a presence to be reckoned with. As deputies they had railway passes and could travel all over the country at state expense and give political talks.

The big winners in 1928 were the Communists, who went from 45 to 54 seats; the SPD did better, as always, with 153 seats and was thus the largest party in the Reichstag. Between them the Marxists could claim over 200 seats and, had they been able to work out an alliance, would have been a force the Nazis would have found almost impossible to beat. As it was, the Comintern—that is, the Communist Party in Moscow—determined that any such coalition with the SPD was out of the question. Already in the spring of 1928 the SPD, one of the main supporters of democracy in the country, were harshly branded by Soviet leaders as "Social Fascists."

The new line from the Kremlin was adopted at the Sixth World Congress of the Comintern in July–August 1928. The theory was that the growth of Fascism had infected not only Italy and Germany but also workers' parties like the SPD. Moscow detected a rising threat and called on Communists everywhere to fight against Socialist parties. A *Pravda* report from the Comintern meetings in July 1929 stated that the Social Democrats were "a component part of the fascist system" and had to be defeated.[18] The KPD was thus compelled, under instructions from Moscow, to turn against the SPD. The Nazis scoffed at their bitter divisions and put all Marxists into the same pot.

And yet the divisions within the working-class movement helped the Nazis to grow. Hitler and Himmler began publishing and distributing "propaganda guidelines" in March 1927. These were written mainly by Himmler, who helped create and run the propaganda machine for which Joseph Goebbels is usually given credit.[19]

In July 1928, Fritz Reinhardt, gauleiter in Upper Bavaria–Swabia, set up a "speakers' school" that began by offering correspondence courses. Himmler urged Party leaders to participate. All were offered some basic theory, told to practice in front of a mirror, given several set talks to memorize, and even provided with answers to likely questions. Speakers had to know what they were talking about and were introduced to the most up-to-date material on social and political matters. The goal was for ordinary people to become interested enough to make the trip to the district capital, where they would hear better-trained *Gau*-speakers and perhaps even national Party leaders.[20]

The speakers' school was officially recognized on May 6, 1929. Thereafter, each district nominated two people per course. Once they completed the instruction, they were designated as official Party speakers. Every two weeks they received published reading material, as Reinhardt said, "in a way similar to the information service of the Communists and Socialists." The number of trained Nazi speakers has been estimated at around six thousand by Hitler's appointment in January 1933. Most still drew only small audiences, but together they conveyed the impression of enthusiasm, commitment, and tirelessness. Their activity was the best answer to the fears about the Communist Party. Many worked without pay, and only as the Party's membership drive began to succeed were some given a salary.[21]

The Party made innovative use of the new film medium. It was also skillful in presenting itself on the radio. In October 1928 it created a weekly picture magazine, the *Illustrierter Beobachter* (Illustrated Observer), taking its title from the Party's national newspaper. A Nazi version of *Life* magazine, it combined stories with lavish pictures and would become an institution in the Third Reich. All these innovations were only just getting off the ground in 1928, but later paid dividends.[22]

In the meantime, everything was done on a shoestring budget. There was not even enough money in the coffers to hold a Party rally in 1928, a sign the membership drive was not going that well. The consequences of failure in elections and recruitment were hammered out at long meetings in Munich. But in August Hitler reported the Party had a hundred thousand members and 1,124 "local groups." Although the police said these numbers were "greatly exaggerated," in fact they were not that far off.[23]

In September there was an announcement of the Party structure: new districts were defined, some new leaders put in place, and the importance of the *Gau* highlighted. There were twenty-four *Gaue* outside Bavaria, which had eight "independent *Untergaue*" of its own. Most of the gauleiters were strong believers who remained in office for much of the Third Reich. If they moved, they usually went to equally important posts elsewhere.[24]

Although the Party devoted great energy to reorganizing, improved election results were slow in coming. Indeed, the Prussian state government concluded that Hitler no longer posed a threat and at the end of September 1928 lifted the ban on his public speaking. Daringly enough, the leaders of the Party scheduled a giant rally for November 16 at Berlin's Sportpalast with Hitler as the main attraction. The Party press said eighteen thousand paying customers packed the place, a slight exaggeration but still a massive gathering that demonstrated how the movement might be getting stronger.

Introduced briefly by Goebbels, Hitler showed that on a national stage he easily put the leaders of all other parties in the shade. He was often interrupted by "thunderous applause" and left them cheering wildly.[25]

They were all elated to see Hitler at his full powers for an hour and a half. He hit the nationalist and economic themes, underlining how the country had been weakened and shut out of international affairs. He told his usual story about the World War and how Germany was falsely accused of causing it.

Hitler said he wanted to rise above politics and social classes, to speak for the creation of a "community of the people" based on "pure blood." He trotted out his favorite hobbyhorse—that racial mixing led to national decline—and branded democracy an "error." Marxism and class conflict had to be overcome, "not in order that the bourgeoisie wins, but the German people survive. We want to create space and bread, because now we are slaves of the world economy, slaves on our own soil. We confess that our intention is to give the people land again. On the head of our weapons there is our will, the great weapon, to destroy other philosophies." He was referring not just to Marxism but to parliamentary democracy as well. "The republic persecutes us, takes our freedom and very being, but thereby creates the weapon for the struggle of the Third Reich."[26]

Hitler went back to Munich, where he addressed the National Socialist German University Student Group in November. Under the leadership of twenty-one-year-old Baldur von Schirach, the student organization made great gains in the nationwide university association. Perhaps more important than winning those elections, Schirach brought Nazi ideas to the country's young elite. The Nazi university students were officially organized on January 26, 1926, but only became a force to reckon with two years later.

Hitler was a big drawing card on November 20, and twenty-five hundred or more university students and invited guests packed the Löwenbräu Keller to hear his speech titled "Not Pretty Words, but Deeds." It touched all the themes likely to appeal to such a crowd, particularly nationalism and the need to fight for the fatherland "and for the coming Third Reich." He was looking for recruits who wanted to assert Germany's will abroad and overcome class conflict at home. He took aim at the Communists, who were accused of attacking Party members after his recent talk in Berlin. "We will break the terror of the Communists, because we'll fight terror with terror." He ended with the message that come what may, neither he nor the Party would bend, but would continue the battle. As usual, Hitler's remarks were greeted with great applause.[27]

In preparation for elections Himmler devised propaganda "concentrations," whereby the Party would employ saturation campaigning in one district for a week or ten days. In late 1928 the Party would schedule as many as two hundred rallies in any one district for an upcoming election. The tactic, which has been called "highly sophisticated," was not used in areas already in the fold and avoided places where there was little or no support. Instead, Himmler, Hitler, and Hess directed the all-out drives to areas where breakthroughs were likely. To determine which to target, Himmler would evaluate the incoming monthly reports of the gauleiters and compile a master list identifying where the propaganda "concentrations" should take place.

The scheduling was worked out by the three leaders, in conjunction with Hitler's speaking arrangements and the availability of other top performers. As a follow-up, the SA would visit each village and town that had been hit in order to show themselves in the best light. The net effect was seemingly endless numbers of meetings, a fact that never failed to impress.[28]

Similar procedures determined the topics, including Hitler's. There was little point in condemning Marxism or Bolshevism in a rural area where people did not feel threatened by Socialists or Communists. Similarly, many parts of Germany had no Jewish communities at all and little or no history of anti-Semitism, so there it made little sense to dwell on these matters. Where agricultural issues were of immediate relevance, the Party tried to exploit them. Even in 1928, before its speakers' school began, it had used ten "experts" on agriculture to every one on Bolshevism.[29]

The impression conveyed in Goebbels's diary was that Hitler came up with the ideas and others made things happen. By late 1929 Goebbels and Himmler were cooperating closely on the Party's propaganda.[30]

Voters had no idea about the careful calculations behind the scenes. Certain areas would be selected for a saturation campaign and then overwhelmed. The Party gave the impression that it was a giant movement whose activities made it seem unstoppable and inexhaustible. It used the right "experts" at the right times. Historians, particularly those who interview local people, always report such impressions. The Nazis paid enormous attention to detail, from providing outlines for election posters to suggesting battle songs the SA might sing as the occasion demanded.

OMENS OF THINGS TO COME

The Party's organizational apparatus was in place by the end of 1928. Membership also grew, with the number 100,000 reported in October 1928 and 150,000 in September 1929. Active members were likely around one-tenth less than those numbers, as some people left the movement and others passed away. Finding the right personnel to represent the Party was a continuing problem.[31]

Hitler and his Party could see hopeful signs in 1929 that they would likely do better in the next national elections, even before the Great Depression began. Not only was Hitler a great attraction, but other Nazis addressed ever-increasing audiences as well. For example, Goebbels had a packed house of five thousand in Hamburg's Circus Busch in mid-April 1929. That city had a reputation for supporting left-wing or liberal parties, and for Goebbels to get such a crowd there was encouraging to the Nazis. The same number gathered to hear him in Berlin in September. In various other parts of Germany the story was the same. These mass events took place in a highly politicized atmosphere even before local and state election campaigns got started.[32]

The annual Party rally in early August 1929 was deemed by the Nazis a great success. Police estimated that 26,300 showed up in Nuremberg, whereas the Nazis said the number was 200,000.[33] The event was a social phenomenon, with gatherings that included special sessions led by experts to deal with propaganda, culture, civil servant, peasant, and trade-union issues. The Party already had numerous suborganizations, such as for youth and university students. Newer ones included the Union for National Socialist Lawyers, the National Socialist Doctors' Union, the Union of National Socialist Teachers, and the League of Struggle for German Culture. These organizations directed specific messages to respectable sections of the middle class, and to judge by new Party joiners, the efforts had considerable success.

A number of women's organizations had links to the Nazi Party in the 1920s. These were reorganized by Strasser, and on July 6, 1931, he announced the new National Socialist Women's Group (NS-Frauenschaft). In the 1920s women were drawn to right-wing parties like the Nazis out of revulsion over "everything associated with social-ism—including 'atheistic Marxism.' " Such women preferred "Christian morality" to "Bolshevist license," and Nazism appealed primarily "because of its anti-Left stance."[34] That point would also hold for many men and for various middle-class groups attracted to the movement.

Behind the outward respectability, there was violence. Tumult erupted in the streets between the SA and members of the SPD paramil-itary association during the 1929 Party rally, and a female member of the NSDAP was shot dead. The SA attacked various left-wing groups, and there were stories with headlines like "The Wild West in Nuremberg" and "Red Murder in Nuremberg." Even while Hitler was speaking, rumors went through the crowd that some kind of leftist attack was imminent.[35]

The theme of Hitler's talks was the creation of a "racial state" for Aryans, along the lines of ancient Sparta. The mission was the "reorgan-ization of the body politic" to stop degeneration and hold back the Jews. As always, there was a history lesson. In November 1918 Germany's fate had supposedly fallen to Marxists or bourgeois politicians: "In the name of Socialism they delivered the nation to international high finance, in the name of progress they provided barbarism out of the Middle Ages, in the name of culture they infected art, and in the name of art they destroyed culture." But the new movement would bring regeneration: "The miracle is that against the symbol of the Soviet star, at last there stands a German cross"—the latter being the swastika (that is, the *Hak-enkreuz,* literally "bent cross"). Hitler chalked up a long list of crimes against the republic, as well as the bourgeois and Marxist parties. As always, the speech ended on an upbeat note. "Germany," he assured his audience, was "awakening."[36]

In November–December 1929, the Party did better than ever in state and local elections, particularly in northerly and largely agrarian Schleswig-Holstein, where it earned 10.3 percent of the vote. It did reasonably well (5.1 percent) in parts of Hessen, where it built on the anti-Semitic tradition identified with Otto Böckel in the prewar era. In Protestant Nuremberg, Nazis captured 15.6 percent of the vote in the December 1929 municipal elections, and the Party became the second most powerful in the city, behind only the SPD. The Nazis improved their showing in every major Bavarian city, and even in "Red" Berlin the election brought a dramatic increase. Goebbels was overjoyed.[37]

The Party helped its nationalist profile in late 1929 by participating in the effort, led by Alfred Hugenberg of the German National People's Party (DNVP) and other prominent conservatives, against the Young Plan. The American lawyer and corporate executive, Owen D. Young proposed dealing with the reparations question, which was still plaguing economies since the First World War, in a plan that would make it possible for Germany to pay off its debts in fifty-nine years. In return the Allies offered to withdraw promptly from the Rhineland. The deal was signed but caused a nationalist uproar, and Hugenberg organized a petition drive to force the government to reject it. Enough signatures were collected to hold a national plebiscite, as permitted under the Weimar constitution, which was carried out on December 22, 1929. Although the great majority voted to accept the plan, and thus in effect reject the objections of Hitler, Hugenberg, and others, the campaign put Hitler on the front pages. He came across as the most nationalistic of the nationalists, the man who stood up for Germany no matter what.

On January 5, 1930, Hitler was interviewed by Karl Henry von Wiegand of the *New York American*. Asked to explain why the Party was doing so well, he answered that it was due to efforts to save Germany from Bolshevism. He pointed to recent elections as proof that his message was getting through. In reply to the suggestion that he might be "overrating the danger of Bolshevism," he referred to signs of economic decay that were smoothing the way for the Reds. "The public mind in Germany is in utter confusion. It is in this state of affairs that the National Socialists are raising the cry of home, country and nation against the slogan of internationalism of the Marxian Socialists."

Wiegand asked why anti-Semitism was on the Party's program. Hitler replied, "The people would not understand it if I had not done so. All denials notwithstanding, there is a strong anti-Semitic sentiment, not only in Germany but in other countries as well." He voiced the usual pretense that was simultaneously a threat: "I am not for curtailing the rights of Jews in Germany, but I insist that we others who are not Jews shall not have less rights than they."

Hitler told Wiegand he wanted measures like the restrictions of the U.S. Immigration Act of 1924. It limited new entries to 2 percent of the number of people from any given country already living in the United States in 1890. Hitler said that "the National Socialists want the immigration frontiers of Germany protected as America protects hers." He was interested in more than that, although he hastened to add that he had "no thought of revolution." He pointed to the weaknesses of parliamentary democracy as a system of government, but showed admiration for the powers of the American president, who was "more than a rubber stamp" for decisions made by Congress.[38]

Although Hitler and his more faithful followers like Goebbels expressed satisfaction at the progress they were making in the polls, they were frank enough to admit they were at least three years away from power. Even that timescale would have been overly optimistic had not the Great Depression intervened.

12

NAZISM EXPLOITS ECONOMIC DISTRESS

German agriculture was affected by falling prices in the late 1920s, and the situation was not helped in 1926–27 when the republic signed trade treaties with countries like Poland and permitted imports of foodstuffs at favorable rates. Prices for all major agricultural products fell every year from 1928–29 until 1933–34.[1] Peasants went into debt, and many lost their farms. The German Communist Party tried to recruit these unfortunates, but the link with Soviet Communism and collectivization led to failure. The Nazi Party was far more successful in infiltrating the emerging protest movements among the peasantry and by the end of 1930 established its own Office for Agriculture (*Agrarpolitischer Apparat*).[2]

In the Party's first program for agriculture, worked out by Hitler and Konstantin Hierl and published on March 7, 1930, the agricultural sector's underlying problems were linked to defeat in 1918 and reparations. The Party also blamed the flood of foreign food products. The plight of the peasantry was summed up under four headings: high taxes; false trade policies; unfair profits by middlemen (Jews were mentioned); and steep electricity rates (said to be set by Jewish companies). Farms lost through debt were allegedly scooped up by Jewish financiers. The answer to peasant woes was a law to prevent speculation in land and make it impossible to buy out independent peasants (a law of entailment). Only "German racial comrades" would be allowed to own land; the question of agriculture was a matter of "life or death" for the nation. Although Hitler would not go so far as to regulate the size of farms, he said smaller and medium-sized properties had to be protected. He would confiscate land, but only if owned by non-Germans and in exceptional cases.[3]

The new agricultural program was consistent with his long-held views and the mirror opposite of the one promoted by Stalin at around the same time. In April 1929, as we have seen, Hitler renounced the "Socialist" plank in the Nazi program that talked about "expropriating land," and "clarified" it to make it applicable only to Jews who speculated in land. Nevertheless, the original "Socialist-sounding" demand left a residue of distrust.

One way around the problem was to send trained experts to speak in the countryside. By 1930 the Nazis had perfected their approach and could put on a real show, complete with bands, parades, and movies. Crowds were entertained while waiting for the main event. There was the usual entrance fee to the tent or the hall, and for those times the price of admission was substantial. Having to pay to hear a speaker posed the question "How important is your future and the future of the country to you?"[4]

There was a pronounced racial component in the new Nazi agricultural policies. Walther Darré, who took over the leadership of the agricultural department of the NSDAP in 1930, had not been involved directly in formulating the new program, but he accepted the principles and was known for publications like *Neuadel aus Blut und Boden* (1929; New Aristocracy from Blood and Soil). Darré caught Hitler's eye when he was looking for farming experts to tap rural votes. He became Hitler's minister of agriculture in June 1933.[5]

For Hitler the peasantry was vital to the realization of his ideological aims. In this context, the concept of "blood" conveyed the determination "to strengthen the racial basis of our people," while "soil" expressed the goal of conquering "living space," that is, foreign lands in Eastern Europe.[6] No doubt what appealed to many farmers were specific promises to deal with economic problems, but they were attracted by aspects of Nazi ideology, including belief in a harmonious "community of the people." Frequently the Party's pronouncements contained open or thinly veiled anti-Semitism. Hitler's March 7, 1930, speech setting forth the new program for farmers ended on a high-sounding note: the "crisis of the agricultural population is one part of the crisis that involves the whole population, and the National Socialist movement is fighting to free the whole country."[7]

FROM REPUBLICAN DEMOCRACY TO "SEMI-DICTATORSHIP"

The economic crisis in the countryside was overtaken and deepened by the Great Depression, which began with the Wall Street crash on October 24, 1929. Germany had experienced unprecedented inflation only six years earlier, and now it was faced with chaos once again. As the economy unraveled, even those who were fairly secure wondered how long they could hold on.

The government was reliant on loans from America, and when these were called in, it ran into trouble. The president of the Reichsbank, Hjalmar Schacht, said he would agree to borrow the money to pay the debts, but only if the chancellor would put forward a long-term plan to put the financial house in order. This condition and other issues that arose began an acrimonious debate in the Reichstag that ultimately brought down the government of the "Great Coalition" of five parties under Chancellor Hermann Müller.

The immediate cause had to do with budgetary disputes, most notably unemployment insurance. Were workers going to pay more for their insurance and get smaller benefits, or were the employers and the state going to carry more of the burden? Was Weimar's welfare state to be maintained or dismantled? No agreement could be found among the coalition partners in the government. President Hindenburg would not back Müller by using the emergency powers under article 48 of the constitution.

Thus on March 27, 1930, the chancellor resigned on what was long called a "black day" for the republic. In retrospect it marked the end of "relative stability" and the beginning of the dissolution phase of democracy.[8] Müller's ouster had been under active consideration by Hindenburg and a number of his influential advisers for months. They had grown weary of the SPD at the helm and wanted to move to the right. They ushered Heinrich Brüning, a political economist, of the Catholic Center Party into office. A lifelong bachelor who seemed distant, cold, and secretive, he stood for belt-tightening and reduction of expenditures, particularly of the civil service, policies that were described by Sebastian Haffner as "Operation successful, patient died." Brüning introduced what Haffner called a novel form of government: a "semi-dictatorship in the name of democracy and in defense against a real dictatorship." Short of an economic miracle, however, the chancellor was bound to fail.[9]

Hindenburg had already seen enough of parliamentary democracy and expected Brüning to carry on without the backing of the Reichstag if push came to shove. On April 3 there was a first vote of nonconfidence, but the government stayed in office. The chancellor proposed measures to keep the economy afloat, but they had the effect of reducing what citizens had to spend. The new approach was pushed through by presidential emergency decree on July 16. There followed a renewed motion of nonconfidence. The Nazi Party joined with the SPD and KPD and others to protest what the Communists called the "hunger government."

Thus began the transition to an openly presidential government that would culminate in dictatorship. To be sure, new elections were called for September 14, but democracy was already under threat. Apart from the breakdown of the republic's institutions, there were telltale signs the Nazis and Communists would make major gains at the next polls.[10]

Fueling their rise was the economic crisis. A full year before the Depression hit, unemployment was high. In 1929, on average 8.5 percent of the "employed population" was without work. The figures jumped to 14 percent in 1930, 21.9 percent in 1931, and 29.9 percent in 1932. Trade unionists suffered even higher rates, with the result that the Depression crippled their movement.[11] One recent estimate suggests that in the winter of 1932–33, almost 40 percent of all workers and white collar employees were unemployed.[12] Total industrial production, pegged at 100.1 in 1929, went to 70.1 in 1931 and 58.0 in 1932. In effect the economy was grinding to a halt.[13]

Contrary to some assertions, unemployment was still rising when Hitler was appointed. From 5.1 million in October 1932 it stood at just over 6 million in January and February 1933. The situation only began to improve significantly in May, June, and July 1933, namely on Hitler's watch.[14]

Unemployment became the dominant fact of life during the years of the Brüning government and beyond. It clawed back social insurance measures, like the new system introduced in 1927, when the country was reasonably stable. It also kept reducing the period a person could collect, which left those affected little choice but to join the swelling welfare rolls.[15]

The sense of despair was reflected in suicide rates for 1932, which were more than four times higher than those in Britain at the time and nearly double what they were in the United States.[16] There was a broad perception that the country was experiencing a breakdown of cultural and moral values. Large families were becoming a thing of the past, and more women were going to work; abortions were thought to be reaching alarming proportions; and prostitution, sexual deviancy, and venereal diseases were presumed to be spreading.[17]

NAZI POLITICS AS CRUSADE AGAINST THE REPUBLIC

For the 1930 elections, the Nazis announced they would use a thousand specially trained speakers and hold no fewer than thirty-four thousand electoral meetings. These were scheduled for a campaign to last around six weeks. The price of admission (discounted for some) to hear the better-known, particularly Hitler, helped finance the campaign. In just three speeches Hitler gave at Berlin's Sportpalast, the Party netted at least thirty thousand marks. It was a similar story elsewhere. He had become a fund-raising machine. Most parties used amounts like that to finance an entire local campaign.[18]

Most of these Hitler routines began with a lengthy historical sketch tracing the ultimate source of all Germany's problems to November 1918, the revolution, the armistice, and the Treaty of Versailles. He never tired of repeating this story, and his audiences were always eager to listen to it yet again. To mention just one example: the address he gave in Cologne on August 18 was titled "The November Crime and Its Consequences." There was no need to ask, "Which crime?" or "What Novem-

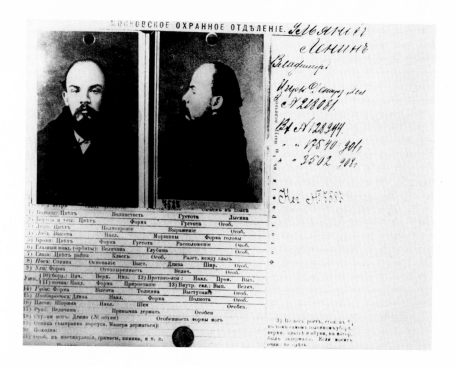

ABOVE: Vladimir Lenin's mug shot kept in Moscow by the Russian
Secret Police (Okhrana) in 1895. He was arrested
at the end of the year in St. Petersburg.
BELOW: Red Guards in front of the Smolny Institute
at the time of the Bolshevik Revolution. (1917)

Vladimir Lenin (*front row, middle*) with Joseph Stalin
to his right and Mikhail Kalinin on his left. (1919)

ABOVE: The Red Army marching in primitively bound shoes
during the Russian Civil War. (1919–20)
BELOW: White Guard Cossacks posing with their victims. (1919)

Lenin and Stalin at Lenin's dacha in Gorky
in 1922. Suspicions that Stalin had himself super-imposed
in the picture have been disproved since the opening of the archives.

LEFT: Lenin at the second world congress of the Comintern. Directly behind him stands Maxim Gorky. Grigory Zinoviev is on the right, and Karl Radek on the far left, next to whom is Nikolai Bukharin.
BELOW: Stalin at the funeral of Feliks Dzerzhinsky, first head of the Cheka. *Left to right:* Aleksei Rykov, Genrikh Yagoda, Mikhail Kalinin, Leon Trotsky, Lev Kamenev, Joseph Stalin, Mikhail Tomsky, and Nikolai Bukharin. (1926)
BOTTOM: Stalin and some of his competitors before their fall. *Left to right:* Stalin, Aleksei Rykov, Lev Kamenev, and Grigory Zinoviev. (early 1920s)

ABOVE: Soviet leaders in 1935 reviewing the annual celebration of the October Revolution. *Left to right:* Anastas Mikoyan, Andrei Andreyev, Nikita Khrushchev, Lazar Kaganovitch, Vyacheslav Molotov, Joseph Stalin, Yan Rudzutak, and Mikhail Kalinin.
BELOW: A Russian kulak who was deported to the forests of Karelia for compulsory labor in 1932.

Compulsory collectivization in 1929 in the Soviet countryside.
The banner reads: Peasants, read books! The Book is the best friend of
those on the land. It teaches how to carry out agriculture properly.

ABOVE: Gulag labor and the construction of the Fergana Canal
in Uzbekistan in summer 1939.
BELOW: Gulag prisoners work on the Belomor Canal in 1933.

ber?" The crowd knew the story by heart, and twenty thousand packed the Rhineland Hall to hear it. He offered no well-aimed attacks on government policies followed by concrete counterproposals. Instead, the audience was treated to a condemnation of the republic from top to bottom.

He wanted to start a "regeneration process" of the body politic and rekindle hope that the nation was not "at the end of its days but at the beginning of a new era." Part of the standard fare was that the Nazi movement had grown from an alleged "seven-man group" into one embracing tens of thousands at first, then hundreds of thousands, and finally millions. He attacked all other parties for representing specific social classes or interests. "They talk about the people, but know only splinters of it."[19]

Sometimes Hitler spoke about the adverse economic situation and the government's mistaken efforts but did not dwell long on them. He mentioned Brüning's name only four times altogether. Finance Minister Paul Moldenhauer's tax proposals were briefly held up to scorn. Next to nothing was said about the Wall Street crash, and few details were given about unemployment and how to cure it. The fundamental blame for almost all ills was placed on the Marxists and on parliamentary democracy.

The aim was to appear to be above parties and special interests and in favor of the nation (das Volk) as a whole. The Jews were occasionally mentioned, such as in the context of being behind the machinations of capitalism. Selections taken straight out of Mein Kampf were published as articles during the election. Hitler also repeated one of the favorite themes from that book, namely that Germany had to expand to the east or die. So the end of democracy and eastward expansion were on the agenda. However, he was trying to reach out to groups he had not already won over, so he hammered away not on the anti-Semitic and racist themes but on the nationalist one.

He said repeatedly that he considered the elections a farce, but the Nazis were nonetheless going to fight them with all the resources they could muster. He vowed that the first day after the next elections, the Party would commence the battle for the German nation all over again. Although he did not say he wanted a revolution, no one who heard these remarks or read them in the press could doubt that he was intent, once in power, on getting rid of the parliamentary system.

All these Hitler meetings had packed houses. In Frankfurt on August 3 he drew twenty-five thousand at what was called the largest public event ever held there. In Berlin on September 10 he attracted a minimum of sixteen thousand to hear him speak on Germany's "awakening." In Breslau two days later some twenty to twenty-five thousand gathered for a talk on overcoming class conflict. There, as in most of his other appearances, however, the note struck was nationalism.

These speeches did not take a "shopping list" approach by trying to offer something for every social class or region, but sought to appeal to the national interest. By refusing to make more empty-sounding promises, the Party came across as novel and interesting. Because more than a dozen parties ran in the election, as usual the vote was hopelessly split. Nevertheless, the shock was that the Nazi Party became the second largest in the country with 107 seats out of a possible 577. It won 18.3 percent of the vote, which was taken from all sides of the political spectrum.

Almost as astonishing as these gains were those of the KPD, which garnered 13.1 percent of the ballots and got 77 seats. As expected, the SPD lost about 5 percent compared with the previous election, but still had 24.5 percent of the vote and 143 seats. Nobody really "won" this election, but the extremists and antirepublicans made great strides.[20]

Hitler was triumphant in his postelection speech, "Our Solution: After the Victory the Struggle." He said winning so many seats was fine, but not to forget, the Party rejected parliament in principle. The many new Reichstag seats merely gave it new weapons to continue the fight. The goal was neither a conventional political revolution nor a putsch, "but a revolution of the German soul, conquest of the German person. Then we will leave it to the sovereign German people to settle accounts with the seducers."[21]

For Chancellor Brüning, the election was a disappointment, but he had had no clear electoral strategy. Until President Hindenburg (and his advisers, like General Kurt von Schleicher) finally lost confidence in him and forced him out, Brüning put together two cabinets whose members had little popular support. Brüning earned his title as Germany's "hunger chancellor" when unemployment skyrocketed. As bad as it was in the United States and Great Britain in 1932, it was almost exactly twice as bad in percentage terms in Germany.[22]

Hindenburg and his advisers, led by his son Oskar and General von Schleicher, grew weary of Brüning, whose resignation was demanded on May 29, 1932, and given the next day. In classic understatement, Hindenburg said he would not support the chancellor's government any longer and it had to go as quickly as possible "because it is unpopular."[23]

The next day Franz von Papen was named the new chancellor with a "Cabinet of the Barons," so called because seven of its ten members came from the nobility. Papen announced his plan two days later, not as was customary to the Reichstag, but over the radio. Claiming that parliament had ruined the economy by turning the state into "a kind of social welfare institution," he sounded like a "distillation of darkest reaction" compared to even the kaiser's prewar governments.[24]

Papen pushed a right-wing agenda, including resistance to what he called "cultural Bolshevism," and on June 14 he had Hindenburg sign the first of many emergency decrees. It cut unemployment insurance payments by an average of 23 percent and restricted the period someone could collect to six weeks from thirteen; it also reduced welfare payments by an average of 15 percent. The economy needed some pumping up, but these measures were bound to have the opposite effect.[25]

Papen and supporters around Hindenburg called for new elections for July 31, which they thought might give them more support but which benefited only the extremist parties. Hitler's Party emerged as the overwhelming winner, obtaining 37.4 percent of the total and 230 seats. The Nazis more than doubled what they had obtained in the previous election. Support varied by region and social group, with Catholic areas and Communist urban ones generally immune to the Nazis. Hitler's Party did better in rural areas than in the cities, and much better in Protestant districts.

Unemployment was a crucial factor, but it usually had an indirect effect on the vote for the Nazis, as unemployed workers tended to go left rather than right and so voted Communist. As the stock market went down, therefore, the vote for the KPD went up, a doubly alarming development for the middle classes and elite, who were not themselves unemployed. Anxieties about the twin threats of economic collapse and Communism made these groups psychologically "ready" to vote for Hitler's Party. Many lost faith in liberal and moderate parties, who seemed out of touch.

Some workers also began to vote Nazi, but they tended to be in areas outside the major urban-industrial centers. Women voted for Nazis as well; for the first time in July 1932, they did so in numbers that might have exceeded men's.[26] (That trend was to become more pronounced once Hitler was appointed chancellor.) New voters added to the total, so that they picked up enough support across the social spectrum to be able to claim they were a "people's party of protest."[27] By comparison, all the others were tied to specific classes, regions, interests, or religions.

The social composition of the Party, especially the new joiners in 1930–32, was similar to its voters. The NSDAP prided itself on giving out membership number one million in April 1932, and Hitler liked to boast (falsely) that his was the largest organization in German political life. The real membership was below a million, and registered 849,009 on January 1, 1933.[28]

The SPD, which had created the Weimar Republic and was most identified with it, came in a distant second in the elections, with 21.6 percent of the vote and 133 seats. What alarmed the middle classes was that the Communists finished a strong third, taking 14.6 percent of the vote and 89 seats. The extremist parties, which would include the German National People's Party (DNVP), along with the Nazis and Communists, could have formed, at least in theory, a majority to get rid of the republic.

Not only were the enemies of democracy growing, but the institutions of the republic were crumbling. In 1930–32, Germany was in the process of changing from a democracy into what was close to a presidential dictatorship. In 1930 Hindenburg issued five emergency decrees; in 1931, forty-four; and in 1932, sixty-six. The relevance of parliament declined almost to insignificance. In 1930 the Reichstag passed ninety-eight laws; in 1931, thirty-four; and in 1932, only five.[29]

STREET VIOLENCE

The end of democracy resulted not just at the polls during elections but from broader social developments. The years since 1918 had seen more violence in the streets than was ever the case before, much of it involving clashes between uniformed bands of men linked to political movements of the right or left. Paramilitary groups of one sort or another engaged in pitched battles that created an atmosphere the very opposite of the law and order so respected by Germans.

By the late 1920s hundreds of thousands joined these organizations, carrying on politics in a new style. Most alarming for "good citizens" were the Communists. In 1924 the KPD founded the Rotefrontkämpferbund (Red Veterans' League), and three years later had 127,000 members. However, the organization was poorly run, and numbers fell by more than half in the last years of the republic. To take up the slack, local Communist "self-defense" groups (mostly non-uniformed) had a membership estimated at around 100,000. The SPD's Reichsbanner Schwarz, Rot, Gold (Reichflag Black, Red, Gold) was also formed in 1924 and soon boasted as many as 3.5 million members. By the early 1930s, the SPD recruited Schutzformationen (Protective Formations, or Schufos) for speakers and marches. There were about 160,000 members in the Schufos in early 1931 and some 250,000 a year later.[30]

Membership in the SA went up with unemployment: there were around 60,000 in November 1930, and in 1931 the ranks more than quadrupled to 260,000. That figure had nearly doubled again to 445,000 by August 1932.[31] A percentage of Nazi Party dues went to the SA, but it was largely self-financing. Members had to buy their own uniforms and, when they could not, find someone else to pay the bill. Beginning in 1929 the organization even sold its own brands of cigarettes and other items to raise money.[32]

Himmler's SS had nearly 25,000 members in August 1932 and around 52,000 in January 1933. Although not as involved in street violence, the SS was generally supportive of SA hooliganism. The Nazis often allied with the nationalist Stahlhelm (Steel Helmet), a right-wing veterans' group, which had around 400,000 members in 1932. All in all, the Nazis could put a large number of uniformed men on the streets whose unruliness and brutality became legendary. As disruptive as some "legalistic" citizens might have found them, there was consolation in knowing these bullies were there to fight the left when no one else was going to do so.

The SA tended to be more radical than the Nazi Party, preferring violence and a direct assault over elections. Thus, Hitler's decision for a legal route did not always sit well. Tensions reached critical dimensions in late August 1930, when the SA demolished Berlin Party headquarters and Hitler had to sort out the "rebellion." In a speech to the Berlin SA, he proclaimed himself head of the SA and SS and demanded total loyalty.[33] Ernst Röhm, one of Hitler's old friends, was called back from Bolivia and named chief of staff of the SA on January 1, 1931.

The government could dissolve threatening organizations like the SA, and to forestall such a move, Hitler "purged" leaders like Walter Stennes and some five hundred of his followers in northern and eastern Germany on May 21, 1931.[34]

Presidential elections were slated for 1932, and Hitler was undecided whether to run. Here the lowly corporal would be against the vaunted field marshal Hindenburg, hero of the First World War. In the end, the drama of the situation was too much to resist, and Hitler announced his decision to enter the race to an ecstatic mass meeting in Berlin.[35]

His appearances in the election campaign emphasized Germany's misfortune since the revolution of November 9, 1918. Again he gave something like history lectures, retelling the familiar narrative of the weak republic. He asked Hindenburg, "the old man," to "step back, you can't cover the ones we want to destroy," but took pains not to offend or attack the man personally. The victor in the election, he said, had to "revitalize" the nation, for only out of a "healthy people" would it be possible for a "healthy economy" to grow.[36]

Hindenburg got 49 percent of the votes in the first round; Hitler came second with 30 percent. Joseph Goebbels, who had been promoted to Reich propaganda leader in April 1930, made Hitler the main attraction. In the second round Hitler used an airplane to cover the country, but Hindenburg won. Hitler's showing, with over thirteen million votes (37 percent), was sensational, and his stature grew beyond that of every other politician in the country.[37]

In an interview with the London *Times,* Hitler said he never actually wanted to be president. He decided to run against Hindenburg "on the sole ground that this system, which we have sworn to overcome, was taking refuge behind his reputation and popularity." The reporter said that some suggested as many as a million Communists had voted for him, a fact that Hitler doubted. If it were true, however, that would be a feather in his cap because one of his objects was to annihilate the Reds, and if that "could be effected by conversion and absorption the ideal solution to the problem of national unity would have been found."[38]

Hindenburg was persuaded only three days after his reelection to ban the SA and SS. There was concern among authorities at the state level that the elections to follow on April 24 would be disrupted and worse. Nevertheless, Hitler threw himself anew into the battle, addressing hundreds of thousands in more than two dozen major speeches. He again used an airplane to make as many personal appearances as possible.

Once more he said little about the Jews and not much about the Marxists. Rarely did he mention opponents by name. Occasionally he admitted he would get rid of all the political parties to bring the country together, or said the peasants or some other group needed help, but that was the exception. He presented himself as the charismatic leader, above politics, bringing the positive message of national unity. The Party did well in the state elections, though it had no great breakthroughs.[39]

The officer corps began to assume a still more prominent role in politics at this time. General Kurt von Schleicher had met with Hitler on May 7, 1932, and informed him that Brüning was going to be dropped and new elections called. Hitler agreed to support the new government (already selected) of Franz von Papen if they would lift the ban on the SA and SS, and they did so on June 16, 1932. Legalized again, the SA renewed its violent ways in the streets.

The number of SA casualties rose like a barometer of violence: 2,506 in 1930; 6,307 in 1931; 14,005 in 1932. These injuries were covered by the SA's own insurance company.[40] Violence reached a new level during the July 1932 elections, the bloodiest ever held, in which eighty-six people were killed, a figure that included thirty-eight Nazis and thirty Communists. There were 461 "riots" in Prussia alone in July. It felt like the country was on the edge of social calamity.[41]

In big cities there were pitched battles, with passersby killed in the cross fire, as happened when sixteen people were shot on "Bloody Sunday" (July 17, 1932) in Hamburg-Altona; two more died later. The police intervened to break up the fighting, but favored the Nazis.[42]

Violent clashes, mostly involving the Nazis and the Communists, became a common feature all over the country. In Hamburg on July 2, 1931, for example, Jews returning from religious services were attacked. The Nazi version of the story was that the Jews had been assaulted by Communists and had to be rescued by the SA, who happened to be passing by. There was a meeting of Nazi students several weeks later on the theme "Hitler or Stalin?—the Bankruptcy of Bolshevism." It ended in a melee between Nazis and Communists.[43]

The incidents took place not only in the big cities and industrial centers. Even more tranquil areas like Baden in the southwest, famous for its wines and two universities, saw a dramatic increase in street violence. Communists there were few, recruited, according to the police, mainly from the unemployed, but augmented by outsiders. Though the "Bolsheviks" were no real threat in such places, the Nazis played up the theme anyway.[44]

Hitler sanctioned what the SA did even when it led to murder. This was the case in the village of Potempa in Silesia, where members of the SA broke into a home at 1:30 in the morning of August 10, 1932, dragged out a Communist sympathizer, and trampled him to death. What set this killing apart was that five SA men were eventually sentenced to death for it. The Nazi Party had held up the accused as martyrs and, upon hearing the verdicts, started a riot that led to the vandalism of Jewish shops. To the Nazi mind, there was a straight link between Communists and Jews. The "enemy within" was both Jewish and Marxist. Hitler did not condemn the killers; rather, he protested the verdicts. Chancellor Papen commuted the sentences, supposedly to avoid giving the Nazis "propaganda material."[45]

13

"ALL POWER" FOR HITLER

The July 1932 elections showed Hitler with by far the largest following of any politician in the country. He was the message, a social phenomenon, the führer who enthralled millions by telling them what they already knew or wanted to hear. He could draw crowds of twenty-five thousand or more almost anywhere, even as he steadfastly refused to make any specific promises of what he would do to cure Germany's many problems.

Hitler's quandary after the elections was what to do next. He made an appointment with Kurt von Schleicher, Hindenburg's most important adviser and the power broker of the moment. Goebbels wrote in his diary it was to be "all power or nothing." Hitler felt "the Barons" would yield, but was unsure about the president, "the old man."[1]

On August 6, Hitler conferred with Schleicher just outside Berlin. After hours of discussion Schleicher agreed that Hitler had to be named the new chancellor, with several key ministries also going to the Nazis.[2] Schleicher's hope was to use the numerically strong SA against the Marxists and avoid a clash with the army. Goebbels's diary entries for this period are filled with stories about the rising "wave of terror" of the

Marxists and the widespread perception of a threat from the left. He spoke of Hitler waiting at the very "doors to power" and was convinced "the great moment is here."[3]

Not only Schleicher but Papen, who spoke with Hindenburg on August 10, felt it might be useful to name Hitler as chancellor. At this decisive moment in time, however, "the old man" turned out to have ideas of his own and said it would be a bit much for him to name a mere "Bohemian corporal" to be chancellor.[4]

Hitler met with Papen and Schleicher on the morning of August 13 and was told that the most he could hope for was the position of vice-chancellor. But he wanted nothing less than an appointment like Mussolini's. That afternoon Hindenburg spoke to him directly. He said that his responsibility to God, the fatherland, and his conscience would not allow him to accede to Hitler's wishes. He appealed to the Nazi leader's patriotism to take a lesser post and to cooperate with the government, but was stiffly refused. The official communiqué issued about the negotiations deliberately made the president appear the noble statesman and Hitler a selfish politician not content merely to be brought into the cabinet, but a man who wanted the "entire governmental authority."[5]

This turn of events was Hitler's greatest political defeat since the attempted putsch in 1923. Papen toyed with reckless steps, such as restricting the vote or ruling without the Reichstag, but such measures would have caused wholesale social upheaval. He apparently gave serious thought to establishing a military dictatorship.[6]

The Reichstag session on September 12 ended with a vote of nonconfidence, which was put by the Communists and carried by a great majority. The government was revealed as a tiny clique of reactionaries devoid of support. Papen had to call elections yet again, in effect the fourth federal election in 1932 if we include the two for president.[7]

Hitler's campaign differed from previous ones. He had been thrown onto the defensive by the government's claim that he had been offered a major cabinet post but wanted the entire government. He came across as power hungry, not having the nation's best interests at heart, and as just another politician.

ANTI-SEMITISM IN WORD AND DEED

Anti-Semitism was never far beneath the surface in any of Hitler's speeches, but this time it was offered in a code all his listeners recognized. All he had to do was mention the well-known name of "the Jew" Jakob Goldschmidt, an illustrious banker until the crisis of 1931. Hitler talked of him and Papen as the "marriage" of the "Berlin Jews and the Gentlemen's Club."[8] His most common criticism of Papen's economic program was that its "spiritual father" was Goldschmidt. In the short campaign, Hitler used Goldschmidt's name more than a dozen times to convey the anti-Semitic message.

Hans Mommsen points out that during the Weimar years "anti-Semitic feelings, particularly toward non-assimilated Jewish groups, began to pervade German public life as a whole." Anti-Semitism was "a clear indicator of the increasingly antiliberal character of German political and intellectual life."[9] There were several open assaults on the Jews, some that were not so small, like the attacks in the Scheunen quarter of Berlin in November 1932.

Anti-Semitism and anti-Bolshevism were inextricably entwined in contemporary discourse, and not just in the Nazi Party. In out-of-the-way places, like the Catholic and rural Black Forest, which had no tradition of anti-Semitism (or Communism) and where few Jews lived, the Nazi Party "adapted" to local circumstances and soft-pedaled anti-Semitism. According to a recent study, it was above all "the profound fear of Russian Bolshevism" that was "the most important, perhaps most decisive reason for the success of the Nazi Party in the Black Forest region, and possibly in other regions as well."[10]

Some people supported the Nazi Party because of its anti-Semitism, some did so despite the anti-Semitism, and some may have ignored it. Precisely what the mix was varied infinitely, even in the mind of a single individual. There can be no doubt, however, that Hitler and his Party had been rabidly and openly anti-Semitic from 1920 onward, and anyone who paid Party dues, read the Party press, or voted for the Party would have been aware of that fact.[11]

In 1934 Professor Theodore Abel of Columbia University sponsored an essay contest for Nazi Party members. Advertisements were placed in

Nazi newspapers inviting members of the Party to submit their autobiographies, with prizes awarded the best. Abel analyzed and quantified the content of the essays. One of his findings was that of the six hundred essays received, 60 percent made "no reference whatsoever to indicate that they harbored anti-Semitic feelings." Abel assumed some respondents said nothing "because membership in the National Socialist party implied that they opposed the Jews." This data has been used repeatedly to suggest that most Nazis were at best indifferent about anti-Semitism and some of them even opposed to it. But they were writing for an American professor who, for all they knew, might be Jewish. In any case, there would be an inclination to emphasize the positive aspects of their movement, their reasons for joining, and not mention its overt racism.[12]

It is obviously true that anti-Semitism, like all motives for supporting Nazism, varied from place to place. In some areas Nazi anti-Semitism was so blatant as to make the two synonymous. Yet the issue was a nonstarter politically in localities with no tradition of anti-Semitism. Jews in Germany felt the country was a better place to live than anywhere else, and their support for Zionism was weak compared with that of Jews in Central European countries.

Another approach to the role of anti-Semitism was taken by studying the "enemy groups" pictured in Nazi posters used in the five national elections between 1928 and 1932. As in all such representations, the messages are mixed and full of subtexts and suggestions. Six of 124 posters were aimed specifically at the Jews. The primary "enemy" pictured (39 in all) was the SPD/Marxism. However, this does not "prove" the Nazis did not push anti-Semitism as well, given the link they always made between the Jews and the Marxists. For the Reichstag elections of November 1932, one of the most appalling posters showed a colossal, animalistic Red Army soldier. The motto was that only Hitler could rescue the country from such a Bolshevik beast. Other posters used the motif of an attack against the "Bigwigs and Nobles' Club," which was explicitly associated with Jews. Jews were frequently linked to the Weimar "system" and the "November parties." These and others, therefore, were not without hints of anti-Semitism.

One of the most graphic and colorful posters from 1930 showed a large serpent emitting poisons, including Bolshevism, inflation, "war guilt," Versailles, and terror. The head of the snake, itself a symbol of evil, was marked with the Star of David. It was pierced through by a sword with the implication that stopping the Jews (perhaps killing them) would solve all problems.[13]

Some of the intellectuals in the Party like Werner Best said they did not believe in the "absolute inferiority of the Jews." However, Best still held that anti-Semitism had to prevail in Germany as "political, economic, and cultural self-defense." There had to be a struggle to free Germany from what he termed the "overdominance of foreign people." Not unlike Hitler, he called for a "rational," as opposed to only emotional, anti-Semitism. He would later become a key member of the SS and the secret police.[14]

It was not just what Hitler said but what members of the movement did that made people aware of the stance on the "Jewish question." In eastern Germany in August 1932, bombs and hand grenades were thrown at Jews or their property, leaving the victims to rely on the police for protection.[15]

There were two especially notorious anti-Semitic events in these last years of democracy. On October 13, 1930—the day the Reichstag opened after the latest elections—the SA wanted to use the occasion to protest the government's decision to ban their wearing uniforms. The Nazis met at the Reichstag, and then made their way to a nearby business district, where they systematically smashed the windows of mainly Jewish firms, including prominent department stores. Here was an unprecedented example of the SA's anti-Semitism that combined with its anti-plutocratic attitudes. A similar but even larger outburst of these destructive urges took place on September 12, 1931. The scene was on Berlin's Kurfürstendamm, the upscale shopping area. Five hundred SA men marched down the Ku'damm screaming, "Long live Hitler!" and "Germany, awake, and death to the Jews!" This was on the Jewish New Year (Rosh Hashanah), and the SA attacked anyone who "looked Jewish" near the synagogue.[16]

Thus, contrary to the assertions in older literature, anti-Semitism in word and deed by no means became a "marginal phenomenon" in this period. On the contrary, in the last years of the republic, there was a discernible increase in anti-Semitism from the far north to the south of the country. The most obvious expressions were these SA attacks.[17]

Apart from taking out their spite on the Jews through these and many other individual acts of violence, the Party, the SA, and the SS agreed (as did the nationalist DNVP to some extent) that the legal rights of the Jews were going to be curtailed if and when Hitler became chancellor.

HOLDING OUT FOR POWER

Time dragged on, and still Hitler was not in power, but he continued to campaign. In left-oriented Essen—in front of fifty thousand on October 30, 1932—he said his aim was to unify the "body politic" (*Volkskörper*), overcome all social divisions, and create the racially based "community of the people." He had to succeed because "Germany had to be German or it will be Bolshevik."[18] The goal was to create a new and unified Reich. One half of the nation could not rule the other nor terrorize it into submission. The entire "community" had to be in agreement.[19] On November 5 in Munich before ten thousand, he insisted: "One cannot construct from the top down, nor from the top down falsely invent a constitution, but it has to grow naturally out of the community." His aim was to attract "the broad masses that are difficult to conquer because they are thickheaded and stubborn." Yet "in times of need they are the basis on which one could build."[20]

What about the constitution? He said what he had in mind—and did so under oath—at a famous trial of three army officers in September 1930. They were charged with propagating the idea in the army that they would support a Hitler coup by refusing orders to put it down. Questioned at length about his plans, Hitler summed them up: "The National Socialist movement in this state seeks its goal by using constitutional means. The constitution determines our methods, but not the goal. We will use constitutional ways to achieve the relevant majorities in the legislative bodies. However, the moment we achieve that goal, we will mold the state into the shape we hold to be suitable."[21]

Hitler often claimed that his model was Benito Mussolini, whom he lauded for creating a system that stopped Bolshevism. Questioned in court on this point earlier in 1930, and on Mussolini's violent methods, Hitler answered that the Fascists did not bring about a revolution like the one in Germany in 1918, but "rescued the future of the Italian people." They used violence not against the state but against the "terror elements of the street that the state could not master."[22]

In his New Year address in December 1932 Hitler said it was coming down to a fight to the finish with the Reds. He exaggerated the threat of Bolshevism and claimed that the Communist Party in Germany had 6 million supporters. The KPD in fact had won 5.9 million votes in the last election, but the Party membership at the end of 1932 was around 360,000, of whom 252,000 were dues paying.[23]

Hitler's exaggerations aside, many "good citizens," not just supporters of the Nazi movement, believed that the "Bolshevik danger was enormous." Hitler as always sought to identify the real instigator behind Bolshevism: the "Jewish-intellectual leadership of the world revolution that had just conquered Russia" and who had "exterminated the earlier leading spiritual non-Slavic upper class."[24]

Although he continued to draw large and enthusiastic audiences, the November 1932 election results were disappointing. Overall participation was down by over three points and the Nazi vote by over four. Goebbels surmised that some were put off by Hitler's refusal to take the cabinet position offered him, but saw reason for hope: "hardly 10 percent of the people stand behind the government," and so it would not be able to hang on for very long.[25]

Hitler was undaunted, and with 11.7 million votes and 196 seats (a drop of 34) the Nazi Party was still far ahead of all others. The DNVP, led by Alfred Hugenberg, won back some support lost to the Nazis in recent elections and added more seats. The vote for the second-place finisher, SPD, was down slightly, and it lost 12 seats to 120. Communist Party support grew yet again, as it had in every federal election since 1924. They now had 100 seats, 11 more than in the previous Reichstag.

The country was stuck in a political deadlock. Gregor Strasser, the second most powerful man in the Nazi Party, began to have doubts about the wisdom of Hitler's all-or-nothing approach. Certainly a violent seizure of power on the Leninist model was out of the question. Hitler's aim was to get enough support to be appointed by the head of state, on the model of Mussolini, but President Hindenburg stood stubbornly in the way.

Strasser thought it a mistake for Hitler to have rejected the offer of a position in the government. The momentum of the Nazi steamroller seemed to have slowed to a snail's pace; the coffers were empty; many were giving up their memberships; and some local elections showed support slipping away.[26]

Putzi Hanfstaengl, who was close to Hitler in these months, expressed a different view. He said Hitler's behavior during 1932 was not that of "a politician in the ordinary sense. He did not concern himself with the day-to-day kaleidoscope of the political scene. He was not looking for alliances or coalitions or temporary tactical advantage. He wanted power, supreme and complete, and was convinced that if he talked often enough and aroused the masses sufficiently, he must, in due course, be swept into office."[27]

Hitler tried again to obtain the chancellorship in negotiations with Hindenburg and Schleicher, demonstrating, according to Goebbels, both strong nerves and determination. The effort again came to nothing, but the propaganda expert was relieved there was no repeat of the August 13 debacle that cast Hitler as just another ambitious politician.[28]

A showdown between Hitler and Strasser took place in Weimar on November 30 when Strasser argued for participation in a coalition government. Hitler—backed by Goebbels and Göring—rejected the idea. Hitler was for holding out against Schleicher and those trying to lure him into accepting a role in the cabinet instead of giving him the chancellorship. He won the argument but seemed to be losing the war, as the Nazis promptly suffered a setback in the municipal elections in Thuringia on December 4.

ON THE EVE OF VICTORY

Two days before these elections, Schleicher was named chancellor, a decision Goebbels thought was favorable to the Nazis, as it was the last card Hindenburg could play before having to turn to Hitler. In a meeting with Schleicher and Hindenburg, Strasser was told by the old man that he would never appoint Hitler chancellor. Strasser was himself offered the vice-chancellorship, in hopes of splitting the Nazi Party. The negotiations came to nothing, but Hitler grew convinced his once loyal follower was conspiring against him, and on December 8 Strasser, disheartened and demoralized, resigned all his posts. In a letter to Hitler he said that the movement was wasting away in "useless opposition." He thought it mistaken to place so much emphasis on anti-Marxism and wanted the Party to take its "Socialism" seriously.[29]

Hitler would not yield on these vital issues and convinced Party leaders to stay the course. Strasser found himself distrusted and isolated, and left for vacation in Italy.[30] Although Strasser played no further role in the history of his times, Hitler had him killed during the so-called night of the long knives on June 30, 1934. In the meantime, Hitler took over all Strasser's posts himself, but otherwise carried out no purges. Quite to the contrary, he visited regional leaders to mend fences and give assurance all was in order.

Chancellor Kurt von Schleicher's strategy of trying to split the Nazi movement had failed. The new Reichstag was adjourned, and the political deadlock continued into January. Although it was long thought that Hitler negotiated behind the scenes with major industrialists, his contacts with them had been limited, and there was no great breakthrough in early 1933. Some industrialists had given funds to the Nazis but, covering their bets, gave as much or more to other right-wing parties.

When word leaked out that a meeting had taken place on January 4 between Hitler and Kurt von Schröder, a well-connected businessman, along with Papen, the left-wing press jumped on the story. For both Communists and Socialists, the meeting confirmed what they had long asserted: Hitler was the "agent of big industry." This story line has informed the understanding of Nazism ever since for many on the left. However, Schröder did not represent all or even most of Germany's industrialists, but some who belonged to Wilhelm Keppler's circle of friends. The latter was a limited group of capitalists who, with the well-known exception of Fritz Thyssen, did not include any of Germany's big names. Papen insisted that he himself had been falsely charged with arranging the financing of the Nazi Party. Recent accounts have backed up his claims.[31]

Hitler's famous speech to the Düsseldorf Industrial Club on January 26, 1932, had suggested his ties to the mighty capitalists. Invited by Thyssen to address the club, Hitler did his best to allay fears and win over the seven to eight hundred who showed up to hear him talk about topics dear to his heart like the Darwinian "struggle for survival" and the "threat of Bolshevism," cast as a danger for the German economy. He strongly supported private property.

He boasted that the men in SA and SS uniforms, fighting on their behalf, were still paying their own way, buying their own uniforms, shirts, emblems, and flags. These men had the new ideal he wanted the industrialists to share. If the speech was not a complete triumph, it went some distance toward convincing them he was not going to nationalize industry. If they did not know it already, he made it abundantly clear that he was a die-hard opponent of Communism.[32]

Was Hitler's star falling in January 1933? He had a chance to show it in yet another state election on January 15, this time in Lippe-Detmold, a tiny state with a total population of around 160,000. An election there could have enormous political significance if the Nazis lost, and so they threw themselves into it with a vengeance. They did not get funds from the industrialists with whom Hitler supposedly had made a pact. The Nazis gained less than 5 percent (up to a total of 39.5 percent) from their last showing, but the results were positive enough for the Party newspaper to scream: "Resign, Mr. Schleicher! — Hitler Wins in Lippe!"[33]

Hitler's determination to see the struggle through, when nearly everyone around him despaired, was remarkable. His intransigence can be followed almost daily in Goebbels's diaries.

During the two weeks that followed, the power brokers in Berlin went to work behind the scenes. When Schleicher found he could not after all put together a government Hindenburg would approve, he began toying with the idea of trying to have the Reichstag dissolved and the elections postponed until the autumn, a course of action that could have led (as he had argued himself on earlier occasions) to a general strike at best and a civil war at worst.

He ran out of time and resigned on January 28. He informed the president that there were then only three options: a majority Hitler cabinet; a minority Hitler cabinet; or for him to carry on. Hindenburg turned for advice to Papen.

Papen and Oskar von Hindenburg, along with other close advisers, had been seriously negotiating with Hitler since January 18, but he kept insisting he would accept nothing short of the chancellorship. Hindenburg proved to be almost as stubborn. Ultimately, Papen recommended Hitler, on condition that he himself would be named the vice-chancellor. Hitler agreed with the arrangement and was willing to have only a limited number of Nazi ministers. The president decided after all to appoint the "Bohemian corporal" the new head of government.[34]

The Hitler cabinet was, except for two posts, dominated by conservatives. One of these, Alfred Hugenberg, almost brought the negotiations to a standstill by refusing to accept Hitler's one remaining condition, namely new federal elections. He argued until moments before 11:00 a.m. on January 30, when they were received by Hindenburg for Hitler's official appointment. Hitler was still willing to go to the brink, and at the last minute Hugenberg relented. Hitler got the chancellorship and new elections as well. After swearing in the cabinet, Hindenburg closed the brief ceremony with the words "And now, gentlemen, forward with God!"[35]

The legality principle that got Hitler into power would also make resistance to him difficult. The feeble last-minute efforts of the KPD and SPD to work out a united front came to nothing. There would be no general strike or any real resistance. The left did not want to give the Nazis an excuse to use the police or the army, and waited in vain for them to do something patently illegal to mobilize opposition.

Just over a week before his appointment, Hitler spoke to a typically large audience of twenty thousand in Berlin. He claimed he already had 50 percent of the people behind him. What he wanted was to gain the participation "in a few years of 60, 70, 80, and finally 100 percent of the nation." As he never failed to repeat, the lessons of 1918—the German revolution and defeat in the war—showed what happened when the people were not really behind the state.[36]

Whereas Hitler was emphasizing popular support, Franz von Papen, with little understanding of the dynamics of the Hitler revolution, was convinced that he and other experienced politicians would have an easy time of it with the corporal. He exclaimed to Minister of Finance Lutz Graf Schwerin von Krosigk, "We have hired him!" He asked a doubting acquaintance, "What do you want? I have Hindenburg's confidence. Within two months we will have pushed Hitler so far into a corner that he'll squeak."[37]

On the night of Hitler's appointment, Hermann Göring sounded a bold note: "We are closing the darkest era of Germany's history and are beginning a new chapter."[38] At almost the same time Goebbels recorded his impressions of the Nazi "Revolution":

It seems like a dream. The Wilhelmstrasse belongs to us. The führer is already working in the Reich chancellery. We stand in the window upstairs, watching hundreds of thousands and hundreds of thousands of people march past the aged Reich president and the young chancellor in the flaming torchlight, shouting their joy and gratitude. . . . Germany is at a turning point in its history. . . . Outside the Kaiserhof the masses are in wild uproar. In the meantime Hitler's appointment had become public. The thousands soon become tens of thousands. An endless stream of people floods the Wilhelmstrasse. . . . The struggle for power now lies behind us, but we must go on working to retain it. . . . Indescribable enthusiasm fills the streets. . . . Hundreds of thousands and hundreds of thousands march past our windows in never-ending, uniform rhythm. The rising of a nation! Germany has awakened! In a spontaneous explosion of joy the people espouse the German Revolution. . . . The new Reich has risen, sanctified with blood. Fourteen years of work have been crowned by victory. We have reached our goal. The German Revolution begins![39]

Papen, initially so distant and pompous, soon became swept up in the revolutionary enthusiasm. Later he recalled that on the evening of Hitler's appointment he was in the room with the chancellor as the crowds streamed by in the streets below:

We watched an endless procession of hundreds of thousands of delirious people, from every level of society, parading with lighted torches before Hindenburg and the Chancellor. It was a clear, starlit night, and the long columns of uniformed Brownshirts, SS and Stahlhelm, with their brass bands, provided an unforgettable picture. As they approached the window at which the old Reich President appeared to the crowd there were respectful shouts. But about a hundred yards further on, Hitler stood on the little balcony of the new Reich Chancellery. As soon as they saw him, the marchers burst into frantic applause. The contrast was most marked and seemed to emphasize the transition from a moribund regime to the new revolutionary forces.

I had preferred not to put myself forward and was sitting quietly in the room behind the balcony, leaving Hitler and Goering to take the salute. But every now and then Hitler turned round and beckoned me to join him. The fantastic ovation had put even these hardened party chiefs into a state of ecstasy. It was an extraordinary experience, and the endless repetition of the triumphal cry "Heil, Heil, Sieg Heil!" rang in my ears like a tocsin. When Hitler turned round to speak to me, his voice seemed choked with sobs. "What an immense task we have set ourselves, Herr von Papen—we must never part until our work is accomplished." I was happy to agree.[40]

"LEGAL REVOLUTION"

"Revolution" is usually defined as "a complete and forcible overthrow of an established government or political system," and therefore illegal. However, Karl Dietrich Bracher suggests that we think about Hitler's actions after his appointment as a "legal revolution." Hitler avoided Lenin's methods because of "the German people's deeply rooted aversion to and mistrust of overt revolution." For Bracher, this legality tactic "played a decisive role" in what would become a new type of dictatorship.[41]

The aim of Hitler's revolution was a dictatorship by popular consent, whence he could achieve legal recognition for his relentless war on democracy, Communists, and Jews. Lenin and Stalin, schooled in Russian terrorism, saw revolution as justified insurgence against tyranny. Confident as they were in the vanguard of world revolution, guided by the Marxist idea of the class struggle, anticipating some kind of final and bloody showdown, and already used to the illegal methods of the underground, they took it for granted that something akin to civil war would be needed to secure the revolution. They had no interest in waiting on ordinary people or wooing popular opinion. The Soviet peoples would, in all their diversity and economic backwardness, be dragged kicking and screaming into the future.

PART FIVE

STALIN'S REIGN OF TERROR

14

FIGHT AGAINST THE COUNTRYSIDE

In 1930–31 Stalin's regime carried out a dekulakization program in two waves, which together deported 1.8 million people accused of being kulak or "kulak-like" (*podkulachnik*). As we have seen, many were sent to the Gulag system or exiled to "special settlements" in distant parts of the country. By January 1932, the OGPU estimated that close to 500,000, or nearly 30 percent of these people, were dead or had run away.[1] Two million more who had been slated for deportation within their region (category-three kulaks) joined the exodus to the cities involving a total of twelve million people.[2] This disruption of normal life had fatal consequences for vast numbers of innocents.

The peasantry was resilient and resisted collectivization away from the glare of the police and in surreptitious ways. According to available statistics for 1930, 55 percent of all peasant households may have been on collective farms in March, but the percentage had fallen by more than half by June. In some areas (like the central Black Earth region), over 80 percent of those collectivized in March fell to just over 15 percent in June. Thus, when they had a chance and a choice, all but the poorest—who might benefit by joining such a venture—left collective farms in droves.[3]

RENEWED ASSAULTS ON THE PEASANTRY

Shortages began to spread, and on January 13, 1931, the state introduced a rationing system for essential food and commodities. The exclusion from the provisioning system of the peasantry and those considered disenfranchised meant that 80 percent of the country had to fend for themselves.[4]

Given population growth and the move to the cities by millions, the state needed to collect more grain for 1931 than it had the previous year, and still more in 1932. This was a futile task and led to desperate protests from the peasants. They stole or slaughtered livestock and ate the meat before it could be taken from them. Rumor was that no one on the collective farms would get any. This turn of events was an economic disaster, since farms could not operate without farm animals in an era when most had no tractors.

The regime renewed the collectivization drive to force peasants onto industrial-scale operations and increase production, and in 1932, with famine already in the air, just over 60 percent of all peasant households were back on the collective farms. That figure would grow to 89.6 percent by 1936 and include virtually all peasant households in the main agricultural regions.[5]

On June 16, 1932, the Politburo discussed calls for help from Communist leaders in Ukraine and agreed to send them unused oat seed, corn, and grain.[6] Two days later, in a letter to Kaganovich and Molotov on behalf of the Politburo, Stalin acknowledged reports of "impoverishment and famine" but took no responsibility, nor did he admit that quotas were too high. He blamed the famine on the personal failings of those directly in charge, particularly the first secretaries of the Party in Ukraine and the Urals, who had supposedly divided the total quota among all localities and collective farms in a "mechanical equalizing" way, instead of demanding more from better-producing areas to compensate for poorer ones. He castigated officials for being too preoccupied with new industry, when they should have been keener to secure a prosperous agriculture, which was needed to support industrial development.

Stalin wanted the Five-Year Plan fulfilled "at any cost," and he suggested having a meeting with regional authorities and instructing them on how to improve. They were to be held personally responsible for any shortcomings.[7]

Some food assistance was offered to the starving. By July, Stalin was willing to reduce the demands for grain from Ukraine, but only for collective farms and individual peasants who had "especially suffered." In a follow-up note on August 5, he blamed "the main shortcoming" on the "organizational lapses" of the Commissariat of Agriculture and outlined needed changes.[8]

He also ordered an end to "sabotage." On July 20, 1932, he wrote to Lazar Kaganovich, by then the third most important man in the Party after Stalin and Molotov, and complained about thefts in the countryside by "dekulakized persons and other antisocial elements." He believed there had to be a new law that treated certain thefts as "counterrevolutionary." He was incensed about robberies from freight cars, collective farms, and cooperatives and demanded they be punished by "a minimum of ten years' imprisonment, and as a rule, by death." He also wanted the OGPU to introduce stricter surveillance. As for profiteers, he said bluntly: "We must eradicate this scum" and send "active agitators" to concentration camps.[9]

The note to Kaganovich led to the notorious law "On the Protection of the Property of the State Enterprises, Collective Farms, and Cooperatives and the Strengthening of Public (Socialist) Ownership," which went into force with its publication in *Pravda* on August 7. This law, designed to be used against hungry peasants who stole grain from the fields, was known as the "law on the five ears of corn." In the first months alone, tens of thousands of starving people were found guilty of the crime of "counterrevolutionary" theft. Of that number, an estimated five thousand were sentenced to death, and many thousands more were given ten-year prison sentences.[10]

On August 11, Stalin suggested softening the law. Those executed should be guilty of systematic thefts, not petty ones, but the repressive process had a momentum of its own. District-level officials continued to be more radical than Stalin and fired judges who would not prosecute to the full measure of the law. Mass repression, beatings, and vigilante acts continued in many parts of the country.

Stalin admitted to Kaganovich that the crisis in Ukraine was the "most important issue" facing the country. He said they might lose the great grain-growing region "unless we begin to straighten out the situation."

He was reminded by some fifty district committees from the area that the grain procurement plan was "unrealistic." He refused to budge and, determined to move ahead on the backs of the peasants, stubbornly held to the idea that the problem was poor leadership combined with resistance by "counterrevolutionaries." His solution was to make organizational-administrative changes and to install new leaders in Ukraine who would turn it "into a real fortress of the USSR, into a genuinely exemplary republic."[11]

Stalin was by no means alone in his unbending attitude. The Politburo sent Kaganovich and Molotov to lead commissions to the North Caucasus and Ukraine on October 22, 1932, and like Stalin, they blamed the problems on sabotage organized by "kulaks," "counterrevolutionaries," "saboteurs," or "foreign elements."

Raids were used to search for kulak grain—but in fact most such people had long since been deported. The assault was actually on collective farms not meeting quotas and thought to be holding back. Even regional and local Party leaders felt the men in the Kremlin were demanding too much. Moscow's response in the North Caucasus was to arrest five thousand "criminally complacent" functionaries, along with fifteen thousand collective-farm workers. The Cossacks still in the area were again victimized. Molotov followed a similar pattern of repression in Ukraine, and other grain-producing areas soon did so as well. In 1932, tens of thousands were deported to the Gulag, and more followed the next year.[12]

CAUGHT BETWEEN VILLAGE AND CITY

In November 1932 the Politburo ordered local authorities who had not fulfilled their quotas to carry out new raids. They sent activists, like the infamous 25,000ers they had used earlier against the kulaks, to get grain from peasants "at any cost." These "thousanders" used all forms of terror to achieve their goals. Stalin told the Politburo that "certain groups" of collective farmers and peasants had to be dealt a "devastating blow." Communists suspected of being in cahoots or sympathizing with them were condemned; in some places, such as the North Caucasus, half the Party secretaries were expelled on Kaganovich's orders.[13]

There is extensive evidence on the deteriorating situation in the countryside. Lev Kopelev, a young and enthusiastic Communist and a "thousander" who took part in these raids, left a memoir. He accepted Stalin's views and recalled how he "was convinced that we were warriors on an invisible front, fighting against kulak sabotage for the grain which was needed by the country, by the five-year plan." He thought he had a mission to save "the souls of these peasants who were mired in unconscientiousness, in ignorance, who succumbed to enemy agitation, who did not understand the great truth of communism."[14]

The "thousanders" believed the peasants had plenty of grain stashed away. To get at these "private reserves," the raiders used what they called "undisputed confiscation," which is to say, they took everything else from a household, including clothing, religious objects, and even family pictures. Kopelev says it was "excruciating" to hear the screams of protest, but he had persuaded himself not to give in "to debilitating pity. We were realizing historical necessity. We were performing our revolutionary duty. We were obtaining grain for the socialist fatherland."[15]

Kopelev's commitment to Communism and Stalin was coupled with disdain for peasants, an attitude common already in Lenin's time. Kopelev persisted in the ritual of praising Stalin as

> the most perspicacious, the most wise (at that time they hadn't yet started calling him "great" and "brilliant"). He said: "The Struggle for grain is the struggle for socialism." And we believed him unconditionally. And later we believed that unconditional collectivization was unavoidable if we were to overcome the capriciousness and uncertainty of the market and the backwardness of individual farming, to guarantee a steady supply of grain, milk and meat to the cities. And also if we were to reeducate millions of peasants, those petty landowners and hence potential bourgeoisie, potential kulaks, to transform them into laborers with a social conscience, to liberate them from "the idiocy of rural life," from ignorance and prejudice, and to accustom them to culture, to all the boons of socialism.[16]

Victor Kravchenko, another activist for a time enthralled by Stalin, remembered on his rounds that "despite harsh police measures to keep the victims at home, Dniepropetrovsk was overrun with starving peasants. Many of them lay listless, too weak even to beg, around railroad stations. Their children were little more than skeletons with swollen bellies. In the past, friends and relatives in the country sent food packages to the urban districts. Now the process was reversed. But our own rations were so small and uncertain that few dared to part with their provisions."[17]

In Ukraine, which was the worst affected in the USSR, the level of urban mortality was 50 percent higher in 1933 than in 1932, but in rural areas it was nearly three times as high. By contrast, mortality rates in the areas around Moscow and Leningrad were largely unchanged in 1932–33. Outside Ukraine, there were areas like the lower Volga where mortality rates also jumped, indicating that more than one nationality suffered in the famine and that epidemic illnesses also played a role.[18]

Hundreds of thousands tried to escape to the cities to look for food or get on ration lists. To cut off the exodus, the government introduced internal passports on December 27, 1932. The passports, a despised feature of tsarist Russia, were issued to most townspeople over the age of sixteen—with the exception of the thirty or more groups officially "without rights," the *lishentsy*. But no passports were given to peasants. The stamp in the passport (*propiska*) became a matter of life and death, a novel form of persecution.[19]

Furthermore, Stalin and Molotov issued orders on January 22, 1933, to restrict the sale of railway tickets. Those caught trying to flee the famine were forced to turn back. Some were simply taken outside the city limits in open wagons and told to fend for themselves.[20]

Miron Dolot's memoir tells of his experiences as a young boy in Ukraine. He writes that his village was forcibly collectivized and that while they already suffered food shortages in 1931, the next two years brought full-scale famine. He remembered the "thousanders" who came for grain, not from the kulaks, but from the poor villagers now working against their will on the collective farms. Much that happened was senseless. Horses, once valued workmates of the peasants who cared for them, had been rounded up by the state and placed on collective farms without first taking steps to ensure they would be properly housed and fed. In the midst of the famine, the horses, now looked upon as "useless eaters," died from starvation and neglect before the promised tractors were there to replace them.

The villagers asked "Comrade Thousander" why their homes were searched for food when none existed. They were told the mere fact they were still alive proved there was food to be found. Although the harvest was good in 1932, the state took everything, and starvation grew rampant in the countryside.

Dolot and his mother left for town in January 1933 to exchange two medallions of gold she had saved. On the way they saw death everywhere. He remembered how the open spaces "looked like a battlefield after a great war. Littering the fields were the bodies of starving farmers who had been combing the potato fields over and over again in the hope of finding at least a fragment of a potato that might have been overlooked or left over from the harvest. They died where they collapsed in their endless search for food. Some of the frozen corpses must have been lying out there for months. Nobody seemed to be in a hurry to cart them away and bury them."[21]

By the next spring Dolot's village was a ghost town. It

> had become a desolate place, horror lurking in every house and in every backyard. We felt forsaken by the entire world. The main road which had been the artery of traffic and the center of village life was empty and overgrown with weeds and grass. Humans and animals were rarely seen on it. Many houses stood dilapidated and empty, their windows and doorways gaping. The owners were dead, deported to the north, or gone from the village in search of food. Once these houses were surrounded by barns, stables, cattle enclosures, pigpens, and fences. Now only the remnants of these structures could be seen. They had been ripped apart and used as firewood.[22]

The peasants died in the hundreds of thousands. Some went quietly, others died of poisoning when they ate things unfit for human consumption, and an unknown number committed suicide. Vasily Grossman describes it as follows:

> In one hut there would be something like a war. Everyone would keep close watch over everyone else. People would take crumbs from each other. The wife turned against the husband and the husband against the wife. The mother hated the children. And in some other hut love would be inviolable to the very last. I knew one woman with four children. She would tell them fairy stories and legends so that they would forget their hunger. Her own tongue could hardly move, but she would take them into her arms even though she had hardly any strength to lift her arms

when they were empty. Love lived on within her. And people noticed that where there was hate people died off more swiftly. Yet love, for that matter, saved no one. The whole village perished, one and all. No life remained in it.[23]

Some of the collectors took advantage of their position to exchange food for sexual favors.[24] Reports of the Ukrainian OGPU in May 1933 suggest that cannibalism became common.[25]

Protests about the excesses committed by the "thousanders" and others were sent to Moscow from many sources, including letters from the novelist Mikhail Sholokhov (later a Nobel Prize winner), whose book *Virgin Soil Upturned* (1932) was based on research into the collective-farm system on the Don. Stalin knew Sholokhov and recommended the book to Kaganovich. He said the writer might not have been all that talented, but was "profoundly honest" and wrote "about things he knows well."[26]

Sholokhov sent Stalin two letters in April 1933 describing what he saw in the North Caucasus. He detailed the tortures used to get grain and worried that such methods would discredit the idea of the collective farm. Stalin responded and told the novelist not to be deceived. If some activists were sadistic, they would be punished, but he should not lose sight of the fact that those who withheld their grain, far from being "innocent lambs," were engaged in sabotage and prepared to have the Red Army and workers go without food. "The fact that this sabotage was silent and appeared to be quite peaceful (there was no bloodshed) changes nothing—these people deliberately tried to undermine the Soviet state. It is a fight to the death, Comrade Sholokhov!"[27]

Nevertheless, Stalin had the allegations investigated, and the Politburo gave grain to the two districts mentioned by Sholokhov. The Politburo approved additional small amounts of grain, some of which was supposed to go to areas of Ukraine, but precisely who received that food remains uncertain.[28]

The famine was the result of disastrous farm policies, coupled with wasteful collection measures, so in that sense it was man-made, not simply the result of natural catastrophe.

Moreover, the regime exacerbated the already dreadful situation because it continued grain exports. These went up dramatically in 1930 over 1929 and rose again slightly in 1931. Thereafter, exports were reduced, but not before the famine had already set in.[29]

FATALITY RATES

Historians have given varied answers concerning the fatalities of the famine, partly because the statistical evidence is flawed. Mortalities were not always recorded, and the dead were often left where they fell. It was also true that deaths related to the famine continued long after, because survivors whose health was seriously undermined died prematurely. Kazakhstan went through a demographic catastrophe in this period, part of which involved a typhus epidemic, and another epidemic in the lower Volga had similar consequences.[30] A scholarly account based on newly opened Russian archives concludes that the "excess mortality"— that is, the deaths above and beyond "normal" statistical projections— was between four and five million. These figures can be taken as a minimum.[31]

Kazakhstan in central Asia came under the yoke of collectivization, even though no more than 25 percent of the population was engaged in agriculture and a small percentage of those in grain growing. The mostly Islamic people were either nomadic or seminomadic—that is, they migrated with their herds in summer. Soviet experts advised against trying to collectivize this region, but under the Five-Year Plan the Kazakh Communist Party forged ahead, and the people resisted by slaughtering their livestock. The experiment failed, and a famine, coupled with typhus, resulted.

Nicolas Werth estimates a total of six million deaths in the 1932–33 famine: four million in Ukraine, one million in Kazakhstan, and another million in the North Caucasus and the Black Earth region.[32] Robert Conquest suggests five million died in Ukraine, not four million, but otherwise is in agreement with Werth on the effects of the famine.[33]

The dekulakization campaign, which began in 1929, was separate from but sometimes overlapped with the famine. Those labeled kulaks suffered from persecution, and an unknown number of them sent to the camps died as a direct result of the famine.

Between 1930 and 1933 over a million kulak households were affected by dekulakization. Approximately 2.1 million accused of being first-category kulaks were exiled outside their own region as "special settlers" (*spetsposelentsy*), but went to work in camps and settlements of the OGPU. In addition, between 2 and 2.5 million were branded second-category kulaks and exiled to somewhere away from their homes, but remained (for a time at least) in the same region. A final group, estimated at between 1 and 1.25 million, "dekulakized themselves," that is, left their homes and fled. According to what are called "official records," 241,355 died in exile, and 330,667 "escaped and were not recaptured"—all of this just in 1932–33. The famine continued into 1933–34, the result not of drought but of the state's brutal grain extraction program.[34]

We should be skeptical about Soviet statistics, which inflated production figures "under pressure from politicians" to make the system appear to be prospering. Intimidation was likely also applied to reduce figures on mortalities, lest the system look the failure it was. There can be little doubt that the famine as a whole was one of the worst disasters in modern European history.

THE STATE INVADES THE COUNTRYSIDE

Stalin said over and over that the problems of agriculture lay in its poor organization, and he put forward detailed proposals, including the deployment of the Machine Tractor Station (MTS). The theory was to pool machinery and utilize it on the great expanse of collectivized land.[35] In January 1933, his proposals began to be implemented. The MTS also had political sections (*politotdels*), representatives of the central authorities "specifically chosen" from the urban Communist Party. They were sent "to direct the political and economic reorganization" but were independent of the local (*raion*) Party. With exclusive rights to direct political work on the collective farms, they had links all the way to Moscow. To reinforce the surveillance and control from the center, the deputy of the *politotdel* was a member of the OGPU.

Although the political sections of the MTS changed over time, they carried forward the Party's message and led recruitment drives. The MTS went on to boast enormous gains in terms of machines available. The production and procurement of grain crept upward only slowly during the remainder of the 1930s, and there was no great breakthrough. What was crushed in the process was the last shred of peasant independence.[36]

The relationship between the Stalinist regime and the peasantry was not governed only by repression. To get them to bend, Moscow cooled its missionary zeal in the countryside. To entice them to join the collective farms, the government left them some room to work on small plots of land. The peasants manipulated this hybrid system as best they could and over time even accommodated themselves to the collectivization as a whole.[37]

Stalin may have hoped his image among the peasants would become something between the "good tsar" and the "leader" who dispensed justice and provided rewards for hard work. But memories of collectivization remained raw, and peasant attitudes toward him in the late 1930s were generally "sour and wary."[38]

Andrea Graziosi thinks Stalin won more grudging support. She suggests that the victory in the battle for grain was "also Stalin's *personal* victory. Many peasants now 'recognized' him as a stern, master-like 'father' whom it was impossible to disobey (even though one could still 'cheat' him of a small part of the harvest)." Graziosi believes that this attitude was "one of the roots of the indubitable hold of Stalin's cult from the mid-1930s onward also in the countryside."[39]

The tough-minded peasants had little choice but to recognize Stalin as their master, since his power of life and death over them was a fact they could not change. Joining in the celebrations associated with the Stalin cult would have been a prudent act for a countryside beaten into submission by a tyrannical and murderous "father."

FROM BRIEF "THAW" TO GREAT TERROR

At the beginning of 1934 Stalin signaled victory in the war against the countryside and a "thaw" in militant Communism. The OGPU was dissolved on February 20, 1934, and incorporated into the new Union People's Commissariat for Internal Affairs, the NKVD. Unlike its predecessors, the NKVD initially did not have the power to execute people on its own authority. Cases of treason would henceforth go before the courts. A symbol that police terror might be ending was the death on May 10 of Vyacheslav Menzhinsky, chairman of the OGPU.[40]

Genrikh Yagoda, known to be somewhat less of a hard-liner, became the head of the NKVD. The "thaw" or "retreat," such as it was, hardly lasted a year. It ended on December 1, 1934, with the assassination of Sergei Kirov, the dynamic Party leader in Leningrad and supposedly beloved by Stalin.

Suspicion circulated, especially within dissident circles, that Stalin ordered the assassination because Kirov had become a rival, identified with a more liberal course. No conclusive proof has emerged. If in fact Stalin ordered the killing, it might indicate that he wanted a clampdown on more liberal-minded Party members, perhaps that he meant to touch off events like the terror that would sweep through all sectors of society in 1937–38. Whatever the hidden truths, Stalin used Kirov's murder to his political advantage and set in motion a process that developed into the Great Terror.

The Kirov assassination forms part of the backdrop for the mass crimes that followed. Young activists, particularly those who rejected "the tyrant in the Kremlin," recognized the murder as an excuse for Stalin and his "gang" to launch a campaign "of extermination against the dissenting sector of the Party." Thus they saw Kirov's death as the end of the last hope for democracy in the Party, a signal that Russia would soon "be bleeding to death."[41]

Stalin ostentatiously went to Leningrad to investigate and eventually even questioned some of the suspects. The Politburo passed a decree, formulated by him on his trip, which became the notorious law of December 1, 1934. Investigative agencies were to speed up the cases and not to wait to consider the possibility of pardon. The NKVD was permitted to execute immediately. In sum, this decree provided the legal basis for the police terror and purges to come.[42]

Stalin handed over the investigation of Kirov's assassination not to Yagoda but to Nikolai Yezhov, one of the rising stars in the NKVD. Although Kirov's murderer was a disgruntled Party member who was caught on the spot, Stalin insisted there was a conspiracy involving his former opponents Kamenev, Zinoviev, and perhaps others. This was the line of investigation the relentless Yezhov now pursued, and he came up with the desired results.

Yezhov reported directly to Stalin and maligned the leadership of the NKVD for its lack of professionalism and readiness. With Stalin's support, Yezhov moved up in the police and began talking about "idleness" and "complacency." He said Kremlin security was so lax that it was possible for assassins to get at Stalin and laid this "failure," too, at Yagoda's door. It was no surprise on September 25, 1936, when Stalin wrote to members of the Politburo and demanded Yagoda's dismissal. The grounds were that the man was not "up to the task in the matter of exposing the Trotskyite-Zinovievite bloc" supposedly responsible for Kirov's murder.[43]

Some impressionable idealists were inclined to take Stalin and Yezhov at their word, to believe that there was a "new counter-revolutionary underground" afoot and that "terror was indispensable."[44] Their convictions were about to be tested.

15

TERROR AS POLITICAL PRACTICE

Soviet law enforcement in the 1920s and 1930s was far from being ever present and all knowing. At the beginning of the 1930s the police numbered half what they had been under the tsar during the Great War. There were even fewer in the countryside, where often vigilantes were the ones keeping a semblance of order. In the cities enforcement favored the use of roundups or sweeps of likely areas. The new passport system provided a means of separating out the "undesirables."

FORMER PEOPLE

The "passportization" law, introduced in December 1932 to stem the flow of peasants from the countryside, took a year to implement. Lev Kopelev later remarked how the obligatory registration of all citizens "laid an administrative and juridical cornerstone for the new serfdom; it provided one of the foundations for an unparalleled state totalitarianism."[1] By mid-1934 around twelve million residents in "regime" cities had passports, which more or less guaranteed or "privileged" supplies. Almost fifteen million had them in "non-regime" and less fortunate cities.[2]

The passports singled out those who did not fit the image of the model Soviet citizen. Specific groups were not just denied the crucial documents and food rations, but could be expelled from cities, like kulaks or dekulakized persons. Also banished was anyone with a criminal record; most refugees from abroad; the *lishentsy,* or "former" people, like former policemen, nobles, and merchants. The relatives of all of the above could also be denied the right to live in the city.[3]

Disenfranchised people could flee and change their identities and were hard to keep track of. For the electoral campaigns of the late 1920s, the Russian Federation reported as disenfranchised 3 to 4 percent of the rural electorate and 7 to 8 percent in cities.[4]

Stalin removed the status of *lishentsy* in 1936, but old identities proved almost indelible, and many "formers" were among the first caught in 1937 by secret police order No. 00447. The authorities pursued "former kulaks," "former members of anti-Soviet parties," "former Whites," "former tsarist bureaucrats," and other such groups. One official argued that the senselessness of the idea of "formers" was reason to drop it: "At one time we had former people; now it turns out we have the children of former people. It looks like soon there will even be the grandchildren of former people's children. How far will this go? . . . If a man is 74 years old and he is the son of a former trader, then surely he is not himself a former trader . . . children of former people, grandchildren of former people, great grandchildren of former people—we can't carry on like this."[5]

SOCIALLY DANGEROUS AND SOCIALLY HARMFUL ELEMENTS

In early 1933 Stalin had signaled a new wave of terror against the "last remnants of the moribund classes—the private manufacturers and their servitors, the private traders and their henchmen, the former nobles and priests, the kulaks and kulak agents, the former White guard officers and police officials, policemen and gendarmes, all sorts of bourgeois intellectuals of a chauvinist type, and all other anti-Soviet elements—have been thrown out of their groove."

The Five-Year Plan, said Stalin, allowed these has-beens to worm "their way into our plants and factories, into our government offices and trading organizations, into our railway and water transport enterprises, and, principally, into the collective farms and state farms. They have crept into these places and taken cover there, donning the mask of 'workers' and 'peasants,' and some of them have even managed to worm their way into the Party."

He called for extreme vigilance. The full measure of revolutionary law had to be used "against thieves and wreckers in the public economy, against hooligans and pilferers of public property. . . . A strong and powerful dictatorship of the proletariat—that is what is now needed, to disperse the last vestiges of the dying classes and to frustrate their thievery."[6]

This mandate led the secret police to sweep through markets, train stations, and poorer parts of cities. In Moscow between January and August 1933, 65,904 were denied passports and driven out. In Leningrad for the same period the number was 79,261. Once word spread, as many or more left these cities of their own accord and in desperation. Yagoda urged police to "clean up" the cities, and hundreds of thousands were expelled. On April 28, 1933, the passport decree was extended to all urban and semi-urban areas, which caught still more in the dragnet. The fate of the expellees varied, but being forced to leave the city turned into a death sentence for tens of thousands.[7]

On August 13, Yagoda issued guidelines for "nonjudicial repression" of passport violators, by which special troikas reviewed cases and passed sentences on the *lishentsy*, the kulaks, those deemed not gainfully employed, and "criminals and other antisocial elements." The first three types were transported to penal resettlement colonies, while the last group was sent to a work camp for a minimum of three years, sentences given to all repeat offenders. In 1933 the OGPU troikas dealt with 24,369 cases and "convicted" around 7,000.[8]

The police were concerned about "socially dangerous elements," loosely defined as having "two or more past sentences," as well as any-one with four arrests on suspicion of crimes against property or individ-uals. Included here were those with records of "hooliganism," pimping, and other such activities. The secret police prosecuted them all outside the jurisdiction of the courts, as they had done in more limited fashion during the 1920s.[9]

By the early 1930s the concept of "socially dangerous elements" had partly been overtaken by "socially harmful elements" (*sotsial'no-vrednye elementy*). It became a catchall for repeat offenders, and police wanted to use their own authority to quarantine them.[10]

Such an approach hit innocent people like the mother of Stepan Podlubny, who was attending an institute of higher learning in Moscow. She was whisked away because her papers were not in order. They had lived since 1931 in Moscow, where she had a respectable position and he was in the Komsomol, but there were kulak connections in their past.

By the time Stepan found her, she had been sentenced to eight years by an NKVD troika for "concealing her social origins" and branded a "socially dangerous element." She was sent to a concentration camp in the Urals. Although Stepan was allowed to continue his studies, the stigma was now on his record, and he lost his state funding. The damage caused by his origins could never be entirely undone.[11]

A Central Committee directive of May 9, 1935 (order No. 00192), defined "harmful elements" as people with previous convictions and "continuing ties" to the criminal world. Those without a regular job were also singled out, as were "professional" beggars. People who offended the passport laws in some way, and even children (over twelve) "caught in a criminal act," were all covered by the broad concept of "socially harmful elements." By the end of 1935, the police netted at least 266,000 such "elements."[12]

The Politburo sought to cure the problem of juvenile delinquency and homelessness and on April 7, 1935, decreed that "the full force of the law" should be used against young offenders. Whereas the older penal code did not permit executing anyone under twelve, the government announced a few days later that the death penalty could be used even against even younger adolescents. A new series of "work colonies" was established for minors. The scope of what happened can be gathered from the fact that between 1935 and 1939, more than 155,000 minors were sent to these colonies. As of April 1, 1939, more than 10,000 children were confined in the Gulag.[13]

"ANTI-SOVIET ELEMENTS"

Stalin personally inaugurated an escalation of repression on July 3, 1937, with a note to Yezhov dealing with what he called "anti-Soviet elements." He stated it "had been observed that a large number of former kulaks and criminals" who had been deported were beginning to return and were engaging in "sabotage." They were undermining the collective farms, transportation system, and industry. On Stalin's orders, "the most hostile" were to be "arrested and executed" by a troika and the less dangerous deported.

On July 30, 1937, Yezhov issued order No. 00447 concerning "anti-Soviet elements," which included more groups than those mentioned by Stalin. "Investigative materials" supposedly revealed nine different groups; topping the list were the former kulaks, followed by "socially dangerous elements," namely former Whites, gendarmes, bureaucrats, bandits, gang abettors, and political opponents.

Order No. 00447 spelled out in advance — as Stalin had instructed — the two categories of "elements" that were to be found. These were then broken down into separate groups, "the most active" and the "less active but nonetheless hostile." All those in the first category were to be executed, after what was called "consideration of their case" by a troika. Those in the second category were subject to arrest and confinement in a prison or concentration camp "for a term ranging from eight to ten years."

The order set a quota for both types across the country. For example, the Leningrad region was given a quota of four thousand category-one persons (to be executed) and ten thousand category-two (to be arrested and confined for years in a concentration camp). The Moscow region had five thousand in category one and thirty thousand in category two. Even the smallest districts were given quotas.[14]

The order also determined for execution a quota of ten thousand already in the camps, a figure soon raised. At Solovki, for example, the initial quota was twelve hundred, but from October 1937 to February 1938 eighteen hundred were executed.[15]

These campaigns made no effort to "terrorize" individuals into changing their minds or behavior. There was no discourse with the offenders, no attempt to win them over, for they were deemed beyond redemption.

There was also no point to the old fiction that work might "liberate" them. They were given nothing more than a shot in the back of the head. Most were chosen by quota as members of mythical collectivities.

Far from being forced into this by Stalin or Yezhov, local officials tried to outdo one another. Thus, when officials from western Siberia were told they were second in the entire country in the number of liquidations they had carried out, their mood—so one of them later said—"reached ecstasy." In Karelia, there was "exceptional competition between the NKVD and the local organs to reach quotas."[16]

Yezhov came to believe that quotas might be too small and issued a blank check to officials like the new head of the NKVD in Smolensk in October 1937: "Imprison whomever you should." Yezhov's view was that it was better to go "too far than not far enough."[17] Some police used scandalous pretexts to meet their quotas—for example, arresting everyone who one day happened to witness an industrial fire or was accused somewhere else of being involved in a forest fire. Police made these allegations to get a "supplementary quota of 3,000, of whom 2,000" were shot.[18]

The Politburo, assailed by requests, showed no qualms about raising "limits" on a weekly basis, including expanding the numbers to be executed. On February 17, 1938, the Central Committee gave (yet again) permission for the NKVD "to carry out supplementary arrests of kulak and other anti-Soviet elements and to submit the cases for consideration by the troikas, having increased the quota for the NKVD of the Ukrainian SSR [Soviet Socialist Republic] by THIRTY THOUSAND."[19]

The troikas went through hundreds of cases on a daily basis. The Omsk troika decided no fewer than 1,301 cases on a single day. These were hardly "hearings" since as usual the accused was not present, but, as more than one member of these courts admitted, there was not even time to read the files. On average in Moscow they went through 500 cases a night.[20] In 1938 alone, the Dalstroi troika sentenced 12,566 people, of whom 5,866 were condemned to death.[21]

Dalstroi was an acronym for Far Northern Construction Trust, which itself at one time controlled 130 camps with 163,000 slaves ranging over a region larger than the landmass of Western Europe. It was part of the Gulag, and the terror within the terror of Dalstroi during the late 1930s crippled its economic output. Indeed, the repressive inclinations of Stalinism "consistently undermined its own economy."[22]

Grigorii Gorbach, the ambitious chairman of the NKVD in Omsk, was not satisfied with the "allotment" of 2,438 he was given on July 9 and asked Moscow (no reason given) for a higher one on August 4 even before operations began. Twelve days later he reported his men met and exceeded a quota of five thousand executions, and asked for a new target of eight thousand. Stalin himself wrote in the margin of the telegram that he favored granting this request. Gorbach's feats did not end there, but he brought the same zeal to his work when transferred to the western Siberian province.[23]

Another local police official wrote Stalin on October 28, 1938, to say he had just left one locality "where they had already spent all their 00447 allowance, but there were still over 2,000 elements in prisons, whose time limit has been over long ago. All these elements are counter-revolutionary kulaks, members of bourgeois parties, clerical activists. The instruction of their case is over, prisons are overcrowded. . . . They asked me for a further allowance for 2,500, a demand that I hereby report to you."[24]

The NKVD needed no explanation for Stalin because it was dealing "the last blow" against well-known enemies. This operation was planned to last four months but was repeatedly extended and ran from August 1937 to November 1938.

Local officials came up with their own numbers, informed Moscow, and overfilled their quotas. Briefings would be held for regional heads of the NKVD, and a sweep would go off like a surprise commando attack. The camps were turned into places of extermination, to use the term applied by one of Russia's leading historians today. The Soviets did not use gas chambers, but they murdered on a vast scale. Under order No. 00447, no fewer than 767,397 were sentenced by troikas, of whom 386,798 were given the death penalty.[25] This figure does not include the thousands sent to the Gulag. Even though the number of camps kept growing, so many people were sent to them in 1937–38 that overcrowding resulted in a 200 percent increase in mortality rates.[26]

The ripple effects of operation 00447 can be seen in a letter of Party member V. Antipov to the Central Committee of the Communist Party on December 12, 1938. He said "thousands of families" who had been banished were forced to seek shelter near railroad stations. The Novgorod NKVD was particularly zealous and in two weeks during late October 1938 exiled one thousand families for the "crime" of being related to someone who was once on trial. The families were given twenty-four hours to depart and sold what they could. Everyone had to leave, the elderly, the infirm, and the children.

Antipov thought that the relatives of those convicted should be deported to places away from the border, but questioned whether it was right to banish "absolutely everyone" associated with some wrecker. The exiles were compelled to move around; they had no housing or jobs. And so the tragedy of operation 00447 kept unfolding.[27]

NKVD leaders in Leningrad and Moscow resorted to killing off physically handicapped prisoners who, for a variety of reasons, were tarred with the brush of operation 00447. In Moscow the prisons were overcrowded, and Gulag officials balked at taking eight hundred prisoners already sentenced but considered invalids. In February and March 1938 special hearings sentenced at least 163 to be shot. The police framed them for the crime of "anti-Soviet agitation" when as often as not the victims were simply in the wrong place at the wrong time.[28] There is no telling how widespread these practices became.

The "criminalization of the unpopular, uncontrollable and disruptive activities" by the party-state might have struck a responsive chord among the population. As the "virtual civil war" raged, citizens learned how to cope and also how to benefit from it personally by carefully aimed denunciations of colleagues, neighbors, or functionaries.[29] Sarah Davies, writing about Leningrad, notes some sympathy for the unfortunates but also says that "many workers clearly welcomed" the policy of expelling those without passports and "criminal elements" and even "questioned why such undesirable groups had continued to live in the city for so long." She goes so far as to suggest that "much of the available material points to popular indifference to, and even approval of, the terror."[30]

Ordinary people might well have had little sympathy for the terrorized members of the elite. We need more evidence before we can say how they felt about the terror in general, especially when it happened to people not unlike themselves.

CHURCHES UNDER THE HAMMER AND SICKLE

Religion and the churches had been the object of Communist hostility since 1917. For Marxists, religion was the "opiate of the masses" in that it encouraged people to adjust to the world as it was, not struggle against it.

Numerous religions were represented in imperial Russia, but the religion of the majority was the Russian Orthodox Church. The first step against it was a decree of January 20, 1918, on the separation of church from state and school. It was modeled on a similar decree passed by the Paris Commune in the nineteenth century and (with no irony intended) usually publicized as the Decree on Freedom of Conscience.

The Soviet measure removed religious symbols from public buildings and allowed for the confiscation of properties. The Communists closed the seminaries and most monasteries immediately, and the Cheka arrested members of the clergy suspected of being political opponents. However, there was no wholesale roundup, and citizens as individuals were allowed to continue their religious faith, at least for the moment.[31] In the context of the revolutionary upheaval, it was not yet possible to put together a concerted campaign to eliminate religion altogether.

After the revolutionary period, the Orthodox Church (and other forms of religion as well) came under assault in three distinct waves: the first at the end of the civil war in 1922; the second during collectivization (1928–32); and the third during the Great Terror (1936–39).[32]

Lenin struck the first and typically harsh blow during the famine of 1922 and set the murderous tone. He wrote Molotov and the Politburo on March 19, 1922, that the famine presented an ideal opportunity to "smash the enemy's head with a ninety-nine percent chance of success."

"It is precisely now and only now, when in the starving areas people are eating human flesh, and hundreds, if not thousands of corpses are littering the roads, that we can (and therefore must) carry out the confiscation of the Church valuables with the most savage and merciless energy, not stopping [short of] crushing any resistance." Lenin referred with approval to Machiavelli, who "rightly said that if it is necessary to resort to certain brutalities for the sake of realizing a political goal, they must be carried out in the most energetic fashion and in the briefest possible time, because the popular masses will not endure prolonged application of brutality." Following Machiavelli, he came to the conclusion that they must now "give the most decisive and merciless battle to the [reactionary] clergy and crush its resistance with such brutality they will not forget it for decades to come."[33]

Lenin was concerned that Jewish members of the ruling elite distance themselves from the persecution, lest they provoke an anti-Semitic backlash. His letter to Molotov concluded as follows about the orders that should be formulated at the next Party congress:

> At this meeting, pass a secret resolution of the congress that the confiscation of valuables, in particular of the richest abbeys, monasteries, and churches, should be conducted with merciless determination, unconditionally stopping at nothing, and in the briefest possible time. The greater the number of representatives of the reactionary clergy and reactionary bourgeoisie we succeed in executing for this reason, the better. We must teach these people a lesson right now, so that they will not dare even to think of any resistance for several decades.

This letter, written when he was already gravely ill, shows how Lenin's penchant for ruthlessness persisted. He ordered the secret police, for tactical reasons, to keep their hands off Patriarch Tikhon, the head of the Russian Orthodox Church. The immediate consequence was that twenty-seven hundred priests and five thousand monks and nuns perished, and across the country there were an estimated fourteen hundred clashes between loyal parishioners and the police, with two hundred show trials. What happened to the clergy in the camps defies the imagination, with every cruelty and torture imaginable heaped on them.

As for Patriarch Tikhon, he was indicted on March 20, 1922, threatened, held in detention, and harassed until his death just over three years later. His successors were intimidated, and to the extent the Orthodox Church continued to exist, it was all but taken over by the state.[34]

Officials down the line showed their own antireligious enthusiasm. For example, Petr A. Krasikov, in the Russian Federation's Commissariat of Justice, organized the confiscation of Church valuables in 1922 and advocated closing as many churches as possible. Over the years, the League of Militant Atheists, among others, padlocked churches in the capital city and elsewhere. Major houses of worship were demolished in the capital, the most important of which was the seventeenth-century Church of the Blessed Virgin. It was replaced by a political statue.[35]

There was symbolic value to turning former cathedrals of the Solovetski Monastery into concentration camps, with the floors covered in plank "beds." The facilities were completely unsuited to housing prisoners, who suffered from the cold, lack of space, and deplorable conditions.[36]

A second wave of religious repression came in the context of collectivization and was particularly ruthless in Ukraine. Churches were destroyed and the clergy shot on trumped-up charges. In addition, there was the continuing campaign to inculcate Communist ideals, to socialize the population and increase literacy.

The Cultural Revolution that began in 1928 witnessed more repressive policies toward religion. The Party concluded that anyone who identified with Communism was enlightened and progressive, while those who held on to a belief in God were backward and even counterrevolutionary. In the 1930s, merely talking to a priest could be grounds for concluding a person was an anti-Soviet element who should be "repressed," that is, arrested or sent to a camp.[37]

During the 1930s, the destruction of sacred places, including venerated cathedrals, continued. The most significant of these actions, backed by Stalin and the League of Militant Atheists, was the leveling of the Cathedral of Christ the Redeemer. Besides getting rid of these reminders of a despised past, the object was to destroy popular religious faith and replace it with secular loyalty to Communist ideals and specifically to the Soviet regime.

There was a shock, therefore, when the 1937 census showed nearly 60 percent of the population answered yes to the question "Are you a believer" in religion? Seventy-eight percent in their fifties still felt the pull of religion, and as many as 45 percent in their twenties admitted to some religious faith. The question itself, particularly given the context of the times and the raging terror, had to make people nervous. There would have been pressures to give the regime-approved answer to a census taker at the door, so it seems likely that even more people than indicated by the results held on to their religious faiths.[38]

Georgy Malenkov of the Central Committee Secretariat wrote to Stalin in April 1937: "The time has come to finish once and for all with all clerical organizations and ecclesiastical hierarchies." This exchange signaled the third wave of repression. Priests, bishops, and nuns were arrested in the thousands and sent to the camps, where they were executed or subjected to the worst possible treatment. Out of an estimated twenty thousand churches and mosques functioning in 1936, fewer than one thousand were active in 1941.[39]

TERROR AS SOCIAL PROPHYLAXIS

Terror was used in the 1930s to maintain Stalin's dominant position and undermine opposition. It was also employed with the intention of forcing through the transformation of society. Stalin used the most brutal means to get rid of what remained of old Russia, including the remnants of capitalism, the independent peasantry, and the clergy.

As well, the Stalinist use of terror had the function of being a social prophylaxis. "Real" opponents would be liquidated and society purified and cleansed of anyone who might become an opponent in the future. "Former" people, women and men whose social backgrounds left indelible traces, could not simply shed their old identities. Social background and old political associations could never be erased, and for hundreds of thousands there could be no redemption. They would be eliminated or sent to concentration camps from which they would never emerge.

The Nobel Prize winner and former Gulag prisoner Aleksandr Solzhenitsyn provides an instructive quotation about prophylactic terror from Lazar Kogan, one of the bosses of the Gulag, who said to a prisoner: "I believe that you personally were not guilty of anything. But, as an educated person, you have to understand that social prophylaxis was being widely applied." In this instance "understand" meant that the "educated person," completely innocent as he was, should nonetheless accept that the punishment he received was just from the perspective of Communism, a system they all presumably revered.

Solzhenitsyn mentions several cases he knew to illustrate just what this form of terror was all about. In Moscow in the 1930s a group of young people gathered for a musical evening, but without getting written approval beforehand: "They listened to music and then drank tea." This event, it was alleged by the secret police, "was a cover for counterrevolutionary sentiments," and the money was to be used not to buy tea, as they claimed, "but to assist the dying world of the bourgeoisie." These charges would seem laughable, but not in the context of those times. All the participants were arrested and given between three and ten years in the Gulag. Most of the organizers would not confess and were shot.[40]

Molotov provides other examples of how the various strands of terror were entwined. He insists, even looking back from the post-Soviet period, that the terror was "necessary" to maintain Leninism. Even if innocent heads rolled, "there could have been sympathizers among them."

Felix Chuev, in conversation with Molotov, asked him about the tortures to extract confessions, how clearly innocent family members were killed for nothing, and why it never seemed to occur to Stalin "that we could not possibly have so many enemies of the people" inside the Soviet Union itself. Molotov's best answer was:

> It is certainly sad and regrettable that so many innocent people died. But I believe the terror of the late 1930s was necessary. Of course, if we had used greater caution, there would have been fewer victims, but Stalin was adamant on making doubly sure: spare no one, but guarantee absolute stability in the country for a long time—through the war and postwar years, which was no doubt achieved. I don't deny that I supported that view. I was simply not able to study every individual case. . . . It was hard to draw a precise line where to stop, [and so no lines were drawn at all]. . . .
>
> That policy of repression was the only hope for the people, for the Revolution. It was the only way we could remain true to Leninism and its basic principles. Today that policy would be out of the question, of course.[41]

16

"MASS OPERATIONS"

With Hitler's rise in the West in the 1930s, Stalin became suspicious of Germans living in the Soviet Union. He hastily wrote at a Politburo meeting on July 20, 1937, an order for the arrest of all Germans then working in war-related industries everywhere in the USSR. He thus initiated a process that would be fateful for hundreds of thousands. The order was soon followed by others that affected many other national minorities.

AGAINST NATIONAL MINORITIES

In a follow-up to Stalin's instructions on July 20, Yezhov signed operational order No. 00439, outlining that Germany had organized a network of "spies and wreckers" in the defense industry and other strategic sectors. He ordered the NKVD to draw up lists and make arrests of German nationals. There were only about four thousand such people in the Soviet Union, but the suspects grew exponentially when police included those who had become Soviet citizens. German refugees, even members of the Communist Party, were closely scrutinized. Soviet citizens who had ever had ties with "German spies, wreckers, and terrorists" were particularly vulnerable.[1]

R. M. Traibman, former member of the Moscow NKVD, recalled being given "barely two days" to "uncover a counterrevolutionary, nationalist formation among young Germans." The NKVD invented charges and extorted confessions to implicate about fifty children of German émigrés, aged sixteen to twenty-five. Traibman later (in 1957) admitted that he was "especially outraged" by the incident, typical of the time.[2]

Operation 00439, signed by Yezhov on July 25, 1937, was supposed to last three months, but continued until November 1938. Whenever local and regional authorities found the number of suspects "too thin," they would go after non-Germans. In total, 55,005 were condemned by the "extrajudicial" troikas, and of those 41,898 (76 percent) were shot.[3]

Other national operations followed a similar course. Foreign nationals or former foreign nationals singled out included Afghans, Bulgarians, Chinese, Estonians, Finns, Greeks, Iranians, Koreans, Kurds, Latvians, Macedonians, and Romanians. Still other groups or people associated with them were also arrested.

The complete story of what happened remains to be told, but these national operations had no quotas, and the NKVD, given a free hand, everywhere exceeded expectations. Party Secretary Sobolev for Krasnoiarsk bluntly told them to get on with the job and "stop playing internationalism." His instruction was that "all these Poles, Koreans, Latvians, Germans, etc. should be beaten, these are all mercenary nations, subject to termination . . . all nationals should be caught, forced to their knees, and exterminated like mad dogs."[4]

Operation 00485 aimed to liquidate the "Polish diversionist and espionage groups and organizations of the Polish Military Organization (POV)." Even though POV had already been disbanded, its networks allegedly continued. The Poles were accused of being spies who had infiltrated Soviet society and economy. The operation began on August 11, 1937, on Yezhov's orders, two days after it had been approved by the Politburo.[5]

The net was soon cast to include all Polish refugees, political exiles, former members of the Polish Socialist Party, former Polish prisoners of war who stayed in the USSR, and even all Soviet citizens who had contact with Polish diplomatic, consular, military, commercial, or economic representatives in the USSR.

In Moscow the NKVD came up with cases by reading the telephone directory for foreign-sounding names indicating that the person might be Polish, Latvian, Bulgarian, or some suspect nationality. Such methods confirm the arbitrariness of the police terror.[6] The leadership of the Polish Communist Party was thought to be involved in an anti-Soviet conspiracy, and suspicion even fell on ex-NKVD agents or informants dealing with "Polish Affairs." All Soviet citizens with "family or other suspect ties" in Poland were included, as were all Soviet "clerical elements"—that is, the Church—with connections to Poland.

Stalin was pleased with a preliminary report submitted by Yezhov for September 1937, even though the program was just starting. He noted on the report: "Very good! Dig up and purge the Polish espionage mud in the future as well. Destroy in the interest of the USSR." With that encouragement the NKVD promptly extended the operation to include family members of arrested Poles.[7]

According to the census for 1937, there were 656,220 Polish people with Soviet citizenship, and sifting through so many was difficult. Around 140,000 were arrested in the Polish operation, of whom just over 111,000 were executed and nearly another 29,000 sent to concentration camps. In the Greek, Finnish, and Estonian operations, the percentage of those executed was still higher.[8]

To facilitate confirmation of verdicts by Moscow, Yezhov and Procurator General Vyshinsky adopted the "album method." Staff copied into an album a brief summary of each "crime" and suggested punishment. When it was full, it was sent for countersignature by Yezhov and Vyshinsky, who took to signing the bottom of the page and approved whole albums at a time. Even so, they could not keep up. Hundreds of albums streamed in and caused long delays before sentences were carried out.

By July 1938 more than 100,000 cases were "pending." In the meantime, prisons were filled to overflowing. The Politburo decided in September to end the "album procedure" and dispense with the illusion that the NKVD could not execute as it wished. Special troikas went through the pending cases (for operation 00447 against the "formers") in two months; of the 105,000 people whose cases were reviewed, 72,000 were shot, with most of the remainder sent to a concentration camp. Only 137 were released.[9]

The final count of all the national operations is staggering. Around 350,000 people were arrested and 247,157 executed. Another 88,356 ended up in prison or a concentration camp.[10] In addition, countless family members suffered, with children taken away and sent to orphanages.[11]

Recently published documents may underestimate the numbers. For example, many men and women were tortured to death in the process of investigating their cases. The demise of these "suspects" in "investigative custody" was likely not counted among the executed. Moreover, those who died in transit to camps, and there were considerable numbers of them, were not included on the final murderous balance sheet.

GROWTH OF THE GULAG

The Gulag was already a reality in 1930 and contained 179,000 prisoners. But the number soon grew, and in 1934 there were 510,307; by 1937, 820,881; and in 1940, 1.3 million.[12]

At first the main "business" of the camps was logging in the far reaches of the taiga forests. The production of lumber by prisoners came to be regarded by foreign countries as "unfair competition," and the U.S. Congress considered boycotting goods produced "by convict labor." The threat forced the Soviets to employ prisoners in areas of the economy beyond lumbering where they could be hidden—as in the gold mines in the Far East at Kolyma—or where "their presence could be celebrated" as contributing to the public good.[13]

Stalin became involved in the "Socialist reconstruction" of Moscow in 1930 and was drawn to the idea of using Gulag prisoners on giant construction projects. The Moscow-Volga Canal that would link the capital city with the Volga River had been a dream of Russian rulers. After lengthy planning, the Politburo resolved to go ahead on May 23, 1932, and work began in June. It would use workers and the same secret police supervisors available when the White Sea–Baltic Canal (Belomor) was completed. The Moscow-Volga Canal (or the Dmitrovsky

Canal, as it went through the city Dmitrov) covered roughly a hundred miles, and in digging it, Gulag workers displaced more cubic meters of earth than the building of the Suez Canal. It was a nightmare. The canal had to go uphill more than half the way, necessitating locks, dams, and reservoirs, and, on Stalin's orders, had to be built quickly (about two years) and cheaply. Work went on around the clock by *zeks*—the slang name given to Gulag prisoners—most of it done by hand and without machinery.[14]

The project was presented in the press as an opportunity for the rehabilitation of many "criminals" who "burned with creative fever." The slogan of one camp newspaper, called *Perekovka* (Reforging) was "Let us drown our past on the bottom of the canal." The message was that hard labor would transform "criminals" into good citizens, the same rationalization for the camps as in Lenin's time.[15]

The press in the West, including in Germany, France, Great Britain, and the United States, continued to report on conditions in the camps, most often in condemnatory articles. Molotov, given the task of counteracting the foreign-press campaign, did not deny the use of forced labor, but said it was not slavery. On March 8, 1931, at the Sixth Congress of Soviets, he put the matter as follows: "The labor of those deprived of liberty who are healthy and capable of working is being used by us on certain communal and highway tasks. We did this before, we are doing it now, and we shall continue to do so. This is profitable for society. This is beneficial for the culprits, for it teaches them how to work and makes them useful members of society."[16]

The Moscow-Volga Canal opened, somewhat behind schedule, in July 1937 to great fanfare, but without a word about the thousands who died building it. Nor was anything said about the thousands who perished while working on Belomor.

Recent analyses by economists show that the entire Gulag forced-labor system was uneconomical. It was not just a matter of the unneeded railway lines to nowhere and shallow canals that soon went all but unused. The Gulag "promoted the wide proliferation of padded statistics and false reports." Cheap slave labor "became a kind of narcotic for the economy, which it found increasingly difficult to give up by replacing prisoners with civilian workers." Thus, the overall effect of the Gulag was to corrupt what remained of the "free" economy.[17]

"FIRST ARCHITECT"

The Soviet Writers' Congress held in 1934 gave credit to Stalin for the new concept of socialist realism and adopted it as its guiding principle. The theory posited that authentic works of art in a workers' state had to spring from and reflect Socialist experience. In practice it demanded that artists give up any remnants of independence from state authority and, in strict conformity with Party dictates, focus on creating works of art meant to glorify Communist ideals.

Not long after the congress, the All-Union Congress of Soviet Architects hailed Stalin as "the first architect and builder of our socialist motherland," and embraced socialist realism as the great breakthrough in giving expression to a truly Socialist culture. Their building projects would be "guided by the great ideas of Lenin-Stalin." They expressed their willingness and duty to take their cues from Stalin as the paragon of good judgment and wisdom: "We, the architects of the USSR, gathered at this All-Union meeting, greet you, the first architect and builder of our socialist motherland, organizer of the greatest historical victories of the working class, beloved leader of the world proletariat, and best friend of the Soviet intelligentsia."[18]

Stalin's interests in architecture developed with the first Five-Year Plan. During the first eight years of the Soviet Union, ten thousand buildings were protected by the state because of their special interest, and just under one-third of them were restored. From 1928 the emphasis changed, and numerous historic buildings were torn down. These included the Church of Savior in the Wood (1330) and other religious structures inside the Kremlin itself.[19] Nothing was sacred but the grand historical mission as Stalin defined it. He turned to transforming Moscow into the world's great beacon of modernization. By 1931, he had backed three big projects in Moscow: the subway, the canal, and the Palace of Soviets. He usually made final decisions himself about which proposals would be accepted from the architects. He insisted the palace had to be "a little taller" than the Empire State Building in New York. A Lenin statue was to adorn its top and had to be triple the size of the Statue of Liberty.[20]

Stalin wanted the Palace of Soviets on the site where the famous Cathedral of Christ the Redeemer then stood. The cathedral was the largest house of worship in the USSR, created from contributions of ordinary citizens to celebrate victory over Napoleon, but now it was leveled. Distraught clerics who protested were dragged off and shot the same night.[21]

But publicists hailed the coming palace as "a symbol in the people's eyes of all the achievements of socialism."[22] There was an ironic truth in this boast, because the palace was never built. While the foundations were being poured, it was discovered that the land could not hold such a massive building and that water seepage into the foundation could not be stopped. Construction was halted when the war came, and eventually the site was converted into a swimming pool. After the end of Communism, the Cathedral of Christ the Redeemer was rebuilt in record time and stands today as a symbol of Moscow's rejuvenation.

Stalin also pressed ahead with the White Sea–Baltic Canal (Belomor), in one of the most inhospitable regions of the country. Again he wanted to use only Gulag labor.

The Politburo had approved the project on May 5, 1930, and it began in February 1931. New camp sites were created as the project moved forward, with prisoners living in horrendous conditions. Solzhenitsyn reports the rumor that a hundred thousand died during 1931–32, the first winter of the project. Even if this number is exaggerated, death was common and bodies were left unburied, their bones eventually interred in the canal.[23]

In August 1933 the canal was ready for Stalin to take a maiden voyage. He was followed by a group of writers led by Maxim Gorky, who had already written in praise of the concentration camps upon his visit to Solovki in the summer of 1929. Solovki had been readied at that time for Gorky to "inspect," and he triumphantly proclaimed the camp an unqualified success. "If any so-called cultured European society dared to conduct an experiment such as this colony, and if this experiment yielded fruits as ours had, that country would blow all its trumpets and boast about its accomplishments."[24] The winter that followed Gorky's visit was especially hard for Solovki. Another twenty thousand men arrived at the already overcrowded camp; given the woeful sanitary conditions, typhus broke out "and many thousands died."[25]

On August 17, Gorky led an outing of 120 authors on a visit to the newly completed canal. We have their impressions in a book they published. Written by an authors' collective, *The White Sea–Baltic Canal* gave everything the highest grades, especially the concentration camp—

a veritable "torch of progress." They were impressed by forced labor, which, they asserted, worked miracles and transformed what they called "human raw material."

The authors repeated the line about the causes of crime and the need for labor camps: "Criminals are the result of the repulsive conditions of former times, and our country is beautiful, powerful and *generous,* and it needs to be *beautified.*" Those compelled to work on the canal would be "reforged." No longer was a sentence in prison merely time behind bars, because forced labor led to the "restructuring of the consciousness and the pride of the builder." Gorky and his authors' collective did not mention a single person who had died on the Belomor canal.[26]

George Bernard Shaw came to see the wonders of the Socialist experiment in 1931 and was ushered through the camps, buffed up only hours before. He was impressed and heartily recommended Stalinist Socialism to his friends Sidney and Beatrice Webb, who were equally taken on their visit that year.[27]

The Gulag had fifty-three camps in 1940, some of them enormous. The Bamlag, for example, was another "moving" camp given the task of building a two-thousand-kilometer-long railway line from Baikal to Amur in the east. The prisoners, numbering 260,000 in 1939, had the impossible task of finishing the railway in four months, not only in the absence of proper machinery but also without adequate clothing and even shoes. Once again, the deaths of the *zeks* ranged in the tens of thousands.[28] The same general lack of utility and wastage of human lives was in evidence in these massive railway construction projects as in the canals.[29] The former earned the dubious title of "dead railroads" in every sense of the term. Despite the enormous effort, the results "were insignificant."[30]

For a long time the number of Gulag prisoners was top secret, but recently we have found the official figures. Caution is advised because Soviet record keeping was so sloppy. Historians now add together the populations of the Gulag camps with those in "labor colonies." Thus, in addition to the Gulag prison population we have already mentioned, many were confined in these places. The figures we have show that from 1935 onward, there was somewhere between 240,000 and 885,000 in the colonies. In 1938 there were close to 2 million in the Gulag and colonies combined.[31]

If we want to imagine a complete picture of how many people were affected, we have to keep in mind what statisticians call "in-out migration," that is, people who were released (because they were sick or too old) and who were replaced each year. Thus, if 400,000 left the camps and the same number of new prisoners were sent to them in any given year and if we only note the camp population on the first day of the year, we overlook the fact that 400,000 additional people had endured the ordeal. It is, therefore, difficult to say for certain how many passed through the camps.

The great majority were men between the ages of nineteen and forty. In the 1930s women made up on average 6.7 percent of the camp population.[32] The fate of women was horrendous. They were assaulted by guards and other prisoners alike; rape and sexual abuse were daily occurrences, and many had to make deals with one or more men who would protect them in return for sexual favors.

The Gulag knew no age limits. Juveniles aged up to eighteen could be sent to the camps or the colonies for many "crimes," including being homeless or abandoned, breaking passport laws, or being petty thieves.

"Members of the family of repressed persons" (chlen repressirovannogo), including children, were not spared in the terror. What happened to them, even young Communists devoted to the cause, can be seen in the case of Anton Antonov-Ovseyenko. His father, Vladimir, was an Old Bolshevik who stormed the Winter Palace in 1917, served as a Red Army commander in the civil war, and for twelve years was a Soviet ambassador abroad. He was recalled in 1937, arrested like so many other Old Bolsheviks, and executed. His son Anton was seventeen at the time, a member of the Komsomol, and a true believer. He could not accept the guilt of his father, but still believed Stalin's name "was sacred." His father's arrest tainted him, and he was arrested in 1940, released, but arrested again the day after the German invasion in June 1941. He endured the next twelve years in the Gulag. That happened even though in the spring of 1938 Stalin had made the famous statement "The son does not answer for the father."[33]

GLIMPSES OF THE GULAG FROM THE OUTSIDE

The industrial engineer Victor Kravchenko escaped the purges and clutches of the local NKVD in Ukraine. He was never arrested, but transferred as a plant manager to Pervouralsk in the Urals near Sverdlovsk (formerly Yekaterinburg), where he found the system of favors, the NKVD, which meddled in everything, and the concentration camps. He wrote as follows about the short drive from the railway station:

> I suddenly saw the barbed-wire fence of a concentration camp a few hundred meters off the road. We stopped the car so I could take a better look. The camp, acres and acres of bleak barracks in a huge clearing in the woods, seemed deserted, silent as death. It was six-sided and at each of the six corners there was a watchtower, equipped with big search-lights and machine guns.
>
> "Where are the prisoners?" I asked my companion.
>
> "At work this time of the day," he said. "A few of them are in our own factory, the rest in other plants, mines and on construction jobs. Victor Andreyevich, I see you're new to the Urals. You'd better get accustomed to the prisoners everywhere."[34]

One day Kravchenko went with a colleague on an outing and soon "came across a dismal stretch of marshes where perhaps three hundred prisoners, many of them women, were at work. All of the unfortunates were indescribably dirty and grotesquely clad, and many of them stood up to their knees in muddy water. They worked in absolute silence, with the most primitive tools and seemed utterly indifferent to the two strangers."[35]

In the summer, Kravchenko took two visitors, both members of the Party, to see the beautiful river nearby. They found themselves "on a hillock looking down on the barbed-wire enclosure, in a forest clearing several hundred yards from the river's edge. As usual, there were the four towers at the corners of the quadrangle. Guards with fixed bayonets were in evidence. At the farther end of the enclosure several hundred prisoners, men and women, were working on the construction of a new row of barracks. Our expedition was ended there and then. All desire to see more of the river left us and we drove back to Pervouralsk in silence."[36]

The region around Sverdlovsk, as Kravchenko soon discovered, was one of the areas where concentration camp labor was most heavily used. It seemed that there was a camp with two thousand prisoners or so in all directions. They had to tramp six or seven miles to work sites each day and in all weather.

There were concentration camps in the nearby city of Magnitogorsk, the industrial center created from scratch in the context of the Five-Year Plan. Former kulaks lived in a special labor settlement (*spetstrud-poselok*). In the early 1930s, there were somewhere between thirty and fifty thousand of these unfortunates kept behind barbed wire in the city. Over the winter of 1932–33 the kulaks had to live in tents, and an estimated four or five thousand workers died. No children under ten survived. The dead were replaced each year by a stream of newcomers, so the population of the colony stayed the same. By the end of the 1930s an estimated thirty thousand were still in this camp.[37] During the 1930s the kulaks made the most of their bad situation, and eventually the barbed wire came down and the armed guards were removed. They still lived in "wretched" wooden barracks and had to repay the government for the cost of constructing these camps.[38]

Although the kulaks in Magnitogorsk regained the right to vote, only about one-quarter obtained passports, so that 75 percent of them could not leave town. Over the years, when ordinary people suffered during times of shortages, the former kulaks, as social outcasts, had it far worse.[39] Officially, 389,521 of these "special settlers" died between 1932 and 1940.[40]

Also in Magnitogorsk was a separate corrective labor colony (ITK) that belonged to the Gulag and held "harmful elements."[41] One day the American John Scott, a Communist fellow traveler, came upon "a curious sight" of forty or fifty Orthodox clergy "wearing dirty, ragged, black robes." Scott noted distantly how "they were hard at work with pick and shovel, digging away a little hill. A pug-nosed plowboy sat on a near-by knoll with an old rifle on his lap and surveyed them placidly. I asked one of them what he was there for, but he did not even answer me."[42]

Scott did not empathize with the forlorn and seemed unmoved upon hearing that they "had been charged with burning grain or some such semi-criminal, semi-political offense."[43]

In the few years of its existence through 1933, the ITK in Magnitogorsk "officially" received 26,786 settlers. Their treatment was reflected in their physical condition, which was so bad that they stood out; they were easily recaptured when they tried to escape.[44]

In all of the Soviet Union in 1940 there were 425 of these corrective labor colonies with a population numbering 315,584. The original intention was for them to hold men and women who were serving short sentences, but that rule varied. The Soviet gospel on crime was that people had to work to find a "cure," but in fact they were fed so badly and worked so hard that many died.[45]

Stalin and other leaders were bombarded with requests from the commissariats for more "cheap" Gulag labor. At the meeting of the All-Russian Central Committee of the Party in July 1940, Stalin raised objections. He found the use of such labor in remote places acceptable but was less certain about the cities, "where a criminal is working on the side, and then a non-criminal is working there. I don't know about that. I would say it's very impractical and not altogether proper." His quibbles were minor and had no effect. Forced labor continued to be used on projects Stalin thought improper.[46]

The Gulag was by no means confined to the north or the east but located all over the country. The census for 1939 registered more than 100,000 inhabitants of the Gulag in or near the capital, which included 16,551 "prisoners of camps, prisons, and colonies" under the Moscow NKVD, and another 91,080 under the NKVD of the Moscow region.[47] The country was covered from one end to the other.

"MEASURING" TERROR

One way of calculating the extent of the terror in the 1930s and before the war in 1941 is to look at recently revealed statistics on prisoners in the Gulag. These include the census of the camps, taken on the first day of January each year. The system grew annually with the notable exception of 1937, the year of the Great Terror, when so many were executed. The highest number of prisoners in NKVD corrective labor camps was reached on January 1, 1941, when a census counted 1,500,524 prisoners. There were another 429,000 in labor colonies and some 488,000 in prisons.

The Gulag system, in all its divisions, held a total of four million as of June 1941, with another two million involved in corrective labor. They were entitled to only a small part of their salaries, most of which was withheld by the state. They lived in constant dread, since even a minor infraction of the rules could mean incarceration.[48]

Apart from being sent to the Gulag, approximately 20 million (including some repeat offenders) were "convicted" in one way or another between 1930 and 1941. We might recall that the 1939 census counted 37,500,000 families, and 4 million single adults. If we match the "convictions" to these population figures, we can see that one or more members of every second family suffered arrest, execution, or detention.[49]

Imposing work discipline was yet another side of the terror. It became mandatory to fire and to evict workers from company housing in 1938 if they were late for work on three occasions. In 1939 the effort was stepped up by criminalizing misbehavior at the workplace. A compulsory workbook was introduced to keep tabs on employees.[50]

In June 1940 a decree was passed "on the adoption of the eight-hour day, the seven-day working week, and the ban on leaving work of one's own accord." Employees more than twenty minutes late (including people like schoolteachers) could be punished by six months of "corrective work." Moreover, they would be docked 25 percent of their wages and might be sent to prison for up to four months. This decree, which pressured everyone, was one of the most hated.[51]

On August 10, a new decree increased the punishment for offenses like shoddy work, petty theft, and "hooliganism." Culprits could be sent to the camps for up to three years or subjected to other punishments. Given the high-handed and often corrupt ways of supervisory officials, in tandem with the arbitrary police, the new decree made ordinary citizens more vulnerable than ever to the vagaries of the system.

The commissar of armaments, Boris Vannikov, persuaded Stalin that these measures were needed to control the workforce. The Great Terror had undermined the authority of managers, he said, and discipline had to be restored.[52] Stalin went along but was uneasy. As he suspected, the new regulations were unpopular, and prosecuting undisciplined workers swamped the court system. In the first year the decree on tardiness led to the prosecution of three million (approximately 8 percent of the total workforce), with half sentenced to imprisonment. Lesser punishments were also devised for the tardy—for example, forcing surface workers in the coal fields to work down in the mines.[53] The number of "hooligans" sent to the camps doubled in 1940 what it had been in 1939.[54]

According to Wolfgang Leonhard, a true-believing Communist and student who lived in Moscow at the time, the new decrees "came to occupy so central a position in the life of every inhabitant of the Soviet Union, that others were hardly noticed at all. The collapse of France, the air battles over England, the occupation of the Baltic states by Soviet forces and their conversion into Republics of the USSR, the annexation of Bessarabia and the northern part of Bukovina to the Soviet Union—all paled into insignificance in comparison with the struggle against the so-called shirkers, idlers and disruptive elements."[55]

At the beginning of the Nazi invasion, the NKVD reported some Moscow workers as defiantly saying, "When Hitler takes our towns, he will put up posters saying 'I won't put workers on trial, like your government does, just because they are twenty-one minutes late for work.' " Such remarks were mixed in with calls to get rid of the Communists and the Jews, revealing again some of the fatal ways anti-Semitism and anti-Bolshevism became entangled in these dangerous times.[56]

Stalin worried about the productivity of the countryside. When he heard of continuing problems, he was usually told that the collective farmers paid more attention to their tiny private plots than to the large enterprise. In 1939 an investigation led by A. A. Andreyev reported at the end of May that peasants were undermining collective farms to devote time to their own pursuits. Many did not work full-time on the collective at all, some put in a few days, while others did piecework for money. Stalin and other leaders were appalled, and in the discussion of Andreyev's report the terms that kept coming up were "compelling," "obliging," "limiting," "forcing," and "nationalizing" to describe the method to get peasants to produce more.[57]

17

"CLEANSING" THE SOVIET ELITE

L enin began the tradition of purging the Party of those who disagreed with him. In 1919, 10 to 15 percent of Party members were
expelled, though some who showed self-criticism were allowed to
rejoin. On September 20, 1921, Lenin purged what he called the "rascals,
bureaucrats, corrupt or fickle Communists, and Mensheviks who put a
new coat of paint on their 'facade' but are still Mensheviks at heart."[1]
This purge, the greatest of all (in percentage terms), led to the loss of 25
percent of the members. It was followed by five others in the 1920s,
which expelled between 3 and 13 percent in either a "verification"
process (*proverka*) or "cleansing" (*chistka*).

Grounds for being ejected varied, but high on the list was hiding one's
social origins. Corruption was considered a major offense, as was violat-
ing Party discipline, but even "passivity" was frowned upon. The tradition of purging various "elements" continued into the 1930s, when its
political significance grew because Party members by then occupied
leading positions in society.

PARTY PURGES UNDER STALIN

The Party itself became massive, and in 1929, the beginning of the first Five-Year Plan, membership reached 1 million, not counting candidate members, usually representing between one-third and two-thirds of the regular membership. By 1933, there were 2,203,951 members and 1,351,387 candidate members. The Party was underrepresented in the countryside, reflecting the generally negative attitude of peasants to Communism. Women were also underrepresented, likely a result of persistent social attitudes that resisted putting them on an equal footing with men. Still, by 1932, there were nearly half a million female members, or 15.9 percent of the total.[2]

Purges were generally conducted within and by the Party itself, with directives issued from Moscow. Some local leaders wanted to avoid overheating the atmosphere, however, as is shown in a letter of the Smolensk City Party Committee, which said in the midst of the 1935 events that it did not want the Party to "transform the work of verifying party documents into a campaign of unmasking." The aim should be to raise "party awareness" and foster "integrity" in the ranks by "sweeping them of all alien and corrupt elements." Such a process was in practice difficult to control.[3]

The secret police was more involved in the 1935 purge, with its boss, Yezhov, in charge of the "verification of party documents." He reported in December that 177,000 members (just under 10 percent of the total) had been expelled. Some 15,218 were arrested.[4] Stalin said Yezhov might have gone too far, but in fact he wanted deeper cuts.

Stalin was informed in early 1936 that Trotsky, living in exile since 1929, working through sympathizers, was still trying to influence events in the Soviet Union. Several top leaders were arrested for being part of this "conspiracy," which allegedly included the already incarcerated Kamenev and Zinoviev. On July 29, 1936, the Central Committee informed local and regional committees that a "Trotskyist-Zinovievist" plot had been uncovered, the aim of which was to assassinate eight national leaders, including Stalin, Kliment Voroshilov, and Kaganovich. The Party was called upon to exercise "proper Bolshevik vigilance" and stop those who operated "under cover of their Communist rank."[5]

Letters of denunciation flowed in from the regions as they discussed this Central Committee note. Moscow's response was to "focus the attention of all members of the Party on the struggle against the last vestiges of the villainous enemies of our Party and of the working class, to focus their attention on raising Bolshevik revolutionary vigilance with every means possible."[6]

SHOW TRIALS

That note set the stage for the first major show trial in Moscow on August 19–24, 1936. Zinoviev, Kamenev, and fourteen other major Party leaders were charged with organizing a "terrorist" center on Trotsky's instructions. Behind the scenes, Stalin worked out the details of what was to happen. He had plenty of willing accomplices. Kaganovich, on vacation as the trial approached, wrote to Stalin on July 6 that, having read the interrogations, he was sure that the "main instigator of this gang is that venal scum Trotsky. It is time to declare him an outlaw, and to execute the rest of the lowlifes we have in jail."[7]

One feature of the trial was that all the accused openly confessed to crimes most observers regarded as preposterous. They also implicated others, such as Bukharin, Aleksei Rykov, and Mikhail Tomsky (that is, leading rightists), as well as Karl Radek (a well-known leftist) and several generals. All were not tried at once. Tomsky committed suicide the day after his name was mentioned by Procurator-General Vyshinsky.[8]

Suicide became one way to cope with accusations, but at the Central Committee meetings in December 1936 Stalin said that those who chose that option were admitting their guilt. They were trying to "cover their tracks," to "distract the Party, undermine its vigilance, and deceive it one last time before they died." Far from being victims, Stalin told the committee, they took their lives out of fear "that everything would be discovered." He said suicide was a simple method to "spit on the Party for the last time, and deceive the Party."[9]

Many rank-and-file members adopted this coldhearted interpretation. A director of a machine-building factory in the Urals, for example, said of the death of a local official in early 1937: "These days we cannot believe suicide notes—even these may well turn out to be false. In committing suicide an individual is trying to threaten the Party, to tell it that by mistreating those who commit political crimes, the Party cripples people and forces them to put revolvers to their own heads." He concluded that in this case as well "a suicide has to be regarded as an anti-Party gesture."[10]

Stalin's correspondence with Kaganovich reveals his part in the show trials. He helped phrase the charges, decided on the slate of defendants, crafted the evidence, and prescribed the sentences. He even dictated Vyshinsky's emotional speech as the grand finale of the trial and polished its style.[11]

Stalin wanted a public trial to convince the world and Soviet citizens that these former "oppositionists" aimed at counterrevolution and acted as the agents of foreign governments. The press frenzy reached its climax on the last day of the trial with the headline "Crush the Loathsome Creatures! The Mad Dogs Must Be Shot!" Each of the unfortunates made his plea for mercy. Kamenev went so far as to say, "No matter what my sentence will be, I in advance consider it just." He told his sons not to look back, but to "go forward. . . . Follow Stalin."[12]

Lev Kopelev, later a dissident, was credulous. He stopped talking to people he knew were innocent when their exclusion "had been decided by a higher necessity." Despite second thoughts "the rule remained: unswerving loyalty to the idol," namely to Stalin and Communism, "the graven image" he had helped to create.[13] What was called "Bolshevik party-mindedness"—a mystical concept—meant repression of doubts, "iron discipline and faithful observance" of the Party's dictates and rituals.[14]

Even as this first major show trial was proceeding, Stalin and his henchmen were preparing the next. Georgy Pyatakov, deputy commissar of heavy industry, was arrested on September 12. Stalin's longtime ally and fellow Georgian Sergo Ordzhonikidze, commissar of heavy industry, vainly tried to slow down the repression, but Pyatakov, once a supporter of Trotsky, soon "confessed" his role in the conspiracy supposedly being hatched against Stalin.

Yezhov revealed the "facts" at the December meeting of the Central Committee, and key leaders such as Pyatakov, Radek, Grigory Sokolnikov, and Leonid Serebriakov were arrested. They were allegedly a "backup" to take over once the main conspirators were caught. Yezhov said there were ties between this group and hundreds of Party leaders. Pyatakov was called a "vicious fascist" and a "degenerate Communist." Yezhov insisted "these swine must be strangled."

There was a commotion at the meeting when someone asked about the popular Bukharin. Stalin said Bukharin aimed to restore capitalism, bring back private enterprise in agriculture, and worse. Although Bukharin and other accused on the Central Committee were allowed to respond, they were not convincing, partly because they were in fact critical of Stalin. At the very least they thought the Soviet Union under his aegis was socializing faster than was sustainable. Stalin's concluding speech was calm and cool but left little doubt that he believed Bukharin and his allies to be as guilty as Yezhov had intimated.[15]

What was at the heart of the matter? Stalin wanted a radical transformation of society. He was opposed by Bukharin and "the right" who believed he was going too far and by those on what Stalinists called "the left" (onetime sympathizers with Trotsky) who felt Stalin was not going far enough and had made too many concessions to "capitalism." The debate would start up anew whenever any policies seemed not to be working. The "left" or the "right" opposition picked away at Stalin, and with the purges he struck back.

At the end of 1936 and into the next year many began to feel some kind of national calamity was at hand, be that war or famine or both, their worries fueled by a failed harvest in 1936. That led to breadlines and anxieties verging on panic.[16]

The NKVD intercepted letters, from which they extracted strident views of the situation. These included:

"I wish that a war would start. I would be the first to go against the Soviet government."

"Tsar Nicholas was stupid, but bread was cheap and white, and you didn't have to stand in line for it. You could have as much as you wanted."

"The Soviet government and Stalin act like we are serfs. Just like before, when the peasants worked for landlords, now the kolkhoznik [worker on a collective farm] works until he drops—nobody knows for whom, but he does not get bread."

"What a life! If Trotsky were the leader, he would rule better than Stalin."

"Hitler will not only take the Soviet Union, but the whole world will be under his power—then we will begin to live. But now only the leaders have a life."[17]

These disorganized voices of discontent hinted at support for Stalin's enemies, so eliminating potential leaders was one way to solidify his dictatorship beyond all possible threats.

"ACCOMPLICES" OF FASCISM?

The second great show trial was conducted in Moscow between January 23 and 30, 1937. In the dock this time, besides Pyatakov, Radek, Sokolnikov, and Serebriakov, were more than a dozen others. The prosecutor Vyshinsky met with Stalin to work out how to proceed, even jotting down how to mimic Stalin's tone. Vyshinsky was told not to let the accused "babble," but to "shut them up."

The defendants again confessed their guilt and did not even ask for mercy. One said: "I do not need leniency. The proletarian court should not and cannot spare my life. . . . I want one thing: to calmly mount the execution block and wash away the stain of a traitor of the Motherland with my blood."[18]

To give the show trial another prop, defense counsel was added. One plea is worth noting as an illustration of what a show trial was about. Ilya Braude's remarks went as follows:

Comrade Judges, I am not going to conceal from you the exceptionally difficult and immeasurably hard position a counsel for the defense finds himself in this case. After all, a counsel for the defense, Comrade Judges, is first and foremost a son of his Motherland, he is also a citizen of the great Soviet Union, and the feelings of great indignation, wrath, horror which all our country, both young and old, are now seized with, these feelings are inevitably shared by the counsels for the defense as well. . . .

I am defending I. A. Knyazev, the head of the railway, who in order to please the Japanese Intelligence Service derailed trains carrying workers and Red Army men. I shall not conceal that as I was reading over the materials of the case, as I was leafing through the documents, as I was listening to Knyazev's testimony, I imagined the crash of the carriages as

they were being derailed and the groans of the dying and injured Red
Army men.... Driven into a corner, Knyazev agreed to join the
counter-revolutionary Trotskyite organization. Thus began the first page
of Knyazev's despicable actions which had been dictated to him by the
Trotskyite terrorist organization.[19]

The outcome was a foregone conclusion. A crowd of 200,000 demonstrated their bloodlust in Red Square on January 29, despite the −27°C
temperatures. They carried banners reading: "The Court's Verdict Is the
People's Verdict."

Nikita Khrushchev, one of Stalin's most vicious enforcers, addressed
the crowds and passionately denounced the "Judas-Trotsky." The guilty
"raised their hand against all the best that humanity has, because Stalin
is hope.... Stalin is our banner. Stalin is our will, Stalin is our victory."[20]

Sergo Ordzhonikidze, a longtime Stalin friend, became entangled
himself. He opted for suicide on January 31, an ominous sign of worse to
come for others.

Bukharin's fate was discussed in his presence at the Central Committee plenum beginning on February 23. The shadow cast over the meeting
was the suicide of Ordzhonikidze and the execution of Pyatakov. Molotov demanded Bukharin confess. If he would not, his refusal would be
taken as "proof" he was a "fascist hireling."[21] Voroshilov called his ex-
friend a "scoundrel." Stalin told Bukharin to "ask the Central Committee for its forgiveness."[22] A commission struck to investigate Bukharin's
case and that of Rykov came back on February 27 with the conclusion to
"arrest, try, shoot" both.[23] However, the ever-calculating Stalin suggested that instead their cases be turned over to a special commission of
thirty-six worthies for investigation.

The third major show trial—usually called the trial of twenty-one—
included Bukharin and other important leaders, like Yagoda, of the so-
called "right-Trotskyist bloc." It began on March 2, 1938, with Vyshinsky
descending to new levels to besmirch the accused. Some of the Soviet
Union's great writers and publicists chimed in as well. A Moscow
writer's open letter stated bluntly: "We demand the spies' execution! We
shall not allow the enemies of the Soviet Union to live!" It was signed by
writers as illustrious as Boris Pasternak, Mikhail Sholokhov, and Alexei
Tolstoy. Vasily Grossman, who had been saved by Bukharin's direct

intervention earlier, now shouted: "No mercy to the Trotskyite degenerates, the murderous accomplices of fascism!"[24] Vyshinsky's summation
against Bukharin was that he was a "damnable cross of a fox and a
swine."[25]

Bukharin's professions of innocence were useless. Sentence was
passed on March 13, and two days later he, Rykov, and seventeen others,
including the former NKVD chief Yagoda, were executed. This was the
last of the great show trials, but the terror was operating at other levels
as well.

Lev Kopelev admitted in his autobiography he did not really think

> Bukharin and Trotsky were Gestapo agents or that they had wanted to
> kill Lenin, and I was sure that Stalin never believed it either. But I
> regarded the purge trials of 1937 and 1938 as an expression of some far-
> sighted policy; I believed that, on balance, Stalin was right in deciding on
> these terrible measures in order to discredit all forms of political oppo-
> sition, once and for all. We were a besieged fortress; we had to be united,
> knowing neither vacillation nor doubt. But to most people—the "broad
> masses"—the theoretical differences between left and right within the
> Party were difficult to understand: both sides quoted Lenin and swore
> loyalty to the October Revolution. Therefore, the opposition leaders
> had to be depicted as deviationists and villains, so that the people would
> come to hate them.[26]

Victor Kravchenko, who was more skeptical than Kopelev, agreed in
substance about Bukharin. In his autobiography he recalled that no one
he met in Moscow

> attached the slightest value to their confessions. These men had con-
> sented to serve as puppets in a political morality play not in the least
> related to truth. Stalin was destroying his personal opponents and had
> succeeded in forcing them to participate in their own humiliation and
> extinction. We wondered about the techniques he had used. But even
> Party people were not expected to believe the trial testimony literally.
> To do so would have been tantamount, among Communists, to an
> admission of congenital idiocy. At most we accepted the fantasies in a
> symbolic, allegorical sense.[27]

Given the atmosphere in which conspiracies by foreign powers were being discovered with such regularity, it was "logical" that foreign spies would have to be found inside the armed forces. From the latter part of 1936 the NKVD gathered evidence against some of the most senior officers. Using torture, they gained confessions that implicated (among many others) Marshal Mikhail Tukhachevsky, hero of the civil war and deputy commissar of defense. On May 22, 1937, he was arrested and, with Stalin's express permission, tortured brutally. Stalin's instruction was to find out what the marshal knew: "It is impossible that he acted on his own."

The extorted testimonies were duly presented to Stalin in order to confirm suspicions. He then circulated his opinion to the Politburo for what was by then merely a pro forma "vote" to remove Tukhachevsky and others from the Communist Party. The damning accusation was that he was part of a "Trotskyite-Right [sic]" conspiracy on behalf of Hitler's Germany. On June 11, the one-day military tribunal met and, in keeping with Stalin's instructions, sentenced Tukhachevsky and seven army generals to death. The sentence was carried out early the following morning. Stalin attended to all the details, even seeking to orchestrate popular responses. He sent telegrams to Communist Party officials across the USSR telling them to organize meetings and pass resolutions "about the need to apply the supreme measure of punishment"—which is to say, to call for the execution of the traitors.[28]

In the next nine days 980 senior officers and political commissars were arrested in connection with this "military conspiracy." The wave of repression then struck down an even longer list of officers. A former Soviet general noted how "they were the flower of the officer corps, with civil war experience, and most of them were relatively young. The blow to the Soviet armed forces was immense."[29]

In 1937–38 the officer corps was purged of at least 33,400, of whom a minimum of 7,280 were arrested. Many who perished were among the top command of the army and navy, including three of five marshals, fifteen of sixteen commanders, and sixty of sixty-seven corps commanders. As happened to Tukhachevsky's family, their wives and children were often arrested and killed. The entire affair was pushed by Stalin, but not because he really believed there were plans for a coup. His motivation had more to do with his continuing mistrust of the army.[30] The purges not only caused direct harm to the armed forces but led to doubts, demoralization, and paralysis of will. The USSR would pay the price for this senseless purge with the German invasion in 1941.

The Politburo approved holding forty or so additional show trials across the country in the second half of 1937, and in 1938 another thirty were staged. Local and regional Party leaders and other members of the elite were tried in these cases.

An example of what ensued can be seen in Georgia, where the Party boss, Lavrenti Beria, went after "counterrevolutionaries." Empowered by Moscow in June 1937, he told the head of the regional NKVD, Sergei Goglidze, that those under arrest should be beaten if they would not confess. Goglidze described what happened next: "After this the Georgian NKVD began mass beatings of those under arrest. They were beaten at will. Testimonies against large groups of people appeared in the records and the numbers of those arrested as a result of having been mentioned in the testimonies grew, which led to falsification of cases and a distortion of reality."[31]

The results were tragic. Out of the 644 delegates to the Tenth Party Congress in Georgia held in May 1937, 425 were arrested and shot. Their wives and children were often arrested and tortured as well. The purge of the ranks went into the thousands. According to one witness, the troika in Tbilisi during 1937 "often did not concern themselves with compiling lists and conducting investigations" to send to Moscow for signing. Instead, the troika there "judged guilty and innocent alike according to the law of the Holy Inquisition, and their decision had the power of God."[32]

Raion, or district-level, show trials differed from those in Moscow and did not always rely on public confessions. The most absurd charges were brought, and outlandish plots were alleged. The need for witnesses to back up the charges provided opportunities for the powerless to assert themselves; there was no want of complaints and denunciations from peasants and other citizens. The provincials were more than mere "bystanders gathered to watch a public hanging," as they often were the ones who gave the incriminating evidence.[33]

To some extent the local trials removed one cohort of officialdom, but the basic structure of the system remained. The same point holds for the larger show trials in Moscow. Nevertheless, the trials and purges made possible the entrance of new people into the elite, those more likely than ever to be loyal Stalin supporters.

STALIN'S THEORY OF THE SHOWDOWN

Bukharin was once a favorite in the Party, and getting rid of him represented the last obstacle to Stalin's unchecked dictatorship. The evidence against him was assembled by Yezhov, but before the ax fell, the Central Committee held its plenum in February–March 1937.

Stalin addressed some awkward facts, in particular the question: if Socialism in one country was the great success he kept claiming, why were there so many enemies? One explanation was that the nearer the Soviet Union came to achieving Socialism, the more desperate would be the struggle of the "remnants" of enemy classes. This was a theory he had broached in 1928, and he brought it up again at the plenum of the Central Committee in February–March 1937. As he put it:

> The further we move forward, the more success we will have, the greater fury can we expect from what remains of the defeated exploiting classes, the more intense will be the struggle they put up, the harder they will try to harm the Soviet state, and the more desperate they will become as they grasp at the last resort of the doomed. It must be kept in mind that the vestiges of the defeated classes in the USSR are not alone. They are directly supported by enemies beyond the borders of the USSR . . . and must be aware of this. And so, they will keep up their desperate sorties. This is what history teaches us. This is what Leninism teaches us. We have to remember this and stay on the alert.[34]

This theory derived from the claim that as the class struggle became more volatile, it inevitably led to civil war, because no dominant class ever gave in without a desperate fight. Stalin built on that Marxist-Leninist point by suggesting that the "dying classes" would fight to their last breath. The theory also served to explain why Communists felt compelled to eliminate all the "formers" or the relatives and friends of the "formers." The all-out battle on this "front" against the innocent and defenseless was imagined as the "final showdown" against a vicious and dangerous enemy.

The idea of a showdown or last stand is common in Western culture. Before the "bad guys" or "evildoers" pass away, they muster renewed strength for a last-ditch effort and are at their most dangerous. The final showdown linked the struggles against the whole range of enemies, from kulaks to "socially harmful elements," "anti-Soviet elements," and enemies in the ranks of the Party itself.

The official discourse of the regime was that it was the most popular in the world. The Communist way to explain industrial accidents or deviant social behavior was to attribute the causes to persons who were "alien infiltrators." Those with the "wrong" social or political background had ingrained anti-Soviet attitudes that they had "masked" or hidden. Ultimately, the only way to end their opposition was to kill them or put them in concentration camps, from which they were unlikely to return.[35]

Stalin was the main mover and organizer of the terror, made the key decisions, and often saw their implementation through. He relished hearing the details of the tortures and the last minute pleas uttered by the condemned. Although other leaders like Molotov, Voroshilov, and Kaganovich certainly played their part in the Great Terror, recent research shows that overwhelmingly it was Stalin who was its author.[36] The repression and outright murder of hundreds of thousands of completely innocent people revealed the dictatorship in all its horror. Nevertheless, true believers at the time, and ever since, found ways to rationalize it and to support it in the name of the higher cause.

MAKING WAY FOR NEW PEOPLE

One of the ways people found to participate in this system was by sending letters to the authorities. Letters of denunciation were sent to all the top leaders, including Stalin, who took a keen interest in them. Not just ordinary citizens but leaders down the line wrote to bring a superior or boss to his attention. If Stalin did not like the person who was denounced, he sent the incriminating letter to the NKVD with a note to investigate. If he was more positively disposed, he simply kept the letter for his files. This was the dictator's greatest power.

Party members completely in tune with Stalin became serial denouncers and wrote him so regularly as to win a place in his heart. Polia Nikolaenko, resident of Kiev, is said to have denounced thousands, many of whom paid with their lives. Kiev Party bosses treated her with disdain, but Stalin, under the iron rule that if there was smoke there was fire, came to her aid when she complained of being ignored. Ukrainian leaders were told to "pay attention to Comrade Nikolaenko" and protect her.[37]

Nikita Khrushchev was in some ways typical of how Party leaders became enthusiasts for terror. As Party boss of Moscow, he thundered in August 1937 to a Party conference that "scoundrels must be destroyed." Khrushchev was ruthless; by the time he finished, only 3 leaders were left of 38 in Moscow's city and Party organizations, and 10 Party secretaries in the wider Moscow district remained out of 146. He happily exceeded the quota, set by the Politburo on June 27, of 35,000 "enemies" to be repressed; within two weeks he told Stalin he had already picked up 41,305 "criminal and kulak elements." Out of these, he personally assigned 8,500 "to the first category," as the expression went, that is, they were to be executed.

Khrushchev's reasoning was as follows: "In destroying one, two, or ten of them, we are doing the work of millions. That's why our hand must not tremble, why we must march across the corpses of the enemy toward the good of the people."[38]

Some of the fears that fueled the purges may have been motivated by a panic to eliminate a fifth column of possible traitors in a time when the threats of war were growing. The sheer scale of the repressions indicates, however, that the process got completely out of control and lost any rational foundation it might have had.[39]

The press played up the show trials in the provinces. The coverage seems to have deflected blame away from Stalin and onto the shoulders of lower-range leaders. Even some of the victims blamed the "little Stalins" for what was going wrong.

Unlike the great show trials, local ones easily found plausible charges and gave citizens an opportunity to redress wrongs suffered at the hands of abusive or incompetent administrators. This populist side of the terror targeted the elites and likely won the regime support. Not just political bosses but managers and foremen were called to account. Workforces in factories and on collective farms were brought into the trials to bear witness, and everything possible was done to publicize the events.

Members of the Party or its affiliations who were denounced engaged in "self-criticism" meetings that turned into purges of the soul. Children were cajoled in meetings of the Komsomol to defame arrested parents. Any Communists who might have previously supported Trotsky or Bukharin were endangered and were lucky if they were merely expelled from the Party.[40]

The Commission for Judicial Affairs of the Politburo determined in advance what the sentences would be of the more prominent people. The names of members or leaders of the Party, or well-known figures in industry, the army, or arts and culture, who were brought to court were submitted on lists to Stalin. He personally signed 362 of these lists, as the ultimate judge, juror, and executioner. It should be noted that other members of the Politburo were involved in this practice as well. Thus, Voroshilov signed 195 lists, Kaganovich 191, Andrei Zhdanov 177, and Anastas Mikoyan 62. There were forty-four thousand names on the lists submitted to these men, and thirty-nine thousand were condemned to death.[41]

The Party's Central Committee was hit hard. By the time of the Party congress in March 1939, the 139 members elected in 1934 were reduced to 32 full and candidate members. Ninety-four had been executed; one had been assassinated; four died by their own hand and five of natural causes; and three were still in prison. Members of the Central Committee elected before 1934 (but not reelected that year) went from ninety-five to forty-four during the purge. All in all, close to 70 percent of the entire Central Committee was wiped out.[42]

As for the Party itself, by one accounting, 60 percent of the members in 1933 were gone by the beginning of 1939. Some 1.8 million were expelled, and 1 million new ones were recruited. In the process, the Party was transformed into a more Stalinist institution than ever before.[43] If this was indeed the intent behind letting the purges go so far, Stalin could hardly have been unhappy.

At the local level, this process took on a momentum of its own. Stalin may well have been surprised by the scale of the terror, but he had a hardness and resiliency that defies the imagination, and it certainly fits his profile that he would seize any and all opportunities to outwit his foes and rid himself of troublemakers. The so-called Old Bolsheviks, with their ideas of Party "democracy" or at least of open discussion of the issues, had long been a thorn in Stalin's side. The purges functioned to remove many of them once and for all and to bring in more enthusiastic new people who had the energy needed to carry the revolution forward and in just the way Stalin wanted.[44]

The terror in the 1930s was without precedent. Various estimates of the numbers arrested during that decade range up to 3.5 million and beyond. In 1937 alone, 936,750 people were arrested, of whom 790,665 were "convicted." Astoundingly, 353,074 of these people were shot, and 429,311 were sent to the Gulag or prison. In 1938, the number of arrests fell to 638,509, but the executions, at 328,618, did not decrease significantly. That year another 205,509 people were consigned to the Gulag or prison.[45] These official figures underestimate the full extent of the fatalities in many ways and, for example, do not include the hundreds of thousands who died in the Gulag or in exile.

No single agency counted all the arrests or registered the deaths and executions, so we are still trying to reconstruct what happened. A conservative and careful estimate (that is admittedly incomplete, but based on all the available documents) now puts the number of those killed in the 1930s at around two million.[46]

PART SIX

HITLER'S WAR AGAINST DEMOCRACY

18

WINNING OVER THE NATION

The new Hitler cabinet gathered at 5:00 in the afternoon on January 30, 1933. Some ministers met the chancellor for the first time, but they all knew what he stood for, including racism, anti-Marxism, rabid nationalism, and a desire to rearm. Hitler was permitted to have only two other members of his Party in his cabinet, namely Wilhelm Frick (minister of the interior) and Hermann Göring (who was put in charge of the Prussian Ministry of the Interior). The others were conservative figures, and, interestingly enough, it was from that quarter that the most radical initial demands came.

CABINET CONSENSUS AND POPULAR APPLAUSE

The meeting agreed that if new elections were called (as was all but certain), the composition of the cabinet would remain unchanged. That was a demand of Alfred Hugenberg, head of the German National People's Party (DNVP) and the minister of economics and agriculture. He had insisted on this point as the final condition for agreeing to Hitler's chancellorship.

Hitler's animosity toward the Communists was well known, and without his having to say a word, Hugenberg and others argued for banning the KPD immediately. There was agreement in principle on getting rid of that Party, the only issue being one of timing. On Hitler's advice and out of fear they might spark a general strike, they held their fire. Their goal was to ensure that the government would win the majority needed to pass an enabling law—that is, a measure that would make the Reichstag redundant.

There was an unsuccessful attempt to avoid new elections. At Franz von Papen's insistence, Hitler agreed to negotiate with two leaders of the Catholic Center Party to try to bring them into the "government of national concentration," as it was called. In a meeting on January 31, the Catholics balked when Hitler mentioned a yearlong "adjournment" of the Reichstag. He broke off negotiations, and new elections were on the agenda, subject to President Hindenburg's consent.

Later that day when Hitler told the cabinet of this result, Papen sought assurances "that the coming election to the Reichstag would be the last one and a return to the parliamentary system would be avoided forever." Papen—a man in the cabinet supposedly to keep the radical Hitler in check—had in fact believed for some time that a holiday from democracy was necessary.[1]

Before Hitler and Papen approached the president, they agreed that the new Reichstag would be asked to pass an enabling law, a constitutional change that needed a two-thirds majority. The law would be in effect for four years. They told Hindenburg of this plan and their hope that elections would bring the desired result.

The president agreed to call new elections for March 5, the earliest possible date. Hitler told the cabinet of this decision and presented them with the government's slogan for the campaign, "Attack on Marxism," a call to arms that everyone in the government could embrace with enthusiasm.

What would be different about the March 5 election was that it was designed to mobilize support for the already existing government, not to create a new one. When the Reichstag was dissolved, there was a transition to a novel "experiment" in "dictatorship based on plebiscites."[2] There were, therefore, to be many more elections and plebiscites after

March 1933, but they, too, were opportunities for the nation to acclaim its support for the government. The new regime would become a hybrid, a "consensus dictatorship."

The centerpiece of the Nazi election appeal was the enabling law, supposedly needed to deal swiftly with Germany's dire crisis. The Reichstag could not do so, it was argued, because it was too slow and cumbersome.

APPEALS TO THE NATION

Already by the second meeting of his cabinet, on the evening of February 1, Hitler produced a draft of an address to the German nation, to be delivered on the radio at ten o'clock.

The speech itself revealed something of the government's aims, but it was stock-in-trade Hitler, beginning with the lecture about the "discord and hatred" befalling the people since the fateful day of November 9, 1918. It hit the anti-Bolshevik note from beginning to end: "Fourteen years of Marxism have undermined Germany. One year of Bolshevism would destroy Germany. The richest and most beautiful areas of world civilization would be transformed into chaos and a heap of ruins. Even the misery of the past decade and a half could not be compared with the affliction of a Europe in whose heart the red flag of destruction had been planted." Hitler and the nationalist leaders were not going to let that happen; he declared a "merciless war against spiritual, political, and cultural nihilism. Germany must not and will not sink into Communist anarchy."

There was one vital precondition for the political and economic revival of the nation: "We must overcome the demoralization of Germany by the Communists." That requirement could only be achieved by moving beyond outlawing the Party to reorganizing the economy with two four-year plans. When Papen had first heard these phrases, he had remarked that they sounded too much like Stalin's five-year plans, but Hitler wanted to give a time frame. His two main points were, first, to rescue the German farmer from poverty and secure the agricultural basis of national life and, second, to aid the worker by a "massive and comprehensive attack on unemployment."

This language had to impress desperate farmers and people without jobs who wanted to hear their government commit to programs and deadlines. Hitler offered immediate steps, like introducing a labor service and settlement policy for farmers, and gave them the assurances they wanted. The government would take all necessary measures to get the economy moving and to put state finances on a sound footing.

He also spoke of the public good: "We men of this government feel responsible to German history for the reconciliation of a proper body politic so that we may finally overcome the insanity about class and of class warfare." Sounding like the kaiser on the eve of the First World War, Hitler said: "We do not recognize classes, but only the German people, its millions of farmers, citizens, and workers who together will either overcome this time of distress or succumb to it." He ended with the main election appeal: "The Marxist parties and their fellow travelers had fourteen years to prove their abilities. The result is a heap of ruins. Now, German people, give us four years and then judge us."[3]

The speech was not as vacuous as is often suggested, and many who lived through the times found it so effective that they refused to believe Hitler had written it. They thought someone else, perhaps an obscure backer or someone like Papen, must have put it together. Max Domarus, who at the time collected Hitler's speeches and proclamations, was struck by how often Hitler was underestimated and called it "absurd" to imagine he did not write his own material.[4]

Hitler recorded the speech and had it played on the radio as the "Appeal of the Reich Government to the German People." Within hours of his appointment he was at home among more experienced politicians and statesmen. Far from "forcing his will on a startled Cabinet," as one account has it, there was a remarkable degree of agreement.[5] His colleagues and not just Hitler wanted to eliminate what was left of parliamentary democracy and pursue the Marxists, whose civil and legal rights they were all willing to curtail. Moreover, right from the outset the government had far more backing than is often assumed. The only significant opposition came from the working-class movement, which, thanks to guidance from Moscow to the German Communists, was too divided to be effective.

ELITE SUPPORT FOR THE NEW CHANCELLOR

Within a week, social consensus in support of Hitler's new government was reflected in the officer corps, which was easily won over, despite their conservative Prussian traditions. General Werner von Blomberg, a well-known figure, was made the new minister of defense, chosen by the circle around Hindenburg to look after the interests of the Reichswehr. He was assisted by a new head of the Ministerial Office, Colonel Walther von Reichenau. Although Hitler had nothing to do with these appointments, he could hardly have wished for more. Their support was already a foregone conclusion.[6]

Blomberg was smitten when he first met Hitler in August 1930. His predisposition in favor of National Socialism was influenced by his divisional chaplain, Joseph Müller, and his (then) chief of staff, Reichenau. Blomberg concluded that with the support of the people, Hitler could do for the German army what Stalin did for his, namely turn it into a national institution.

Hitler spoke briefly with Blomberg on January 30, and the two saw eye to eye at once. Blomberg mentioned he had visited the Soviet Union and United States and had become convinced that modern armed forces had to be based on "broad industrial mobilization." In future, he said, the air force would play the dominant role—even at the cost of the regular army. Reichenau was even more sympathetic to Nazism and had talked earlier with Hitler. Blomberg and Reichenau were reputed to be "the most gifted and modern-thinking senior officers" in the country, and Hitler was quick to see the fruitful prospects of having these two in charge, both interested in transforming the armed forces and sharing his view of a National Socialist future.[7]

It was an illusion for Hindenburg to believe that making Blomberg the defense minister would put the Reichswehr in the hands of an "apolitical" officer.[8] In fact the old man himself had already been won over, and he vouched for Hitler on February 17 in a meeting with Fritz Schaeffer of the Bavarian People's Party. Schaeffer was concerned that the new chancellor might try to remove the individual German state's rights, but was assured the country was in good hands. Hindenburg said that "after initial reservation, he had in Herr Hitler come to know a man of the most honorable national will and he was now quite happy that the leader of this great movement was working with him and the other groups of the right."[9]

The officer corps as a whole responded warmly to Hitler's appointment. Young officers in particular accepted it either with "satisfaction" or with "enthusiasm." They were pleased that a "military-friendly" government would be in power and concentrate "all national elements." Hitler's political program, from the battle against Marxism to the renewal of Germany as a great power, matched perfectly with the wishes of the armed forces.

Grand Admiral Erich Raeder thought his own response was typical. He testified after the war: "I welcomed the energetic personality, because he was clearly very intelligent; he had at his disposal incredible willpower, and was a master in leading men. In my opinion he was a great and talented politician in the first years, whose national and social aims were already known for years, and which found an echo in the armed forces as well as among the German people."[10]

The enthusiasm of many younger officers can perhaps be gleaned from an incident in Bamberg, a small Bavarian town, on the evening of January 30, 1933. An enthusiastic parade formed, celebrating the Hitler government, when a young lieutenant in uniform joyfully jumped out in front of the crowd to lead it. He was later mildly reprimanded by his superior officers, but boasted to his comrades "that the great soldiers of the time of the Wars of Liberation [from Napoleon] would have shown more sympathy with such a genuine rising of the people." The young lieutenant was Claus Schenk Graf von Stauffenberg, the man who, as part of the resistance movement eleven years later, tried to assassinate Hitler.[11] In January 1933 and well into the Third Reich, however, it was taken as a given that young officers like Stauffenberg supported the new government, including its nonmilitary goals. A distant relative remembered being surprised when she heard of his involvement in the assassination attempt in 1944, since she had considered him "the only real National Socialist in the family."[12]

The senior ranks of the military were somewhat disconcerted by Hitler's lowly social origins, political style, and violent methods, and his revolutionary aims did not fit with their conservatism. However, they put their reservations aside to have, as they said, a "real chancellor" again. They wanted someone like Hitler to restore what they called a "power state." Hence the attitude even of many older officers has been described as "positive-friendly, largely uncritical" toward Hitler's appointment. "National" to the military had meant "standing on the right," and with an extreme right-winger in power they were bound to be sympathetic. Opinions no doubt varied and changed over time, but through all such differentiations Blomberg's and Reichenau's attitudes were quite representative.[13]

On February 3, Blomberg briefed a meeting of group and district commanders in the Defense Ministry and mentioned the "frenzy of enthusiasm" (*Begeisterungsrausch*) engulfing Germany. As he saw it, the cabinet was an "expression of broad national will and the realization of what many people have been seeking for years. Admittedly, it only represents a minority of the nation, but a firmly formed minority counting millions, who are determined to live and, if need be, to die for their idea. Great possibilities result from this if the leading figures show firmness and skill."[14]

At a dinner held that same evening at the home of the commander in chief of the army, General Kurt von Hammerstein-Equord, Hitler spoke for two hours and gave what was in fact an abbreviated sketch of the Third Reich to come. His domestic aim was to "exterminate Marxism root and branch" and create the "tightest authoritarian state leadership." He yearned to remove "the cancer of democracy." The people as a whole and especially youth had to become aware that "only struggle can save us and that everything else must be subordinated to this idea."

He wanted to reintroduce a military draft. This he saw as crucial to building up the armed forces, but it also had to be linked with a program of toughening up German culture. He told them the country had to get rid of pacifist, Marxist, Bolshevik ideas that corrupted the spirit of the men even before they were drafted. He was firmly in favor of the army; there would be no fusion with his Party's SA. He also said they had a choice about how to use the renewed military: either fighting for new possibilities for exports or, better still, making Germany into a "continental great power." The new military should be used for "the conquest of new lebensraum in the east and its ruthless Germanization."[15]

The idea of "ruthless Germanization" was vague, but it sounded the first note of far-reaching plans for the east. Hitler left Germany's top generals in no doubt about his agenda, which went well beyond tearing up the Treaty of Versailles. His words suggested that he already wanted a racial war of aggression in the east: What else would "ruthless German-ization" mean?[16]

On February 20 he gave another presentation to around twenty-five leading industrialists who had been invited to Göring's official residence for a chat. This time the focus was on economics and the domestic scene. Industrialists like Gustav Krupp von Bohlen and Halbach of the Krupp steel and coal works went along. Hitler wanted to be clear about where he stood on economic issues: like them, he was for private property, free enterprise, and the role of the "selected" in society, and he shared his guests' grave concerns about Socialism and especially Bolshevism. He said the turning point in Germany's history had arrived; the country had to decide whether it was going to support the existing order or go Communist.

Domestic peace and economic recovery would come about only

> if Marxism is finished off. Therein lies the decision that we have to face and where the struggle is still so difficult. I put my life into the struggle daily, as do those who stand with me in this struggle. There are only two possibilities: either we drive the enemy [Marxism] back on the basis of the constitution—hence for that reason the current election—or the struggle will have to be fought with other weapons that perhaps will cost more victims. I would really like to see this avoided. Hopefully the German people will recognize the importance of the moment, because they will decide over the next ten, yes, perhaps one hundred years.

Krupp replied that it was "high time to create clarity on domestic political questions in Germany" and that a strong state would foster the economy. There was no hint of disagreement, and any that did exist would have paled in the face of the mounting concern they all shared about the dangers of Marxism.[17]

When Hitler left, Göring asked for financial help for the coming elections. He pointed out that the SA was involved in street fights with the Communists and getting killed and suggested that the industrialists could help out with funds.

It was a milestone meeting and "the first significant material contribution by organized big business interests to the Nazi cause." Giving the money may have been less than "wholly voluntary," but it is an overstatement to suggest it was a "mild foretaste of the political extortion" to come. Their responsibility was hardly "mitigated" because they did not realize a one-party dictatorship was in the plans. In fact, Göring told them the election would be the last for many years.[18] Krupp and many other industrialists were comfortable with Hitler on most issues and found ways to work with his regime to their mutual benefit. The Krupp firm began to show profits again, and the rearmament program, a cornerstone of Nazi economic policy, paid handsome dividends for firms that were part of it.[19]

Many German princes and other aristocrats supported the Party before and after 1933. A recent study shows the names of 279 members of the high nobility, some of recent vintage, in the Party, and that list is by no means complete. Although after 1945 many came up with exculpatory reasons for their commitment, it was likely the case that they, like Prince Philipp von Hessen, joined up "in an outpouring of idealistic sentiment according to the so-called National Socialist world view—something along the lines of Hitler's speeches, Hitler's *Mein Kampf*," and other Nazi writings. The ostentatious appearance of so many from high society in Nazi garb likely helped to give the Party and the Third Reich an added air of respectability.[20]

THE BROADER PUBLIC

There was no organized protest and little unorganized resistance to Hitler's appointment and the beginning of the new regime. Many conservatives were fed up with the old Socialist-inspired system, an economy in shambles, and disorder on the streets, and they looked forward to a more disciplined society. It was certainly true that "many apolitical Germans were relieved that the long-drawn-out government crisis was over, and no doubt greeted its resolution with hopeful expectations."[21]

Middle-class professional groups such as physicians welcomed "the new regime with high hopes, expecting it to redress anomalies left over from the health administration of the Weimar Republic." The Great Depression badly affected the medical profession, particularly young doctors trying to set up their practices. The Third Reich was going to be race and health conscious, and the doctors guessed they would prosper. Their chances of doing well went up further in 1935, when Jewish physicians were forced out. It was no accident that doctors rushed to join the Nazi Party with greater alacrity than members of any of the other professions.[22]

During the election campaign Hitler presented a rosy picture of the future and tried to pump up spirits. On February 11 he addressed the International Automobile and Motorcycle Exhibition in Berlin, the first time anyone as important as a chancellor had opened such an event. He said the automobile industry would, with the airplane, lead the way into the future. His plans to help included giving tax relief, building up Germany's highway network, and backing motor-sport events. The image he presented here was of the progressive thinker. He said he was not just business-friendly, but had a vision of a technologically based economy that would be good for all.[23] He reminded these industrialists about what they owed Germany's unemployed people and told them he took no salary as head of government. By May 1 he had announced a road-building scheme and by the end of June had put Fritz Todt in charge. He swept aside objections, latched onto plans, and pushed them through. As America showed, the automobile and highways caught the imagination and were enormously popular.[24]

He vindicated the support of companies like Daimler-Benz, whose chairman wrote in May 1932: "We have no occasion to diminish the attention which we have until now afforded Herr Hitler and his friends; he will be able to rely on us in the future, as in the past."[25] Hitler had plans for introducing the Volkswagen, the people's car. If none went into mass production at this time, his grand visions got people hoping again.[26]

He continued to hammer away on the theme of fighting and beating Communism. There was a broad anti-Communist consensus among the middle classes, and it extended into rural areas as well.

Alfred Hugenberg took immediate steps to help farmers, many of them DNVP supporters. Hitler himself had long maintained that a healthy agricultural sector was vital to the well-being of the country. There would be no Bolshevik-style nationalizations here. The landowners' main interest group, the Reichslandbund (Reich Agrarian League), was already predisposed to Hitler's Party, and the new regime almost immediately raised import duties on food and helped indebted farmers. That won even more support.[27]

The anti-Communist sentiment in the air was embraced by the

Catholic faithful, who nevertheless withheld their vote from the Nazi Party in March 1933. There was considerable support for Hitler in the working class, certainly for solving economic problems and curing unemployment. There was near-universal agreement on dealing with the great national issue plaguing the country since 1919, namely the Treaty of Versailles.

Some people were of two minds, pulled in one way by hope, pushed in another out of fear of what might come next. There was no unitary response to Hitler's regime at the beginning, but a common theme in the diaries and letters of the time was that he should be given a chance.

The reaction on the radical left was the exact opposite. In Berlin at the conclusion of the triumphal Nazi procession on January 30, there were clashes with the Communists, and one SA leader and a policeman were killed. In other parts of Germany, Communists demonstrated the next day. Sometimes things got out of hand, and outbursts of violence had to be broken up by police. These were isolated acts and not part of a centrally directed campaign.

"STRUGGLE AGAINST THE RED TERROR"

On January 31, in a meeting with Goebbels, Hitler laid down guidelines for the "struggle against the Red terror." In the short term, "we want to avoid direct countermeasures. The Bolshevik attempt at revolution must first flame up. At the appropriate moment we will then strike." Hitler was biding his time in expectation that Communists, lulled into a false sense of security, would take provocative steps. He would then have the authority to react harshly and would eliminate them and all other "Marxists." He believed that the same kind of approach had to be taken to any resistance from state and local governments in Germany, as well as the "Jewish press." Responding to such provocations in the name of law and order would be widely applauded and politically successful.[28]

The Nazis played up the significance of clashes between the SA and the Communists. On February 5, Hitler, Goebbels, and other top Party officials attended the Berlin funeral of the SA leader and the policeman who had been shot by the Communists on January 30. It was a cold and rainy winter day, but an estimated 600,000 people lined the streets for the funeral. It was, Goebbels noted, the first time that the SA and the police stood together.[29]

Göring could not resist moving against some police leaders and pushed out those unsympathetic to the Nazi cause. He banned demonstrations by Communists and suspended the Socialists' main newspaper for three days. Besides harassing the opposition, he tackled the state's institutions, but there was no "purge" of the police on the Soviet model. Most of those forced out were replaced not by die-hard Nazis but by "conservative and nationalist government experts, and to some extent conservatively inclined landowners from the nobility, former officers, and industrial managers."[30]

Göring suggested the cabinet take immediate action to rein in the Communists, whose violence in the streets was increasing, and on February 4 they agreed to issue an emergency "Decree of the Reich President for the Protection of the German People." It had been substantially prepared by the Papen government and imposed strict regulations on public meetings and demonstrations of all kinds. Suspects could be held in custody for up to three months. The application of this decree was still limited, but it marked the beginning of the erosion of civil and legal rights.[31]

On February 15, Göring instructed Prussian police to stop keeping Nazi organizations under surveillance. A week later he authorized the creation of "deputy police" (*Hilfspolizei*) from the ranks of the SA, the SS, and the Stahlhelm. News stories said measures had to be introduced to protect public security and private property against Communism. But soon the KPD and SPD were faced with Nazis who had been deputized as police.[32]

The Reds waited for the Nazis to do something patently illegal, but nothing happened to justify calling a general strike or even mass demonstrations. The hand-to-hand fighting with the SA continued in February much as before, and there was no sudden switch to "Nazi terror" or open "murder" of working-class activists. Certainly some members of the KPD and SPD were killed in street battles, and so were some innocent bystanders. It was surely the case that police intervened with relish against the KPD, even opening fire on the crowds when (rarely) the occasion demanded. But the police were by no means under Nazi control from the outset.[33]

It was already long past midnight when Communist Party leaders finally tried to reach agreement with the Socialist Party, but the efforts to form a united front failed. A last try by the KPD leader, Ernst Thälmann, in an open letter of February 27 "to the Social Democratic and Christian workers of Germany," was ignored. The years of bitter struggle and acrimony within the working-class movement made cooperation impossible. The Socialists thought a strike would be used as an excuse by the government to destroy the trade unions and other workers' organizations. In the end one left-wing party blamed the other for making Hitler possible.[34]

The critic Carl von Ossietzky wrote that the supporters of the republic lost because they lacked the will to live. He said that the political right outmaneuvered the left by its "cold, hard will to power and its feel for the issues that really matter." Thus the right "conquered the high ground without having to fire a shot."[35]

The liberal middle classes may have been struck by "icy horror" when they heard Hitler was appointed, but some consoled themselves that he could not last long. They wrongly concluded that Hitler had been "captured" by more experienced politicians and badly miscalculated his popular support.[36]

In the March elections Hitler used the office of chancellor as a prestige factor and presented himself as Germany's savior. His campaign echoed all the themes of the previous two or three years, with even stronger emphasis on the war with Marxism. The gatherings were packed wherever he went, and the speeches were often carried live on national radio. He talked about creating a "community of the people" in which the German worker was no longer a stranger, and he appealed to those who might be fleeing from the Nazi Party. He was sure he could turn them around once they saw that what he really wanted was in their best interests.[37]

19

DICTATORSHIP BY CONSENT

The door was opened for the establishment of one-party rule in Germany when, late on February 27, 1933, a fire broke out in the Reichstag buildings. Police arrested Marinus van der Lubbe, almost certainly the lone culprit, although there has been speculation ever since about who might have set the fire. Whoever did it and whatever the reason, the arson came at a time most favorable to the Nazi cause.

Hitler, Göring, Goebbels, Papen, and the Berlin police chief, Wolf Heinrich Graf von Helldorf, rushed to the scene. According to Rudolf Diels, head of the Prussian Political Police, they seemed sincere in the belief that the arson was an attempt to create chaos and confusion. Göring was filled with emotion. Diels remembered him saying that it was the beginning of a "Communist coup." He also recalled Hitler shouting: "There are no more grounds for mercy; anyone who gets in our way will be slaughtered. The German people will have no understanding for mercy." Overcome with rage, Hitler added that "every Communist functionary will be shot where he is found. The Communist members of parliament must be hanged this very night." He also wanted to pursue the Socialists.[1]

Hitler did not follow through on the threat. Instead, early the next day he prevailed on President Hindenburg to declare a state of emergency and had new measures ready for the cabinet. The Reichstag-fire decree, as it became known, took immediate steps "in defense against Communistic violence endangering the state."[2] This measure suspended constitutional guarantees of personal liberty; allowed police to detain anyone they wished; and imposed restrictions on freedom of expression, assembly, and association. The powers of the national government were extended over the states. The decree also provided the legal basis for creating the secret state police, or Gestapo, as well as the concentration camps. The latter emerged soon after the March elections. In the meantime, state-sponsored violence was used against the paramilitary forces of the Communists and the Socialists.

THE CREATION OF THE ONE-PARTY STATE

The elections held on March 5 did not produce the majority Hitler hoped for. The Nazis won by far the most votes (43.9 percent), and collected 288 seats out of 647. Their allies in the election, the DNVP (Hugenberg's party), picked up 8 percent of the vote and 52 seats. The NSDAP-DNVP coalition thus had a slim majority.

Voters held to the big blocs. The SPD and the two Catholic parties (Center and Bavarian People's) received almost the exact number of votes as in the last elections. Despite pressure on the Communists, they managed to hold on to 81 seats.

It is hard to estimate the extent the votes for the big bloc parties were "against" the Nazis and how many simply reflected traditional loyalties. Safe to say, there was widespread yearning for much that Hitler stood for. He was by far the most popular leader in the country, its most militant anti-Marxist, and viewed by many as the only one able to hold back the Red tide. He also embodied the hope for better times. He won more votes than any party had received since 1920, and the massive numbers in his favor gave the government "plebiscitary legitimacy, which was all the more important in terms of moral backing."[3]

Goebbels considered the election results "fantastic and unbelievable," greater "than we dared to hope." He summed up the enormous support for Hitler and National Socialism as: "The people want it!" On the afternoon of March 6, he met with Hitler to work out details for his ministry, one of the few new ones added in the Third Reich. It was formally called the Ministry of Popular Enlightenment and Propaganda and comprised separate chambers for the press, radio, film, theater, music, the visual arts, and literature. The ministry came to play a considerable role in winning over those citizens who were not already on the Party's side.[4] Hitler's view was that the propaganda would "channel all the energies of the people toward the purely political." It would take time for economic policies to come into effect. In the meantime, he did not want the people to slip into apathy.[5]

The Enabling Law had been on the table since at least November 1932, and it was no secret that the elections of March 5 would be the last for some time. Hitler said at the March 7 cabinet meeting that he regarded the election "as a revolution. Ultimately Marxism will no longer exist in Germany." Papen reported that the leader of the Catholic Center Party was "prepared to let bygones be bygones" and had offered to cooperate in getting the Enabling Law passed.[6]

The arrest or flight of Communist members of the Reichstag made it easier to get the two-thirds majority needed to bring in the Enabling Law as a constitutional amendment. Discussions with the Catholic Center and Bavarian People's parties led to agreement on the new law on March 20, and three days later it was presented to the first meeting of the new Reichstag. To assure support, Hitler promised to respect the rights of the Catholic Church.[7]

The Reichstag opened on March 21 in Potsdam in the famous Garrison Church. The pomp and ceremony of the old president next to the young chancellor conveyed a sense of continuity and hope. The first real business took place on March 23, when Hitler presented the Enabling Law in a special session held at the Kroll Opera House in Berlin. The government declaration began by saying what had gone wrong, above all since November 9, 1918. Just as in Hitler's speeches, it promised a rebirth by way of cleansing the "body politic of its internal defects." The burning of the Reichstag was taken as a failed signal to start a Communist revolution. The government would not stop until such threats were completely "exterminated and destroyed." The ultimate goal was to end conflict and create a "genuine community of the people."[8]

Passage of the Enabling Law meant the end of the constitution, states' rights, and other pillars of democracy. The Catholic Center Party went along. As one of its leaders explained, the "Fatherland is in the gravest danger. We dare not fail."[9]

The government allowed two hours for the Reichstag to decide and granted the right to speak to anyone who disagreed. Only Otto Wels of the SPD took up the challenge. The vote was 441 in favor and 94 against the law. It was to remain in force until April 1, 1937, when it had to be renewed.[10]

Goebbels observed in his diary: "Now we are also constitutionally the masters of the Reich." Not only was the Reichstag redundant, but within the cabinet Hitler's authority was soon accepted by acclamation. As early as April 22 — referring by then to Hitler as the führer — Goebbels noted that there was no longer any voting in the cabinet. "The führer decides. Everything is going much faster than we had dared to dream."[11]

Once the Enabling Law was passed, the political parties were soon dissolved, beginning in mid-March on the left wing of the political spectrum with the KPD. On April 17, Hitler met with Goebbels and opted to take on the trade unions, long the pillar of the Socialist working-class movement. The May 1 holiday tradition to celebrate the struggles of ordinary workers would go ahead, but instead of highlighting class struggle, it would be modified to celebrate all Germans and to give them a chance to express their national will. Immediately following the holiday, the unions would be taken over. Goebbels noted that there might be some "noise" for a few days, but that would pass, and "then they belong to us." Moreover, "once we have the unions in our hand, then the other parties and organizations will not be able to hold out for long." He expected no resistance, and next to none took place.[12]

A flimsy excuse was found to ban the SPD on June 22. By the end of the month the two remaining liberal parties and even Hitler's DNVP partners, recognizing the inevitable, had disbanded themselves. Finally, on July 5, the Catholic Center Party followed suit.[13]

July 14, 1933, can be taken as the day of the last steps in the "coordination" process and was meant to mark the end of a long era dating back to the storming of the Bastille on July 14, 1789. The day was celebrated as the beginning of the French Revolution and became the symbolic opening of the modern era of the "brotherhood of man." The universal ideals of "liberty, equality, and fraternity" proclaimed by the French also inspired Lenin, Stalin, and the Bolshevik Revolution.

It was therefore something of a statement that on July 14, 1933, the Hitler cabinet reeled off forty-two laws, meant to spell the end of the "brotherly" era. Also passed was the Law for the Prevention of Defective Offspring, which formed the basis of a new sterilization program.

In addition, a new law on plebiscites was enacted. This mechanism made it possible to pass laws and other measures by direct appeal to the people. The events became devices Hitler used to show his popular backing, and they encapsulate the concept of his "plebiscitary dictatorship."[14]

TERROR AND ACCOMMODATION

Concentration camps, initially for Communists, were widely publicized and designed to appeal to the strong anti-Communist phobia in the country. Even Socialists, longtime rivals for the hearts of workers, were "full of enthusiasm for the struggle against Communism and Bolshevism, with which they identified the creation of anarchy."[15] The anti-Communist campaign was supplemented by an attack on hard-core criminals. Hitler shared the popular distaste for sex offenders and the like, and by cracking down on them, he appealed to the German tradition of law and order.

How much terror was there in the beginning? If we include temporary sites where victims were held briefly and tortured but not necessarily arrested, the number of victims was large. One recent account lists over 160 places used in 1933.[16] We can only guess how many were dragged through them. In the first wave of arrests in March and April 1933, an estimated twenty-five thousand people, mainly Communists, were picked up in Prussia alone.[17] It is likely that there were as many again in the rest of the country. A small number of women, mostly Communists, were sent to the camps beginning in March 1933 and held in Gotteszell (Baden). There were two Communist women at another camp in Moringen, near Göttingen, in early June 1933, and by autumn there were seventy-five women prisoners.[18]

In the summer of 1933 a new wave of arrests picked up some leaders of recently disbanded political parties. On July 31 a camp census counted a total of 26,789 prisoners. Suspects, most in left-wing parties, were taken to a concentration camp for a short time, mistreated, and released. A total of about 80,000 spent time in a concentration camp in all the early camps. These figures do not include the many who were beaten by the SA or Party radicals in improvised torture cellars, which were soon dissolved. Most of the victims, like those sent to the early camps, had been involved in the Communist Party and, to a lesser extent, the Social Democratic Party or the trade unions.

There were fatalities, but these were "relatively few," and, with the emphasis on one group, namely the Communists, they make it hard to agree with those who insist that the Third Reich was established and maintained by terror. Karin Orth's recent study shows that even now it remains difficult to determine the exact number killed in the early camps of 1933–34, but she—as well as most other specialists—puts the figure at "several hundred."[19]

Coercion and violence were limited and predictable and thus different from the arbitrary and sweeping terror of the Soviet Union. Hitler set out to combine popularity and power and aimed terror at specific groups of "outsiders." Those who came to support his regime, and that was the great majority, accepted the harsh approach to these "others" as part of the bargain. Citizens could read the abundant stories in the press, and even if they assumed these were cleaned-up versions of the truth, it was easy to look the other way and give the government the benefit of the doubt. The Soviet Union, on the other hand, endured massive terror from the outset, then a civil war, followed by sustained terror.

The images of the German camps portrayed in the press as anti-Communist institutions helped to ease popular accommodation to the new system. While some worried about them, concerns were partly allayed because of the perceived Communist threat and breakdown in law and order.

The Nazis had grown so confident about their support from the population by the end of 1933 that they seriously considered getting rid of both the Gestapo and the camps. Hitler played down the "excesses" in the camps and only said some enemies had had to be interned to stop them from interfering with Germany's political rebirth.[20]

The numbers confined were steadily reduced until the end of 1934, when there were "at most" three thousand prisoners. That was the lowest point they would ever reach.[21] Nearly all camps had closed by 1934–35, when Hitler's dictatorship was firmly anchored.

How did ordinary citizens as a whole react to this first wave of arrests? Apart from those directly threatened, as Ian Kershaw concludes, "the violence and repression were widely popular." It did not bother many Germans that the Reichstag-fire decree took away the rights of Communists. In fact, the decree was "warmly welcomed."[22]

"MARCH CASUALTIES"

Sebastian Haffner, who lived in Berlin during those times, believes that if there had been elections only three weeks after March 5, the Nazis would have obtained "a true majority." Many Germans were shifting their support to the Nazis. Haffner's observations are backed up by the fact that millions were rushing to join the Nazi Party or one of its associated organizations.

This increase in support, according to Haffner, was not "the result of the terror, or intoxication resulting from the constant festivities (though the Germans like being intoxicated by patriotic celebrations)." Apart from the bandwagon effect, and the attractiveness of getting in on the spoils, some wanted to be part of a larger movement, to be unified at last and comrades in a mighty cause. The snobbish Haffner looked down on the "more primitive, inarticulate, simpler souls" who switched sides when their "tribe" was beaten. "Saint Marx," in whom workers and other folk once believed, he said sarcastically, "had not helped. Saint Hitler was obviously more powerful. So let's destroy the images of Saint Marx on the altars and replace them with the images of Saint Hitler. Let us learn to pray: 'It is the Jews' fault' rather than 'It is the capitalists' fault.' Perhaps that will redeem us."[23]

In 1930 there were 129,583 Nazi Party members, but registration jumped in early 1933 to 849,009 until in May the Party itself called a (temporary) halt and would accept no new members. When the ban was later lifted, a steady stream from all classes signed on, and by the early war years there were more than 5 million card-carrying members.[24] There was a flood of joiners to the other Nazi mass organizations, such as the storm troopers (SA). There were nearly a half-million members in August 1932; exactly two years later that number approached three million.[25]

Women joined the National Socialist Women's Group (NS-

Frauenschaft), which was more of an elite organization. At the end of 1932 it had a membership of 110,000, which grew to almost 850,000 a year later and increased to over 1.5 million in the course of 1934. The mass-oriented German Women's Enterprise (Deutsches Frauenwerk) was founded in September 1933 as an umbrella organization for all other women's organizations that had been dissolved. It had 2.7 million members by 1935, and by 1938, with nearly 4 million, it was the largest non-compulsory organization in the country.[26]

Women adjusted quickly to the new regime and, despite some grumbling, became one of its pillars.[27] In a few years they surpassed men in the degree of their support of the Third Reich.[28] Hans-Ulrich Wehler points out that contrary to what many have been saying for decades, by 1938, if not earlier, the "consensus state" was attained in Germany.[29]

LEGITIMIZING THE NEW REGIME

Hitler had to address several areas of popular concern in order to combine power and popularity. The top priority was to solve the economic problems. As unemployment went down, support for Hitler went up. In fact, with few exceptions, the jobless rate declined every month after Hitler's appointment to November 1938. The Depression had been beaten by 1936, when there even began to be labor shortages.[30]

People in numerous government offices and many ministries were involved in decisions leading to this turnaround, but it all happened on Hitler's watch, and he was given the credit. Jobs and incomes bounced back, and hope was restored, especially among young men and women, who were also offered new state-sponsored programs. In 1935 conscription was reintroduced, and that drew working-age men from the labor market and helped reduce unemployment.[31]

Although there were special new contributions workers had to pay, these were more than offset by new programs. Vacation days went up steadily, from the usual three, to six, and eventually in some cases to fifteen, making German workers on that score the best off in the world. The social insurance schemes (old age, sickness, accident) were retained, improved, and extended to many not previously covered. The new Strength Through Joy organization offered holidays abroad that were heretofore unthinkable for people of the working classes. This became the most popular of all the Nazi programs. It played a role in helping to create "a durable popular legitimacy despite intermittent and deeply felt expression of discontent." What impressed so many was "the attentiveness to the popular quality of life." The regime even tried to clean up and brighten the workplace, and such measures were taken as showing respect for workers.[32]

New government measures combined economics and ideology—for example, the marriage loan scheme brought in for racially fit couples as part of the law on the reduction of unemployment (June 1, 1933). Generous loans were provided on condition that female spouses leave their jobs; the expectation was that a position would be opened for an unemployed male. Women were of central interest to the regime, not simply as potential mothers, as in Fascist Italy, but as mothers of the German race.[33]

Oral histories of the time invariably point to the importance of employment and order as the keys to support for Hitler.[34] Grumbling did not cease but good times were on the way back.[35]

Workers who were in the KPD were harassed. Of the 300,000 members in the KPD in 1933, about half would experience some form of persecution in the course of the Third Reich. The others either changed sides or resigned themselves to the facts and retreated from politics. The SPD and the organizations linked to it (such as the free trade unions) had many more members but, taken together, suffered far less persecution than Communists. Both parties continued to a limited extent in the underground but posed no threat to the regime.[36]

The workers' attitudes were influenced by the return to full employment and the successes Hitler chalked up in foreign affairs. By 1936, he had reached new levels of popularity, also among workers.[37] A handful in the working-class movement engaged in resistance, but only deeply committed radicals continued their rejection of Nazism. Workers despised the Versailles Treaty, and as Hitler tore it up, he undoubtedly hit a nationalist chord among all classes. Recent studies of the resistance have underlined that there was "a great willingness for consensus with the NS-regime, also among the working class."[38]

Facing and defeating the Communist threat in itself gained Hitler a great deal of support. Many believed Communists had attempted to seize power illegally again when they (allegedly) burned down the

Reichstag in 1933. Victor Klemperer, a German-Jewish professor who lived in Dresden at the time, noted in his diary on November 14, 1933, that "all Germany prefers Hitler to the Communists."[39]

LAW-AND-ORDER ISSUES

Many citizens, and not just those in the conservative, religious, or Nazi camps, saw the liberal Weimar Republic as a degenerate society and believed their country was on the road to ruin.[40] Hitler appealed to a longing among good citizens for a more disciplined society of the kind they identified with the era before 1914.[41] From their point of view, the Third Reich marked a pleasant change from the days of disorder.

Some civil servants had their reservations, but with rare exceptions they stayed at their desks. Hitler and others in the Nazi hierarchy feared the civil service might adopt a passive attitude, making their tasks more difficult. The concerns were unfounded; as Hans Mommsen puts it, "There can be no doubt about the willingness of the broad mass of civil servants to serve the new government loyally."[42]

In fact it was the Nazis who acceded to the wishes of the civil service when, on April 7, 1933, the government introduced the Law for the Restoration of the Civil Service. Lurking behind the notion of "restoration" was the thought, shared by many in it, that the institution had been subjected to political tampering. What the civil service wanted was a return to an idealized past in which they served society through apolitical work, undisturbed by politicians. In order to achieve that, they were prepared to accept as a necessary evil that there would be some illegalities in the short term, but only to clean out the bureaucracy.

In practical terms the new law came in handy to dismiss a few political appointees, but it was mainly used to get rid of the Jews. What happened in the Ministry of Justice gives a good impression of the broader developments. There were 45,181 tenured positions in the Prussian justice system in April 1933, of which 1,704 were filled by Jews. In March 1934, when the purge was largely complete, 331 Jews remained—mainly (and temporarily) because of Hindenburg's intervention.[43]

German judges do not seem to have been unusually concerned. While some tried for a time to keep up contact with dismissed colleagues, most were indifferent, as the Nazis calmly moved more "nationally reliable" judges into place.[44] In a country where the civil service plays an important part in everyday life, the "restoration"—not revolution—of its rank and file conveyed the impression of "normality."

The Criminal Police, or Kripo, were given new powers to fight crime. In keeping with Hitler's wishes, a Prussian decree and a federal law in November 1933 dealt with "dangerous habitual offenders." The Kripo could put suspects in "preventive custody" almost at will,[45] and arrest quotas were set for each district.[46] The federal law gave judges power to order the "preventive detention" of persons deemed likely to re-offend, as well as the sterilization of those defined as "dangerous morals offenders" or "dangerous habitual offenders."[47]

In 1934, the first year the new measures came into force, judges ordered the preventive detention of 3,723 habitual criminals. The numbers fell slowly until 1938, when they picked up again.[48] Between 1934 and 1939, judges alone used their new power to incarcerate 26,346 (without trials).[49]

Life on the inside of prisons became far tougher, but this "legal terror" created little alarm among good citizens who generally believed that prisoners should do hard time. The days of "coddling" criminals were over. Police went after the loosely defined group called the "asocials"—or antisocial elements—whose way of life, or even unkempt appearance, offended middle-class values and "wholesome popular sentiment."[50]

Many who lived through the times recall that "specifically when it came to sharper policies toward criminals, there existed between the people and the National Socialist regime a *consensus.*" This conclusion comes from a man (born in 1925) who had a minor brush with the secret police but who later served in the Wehrmacht.[51] There is overwhelming evidence that "fighting crime" and reestablishing "good order" won considerable support for Hitler and his regime.

THE BLOOD "PURGE"

One of the great contrasts between the Nazi and the Russian revolutions was the near absence of purges in Hitler's Germany. His hold on the Party, the state, and the nation was such—and their identification with his ideas so strong—that there was little need to kill off opponents. In the early years, moreover, his ambitions, insofar as they were known, were modest and most Germans agreed with them.

There was one purge of the SA. The organization's unruliness and violence had been an advantage prior to 1933; thereafter such behavior ran up against citizens' concerns about law and order. The nation did not appreciate the vigilante-style operations of the SA as deputy police, and the elites in the military and the economy pointed accusatory fingers at the SA for wanting to become part of the army or for being too "Socialist."

At a meeting on July 6, 1933, Hitler reminded the Reich governors (*Reichsstatthalter*) that revolution was "no permanent condition" and that the revolutionary current had to be "channeled into the secure bed of evolution."[52] In August the role of the SA as deputy police was abolished and funding cut off. This step helped reassure citizens but did not quench the thirst of some in the SA for revolution. But after six months or so in office, Hitler's regime had nothing more to fear from organized resistance, and the immediate worry was how to curb its own radicals.

On February 1, 1934, Ernst Röhm presented plans to the military that would have transformed his SA into an institution akin to a militia alongside the army. Minister of Defense Blomberg was completely opposed. To show his heart was in the right place, and without any pressure being exerted, Blomberg introduced both the swastika and the "Aryan paragraph" into the army—thereby forcing out seventy men presumably "suspect" for being Jews. Hitler informed the SA he would not accept Röhm's plan, and at the same time he asked the secret police to begin assembling information on him.[53]

The issues with the SA festered. On June 17, 1934, former chancellor Papen told an audience at Marburg University that inner peace in Germany had to be restored: "No nation can live in a continuous state of revolution, if it wishes to justify itself before history."[54] Papen may have wanted to mobilize conservative opposition to Hitler, but the chancellor avoided being hemmed in.

Blomberg urged Hitler to do something about the SA when they met briefly on June 21. The most opportune time to act would be before the

SA returned from leave on August 1. The planning was more or less complete on June 28, and early on June 30 Hitler flew from the Rhineland to Munich. He and his entourage went to the hotel on the Tegernsee where Röhm and other SA leaders were staying. Röhm and his men were arrested and not long afterward shot.[55]

An assorted group of others were also executed during what was dubbed the "night of the long knives." Hitler settled scores with former chancellor Kurt von Schleicher and his wife, whose assassination was presented to law-abiding German citizens as necessary to stop an alleged revolt. This claim was baseless, but the killings put an end to any threat to Hitler's near absolute power.

This was the first mass murder in the Third Reich, and no effort was made to conceal the fact that the killings were without a semblance of a trial. Most Germans accepted that Hitler "sentenced" a hundred or so culprits to death.[56] The SA was given a new leader, and while the organization continued to exist, its membership was allowed to dwindle.

Reports on public opinion were unanimous in their approval.[57] Hitler had managed to signal the arrival of political stabilization, and he granted a selective amnesty on August 10. Basking in the goodwill all around him, he used the occasion of Hindenburg's death to publicize the "unification of the office of Reich president with that of Reich chancellor."

Citizens were given an opportunity to express their opinion on August 19, in a plebiscite on Hitler's decision to unite the two offices. Voting in favor was 89.9 percent. The underground opposition was bewildered by the positive popular responses: "(1) The broad mass has not grasped the political meaning of the events. (2) Large, obviously very large sections of the population even celebrate Hitler for his ruthless determination, and only a small section has started thinking or been shocked. (3) Also large sections of the working class have fallen into an uncritical deification of Hitler."[58]

Although Germans could only guess at how many were murdered on the night of the long knives, Socialist underground reporters admitted that the event increased support for Hitler. The action no doubt undermined respect for the law but appealed to those who had "strong sympathies for 'summary justice' and as hard a punishment as possible." As usual, the Socialists chalked up the reaction of the people to "false consciousness."[59]

FIRST FOREIGN POLICY MOVES AND POPULAR OPINION

Hitler's rivals on the international stage could not imagine how wide his ambitions ranged.[60] On October 14, 1933, he took the country out of the League of Nations and used a radio address not only to explain the decision but to contrast the Nazi revolution with the French and Russian revolutions in which countless people were slaughtered. In his revolution, he said, there was so much respect for private property that "not a single pane of glass in a shopwindow was broken, no business was plundered, and no house damaged."[61]

Typical of this "plebiscitary dictatorship," the decision to leave the League was put to the people exactly a month after the event. A resounding 95.1 percent were in favor. This was not a free vote, but even anti-Nazi observers agreed that the results reflected "genuine national enthusiasm." To their chagrin they had to admit to themselves there was "real consensus."[62]

It is worth citing one of the first underground Socialist reports about the plebiscite. Here was what Hitler's opponents had to say about the overwhelmingly positive result:

> Because of the extraordinarily high number of votes in favor of the regime even critical foreign observers were tempted to assume that the numbers had been faked or resulted from direct force and terror. Those assumptions, however, are based on a mistaken perception of the real and profound influence fascist ideology has upon all classes of German society. . . . Careful observations . . . show that the results of the election in general are a true indicator of the mood of the population. Particularly in rural districts and in small villages there may have been many "corrections." The general result indicates an extraordinarily rapid and effective process of fascistization of society.[63]

Another foreign policy success came in early 1935. At Versailles in 1919 the Saarland had been cut off from Germany in the expectation it would join France. The matter was to be decided on January 13, 1935, by a plebiscite among Saarlanders, including Communists from the area who were released from concentration camps to vote (they testified later they were allowed to vote as they wished). The election, run by Swedes to ensure fairness, showed that 90.8 percent favored rejoining Germany, even though they would have known what the Third Reich stood for. There may have been some pressure, but at worst it was moderate and indirect. The result was an important symbolic victory. How bad could it be to live in the Third Reich when Saarlanders voted in such numbers to join it? The return of the Saar soon followed with great pomp and ceremony.[64]

Another symbolically important decision that year was taken on March 16 to introduce the military draft; the expressed intent was to create an army of thirty-six divisions. Germans had felt humiliated at being limited by the Versailles Treaty to an army no larger than a hundred thousand men. Even former supporters of the SPD saw advantages of calling the men to the colors: it would free up jobs for the unemployed, and the expanding army would increase demand for goods and thus help the economy to recover.[65]

Hitler's reintroduction of conscription was greeted the next day by a spontaneous and massive demonstration in Munich. The underground Socialist report reeked of consternation: "The enthusiasm on March 17 enormous. All of Munich is on its feet. One can force a people to sing, but one cannot force them to sing with such enthusiasm. I experienced the days of 1914 and can only say that the declaration of war did not make such a great impression on me as the reception of Hitler on March 17. . . . The trust in the political talent and honest intentions of Hitler is growing ever greater, just as Hitler has again won extraordinary popularity. He is loved by many."[66]

Almost exactly a year later, on March 7, Hitler sent his army across the bridges on the Rhine into what was supposed to be an area free from the German military. France had hoped this part of the Rhineland would be a buffer zone between the two countries. Hitler now boldly broke the terms of the treaty, and the French did nothing. A Reichstag election followed on March 29—another exercise in plebiscitary dictatorship, in which 99 percent gave their support to Hitler. Even if the voting was rigged, there was no question that most of the country embraced the beginning of Germany's return to great-power status. Numerous reports, even from the skeptical Socialist underground, saw nothing "artificial" about the reaction and thought the consensus in favor of Hitler massive.[67]

Hitler took the occasion of the outbreak of the Spanish civil war to remind the nation of the continuing threat of Soviet Bolshevism. Germany supported General Francisco Franco in Spain, while the Soviets took the side of Republicans. At the Nuremberg Party rally on September 9, 1936, Hitler spoke about the Soviet "wire-pullers" and said he was going to make Germany as secure against an attack from the outside as he had made it secure within.[68]

He also announced a four-year plan to prepare for war. He derided the Soviets, who were at the time putting enormous efforts into building a subway system. He said that in the time it took them to build eleven kilometers of subway, Germany built seven thousand kilometers of the autobahn. He scoffed that the Communists could not feed the people, even though Soviet lands were blessed with vast natural resources. The anti-Communist majority in Germany liked to see Hitler running down Stalin.[69]

Behind Hitler's words there was the threat of action. Having evaluated the international situation, he began to press on with his plans. On March 12, 1938, he ordered troops into Austria and brought that country "home into the Reich." Britain, France, and the League of Nations reacted as they had to all previous violations of the Versailles Treaty: they did nothing more than raise a timid protest. The German Socialist underground was doubly disappointed. "It is unfortunately true," they wrote, "that the German people lean toward the use of force. It is also true that the victor-powers of the First World War do everything possible to strengthen their belief in the use of force."[70]

A plebiscite was held on April 10 to give Germans and Austrians an opportunity to express themselves. Ninety-nine percent of Germans and Austrians were in favor of the "reincorporation." The Socialists conceded that the event had "raised and strengthened" Hitler's regime. Even Hitler's former left-wing enemies were pleased. The oppositional Socialist report added, "The national high mood that is registered from Germany is real [echt]."[71] For many Hitler had become "the statesman who completed Bismarck's work."[72] That was the highest compliment good citizens could bestow.

This was not the last of Hitler's bloodless conquests. By September 1938 his demands to "protect" Germans in the Sudetenland—that is, in western Czechoslovakia—had brought Europe to the brink of war. However, Britain and France carried their appeasement policies to the

Munich conference held on September 29–30, where they agreed to Hitler's demands and ceded the territory.

The German people did not want war, and their joy was all the greater when Hitler pulled off the miracle. The Socialists reported that many of their comrades were depressed. With every victory, Hitler dampened worries and created the impression he could demand what he wanted and get it without war. With resignation and despair the Socialists observed that the people had begun to think he was infallible.[73]

German nationalism, which had suffered one setback after another since 1918, underwent a renaissance. Hitler's status rose into the stratosphere. His charisma was self-evident, and he basked in glory, even in parts of the country known to be reserved about him on his rise to power.

The dreadful irony was that Britain and France, which had done next to nothing to help the democratic Weimar Republic, now made Hitler look like a genius. By the spring of 1939 the identification with him existed "over broad segments of society."[74]

20

PERSECUTION OF THE JEWS IN THE PREWAR YEARS

L ong before Hitler came to power, Jewish leaders had worried that their community was fading away through conversion or intermarriage. On Hitler's appointment, just over a half million "believing Jews" lived in Germany, less than 1 percent of the population. Hitler represented a much more immediate threat, because he had sworn for years that there was no place for Jews in the country.

The new chancellor said relatively little in public about the Jews in 1933 and 1934. He would not, at least in the beginning, pursue ideology if it cost jobs and would lose support, so anti-Semitism was not emphasized.

Nevertheless, after the March 1933 elections, the Party and SA boycotted or damaged some Jewish shops and businesses, and occasionally assaulted Jews openly.[1] Hitler had fanned the flames for so long that he could hardly disavow the radicals, but the attacks did not sit well with most citizens. The American Jewish Congress threatened a worldwide boycott of German goods, and that warning gave Hitler even more pause. On March 26 he spoke with Goebbels, and they decided on a "nonviolent" boycott of Jewish businesses. The move would send a signal to the international Jewish community, and in Germany it would channel the illegal and unpopular "excesses" of the SA in a semi-legal direction.[2]

BOYCOTT OF THE JEWS

On March 30, the cabinet met and for the first time made decisions on the basis of the Enabling Law. Hitler talked about "defensive measures" to be introduced shortly against "Jewish atrocity propaganda abroad." He said these steps had to be organized by the regime; if they came "from the people," they might take on "undesired forms." The ominous note came at the end of his brief statement: "The Jews have to recognize that a Jewish war against Germany will hit the Jews in Germany with all sharpness."[3]

The boycott on April 1 had ripple effects even in Berlin's high court, the Kammergericht. Young Sebastian Haffner, training to become a lawyer, recalled the dignified setting, the black gowns and serious people going about their jobs. He was in the library, which "was full of extreme silence, a silence filled with the high tension of deeply concentrated work. . . . No breath came in from the outside world; here there was no revolution."

An uncustomary disturbance then intruded, doors were banged, jack-boots heard in the hall, orders given. The silence in the library was broken when one of the lawyers whispered, "SA." Another voice said, "They're throwing out the Jews." In response a few people giggled. "At that moment," Haffner recalled, "this laughter alarmed me more than what was actually happening. With a start I realized that there were Nazis working in this room. How strange." Someone from the court soon said it might be advisable for "the Jewish gentlemen to leave."

The dramatic moment came when the door of the library burst open and men in brown uniforms filled the room. They told "non-Aryans" to get out. Haffner wondered what to do, when one of the Nazis came to him and barked: "Are you Aryan?" Without thinking, Haffner blurted out immediately: "Yes!" His answer was correct, but he never forgave himself for saying it. As he wrote later: "I had failed my first test. I could have slapped myself."[4]

The boycott of the Jews reverberated through German society. The new regime was clearly intent on pursuing Hitler's anti-Semitic aims.

Nevertheless, the immediate priority was curing unemployment, and compromises had to be made. Thus, the department stores—almost all of them in Germany owned by Jewish merchants—were allowed to stay in business. Hitler had promised to get rid of them, but he could not do so if it would cost jobs. In mid-1933, he assented to a loan for the Tietz group, a large Jewish store chain. The government did not want to risk fourteen thousand jobs and helped to bail out the company. Behind the scenes, however, the pressure against the owners persisted, and within a year Georg and Martin Tietz were forced to sell. It was one of the first major cases of "Aryanization," a process of taking over Jewish-owned firms introduced gradually until November 1938, when it became sweeping.[5]

Germany did not have a pogrom on April 1, or anything approaching it, but there were reports of violence and arrests, and several Jews were murdered.

The great majority of citizens were opposed or indifferent to the boycott. Some made a point of shopping at Jewish stores. The Nazis themselves considered the boycott a failure.[6] Germans did not show the anti-Semitic zeal of their leaders, and the cabinet called it off.[7]

Jews were not social outsiders when Hitler came to power. They had opportunities to be professors, judges, and politicians that would have been unthinkable at the time in many parts of the United States. German Jews were also patriotic and generally unresponsive to the early Zionist movement. The April boycott, though it failed, left even optimists in the Jewish community feeling under threat.

On April 4, President Hindenburg made a plea to Hitler not to take any action against Jewish war veterans. Hitler's response was the longest note he wrote on Jewish affairs. He said anti-Semitic policies were needed because "*Germans*" had been excluded from certain professions, like law and medicine, where Jews took up so many positions. He said the state was weakened by having a "foreign body"—the Jews—dominate the business world, and he reminded the president of the officer corps' long-standing policies of not admitting Jews. Hitler agreed for the moment to hold off action against war veterans in the civil service and elsewhere.[8]

The April 7 Law for the Restoration of a Professional Civil Service contained an "Aryan paragraph" that excluded most Jews. Millions were affected by the questionnaires and investigations that were part of the law. Subsequent purges took their cue from this law. Jewish professors were forced out, and Jewish students subjected to a "numbers" clause restricting admission. They were soon excluded from the arts, press, and free professions.

"INDIVIDUAL ACTIONS" AND THE NUREMBERG LAWS

After the boycott the Jews suffered a steady stream of "individual actions," a code word of the day for violence and destruction of property. The vigilante-style assaults resulted in several cases of murder. Contrary to what we might assume about Hitler's dictatorship, violence was not ordered from Berlin, but took place on local initiative.[9]

If forcing Jews from the economy was generally popular, most Germans were reserved about violence and these "individual actions."[10] Jews were torn about staying.[11] They were particularly demoralized that some neighbors and acquaintances took it upon themselves to inform the Gestapo, the police, or the Party about Jews' "undesired" if not yet expressly "illegal" behavior. People thought to be "friends of the Jews" were open to attack as well, with defamations painted on their front door that they were a "Jew Servant" or "People's Traitor."[12]

The population in some places showed disdain for these denouncers. Nonetheless, in Berlin in June 1935 "race defilers" were marched through the streets by Party activists in civilian clothes. The Berlin Gestapo noted in August 1935 that 208 persons were reported for "race defilement."[13]

This was the "popular" background Hitler was looking for to introduce race laws. In *Mein Kampf* and in countless speeches he had said that "blood mixing" led to the decline of a nation. In September 1935, having directly or indirectly fostered anti-Semitism during the previous months, he announced new laws at the Party rally.[14]

The Nuremberg Laws, or Law for the Protection of German Blood and German Honor, outlawed new marriages between Jews and non-

Jews; forbade extramarital sexual relations between them; made it illegal for Jews to employ non-Jewish women under forty-five as servants; and made it a crime for Jews to raise the German flag. Hitler asked that laws be prepared for him to sign. The definition of who was a Jew was vague. At the last minute, he considered a broad version of the law to apply to those of "mixed race" but backtracked when he sensed that the German public thought that too sweeping.[15] Jews were shocked, as their legal status reverted to what it had been long before.

The response to the laws ran the gamut. They were welcomed by some people who hoped for an end to violence. Others began to feel sorry for Jews, but some felt the laws did not go far enough.

A Gestapo report for Berlin said Jews were now shut out of the "community of the people." The new laws created a kind of invisible ghetto and opened the door to the denouncers to lay ever more charges, often for personal gain. The participation of ordinary citizens made the enforcement of the Nuremberg Laws possible.[16]

FROM OLYMPIC BROTHERHOOD TO NEW ASSAULTS

For 1936 Germany was awarded the Winter Olympics, held in Garmisch-Partenkirchen (February 6–16), and the Summer Olympics, hosted by Berlin (August 1–16). The discriminatory measures, concentration camps, and secret police were all well known. American and British members of the International Olympic Committee tried to pressure German colleagues into letting Jewish athletes compete for their team. Led by the American Avery Brundage, however, the IOC rejected the boycott proposed by some of his countrymen against the 1936 Olympics. Late in 1935 the United States signed on, and other countries quickly followed suit.[17]

Merely holding the games was a great victory for Hitler because they gave him a chance to show that things were not as bad in Germany as some said. (The IOC awarded the Winter Olympics to Germany for 1940 and to Italy for 1944. They were not held.) In 1936 the German government had the more obvious aspects of its racism cleaned up. Signs like "Jews Are Forbidden" posted at city or village gates were removed.

One bewildered Jewish citizen of Berlin was asked by visitors from England and France, "What do you really want; why are you so against the regime? We were treated wonderfully here."[18] But the Olympics were hardly over when the inexorable pressure on the Jews began again, including violence against persons and property.

On the fourth anniversary of his appointment, Hitler addressed the Reichstag. He spoke about what had happened since the "revolution of all revolutions" and was proud to report that surely "the greatest transformation in our nation was carried through with a minimum of victims and losses." The Nazis struck only where "Bolshevik lust for murder still believed in victory or to be able to hinder the realization of National Socialism."

He alluded to the Four-Year Plan (announced in September 1936), to say how important it was to stop the "poison" of Communism. He claimed that if Germany had lost to that "barbarism," the West would have been threatened. With satisfaction he noted that all cultural activities of the Jews had been ended and they had been removed from the press, theater, film, science, and other areas. Far from the ruination that had been predicted, he insisted that cultural life was blossoming as never before.[19]

The verbal assault on Jews and Communists coincided with a new wave of anti-Semitism at the grass roots. One district official in Bavaria reported in February 1937: "Jews and Bolshevism are two inseparable concepts, and for that reason I do not want to see another Jew in my town."[20] The emphasis was on cajoling Jews into emigrating, but most accounts concluded that the process was going too slowly.

In his closing speech to the Nuremberg Party rally on September 13, 1937, Hitler hurled virulent anti-Semitic charges. He saw the world in the midst of a great and all-encompassing insurrection "whose spiritual and technical preparation and leadership, without any doubt, comes from Jewish Bolshevism in Moscow." This was no ordinary attack, for the world had seen nothing like it "since the rise of Christianity, the crusade of the Mohammedans or since the Reformation." The aim was at the entire social order, including its culture, traditions, and very substance of the people. Hitler repeated his theory that the small Russian ruling class had been overthrown by Jews, who had created a "brutal dictatorship." He purported to have statistics revealing that "over 80 percent of the leading positions" in the Soviet Union were held by Jews.

"That means, therefore, not the dictatorship of the proletariat but the dictatorship of the [Jewish] race." Once they had secured power there, they wanted to expand to the West: "The final aim is then a complete Bolshevik revolution."

He recounted seeing this struggle during the Munich republic in 1919. "They were all Jews!" he asserted. The same was true for Hungary at that time, and it was currently happening, he said, in Spain. That was why Germany was there to help General Franco. "We see in principle every further spread of Bolshevism in Europe as tipping the balance of power." He was willing to deal with other European "cultural nations" like Britain or France, but when it came to the Soviet Union, that was the "Bolshevik plague," "Jewish World-Bolshevism," and "an absolute foreign body that makes not the smallest contribution to our economy or culture."

Hitler's attack on the "Jewish-dominated" Soviet Union thirsted for blood. "The time," he said with reference to Germany, "in which one could do whatever one pleased with a defenseless people" was over. Anyone hearing this several-hour-long tirade, which included threatening the USSR militarily, would have concluded that war was in the cards. That conflict would clearly also be against the Jews, as the two were so closely identified in Hitler's mind.[21]

The themes of anti-Semitism and anti-Bolshevism were played up in the press, but anti-Semitism was also linked to anti-Americanism. The Nazis highlighted the decay and degeneracy of American lifestyles, and Hitler grew convinced of the racial and social problems in the United States.[22] Just before and into the war years, the anti-American speeches of leading Nazis played up anti-Jewish themes.[23]

Not all German citizens accepted the anti-Semitism. There were numerous reports from many parts of the country, particularly in rural Catholic areas, where both spiritual and material assistance was offered Jews. On the other hand, it was also true that many religious leaders, and not just those in Germany, who had reservations about some aspects of the new regime, agreed with Hitler's stance against atheistic Bolshevism.[24]

FIRST "NATIONAL OPERATION"

By 1938 harassment had caused many Jews to leave, but approximately 360,000 remained. The SD (Security Service) estimated that "reincorporation" of Austria in the so-called *Anschluss* in March meant the gain of "around 200,000 Religion-Jews" and brought Germany's new total back to what it was in 1933. The SD said there were really many more, but they were concealed because they had converted to other religions.[25] In Austria, anti-Semitic persecution, which was brutal from the start, dramatically accelerated. By late March, Viennese Jews were driven to such despair that more than eighty committed suicide.

The anti-Semitic violence in Austria "started before the Wehrmacht crossed the border; despite official efforts to curb its most chaotic and mob-like aspects, it lasted several weeks." Public humiliation of Jews became a popular sport, and many people enriched themselves through theft and extortion.[26]

In Germany, Aryanization of Jewish business moved forward inexorably. By the summer of 1938 an estimated 75 to 80 percent of all businesses that had been Jewish as of 1933 had been liquidated.[27] Firms were ruined when customers began to avoid them. Moreover, any misstep by a Jewish firm brought home its precarious legal position. But it was the regime itself that opened the door to the robbery by providing a "legal basis."[28]

In Austria the process was put into high gear immediately. For example, of thirty-three thousand or so Jewish businesses in Vienna in March, all had been either "Aryanized" or "liquidated in an orderly way" by May. Anti-Semitism was more popular in Austria than in Germany, according to police accounts. The notorious Adolf Eichmann was in Vienna on March 16, only four days after the Wehrmacht walked into Austria. His task was to take charge of Jewish affairs. Soon, however, as David Cesarani shows, "Viennese Jewish leaders came up with the idea for a centralized emigration office, and they provided the staff to make it work. It was the first example of a 'Jewish council' operating under Nazi control which at its extreme fringes appeared more like collaboration."[29]

Many Jews were plundered of everything they owned and had neither the funds nor the wherewithal to get out. They needed help to leave, and to obtain it they had to work with people like Eichmann. By August the Nazis had created the Central Office for Jewish Emigration, and by the time Eichmann left Vienna in May 1939, he bragged that he had deported a hundred thousand or more. To facilitate matters, sometime in October 1938, Himmler had ordered all Austrian Jews to be concentrated in Vienna.[30] Eichmann's forced deportations now became the model of the moment for solving the "Jewish question."

The United States responded to the growing refugee problem by convening a conference in Évian, France. It met July 6–14, 1938, but the assistance offered Jews by the world community was almost insignificant. Not only America but countries like Canada and Australia showed little compassion. The unwillingness to do much was played up cynically in the German press. Far from shaming the Nazis into relenting, the Évian conference encouraged them to continue their exclusionary policies.[31]

Celebrations in Germany about taking Austria sometimes degenerated into anti-Semitic violence, even in places known to be reserved about Nazism. In April and May "individual actions" against Jews were reported "in almost all parts of the Reich."[32]

On April 26, 1938, a decree forced all Jews (and their non-Jewish spouses for those in mixed marriages) to register their worldly wealth. Into the summer, violence and aggression aimed at Jews increased noticeably. The security authorities said that "actions against the Jews" and local boycotts were common, even when officially forbidden. Businesses were taken away, and sympathizers with the Jews were sometimes attacked by a mob and had to be rescued.[33]

The Socialist underground reporters held on to their conviction that most citizens did not support what the Nazis were doing, but admitted that "as a result of the long anti-Semitic campaign many people had themselves become anti-Semitic."[34]

Hitler added fuel to the fire in another speech at the Nuremberg Party rally in September. Although international tensions were rising and the issue of the German minority in Czechoslovakia dominated his main address, he made a point of mentioning the Jews. The world complained that Germany "was trying to get rid of its Jews," but when the international community had a chance to open its doors, it would not. He said that Germany was overcrowded, but the "democratic empires"—presumably Britain and the United States—had no space for Jews. He did not call for violence, but gave every sign he wanted Jews out.[35]

A national SD report for that month alleged that some Jews were being "rude in public" in hopes of fueling international tensions as a way to focus the world's attention on their plight. Most Jews, however, worried that in the event of war they would "be placed in concentration camps or in some other way finished off" (*unschädlich gemacht*). The national SD report for October noted the deteriorating economic position of the Jews through "Aryanization" and the "increasingly anti-Jewish stance of the population." It was a backlash whose "strongest expression" took the form of "actions." The events were fostered by the Party or the SA and "in the south and southwest of the Reich took on the character of a pogrom."[36]

Germany was handed the western part of Czechoslovakia (the Sudetenland) at Munich in September 1938, and it took the rest of the country in short order (March 14–15, 1939). It thereby acquired yet another Jewish community of ancient standing. According to the criteria of the Nuremberg Laws, there were 118,310 Jews in the newly proclaimed Protectorate of Bohemia and Moravia. Here, too, emigration—or forced deportation—became the favorite option for solving the "Jewish question."

In this context, note should be taken not only of what Eichmann was doing in Vienna but also of the German decision to deport Jews of Polish nationality. Some Polish Jews had been living for decades in Germany. Many of them were born there but not allowed to become citizens. The Polish parliament passed a law on March 31, 1938, to withdraw citizenship of many of the Poles living in Germany (nearly half of whom were Jewish) by November 1. The German government responded to the "provocation" by organizing a forced deportation.[37]

German authorities sent home all male Jews of Polish nationality. The total number forced out in three days (October 27–29) was estimated at seventeen thousand. Himmler thought the women would follow the men of their own accord. The SD expected that a total of seventy-five thousand Jewish Poles in Germany would be affected. Those who were shoved over the border were caught in a no-man's-land, driven back and forth before being allowed into Poland. Some were permitted to return briefly to Germany to sell off their property.[38]

The SD followed the reaction in cities where the Polish Jews were assembled before deportation. In Düsseldorf around three thousand were sent back. Jews of other nationalities regarded the action as a "trial balloon" for the German government to see how foreign countries would react. Families were torn apart when fathers were compelled to leave.[39] This event was the first major "action" that forced Jews out of Germany. It was the closest thing yet to one of the "national actions" being carried out at about the same time in the Soviet Union.

POGROM

Given the violent attacks on the Jews through the summer and into the fall of 1938, as well as what was happening in Austria and Czechoslovakia, the smell of a pogrom was in the air by October. Observers in the Socialist underground began their long reports with the chilling phrase "The campaign of annihilation of the German Jews is by all appearances entering its final stage."[40]

The attack on the Jews, labeled sarcastically at the time by persons unknown as the "night of broken glass," took place November 9–10. *Kristallnacht* began when seventeen-year-old Herschel Grynszpan fatally shot a minor official (Ernst vom Rath) in the German embassy in Paris on November 7. Grynszpan's parents were among the Polish Jews recently deported from Germany. On November 8, when he heard of the shooting in Paris, Goebbels noted: "If only we could unleash the wrath of the people!" Attacks on the Jews were in fact already under way in some places (like Hessen), as he noted in his diary. As word of the assassination reached other localities, violence erupted.

Late on November 8, Goebbels was with Hitler to celebrate the anniversary of the attempted putsch of 1923. All the Nazi bigwigs were in Munich for the annual commemoration of the "fallen."[41] On the evening of November 9, Hitler was due at a reception. Vom Rath died in the afternoon, and Hitler was informed immediately. When he entered the reception, he spoke briefly with Goebbels and left. This was stage-managing to make it look as though Hitler were rushing off after having just heard the news. Goebbels only then announced vom Rath's death, but Hitler had already decided the demonstrations under way should "be allowed to continue."

Hitler felt a pogrom could be politically useful, noting to Goebbels that "the Jews should for once feel the anger of the people." Goebbels gave the orders to those at the meeting. He told them that Hitler wanted up to thirty thousand arrested. He beamed with delight as reports streamed in that synagogues were burning all over Germany and that the property of the Jews was being destroyed. In his diary he wrote triumphantly, "Bravo! Bravo!" to it all.[42]

Although they decided to stop the pogrom on November 10, Goebbels said Hitler's view was "completely radical and aggressive." The Jews were to put their businesses in order again (at their own expense), and then be forced to sell them. The insurance companies were not to be asked to cover the damages.

The pogrom was the first major violent event experienced by the Jews in Germany in centuries. The riots swept cities and the smallest villages, and there were various reactions. Many people were actively or passively involved in the persecution. But local citizens did not always turn on their longtime neighbors, and some hid Jews or helped them.[43]

About thirty thousand were arrested and more than a hundred killed.[44] Out of despair and as a last gasp of resistance, between three and five hundred committed suicide.[45] Around ten thousand Jews were sent to the camps at Dachau, Buchenwald, and Sachsenhausen. Most were released within weeks.[46]

On November 12, Göring chaired a meeting to deal with the follow-up to *Kristallnacht*. In keeping with Hitler's wishes, a collective fine was levied on the Jews to pay for the damages. Reinhard Heydrich said that Eichmann (also at the meeting) had achieved considerable success in Vienna by forcing the emigration of fifty thousand Jews. In the same period only ten thousand left "old" Germany. Heydrich now wanted to employ the "Vienna model."[47]

POPULAR REACTIONS

In a lengthy report of December 7, 1938, the SD Main Office said the pogrom was carried out by the SA, the SS, and the Nazi Party. It stated that plundering took place, but was kept to a minimum. Some 360 synagogues were destroyed and thirty-one department stores burned down or demolished.

According to the report, the population initially agreed with the action but changed their minds once they saw the damage. People wanted something done about the murder of vom Rath but believed it wrong to destroy businesses and homes. Mainly Catholic areas were especially opposed to the attacks on "the houses of God." Elsewhere, caustic remarks were directed at collectors for Nazi charities. Some ostentatiously showed sympathy for the Jews by shopping at the Jewish stores still operating. In the Ruhr a leaflet circulated proclaiming that those responsible should be stood against a wall.

The SD report concluded that the pogrom and series of restrictions sent out by all branches of government "aimed at the complete exclusion of the Jews from all areas of life, with the final goal [*Endziel*] their removal from the area of the Reich by all means and in the shortest possible time."[48]

In countless other reports the pogrom was said to be "regarded with satisfaction" or even with the "greatest satisfaction."[49] Reading between the lines, however, one can see that public opinion was ambivalent and divided. The mayor of Bielefeld, for example, stated that "understanding existed for the struggle against the Jews and that in general it was taken as obvious that if the Jews were to be rendered harmless, very sharp measures would have to be used." Nevertheless, he said what was "generally not understood" was the wanton destruction of property.[50]

Many Germans evidently began to feel sorry for Jews. The mayor of one small town commented, "The population had mostly not understood the action, or better, they did not want to understand it. The Jews were also pitied, particularly because of the damage inflicted on their worldly possessions and because the male Jews were led off to a concentration camp. This attitude of the population was perhaps not widespread, but I estimate that here at least 60 percent of the population so thought."[51]

In Kochem, the Catholic clergy and population "in many cases expressed pity for the Jews." A small town in Baden summed up the "general" reaction with the statement "The poor Jews!!!" Even in places that supposedly welcomed the uproar, the population "for the most part pitied the Jews." One town was said to agree with the arrest of male Jews when it heard news of the Paris murder. "However, as the numerous rumors about the mistreatments that followed leaked back, particularly from places outside the locality, and as the public transport of the more or less miserable-looking figures followed, the sympathy of the population no longer favored the action. The population was serious and depressed. Here and there were clear signs of pity." Some said the event was inconsistent with Germany's reputation in the world.[52]

Although some reports "applauded," many reveal only silence on the topic. "Seldom did anyone give an opinion," and many felt ashamed, ran some accounts. There were those who thought the vandalism and arrests "were still too mild." However, the "far greater majority" considered the destruction of property wrong and believed that those responsible should be held to account.[53]

The SD-West's annual report for 1938 pointed to the mixed reactions as well. The Rhine-Ruhr stated that the population rejected the pogrom, although many people agreed the "Jewish question" had to be solved. Even the supposedly "reliable" part of the population, which wanted Jews out of the economy, did not agree, and there was almost universal condemnation. The reasons varied from religious to humanitarian concerns. Opinions were divided in the east as well, where the SD-Elbe said some workers and the lower middle class accepted the pogrom but did not like the destruction of goods. "Educated" people condemned the whole episode. The general conclusion was that the pogrom, "like the boycott of the Jews" in April 1933, was a "tactical mistake." The Jews themselves, as everywhere in Germany, were devastated, not only materially, but psychologically.[54]

The SD report from the north was even more negative. The attitude of the population in the Stettin area "left much to be desired" on anti-Semitism: "In the rejection of the measures against the Jews, everyone was united, only the basis for this attitude varied somewhat."[55]

The national report registered condemnations from across the political spectrum. Liberals described the action as "barbaric" and "devoid of culture" and the destruction of synagogues as "irresponsible." The phrase quoted was of "the poor repressed Jews." The movement on the right "unanimously" said the measure was "unjustified and unworthy of a people of culture." The Socialists condemned it in different ways. Some said that the persecution of Christians would follow.[56]

There were relatively few objections to what happened as a matter of principle. Germans did not generally object to anti-Semitism as such. They did not say much about how despicable it was for the regime to be persecuting the Jews. Some historians have taken the general failure of the populace to address such issues as indicating that most Germans were more concerned about property than about the Jewish people.[57] At the same time, recently published documents show far more sympathy for Jews than is often supposed. There is plenty of evidence in the private diaries of non-Nazis that the riots and the arrests were highly disturbing to many Germans.[58] The Socialists insisted that the overwhelming majority "abhorred" the excesses of November and the "continuous pogrom" since then.[59]

It has been argued that at the time it would have been highly imprudent for ordinary Germans to criticize the regime on the central issue of anti-Semitism and that some, if not many, people were indirectly expressing their displeasure at the pogrom through their criticisms of the wastefulness.[60]

The mass of Germans broadly agreed with significantly reducing the number of Jews in prominent positions, and many accepted the Nazi strategy of eliminating their civil rights. That does not mean people did not pity individual Jews or have empathy with them as human beings. But as Jews, they were in effect consigned to the fate that awaited them.

The Socialist underground was convinced that Nazi policy aimed at mass murder. Their report of February 1939 even brought up the comparison with the slaughter of the Armenians carried out by the Turks during the Great War.[61]

PROPHECY OF DOOM

Hitler's first speech after the pogrom occurred on January 30, 1939, the anniversary of his appointment as chancellor. He began by talking about the international situation and said that the German people had nothing against England, America, or France. He then turned to the Jews as the real "world enemy." He charged them with wanting to bring the nations of the world to war. They had been "overcome" in Germany, he said, and they would also go down to defeat everywhere. He noted that other nations might pity the Jews, but no one would take them in. At this time he thought it might be possible for the European powers to clear up the "Jewish question" through negotiations. He suggested that there was enough space in the world for the Jews, but he wanted an end to what he called the belief that they had a God-given right to "exploit" the productive work of other nations.

Having set this scene, Hitler issued what became a notorious threat:

> I have often been in my life a prophet and was mostly laughed at. In the time of the struggle for power it was in the first instance the Jewish people who merely heard my prophecies with a smile, that I would one day take over the leadership of the state and thus of the entire nation, and then along with much else also bring the Jewish problem to a solution. I believe that the loud laughs have stuck in the throat of the Jews in Germany.
>
> I want to be a prophet again. If international Jewry inside and outside Europe should succeed, once again, to bring the nations into a world war, the result will not be the Bolshevization of the globe and thereby the victory of Jewry, but the destruction of the Jewish race in Europe.[62]

He identified the Jews with the spirit of Communism. He referred to the famous phrase at the end of *The Communist Manifesto* (1848) by Marx and Engels, "Workers of the world unite," as "Jewish words." Hitler suggested an alternative motto: "Productive members of all nations recognize your common enemy!"

In this diatribe he emphasized once more the purported links between the Jews and the Bolsheviks. They were one enemy, with the Jews supposedly behind the threat of war. But it was he above all who wanted war and worked to make it come about. Indeed he was disappointed to be deprived of it at the Munich conference in 1938.

The World War would soon enough come and by Hitler's design. It would give him the pretext he yearned for and believed he needed to set about the destruction of both the Jews and Bolshevism.

21

"CLEANSING" THE GERMAN BODY POLITIC

Hitler believed in the popularized theory of eugenics, a concept coined in the 1880s by Sir Francis Galton, a half cousin of Charles Darwin. Galton concluded that "physique, ability, and character" were hereditary, as were "intellect, zeal, and devotion to work." He and his successors in this field thought that inheritance needed help, however, and proposed offering assistance to couples likely to bear fit children. The other side of this program was to prevent the "dysgenic," or unfit (mentally, physically, behaviorally), from propagating.

The eugenics movement was international in scope and varied from place to place. In the United States, programs based on eugenics were backed by Presidents Theodore Roosevelt and Woodrow Wilson. Beginning in 1899, ten states followed Indiana, which began sterilizing the mentally handicapped to ensure that the "inferior" did not gain the upper hand. German scientists were impressed by America's compulsory sterilization, a practice upheld by the U.S. Supreme Court in 1927. The annual rate of such procedures until 1930 was around two hundred to six hundred per year, but in the next decade grew to two thousand to four thousand per year.[1]

In the Soviet Union during the 1920s, A. S. Serebrovsky, a Marxist proponent of eugenics, thought that central planning would make it possible to breed desirable qualities. He invented the concept of the "gene pool" and suggested that "one talented and valuable producer could have up to 1,000 children."

That theory was taken up by Hermann J. Muller, an American scientist who moved from Texas to the Soviet Union in 1933. A great admirer of Stalin, Muller considered the USSR the ideal place to apply eugenics and in 1935 revived Serebrovsky's artificial insemination schemes. He thought it possible for the majority of the population to acquire the "innate quality" of men like Lenin, Newton, and Leonardo.[2]

Writing to Stalin in May 1936, Muller professed great confidence "in the ultimate Bolshevik triumph throughout all possible spheres of human endeavor." He declared it feasible to reproduce "transcendently superior individuals" and guarantee the triumph of Bolshevism. Stalin was not impressed. But a group around T. D. Lysenko, an unqualified quack and a leading light in Soviet science thanks to Stalin's patronage, concluded that eugenics, genetics, and Fascism were all cut from the same cloth. Stalin had had enough. Muller had to flee and decided to say nothing about his experiences in the USSR "for fear of alienating Western leftists from his eugenics."[3]

In the Third Reich eugenics came to inform a wide array of policies, from welfare and family planning to fighting crime, social problems, and chronic-care patients. It would be used to mold the racially fit society and be accompanied by anti-Semitism, which would drive out the Jews.

RACIAL HYGIENE

The German variation of eugenics, called racial hygiene, was formulated by Alfred Ploetz at the beginning of the twentieth century. A physician who had practiced in the United States, Ploetz concluded that disease and defects of character were hereditary. He decided to work in this area instead of pursuing the "Sisyphean labor" of treating medical problems after they arose. Like many who believed in eugenics, he thought that social welfare and health insurance made the situation worse by helping the weak. He worried that indiscriminate marriage would lead to social and biological degeneration. Long before the Nazis came to power, racial hygiene had already "become a scientific orthodoxy in the German medical community."[4]

In *Mein Kampf,* Hitler wrote that "incurably sick people" should not be allowed "to contaminate the remaining healthy ones" and that "defective people" should be prevented from propagating.[5] He spelled out how he would use eugenics. In 1929 at the Nuremberg Party rally he called it disastrous for the state to interfere in the process of natural selection. He was appalled that the mentally handicapped and criminals were allowed to procreate and that "degenerates" were helped to survive. "Thus we slowly raise the weaker and kill off the stronger." This "false pity" had to stop. His inclination was to destroy the weak, as supposedly had been done in ancient Sparta. But euthanasia was too radical for German public opinion and had to wait until the war years before it was tried.[6]

Sterilization was illegal in Germany until July 14, 1933, when the Law for the Prevention of Offspring with Hereditary Diseases was enacted.[7] It can be traced, almost verbatim, to the California sterilization act of 1909.[8]

In Germany the law applied initially to congenital feeblemindedness, schizophrenia, manic depression, hereditary epilepsy, Huntington's chorea, hereditary blindness or deafness, serious physical deformities, and severe alcoholism. The German government set up "hereditary health courts" consisting of a judge and two doctors. They read the files but did not examine the person. Approximately 200,000 women and the same number of men were sterilized in the course of the program, nearly all against their will. Some 5,000, mostly women, died as a result of the procedures. Not only medical but social criteria were used in the decisions, and factors like undesired behavior, even unruliness or promiscuity, could lead to sterilization.[9]

Long before he achieved power, Hitler wanted to sterilize criminals, particularly repeat sex offenders. He was persuaded to promulgate a separate law in November 1933. In the meantime, the radical eugenicists Arthur Gütt and Ernst Rüdin (medical experts in the Ministry of the Interior) fought to extend the sterilization program to those considered to have a "hereditary criminal disposition." They argued for a broadened concept of feeblemindedness to include not only the criterion of intelligence but also "disturbances in emotions, will, drives, [or] ethical sentiments." Anyone deemed suffering from "ethical defects" or "inability to develop a proper understanding of the order of human society" could be considered feebleminded, and sterilized.[10] Twenty-five percent of the men sterilized under the program had a criminal record.[11]

Eugenics found its way into a wide array of public policies and was propagated by a host of new institutions and professionals. The police gave particular attention to the work of Dr. Robert Ritter, who took for his field of study the racial-biological makeup of criminals and later grew interested in Gypsies and Jehovah's Witnesses.[12]

In the United States, *Fortune* magazine reported that 66 percent of those surveyed in 1937 favored compulsory sterilization of habitual criminals.[13] In Germany the principle of sterilization was rejected by many Catholics, although more generally the law was believed to be a good remedy for dealing with habitual criminals or sex offenders. There was reluctance to see these measures applied across the board.

Some eugenics programs, however, were received positively, as can be seen in the acceptance of marriage loans introduced in an act to reduce unemployment on June 1, 1933. Couples were offered on average six hundred Reichsmarks interest free. That was a sum industrial workers would earn in four or five months. The money would be paid on condition that the couple passed racial and medical tests and that the female spouse left her job. Not long after, with the aim of encouraging larger families, the regime added that the debt would be reduced by one-quarter on the birth of each new child.[14] Between August 1933 and January 1937 alone, 700,000 couples took out the loan. The birthrate, about which population experts were long worried, grew every year from 1933 to the outbreak of the war. British experts at the time said this development was "spectacular," particularly because birthrates were falling in so many countries. Not only did organizations for women become the largest voluntary ones in Germany, but the birthrate as well offered an even "surer measure of the popularity of the regime's policies towards women and the family."[15]

"ANTISOCIAL ELEMENTS"

Hitler's regime pursued an array of individuals, including beggars, the chronically unemployed, charity cases, alcoholics, tramps, and others on the margin of society. What was new was not so much the attitude of the government and German society as the Third Reich's determination to act. The more hard-nosed approach to all "crime" won the regime a great deal of support.

The Nazi police and justice system grew more radical over time. On December 14, 1937, the Ministry of the Interior issued a "fundamental decree on the preventive police battle against criminality"; the community had to be protected "from all parasites." The newly reorganized Kripo was empowered to put in "preventive custody" any persons deemed "asocial" or "professional or habitual criminals."[16] In early 1938 the Kripo began to assert independence from the courts. It claimed to be carrying out the will of the führer and to require no further authorization.

The definition of the asocials kept expanding and by April 1938 included all those "who through minor, but oft-repeated, infractions of the law demonstrate that they will not comply with the social order that is a fundamental condition of a National Socialist state, for example, beggars, vagrants, (Gypsies), prostitutes, drunkards, those with contagious diseases, particularly sexually transmitted diseases, who evade the measures taken by the public health authorities." Also falling under the definition were "persons, regardless of any previous conviction, who evade the obligation to work and are dependent on the public for their maintenance, for example, the work-shy, work evaders, drunkards." The Gestapo carried out the first "asocial action" at the end of April 1938 and sent about two thousand to the Buchenwald concentration camp.[17]

In June 1938 the Kripo "asocial" campaign apprehended around fifteen hundred Jews, the first time such a large group was singled out and sent to a concentration camp.[18] Between June 13 and 18 the Kripo arrested a minimum of two hundred non-Jews in each police district, including tramps, beggars, Gypsies, and pimps.[19] As usual the police exceeded the quota of three thousand and arrested well over ten thousand.

These actions conformed to Hitler's wishes, but economic considerations also played a role. The cheap labor of the long list of asocials and others would be used in concentration camps to finance the burgeoning SS empire. The push to use prisoners in new SS enterprises—such as the German Earth and Stone Works, founded in April 1938—came from an agreement reached between Himmler and Albert Speer, the general construction inspector.[20] It is possible that Hitler brought Himmler and Speer together at the end of 1937 or early in 1938, but Speer in any case was anxious for the provision of cheap building materials and saw the opportunity, through the SS exploitation of prisoners, to get it.[21] The combination of ideology, racism, economics, and raw ambition had deadly consequences for untold thousands who eventually slaved in SS camps.

"SEXUAL PERVERSIONS"

Hitler was prudish in his abhorrence of the "sins" of the modern big city, like pornography, homosexuality, and even immodest dress. He wrote of these matters as the "political, ethical, and moral contamination of the people" and the "poisoning of the health of the body politic." In *Mein Kampf* he promised "ruthless measures" to stop syphilis, and that meant combating prostitution.[22]

Police were ordered from the onset of the regime to use all measures on the books (such as laws on spreading venereal diseases) to eliminate street prostitution and take control of brothels. There were sweeps of the red-light districts, with thousands arrested. Health, welfare, and youth officials helped the police. It was common to demand forced sterilization of "loose" women who were considered threats to the racial community.[23]

According to old friends from his time in Vienna, Hitler turned "against [homosexuality] and other sexual perversions in the big city with nausea and disgust."[24] Homosexual acts were criminalized in Germany in the nineteenth century, and the Third Reich stepped up enforcement. Although lesbianism was frowned upon, it was not perceived as a "danger to the nation's survival," and there was no systematic campaign against it.[25] Persecution of homosexuality was reflected in court verdicts. In every year after 1933 the number of arrests increased: 948 in 1934; 2,106 in 1935; 5,320 in 1936; 8,271 in 1937; 8,562 in 1938. In the war years the numbers declined steadily, likely because so many young men were drafted.[26]

SINTI AND ROMA

In 1933 there were around twenty thousand Sinti and Roma, or Gypsies, in Germany. Most lived as wanderers who wanted neither a fixed home nor a regular job. Their image in Europe was not a wholesome one, for they were viewed as living off crime and having no permanent abode.

Police used measures already on the books, but they received plenty of suggestions from locals who wanted to get rid of "their Gypsies" and demanded they be sent to Dachau. Between 1935 and 1939 new "Gypsy camps" were set up in Cologne, Düsseldorf, Essen, Frankfurt, Hamburg, Magdeburg, and Berlin. These were less severe than concentration camps, but more than unpleasant.[27]

In October 1938 the Kripo created a new branch to deal with what Himmler called the "Gypsy plague." According to Dr. Robert Ritter, there were two kinds of Gypsies, those of "mixed race" and "pure breeds," and each had to be dealt with separately. That was the first time Gypsies were officially considered a race.[28]

The registration of the Sinti and Roma in Germany had been completed before the war. There were isolated attempts in October 1939 to attach additional train cars to the first deportations of Jews to the Lublin region of Poland. These hit-or-miss efforts were stopped by Himmler.[29]

Ritter's research had concluded by early 1940 that about 90 percent of all Gypsies in the Reich were of mixed race, and hence the "worst" kind. He recommended that the "bulk of the asocial and useless Gypsies of mixed race" be forced to work in "large, migrating work camps" and be hindered from further propagating. The Gypsy population would gradually fade away, and, according to Ritter, "only then will the coming generations of the German people be really freed from this burden."[30]

The Ministry of the Interior suggested to police on January 24, 1940, that the sterilization of Gypsies, including those of mixed race, was the "ultimate solution of the Gypsy problem."[31] Nothing came of this suggestion, so on April 27, 1940, the Kripo was ordered to begin "resettlement" operations. These were held up for a time but soon continued.

CONCENTRATION CAMPS AND ASOCIALS

The concentration camps seemed to be fading away in 1934; at the end of that year at most three thousand prisoners were still in the camps. By September 1935, Himmler had come up with new missions for the camps. A sign of things to come was given by Hitler at the Nuremberg Party rally of September 1935.

That rally was infamous because it introduced new laws banning marriage between Jews and non-Jews. Hitler also announced by proclamation a "struggle against the internal enemies of the nation," one of his favorite themes. This time the "enemies" were defined as "Jewish Marxism and the parliamentary democracy associated with it"; "the politically and morally depraved Catholic Center Party"; and "certain elements of an unteachable, dumb, and reactionary bourgeoisie." Radical steps were purportedly needed, even though the speech also claimed that Germany enjoyed greater security and tranquillity than ever. Hitler even highlighted improvements since his accession to power, when the country suffered the "ferment of decomposition" and "signs of decay."[32]

On October 18, Hitler and Himmler decided to broaden the concepts of "enemy" and "crime" that the new secret police were supposed to fight.[33] The concentration camp system and the numbers of prisoners grew thereafter.

Prior to the war, the camps held two main groups: "enemies of state" and variously defined social outsiders. In the war years the Jews would become the primary target and would endure great suffering. But in the years leading up to the war, Jews were a minority of the camp prisoners.

In Buchenwald there were 10,188 prisoners at the end of October 1938, including 1,007 "professional criminals" and 4,341 "asocials." The Gestapo's prisoners in the camp (3,982 persons) were Communists and other political enemies, but these included an unknown number of criminals and asocials.[34]

Sachsenhausen, the large camp north of Berlin, had a similar prisoner population. Between June 1938 and September 1939 the number in the camp varied from just under 6,000 to a high of around 9,000. That changed briefly in December 1938, when there were up to 12,622 people, many of whom were Jews sent there as part of the November pogrom.[35] At any one point in this period more than half the prisoners were asocials. No complete figures survive of those held in preventive detention in subsequent actions, but a partial reconstruction shows 12,921 at the end of 1938; 12,221 at the end of 1939; and 13,354 at the end of 1940.[36]

The main camp for asocials was at Flossenbürg in northeastern Bavaria. It was founded in late April–early May 1938, when the Gestapo and Kripo picked up thousands of asocials. This place was designed for "non-politicals" like repeat offenders, pimps, tramps, beggars, and alcoholics. The camp was also supposed to help finance Himmler's SS empire.[37] Physically fit males, removed from one institution or another, or arrested on the street, were sent there and forced to work in the rock quarry.[38]

The population of the camp became more heterogeneous over time.[39] A survey of February 8, 1943, the last one before the camp was inundated with evacuees from camps to the east, indicated just over four thousand prisoners. An estimated one-third were Germans, while most of the rest were slave workers from the east. Like all other main concentration camps, Flossenbürg eventually had its own empire of sub-camps, and by 1945 ninety-two of them were linked to the main camp.[40]

There were small numbers of Jews in this camp in mid-1940, but most came later, between August 1944 and January 1945, when at least ten thousand arrived from Poland and Hungary. They were sent primarily to the sub-camps of Flossenbürg, where thousands perished.[41] By the end of 1944 the camp population had doubled to eight thousand and in February 1945 stood at eleven thousand.[42]

A census of the Flossenbürg system at the end of February 1945 shows that the population had become internationalized. Poles made up the largest contingent (38.2 percent) of the twenty-two thousand prisoners, followed by Soviets (23.2 percent). Among the thirty nationalities were many Hungarians, especially Hungarian Jews (9 percent), but also many French (6.7 percent), Italians and Germans (each with 5.5 percent), and Czechs (with 4.8 percent). At that point the Flossenbürg system as a whole contained forty thousand prisoners, of whom twenty-nine thousand were male. By the time the system collapsed in 1945, the population had grown to around fifty-two thousand.[43]

That camp had fifteen hundred recorded executions in the year April 1944 to April 1945. At times, it killed up to ninety people per day, including Germans involved in resistance activities like Pastor Dietrich Bonhoeffer and General Hans Oster.[44] There were no gas chambers at this camp, no assembly-line killing, but in little-known Flossenbürg and its sub-camps at one time or another at least a hundred thousand were incarcerated, of whom perhaps one-third died.[45] That was more people than were killed in the bloodiest period of terror in the French Revolution.[46]

CONCENTRATION CAMP SYSTEM IN THE WAR

At the end of 1933 it seemed concentration camps would be closed down, but on March 20, 1936, Hitler agreed to new plans to expand them again that were put to him by Himmler. The idea was to cover Germany with five large camps.[47]

Himmler and Oswald Pohl, chief of SS administration, were keen to exploit cheap labor, and in 1938 they founded the first of many SS-owned companies, the German Earth and Stone Works, which set up rock quarries and brickworks. Economic considerations partly determined the locations of new camps in 1937–38, when Flossenbürg (in northeastern Bavaria), Buchenwald (near Weimar), and Mauthausen (in newly annexed Austria) were built. Two more major camps at Gross-Rosen (Lower Silesia) and Natzweiler (in Alsace) were built in 1940, all near sources of raw materials.

The number of prisoners increased from 21,400 in August 1939 to 32,120 in October, as suspect persons were picked up around the outbreak of the war.[48] Pohl reported on April 30, 1942, that the six main camps had 44,700 prisoners. The purpose of the camps shifted away from merely holding certain prisoners "to the economic side. Mobilization of all prisoner labor took place, initially for war purposes (increase of arms production) and later for peacetime building work."[49]

Like most of the people sentenced by the notorious People's Court, only a minority of the prisoners in camps were German. The number in all the concentration camps grew dramatically over time. By August 1943 (despite astoundingly high death rates) the figure had gone up to 224,000. A year later the prison population stood at 524,268, and it continued to expand.

Albert Speer met with Hitler on September 20 and 22, 1942. There was a deepening labor shortage, and the regime faced an awkward choice: either move factories to the camps (as Himmler wanted) or move prisoners to the factories. Speer and others argued for the latter and for private enterprise.[50] Decentralized production facilities would have an additional advantage in the face of growing air raids.[51] Hitler agreed with Speer, and the result was enormous transformation of the camp system, which spread like a cancer into nearly every corner of the country.

Germany became covered in a network of hundreds of concentration camps and many other kinds of punitive facilities. Dachau eventually had 197 sub-camps; Sachsenhausen administered 74; Buchenwald had 129 sub-camps by war's end; Flossenbürg controlled 97; Mauthausen in Austria eventually had 62; Ravensbrück had 45; and Neuengamme had 90 outer camps. Gross-Rosen eventually had a total of 118 sub-camps, and the main camp at Mittelbau-Dora had 32.

Many of these sub-camps, it should be noted, were larger than the biggest prewar main concentration camps, some with tens of thousands of prisoners. It would have been impossible for citizens not to know about these, not only because they were widely publicized in the German press of the day, but because there were so many hundreds of them. They were located in practically all cities and on the premises of factories of any size. The national composition of the camp system was overwhelmingly non-German, with prisoners drawn from all over the vast reaches of the Third Reich, especially from Eastern Europe.

PART SEVEN

STALIN AND HITLER:
INTO THE SOCIAL CATASTROPHE

22

RIVAL VISIONS OF WORLD CONQUEST

Soviet leaders were disappointed by the failed revolutions after the First World War, particularly in Germany. The Communist International (Comintern) was created in early 1919 to win support among left-wing radicals in the West for the revolution in Russia and to spread it worldwide. In 1920 Lenin tried to carry Communism westward on the bayonets of the Red Army, but the Poles stopped the invasion outside Warsaw. The Soviets reverted to political methods, but there was no doubt that the aim was to create dictatorships along the lines of the Leninist model.

At the opening session of the Comintern, Lenin and Trotsky described the epoch as "one of disintegration and collapse of the entire world capitalist system, which will involve the collapse of European civilization as a whole." Capitalism had to be destroyed, and workers of the world should seize power and create a "new apparatus of power"—namely the dictatorship of the working class. "It should be used as an instrument for the systematic suppression of the exploiting classes and their expropriation." The goal was decidedly *not* to introduce "a false or bourgeois democracy." The latter was nothing more than a "hypocritical form of the rule of the financial oligarchy." The bourgeoisie would have to be disarmed, and "open armed conflict with the political power" carried through to victory. The Bolsheviks had no patience even with the Socialists and branded them "social-traitor parties." The ambition was to establish worldwide Communism. Stalin was forced to take up alternative approaches, but would relaunch the drive to bring about the millenarian dream at the earliest moment.[1]

COMMUNIST PLANS FOR WORLD CONQUEST

Stalin had become convinced by the early 1920s that capitalist imperialism from the West and the East automatically implied "the inevitability of armed collisions." Sooner or later these would culminate in armed conflict on the scale of the First World War. His pragmatic approach was to do what was possible to have the "imperialist" countries war among themselves and ensure they not join in an anti-Soviet alliance.

His strategy was the ancient one of "divide and rule." As the U.S. ambassador George F. Kennan put it, this approach "consisted in the instinctive effort—the same to which he was so addicted in personal life—to divide his opponents, to provoke them to hostile action against each other, to cause them to waste *their* strength in this way, while he conserved *his.*"[2]

At the plenary session of the Central Committee on January 19, 1925, Stalin said the Soviet Union would inevitably be affected by a major clash of arms: "If war comes we will not be able to sit back and relax. We will have to make a move, but we will be the last to act. We shall throw our weight onto the balance, and that might tip the scales."[3] He said repeatedly that he was not giving up on world revolution. In May 1925 he insisted it was important to focus for the time being on making the revolution a success at home, but that would be the first stage in the global struggle.[4]

For Stalin, spreading Communism was a crucial part of the Leninist mission to "save" the proletariat, but he also conceived of it as a defensive measure against a hostile world. In his address to the Seventeenth Party Congress on January 26, 1934, he said that the next major war would be aimed at the conquest and division of the USSR and the country had to prepare itself appropriately. He even alluded to his own terror

ABOVE: The accused and their lawyers at the Hitler Trial. *Left to right in uniform:* Friedrich Weber, Hermann Kriebel, Erich Ludendorff, Hitler, Wilhelm Brückner, Ernest Röhm, Heinz Pernet (in civilian clothes, later Minister of the Interior), Wilhelm Frick, and later Gauleiter Robert Wagner. (1924)
BELOW: Hitler and Goebbels pose with local Party officials in Hattingen. (1926)

LEFT: Adolf Hitler with SA-leader Pfeffer von Salomon at an event in Munich in 1927. Between the two, partly hidden, is Rudolf Hess. On the left in a hat facing the camera is Alfred Rosenberg.

BELOW: Chancellor Adolf Hitler greets President Paul von Hindenburg on the occasion of the opening of the Reichstag in Potsdam on March 21, 1933.

Adolf Hitler poses with members of his new government soon after his appoint-
ment. *Left to right:* Walther Funk, Hans Heinrich Lammers, Walther Darré, Franz
Seldte, Franz Gürtner, Joseph Goebbels, unidentified, Hitler,
Hermann Goering, unidentified, Werner von Blomberg, Wilhelm Frick, Constantin
Freiherr von Neurath, Hjalmar Schacht, Lutz Graf Schwerin von Krosigk,
Johannes Popitz, Franz von Papen, and Otto Meissner. (February 1933)

ABOVE: A crowd gathers in front of a Jewish-owned store
in Berlin on the first day of the boycott on April 1, 1933.
BELOW: Himmler and police colleagues. *Left to right:* Franz Josef Huber, Arthur
Nebe, Heinrich Himmler, Reinhardt Heydrich, and Heinrich Müller.

Visitors line up to attend the opening of the
Great Anti-Bolshevism Exhibition of 1937.

ABOVE: Officials at the opening ceremonies of the 1938 Party rally in Nuremberg. *Left to right:* Joseph Goebbels, Robert Ley, Heinrich Himmler, Victor Lutze, Rudolf Hess, Adolf Hitler, and Julius Streicher.
BELOW: Leaders at the Munich Peace Conference in September 1938. *Left to right:* Neville Chamberlain (Britain), Edouard Daladier (France), Adolf Hitler, Benito Mussolini (Italy), and Count Galleazzo Ciano (Italy).

Hitler's speech to the Reichstag in which he first mentioned his "prophesy" of what would happen to the Jews should "they" bring about another world war. (January 30, 1939)

ABOVE: Soviet Foreign Minister Vyacheslav Molotov signs the German-USSR non-aggression pact in Moscow. Standing directly behind him is Joachim von Ribbentrop and Joseph Stalin. (August 23, 1939)

BELOW: At the headquarters of the German army in East Prussia, June 30, 1941. *Left to right:* Walther von Brauchitsch, unknown, Wilhelm Keitel, Adolf Hitler, and Franz Halder. In the background is Walter Warlimont.

and purges to come, which were supposedly needed to root out would-be traitors. Despite the great successes that had been achieved, he warned, they had to be wary of being overconfident.[5] His view was that after the next war the Soviets might bring Communism to Europe—and perhaps beyond.

Stalin's speech to the plenum of the Party's Central Committee on March 3, 1937, underlined the deteriorating international situation as sufficient justification for the mass terror and the show trials. "Is it not clear," he asked rhetorically, "that as long as there is capitalist encirclement, we will be infiltrated by wreckers, spies, diversionists, and assassins sent to us by foreign states?"[6]

The entrenched worry about capitalist encirclement, an unquestioned "truth" since Lenin's time, was magnified many times over by Hitler's successes. From the Soviet point of view, the Western democracies were complicit since none tried to stop Hitler or to join in the collective security agreements Stalin proposed.

At the Eighteenth Party Congress on March 10, 1939, he said the long anticipated imperialist war was already under way. It had not yet become universal, but pitted Germany, Italy, and Japan—the "aggressor" states—against the United States, Britain, and France. The latter still would not embrace collective security, as recommended by the Soviet Union, but tried to appease the aggressors. Stalin felt these "non-aggressor" states were much stronger than their enemies, so why did they not resist? The reason was simple: the United States, Britain, and France were conspiring to have Japan become embroiled with China, and to set up Germany and Italy for a war against the Soviet Union. These nations would be encouraged to make war and thereby would "weaken and exhaust one another, and once they had become weak enough," the West would "arrive on the scene with new-found strength, 'in the interests of peace' of course, and to dictate conditions to the weakened belligerents. Cheap and easy!"[7]

Stalin was convinced he saw through the machinations designed "to poison the climate and provoke a conflict" between Germany and the Soviet Union from which the West would ultimately gain. His worst nightmare, one that haunted him throughout the war to come, was that Western democracies like Britain and France might join Germany in an anti-Soviet crusade.

His strategy at the end of August 1939 to deal with that worst-case scenario was to encourage (or at least not hinder) Germany's attack on Poland, which might lead Britain and France to come to Poland's aid. There was no reason to expect such a war would be a quick victory for Hitler, but it might well drag on and weaken all the enemies of the Communists. Ultimately the war in the West would make it possible for the Soviet Union to break out of the capitalists' encirclement. At the very least it would allow the Soviets to reclaim lands lost at the end of the First World War.

When Stalin signed the nonaggression pact with Hitler in August 1939, he was in effect reviving the internationalist side of Leninism. He told a meeting of his intimate circle on September 7: "A war is on between two groups of capitalist countries . . . for the redivision of the world, for the domination of the world! We see nothing wrong in their having a good hard fight and weakening each other. It would be fine if at the hands of Germany the position of the richest capitalist countries (especially England) were shaken." Stalin boasted he was playing these powers off against each other.[8]

Historians have said Soviet foreign policy under Stalin was driven either by "revolutionary" ideological expansionism or by "traditional" great-power political considerations.[9] In fact the approach varied over time, but either way, the coming of the Second World War opened expansive possibilities.

HITLER'S ANSWER TO THE COMMUNIST CHALLENGE

Hitler's worldview was worked out in opposition to the Communism he saw stalking the streets in Germany after the First World War. He also developed plans that were much more than idle daydreams. When he spoke to German army officers about his vision of the future, they were impressed and for the most part also convinced. The assertion that Hitler's plans were little more than "objectless" fantasies is no more convincing than the claim that he "notoriously" exhibited "inner insecurity in all fundamental questions" and should be labeled a "weak dictator."[10]

One of Germany's leading military historians takes Hitler's ideas on foreign policy and his "program" far more seriously. "It is a mistake," Manfred Messerschmidt writes, "for anyone to suppose that these ideas of Hitler's were not more than simple reflections of a purely abstract nature. That is to miss the direction of his thought. We should not over- look its affinity with the 'philosophy of war' that became widespread after 1918. Hitler's ideology and foreign policy objectives, as his later statements show, combined to form a thoroughly effective basis of polit- ical action."[11] Hitler had no difficulty in explaining his position to lead- ing officers when he met with them only days after his appointment as chancellor.

To say that he had a "theory" or "philosophy" is not to claim that he planned everything in advance. He also made tactical compromises, and at crucial points in the war he even broke some key principles.

The idea of struggle was integral to Hitler's thinking, particularly in foreign policy. He said in a speech at Erlangen in 1930, "Every form of life seeks to expand, and every people strives for world domination."[12] The "stage plan" to world conquest he put forward in his writing before he came to power postulated that the first step for a new Germany was to reassert itself in foreign affairs and regain its rightful place as the dominant power on the continent. The initial period would be the most dangerous because the country would be vulnerable. But Hitler would never be content merely to tear up the Treaty of Versailles, put France in its place, and return Germany to what it was in 1914. In his view, the nation would have to prepare for war with the Soviet Union, but, so his thinking ran, it would do so with Britain's support or at least with its neutrality.

Purges in the Soviet Union in the 1930s helped to reinforce Hitler's determination, because the Red Army—most people in the West agreed—was so depleted that victory would come easily. Hitler believed that Germany would gain continental hegemony and lebensraum (living space) in the east. With that platform, Germany could then expand on a global scale and acquire a navy and colonies.[13]

Hitler thought it would be possible in his own lifetime to make Ger- many one of the "big four" powers in the world, alongside Britain, Japan, and the United States. He said little about America, but it was vir- tually inevitable that after wars against France and the Soviet Union, there would eventually be something akin to a "battle of the conti- nents." War against the United States might not happen in Hitler's gen- eration, and in any case it would also take time to foster the master race. He was convinced, however, of the "racial supremacy of the German people" and believed that ultimately, "like a god, the new human being would protect the world domination of the Germanic blood from all change."[14]

Hitler thought of America in the 1920s as an economic giant but knew little about it. He said America's decision to enter the war in 1917 was the result of Jewish influences. He liked U.S. immigration laws; he said they were based on racism and designed to ensure the survival of "Aryan" supremacy. In the 1930s, however, he began to view the United States as weak because its leaders stemmed from the "wrong side" of the U.S. Civil War. He said there was too much interbreeding—which in his books meant degeneration and decline—so that America had become a "mongrel society." From this point on, he also badly underestimated or ignored American economic and military potential.[15]

Right from the beginning of the Third Reich, Hitler started preparing for war and soon chalked up impressive foreign policy victories. By the time he met with the heads of the German armed forces on November 5, 1937, his resolution for war was firm. According to notes taken by Colonel Friedrich Hossbach, Hitler said the nation was close to full military capacity, but at a certain point (1943–45) its advantages would begin to slip away. He had frequently said Germany should head east first and tackle the "Jewish-Bolshevik" Soviet Union, with Britain as either an ally or neutral. To the consternation of the military leaders present, Hitler now held he was willing to risk war, even against Britain and France, in order to further his program. Some of the military thought peaceful means could be used to gain much of what Hitler claimed the German people needed. But no one really argued with either his short-term or his long-term goals. They objected mainly to the risks.[16]

This Hossbach memorandum was secret, but Hitler said more than enough in public for the European powers to know what he had in mind. Goebbels later spoke about this matter to a small circle of invited press people on April 5, 1940, just before the opening of the offensive against France. With a triumphant air he boasted that they had kept their foreign policy aims vague until that moment. Goebbels said their neighbors should have gotten rid of Hitler while they had the chance. Instead, they waited until he was better armed than they were and had made it through the most dangerous period, and only then they declared war. To the propaganda minister it was ridiculous.[17]

NEW KIND OF WAR ON THE HORIZON

The Munich conference of late September 1938 involved the prime ministers of Britain and France, along with Mussolini and Hitler. It was a great victory for Hitler. "General Bloodless," as Germans fondly nicknamed him, continued to win without a fight. The peaceful outcome of the conference left him dissatisfied, however, as he wanted a short war with Czechoslovakia to parade as a conquering hero. Sir Nevile Henderson, the British ambassador to Germany and a participant at Munich, shrewdly observed that the moment Hitler signed the agreement he regretted it. Hitler believed that he had accepted less than he could easily have taken.

Henderson was of the opinion that Hitler saw himself not as an ordinary politician but as someone who listened to an otherworldly voice. Henderson capitalized "Voice" and said of Hitler that "his Voice had told him that there would be no general war, or that, even if there were, there could be no more propitious moment for it than that October; and for once he had been obliged to disregard that Voice and to listen to counsels of prudence."[18]

At Munich, Hitler promised to guarantee the independence of what remained of Czechoslovakia. On September 30, after a separate meeting with the British prime minister, Neville Chamberlain, he grudgingly signed a resolution that the two peoples would never go to war against each other. Chamberlain waved this document to the crowds on his return to Britain, but Hitler attached no importance to it whatsoever.[19]

Only three weeks later, he issued directives to the army to prepare a surprise attack on what remained of Czechoslovakia.[20] In a short campaign on March 14–15, 1939, he crushed his smaller opponent.

Before the dust had settled, he demanded the return of Danzig, which had been lost to Poland in the Versailles Treaty. Thus he began to lay the groundwork for the coming war against Poland—which was merely a stepping-stone to the conflict he wanted with the Soviet Union. On March 23, he simply annexed the Memel territory from Lithuania, another challenge to which Britain and France failed to respond.

Hitler long held antipathies toward the Polish people, and conquering that country was part of gaining lebensraum in the east. In a communication to Walther von Brauchitsch, commander in chief of the army, on March 25, he said the issue would be solved when political conditions were right; Poland "ought to be beaten down, so that it will not need to be taken into account as a political factor for the next decades."[21]

Only after Hitler's high-handed conquest of the remainder of Czechoslovakia and the threatening sounds he began to make toward Poland did Western democracies finally realize that he could not be appeased. Chamberlain, with the unanimous agreement of the House of Commons and the staunch support of the public, had finally had enough. On March 31, he announced that the government "had undertaken an obligation of mutual assistance to Poland in the event of any aggression which might endanger the independence of that country." The French followed suit, so that, as Henderson observed, "war would be the inevitable outcome of the next aggression by Germany."[22]

Threatening Hitler with dire consequences, however, was completely meaningless. Far from being deterred, he was disgusted and in angry reaction had war directives drawn up by the military. He issued these orders on April 11 for preparation of Operation White, a surprise attack on Poland that was to begin anytime after September 1. There would be no declaration of war, and he hoped a swift victory might not lead to anything more than a local action.[23]

On May 23, when Hitler addressed senior military leaders, he knew a general war was a distinct possibility. He wanted to conquer Poland, not only to take lebensraum, but also because he saw it as having too little substance to act as a bulwark against Bolshevism. He reckoned it would be difficult to avoid war with England and a repetition of the easy victories was unlikely. In case matters would get that far, he wanted to be prepared for England, and his aim was as "always" to bring that country "to its knees."[24]

The SS also were drawn into the plans for operations against Poland. The SD Main Office created a new office, SD II P (Poland), on May 22 to assemble intelligence on everything "of an ideological-political, cultural, propagandistic, and economic nature." It was also to collect "complete" accounts of the Jews in Poland. This information was to be given to the still to be formed Einsatzgruppen (action groups). On July 5, Heydrich held a first central conference of key police and intelligence officials as part of the preparation. Initially there were to be four, but eventually there were five Einsatzgruppen of about five hundred men each, divided in turn into smaller Einsatzkommandos of a hundred or so. Led by experienced SD officers, the groups were composed of members mostly from the Gestapo; the Kripo (Criminal Police), and the SD. Another twenty-four thousand from the SS Death's Head Units were available by the time of the Polish campaign, comprising men trained by Theodor Eicke to run concentration camps.[25]

Guidelines for the security police (that is, the Gestapo and Kripo) and SD to cooperate with the High Command of the Wehrmacht (OKW) were established on July 31, 1939. The task of the Einsatzgruppen was "combating of all elements hostile to the Reich and Germany in enemy territory behind the fighting troops." The decision was made for an "initial sweep" to pick up ten thousand "enemies," with double that number arrested in a second round. They were not to be shot out of hand, but sent to concentration camps, so the agreement did not amount to a deal between Heydrich and the OKW for mass executions or deportations. It would soon become clear, however, particularly with respect to Jews and Poles, that the SS leadership had no intention of keeping to these rules and did everything in its power to get around them from the first day of the war.[26]

In mid-August, Heydrich held meetings with the leaders of the Einsatzgruppen at Gestapo headquarters in Berlin. They were given a free hand to shoot people from a long list, including those who had supposedly persecuted the German minority in Poland, the intelligentsia, the resistance, "partisans," and Jews. Heydrich told a colleague in July 1940 that prior to the war against Poland, he was given an "extraordinarily extreme" order by Hitler. He was instructed to "liquidate" various circles of the Polish leadership "that went into the thousands." Before the war began, the names of enemies were compiled with the cooperation of German military intelligence.[27]

Already from early 1939 special "schooling pamphlets" that were regularly sent to the troops of the Wehrmacht told them what to expect. The aims of the regime were said to include: "(1) the elimination of all after-effects of Jewish influence, above all in the economy and on spiritual life; (2) the struggle against world Jewry, which seeks to set all the people of the world against Germany." This enemy was to be fought "as we struggle against a poisonous parasite; we hit him not only as an enemy of our people but as a plague on all peoples." There was an abundance of such material, and it no doubt helped to persuade many in the armed forces that the Jews were the deadly enemies of the "master race." It should be noted that these ideological and expressly anti-Semitic messages were conveyed by the High Command of the Armed Forces, not the SS. There appears to have been a consensus on this matter; at least there is no evidence that officers raised any objections.[28]

On August 22, Hitler revealed his attitudes about the coming war at a meeting with about fifty leaders of the armed forces at the Berghof, his mountain retreat. Notes of what was said were offered in evidence at the Nuremberg trials in 1945–46. Army Chief of Staff General Franz Halder also made entries in his diary for the day.

Hitler made the decision about Poland in the spring. In his view, there were compelling reasons for doing so: he was getting on in years and felt the pressure of time; and the German people backed him—and "no one will ever again have the confidence of the whole German people as I have." Mussolini's support was also decisive. "If anything happens to him, Italy's loyalty to the alliance will no longer be certain." There were uniquely favorable conditions as well. Britain was unprepared for a land war, while France had declined as a military power. British and French leaders were "no masters, no men of action" and could not live up to the promises they had recently made.

Hitler's initial plan was to have a short war in the west (France) before going east; he changed his mind because the relationship with Poland had become "intolerable." Even if Britain and France kept their word to Poland, the war would not last long, as they did not have the military force to back up their commitments and were hoping Russia might do their fighting for them. Hitler proudly announced he had just come to terms with Stalin. "Our enemies are small-fry; I saw them in Munich."[29]

The cryptic notes show how firmly he held to the "lessons" of the First World War: "The nation collapsed in 1918 because the spiritual prerequisites were insufficient." Now Germany needed internal unity and firm leadership. "Crises," he said, "are due solely to leaders having lost their nerve."

The war aims he enunciated were unprecedented:

Destruction [*Vernichtung*] of Poland the priority. The aim is the elimination [*Beseitigung*] of active forces, not to reach a definite line. Also if war breaks out in the west, the destruction of Poland remains the priority. In view of the season, a quick victory. . . . Close your hearts to pity. Act brutally. Eighty million people must obtain what is their right. Their existence must be made secure. The stronger has the right. The greatest harshness. . . . Every newly awakening Polish active force is to be destroyed again immediately. Continuous demolition. . . . The complete demolition of Poland is the military goal. Speed is the main thing. Pursuit to the point of complete annihilation [*völlige Vernichtung*].[30]

Nicolaus von Below, Hitler's adjutant, recorded that although some generals had doubts about such matters as the likely response of the United States, they posed no questions and did not offer counterarguments. Because Hitler, to everyone's surprise, had secured the non-aggression treaty with Stalin, the leaders of the armed forces were speechless.[31]

Another of the note takers quoted Hitler saying "Genghis Khan had sent millions of women and children to their deaths, and did so consciously and with a happy heart. History sees in him only the great founder of states." He had already issued orders to the SS Death's Head Units "mercilessly and without pity to send every man, woman, and child of Polish ethnicity and language to their deaths. . . . Poland will be depopulated and resettled with Germans. . . . Be hard, spare nothing, act faster and more brutally than the others." When Western Europeans heard about the horrors, they would "shake with fear. That's the most humane way of war."[32]

STALIN, HITLER, AND THE NAZI-SOVIET PACT

Stalin's address to the plenary session of the Party congress on March 10, 1939, said the three democracies seemed to be encouraging Hitler to start war on the Bolsheviks, and everything will be all right.[33] He warned that the USSR should not be underestimated but admitted it was going to take ten to fifteen years "to catch up economically with the advanced capitalist countries." That point was duly noted by Germany's ambassador to the Soviet Union.[34]

Hitler was not to be stopped with veiled threats, and even as Stalin was speaking in Moscow, Hitler seized Memel and the rest of Czechoslovakia.

Stalin ordered his foreign minister, Maxim Litvinov, to inform the German ambassador of the displeasure of the Soviet government.[35]

In May 1939, Stalin had removed Litvinov, who was Jewish, as the commissar of foreign affairs and replaced him with Vyacheslav Molotov, who later recalled Stalin telling him to "purge the ministry of Jews," suggesting a turnabout on official anti-Semitism. Molotov said he was happy to comply.[36] For Hitler this move indicated Stalin's interest in talking, but all the while Stalin kept trying to form a triple alliance with Britain and France and resisted German entreaties. The Soviets were circumspect, but their suspicions grew with the dilatory approach Britain adopted to negotiations in 1939, which dragged on from April 15 into mid-August.

Britain and France sent a military delegation to Moscow to negotiate, but Stalin was infuriated that the officers were of low rank and traveled by ship instead of by plane. The Soviet secret police chief, Beria, prepared a dossier on each of the negotiators, and as soon as Stalin read the files, he remarked: "These people are not serious. These people can't have the proper authority. London and Paris are playing poker again."[37]

At the meetings the USSR said it was prepared to put up 120 infantry divisions in the event of war with Germany, and the British and French would have to contribute at least 86. In fact, the British army was completely unprepared and had—by Hitler's estimates, which were not far off the mark—something like 3 divisions it could deploy in Europe. For Stalin the British admissions made the negotiations a joke. Even if the French had more men, they had nothing like as many as the Soviets thought necessary. If war came, the Soviets would be left facing the military wrath of Germany more or less on their own.

Stalin had had enough of these vacillations, so that when the German ambassador in Moscow conveyed his government's wish to improve relations on August 15, Molotov answered within two days that a nonaggression pact might be useful. On August 18, Hitler wrote Stalin to request that his foreign minister, Joachim von Ribbentrop, fly to Moscow immediately for talks. He was willing to negotiate spheres of influence, but emphasized the urgency in view of the fact that "an early outbreak of open German-Polish conflict is probable."[38]

Hitler sent his acceptance of the pact two days later and expressed his willingness to sign Stalin's supplementary protocol—with demands in it he had not even seen. Stalin underlined the phrase in Hitler's telegram that said "a crisis may arise any day." Hitler urged Stalin to meet with Ribbentrop as soon as possible and assured him his minister would have "the fullest powers to draw up and sign the nonaggression pact as well as the protocol."

Before Stalin had the fateful meeting, he read everything his minions could assemble for him about and by Hitler. He underlined passages about Germany's "eternal ambitions" in the east and Hitler's attitude toward Russia. Stalin was playing for time and also following his long-standing view that it was preferable for a war to begin among the Western powers. He could then, at the right moment, intervene to tip the balance.

He was wary enough of Hitler and recognized how easily he had been able to wipe out the Communist and Socialist movements in Germany. Later he mentioned how Hitler "took the people with him" into the war, a dictator with the citizens behind him, making him all the more dangerous.[39]

On August 23, Stalin and Molotov met with Ribbentrop and repeated their view that the British wanted to foment war between the Soviet Union and Germany as a way to maintain their own empire. At the end of a long evening there were toasts all round, ending with Stalin giving "a guarantee on his word of honor that the Soviet Union would not betray its partner."[40]

The nonaggression treaty was a conspiracy to wage war on Poland. The "secret additional protocol," added at Stalin's urging, assigned each country a "sphere of interest" in the event that a "territorial and political transformation" should take place in Poland. In plain English that meant Germany would take the western part of Poland and the Soviet Union the eastern part. Stalin wanted the Soviet sphere to include Finland and the Baltic States (Estonia, Latvia, and Lithuania), all the way to Bessarabia in the far south.[41]

Hitler needed the pact with Stalin so as not to worry about his rear if the British and French called his bluff. For Stalin the agreement was of monumental importance. It opened a new chapter in his career and revealed that his ambitions had moved beyond the Soviet Union. His "program" from the mid-1920s was being extended, from building Socialism in one country to breaking out of capitalist encirclement and now even seeking ways to expand the Soviet Union and spread Communism. Stalin later told the British ambassador Sir Stafford Cripps that he had signed the pact with Hitler because both of them sought "to destroy the old balance of power that existed in Europe," whereas Britain and France were trying to maintain it.[42]

The change of direction was a shock to Communists everywhere, and it took a few days for Stalin to work out a new "line." On September 7 he met with Molotov, Zhdanov, and Georgi Dimitrov, the head of the Comintern. He observed that it would "not be bad" if Germany and the capitalist countries were weakened: "Hitler, without understanding it or desiring it, is shaking and undermining the capitalist system." Stalin said the pact was "helping Germany," but next time the USSR might support the other side.[43]

The new Communist position went as follows: until the war it was right to see a difference between democratic and Fascist regimes, but now that the war was on, the old distinction no longer made any sense. Communist parties the world over were told that they were witnessing a war among imperialist powers and that there was a possibility, if Communists played their cards right, to make progress toward the destruction of the slave-based system of imperialism once and for all. They could step in when a country—Poland, for example—was suffering the agonies of defeat and turn it into a Soviet republic. Poland was now described as a "Fascist state that enslaves Ukrainians, Byelorussians, and other Slavs"; if it fell, the world would have "one less bourgeois Fascist state. Would it be so bad if we, through the destruction of Poland, extended the Socialist system to new territories and populations?"

The Comintern promptly issued a worldwide directive to the faithful. Instead of being against Germany, Communists in countries engaging the "Fascists" had to take an antiwar stand. Even in neutral countries like the United States, Communists were instructed to come out against intervention. The activists in France, England, Belgium, and America in particular were told they "must immediately correct their political line."

François Furet, once a member of the French Communist Party, writes that the Communists, faced with Stalin's directive, showed an "extraordinary discipline, unique in the history of humanity." Once the new line was issued, there was a "sudden reorientation of such a vast army of militants toward a policy diametrically opposed to the policy of the day before." Communists, whether in Britain, France, America, or out in the far corners of the world, who had been screaming for war against Hitler one minute, now had to come out just as enthusiastically against it.

Mao Tse-tung, who had been instructed to oppose Japanese aggression, went so far in reverse as to see the advantages of Stalin concluding a nonaggression pact with Japan that would divide China. Mao wanted a "Polish solution" for his own country. His thinking was that the Soviets would make him head of a puppet government, and he was ready to consign half the country to the Japanese occupation. In September 1939, Mao was prepared to collaborate with the Japanese, hoping that at the very least they would strike down his nationalist enemies.[44]

Most Communists fell into line with alacrity. In the United States, the Communist volunteers who dominated the Veterans of the Abraham Lincoln Brigade had fought in Spain against Franco, who was staunchly backed by Hitler and Mussolini. The Communists gave up their anti-Fascism and marched in New York in opposition to the American entry into the war.[45]

23

GERMAN RACIAL PERSECUTION
BEGINS IN POLAND

Hitler was deeply concerned that dissenters and defeatists on the home front might stab the battlefront in the back—as supposedly had happened in 1918. It was a fear shared by many leading figures in the Third Reich. In August and early September 1939, the regime took steps against a wide array of such potential "enemies."

In fact the coming of war led to the complete revolution of the terror system, which grew harsher by the day. Concentration camps and prisons filled, as Communists and others were arrested. The transformation of the camp system, which eventually held hundreds of thousands of prisoners, was under way.

The regime also embarked on more radical aspects of its racist agenda in the war against Poland. Hitler saw the Polish people as consisting of "terrible material" and the Polish Jews as "the most dreadful that anyone can possibly imagine."[1]

THE NAZI INVASION

Hitler's decision for war was firm on August 22 when he spoke to his generals and called for "iron nerves, iron resolution." The immediate goal was Poland, but that was merely a springboard to the USSR. The nonaggression pact with the Soviet Union did not mean he had given up his hatred of "Jewish Bolshevism." As he said to one of his generals, it was a "pact with Satan to drive out the devil."[2]

Nevertheless, he was concerned relations with Britain were not working out as he had hoped. According to his program for action in the east, that country was to be either an ally or a neutral, but instead war was imminent.

Despite reservations, he ordered mobilization for noon on August 25, but then delayed it to 1:30 p.m. His uncertainty led him to postpone the attack an hour at a time until he finally canceled it. He was still hoping the British and French would agree not to back Poland. There followed some frantic meetings with Sir Nevile Henderson, the British ambassador, who was still trying to appease Hitler in hopes of avoiding the calamity of war. For his part the chancellor kept insisting that he wanted to maintain good relations, but not at the cost of German interests.[3]

On August 30, he set the attack on Poland for September 1. He still left room for another postponement, but forged ahead and the next day issued directive No. 1 for the conduct of war. A surprise attack was finally planned for September 1, at 4:45 a.m.[4] Britain and France responded on September 3 and, in keeping with their treaty obligations to Poland, declared war on Germany. Hitler decided to hold off the attack in the west and go for "the speedy and victorious conclusion of operations against Poland."[5]

The Polish armies refused to retreat and were vulnerable to encirclement. General Halder noted in his diary on September 5, "Enemy practically defeated," and on September 10 recorded that German troops were crossing the Bug and the San rivers, or what would be the eastern frontier with the Soviet Union. Thus, in barely ten days the Germans had reached their goal in eastern Poland.[6]

This was the first blitzkrieg, or lightning war, with the emphasis on motorized attack, airpower, and rapid movement. The air force, after taking out strategic targets, worked in tandem with the army to compel the Polish forces to retreat. By September 17 the German High Command had set up a demarcation line. To the horror of the Poles, the Red Army attacked them from the east that very day.

The objective was to capture Warsaw, which was pounded by the Luftwaffe on September 25. Three days later Poland sued for peace, and on October 4 Hitler issued an amnesty to any of his troops who had committed indictable offenses in the fighting up to that point "out of bitterness against the Poles' atrocities." The cynical basis for freeing Germans held in prison or before the courts and dismissing the charges—the supposed cruelties committed by Poles against Germans, not the other way round—revealed that he did not mean for his troops to be hemmed in by the conventions of war.[7]

The short conflict was terrible enough. Some 70,000 Poles were killed, 133,000 wounded, and 700,000 captured. Germany suffered 11,000 dead, 30,000 wounded, and 3,400 missing in action. The Red Army, which attacked the Poles when they were already on the edge of defeat, killed 50,000 and took 300,000 prisoners, at a cost of far fewer casualties. It was an uneven fight.[8]

Soldiers of the Wehrmacht became involved in war crimes, such as happened on September 9 near the town of Ciepielów. Germans in the Fifteenth Motorized Infantry Regiment came under fire and suffered fourteen casualties before the Polish troops surrendered. A Colonel Wessel of the Wehrmacht was infuriated and, according to the diary of a German eyewitness, ranted about the dead and the "partisans," even though his three hundred Polish prisoners were in uniform. He ordered them moved down the road, and all were shot, their fate even caught on camera. Subsequent investigations showed a minimum of sixty-four additional occasions when German soldiers—not the SS or security police—shot Polish prisoners of war, sometimes en masse.[9]

The total number of German-ordered executions in September has been estimated at sixteen thousand, but the exact figure remains unknown.[10] Reprisal policy was: if locals shot at the Germans, the invaders would select intellectuals, politicians, and other notables for execution.

ETHNIC CLEANSING IN WESTERN POLAND

On September 7 in conversation with Walther von Brauchitsch, commander in chief of the army, Hitler called for a *"völkisch-politische Flurbereinigung,"* or "ethnic cleansing," of the conquered area. Admiral Wilhelm Canaris of military intelligence (*Abwehr*) soon learned of this and on September 12 mentioned his concerns about the "extermination of the nobility and clergy" to Wilhelm Keitel, the head of the Wehrmacht High Command. Keitel said the "matter has already been decided by the führer." If the army chose not to participate, it would have to tolerate the "ethnic extermination" (*volkstümliche Ausrottung*) going on around them.[11]

Jews were singled out from the start, with looting, burning of synagogues, and public humiliations all part of the routine. In reprisal for resistance of any kind, or simply on a whim, troops lashed out, and in some localities they clearly preferred to kill Jewish Poles.[12]

Halder confided in his diary on September 10 how an SS artillery unit "herded Jews into a church and massacred them." The men were court-martialed and some given a year's sentence. They were almost certainly freed by Hitler's amnesty in early October.[13] The main killers of the Jews were the Einsatzgruppen of the security police and SD. The twenty-seven hundred men in these groups were under the command of Reinhard Heydrich. On September 3, Heinrich Himmler gave them shoot-to-kill orders that concluded: "In every area where insurgents are encountered, leading figures from the local Polish political administration are to be taken as hostages. If it becomes necessary to shoot hostages in order to prevent attacks by insurgents, it is to be reported to me immediately so that I may render a decision."[14]

More was involved than dealing with insurgents and hostages, as Heydrich made clear on September 7. He told the heads of the Gestapo, Kripo, and SD that Poland would be wiped out and what remained administered by Germany: "The leading population groups in Poland will be neutralized [*unschädlich gemacht*] as much as possible. The remaining, lower population will not retain any of their own schools, but be repressed one way or another." Under no circumstances was the ruling class to be allowed to remain in Poland, but sent to German concentration camps, whereas the "humbler" classes should be sent to provisional camps on the border. "Polish plunderers" were to be shot on the spot.[15]

When Heydrich found out that two hundred executions were taking place each day, he complained that the responsible military courts were working "far too slowly." He wanted the accused shot or hanged immediately. He agreed to spare "the little people," but the nobility, the heads of the Church, and Jews "must be killed."[16]

A particularly gruesome atrocity began on September 7 when Lothar Beutel of Einsatzgruppe IV reported that eighteen ethnic Germans were killed by Poles in the town of Bromberg (Bydgoszcz). There was a rumor that many ethnic Germans who had lived in the town had been killed on September 3. With each retelling, the number in this "Bromberg massacre"—sometimes also called "Bloody Sunday"—grew exponentially. When word reached Hitler, he flew into a rage and instructed Himmler to order a large-scale reprisal. Beutel's men executed five hundred known Communists or members of the intelligentsia, and the military or police killed almost as many. Far from standing in the way, the local military commander aided and abetted the killing and ordered additional executions when several more of his men were shot. The action continued over the next several days, and ultimately the security police and Wehrmacht murdered an estimated one thousand Polish civilians in revenge for Bloody Sunday. Nearly half were also involved in some form of resistance and, from the army's point of view, were killed as part of the "pacification policy."[17]

What the Germans did in western Poland was nearly as horrendous as what the Soviets were doing at the same time in eastern Poland. Jan Gross estimates that in the two years of occupation the Germans killed around 120,000—notably before the mass murder of the Jews began. In that short time, Gross claims that the Soviets "killed or drove to their deaths three or four times as many people as the Nazis from a population half the size of that under German jurisdiction." Many Jews who left for the east when the Germans arrived began to "vote with their feet" when they experienced Soviet occupation and went back to the western zone.[18]

MASS MURDER AND EUTHANASIA

Hitler had long believed that the coming war would provide an opportunity to "cleanse the body politic" with complete disregard for legal conventions and public opinion. From 1933 onward, he told confidants that he favored "euthanasia," in the sense of killing the chronically ill and certain kinds of asocials.[19]

The decision to launch euthanasia in Germany with children came about following a chance petition to Hitler in the winter of 1938–39 from a man named Knauer, who wanted his severely retarded child to be granted a "mercy death." This was but one of many requests from parents to have their "idiotic children" put to death. The letter ended up on the desk of the impressive-sounding Chancellery of the Führer (KdF)— which had little real power and was seeking a mission. The letter was shown to Hitler, who ordered an investigation by his physician Karl Brandt and eventually granted the Knauer family's wish. Indeed, the killing of such children began several months before Hitler gave euthanasia his official authorization.

In May 1939 he had ordered the creation of the Reich Committee for the Scientific Registration of Serious Hereditarily and Congenitally Based Illnesses. His resolve was strengthened by advice from his personal physician Theo Morell, whose investigations of public attitudes in the summer of 1939 concluded that few close relatives would be opposed to the "mercy killing" of their chronically ill children.[20] By August 18 the Reich committee prepared circulars and sent them to regional authorities in search of information on "deformed births etc."[21] Those children were eventually transferred to one of thirty or so special clinics, where they were starved to death, given lethal injections, or murdered in some way. Altogether, some fifty-two hundred had been killed under this program by the end of the war.

Hitler's aims went well beyond dealing with malformed or mentally ill children, for in June or July 1939 he told Dr. Leonardo Conti (the new Reich health leader), among other top officials, that he wished to get rid of adult psychiatric patients who were seriously ill during the coming war. His attitude was firmed up by another report that he interpreted as concluding that "unequivocal opposition from the Churches was not to be expected."[22] Hitler put the euthanasia program under one of his own offices, the KdF, with Philipp Bouhler and Viktor Brack taking the leading parts.

Sometime in October 1939, Hitler issued an authorization to empower certain doctors to give a "mercy death" to those whom they regarded as incurably ill. He backdated the short note to the first day of the war in 1939. Together with other decisions we have already seen, this timing suggests that the coming of the war represented a significant turning point in Hitler's mind.

He may have been slow to start this program in Germany, but he quickly determined that people in chronic care in Poland would be murdered. Even so, orders did not always descend from Hitler or Berlin, for the zealots in the provinces were given free rein and did not wait for instructions once they became aware of what was expected.

On September 19, Hitler paid a victory visit to Danzig and came close to offering peace to Britain and France. Claiming to have no war aims against either, he said they should not be deluded by reports that the German people were not as enthusiastic as in 1914. To the contrary, he said, they were behind him and totally determined.[23]

To Danzig, Hitler took along the euthanasia advocates Bouhler, Brandt, and Conti, as well as other top Nazi officials like Himmler and Martin Bormann. He held discussions with Gauleiter Albert Forster, and the Berlin killing experts conferred with the Danzig specialists. Three days later a special commando under SS Major Kurt Eimann (which had already been formed) began clearing the mental hospital at Conradstein (Kocborowo), south of Danzig. In fact, mass graves had been dug even before Hitler arrived, so the decision to kill must have already been taken. Most patients were brought to a forest and shot, after which new patients were then escorted to Conradstein; the process continued into December, and by that time seven thousand had been killed.[24]

The same procedure took place near Gdynia (Gotenhafen), north of Danzig. In total, ten thousand were shot there by members of Einsatzkommando 16 in an operation that ran to December 1939. The well-organized campaign killed another two thousand at a site near Konitz (Chojnice). In late October 1939, the war on the chronic-care patients spilled over into Pomerania. Gauleiter Franz Schwede-Coburg wanted to capitalize on the mood and came to arrangements with Himmler; an estimated fourteen hundred hospital patients were shot by Kurt Eimann's SS commando.[25]

In October and November the killing of hospital patients continued in the Warthegau, likely at the request of Gauleiter Arthur Greiser. The recently created district, Reichsgau Wartheland, usually called the Warthegau, had a population of 5.9 million at the start of the war, and was to be cleansed of all Jews and Poles and incorporated into the Reich. Poles made up over 80 percent of the people, and Greiser wanted them removed. His special wrath was directed at the 385,000 Jews. Turning this area into a Germanic paradise was going to involve wholesale ethnic cleansing and mass murder.[26]

Part of this transformation entailed a euthanasia program. A new concentration camp in Posen (Poznan) used old Fort VII, as it was known. Its gas chamber was built and operating in mid- to late November 1939 and used carbon monoxide to kill. Himmler himself witnessed one of these gassings on December 13. Far from being sickened, as was claimed after the war by members of the SS, he regarded such events as the "high point" of his inspection tours.[27]

The killers sought and found a still more efficient and secretive killing process; they invented the first gas van, which began operations in the Warthegau on January 15, 1940, under Herbert Lange. The mobile killing machine made its rounds in the Warthegau and Pomerania and executed thousands of Polish and German patients as it went. It continued its grim work into West and East Prussia. The first wave in the euthanasia program was designed as part of the overall ethnic cleansing of these areas as laid down by Hitler, Himmler, and Heydrich. The slaughter in these eastern borderlands was not as systematic and "tidy" as the program under the KdF in "old" Germany, but was also not the random murders sometimes pictured in the literature.[28]

Most of the hospitals and clinics, once rid of their patients, were used by the Wehrmacht and SS, not the incoming ethnic German settlers from the east. Contrary to the claims made by some, the object of the killing was not to free up needed beds but to pursue the ideological and racist goal that Hitler had long preached of "cleansing the body politic."[29]

Inside Germany the euthanasia program moved ahead as well. Some time before July 1939, a meeting of experts led by Bouhler and Brandt concluded that 20 percent of the 300,000 or so of Germany's "chronically ill" patients should be disposed of. They expected some "difficulties" with public opinion but ruled out eliminating one person at a time. By early October they had decided to create killing centers.

The strategic plan was presented on October 9, 1939, by Viktor Brack, one of the main leaders of the T-4 operation. He calculated how many should be killed across the Reich by the formula 1,000:10:5:1. That meant that for every 1,000 people, 10 would need psychiatric care at some time in their lives, of whom 5 would be hospitalized; and of those, 1 patient would be killed. Given the German population of sixty-five to seventy million, the result would mean that between sixty-five and seventy thousand would be eliminated.[30]

The operation soon grew too big, and organizers moved into new headquarters at Tiergartenstrasse 4—with T-4 as the code name for their program. The public began to learn what was happening, and some family members went to hospitals and asylums to remove kin. Concerned relatives sent letters to the authorities in search of information about the program and the process. One woman whose two siblings died within a few days of each other wrote that she accepted the Third Reich but worried whether what was happening was legal. She wanted to know if there was some kind of law that made it possible to "relieve people from their chronic suffering."[31]

The program carried on until 70,273 people were killed, just beyond the target figure calculated by Brack before it began. This number does not include those murdered in operations in the newly annexed areas. Hitler called a temporary halt on August 24, 1941.[32] He did so, according to some accounts, because of public disquiet and condemnation of it by the Catholic bishop Clemens August von Galen, who spoke on the topic in his sermon on August 3.[33] The bishop suggested that the murder would spread to include invalids, the incurably sick, injured soldiers, or merely the unproductive. Although that sermon and isolated individual complaints may have played some role in halting the operation, they were not decisive. In fact, the T-4 personnel were needed in the east, where their expertise would be used in the mass murder of the Jews.[34]

The campaign against infirm children did not stop, and a second phase of the program began in places like Hadamar in August 1942.[35] Chronically ill patients were killed, and in isolated instances handicapped or even socially unruly people were murdered.

The operation shifted away from hospitals and asylums to concentration camps. Himmler had approached Bouhler in early 1941 to use T-4 gassing facilities to get rid of the "human ballast" in concentration camps.[36] By September 1941, SS doctors and the Gestapo in camps such as Dachau, Mauthausen, Ravensbrück, Buchenwald, Flossenbürg, and Neuengamme made preliminary selections of prisoners, and panels of visiting T-4 physicians picked the victims for gassing in an operation code-named Action 14f13. The first group selected were asocials, but any Jews in the camps were especially vulnerable.[37] Up to twenty thousand were gassed in T-4 facilities at Bernburg, Hartheim, and Sonnenstein in this action alone.[38] On March 26, 1942, as more people were needed to work, Himmler reminded camp authorities to pay attention to labor needs before sending prisoners to their deaths, and on April 27, 1943, he restricted the killing to the mentally ill who could not work.[39]

The organizers of the program told justice officials in April 1941 that 80 percent of the relatives of those killed "agreed" with what happened, 10 percent "protested," and the other 10 percent were "indifferent."[40] Subsequent historical research supports that conclusion.

NEW VISIONS OF THE FATE OF THE JEWS AND POLES

Nazi radicalism against the Jews kept escalating as Hitler or his henchmen altered their aims as they went. On September 14, 1939, Heydrich informed the relevant authorities in the secret police and SD that Himmler had made suggestions to Hitler on the "Jewish problem in Poland." The top brass confronted new issues with the conquest of that country. On September 19, in a meeting in Berlin of the Ministerial Defense Council, mention was made of possibly moving Germany's Jews to some place in Poland.[41]

Another meeting that day between Quartermaster General Eduard Wagner and Heydrich referred chillingly to what should happen to the Jews and Poles: "complete cleansing: Jewry, intelligentsia, spiritual leaders, nobility." Wagner did not object in principle, but said the operation should take place after the army withdrew from Poland.[42] He reported to Brauchitsch to prepare him for a meeting the next day with Hitler. The führer presented his expanding plans to the heads of the German military on the "resettlement" of the area. Poles and Jews would be driven from the western zones of Poland, and the Jews put into ghettos.

Brauchitsch raised no objections but wanted to delay implementation until military operations ended. In the meantime, so General Halder said, the situation would be studied to decide "which population groups must be resettled and where."[43]

In a follow-up meeting of his own on September 21, Heydrich called together the heads of the Einsatzgruppen and others, including Adolf Eichmann, the specialist in forced deportations of Jews in Austria and Czechoslovakia. The plan was to Germanize those provinces that had been formerly Germany but part of Poland since 1919 and to set aside a district farther east for non-Germans. Heydrich said the "problem of the Poles" was to be solved by "neutralizing" (*unschädlich machen*) the leadership class or by sending them to concentration camps. "The primitive Poles" who remained should be integrated into the labor process but eventually removed from the German-speaking area. He kept changing his mind about what should happen to these "primitive Poles." Should they be sent into an eastern area, as would the Jews, or brought to Germany as slaves? In no case, however, was a recognizable Polish state or a Polish nation—that is, a culturally identifiable entity—to exist.

Heydrich said Hitler authorized the deportation of the Jews to the same dumping ground in the east. Inside conquered Poland the Jews were to be forced into ghettos in larger cities as quickly as possible. Heydrich said the Jews in the Reich would also be sent to Poland, together with the remaining thirty thousand or so Gypsies. What Heydrich called the "final aim" (*Endziel*) of anti-Jewish policies was at this stage a territorial solution of some kind. The future fate of the Jews, Gypsies, and others was still up in the air.[44]

This meeting was significant because it revealed a shift of emphasis in anti-Jewish policy from what had been ordained by Hitler after the "night of broken glass." Earlier he had said he was aiming at eliminating the Jews from Germany by deporting them out of the country, and preferably out of Europe. Under the conditions of war, deportation by ship was impossible as most ports of exit were closed. The new "final aim" formally approved by Hitler and mentioned by Heydrich on September 21—was to send the Jews, including those from Germany, to a "Jewish reservation" in the east. They would be joined there by other "unreliable elements," but no timetable was mentioned.

A particularly diabolical aspect to the plans Heydrich mentioned on this day pertained to the formation of "Jewish councils" (*Judenältesten-räte*) in Poland. Every Jewish community was to form a council of twenty-four members or so, drawn from among the rabbis and other important personalities. Instead of the Germans passing orders directly to the Jews, all instructions were to be channeled through these councils, whose members were to be held "fully responsible" for carrying them out. They were to begin with a census, convey all instructions to the Jews on resettlement, including the times and places of departure, take responsibility for the housing and feeding of the population, and generally see to it that all German orders were obeyed.[45]

Heydrich met with Brauchitsch and Quartermaster Eduard Wagner on September 22 to smooth out ruffles in the relationship between the Einsatzgruppen and the military. The Wehrmacht was the only institution left in Germany that could have raised objections about the ethnic cleansing in Poland. The single reservation was that the resettlement plans ought not to hinder the movement of the military.

By the end of September 1939, Hitler had made up his mind that former Poland was to be divided into three zones. "All the Jews (also those from the Reich) as well as unreliable elements"—including the latter from Germany—were to be deported to the most easterly zone. According to notes taken by Goebbels, they were to be given a chance to see if they could construct anything there. The zone closest to Germany was to be Germanized and colonized and made the new breadbasket for the nation. Between these two zones there would be a third, something not quite a state and not simply a dependency, a territory whose very existence was to mark the physical separation of Germany from Russia. It would be called the General Government (*Generalgouvernement*).[46]

Fresh from his victory parade in Warsaw, Hitler told the Reichstag in Berlin of the "aims and tasks" resulting from the collapse of the Polish state. The entire area had to be secured and restored. The "most important task" was to create "a new order of ethnographic relations," and that meant "a resettlement of the nationalities." This was a problem of concern to the entire east and southeast of Europe, where German minorities were scattered. "It was utopian to think that in an age of the nationality principle and of racial thought, one could leave these representatives of a higher-valued race simply to be assimilated." There would be population transfers of ethnic Germans back to the fatherland. Germany would never permit, he said, "what remained of Poland" to disturb the peace with the Soviet Union.

In the context of solving minority problems in the new German lebensraum, Hitler mentioned the Jews briefly. He said only that there would be an effort to bring "order to and regulation of the Jewish problem."[47]

Goebbels's notes behind the scenes provide an invaluable record. The propaganda minister deduced from what Hitler said that the Jews were "not people anymore." They were rather like "beasts of prey equipped with a cold intellect." He admitted the "Jewish problem will likely be the most difficult to solve." He wrote that Hitler's assessment of the Poles was not to assimilate them with the German people. Poles were "more animals than people." He went to Poland to see for himself, and his film crew came up with material for anti-Polish and anti-Jewish campaigns. After viewing the film later, Goebbels confided to his diary: "This Jewry must be destroyed." His impression was that the occupation administration was "too German. We do not want to put the Polish house in order."[48]

Goebbels visited the Lodz ghetto, where everything he saw reinforced his prejudices: "They are not people but animals. And for that reason, they are not a humanitarian but a surgical task. We have to take steps here, and quite radical ones. Otherwise Europe will go to its doom on the Jewish disease." He said his conclusions won Hitler's "full support. The Jews are trash."[49] At the end of November he visited Posen and had equally harsh things to say.[50]

Hitler needed no coaching. In discussions with the head of the OKW, Keitel, on October 17, he had explained what he had in mind. Poland was not to be "a model province or model state along the lines of German order." Rather, it was to remain leaderless and be allowed to deteriorate into chaos, its living standard kept low. Its people were to become a source of slave labor for Germany. Carrying out this program, Hitler said, would require "a hard ethnic struggle, which follows no legal norms. The methods will have nothing to do with our usual legal principles." Any hope of Poland reemerging "must be eliminated." He added that "the leadership in this area must make it possible to clean out the Jews and the Polacks from the Reich proper."[51]

GERMANY'S DEPORTATIONS FROM
NEWLY INCORPORATED AREAS OF POLAND

The "cleansing" of western Poland was to take place by deporting Jews and Poles to the General Government, but the operation proceeded by fits and starts. Eichmann met with Heinrich Müller, the head of the Gestapo, on October 6 and received the mission to deport around 70,000 Jews from the annexed Polish territories. The experimental deportation, involving only males of working age, took on a momentum of its own. Soon the program aimed to expel 300,000 Jews over perhaps a nine-month period from nearly all areas conquered by the Wehrmacht, including the "old" Reich (that is, Germany), as well as Austria (the Ostmark) and the newly created Warthegau (that is, the northwest part of the former Poland that bordered on Germany). At a meeting with Arthur Nebe, the head of the Kripo, on October 12, Eichmann was asked when it would be possible to send east at least the "Berlin Gypsies" as well. Nebe was told they might be able to attach one wagon for Gypsies to each of the deportation trains. Eichmann opted for the Nisko, across the San River, as the place where the Jews would be dropped off.

This project was barely under way one week before it was stopped on orders originating from Himmler, mainly because the trains were needed for the resettlement of ethnic Germans coming, as per agreement with Stalin, from the Soviet zones of occupation in the east. Tens of thousands were brought west beginning on October 18, and Himmler, who was in charge of this operation, gave it priority over deporting Jews and Poles. Eventually to be moved from the Baltic States were around 110,000 re-settlers; close to 77,000 from Romania; and some 140,000 from various areas of the Soviet Union. These ethnic Germans were to be settled in the western areas of occupied Poland and sometimes brought to Germany proper.[52]

On November 28, 1939, Heydrich informed police leaders in Cracow, Breslau, Posen, and Danzig about another "short-term plan" (*Nahplan*) and a "long-term plan" (*Fernplan*). The need was to make room for incoming ethnic Germans, especially in the Warthegau, by moving out eighty thousand Poles and Jews. The long-term plan, which has never been found, apparently involved "removing the Jews and the Poles from the eastern provinces" to the General Government.

What was new in the plan was the proposal to use some Poles, those who could be termed "racially good," as slave labor in Germany rather than send them to the east. No mention was made of the Jews in Germany and Austria.

The plan was partially implemented between December 1 and 17, 1939. The authorities exceeded their quota, sending eighty-seven thousand Poles and Jews to the east. The broad nature of the racist agenda can be seen from the fact that these deportees included "politically dubious Poles, Jews, Polish members of the intelligentsia, and criminal and asocial elements." The unfortunates were transported in freight cars at a time of year when it was already bitterly cold.[53]

"The final solution of the German Jewish problem" was the subject of another plan, this time formulated by the Jewish affairs specialists of the SD in Berlin. On December 19, 1939, they used the concept of the "final solution" (*Endlösung*) for one of the first times. The document indicates that this term did not yet mean mass murder. The goal at this point was some kind of "reservation." Confusion and lack of certainty prevailed, however, and the approach to Jewish policy was haphazard and meandering.[54]

Heydrich revised plans yet again at the end of the year and made them known on January 30, 1940. The underlying principle was the same, namely to get rid of as many Jews and Poles from the newly incorporated areas as possible and replace them with ethnic Germans. He brought out a point Hitler had signaled earlier. Instead of sending the Poles in the new German areas to the east, he now proposed importing between 800,000 and 1 million of them into Germany, where they would be used as slave labor. Some Jews (40,000) and more Poles (120,000) would be sent to the General Government to make room for incoming ethnic Germans. After that he foresaw moving the remaining Jews from the eastern districts, along with 30,000 Gypsies from Germany and 1,000 Jews from Germany. All would be sent to the General Government. These plans were modified again, with the search still on for some kind of territorial solution to the "Jewish question."[55]

24

HITLER AND WESTERN EUROPE

lways one to be on to the next target, Hitler called a conference on September 27, 1939, the day Warsaw surrendered, to demand the immediate preparation of plans for an attack on France. General Halder was struck that Hitler underlined how time "will, in general, work against us if we do not use it wisely. The economic resources of the other side are stronger. The enemy can purchase and transport. Nor is time working for us in the military sense." The most likely option was that the war would continue, and the implications were obvious: "The goal is to bring England to its knees, to demolish France."[1]

DOUBTERS AND ASSASSINATION ATTEMPT

Hitler ordered preparations for an early attack in the west, notwithstanding the peace offer of sorts he made on October 6 in a speech to the Reichstag. British Prime Minister Chamberlain dismissed the halfhearted overtures, and within days Hitler informed his military leaders of his decision to go ahead. On October 16 he said the strike would likely come between November 15 and 20.[2]

Behind Hitler's back more cautious military leaders, particularly the High Command of the Army (OKH), began wondering aloud about the wisdom of their leader. Several groups started to hatch a conspiracy, even raising the possibility of deposing Hitler. They were not yet prepared to assassinate him.

Brauchitsch and Halder both had doubts about the west offensive but shied away from confronting Hitler. Brauchitsch made one attempt on November 5 to dissuade Hitler, who did not back down but angrily browbeat him into silence before storming out. Halder got cold feet waiting in the adjoining room. The army was divided, and on balance Hitler had far more support than any opponents among the leading officers. On November 12 he issued the order for the attack—code-named Case Yellow.[3]

This process was rudely interrupted by an assassination attempt. There was shock across the country on November 8, when a bomb went off in the Bürgerbräukeller, narrowly missing Hitler. This was the beer hall where the Nazis annually celebrated their attempted coup of 1923. Georg Elser, the man who planted the explosive device, hollowed out the stone pillar next to where the führer was to speak. Elser timed the bomb to go off at 9:20 p.m., in the middle of Hitler's speech, which usually ran from 8:30 to 10:00. Because of the wartime situation, Hitler decided to leave early and narrowly missed the explosion, which killed eight and injured sixty-three more, some of them seriously.[4] Newspapers spoke of the "spiritual" links to the event of both England and the Jews, although, as it turned out, Elser worked alone and was not Jewish.[5] He had been a member of the Communist Party, however, and, obsessed with trying to stop the war, he finally opted for an assassination of the Nazi leader.[6]

According to official public opinion surveys, the "love of the German people for the führer had increased more than ever, and also the attitude to the war had become still more positive among many as a result of the attempted assassination."[7] The Socialist underground reports agreed that regardless of who planted the bomb, it was "the Nazis who reaped the success." Some thought Hitler's death would only have benefited the enemy. The Socialists concluded that "according to our general observations," the attempt to kill Hitler led "to a strengthening" of national "determination" to go forward with the war, and "we recognize by that fact once more that there is only one possibility" of getting rid of Hitler, and that was "the convincing military defeat of the Reich."[8]

A popularly supported leader, one who had recently chalked up an easy victory in Poland, proved to be too much for would-be opponents in the military. Although they worried about the spread of war, they could not agree on what should be done. The western offensive did not go ahead immediately, but there were repeated delays caused by poor weather.

Halder, when pressed by Hitler's opponents, kept saying that it was "impractical" for the army to attempt a coup. Foreign powers would give no assurances what they would do if Hitler were toppled. Perhaps even worse, "opinion among the population and the younger officers (major and below) was not 'ripe,' " which is to say, would not tolerate an overthrow of the government. This was clearly what Halder meant by the "unfavourable" public opinion of the moment. Like the Socialists, he recognized Germans were behind Hitler, and they would only begin to change their minds, if at all, when the country faced military defeat.[9]

For the moment Hitler had the show of support he relished when facing division and dissent in the ranks. He decided to take on the doubters in the military in one fell swoop, not as Stalin would have done, by ordering their mass execution, but by bringing them in for a talk. On November 23, he ordered all the principal leaders (about two hundred in all) to come to the Reich chancellery for a special conference.

They were treated to the well-worn narrative of Hitler's rise from 1919 and how he had proven every naysayer wrong. He reminded them of his successes since taking over in 1933, most of them military victories, and he laid before them what they all saw as a stark fact, namely that Germany's rising population needed greater lebensraum. The alternative was either to take the "cowardly way" of killing children (abortion) or to fight to expand the room available. "No calculated cleverness is of any help here, solution only with the sword. A people unable to produce the strength to fight must withdraw. Struggles have become different from those of a hundred years ago. Today we can speak of a racial struggle. Today we fight for oil fields, rubber," and so on.

He said with pride that no one had predicted the quick victory over Poland, but the issue was not settled; the stronger foe remained in the west, where there was neither peace nor war, a situation that could not last for long. For Hitler, the moment to strike could not be better: if Germany attacked, this time they would have no enemy in the east. How long could the USSR be expected to live up to its treaty obligations, he asked? At a certain point it was bound to make a move. Thus, Hitler's rationale for dealing with the west as soon as possible was to free up the military for the east. He felt the Soviet military was weak and would remain so for a year or two. In his view, even a delay of six months would see the whole situation change.

Hitler intended to attack in the west "at the earliest and most favorable moment. Breach of the neutrality of Belgium and Holland is of no importance. No one will question that when we have won." That was his old refrain, as was his observation that there were no guarantees of success. Essential to victory in his mind—and presumably that was why he had gathered all these officers around him—was that "the leadership must give from above an example of fanatical unity. There would not be any failures if the leaders of the people always had the courage a rifleman must have." There was only one way to stop the war, and that was to attack and win. There was going to be no repeat of 1918—another of Hitler's favorite themes—because this time Germany had numerical superiority.

He ended with the usual all-or-nothing note: "If we come through this struggle victoriously—and we shall come through it—our time will go down in the history of our people. I shall stand or fall in this struggle. I shall never survive the defeat of my people. No capitulation to the outside, no revolution from within."[10]

He played up his popularity with the nation against the theoretical objections of some of the higher officer corps. These men could not stand up to him. Ian Kershaw correctly observes that "Hitler enjoyed a level of popularity exceeded by no other political leader of the time."[11]

What was involved, however, was not simply a popularity contest, because the great majority identified with Hitler's ideas and savored his triumphs as their own.

On January 16, 1940, after many cancellations of the attack on the west, Hitler finally postponed it until the spring. This development meant the armed forces had more time and their chances of success improved. The military leadership was in any case not so much opposed in principle to a west offensive; it had worried more about its lack of preparation.[12]

OPENING THE WAR IN THE WEST

In early 1940 the situation faced by Germany and the Allies was brought to a head. Winston Churchill, who was then the first lord of the admiralty, decided—at almost the same moment as Grand Admiral Erich Raeder—that the strategic position of Norway and Denmark was such that those countries could not be left open to the enemy. As both sides saw, if Norway was taken by the British, Germany's imports would be vulnerable. Raeder put the case to Hitler, who on March 1 issued a directive for the attack—code-named Weserübung (Weser Exercise)—for April 9. Again there was a coincidence with the British who on April 7 began to embark troops for the occupation of Norway and the next day began mining the waters around Narvik. The German invasion of Norway and Denmark went ahead as scheduled, catching the latter completely by surprise. In Norway they encountered far more resistance. Nevertheless, by June 10 the Norwegians sued for peace. The Allied forces in Norway had been withdrawn earlier to help meet the even bigger crisis of the German invasion of Western Europe.

Even before the battle for Norway was over, on May 10, the German offensive against the main enemies in the west began. The delays in the attack had given Hitler and his military leaders time to work out more innovative approaches. They found the plan put forward by the Army High Command, which envisioned a sweeping attack from the northwest, to be unimaginative and predictable. Instinctively, Hitler felt uncomfortable with the initial Case Yellow, as did Generals Erich von Manstein and Gerd von Rundstedt and the tank specialist Heinz Guderian.

The final version of Case Yellow was to begin (more or less as the Allies expected) with surprise strikes, led by General Fedor von Bock, to the north, through Holland and Belgium. The aim was to mislead the British and French into thinking these attacks were the main invasion. In fact the nasty surprise was in the south, where Manstein and Rundstedt had concentrated armored and motorized forces. Their attack would not sweep toward Paris, as would be anticipated, but instead drive through the Ardennes to Sedan and across the river Meuse. Then, again contrary to what would be expected, it would not head south to Paris but turn west and north, driving at full speed for the coast at Calais. That movement, later likened to a sickle cut, would isolate the Allied forces rushing northward to repel Bock's attack and cut them off from their armies in the south. The Germans would catch the Allies from behind and in front, leaving them little choice but to retreat to the coast in hopes of avoiding capture.[13]

The German attack, much of it inspired by Hitler's strategic thinking, with sound advice from Manstein, was a spectacular success. Within ten days, German troops were on the Channel coast. The Allied debacle was partly the fault of their own mistakes, perhaps above all their failure to work out a command structure and to integrate their forces with the Belgians and the Dutch. As one account sums up what happened, "A poorly led and badly coordinated Allied force was pierced at a critical point by concentrated German armor and was never able to regain even its balance, to say nothing of the initiative."[14]

The Allies realized they could not link up with their troops to the south; the British Expeditionary Force began its own march to the Channel with the aim of evacuating as many as possible near Dunkirk. Hitler let himself be persuaded by Rundstedt to stop the advance on May 24, mostly because Rundstedt thought the terrain in Flanders was too soggy for tanks, which in any case needed refurbishing. Generals Halder and Brauchitsch strongly favored chasing down the retreating forces but were overruled. Halder observed sarcastically in his war diary that his troops were stopped with no opposition in sight and on Hitler's direct orders.[15] As it was, the Wehrmacht was but fifteen miles from capturing or killing a substantial proportion of the Allied armies, and that might have had an important effect on the British decision to continue the war.

Many explanations have been given for the mistake of letting escape 220,000 British and 120,000 French soldiers. The myth of Hitler's magnanimity is completely without foundation; he was persuaded to stop the advance by Rundstedt on technical grounds. Göring also led him to believe the air force could finish the job, but his boast was mistaken. It was also true that Hitler wanted to redeploy, first to the south, where some fighting continued. He changed his mind when he saw so many get away at Dunkirk and within forty-eight hours commenced the attack again. Rundstedt turned his forces to the south and headed toward Paris. The German passion was to win as quickly as possible. The attack opened on June 5 and was over in less than three weeks.[16]

In Hitler's view, the escape of the Allied troops seemed of little consequence compared with the overwhelming victory. German units rolled forward almost without stop, entering Paris on June 14. A week later Hitler demanded that the French government agree to an armistice near Compiègne. He also insisted on getting the same railway car and signing the documents in the same place where the Germans had been forced to sign an armistice in 1918. That event was seared into Hitler's consciousness as the day of the ultimate national humiliation. The repetition of the same event, with a different outcome, ended part of Hitler's trauma about the last war.

His vision went far beyond undoing the "shame of 1918" and recouping the territorial losses. He strove for more. In a matter of months he had been able to beat France, Germany's traditional foe, and push the British off the continent. Germany controlled all of Western Europe and, in the east, most of Poland, all of Czechoslovakia, and Austria. The economic potential of this vast area was greater than the dreams of the most voracious imperialist.

All of that meant little in itself to Hitler. He was still fixated on crushing what he called the "Judeo-Bolshevik" threat. In fact, his explanation for the attack on the west was connected to his military plans against the Bolsheviks. He wanted to make sure that "early in the year [1940] he would have his own army free again for a great operation in the east against Russia."[17]

It was in the autumn of 1939, even before the victory over Western Europe, that his adjutant first heard Hitler mention Russia in this way. By late May and early June 1940, Hitler had realized France was on the verge of defeat and Britain might soon have to sue for peace. He promptly began talking with his generals about settling accounts with Bolshevism.

Hitler must have smiled wryly on receiving Soviet Foreign Minister Molotov's "warmest congratulations" when German troops entered Paris. French Communists might have had a difficult time explaining those hearty salutations to their people deeply saddened at what was commonly regarded as a great national tragedy.[18] Molotov's sugar-coated words were completely lost on Hitler and did not give him a moment's pause in his determination to invade the USSR.

Hitler took little more than a perfunctory tour of Paris, hardly long enough to relish the spoils. He told Albert Speer, who was with him: "I am not in the mood for a victory parade. We aren't at the end yet." He asked Speer to "draw up a decree in my name ordering full-scale resumption of work on the Berlin buildings." He had given some thought to destroying Paris but opted not to, because "when we are finished in Berlin, Paris will be only a shadow." Speer visited Hitler later and vividly recalled overhearing a conversation he was having with the military leaders Alfred Jodl and Wilhelm Keitel. "Now we have shown what we are capable of," Hitler was saying as Speer approached. "Believe me, Keitel," Hitler continued, "a campaign against Russia would be like a child's game in a sandbox by comparison."[19] He was still mulling over options when he returned to Berlin, where he was welcomed like a conquering hero.

At that moment, as numerous contemporary records make clear, Hitler reached a new pinnacle of popularity. The majority considered him without question the greatest leader in Germany's long history. The drive from the railway station to the Reich chancellery was a massive lovefest. The crowds could not throw enough flowers or shout their support loudly enough.

Even as a staunch enemy of the regime admitted, Hitler's latest victories had magnified his popularity, and he was now generally regarded by ordinary Germans as "invincible." The people were certain of his victory over the British and the destruction of London and awaited peace in a matter of weeks. They were only puzzled that the landing of German troops was taking longer than expected.[20]

Within days the public began to notice troop transports heading east and tried to figure out the significance of these moves.[21] On July 31, Hitler informed military leaders that the earliest possible date for the invasion of England was September 15. He observed at the same time that Churchill was hanging on because he thought the Soviets would get involved in the war. "With Russia crushed, Britain's last hope would be shattered. Germany would emerge the master of Europe and the Balkans. Decision: Russia's destruction must therefore be a part of the struggle. Spring 1941." These were the cryptic notes taken by Halder on the occasion.[22]

Hitler was determined to take on Stalin before or as part of defeating the British, even though such an attack went against one of the axioms of his thought—namely the need to avoid a two-front war. He was convinced the British were staying in the war in the belief that the Soviets and perhaps the United States would come in on their side.

The German attack would not only crush the home of "Judeo-Bolshevism," as Hitler long had hoped, but hasten peace with Britain. Defeating Stalin would also relieve Japanese worries about Soviet encroachments, and that would free up Japan to explore options elsewhere, making it likely the United States would have to become involved to check the Japanese. That would draw the attention of the United States away from Europe and continue to give Hitler a free hand there.

All in all, by mid-1940 Hitler had come to believe he had every reason to see a rosy future. He was already so powerful as to be considered by most experts, including many in America, unstoppable. The consensus was that a German attack on the Soviet Union would succeed in three weeks or even less.

25

THE SOVIET RESPONSE

S talin was by no means idle while Hitler pursued the war against Poland and Western Europe. He boasted to Nikita Khrushchev that the Nazi-Soviet Pact of August 1939 gave the Communists a free hand not only in eastern Poland but in Estonia, Latvia, Lithuania, Bessarabia, and Finland. He said, "Hitler wants to trick us, but I think we've gotten the better of him." The boast was that the Soviets also had turned the tables on Britain and France, who had wanted to see the dictators at war with each other. Khrushchev had reservations and after the fact recalled them:

> We had a chance to get our head out from in front of our enemy's rifle, a choice we were pushed into by Western powers. That was our justification for the pact. That is still the way I see it today. However, it was a very difficult step to take at the time. For us Communists, antifascists, a people who stood on philosophical and political ground diametrically opposed to Hitler, to suddenly join forces in this war—how could we? Certainly the average citizen saw it that way. It was even difficult for us to fathom and to digest. But we were forced into it, and we were getting something out of the deal too.[1]

What they got was a chance to run roughshod over their neighbors and to transform those societies into mirror images of the Soviet Union.

THE SOVIET ATTACK ON POLAND

Stalin ordered the attack on Poland on September 17. According to Molotov's brutally frank note to the Polish ambassador, that country had ceased to exist, and the USSR could not "remain indifferent when its blood brothers" there were left to their fate. The Red Army was thus ordered "to cross the frontier and to take under their protection the lives and property of the population of Western Ukraine and Western White Russia." Molotov said they would also "take every step to deliver the Polish people from the disastrous war into which they have been plunged by their unwise leaders and give them an opportunity to live a peaceful life." That is to say, they would impose Communism.[2] On September 28, the Soviets signed a "friendship and frontier treaty" with Germany that recognized a mutual frontier between them running the length of the former Polish state. Both sides then did what they wanted with their spoils.[3]

Poland had not reckoned with this turn of events and maintained only the small Frontier Defense Corps (KOP, with around eleven thousand troops) on the border with the Soviet Union. Before his escape over the border, the supreme commander of the Polish forces ordered cessation of resistance to the Red Army. Communications were in chaos, and some Polish units, including the KOP, opened fire anyway. The result was a disaster. The war against their former Soviet allies cost the Polish armed forces at least 50,000 lives, and an unknown number were wounded or missing in action. Molotov admitted at the time that the losses of the Soviet forces were 737 killed and 1,862 wounded.[4]

The Red Army conquered around seventy-seven thousand square miles and thirteen million or so inhabitants of the former Polish state. The Soviets immediately sifted the population for "enemies." They went after the army and all the "Pans" — or the *beloruchki* (literally those with white hands, that is, people who did not work) — such as landowners, bureaucrats, and priests.[5]

An estimated 130,000 officers and men of the Polish army came under Soviet jurisdiction, but there may have been even twice that many prisoners.[6] Marshal Grigory Kulik, in charge of the invading Soviet forces, wanted to release at least the Ukrainians and Byelorussians, but Stalin disagreed. Security Chief Beria set up ten camps that could hold ten thousand prisoners each. Approximately forty-three hundred were kept in a camp at Kozel'sk; these were the mostly better educated members of the elite. Another camp held six thousand policemen and yet another four thousand, primarily senior officers and members of the educated elite.[7]

On March 5, 1940, a decision was finally taken about what should happen to them. Beria told the Politburo there were 14,700 officers, landowners, and policemen, as well as 11,000 "counterrevolutionary" landowners, allegedly "spies and saboteurs . . . hardened . . . enemies of Soviet power." They were given a troika "hearing," meaning their files would be briefly reviewed. Stalin, Voroshilov, Molotov, and Mikoyan signed the death warrants. Then executioners went to work: one of them shot a daily quota of 250 for twenty-eight nights. The bodies were buried in out-of-the-way places, but in 1943 the invading Germans discovered some in the forest at Katyn.[8]

Soviet occupation authorities "cleansed" western Ukraine and western Byelorussia of all those labeled anti-Soviet elements. The fate of the five million or so Poles living in these areas was dreadful. Ukrainians and Byelorussians resented Poles for their dominant position after the First World War, and the Soviets, far from restraining them, encouraged people to find ways to humiliate and kill. Ethnic hatreds ran wild and a bloodbath ensued. Mixed villages erupted into bouts of frenzy when urged on by the Soviets, who wanted to break the hold of the "rulers" (the Poles).

By early 1940 the repressive system had moved into high gear. The Soviets drew up a list of fourteen different categories of people to classify, screen, segregate, and eliminate. Having learned their sociological approach to dealing with various population "elements" at home, the NKVD set the policy of who was to be deported. One of these lists from Wilno (Vilnius) in 1940 revealed that all the "enemy" types targeted for decades inside the Soviet Union were now dealt with in a matter of weeks. The economic and social elite would be killed or deported and the area made ready for Soviet-style Communism.[9]

Sweeps and arrests in Poland were carried out by quota. There were three waves of deportations during February, April, and June, with more planned. The number of Poles affected ranged between 760,000 and 1.25 million and higher.[10] There are problems with all such statistics, but no disagreement on the scale of the operation. Moreover, in addition to those deported, tens of thousands more were tried and given long prison terms. Whole families were sent to the deep interior of the Soviet Union, often with little more than the clothes on their backs. The men were then sorted out and sent to concentration camps, with their families left to fend for themselves. Even by the summer of 1941, when the invading Nazis drove out the Soviets, an estimated one-quarter of the deportees and concentration camp prisoners were likely already dead. The total number of Polish nationals who died in exile during this brief period has never been established, but estimates go into the hundreds of thousands.[11]

Probably 30 percent of the deported were Jews, the largest nationality among the Poles to be exiled. One historian suggests as many as a hundred thousand died in the process.[12] Nevertheless, during the years of Soviet occupation of Poland the stereotype of "Jewish Bolsheviks" intensified more than ever.[13] Some Jews initially had welcomed the Soviets, but that was not true of many who were businessmen, landowners, members of the professions, intellectuals, or activists in Jewish organizations. And while Jews were substantially represented in the Communist Party in regions like Galicia, it would be incorrect to conclude that they identified with Bolshevism in any great number.

The impact of being deported to Siberia was put this way by one Polish survivor:

> I can describe this in a few words: it was murder of babies and children, banditry, theft of other people's property, the death penalty without sentencing or guilt. One lacks words to speak about the horror of this thing, and who has not lived through it could never believe what happened. Having removed from Polish territories to Siberia those whom they found uncomfortable, the Bolshevik Communists announced at meetings: "This is how we annihilate the enemies of Soviet power. We will use the sieve until we retrieve all bourgeois and kulaks, not only here, but in the entire world." "You will never see again those that we have taken away from you."[14]

Polish Communists hoped for politically inspired behavior from the Red Army but were disappointed: "We waited for them to ask how was life under capitalism and to tell us what it was like in Russia. But all they wanted was to buy a watch. I noticed that they were preoccupied with worldly goods, and we were waiting for ideals."[15]

Nikita Khrushchev was sent off with the Red Army supposedly to protect "fellow Slavs" in western Ukraine, but in fact he was there to expropriate, collectivize—in short to Sovietize the area. To achieve their goals, they used administrative and police methods, selective appointments, and rigged elections. Heavy-handed methods were the norm. The puppet regime sent off the following expression of gratitude to Stalin: "From the kingdom of darkness and boundless suffering which the nation of Western Ukraine bore for six hundred long years, we find ourselves in the fairy land of true happiness of the people, and of true freedom."[16] This "true freedom" would have seemed like a cruel joke to the hundreds of thousands who were deported or locked away in the prisons and camps.

Khrushchev appeared in the propaganda film *Liberation* in a festive mood in which good was shown to have triumphed over evil. What he really had on his mind was to destroy the slightest signs of opposition. Thus, when he met leaders of the NKVD in a village near Lvov shortly after Poland's defeat, he cursed them for being lazy: "You call this work? You haven't carried out a single execution." They made up for lost time soon enough. When not executing, they were arresting people. Khrushchev said his aim was "to strengthen the Soviet state and clear the road for the building of socialism on Marxist-Leninist principles."[17]

Khrushchev embodied the hypocrisy of Soviet Communism and took pride in Sovietizing the area, even when it meant killing scores of people. He looked back on this work in Ukraine as if he had brought freedom to the people, when what they had to endure was the full range of Soviet terror. When he wrote his memoirs, by which time it was fashionable to reject Stalin, he remained an unapologetic apostle of Lenin:

> It was gratifying for me to see that the working class, peasantry, and laboring intelligentsia were beginning to understand Marxist-Leninist teachings and that they all wanted to build their future on that foundation.
>
> At the same time we were still continuing arrests. It was our view that these arrests served to strengthen the Soviet state and clear the road for

the building of Socialism on Marxist-Leninist principles; but our bourgeois enemies had their own interpretation of the arrests, which they
tried to use to discredit us throughout Poland. Despite all the efforts of
the Polish rulers to distort our Leninist doctrine and to intimidate the
people, Lenin's ideas were alive and thriving in the Western Ukraine.[18]

Khrushchev recalled that many Jews did not want to register for a
passport in the Soviet zone, but preferred (and were allowed) to transfer
to the German zone. "They wanted to go home. Maybe they had relatives in Poland. Maybe they just wanted to go back to their birthplaces.
They must have known how the Germans were dealing with Jews."[19] In
fact the Soviets offered these Jews a cruel choice. They could either take
Soviet nationality and remain or be "repatriated" to the German zone.
However, any who opted to return to their homes were deported to distant Kazakhstan.[20]

Sovietization in Byelorussia used similar methods. The Poles and the
native population, including the Jews, all suffered. By early 1940,
according to the recollection of one survivor, the business sections of
cities looked more like cemeteries: "stores closed, street lights unlit,
people afraid to walk at night. . . . Breadlines appeared." Soon people
were ordered to obtain passports and register with the Soviet police.
The better-off, such as those who owned a larger house or business, were
banished from the city. Then the arrests and deportations started, as
cities searched out the "politically incompatible," the "ideologically
unfit," and "socially dangerous elements"—to be sent off to the countryside to work at hard labor. Farmers who owned more than one horse or
cow were classified as kulaks and deported. The Jewish population, survivors said, suffered most of all:

> From cities, they were expelled to towns and villages where they knew
> no one and were treated as "displaced persons" by local authorities. . . .
> Of course, this was better than the ghetto under Hitler, but the compar-
> ison was still unknown there, and the exile meant catastrophe and bro-
> ken lives for many. People were forced to leave their homes without
> notice, to abandon all things they possessed, and to go nobody knew
> where. The humiliation and social discrimination that they were sub-
> jected to were horrifying. . . . During nights loud with cries of horror and
> despair, the peaceful inhabitants were filled with fear of, and disgust for,

the authority which waited for darkness to break into private homes, and which treated victims like cattle.[21]

The treatment of the Byelorussians was such that most wanted nothing to do with the Soviet system. Although the peasants were still allowed to sell goods to the cities, and collectivization was not introduced everywhere, they could see what was coming. One of them recalled:

> When I ask myself why it is that in a very short time there remained no advocates of the Soviet system and—except for an entirely isolated group of men who were like a small island in the sea—no one who would not like a return to the prewar era, my answer is clear. Not because the prewar order [under Poland] was so good that we desired no change. Not because we could not live through a cold and hungry winter.... The true reason is that no one was any longer master in his own home. Somebody had put a gag in our mouth, and spoken in our name. Somebody had intruded upon our life, and begun to boss us, and to push us around at his own will.[22]

Khrushchev, encasing himself in Communist mythology, said that the Ukrainians and Byelorussians "joyfully celebrated the victory of Soviet power." There was a local version of the story that cast blame on the Jews.

The people of Ukraine and Byelorussia, for example, had long held alleged grievances against Jews. They were apparently convinced, as were some in Poland, that their Jewish neighbors enthusiastically supported the Soviet occupation. The evidence here shows that the Jews' reception of Soviet "liberation" was at best mixed; there was nothing like a unified response and certainly no hearty welcome, as some claimed. The myth of Jewish cooperation with the Communists turned deadly after June 1941. When the Soviets were driven out by the Nazis, the alleged Jewish-Communist collaboration became a convenient excuse for locals to carry out brutal pogroms against Jews in many parts of Eastern Europe.

Soviet rule in eastern Poland lasted only from September 1939 to June 1941, when the Russians were forced out by the invading Nazis. In this relatively short time, however, the depredations were particularly severe.

Kazimiera Studzińska wrote down her impressions of the Soviet impact on her hometown of Łuck: "The city, neat and pretty before the war, now assumed an eerie appearance: dirty streets full of mud, lawns walked over and covered with mud, lawn fences and small trees lining the streets all broken down. Display windows, unkempt and covered with dust and cobwebs, were decorated with portraits of Soviet rulers. Store billboards were mostly ripped off, with empty spaces left where they were once attached. All this made an impression of a dying city."[23]

As the German forces approached, Soviet troops and police hastily retreated. Moscow sent orders on June 23, 1941, that no prisoners were to be evacuated, and the Chekists compiled lists of "unreliable elements." The Communists were merciless. They bayoneted people to death and tossed hand grenades into cells. Their inhumanity showed no limits. In Łuck, for example, after the prison was hit by a German bomb, the Soviets prevented escapes. On the morning of June 22 or 23 they informed prisoners that those charged with political offenses had their cases closed and could leave, but when prisoners lined up outside, they were cut down by machine-gun fire from a tank. They were told: "Those still alive get up!" Around 370 stood up; they were forced to bury the victims, after which they were executed as well. Estimates of those massacred at Łuck range from fifteen hundred to four thousand. All the prisoners, including women and children in Dubno's three-story prison, were executed. That was also the pattern across the entire region. The death toll remains unknown, but one reliable account of NKVD murders during the evacuations of prisons in western Ukraine and western Byelorussia in June–July 1941 puts the figure at around a hundred thousand.[24]

On August 31, Moscow ordered the deportation of all Ukrainians of German ancestry. Some 392,000 "ethnic Germans" were vulnerable. The secret police had the males arrested as "anti-Soviet elements" and deported, and the women were supposed to follow. Insofar as the Soviets had the time for a scorched-earth policy as they retreated before the Nazi advance, they carried out wholesale destruction without regard to how the people were going to cope or even survive.[25]

The brief Soviet occupation of the eastern parts of former Poland was a horrific page in history. We should not lose sight of what happened there even though the German occupation to come was going to be even worse.

SOVIET OCCUPATION OF THE BALTIC STATES AND MORE

Under the terms of the Nazi-Soviet nonaggression pact, the Soviets declared the Baltic States to be in their sphere of influence.[26] They worked out treaties of "mutual assistance" with Estonia, Latvia, and Lithuania. In late September and early October, Molotov was empowered to propose that they permit Soviet troops to enter and remain stationed on their territories. In his speech on October 31, 1939, Molotov disingenuously stressed that these treaties would not infringe on the independence of these countries.

Finland was offered such a friendship treaty on October 14 and 23 but, instead of accepting, put up spirited resistance to the invasion of the Red Army.[27] The Soviets attacked with what turned out to be undue confidence on November 30. The Winter War carried on until March the following year. Although the Red Army partly succeeded in the end, its victory was hard won. Molotov reported to the Central Committee that 52,000 Soviet soldiers were killed out of a total of 233,000 casualties.[28] In fact the number of Soviets killed may have been greater, but Khrushchev no doubt exaggerated when he said the Soviets lost a million lives.[29]

The Winter War with Finland revealed to the world and particularly to Hitler that the Red Army had glaring weaknesses in both leadership and armaments. It was Stalin's idea to take Finland to prevent it from falling into the hands of the Germans, who would have been able to threaten Leningrad. However, he and the Soviet military underestimated the determination of the Finns. What made the humiliation worse was the knowledge, according to Khrushchev, that "the Germans were watching with undisguised glee as we took a drubbing." In his view, the flawed effort "encouraged our enemies' conviction that the Soviet Union was a colossus with feet of clay."[30]

It was true that the USSR could boast a rise in the gross national product of 5 to 6 percent in the period 1928–40. That rate of growth, which Western economists have determined after correcting for the exaggerations of the Soviet statistics, was impressive even by international standards.[31] In the 1930s the Soviets made enormous gains in the production of the weapons of war—aircraft, tanks, artillery pieces, rifles, and so on.[32] The quality of these weapons, particularly tanks, was sometimes far superior to that of the German ones. At the end of the 1930s, Stalin showered still more money on the military. Between January 1939 and the German invasion, he created 111 infantry divisions and added three million men and scores of specialized divisions.[33]

But if the Red Army could barely handle Finland, how was it ever going to deal with a massive attack of the kind Germany could mount? Stalin was obviously responsible for many of the military problems, as the purge of the officer corps had eliminated thousands of capable and experienced men.

He demanded to know why the war was going so badly. He accused Commissar of Defense Voroshilov, who found the courage to roar back at him: "You have yourself to blame for all this! You're the one who annihilated the Old Guard of the army; you had our best generals killed!" When Stalin disputed this allegation—which was perfectly accurate—Voroshilov smashed a platter of roast pig on the table. Khrushchev, who witnessed this spectacle, said he never saw anything like it. Finland could not hold out forever, of course, and duly sued for peace. Voroshilov lost his position and was no doubt lucky at that.[34]

Ordinary Soviet citizens were kept in the dark about the weaknesses of the Red Army. They had no idea that their vaunted armed forces had suffered a moral defeat and held on to the illusion that the country was well prepared.

The rapid German advance that drove the British from the continent and then defeated France in June 1940 came as a shock to the Communists. As soon as it looked like Germany was going to do well there, the Soviets decided to take steps in their own sphere of influence to even the balance. On June 14 they made new demands on Lithuania, followed two days later by similar ones on Latvia and Estonia. The curious justification for these moves was the kidnapping of some Soviet soldiers and Lithuanians who had been helping them get established. Similar trumped-up allegations were leveled at Latvia and Estonia. All these countries were left no choice but to agree that Soviet troops would be allowed free entry, which is to say, the Red Army would occupy them all.[35]

By August 1, the USSR offered the people of Bessarabia and north Bukovina in the south, with around 3.7 million inhabitants, most of them Ukrainians and Moldavians, the glorious "opportunity of joining the united family of Soviet nations . . . liberated from the rule of Romanian boyars, landlords, and capitalists." That was how Molotov put it in his address to the Supreme Soviet on August 1. He also spoke of what happened in the three Baltic states. Following elections in each, they decided "in favor of introducing the Soviet system" and incorporating into the Soviet Union. Thus, Lithuania's 2.8 million people, the 1.9 million in Latvia, and the 1.1 million in Estonia, along with the people in the south, meant that 10 million had been added to the Soviet Union. If those from the former eastern parts of Poland were counted, Molotov noted with pride, it meant that the USSR had grown in excess of 23 million people. He claimed that "nineteen-twentieths" of them had formerly been part of the Soviet Union and they had been "reunited."

Molotov boasted, but in what was at best a half-truth, that all of this had been achieved "by peaceful means." That the United States was not pleased with these developments, he added, "causes us little concern, since we are coping with our tasks without the assistance of these disgruntled gentlemen."

He said that despite the great changes already under way, imperialist appetites—obviously excluding his own—were growing. The powers he had in mind were not Germany or the Soviet Union, who had conquered vast tracts in Europe. He pointed the finger instead at Japan and the United States, even though the latter was at that time basking in isolationism. He warned that the Soviet Union had "to be vigilant in regard to its external security" and reminded his audience of Stalin's words: "We must keep our entire people in a state of mobilization, of preparedness in the face of the danger of military attack, so that no 'accident' and no tricks of our foreign enemies can catch us unawares."[36]

Stalin sent representatives to the capital cities of each of the three Baltic states: Vyshinsky to Riga; Zhdanov to Tallinn; and Vladimir Dekanozov to Kaunas. Their mission was by then easy to predict. They would Sovietize each, beginning by dissolving parliaments and local institutions. In July there were new elections, but only Communists were allowed to run. The NKVD moved in quickly, as was standard operating procedure, and arrested fifteen to twenty thousand "hostile elements." Many were executed immediately. It was after such campaigns and the elections following them that each state "requested" inclusion in the Soviet Union.[37]

In Estonia an article published on the anniversary of the Russian Revolution in October 1940 stated the goal of the occupation as follows: "Together with the working people of the entire Soviet Union, the working people of the Soviet Estonian Socialist Republic will freely celebrate the twenty-third birthday of the great October revolution. Under the leadership of the Communist Bolshevik Party, the working people of the Soviet Estonian Socialist Republic have begun the building of a new, free, and happy life, exterminating capitalists and big landowners."[38]

The same article pointed to the Red Army's occupation as "the great day of freedom for the Estonian proletariat." In fact the NKVD began arrests almost immediately, taking into custody around three hundred people a month from August 1940 until the Soviets fled in June 1941. During the year of occupation they undercut and destroyed everything held dear by local culture in the name of bringing about a Communist revolution.

In Lithuania the pillars of the old regime were targeted. Jews were attacked insofar as they were considered capitalists or members of the bourgeoisie. Indeed, it might well be the case that Soviet occupation and deportations proportionally affected Jews more than anyone else as "collectivization was especially hard on traders and small business-men."[39] Local intellectuals and the elite, like Mykolas Römeris, one of Lithuania's leading jurists, grew alarmed. He wrote in his diary: "I myself had considerable Soviet sympathies before I encountered the Soviets, and in any event of the two I preferred the Soviet Revolution over Hitler's National Socialism." Nevertheless, the Soviets set out "to decap-itate Polish and then Lithuanian society by deporting its elites."[40]

Hitler's armies had moved closer with their conquest of Poland, so Stalin determined to root out any possible backstabbers. He met with his security chief on May 7 and 9, 1941, and remarked with his usual cold-bloodedness: "Comrade Beria will take care of the accommodations of our Baltic guests."[41] On May 14, Stalin decided to remove "all criminal, socially alien, and anti-Soviet elements" from these areas. There were nine separate categories of all the "usual suspects." Anyone thought to be politically suspicious or an ordinary criminal was sent to the east. The Soviets pursued those "compromised" by what they or their relatives did prior to the occupation.[42]

Altogether, in the June 13–14 operation alone, 85,716 people were deported, including 25,711 from the Baltic States; the others were from Moldavia, Byelorussia, and western Ukraine. These bare statistics do not hint at what these unfortunates endured. To illustrate what happened during that fateful night, we should note that the NKVD apprehended the following family members in the Baltic region: 11,038 regarded as "bourgeois nationalists"; 3,240 related to former policemen; 7,124 kin of former landowners, industrialists, and the like; 1,649 relatives of former officers; and 2,907 described simply as "others."

The figures of these deportations do not say what happened to the heads of households. The women and children were taken into custody without notice and allowed to bring minimal personal goods and food. They were crammed into cattle cars, fifty in each, for a trip that took from six to twelve weeks. They were deposited in the middle of the barren steppe, usually without even a roof over their heads. Their "crime" was that they were deemed by the NKVD to be "socially alien" elements. Beria planned another such large deportation for the night of June 27–28, but that was stopped only because of the Nazi invasion.[43]

The scope of the disaster for the Baltic peoples during the one year of Soviet occupation can be gathered from the numbers killed or deported. For Latvia, the total has been estimated at 34,250; for Estonia, 60,000; and for Lithuania, 75,000.[44]

Like the Great Terror, the murders and forced deportations were—at least in the minds of the Soviet leaders—designed to prepare the country for war, but they were also supposed to help introduce Soviet-style Communist utopia. That was why, after 1945, when the war was over, the "cleansing" operations commenced right where they left off. Thus in Estonia, to mention but one example, when the Soviets returned, they carried out the largest arrest-deportation action in Estonian history. It took place in 1949, when an estimated eighty thousand were banished, with more following on a regular basis until 1952.[45]

26

THE WAR SPREADS

When Hitler signed the directive for the invasion of the Soviet Union on December 18, 1940, he took a fateful step that would visit on Europe a cataclysm unlike anything ever seen in its long history. The military, economic, and ideological motives for the attack had been fixed in his mind for twenty years, bound together by a combination of anti-Semitism and anti-Communism and summed up in the imperative to destroy "Jewish Bolshevism." He did not want to stop even to celebrate his victory over France and Western Europe before pressing on as quickly as possible against the archenemy in the east. After delays caused by weather and other matters out of his control, he determined the attack should begin as soon as possible in the spring of 1941.

His one reliable ally in Europe, Benito Mussolini, upset the plans. Without any consultation he invaded Greece on October 28, 1940. He not only failed to get a quick victory but opened the door to the British, who were hoping to put pressure on Hitler from the south. By December 5, Hitler had decided to attack Greece the coming March in Operation Marita, though he would thus have to postpone the war on the USSR for at least four weeks. After March 27, with the coup of Prince

Paul in Yugoslavia, a man with whom he was able to deal, Hitler decided that Marita should expand. He told his military leaders to prepare for an immediate operation against that country as well.[1]

By April 6, a joint offensive against both Yugoslavia and Greece had begun. The Royal Yugoslav Army surrendered on April 17, with minimal German losses (151 dead, 392 wounded). Most of the Greek army capitulated a week later, and again the Wehrmacht's casualties were modest (100 dead, 3,500 wounded). They drove the British from Greece and forced them to evacuate around fifty thousand troops. Hitler chalked up two more easy victories, but military leaders were concerned German units were getting overextended.

Initially only parts of Greece and Yugoslavia were occupied, and most of the fighting forces were withdrawn. Four specially trained divisions were created, mainly from Austrians, and they were sent in to pacify and hold the vast area. On April 2, before the campaign had begun, Halder agreed that the security police and SD would deal with "emigrants, saboteurs, terrorists," as well as "Communists and Jews."[2] Germany's ally in Yugoslavian Croatia, the Ustaše, settled old grievances and turned the country "into one great slaughterhouse."[3] Communist resistance began almost immediately, organized and led by Josip Broz Tito, who was inspired by Lenin and Stalin. The partisan movement that developed fought against the occupation until 1945, but it was complicated by the fact that newly independent Croatia, controlled by the Ustaše, was allied with the Axis powers and fought the Communists. In addition, loyalist and nationalist Serbs organized into a force as the Chetniks, opposed the Axis occupation, but also were deeply anti-Communist. The result in Yugoslavia was a combination of the horrors of a foreign occupation, ethnic persecutions, and a three-sided civil war.[4]

THE JEWS AND REPRISAL POLICIES

The policies adopted by the Germans in Eastern Europe toward the Jews and any form of resistance were far more radical than any they were following at the same time in the west. On April 16, the day the Wehrmacht arrived in Sarajevo, it unleashed a massive pogrom. Within the first six weeks, the commander in Serbia, General Ludwig von Schroeder, ordered that Jews and Gypsies be forced to wear a yellow armband and that all their property be subject to Aryanization, or confiscation. Hitler's reaction to reports in August of "partisan activity" led him to issue an open-ended imperative to take the "sharpest measures to restore peace and good order."

Chief of the Supreme Command of the Armed Forces Wilhelm Keitel ordered on September 16 that "50 to 100 Communists" be executed for every Wehrmacht soldier killed. In a brief encounter with partisans that soon followed and cost the Germans 21 lives, Franz Böhme, plenipotentiary commanding general in Serbia, ordered that 100 Serbian prisoners be executed for each "murdered" soldier. The prisoners were already in a camp holding mainly Jews and Communists. Böhme's follow-up instructions on October 10 systematized the reprisal ratio as 100 Serbians for every German killed and 50 for each wounded.

The victims singled out were Jews and Communists, while the executioners were drawn from a variety of sources, initially and mainly from the Wehrmacht itself. Some units that ran into resistance combed through houses afterward and shot the required "quota" in reprisal. The OKW was dismayed at this turn of events, because it would tend to create more insurgents seeking revenge. The occupation leaders soon concluded that not all Serbs were Communists and there should be some investigation before executing them. However, there was consensus that all Jews were by definition anti-German and it was safe to use them to make up the quotas. By October some divisions were reporting that they had a "shortfall" of candidates for reprisals because there were no more male Jews left in Serbia to kill.

The Jewish women and children were confined to a concentration camp at Semlin, across the Sava River from Belgrade. On April 11, 1942, a first request went to Himmler to send a gas van to kill them all, and in early March it arrived. Up to one hundred women and children were forced into the van for each of its deadly trips. It drove through Belgrade while the victims experienced the nightmare, screaming until they died on the way to Avala, ten miles or so outside the city. The van made this trip several times a day (save for Sundays and holidays) over a two-month period. By May 10, its work finished, it had killed seventy-five hundred. Yugoslavia's Jewish population stood at seventy-five thousand in 1939 and was reduced to around twelve thousand in 1945. In addition, an unknown number of Jews who had sought refuge in Yugoslavia were found and murdered.[5]

Almost before the shooting stopped in Greece, the German security police pursued the country's leading figures listed in a "search book." The Greeks remember the widespread cruelties and initial famine. As in Yugoslavia, the resistance was led by Communists, with a great deal of popular support behind it.

The Jews in Greece were endangered until the Italians were given jurisdiction over most of the mainland and the islands in June 1941. However, the strategically important region around the ancient city of Salonika, home to tens of thousands of Jews, was occupied by German forces. The full horror did not begin until July 8 the following year, when the Wehrmacht commander (not the SS) ordered male Jews aged between eighteen and forty-five to register for work. Three days later thousands who gathered in long lines to sign up were attacked and humiliated in scenes that appalled many Greeks who did not share this anti-Semitism.

Eichmann grew impatient at the lack of cooperation from the Italians, the allies in charge, and finally sent Rolf Günther to Salonika in January 1943. He was soon followed by Dieter Wisliceny, another trusted specialist, and given the task of deporting the fifty thousand Jews in the city. The transports began to roll on March 15 and carried on relentlessly. Although the Jews' property was there for the taking when they were deported everywhere in Europe, the priority was rather to organize mass murder. "Wild" or disorganized looting was common in Salonika, as individual Germans helped themselves and sent home truckloads of booty.

The economic side of the operation was so ham-handed, however, that of the two thousand or so businesses, factories, and offices owned by the Jews, just six hundred were inventoried. Confiscations were often so hectic that much was destroyed in the process. There was no neat-and-tidy expropriation, with funds flowing to the German treasury, but instead more of a mad scramble for spoils. Germans handed out businesses as a reward to stool pigeons or on a whim. A large array of people got in on the action, from individual Germans in the various services, to the Greeks, Bulgarians, and assorted others.

A sign of the wastefulness of the process—at least from the point of view of the German treasury—can be seen from what happened to the Jews' homes. These were not neatly sold off, even though Salonika suffered from a chronic housing shortage. The Greek authorities complained that getting rid of all the Jews did not help, because looters broke into homes, tore up the roofs and walls, or dug in basements in search of hidden money and jewels. They made most of the dwellings uninhabitable.[6]

By the end of the war, of the seventy to eighty thousand Jews who had lived in Greece in 1939, fewer than ten thousand remained.[7]

STALIN'S UNCERTAIN COURSE AND REFUSAL TO BE "PROVOKED"

Stalin had signed a pact with Yugoslavia on April 6, 1941, but that hardly deterred Hitler. It was left to one of Stalin's cronies to inform the Yugoslav envoy just two days later that Moscow could not maintain its treaty. In private and in public Stalin adopted an appeasement policy, even though he knew very well what the Nazis were doing in the areas they conquered.

He took steps to strengthen the military. The Red Army had to call up reservists for war against Poland, the Baltic States, and particularly Finland. German military studies pinpointed the glaring weaknesses but also noted that the Red Army had instituted reforms to deal with the problems.[8]

Stalin blamed everyone but himself for the Finnish debacle. On May 6, 1940, he had replaced Commissar of Defense Kliment Voroshilov with Semyon Timoshenko. He also had dismissed Chief of Staff Boris Shaposhnikov, put another in his place, and eventually sacked him as well. On December 24 he finally gave the post to the forty-five-year-old general Georgy Zhukov, the man who would become the great Soviet hero.

The war in Finland had revealed that the Red Army was not as formidable as it looked on paper, but the contrasts with the Wehrmacht were damning. Hitler had swept through Western Europe with such ease that the Soviet leaders were aghast. When Stalin heard the reports, his nerves cracked. He rhetorically asked Molotov, Khrushchev, Beria, and other leaders who were with him when the news arrived, "Couldn't they put up any resistance at all?"

Khrushchev, who transmits this disconsolate remark, remembered how Soviet leaders felt at that moment:

Germany, Italy, and Japan were formidable countries, and they were united against us. The most pressing and deadly threat in all history faced the Soviet Union. We felt as though we were facing this threat all by ourselves. America was too far away to help us, and besides, it was unknown at that time how America would react if the Soviet Union were attacked. And England was hanging by a thread. No one knew if England would be able to hold out should the Hitlerites attempt an invasion across the Channel. . . . We knew very well that we were the next country Hitler planned to turn his army against.[9]

Throughout 1940 the Kremlin prepared for the inevitable, but Stalin vacillated. There were times when he seemed satisfied they were doing what they could and others when he realized they were still far behind.

An example of his conflicted state of mind was evident on November 7, 1940, when the Communist elite gathered to celebrate the Bolshevik Revolution. The distinguished guests drank one too many toasts, and the lunch that started at 5:30 went on until 9:00. Guests were about ready to leave when Stalin, glass in hand, said he wanted to speak. What he had to say definitely put a damper on spirits:

History has spoiled us. We have had many successes with comparative ease. This has led to complacency in many of us, a dangerous complacency. . . . We have a lot of honorable, courageous people, but they forget that courage alone is far from sufficient: you have to know something, you need skills: "Live and learn!" One must be constantly learning and every two or three years relearn things. But around here no one likes to learn. People are not studying the lessons of the war with Finland, the lessons of the war in Europe. . . . We are not prepared for the sort of air war being waged between Germany and England. It turns out that our aircraft can stay aloft for only thirty-five minutes, while German and English aircraft can stay for up to several hours! If in the future our armed forces, transport, and so forth are not equal to the forces of our enemies (and those enemies are all the capitalist states, and those who deck themselves out to look like our friends!), then they will devour us. Only given equal material forces can we prevail, because we are supported by the people, the people are with us. . . .

Look at me: I am capable of learning, reading, keeping up with things every day—why can you not do this? You do not like to learn; you are happy just going along the way you are, complacent. You are squandering Lenin's legacy.

This scolding left the room in silence and some in tears. The head of the Comintern, Georgi Dimitrov, who recorded these remarks in his diary, also wrote that he had never seen or heard Stalin "the way he was that night—a memorable one."[10]

As usual, Stalin blamed all the mistakes on everyone else. His subordinates were at fault; they did not work hard enough. In point of fact, it was he who was most to blame, and contrary to his boast, it was not at all clear that the regime had the people behind it.

One of the most important effects of the Winter War with Finland, according to Dmitri Volkogonov, Russian historian and career officer in the Red Army, was that "an unfamiliar lack of self-assurance" came over Stalin, and "from this moment he was obsessed with the sole idea that, if Hitler were not provoked, he would not attack."[11] Although Stalin forced through changes and expanded the armed forces, his determination to avoid acting in a way that Hitler could interpret as a "provocation" persisted up to and even after the German attack was in full swing.

From mid-1940 until then, he permitted the Luftwaffe to carry out reconnaissance flights over the Soviet Union without hindrance. Beria ordered NKVD border units not to fire on the German planes, but to write up a report. Violations of Soviet airspace became routine and were duly noted, but Stalin essentially disregarded the information.[12] Even if the Soviets wanted to stop the spy planes, their military technology would have had a hard time of it.[13]

Some steps were taken to make improvements in the defense of the country. Military conscription was expanded, and according to a new law of May 1940, service was extended from two to three years. Women were encouraged to enlist, but relatively few did. Reservists began to be recalled as early as August 1939, and the army had grown to 3.4 million by July 1940. Another 800,000 reservists were drafted into service in

May 1941. Even so, on the eve of the German invasion many frontline divisions were only at half strength.

The growth of the army, particularly by using older reservists, did not always work well. Many of them resented government policies (such as collectivization), and mass desertion and discipline problems in the ranks in turn inspired a new disciplinary code in 1940. Stiffer sentences became the norm, harsher than any other country's. In 1939, 112 officers and men were executed for various crimes, and military tribunals sentenced 2,283 servicemen to prison terms. In 1940, 528 officers and men were executed, and the number imprisoned jumped to 12,000, with 7,733 given terms of five years or longer. The use of these terror methods to keep the troops in line underscores the Red Army's lack of combat readiness. The officer corps was understaffed and, compared with other European armies, also younger and less experienced.[14]

The most severe problem was the lack of trained officers at the battalion and company levels. To make matters worse, the belated attempt to equip the army with more up-to-date weapons, including tanks, was incomplete in mid-1941. Often old and new weapons were mixed together in units, and that produced confusion and inefficiency. Even basic items like boots and clothing were in short supply.

Stalin had moved the USSR westward with new conquests in 1939 and 1940. The Soviets opted to leave behind the better-fortified positions they already had and shift their defensive line to the west. The new districts faced hostile local populations that had recently been taken over by the USSR. The upshot was that the Red Army did not have sufficient time to establish effective lines and was not ready for the German attack. The Soviets lacked an operational plan for war or for mobilization. The USSR was thus even less prepared for a German assault in 1941 than it had been in 1939.[15]

Stalin put his faith in the Communist theory that National Socialism was the agent of monopoly capitalism, which was intent on acquiring markets, raw materials, and investment opportunities. According to this view it would make no sense for Germany to attack if the Soviet Union was prepared to give everything it craved. A corollary of this theory was that imperialists would inevitably go to war with each other, and it was Stalin's fervent belief that the USSR had merely to wait for the Western capitalist powers to exhaust themselves in war while he played the role of "the laughing third man" watching the fight. He would take advantage of the situation when the combatants were at an end. This theory did not encourage an all-out drive to prepare for an onslaught that appeared to Stalin to be completely irrational.

He struck a new note on May 5, 1941, in an unusually candid speech to military graduates at a ceremonial assembly in the Kremlin. He repeated what he had said about the poor quality of Soviet weaponry in his assessment of the Winter War with Finland. This time he drew contrasts with Germany and said war with that country was all but inevitable. Summing up why their enemies seemed to be getting the upper hand, he explained that they had been creative in finding new ways of escaping the Versailles Treaty, while Britain and France gloated. "Lenin turns out to be correct when he said that parties and states perish from dizziness and success."

Was Germany invincible? Stalin asked rhetorically. Of course not:

Germany began the war with the slogan "Liberation from Versailles." And it had the support of peoples suffering from the Versailles system. But now Germany is carrying on the war under the banner of the conquest and subjection of other peoples, under the banner of hegemony. That is a great disadvantage for the German army. Not only is it losing the sympathy it once had from several countries and peoples but it is also creating enemies in the many countries it occupies. An army that must fight while contending with hostile territories and masses underfoot and in its rear exposes itself to serious dangers. That is another disadvantage for the German army.

Furthermore, the German leaders are already beginning to suffer from dizziness. They believe that there is nothing they could not do, that their army is strong enough and there is no point in improving it any further. All of which goes to show that the German army is not invincible.[16]

Germans had alienated many of the people they conquered, but the same point held for the Soviet Union. Stalin wanted no "hostile" forces in the new republics, and he used brutal methods to that end. As we have seen, he met with Beria and gave him the go-ahead for wholesale deportations of potential troublemakers.

In May 1941 the Red Army began drawing up blueprints for an offensive against Germany. Historians have argued vehemently about the significance of these plans and other evidence about Stalin's motives at that time.

Some have gone so far as to claim that Hitler attacked in a "preventive war" when he got wind of Stalin's intentions. However, Hitler moved for reasons of his own and had made these clear long in advance. So far as Stalin himself was concerned, an offensive war was not feasible, because the capitalist countries (Germany and Britain) were hardly finished off. Actually, they were only hitting their stride. He worried that if he tried to head west, his worst fear might come true: the capitalists would bury their differences and attack the USSR. The most plausible explanation for Stalin's halting attitude was a vain hope that the inevitable war with Germany could be delayed and fought under more favorable conditions.[17]

Far from planning an attack, the Soviet Union invested vast resources in building up its new defensive positions in the recently annexed lands. Research in the recently opened Russian archives has been unable to turn up convincing proof that Stalin wanted to attack. There is no conclusive evidence of the kinds of preparations that would have been needed to train and turn loose the Red Army.[18] It was true that Stalin did not entirely exclude the possibility of attacking Germany, but only if Berlin faltered. He had Zhukov and Timoshenko draw up plans for such an eventuality. In the first half of 1941, when Hitler swept everything in his path, the Kremlin's priority was to pursue "diplomatic and economic appeasement."[19]

WORD OF THE ATTACK TO COME

Reports from the Soviets' worldwide network of spies sounded warnings of an impending attack. The Soviet embassy in Berlin conveyed similar impressions. One staff member there, walking past the studio of Heinrich Hoffmann, Hitler's favorite photographer, observed how different maps were featured in the shopwindow. In the spring of 1940 there were some of Holland, Belgium, Denmark, and France; in early 1941, there were new ones of Yugoslavia and Greece. In late May the maps were of the Soviet Union. Valentin Berezhkov of the Soviet embassy remarked that it was as if Hoffmann were subconsciously signaling Berliners: "Now it's the Soviet Union's turn."[20]

The information conveyed by the Soviet ambassador in Berlin was toned down because he knew Stalin did not want to hear bad news. The conclusion was still inescapable in his reports that an attack was pending. The information did not cause Stalin the least concern, and business between the two countries continued as usual.

He refused to take his own spies seriously. Instead, he questioned their reliability and motives. As early as eleven days after Hitler signed directive No. 21 for Operation Barbarossa back in late 1940, Soviet spies alerted Stalin to the planned attack. He did not discount what they said, but like Molotov and others he was torn by mistrust and driven by wishful thinking that the news could not be true. As one of the leaders closest to him noted, Stalin became "unhinged" as the shrillness of the warnings picked up.[21]

Winston Churchill had gotten wind of the coming German attack in April 1941 and decided to write Stalin. Later Churchill made much of his having conveyed the information, but there was considerable delay before it reached Moscow. Ultimately it was passed over on April 21 and was at best cryptic, citing as a source "a trusted agent." The news was in fact gleaned from secret Nazi radio messages by the code-breaking ULTRA machine.[22] If the British had said more, word of their abilities might have been leaked to the Germans. As it was, Churchill's message did not spell out when the strike would come and was not as "obvious" as is often supposed. Stalin interpreted the short note as another attempt by the British to manipulate him into joining the war against Hitler. He later asked Churchill why the British had not told him in advance of the German attack.

American intelligence knew as much or more about what was coming, but the U.S. ambassador to Moscow, Laurence Steinhardt, advised Secretary of State Cordell Hull not to convey the information because he believed it would be counterproductive. In his view the Soviets would likely regard it as "neither sincere nor independent."

Stalin continued to worry about being "provoked" into war with Germany. On the other hand, he was also concerned that the British might try to reach a separate peace with Hitler and turn on the Soviet Union. By the time Churchill's note arrived, it had the exact opposite effect of the one intended, because it convinced Stalin of Britain's nefarious intentions. "Look at that," he said to Zhukov, "we are being threatened with the Germans, and the Germans with the Soviet Union, and they are playing us off against one another. It is a subtle political game."[23] Stalin thought he saw through it all, but he was too clever by half. The Soviet people paid the price for these costly errors of judgment.

On June 9, Timoshenko and Zhukov showed Stalin reports of Richard Sorge, one of the most reliable Soviet spies, who gave the exact date of the coming invasion. Stalin ran Sorge's character into the mud and threw the report in their faces. The Soviet military men had no more luck on June 18, when they begged Stalin to put the country on full alert. Once again he refused, brushing aside Timoshenko's warning about increasing German reconnaissance flights and troop movements.

Stalin's psychological makeup was such that in moments of great importance he became overcautious, almost to the point of timidity. From all the information coming in, he should have concluded that the moment of truth was at hand.[24]

STALIN'S VACILLATION PERSISTS

What made Stalin's attitude toward the possibility of war all the more peculiar was that for more than a decade he, and Lenin before him, had said that such a conflict with the West was inevitable. Yet he could not imagine Hitler would really attack and held on to the idea that nothing should be done to offend. At a meeting with Timoshenko and Zhukov only days before the attack, he ridiculed them for being alarmist about obvious German activity near the border and left the room. He stuck his head back in to issue yet another scolding. "If you're going to provoke the Germans on the frontier," he roared at Timoshenko, "by moving troops there without our permission, then heads will roll, mark my words."[25]

A well-proven Soviet spy in the German police since 1929, and later even a member of the counterintelligence branch of the Reich Security Main Office, Wilhelm Lehmann reported on June 19 that the attack would begin at 3:00 a.m. on June 22. This news was brought to Beria's personal attention. Even though Lehmann had been a loyal and trusted agent for more than a decade, Beria dismissed the information as "false and provocative." He did not bother to tell Stalin about it for fear of facing the dictator's wrath.[26]

Molotov recalled the dread Soviet leaders had of making the wrong move: "I think psychologically it was impossible for us to be ready for war. We felt we were not yet ready, so it was quite natural for us to overdo it. But there is also no way to justify that. I personally don't see any mistakes in that. In order to delay the war everything was done to avoid giving the Germans a pretext to start it." He thought the Soviets needed two more years to prepare. Pressed by those who interviewed him decades after the war, he reluctantly admitted that Hitler had surprised them and in passing said that the Soviet leadership took a long-term view about spreading Communism and did not want to act precipitously: "I am sure intelligence reports are still coming in, and something may begin somewhere. That's the nature of intelligence. And it has nothing to do with Marxism-Leninism. Our ideology stands for offensive operations when possible. Otherwise, we wait."[27]

Once Stalin signaled the Soviet Union was not going to war because of the actions of some "victory-drunk German generals" or anyone else, the Red Army bent over backward not to contradict him. When commanders in the Baltic and Kiev special military districts took steps on their own to enhance the readiness of their troops as the sound of coming war became impossible to ignore, their orders were countermanded by the Red Army General Staff. Even blackouts and minimal air-raid precautions were expressly forbidden. Soviet aircraft were neatly lined up along runways without the slightest attempt to camouflage them. Whenever the political administration of the Red Army, in keeping with Stalin's thought, labeled messages of an imminent conflict with Germany "provocative rumors," all field commanders fell silent.[28]

Information continued to pour in, and Stalin just as consistently brushed it aside. Finally, on June 21, three German deserters crossed the lines to tell of the impending attack. They swore it was going to happen within hours. Timoshenko got up the nerve to inform Stalin. There was a meeting in the Kremlin with Stalin on the evening of June 21, and he dismissed the "disinformation" yet again. Doubts began, however, and he finally remarked haplessly, according to Mikoyan, "I think Hitler's trying to provoke us. He surely hasn't decided to make war?"[29]

Other members of the Politburo, as well as Timoshenko and Zhukov, finally prevailed on Stalin to take some preliminary steps. Zhukov was permitted to issue a statement to military districts that told of a possible attack on June 22–23, which could start with "provocative actions." The Red Army was not to respond, lest there be "serious consequences." Nevertheless, the army was to be brought to "full combat readiness." In the night the military district leaders were to move troops into forward defense lines and begin camouflaging aircraft and preparing blackouts. The order, which reflected Stalin's obsession with not wanting to make the first move in the greatest chess game of his life, was utterly ineffective and did not even reach all the troops. He left them completely exposed.[30]

Early in the morning of June 22, 1941, the Germans launched Operation Barbarossa. Some Germans were dismayed, but others, including the foot soldiers, thought the Wehrmacht would be in Moscow in six weeks.

This attack was to prove Hitler's undoing and was disastrous all round. It opened the final and bloodiest chapter in the social catastrophe that marked the first half of the twentieth century in Europe. By the time this war ended, it had become the greatest killer of all time. Its political and psychological reverberations would last into the twenty-first century. It was such a profound crisis, so utterly unprecedented in all its many horrific faces, that it raised questions about the very meaning and future of Western civilization.

PART EIGHT

HITLER'S WAR ON
"JEWISH BOLSHEVISM"

27

WAR OF EXTERMINATION AS NAZI CRUSADE

Only days after sweeping across Western Europe and briefly celebrating his victory over archenemy France, Hitler already had a vision of the invasion of the USSR in mind. Its aim was going to be "the extermination of Russia to its roots" (*Vernichtung der Lebenskraft Russlands*).[1]

Nevertheless, he was still torn between trying to finish off the British and pursuing his long-anticipated war in the east. Foreign Minister Ribbentrop hoped the Soviets could be enticed into joining the Tripartite Pact signed in Berlin on September 27, 1940, by Germany, Italy, and Japan. Molotov came for a visit on November 12–13 to discuss such matters, but his brusque manners, probing questions, and humorless style — which had already made him notoriously difficult for diplomats to deal with — only succeeded in annoying Hitler. The führer told his immediate circle that Molotov had "let the cat out of the bag" by outlining Soviet interests in the Balkans and Finland. These were areas Hitler viewed as vital, so when he heard Soviet demands, he felt "relieved," because he saw at once that the relationship with the USSR could not remain even a "marriage of convenience." He may have had a lingering hope the Communists might be won over to the Tripartite Pact or an anti-British alliance. They might be lured by the prospect of the spoils of the British Empire in the distant south, chiefly in the Persian Gulf, Middle East, and India. But the effect of the talks was to harden Hitler's deep conviction that the interests of Nazism and Communism were implacably opposed, and so reinforced his resolution to invade the Soviet Union.[2]

By the end of 1940, he also had "strategic" reasons to do so, namely he coveted unfettered access to the food resources and raw materials in the east. However, the dominant motive—important to many in the Nazi movement—was connected to Hitler's long-standing obsession with conquering lebensraum, the territory deemed essential to the health, welfare, and expansion of the Aryan race. In his view, Bolshevik Jews threatened to thwart this goal, just as German Jews had been behind the "stab in the back" that had brought the country to ruin in 1918. For Hitler, everything now depended on the assertion of absolute supremacy, and specifically the Nazi annihilation of "Jewish Bolshevism," which he regarded as Germany's principal contender for power on the world stage.

As early as September 1919, Hitler had identified the Jews as Germany's great racial enemy and said they had to be "removed altogether." By April 1920, he was blaming them for the social havoc wreaked by Soviet Communism and warning that Germany had to do something or suffer the same fate. He came to believe that the nation's racial existence depended on its success in driving out the Jews and fighting them in what he saw as their incarnation as leaders of the USSR. The Nazis would not rest, he said, "until the last Jew is removed from the German Reich." His early battle cry had been: either "Soviet star" or "swastika."

This conviction was the driving force of Hitler's foreign policy and dominated his thoughts as he developed his military strategy against the Soviets. In a meeting with his generals on December 5, 1940, he went through the steps to follow in the east, including the invasion of Yugoslavia and Greece (successfully completed in April 1941). He emphasized the need for a "war of extermination" on the Soviet Union and spelled out what that meant. He said the attack "must avoid the risky strategy of simply pushing the Russians back. We must use assault methods that cut through the Russian army and create pockets to be destroyed one by one. There must be a starting position that makes provision for major envelopment operations." The conquest would follow.[3]

On December 18, he issued the directive for Operation Barbarossa, and the clock began winding down.

The day after Hitler launched Barbarossa on June 22, 1941, he would tell Germans the war was defensive and the Soviets were the real aggressors. "Germany had not tried," he said, "to carry its National Socialist ideology to Russia, but the Jewish-Bolshevik power holders in Moscow have unswervingly undertaken to impose their rule—intellectually, but above all militarily—on our and other European people. The results of the activity of this regime, however, were in every country only chaos, misery, and famine."

This was Hitler's familiar account of what would happen should Bolshevism win the day and rule Germany. He said the time had come to take action against the "conspiracy of the Jewish-Anglo-Saxon warmongers and also the Jewish power holders of the Bolshevik Moscow Central." They were supposedly trying to hinder "the creation of the new racial state and drive the new Reich again into powerlessness and misery."[4]

"COALITION FORCES" IN THE CRUSADE

As soon as the war began, the press was instructed to return to the slogan used prior to the Nazi-Soviet Pact of August 1939, emphasizing that the enemy was the "Jewish-Bolshevik Soviet government." Hitler did not quite succeed in creating a Europe-wide "crusade against Bolshevism"—but then again, he never really wanted to share the glory. Italy as one of the Axis powers contributed some troops, as did Romania and Hungary, but Hitler did not put much stock in these or in any other foreign soldiers. Himmler was pleased to welcome "Germanic" volunteers in the Waffen-SS and used the slogan "European crusade against Bolshevism" to recruit the following representatives from "Germanic" nations by the end of 1941: 2,399 Danes, 1,180 Finns, 1,571 Flemings, 4,814 Dutch, 1,883 Norwegians, and just over 150 from Sweden, Switzerland, and Liechtenstein. The crusade drew 6,400 ethnic Germans from Alsace-Lorraine, Luxembourg, Romania, Serbia, Slovakia, and Hungary. People from "non-Germanic" nations, not so highly regarded on the Nazi racial hierarchy, were encouraged to join the Wehrmacht, and by the end of 1941 a total of 24,000 French, Croatians, Spaniards, and Walloons had enlisted. The volunteers wore German uniforms with special nationality badges. Russian émigrés were not allowed to join, nor were Czech nationals. When the quick victory that Hitler and all these volunteers expected failed to materialize, he grew more prepared to accept such foreigners in the ranks.[5]

Hitler's greatest error of omission lay elsewhere. He was unable to persuade Japan to move against the USSR in the Far East. Had the Japanese attacked the Communists, they would have tied down important divisions of the Red Army. Instead, as we will see, Soviet troops were free to leave the east of their country when Japan went after the United States. Hitler also had no luck convincing Turkey to attack the USSR from the south. As a consequence of these two failures, the German invasion came from only one direction, and Red Army troops, scores of well-trained divisions, complete with tanks and an air force that had guarded against Japan, were ultimately available when Moscow was about to collapse in late 1941.[6]

Hitler took for granted that General Ion Antonescu, whom he had helped into power in Romania, would join. The conducator, or "leader"—as Antonescu styled himself—was prepared to place his "entire military, political, and social resources at the führer's command." On June 12, 1941, in Munich he joined the Nazi effort to deal with "the Slavic menace, which had made itself felt periodically for centuries and now must be eliminated once and for all." He committed more than two Romanian armies to the cause.[7] Soon after his return home he drafted his own orders to deal with the Jews: "All the Yids, Communist agents and their sympathizers must be identified . . . so that we will be able to carry out whatever orders I may transmit in due time." He started to deport Jews three days before the German attack began.[8]

Antonescu proclaimed a "holy war" on the greatest "enemy of the world, Bolshevism." That was how he put it on the day the war broke out. The goal was also to win back territory "lost" to the USSR. The common views shared by Romania and Germany were the struggle against the Slavs, hatred of Bolshevism, and "an underlying anti-Semitism."[9] Archibald Gibson, the *Times* of London correspondent in Bucharest, thought most Romanians supported Antonescu.

The Balkan dictator immediately began settling scores with Communists and Jews. Mihail Sebastian, a Jewish writer living in Bucharest, recorded in his diary for June 22 how Antonescu proclaimed "the holy war to liberate Bessarabia and Bukovina and to eradicate Bolshevism." Within hours he got an inkling of what was to follow, from two propaganda posters: "One [poster] depicts Stalin in a white smock that carries traces of bloody hands. The text: 'The Butcher of Red Square.' The second—with the text: 'Who are the masters of Bolshevism?'—shows a Jew in a red gown, with side curls, skull cap, and beard, holding a hammer in one hand and a sickle in the other. Concealed beneath his coat are three Soviet soldiers. I have heard the posters were put up by police sergeants."[10]

Antonescu ordered the immediate execution "of all Jewish Communists," as well as "those found with red flags and firearms." News leaked out about the pogrom in Iaşi. Sebastian, who heard about it in Bucharest, called it "a dark, somber, insane nightmare."[11] It led to the deaths of an estimated ten thousand Jews, one of many such incidents to follow. By August ten times that many had been killed along with Communists who came to hand.[12]

The city of Odessa, with a Jewish population of 180,000, became the scene of gruesome mass murder. The Romanians arrived when the Red Army withdrew on October 16. The headquarters of the Fourth Army was blown up, killing officers and men. In response Antonescu ordered reprisals on the following ratio: for every Romanian or German officer killed in the explosion, two hundred Communists were to be executed; for every soldier, the number was one hundred. For that purpose the Communists were to be arrested, along with one person from each Jewish family, a horrific example of where the persecution of "Jewish Bolshevism" logically led.[13]

Odessa became "the city of the hanged," with gallows everywhere. The bloodbath overwhelmed the Jews, and according to a postwar Soviet investigation around 100,000 were murdered in a process that ran for weeks. Germans were involved, but most of the dirty work was done by Romanians, who showed a penchant for cruelty that sometimes shocked even members of Einsatzgruppe D.[14]

Antonescu said on July 30, in response to a letter of thanks from Hitler, that he wanted to reaffirm his commitment "to the campaign we have begun in the east against Russian Bolshevism, the arch foe of European civilization."[15]

What happened to the Jews in Romania illustrates that the Holocaust was a multinational operation. Its cost in human lives varied according to the extent of native anti-Semitism and the willingness to collaborate with Hitler.

In Hungary, Admiral Miklós Horthy, de facto head of state, was anxious to form a military alliance with Germany. Hitler assigned Hungary only a secondary role in the attack on the USSR. He did not ask them to commit to the war, but wrote the Hungarian government on June 21 to inform them of the imminent attack. He said he was "acting in the spirit of the whole of European civilization and culture in trying to repel and push back this un-European influence," that is, the Soviet Union.[16] Horthy responded enthusiastically "as an old crusader against Bolshevism." He said that for "twenty-two years he had longed for this day, and was now delighted. Centuries later mankind would be thanking the führer for this deed. One hundred and eighty million Russians would now be liberated from the yoke forced upon them by two million Bolsheviks."[17] Even before the Hungarian declaration of war on June 27, they began encroaching on the border with the Soviet Union.

Hitler was grateful, but frankly thought the Germans could go it alone. Döme Sztójay, the Hungarian minister in Berlin, neatly summed up the German attitude as follows:

My judgment of the situation is that the Germans do not really need any substantial military support. To protect their northern and southern wings, and their nickel and oil, they have enlisted the Finns and Romanians. The latter are being wooed by them, as hitherto, by territorial revisions. They are not anxious to negotiate with other states, because they like to keep a free hand for themselves; nevertheless, from the propaganda point of view, they want to have as many countries as possible actively participating in the crusade against Bolshevism. Those who do not participate will feel it on their own skins someday.[18]

Hitler's conversation with Sladko Kvaternik, the deputy head of state in "independent Croatia" since April 10, 1941, was noteworthy not just for the agreement on joining the anti-Bolshevik campaign but for Hitler's uncharacteristic openness about his intentions of settling accounts with the Jews. He mentioned only that they would be sent somewhere and said he did not care where.[19]

Bulgaria's King Boris III led his country down a tortuous path, hoping to avoid antagonizing either Germany or the Soviet Union, its Slavic brethren and neighbor. On March 1, the king's rabidly anti-Semitic prime minister, with the government behind him, signed the Tripartite Pact (between Germany, Italy, and Japan). However, Bulgaria resisted pressure to join the attack against the USSR, though it instituted anti-Semitic measures like the Nazis' Nuremberg Laws.

Bulgaria's record was mixed, sometimes committing atrocities in Thrace and even permitting the deportation of Jews from there. But when it came to Bulgarian Jews, it was not just the government but the nation as a whole—courageously inspired by the Orthodox metropolitan Stephan and other Church leaders—that would not tolerate repeated German demands to deport the Jews. There was no history of anti-Semitism in Bulgaria, and even though King Boris was called by Hitler to give up the Jews, the Bulgarians held firm. Thus the approximately fifty thousand Jews who lived in Bulgaria in 1939 remained at war's end.[20]

Hitler had no time for some would-be crusaders who were anxious to participate in the war against the USSR. The new Vichy government in France repeatedly tried to make arrangements with Hitler, who was not interested in having the country as a co-belligerent. Admiral François Darlan wrote to Hitler on May 14, 1941, that he wanted to offer Germany more than the use of French facilities and bases. He wished to join them in taking the "first steps toward a happier future for our two lands" and to work toward "European cooperation." The Vichy government could claim to be as anti-Communist as the Nazis and showed itself, at least to Jews who were not French citizens, to be almost as anti-Semitic.[21]

On July 6, the Germans said they were willing, with the blessing of President Philippe Pétain, to accept French volunteers from various right-wing groups. The Germans permitted only fifteen thousand to join up, but the French hoped for twice that number.[22] Hitler was upset with a Vichy newspaper's report that "the war against the Soviet Union was Europe's war and that therefore, it had to be conducted by Europe as a whole." He told top Reich leaders, to the contrary, that the conquests in the east were entirely for Germany.[23]

Pierre Laval, another Vichy leader, told Albert Speer on June 19, 1942, that he hoped for a "lasting settlement" with Germany. France would provide "intensive economic aid" and a military alliance for "the heroic struggle in the east." Laval was single-minded in his anti-

Bolshevism. Backed by Pétain, he went to see Hitler on November 11 to try again for a "full alliance," but Hitler turned him down. The führer was looking for soldiers who passed his obscure racial-biological test, and the defeated French nation had failed.[24]

This attitude underlines the importance of ideology in Hitler's calculations. It also indicates in large measure why a broad European crusade failed to emerge. Hitler demanded a free hand in the east; he was arrogant and overconfident and distrusted "non-Germans."[25]

Even so, Vichy cooperated when it came to anti-Jewish measures. Of the 350,000 Jews in France, an estimated 77,000 were deported, about two-thirds of whom were refugees. According to one account, "The public clamored for anti-Jewish measures in the summer of 1940." The French government was quick to act against foreign Jews but proceeded more slowly against Jews who were French citizens.[26]

ORDERS AND PLANS FOR THE ATTACK ON "JEWISH BOLSHEVISM"

Hitler's directive for the attack on the USSR aimed to destroy the Red Army, but the "ultimate objective" was to "establish a cover against Asiatic Russia" by rolling back the country to the east. If needed, the German air force would then eliminate "the last industrial area left to Russia in the Urals."[27]

Even though Hitler said in January 1941 that the Red Army was a "headless colossus made of clay," he could not rule out the possibility that the situation could change. "The Russian," he warned, must not be underestimated. The distances were great, but, he reasoned, no larger than the area Germany had already taken. He was convinced the invasion should go ahead as soon as possible. The mightiest weapons and most brutal methods would be used to "exterminate" the Red Army, take the most important industrial areas, and destroy the rest. Baku, with its major oil fields, also had to be captured. The land conquered would not be incorporated into the fatherland, but merely exploited. Victory in the east would make Germany unassailable and capable of taking on the world at some point.[28]

On March 3, 1941, Hitler discussed a draft plan with the chief of the

Wehrmacht operations staff, General Alfred Jodl. He said the war against "Jewish Bolshevism" was to be no conventional war:

> The impending campaign is more than a clash of arms; it also entails a struggle between two ideologies. To conclude this war it is not enough, given the vastness of the space, to defeat the enemy's forces. The entire territory must be dissolved into states with their own governments with which we can conclude peace. Any revolution of major proportions creates facts that can no longer be expunged. . . . The Jewish-Bolshevik intelligentsia, until now the "oppressor" of the people, must be liquidated. The former bourgeois-aristocratic intelligentsia, insofar as they still exist among the immigrants, is also to be eliminated. They are rejected by the Russian people and in the last analysis are anti-German. . . . Under all circumstances we have to ensure that a national Russia does not take the place of Bolshevik Russia, because history proves that in the final analysis it would also be anti-German.
>
> Our task is to set up, as soon as possible, and with a minimum of military force, Socialist state structures that are subject to us. These tasks are so complex that one cannot expect an army to perform them.[29]

Jodl called his staff to make the revisions Hitler requested. Army administration of the conquered area was to be minimal, with Reich commissars given most of the job. Himmler was to be consulted about whether the SS should be employed in the army's theater of operations, and Jodl thought it was a good idea to give the SS that job because of the "need to render all Bolshevik chiefs and commissars harmless."[30]

Hitler's views found their way into the directives issued on March 13, 1941, by the OKW for Barbarossa. These spelled out that Himmler was given "special tasks on the führer's instruction" arising "from the final struggle between two opposing political systems." In the context of these tasks Himmler was "to act independently and on his own responsibility."[31]

Hitler reminded Quartermaster General Eduard Wagner and Reinhard Heydrich of the SS on March 17 that the Soviet Union was to be dismembered. Wagner reached agreement with Heydrich, even though in the armed forces it was common knowledge what the SS units had done during the invasion of Poland in 1939. Wagner issued draft orders on March 26 stating that the security police and SD would have special missions behind the lines, would "act on their own responsibility," and were empowered to take "executive decisions" with regard to the civilian population. This order already opened the door for cooperation between the SS and the Wehrmacht, also with regard to dealing with Communists and Jews.[32]

Hitler thought that the Byelorussians would welcome Germany "with open arms," but was less sure about Ukraine and the Don Cossacks. Finland would get parts of northern Russia, while Germany would take the Baltic States. He was going to be particularly ruthless with the ruling elite the Germans found in place.

> We must build republics insulated against Stalin's influence. The intelligentsia created by Stalin must be exterminated [*vernichtet werden*]. The power apparatus of the Russian Empire [the Soviet Union] must be smashed. In Great Russia we must use the most brutal force. The ideological ties holding the Russian people together have not yet become strong, and the nation would collapse once the functionaries are eliminated. The Caucasus will be ceded eventually to Turkey, but first must be exploited by us.[33]

The Wehrmacht General Staff raised no objections to these ideological goals. Moreover, Field Marshal Brauchitsch told commanders at Zossen on March 27: "The troops have to realize that this struggle is being waged by one race against another and proceed with the necessary harshness."[34]

On March 30, Hitler spoke to his generals for two and a half hours. He reiterated the debatable strategic point that dealing with Russia would end Britain's hopes. He turned to the conflict between Nazism and Communism. General Halder wrote down the remarks, sensing how important they were to an understanding of the war to come:

> *Clash of two ideologies*: Crushing denunciation of Bolshevism, identified with asocial criminality. Communism poses an enormous danger for our future. We must forget the notion of comradeship between soldiers. A Communist is no comrade, neither before nor after the battle. This is a war of extermination. If we do not understand this, we shall still beat the enemy, but thirty years later we will again be fighting the Communist adversary. We are not waging war to preserve the enemy.

Future political image Russia: Northern Russia goes to Finland. [Germany's] Protectorates: Baltic states, Ukraine, Belorussia.

War against Russia: Extermination of the Bolshevik commissars and the Communist intelligentsia. The new states must be socialist, but must not have intellectual classes of their own. We must prevent the formation of a new intellectual class. A primitive socialist intelligentsia is all that is needed. We must struggle against the poison of disintegration. This is no job for military courts. The individual troop commanders must become aware of the issues at stake and be leaders in this fight. The troops must fight back with those same methods used to attack them. Commissars and GPU men [Soviet secret police] are criminals and must be dealt with as such. This need not mean that the troops should get out of control. Rather the commander must give orders that reflect the common feelings of his men.

Embody in a High Command of the Army [OKH] order: This war will be very different from the war in the west. In the east, harshness today means lenience in the future. Commanders must be prepared to sacrifice their personal scruples.[35]

Eliminating "Jewish Bolshevism" could mean getting rid of Communist leaders, and perhaps even Party members, but did not yet spell out the extermination of all Jews in Europe.

The assembled officers were apparently comfortable with Hitler's assertion that international law and military traditions should not be applied to the war against "Jewish Bolshevism." As one account concludes, Hitler thus succeeded in "maneuvering the army, beyond its strictly military tasks, into a war of annihilation against an ideology [Communism] and its followers, for which the EGr [action groups] in particular were earmarked." The next morning some officers expressed concerns, mainly with the exclusion of the courts-martial, which they thought might lead to discipline problems.[36]

On May 2 conversations were held by state secretaries about the food situation. In the "third year of the war," which was presumably 1941, it was agreed that the "entire Wehrmacht" had to be fed from Russia. The brutal calculation that followed was that "x-million people will doubtlessly starve if we take what is necessary for ourselves from the countryside."[37] This hunger plan was given Hitler's blessing (but not his signature) and was widely discussed among the top ranks of the

Wehrmacht and the bureaucracy. The problem was viewed as straight-forward: the German people had to eat, a priority to keep up morale; Western Europe also had to be fed for political reasons; German troops would have to "live off the land"; and with the disruptions caused by war, there would be a shortfall.

According to what became official thinking on the plan, an estimated thirty million Soviet people, mostly city dwellers, would have to be starved to death. Although there was no written order for the destruction of these people, all kinds of options were heard, including shipping them to Siberia. Given how the Germans knew the Soviet transportation system could not cope with such a huge movement of people, "deportation" was a cover for what would be wholesale destruction.[38]

Thus a plan for the greatest deliberately created famine in world history came into existence. It was concocted primarily by Herbert Backe, soon to be minister of agriculture, but involved and was known to many leading civilian and military figures. The plan proved to be "impractical" because it was impossible to keep so many people away from food; the only groups they managed to starve on any scale were Jews in ghettos and Soviet prisoners of war behind barbed wire. The cruel audacity of the hunger plan and the failure of its creators to anticipate the desperate measures of the starving victims suggest the genocidal mentality of the invaders on the eve of Barbarossa. Numerous German leaders made no secret of what was planned, and Hermann Göring, to mention one of many examples, told the Italian foreign minister, Galeazzo Ciano, in November 1941—without a hint of concern—that within a year twenty to thirty million people would starve in Russia. The impression was that it would not be such a bad thing, for certain nations had to be reduced.[39]

Himmler had already commissioned a "resettlement" plan of his own, and work had been going ahead on what became known as General Plan East. He found the first versions not far-reaching enough, even though they envisaged that of the forty-five million or so people living in the area between Russia and Germany, no fewer than thirty-one million were "racially undesirable" and would be sent to Siberia in the decades following the war. Some experts calculated precisely how many train-loads would be involved. Those who remained in the west would work as slaves for the ten million German settlers in the area. The plan specified the percentages of people to be "deported": all Jews, 80 to 85 percent of the Poles, 75 percent of the Byelorussians, and 64 percent of the western

Ukrainians. Given these numbers, this plan called for nothing less than serial genocides.[40]

There were numerous other such plans. Not just the top Nazis but experts and professors from many fields drew up blueprints of their own for the German "Garden of Eden" in the east.[41]

INSPIRING THE TROOPS WITH HATRED FOR THE ENEMY

Hitler's negative views of the population in the east were shared by leading figures in the Wehrmacht and reflected in guidelines issued for the coming campaign. A draft document was discussed by the OKW on May 6 concerning "the treatment of enemy civilians and indictable offenses of members of the Wehrmacht against enemy civilians in the operational area of operation 'Barbarossa.' "

The guidelines indicated that, unlike the experience in Western Europe, German troops would "encounter an especially dangerous element from the civilian population disruptive of all order, the carriers of the *Jewish-Bolshevik worldview.*" Such people would use their "*weapon of disintegration*" treacherously wherever possible, so it was "the right and duty" of the troops to take all necessary steps. This ideological preface to the guidelines was used to abandon all international rules of law. It meant that "punishable actions committed by members of the army out of indignation over atrocities or over disruptive activities of exponents of the Jewish-Bolshevik system" were not to be prosecuted unless the general discipline of the troops was thought to be endangered.[42]

On May 13, Field Marshal Keitel issued a decree building on a revised version of this draft. In cases where Germans were shot at and the perpetrator could not be identified, officers were permitted to order collective reprisals. Felonies by troops against civilians did not have to be prosecuted. In deciding whether to lay charges, the judicial authority should recall "that the collapse in 1918, the subsequent sufferings of the German people, and the struggle of National Socialism with the countless blood sacrifices of the movement were primarily due to Bolshevik influence and no German had forgotten that."[43]

General Eugen Müller, who had worked on some of these drafts, told General Staff officers and army judges that the battle ahead would be like a return of ancient times when one foe lay dead on the ground and the other was victorious. He declared that the population's right of self-defense, recognized by the Hague Convention on land warfare of 1907, did not hold for the Soviet Union. In his view the concept of a "guerrilla" (*Freischärler*) included "agitators, distributors of leaflets, saboteurs," and anyone who would not follow German orders. Punishment should be immediate. Müller was one among many senior officers who spoke along these lines.[44]

On May 24, Brauchitsch forwarded the decree (with minor quibbles) on the treatment of the civilian population to the officers preparing for the coming attack. The commander in chief of the Army Group Center, Field Marshal Fedor von Bock, wrote in his diary that this measure "was so worded that it virtually gives every soldier the right to shoot, from in front or from behind, at any Russian he takes to be—or claims that he takes to be—a guerrilla." Bock's worry was that the discipline of the troops would be adversely affected, but he had no objections in principle.[45]

On June 4 the "Guidelines for the Behavior of the Troops in Russia" was distributed to troop commanders down the line. The new guidelines were prefaced by the same ideological justification: "*Bolshevism is the deadly enemy of the National Socialist German people. This disintegrative worldview and its carriers constitute Germany's enemies and must be fought.* This battle demands ruthless and energetic measures against *Bolshevik agitators, guerrillas, saboteurs, Jews,* and complete elimination of any active or passive resistance."[46]

Building on these guidelines, the "Commissar Order" was issued on June 6 under the heading "Treatment of Political Commissars." It went as follows:

In the struggle against Bolshevism, we must *not* assume that the enemy's conduct will be based on principles of humanity or international law. In particular, hate-inspired, cruel, and inhuman treatment of prisoners of war can be expected *from all grades of political commissar* who are the leaders of the real resistance.

The troops must be made aware that: (1) In this battle with these elements it is false to show consideration or to act in accordance with international law. That endangers our own security and the rapid pacification of the conquered areas; (2) the originators of barbaric and Asiatic methods of war are the political commissars. Therefore they have to be dealt with immediately and with maximum severity. When in *battle* or *resistance* these persons are to be shot immediately.[47]

Officers at the OKW and OKH were aware that the order to shoot commissars "was an infringement of international law."[48] Some troops would inevitably become involved in war crimes insofar as they selected out members of the Red Army they thought were "commissars" and shot them. Halder knew the consequences, but added laconically in his diary that the troops "must do their part in the ideological struggle of the eastern campaign."[49]

The Commissar Order and the guidelines on the treatment of civilians were all the more remarkable in that they were formulated by the conservative officer corps—including its judicial branch. There was no mention here of the radical SS, who were not involved but were gearing up in their own way for the war that loomed.

The explanation offered for why the officer corps fell into line with Hitler, as given recently by Germany's Research Institute for Military History, runs as follows: There was a "substantial measure of agreement on ideological questions," an amalgamation of anti-Semitism, anti-Slavism, and anti-Communism. The officer corps shared with Hitler and leaders of the Nazi Party the view that the war in 1918 had been lost only through a "stab in the back" by Marxists, Jews, and others. They were convinced that extreme steps had to be taken to ensure history did not repeat itself. No doubt many in the military were also swept along by the tide of Hitler's easy victories and had become true believers in him and, to a shocking extent, also in his ideas. Like him they wanted Germany to attain great-power status and to gain the needed territory and resources in the east. "Many officers therefore accepted Hitler's suggestion on March 30, 1941, and regarded themselves as leaders in the struggle against a hostile ideology, against 'Jewish Bolshevism.' " Thus "the called-for unity of militarism and National Socialism became reality to a high degree."[50]

The affinity of ideas between Hitler and his leading generals can be seen in statements made by a wide range of officers before the battle even began, and so cannot be explained by the heat of the moment or the brutalization of warfare. The following operations order of Armored Group 4 from General Erich Hoepner was issued even before the Commissar Order and the guidelines on treating the civilian population. It shows how many different officers transformed Hitler's ideological statements into concrete orders. On May 2, Hoepner had this to say about the coming clash with the Reds:

> The war against Russia is an essential phase in the German nation's struggle for existence. It is the ancient struggle of the Germanic peoples against Slavdom, the defense of European culture against the Muscovite-Asiatic tide, the repulse of Jewish Bolshevism. That struggle must have as its aim the shattering of present-day Russia and therefore be waged with unprecedented hardness. Every combat action must be inspired, in concept and execution, by an iron determination to ensure the merciless, total annihilation of the enemy. In particular, there must be no sparing the exponents of the present Russian Bolshevik system.[51]

The precise number of civilians who were about to die, commissars who would be shot, and prisoners of war who would be murdered or allowed to die remains difficult to ascertain. The scope of the catastrophe was calculated in broad terms, and it was clear that it would be unlike anything seen in history before.

28

WAR AGAINST THE COMMUNISTS: OPERATION BARBAROSSA

Operation Barbarossa gathered the largest attack force in European history. It deployed just over three million German troops, together with some half million from allied countries. The attackers used 3,350 tanks and 600,000 motor vehicles, but their continued reliance on horses (with 625,000 used in the invasion) revealed that this was not quite the mythical "all-mechanized" attack often supposed. The aim was another blitzkrieg, a lightning war to knock out the enemy quickly. Hitler's great anxiety was that the Red Army might escape capture, but of its defeat he had no doubt.[1]

On June 22, 1941, between 3:05 and 3:30 a.m., as the German war diary noted matter-of-factly, the "surprise attack" began. Using some twenty-five hundred aircraft, the Luftwaffe took on a Soviet air force at least three times as large but caught many planes on the ground. Soviet pilots who got into the air initially proved no match for the more experienced enemy, so that in the first week the Soviets lost thousands of aircraft and the Germans established air superiority. Indeed, by mid-afternoon on June 25, Halder stated that the "enemy air force is completely out of the picture after the very high initial losses (reports speak of 2,000)."[2]

Ordinary German citizens reacted to the first news with a mixture of shock, consternation, and lack of understanding. Within a week reports on public opinion suggested a return of confidence. News from the front and letters home, however, indicated that they were dealing with a tough-minded opponent who was allegedly mistreating German prisoners.[3] The Red Army was taken by surprise, but had deployed along the border an estimated 2.9 million men. They had three or four times as many tanks, artillery pieces, and aircraft as the invaders. They used faulty tactics that made it easy for the Germans to drive ahead at full speed. In places the Red Army fought back ferociously, but it took staggering losses.[4]

The greatest weapon in this war, as it had been when Napoleon attacked, also on a June day, in 1812, was the combination of the resilient people, vast distances, and cruel weather.

The battlefront from north to south covered an expanse of 1,250 miles.[5] Given the state of technology and the resources at the Wehrmacht's disposal, that was far too much territory. German supply lines were under constant attack, and the armies were unprepared for winter war.

Yet Germany's leaders, blinded by their prejudices about the inferiority of "the Russian" and underestimating the Red Army, did not even mobilize many more resources than they had against Western Europe. The Germans had 7,184 artillery pieces for the French campaign, and 7,146 to use against the USSR; in the battle for France the Luftwaffe had 3,530 fighter aircraft, but only 2,510 to employ against the Soviets, and one-fifth of them were not ready for action; in the western offensive they mobilized 142 divisions, but against the Red Army there were still only 150.[6] This does not show the level of readiness needed to fight far greater forces over vast distances under what became in the autumn and winter impossibly adverse conditions.

Initially the blitzkrieg worked even better in the east than it had in Western Europe. Army Group North advanced rapidly through the Baltic States; Army Group Center took the parts of Poland conquered by the Soviets in 1939 and drove straight ahead toward Moscow; and Army Group South swept into Ukraine. Everything went according to plan.

On July 3, in a summary of what had happened to that point, Halder painted a positive picture:

On the whole, then, it may be said even now that the objective to smash the bulk of the Russian army this side of the Dvina and Dnieper has been achieved. I do not doubt the statement of the captured Russian corps Commanding General, that east of the Dvina and Dnieper we would find nothing more than partial forces, not strong enough to hinder German operational plans. It is probably no overstatement to say that the Russian campaign has been won in just two weeks.[7]

What remained to be done, he thought, in the face of the great distances and the nagging resistance would "claim our efforts for many weeks to come." What was needed was to prepare a new jump-off line between Smolensk and Moscow, do the same around Leningrad, and thereafter proceed to conquer northern Russia and Moscow. The attack would then aim at the south and the oil in the Caucasus. Halder, believing the Soviets were as good as beaten, thought the goal now was to prevent Stalin from raising a new army "from his gigantic industrial potential and his inexhaustible manpower resources." He fully expected that once the objective switched from annihilating the Soviet enemy to destroying the economy, the "next task" was to focus again on Britain.

Hitler was equally optimistic and thinking along similar lines. He told Goebbels on July 9 of the "surprisingly positive" situation in which "two-thirds of the Bolshevik army was already destroyed or at least under heavy pressure; five-sixths of the Bolshevik air and tank weapons were as good as destroyed." He was even considering withdrawing the bulk of his forces and leaving a mere fifty divisions to pacify the country. He talked about how "the Bolshevik leadership clique had intended to invade Germany and therefore Europe, and at the last moment, with a weakening of the Reich, to carry out the Bolshevization of the continent that it had planned already since 1917." Hitler was convinced that Stalin had intended some such invasion and suggested that the Soviets might have been preparing to take Romania in the autumn, in order to cut off Germany from its petroleum supplies. He was ecstatic that he was able to thwart all such moves and said that the attack parried a threatening Soviet invasion. He believed the German people were "again thoroughly in an anti-Bolshevik frame of mind," and had never really accepted the rapprochement with the USSR following the nonaggression treaty of August 1939.[8]

What Hitler wanted for the east was reflected in a meeting he called at the Wolf's Lair on July 16, 1941. Present were Wilhelm Keitel, Alfred Rosenberg, Hans Lammers, and Hermann Göring.

Hitler was quoted as saying: "In principle we now have to face the task of cutting up the giant cake according to our needs, in order to be able: first, to dominate it; second, to administer it; and third, to exploit it." West of the Ural Mountains no military power would be allowed to exist, in effect what used to be European Russia would come to an end. He made reference to Stalin's speech of July 3, which called for partisan warfare against the invaders. Hitler said such a rally to the Soviets had the advantage of "enabling us to exterminate everyone who opposes us." Germany would keep its true aims to itself for political reasons, but there would be no "wavering policy."

The conquerors would present themselves as liberators, but they dare not lose sight of their goal: "We have to create a Garden of Eden in the newly won eastern territories; they are vitally important to us. Colonies by comparison were of completely secondary interest." Hitler favored heavy-handed methods, shooting, deportation, or extermination, while others (like Rosenberg) warned about raising the historical conscious-ness of some people (like Ukrainians) by treating them badly. Germany was never going to leave the region it would conquer. Hitler's view was that "this giant area would have to be pacified as quickly as possible; this would best happen if we shoot anyone who only looks sideways at us." However, the false assumption among all those present, as well as many in the Wehrmacht, was that the Soviets were as good as beaten.[9]

Although Soviet collapse was thought to be imminent, by August Halder had come to doubt the Communists would give up that easily. At the beginning of the war German military leaders had reckoned on 200 Soviet divisions, but by early August they had already counted 360. If the latter were not fully equipped, they were still there, and no sooner did the Germans destroy a dozen of them, he said, than another dozen appeared. Even though Germany had captured over three million in early 1942, many Red Army units fought to the death and inflicted heav-ier casualties on the Wehrmacht than expected. The prisoners were being allowed to starve in the hundreds of thousands, a war crime of unprecedented proportions. Rosenberg, minister for the occupied east-ern territories, complained that he could find only a few hundred thou-sand fit to work.[10]

The blitzkrieg effect began to falter in the depths of the Soviet Union.

The Wehrmacht was prepared not so much for a full-scale campaign as for "expeditions" by motorized corps, after which there would be follow-up "sorties" into the Ural Mountains, just as the British Indian Army had supposedly done in the nineteenth century in the Afghan mountains.[11]

The Nazi strategy was to use deliberate brutality to shatter resistance and break the enemy's will. However, the tactic of killing off or starving hundreds of thousands of prisoners had the unanticipated effect of stiffening the resolve of the Red Army, because word of the atrocities soon spread. The invaders also disregarded the popular response. If their arrival was often welcomed, at least by some, as liberation from Stalinist oppression, killing all commissars and practically any Jews alienated more than expected. It was soon evident that the Nazis were coming not as liberators but as even more ruthless oppressors than the Soviets.

Civilians in occupied territories were pressed into labor service and sent to Germany, most against their will, to make up for growing shortfalls. Poles were the first to be forced to work as slaves—complete with a *P* marking on their clothing. They were now followed by *Ost,* or "eastern," workers. Inside Germany both were judged racially inferior and legally prohibited from having sexual relations with a "German-blooded" person. Any such "crime" was subject to the death penalty. Poles and eastern workers found guilty were in fact executed in public inside Germany, while German women involved in these forbidden relations had their heads shaved and were paraded through the streets.[12]

Nazi terror was used with far greater abandon outside Germany, where it became the order of the day in Poland in 1939. It was practiced further in Yugoslavia and Greece and applied with more ferocity still in Barbarossa.

Hitler was remarkably cold when he got news of setbacks or the loss of troops. In this he was not unlike Lenin and Stalin. The lives of their own people, whether civilian or military, were there to be sacrificed for the cause.

Anyone reading his memorandum issued on August 27, 1941, has to be struck by how far Germany was overextended. The memo dealt with fighting in North Africa, the air war over Britain, and the struggle in the Mediterranean, as well as the invasion of the Soviet Union. It conceded that only after the defeat of the Soviets would it be possible to take on Britain. There was a candid admission that beating the Soviets was now the top priority and that it "will not be fully achieved in 1941."[13]

REVISIONS OF THE INVASION PLAN

Hitler and his generals recognized in August that they did not have the reserves to continue to attack the Soviet Union in strength in three directions at the same time. There was disagreement about what the priority should be. The military men Halder, Bock, and Guderian all wanted to aim for Moscow. On August 21–22, Hitler repeated that he cared less about taking that city but wanted to focus on the north, where he would surround and destroy Leningrad, and on the south, by taking Kiev and Ukraine.[14]

Kiev fell on September 25 and at enormous costs to the Red Army. The Germans took hundreds of thousands of prisoners and were generally welcomed by the local population. But the great victory was more apparent than real, because the Germans suffered heavy casualties as well and still had to fight on across long stretches of inhospitable terrain.

Leningrad, the home of Bolshevism, had been partly cut off from the rest of the USSR since July 1941, but the effort to encircle the city stalled. Hitler's orders on August 21 took troops from Army Group Center and sent them north. On September 6 the question arose whether he should accept the surrender of the city.

The option, which was also eventually adopted for Moscow, was to wear the cities down from the outside and use artillery and bombing to level them. Hitler wanted to turn them into living hell to induce the population to leave. Gaps would be left open in the lines so people could escape and sow chaos inside Russia.[15]

Stalin sent Zhukov, who arrived in Leningrad on September 9. As the situation continued to deteriorate, he issued an order typical of his command style and the Soviet approach to the war. As the Germans were tightening their vise around Leningrad, his combat order No. 0064, published on September 18, read in part as follows: "The Leningrad Front's Military Council announces to all commanders and political and line cadres defending the designated line that all commanders, political workers, and soldiers who abandon the indicated line without a written order from the *front* or army military council will be shot immediately."[16]

The Germans closed the circle around Leningrad anyway. On September 16, Hitler spoke with his ambassador to France, Otto Abetz, about what demands should be made of that country. He worried about using French troops because at some point in the future, if a "genius" should emerge, he might lead them in a resistance movement. Hitler also spoke about the east. "The Petersburg [that is, Leningrad] poison well" that had been overflowing into the Baltic for years, as he put it, "had to be obliterated from the face of the earth." In Hitler's terms, it was all or nothing: "The Asiatics and Bolsheviks had to be driven out of Europe." The new border in the east would be the Ural Mountains.[17] On September 22 he ordered the city put under siege, after which his commander was "to erase" it "by means of artillery fire of all caliber and continuous bombardment from the air."[18] Some German officers worried about having to feed the "millions" in Leningrad. Officers and men recognized that would be impossible without taking away food needed for the fatherland. There was also concern about ordering troops to shoot what might be many thousands trying to cross over into their lines; officers searched for an alternative approach, because they thought it would render their men mentally and (morally) unstable.[19]

Momentarily all went quiet on the Leningrad front, and the Germans mistakenly assumed that the Soviets had "accepted their fate" and were withdrawing. Hitler and his generals began to count the city as a victory and, especially given the massive losses sustained by the Red Army, concluded the Communists were finished. Based on these mistaken assumptions, they decided it was feasible to attack Moscow in Operation Typhoon.

MESSAGES TO THE GERMAN TROOPS

Hitler sent words of encouragement to the troops on October 2. He told them to keep the ideological mission in mind and claimed that the invasion was a preventive measure, as Stalin had been about to unleash an assault against Europe. By now, he said sarcastically, German soldiers had themselves become acquainted with "the paradise of the workers and peasants." They were able to see the "unimaginable poverty" in what should have been a land of prosperity, the result, according to Hitler, "of almost twenty-five years of Jewish domination." He denounced Bolshevism as worse than the most exploitative form of capitalism and claimed that in both cases the "carriers" of the systems were the same: "Jews and only Jews." He looked forward to Moscow as "the last great decisive battle of the year."[20]

This anti-Semitic and anti-Bolshevik message was published all over Europe, so few people indeed would have been unaware of what the crusade was all about.[21]

Hitler issued a directive on October 7, repeating that the surrender of Moscow and Leningrad was not to be accepted. German troops should stay outside both. Taking Kiev, which had to be fought for street by street and was full of booby traps, showed how costly urban warfare could be. He wanted to incite chaos, forcing people to flee and bringing general social breakdown. That would make it easier to administer the areas.[22]

He called forth a historical dimension by saying that in defeating the Soviet Union at Moscow, Germany would end the Slavic danger that had threatened Europe for centuries. This was not a war for mere booty, or to make life easier for the German taxpayer, but war against the Jews and Communism and for lebensraum.

Germany's top military figures identified "from the start with the ideological aim of combating 'Jewish Bolshevism,'" and many of them issued statements or orders to their troops to underline the point.[23] Quartermaster General Wagner was aware of growing casualties but on October 5 still expressed complete faith in Hitler's military abilities. "Operational goals are being set," he said breathlessly, "that earlier would have made our hair stand on end. Eastward of Moscow! Then I estimate the war will be mostly over, and perhaps there really will be a collapse of the [Soviet] system. . . . I am constantly astounded at the führer's military judgment."[24]

The Wehrmacht kept encircling vast numbers of Red Army troops and taking prisoners. According to Bock, in charge of Army Group Center, his forces (so he claimed) had taken no fewer than 673,098 prisoners by October 19. They had captured "huge amounts of war material." Even so, the way ahead was long and the going tough as the weather worsened. Rain and sleet turned the land into mud. Soon Bock was complaining about "bottomless roads," and his commanders were saying it was impossible to move forward. Ordinary soldiers wrote home to tell of the horrid conditions.[25]

Hitler was adamant that troops not enter Moscow and, by order of October 13, told his generals again not to accept the surrender of that city, should it be offered. Bock's diary shows that although he kept winning battles, the Red Army would not go away. He drove ahead to see the causes of delays and recognized that mud made the roads all but impassable.

The Wehrmacht had made no provisions for the hundreds of thousands, and ultimately millions, of Red Army prisoners they were taking in the advance on Moscow. The wounded were either finished off or left to die. Bock saw the captured Soviets struggle past his vehicle in silence and noted: "The impression of the tens of thousands of Russian prisoners of war who, scarcely guarded, are marching toward Smolensk is dreadful. Dead-tired and half-starved, these unfortunate people stagger along. Many have fallen dead or collapsed from exhaustion on the road."[26]

Although by the end of October orders kept coming in from headquarters to drive on, Army Group Center was becoming exhausted. Everything seemed to be backfiring. Much German equipment was in disrepair; conditions on the ground were so poor that Bock considered ordering his divisions to leave their motorized equipment behind and go forward on foot. German troops were supposed to form a ring around Moscow forty-five kilometers from the center of the city. Bock realized that such a mission required far more troops than he had.[27] On October 25 he noted that the Red Army was rushing reinforcements from Siberia and the Caucasus, while he was forced onto the defensive.

Hitler and Halder could plainly see the blitzkrieg against the Soviet Union was faltering if not failing. However, they agreed that the attack had to continue, even if by early November the main objective was to establish a basis for operations the next year.[28]

On November 13, Halder held a conference near Smolensk with the chiefs of staffs of the armies and army groups. Bock recorded in his diary that it was fifteen to twenty degrees below freezing. There was concern about how troops would survive the winter, never mind prepare for fresh offensives the following year. Halder said he thought it was still possible to take Moscow in 1941, but was given plenty of reasons to conclude otherwise.[29]

He called the operation Hitler wanted "high-risk." In reality, it was bound to fail because German forces were already at the end of their endurance, supplies, and reserves. On November 21, Bock noted that the ranks of his officers had been so decimated that young lieutenants were leading major units without the necessary training and experience. Nevertheless, he still decided to call on his last reserve division. He confided to his diary: "But it is doubtful if we can go any farther. The enemy can move everything he has to Moscow. But my forces are not up to a concentrated, powerful counterattack."[30] Army Group Center fought doggedly onward even at the risk, as Bock put it to Halder on November 29, "of some units burning themselves out."[31]

FAILURE OF THE BLITZKRIEG AGAINST THE USSR

German formations got within eighteen miles of Moscow, and according to some reports a few may have gotten closer than that. Nevertheless, by December 5 battle commanders felt there was no option but to withdraw because their forward positions were too exposed. At almost the same moment the Red Army launched a surprise attack that broke through the weak lines, just as Bock had predicted. Nearly all German military leaders agreed that retreat was necessary, but Hitler would not hear of it. On December 1 he sacked Rundstedt, commander of Army Group South, for suggesting that in the face of an enveloping attack in great strength by the Red Army, some of his forces take up defensive positions. Hitler was adamant about holding the line and not retreating. Rundstedt said he could not comply with that order, which should be changed or he be relieved of his post. A very agitated Hitler dismissed him at once, but that was not the only expression of his displeasure, for on December 19 he forced out Commander in Chief Walther von Brauchitsch and took over the position himself. On December 17, Bock turned over his command (for health reasons), and Field Marshal Wilhelm Ritter von Leeb, in charge of Army Group North (Leningrad), asked to be relieved on January 15, 1942. Even the best of leaders, like Erwin Rommel in Africa, were at the very same time put under fierce pressure, as the presumably unstoppable Wehrmacht was reaching the end of its resources in practically all theaters.[32]

The Germans still thought they could win, even though the Red Army was not just holding on but attacking again and again. Hitler and his "realistic" military experts were convinced of the superiority of their own troops and leaders, and of their ability to finish the job. They were still sure the enemy was about to collapse. To judge by letters from the front, this was a view held by many ordinary soldiers as well, at least in the early going; some hoped—in August 1941—the best Soviet troops had already been defeated.[33]

The image of the shaky Red Army was colored by the Nazi hatred of Bolshevism and the Slavs. Anti-Semitism played a key role, as the Jews were commonly blamed for creating Bolshevism. Prejudice got the better of Hitler's rational calculations, and the same went for many of his top military men.

In Berlin on November 29, Hitler told Goebbels how "positive" he felt about the eastern front, even though there were some minor retreats. The weather was slowing progress, but he expected more victories and to move closer to Moscow, so it would be wrong to conclude, he said, that the war had reached a stalemate.[34]

The situation on the eastern front was in fact deteriorating. Hitler had scheduled an address to the nation, and on December 11 he repeated how Germany had been forced to attack the Soviet Union to stop its plans for the conquest of Europe. Germany was now the leader of a coalition of European forces, and he named all the allied nations, though without mentioning how small their contributions—a fact well known to the public. He said the broad participation in the east had given the war "in the truest sense of the word the character of a European crusade."

The most important part of the speech was the verbal assault on the United States. He emphasized that the people of both countries had nothing against each other and traced the worsening relations to the Jews who supposedly surrounded and used President Roosevelt for their own purposes. They wanted to create a "Jewish paradise" of the kind German soldiers were seeing with their own eyes in the Soviet Union. He charged the Jews with wanting to "destroy one state after the next." He was going to support Japan, not because it was an ally, but because it was coming down to a question of life or death.

Indeed Japan had attacked Pearl Harbor on December 7 without even informing Hitler. Nevertheless, on December 11 he declared war on the United States, a move not called for by the treaty with Japan. He would have preferred a Japanese invasion of the far eastern Soviet Union, which would have brought immediate relief to German troops. But the entry of Japan into the war was viewed as helpful, since it drew British and American forces away from Europe. However, he underestimated American economic and military capacity, above all the will of the people, just as he had failed to appreciate the strength of the Soviets.[35]

Hitler told Goebbels that the war situation in the Soviet Union ruled out further battles, particularly major attacks. He was talking about the spring of the next year as better suited for the renewed offensive. Both men admitted their worry about the heavy Soviet tanks, against which the Germans had no defense. Even when German anti-aircraft guns were used and hit one of these Soviet tanks, it was considered a "lucky shot" when the shell stopped the tank. On the other hand, they regarded Japan's attack as a stroke of luck. Hitler remained optimistic and convinced of victory—although his dissatisfaction with his generals was palpable.

The picture at home, as reported in detail by the SD, was "fairly gray." The letters from the front, so encouraging initially, were now having a negative effect.[36] There was no denying that Barbarossa had failed and the Wehrmacht, not the Red Army, was close to being shattered. The Germans had lost 918,000 killed, wounded, captured, or missing in action. That was 28.7 percent of the 3.2 million involved in the operation. The losses were so grave that it would be correct to conclude that the Wehrmacht never recovered. The Red Army suffered even higher casualties, but it could draw on the arsenal of the United States and now was buoyed up by the probability that it was only a matter of time before the U.S. armed forces would be heading for Europe.[37]

29

WAR AGAINST THE JEWS:
DEATH SQUADS IN THE EAST

In the propaganda buildup to the war against the Soviet Union and thereafter, the German press hammered home the message that Jews were linked with the Bolshevism of the Russian Revolution and with Stalin's Communist regime, and especially with his terror.[1] Long before the attack on the USSR began—as we have seen in detail—Jews were high on the list of those to be singled out and persecuted in Poland in 1939, in Western Europe in 1940, and in Yugoslavia and Greece in 1941. During Operation Barbarossa, however, the murder campaign broke all previous constraints.

In the first stages of the war against the Soviet Union, the main killers of the Jews were the Einsatzgruppen (EGr). Heydrich had organized similar squads for the invasion of Poland, but the attack was now aimed at the homeland of Bolshevism and was intended to be far more radical. Initially he established three Einsatzgruppen (EGr A, B, and C), one each for Army Groups North, Center, and South. Eventually another (D) was added for the Romanian front and elsewhere. These relatively small units—containing fewer than three thousand members in all— were divided into commandos. They were led by highly educated men— many of them with university degrees, some with doctorates. After the war, the psychiatrists, jurists, and others who interviewed them were struck by their "normality."[2]

It is important to keep in mind that Hitler saw Germany as engaged simultaneously in two interrelated wars: one against the Bolsheviks to eliminate them and gain lebensraum, the other against the Jews, portrayed as the power holders or wire-pullers behind the scenes. From the Nazi perspective, the Wehrmacht's battlefront actions against the Red Army and the Einsatzgruppen's murder of the Jews were two parts of the same mission, namely to wipe out "Jewish Bolshevism" and create a racially pure Germanic utopia.

THE EINSATZGRUPPEN, OR DEATH SQUADS, IN THE EAST

On June 17, 1941, Heydrich told leaders of the Einsatzgruppen that the "immediate" goal was "political pacification" behind the advancing troops, and the "final" goal was the "economic pacification" of the area. They were to follow the orders and instructions as given to the Wehrmacht with respect to executing designated groups like the commissars in the Red Army. On July 2, in a note that survives, he repeated some of what he had said to these leaders immediately before they left for the front. They were to execute "all functionaries of the Comintern (as in general all Communist professional politicians); the senior, middle-level, and radical lower functionaries of the Party, the central committees, the district and regional committees; people's commissars; Jews in the Party and in official positions; assorted radical elements (saboteurs, propaganda people, snipers, those who commit violence against the state, rowdies, and so on)."[3]

He added that "no hindrances were to be placed in the way of . . . self-purging efforts of anti-Communist or also anti-Jewish circles in the new areas to be occupied." These efforts were to be assisted "without leaving any traces." They were given a license to kill practically anyone involved in "Jewish Bolshevism."

On July 25, 1941, Himmler ordered the creation of local police units to aid and abet the relatively limited number of Germans in the police and SS at his disposal. By the end of 1941 there were twenty-six local police battalions, and some 33,000 men enlisted in "protective teams," or

Schutzmannschaften. Within a year 300,000 of these indigenous police were working for the Germans. In sum there can be no doubt the Nazis had sufficient forces on the ground to carry out the ambitious "ethnic cleansing" operations they had in mind.[4] By the end of 1941, alongside the Einsatzgruppen, German security divisions, and SS units, there were German order police battalions in the east. The mass murder of the Jews, though led by Himmler and Heydrich of the SS, involved thousands of "ordinary men" in the sense they were not even in the Nazi Party, much less in the SS.[5]

There were vicious attacks against the Jews throughout the "liberated" area. Some local people, for all kinds of reasons, from desire for personal gain to hooliganism, began to ask as soon as they learned the Germans were coming: "Is it permitted to kill the Jews?" This behavior, reinforced by what the invaders said, was anchored in "an entrenched narrative of alleged Jewish collaboration with the Soviets in 1939."[6]

The Soviets had ruled areas like eastern Poland and the Baltic States for twenty months (from September 1939 to June 1941). Occupation meant terror, repression, murder, and the deportation of thousands. When the Nazis arrived, the myth of Jewish sympathy for the Communists was already full-blown. In the small town of Jedwabne, Poland, local Communist sympathizers were killed as soon as the Soviets left, but so were those whom villagers remembered as having welcomed the Soviets when they arrived in 1939.[7]

The tragedy of this one town was a microcosm of the region and of the times. On July 10, within days of the German arrival, the non-Jews in Jedwabne took it upon themselves to murder all the Jews, fifteen or sixteen hundred people, with little or no prodding from the invaders.[8]

As the German forces passed through, and follow-up operations commenced, some people were reluctant to get involved in actions against the Jews. Others were enthusiastic. Franz Walter Stahlecker, leader of Einsatzgruppe A in the Baltic area, reported (for the period up to October 15, 1941) that it was "surprisingly not simple" to incite larger pogroms in Lithuania. He had to get partisans involved, and in several days, beginning in the night of June 25–26, they burned down synagogues and killed thirty-eight hundred Jews in Kaunas. In Latvia (particularly Riga) it was "much more difficult" to start similar pogroms—said to be explicable because the Soviets had murdered the entire national ruling class. Efforts paid off when the Latvian deputy police and others burned synagogues and killed around four hundred Jews. "As far as possible" films were taken of the murders of "Jews and Communists" carried out by the people of Kaunas and Riga—presumably for propaganda purposes. In Lithuania and Latvia, Stahlecker tried first to recruit those whose family members had been murdered or deported by the Soviets. In Estonia, with its small Jewish community, he said it was not possible to incite pogroms at all, but the Estonians had killed particularly hated Communists.

He noted under the heading "Other Security-Police Work" the murder of chronically ill psychiatric patients—to this point, 748 people. This form of euthanasia (as in Poland earlier) fitted perfectly into the ethnic-cleansing mission.

Stahlecker concluded that it would be impossible to fulfill the orders given prior to Operation Barbarossa—which he interpreted as the "widest possible elimination of Jews"—by way of pogroms. At the end of his report, he provided a table of those executed, with the breakdown as follows: In Lithuania, 81,171 people had been killed, 860 of them Communists, while the vast majority (80,311) were Jews. In Latvia, the figure was 31,868, with 1,843 of those murdered listed as Communists. In Estonia, 474 Jews were shot, somewhat fewer than the 684 Communists. In Byelorussia, all 7,620 people murdered were Jews.

Stahlecker said Jews in larger cities (like Kaunas and Riga) were put in ghettos. These would turn out to be merely holding areas; eventually most Jews there were killed as well. He even noted that the Einsatzkommando led the exhumation of the bodies of "Bolshevik victims," had them identified, and used the stories for propaganda purposes. There was an ongoing search for Communists and partisans.[9] We should note that this is merely one of an entire series of similar such reports.[10]

The onslaught against the Jews was directed at first primarily, but not exclusively, at Jewish men. This point generally held for all the Einsatzgruppen. The order to expand the killing to women and children reached different death squads at various times already in July and August 1941. In addition, entire Jewish communities were wiped out.

Hitler signed no order for the murder of the Jews, or at least no document has survived. It would not have been his inclination to issue a written order. His standard operating procedure was to wait for the opportune moment and then pass on his "wish," as he would have done in this case, to Heydrich or Himmler.

We know that Hitler certainly knew about and approved the murders. Heinrich Müller, head of the Gestapo, telegraphed the Einsatzgruppen on August 1, 1941, that "the führer is to be kept continually informed" about the killing operations. The Wehrmacht (OKW), including Field Marshal Keitel and the quartermaster general, and other leading figures of the regime like Bormann, Ribbentrop, and Goebbels also wanted to be kept in the know.[11]

In the summer of 1941 one of the worst crimes committed by Einsatzgruppe B was in and around Minsk. Their reports talked of eliminating entire subsections of people, like the "Jewish-Bolshevik leadership class," and soon even went beyond that. When the Einsatzgruppe arrived, they began killing around two hundred people a day, most labeled "Bolshevik functionaries, agents, criminals, Asians, and so on." Other cities in the area such as Smolensk were "combed through for members of the Jewish intelligentsia."[12] By mid-November, Einsatzgruppe B reported the liquidation of 45,467 since the beginning of Barbarossa.[13] As of March 31, 1943, according to their own records, they killed 142,359.[14]

The activities of these death squads were frequently aided and abetted by the Wehrmacht, many of whose leaders propagated the idea of a war of annihilation against the "Jewish-Bolshevik complex." Even units like Panzer Group 4 were told on the eve of the war that it was the "defence of European culture" against "Jewish Bolshevism." On July 30 the then commander of the Seventeenth Army, Karl Heinrich von Stülpnagel, ordered "selective" reprisals, not simply against the native Ukrainian population, but especially against "Jewish and Communist people."

Walther von Reichenau, commander of the Sixth Army, issued an order on August 10, 1941, mentioning the "necessary executions of criminal, Bolshevistic, mostly Jewish elements" that would be carried out by the organs of Reichsführer-SS Himmler. On September 12, Keitel fired up the troops with an order stating that "the struggle against Bolshevism demands ruthless and energetic, rigorous action above all against the Jews, the main carriers of Bolshevism."[15]

On October 10, Reichenau summarized the tasks ahead as follows: "The essential goal of the campaign against the Jewish-Bolshevik system is the complete destruction of its power instruments and the eradication of the Asiatic influence on the European cultural sphere." He added that "therefore the soldier must have a complete understanding for the necessity of the harsh, but just atonement of Jewish sub-humanity. This has the further goal of nipping in the bud rebellions in the rear of the Wehrmacht which, as experience shows, are always plotted by the Jews."[16]

Five days later Hermann Hoth, subsequently commander of the Seventeenth Army, mentioned in an order how "two spiritually unbridgeable conceptions are fighting each other: German sense of honor and race, and a soldierly tradition of many centuries, against an Asiatic mode of thinking and primitive instincts, whipped up by a small number of mostly Jewish intellectuals."[17]

On the whole the Wehrmacht and Einsatzgruppen worked well together. Although in Poland in 1939 some commanders had objected to the activities of the SS behind the lines, there were no repeat performances in Barbarossa. There were numerous cases in which units of the Wehrmacht killed Jews, excesses that represented the "anti-Semitic attitude and behavior of a more or less large part of the front troops." For example, in Pinsk at the beginning of August 1941, members of the SS Cavalry Regiment 2 drove thousands of Jews into the streets and shot them. The soldiers of 293 Infantry Division witnessed and discussed this incident. According to a member of that unit, "By no means did everyone, but certainly most of his comrades agreed with what happened."[18]

RESPONSE OF THE TROOPS TO RACE WAR IN THE EAST

An army of millions cannot be driven by a single idea, but is influenced by countless factors. It would seem, however, that many soldiers were psychologically receptive to messages of hate against Bolsheviks, and particularly Jews. As we have seen, in the early days of the war the Wehrmacht became widely involved in "the practice of systematically victimizing Jews and Communists."[19]

The army did not have to be browbeaten into enforcing anti-Semitic measures. Captain Hermann Kremp, a staff officer of a security regiment (attached to Army Group Center), wrote home in the summer of 1941. He expressed himself with an appalling crudity and in a disgustingly jovial manner: "The place is crawling with Jews. We're rounding them all up for work, some to sweep the streets, some to mend them. We've got girls washing and darning and boys to clean our boots. For the last couple of days we've been forcing them all to wear the yellow star. Mind you, to get them to do any of this we had to set an example first, for the Jew elder had insisted the job mustn't be rushed. He refused our demand to hurry up, so we had to shoot him. That got the bastards moving!"[20]

This and other letters show that many soldiers interpreted the war in terms right out of Hitler's speeches, which were often parroted, particularly his "prophecy" about the fate of the Jews. More than one soldier said Jews were getting what they deserved and their efforts to manipulate England, America, and the Soviet Union to help them escape would fail.[21] A noncommissioned officer wrote home in July 1942, saying Bolshevism had nearly conquered Germany but the threat had been stopped: "The great task given us in the struggle against Bolshevism lies in the destruction of eternal Jewry. Once one sees what the Jew has done in Russia, one can well understand why the führer began the struggle against Jewry. What sorrows would have come to our homeland had he allowed this beast of a man to keep the upper hand?"[22]

When they saw poverty and misery, many found not pity in their hearts but confirmation of Nazi propaganda. A private wrote, "If in the past I thought that our propaganda had in this respect [conditions in Russia] somewhat exaggerated, today I can say that it had rather embellished conditions, for reality here is still far worse."[23]

A lieutenant who hoped to be used as a translator wrote in February 1942 from the east, "It is simply impossible to describe what we have experienced. The most satanic and criminal system of all time is the Jewish system in the 'Soviet Paradise'—it is a paradise for Jews."[24] A noncommissioned officer wrote in June 1942: "If one sees what the Russian has done here in Russia, only then does one rightly grasp why the führer began the struggle against the Jews."[25]

Nazi ideology, and particularly the justification for the war, infused this mentality. The Wehrmacht used savage reprisals, including destroying whole villages and killing all the inhabitants. When soldiers wrote home, they talked, as one did in July 1941, not of the horrors perpetrated by the Wehrmacht but of their shock at "evidence of Jewish, Bolshevik atrocities, the likes of which I have hardly believed possible." Another wrote that same month that "everyone, even the last doubter, knows today that the battle against these sub-humans, who've been whipped into a frenzy by the Jews, was not only necessary but came in the nick of time. Our Führer has saved Europe from certain chaos."[26] There is an abundance of similar evidence.[27]

A favored practice of the eastern army during 1941 was to have Jews and Communists topple the monuments of Lenin and Stalin. Heinz Backe, a gunner in the 291 Infantry Division, wrote his parents from the Baltic town of Liepaja: "All the town Jews were got together and put in a room the Bolsheviks had used for their conferences. This room was stuffed full of oversized portraits and busts of Stalin and co., and all sorts of Soviet symbols and paraphernalia. The Jews had to carry the lot out and walk in procession through the town streets to the River Windau (Venta) where a pyre was lit, and the Jews, naturally, were made to feed the flames with all the stuff they had been carting."[28]

Germans and their collaborators killed "partisans," "bandits," "subhumans," and above all Jews and Communists with a sense of fulfilling a greater mission. The Wehrmacht commandant for Byelorussia reported shooting 10,431 prisoners out of 10,940 taken in "battles with partisans" just in October 1941. That these people were powerless to resist, and no real threat at all, can be gathered from the fact that exactly two German soldiers were killed in carrying out the operation against "partisans."[29]

MASS MURDER AS REPRISAL FOR BOLSHEVIK SABOTAGE

In Eastern as in Western Europe, in situations involving reprisals German authorities tended to favor killing Jews and Communists. On July 25, 1941, by order of the Army High Command, Soviet soldiers found behind the lines after August 8 were to be regarded as partisans, whether in uniform or not, and shot. Similar orders were issued later by various army groups. As a related but separate matter, Karl Heinrich von Stülpnagel, commander of the Seventeenth Army in Ukraine, provided guidelines for responses to passive resistance or acts of sabotage when those responsible were not captured immediately: "Collective measures *not* to be taken *indiscriminately*. Where the initial act cannot be attributed to the Ukrainian local inhabitants, the local superintendents are to be instructed to name Jewish and Communist inhabitants in the first instance. By means of such pressure, the population is forced to inform the police." He added that Jews in the Communist Youth Organization "are in particular to be regarded as supporters of sabotage and the organization of gangs."

Stülpnagel was disappointed to report that the harsh methods against the Jews "arouse pity and sympathy" among some Ukrainians. The solution was not to stop reprisals but to step up the "enlightenment" of the population "in order to obtain a resolute and more uniform rejection" of Jews.[30]

Jürgen Förster maintains that the harshness of the collective measures against certain groups "cannot be explained solely by the need of the troops for security in the rear area, or by pragmatic considerations. In truth, the ideological background to these measures is beyond question." He shows that the cooperation between the Wehrmacht and the SS in the destruction of the Jews came down to one key point: "the acceptance by many officers and men of the propaganda image of 'Jewish Bolshevism.' Another was the fact that the differences between military tasks and security policing measures had deliberately been blurred, as Hitler had desired." The Wehrmacht, therefore, became involved in the "final solution" by marking out, hunting down, and forcing Jews into ghettos, and even helping the SS carry out mass executions. The Wehrmacht also cooperated with the SS in "pacifying" areas behind the lines, which invariably led to excesses against the Jews.[31]

These points hold for the three army groups but show up most graphically for the sector of Army Group South in Kiev. In September 1941 the Wehrmacht ran into stiff resistance there. The Red Army withdrew, but not before booby-trapping the center of town, and after only a few days under German occupation the timed devices began to go off. The explosions killed several hundred members of the Wehrmacht, as well as numerous civilians. A fire broke out that was fueled by Soviet partisans and raged for days.[32]

Local and regional Nazi officials, including the head of Einsatzgruppe C, Otto Rasch, as well as the city commandant Kurt Eberhard, decided to launch a massive reprisal and to have a large part of Kiev's Jews pay the price. It was easy to blame the Jews and Soviet secret agents. The Germans as well as Ukrainians lusted for revenge.

The activities of Einsatzgruppe C were already covered in blood. They had carried out numerous executions and incited people against

Jews and Communists. Occasionally local groups, delighted to see the end of Communism, acted on their own initiative. For example, as soon as the Red Army left Lvov (Lemberg), and before the German army arrived, partisans began to take out "revenge" on the Jews and Communists. A militia brought Jews to the former NKVD prison and forced them to exhume buried victims. Violence swept through the streets, but only after almost a week did the Wehrmacht put a stop to the pogrom; by that time, four to seven thousand (described as Jews and Russians) had been killed. Similar events were sparked off with every discovery of NKVD victims.[33]

The pogroms might commence when local hooligans or others went on a rampage. On other occasions, as in Tarnopol, they were incited by German forces. In Tarnopol two hundred NKVD victims were uncovered when German troops entered the city on July 2. Now German security police, with the assistance of a local militia, drove six hundred Jewish men into a "prayer house" and murdered them all.[34]

Kiev itself became the scene of the worst mass murder by shooting committed on Soviet territory. In response to the sabotage, an order was posted. Accordingly, on September 29, the next Monday, before eight o'clock, all the Jews "of Kiev and vicinity" were to report with their documents, clothing, and money for resettlement. General Eberhard wanted the Jews killed, but their execution was left to the Einsatzgruppe. One of its special commandos under Paul Blobel carried out the "action" with the assistance of a company of Waffen-SS, two police battalions, and the Ukrainian deputy police.[35]

The assembled Jews were marched to a nearby ravine. The roadway to the killing site was guarded by soldiers of the Wehrmacht. The mass murder took place in a gully called Babi Yar. By the end of the next day, the number of the murdered stood at 33,771.[36]

The story of the persecutions varied somewhat across the five districts of the newly created Reichskommissariat Ukraine. The Nazis found it easier to incite pogroms in areas that had been former Polish lands and occupied by the Soviets for the two years prior to June 1941. The main Ukrainian collaborators were the nationalists and the auxiliary police. It was the latter, "a minority, but an influential one," that hunted down the Jews. Nevertheless, the historical tensions between the Jews and the Ukrainians, along with an incessant barrage of anti-Semitic propaganda from the German occupation forces, "began to find wider appeal."[37]

The result in the Zhytomyr district, for example, was that between 1941 and 1943 an estimated 180,000 Jews were killed. German officials did not even find it "useful" to consolidate the rural and village Jews into ghettos in the cities, but killed men, women, and children straightaway.[38]

In anticipation of this genocidal thrust to the Nazi war against the Jews, Himmler wondered on August 15, 1941, after he attended a mass execution near Minsk, whether it was now Hitler's policy to kill all the Jews.[39] Himmler was disturbed by what he saw and heard about the effects such killing was having on his men. He asked the head of Einsatzgruppe B, Arthur Nebe, who was with him, to find a "less gruesome" method than shooting. His concern was for the mental and physical well-being of the perpetrators. He gave no thought to the victims.

Himmler visited execution sites near Minsk for the purpose of determining how to deal efficiently with the "Jewish problem." Contrary to earlier views, most historians now agree that he did not then issue an order to murder all Jewish men, women, and children. What seems to have happened was that the killing was gradually extended by the perpetrators on the spot. Brutalized by the first weeks and months of killing, and identifying with Nazi genocidal propaganda, they shed whatever reservations they might have had and, in one place, then in another, adopted the most radical solution imaginable.

30

THE "FINAL SOLUTION" AND DEATH CAMPS

There can be no doubt that the decision to kill all the Jews was Hitler's and that he alone had the power to make it. A recent book from the Soviet archives that is based on postwar interrogations of Hitler's aides mentions that he took a personal interest in the development of the gas chambers, but the account is otherwise silent on the mass murder of the Jews.[1]

Dating the decision to kill all the Jews has been controversial and will probably never be settled.[2] To understand why there likely never was a formal order from Hitler, we should bear in mind that his decision-making style was to give leaders on the spot maximum room to take action "as he would have wished." That was how he put it in one of the long monologues at his headquarters on October 14, 1941—right around the time when, according to many historians, he likely gave Himmler the go-ahead to expand the killing of the racial "enemy" in process in the east: "What would happen to me if I didn't have people around me, men whom I completely trust, to do the work for which I don't have time? Hard men who act as energetically as I would do myself? For me the best man is the man who removes the most from my shoulders, the man who can take 95 percent of the decisions in my place.

Of course, there are always cases in which I have to take the final decision myself." Hitler said he was preoccupied with military matters ten
hours a day and liked to relax by looking at art and architecture before
trying to sleep. Presumably he found time to discuss key matters with
Himmler, who visited that very day, but the record is silent on the topic.[3]

HITLER'S "PROPHECY" AND THE DECISION
TO KILL ALL THE JEWS

Hitler gave a speech on January 30, 1941, as he usually did on the
anniversary of his appointment as chancellor, and reminded the audience
of his "prophecy," initially presented on January 30, 1939. He repeated
that if the "Jews of international finance" managed to bring about world
war, as they allegedly did in the First World War, the result would be not
the Bolshevization of the world, as the Jews supposedly wanted, but
rather the "extermination of the Jewish race in Europe."[4] As he was getting ready to launch Operation Barbarossa, he said he hoped that Germany's enemies would recognize that the Jews were the "greater" enemy
of all the warring parties. These nations, he said, should join in a common
front instead of fighting each other.[5]

He knew that by the beginning of the war at the latest, most Germans
had come to accept that there was a "Jewish question" and agreed with
the exclusion of Jews from national life.[6] The regime now sought broad
acceptance of solutions that went far beyond legal discrimination. Reit-
erating in public his well-known "prophecy" of how the Jews would pay
if "they" started another world war was a subtle way to educate the German people in Nazi ideology and to gain their support for, or at least
acquiescence in, what was happening to the Jews, including those about
to be deported from the country. Those citizens who worried about
moral issues could write off the messages as typical Hitler bombast,
while the genuine anti-Semites could feel elated that he was at last settling scores with what they saw as the Jewish archenemy.[7]

On July 31, Heydrich sought authorization from Göring to draw up
"in the near future an overall plan of the organizational, functional, and
material measures to be taken in preparing for the implementation of
the aspired final solution of the Jewish question."[8] The means to be used

mentioned were "by emigration or evacuation," and it envisioned a "territorial solution." It was not yet a decision for annihilation.

The attack on the Soviet Union had opened a new stage in the genocide. The most compelling recent account suggests it is "most probable that in mid-September Hitler tentatively approved not only the deportations" of Jews out of Germany "but also at least in principle the 'eradication' of the deportees."[9] He must have decided sometime between late September and mid-October 1941 to follow through on the murderous logic of the anti-Semitism he had long espoused. The basis for this conclusion about the timing of the decision is that in those months there was "a qualitative and quantitative jump" into mass murder.[10] Hitler may have communicated his wish directly to Himmler, who was in charge of carrying out the extermination. They met at Hitler's headquarters on numerous occasions at that very time, discussing the Jews, among other issues.[11]

Himmler repeatedly claimed that the annihilation was authorized by a führer order. This was his response, for example, when questioned by Bruno Streckenbach, of the Reich Main Security Office, and by Gottlob Berger, chief of the SS Main Administrative Office.[12] He had responsibility, he would say to Berger in July 1942, for implementing the "very difficult order" that Hitler had placed on his shoulders.[13]

Hitler most likely came to his decision to kill all the Jews at a time, according to Goebbels's diary, when he was in an "extremely optimistic" mood. At Hitler's headquarters on September 24, for instance, Goebbels saw a parade of prominent figures presenting themselves to the "extraordinarily happy" Hitler. While waiting his turn for an audience, Goebbels exchanged views with Heydrich. German Jews had been forced to wear the yellow star from September 15, and Goebbels, as gauleiter of Berlin, said he wanted them "evacuated as quickly as possible" from the city. He expected to be able to do that "as soon as we have cleared up the military questions in the east. They should ultimately all be transported to camps created by the Bolsheviks. These camps were built by the Jews, and what could be more appropriate than that they should now populate them." That sounded ominous, but nothing Goebbels recorded of Heydrich's remarks indicates that anything like a final decision had yet been taken.

Goebbels then spoke with Hitler and noted his leader's high spirits. Hitler wanted Bolshevism, born in Leningrad, to die with the city: "Bolshevism began with hunger, blood, and tears" and would end the same way. When Leningrad was leveled, the "Asiatic Slavs" would no longer have a door to Europe. In the city's place fields would be planted, as would be the case also for Moscow. Most of the fighting would be over by mid-October, after which some German troops could be withdrawn. Hitler thought that when Bolshevism was broken, it would retreat to Asia. He believed Stalin, by then over sixty, might sue for peace, since at such an old age he would not be able to stand the pressure.[14]

For Hitler, the defeat of Bolshevism would be the last card Britain had to play. He did not worry about America, he said, because once the Soviet Union was defeated, "hardly anything can still happen to us." He agreed with Goebbels that the Jews had to be "removed from all of Germany." Goebbels wrote enthusiastically that the first cities to be free from Jews would be Berlin, Vienna, and Prague. He hoped that by year's end most Jews would be gone.

Apart from this conversation, Hitler said little about the Jews in the early autumn at his headquarters. However, on October 17, two weeks after talking to Goebbels, when discussing the need to "sift through" the native inhabitants in Eastern Europe, he brought up the topic. "The destructive Jews" were to be eliminated, and on that score there was a consensus among top Nazi leaders.[15] In conversation with Bormann on October 21, Hitler talked about Christianity and Bolshevism but reserved his harshest words for the Jews—seen as being identical with the leadership of the Soviet Union. He went through the usual list of "Jewish-Bolshevik" crimes and ended by saying that "if we exterminate these pests"—presumably the Jews, Bolshevism, and Christianity— "then we perform an act for humanity, the significance of which our men out there can still not imagine."[16]

Hitler met with Himmler and Heydrich in the evening of October 25, the day after Himmler returned from the front, where he had discussed the shooting of Jews with Field Marshal Bock and others.[17] Hitler began by mentioning his notorious prophecy about what awaited the Jews should "they" start another world war. "This criminal race," Hitler went on, "has the two million dead of the World War on its conscience, and now again still further hundreds of thousands. Let no one say to me: we cannot send them into a swamp. Who then worries about our people? It is good if the terror precedes us, that we are exterminating the Jews. The attempt to found a Jewish state would be a mistake." The latter statement was an affirmation that the search for "territorial solutions" was over.[18]

Up to that point the Nazis had been willing to consider specific areas or places where the Jews could be sent, with the clear implication they did not much care where they went as long as they disappeared from the Reich. That now changed, and on October 23 the Gestapo ordered that all further emigration of Jews from anywhere within the Reich was forbidden for the duration of the war. This secret decree can be interpreted in several ways, but strongly suggests the Nazis were determined not to let any Jews escape.

Many developments converged at the same time. The death squads were in full swing, the great deportations from Western Europe were under way, and beginnings were made for the establishment of the death camps.[19] The implications for the mass murder of the Jews were obvious, and it is hairsplitting today to persist in squabbling about when or if Hitler made the ultimate decision or whether "concrete plans" to kill all Jews existed.

Hitler kept hitting the same notes and sending signals that were impossible to miss. He continually provided assurances for people like Himmler and Goebbels as to what his wishes were. He repeatedly made his resolve clear to the public as well. On November 8, speaking to the Party faithful in Munich, he again denounced the Jews for starting the fires of war.[20] The reaction to this speech in the Nazi press highlighted his attack on the Jews. One news story carried the headline "The Jewish Enemy" and concluded that "the war against the Jewish international is a life-and-death struggle that must be ruthlessly fought to the end."[21]

The German people heard about the notorious prophecy again and again, not just from Hitler, but also from Goebbels, who referred to it in newspaper stories on several occasions, the first time on November 16, as he tried to justify the decree that Jews wear a yellow star. He mentioned the dreadful prophecy was coming true. Many Germans apparently agreed that the Jews started the war, at least if official surveys from that period can be believed.[22] Goebbels repeated his message in early December 1941, and at the end of an address before distinguished guests at Berlin University he calmly spoke of "the historical guilt of the Jews," this when trainloads of helpless German Jews were being sent to the east. He recalled for the audience Hitler's prediction of what would come to pass should the Jews "yet again" plunge the world into war. He added, apparently without needing to be more specific, that "we are just now experiencing the realization of this prophecy."[23]

In the meantime, preparations went ahead for the genocide. By November 1, 1941, on Himmler's orders, construction had begun at what would be the death camp at Belzec. Heydrich saw the possibilities of using gas vans to kill large numbers and in late October ordered more. They would be used in many places, as far away as Yugoslavia. In the last weeks of October, Himmler and Heydrich considered creating gassing facilities at other sites, including Mogilev, Sobibor, and Chelmno.[24] Auschwitz already existed as a concentration camp, but in October a large crematorium was ordered for it. Hans Frank, head of the General Government (part of former Poland), was also making plans for the destruction of Jews. All these and other events came within such a short period that they would have been impossible without a decision from Hitler.[25]

HITLER AFFIRMS GENOCIDAL RESOLVE AGAINST THE JEWS

On December 12, the day after declaring war on the United States, Hitler held a meeting with his gauleiters, the regional Nazi Party bosses whose political loyalty he came to value more than ever. He thought it was just as well that he had decided on war with the Americans: sooner or later they would have been forced into it because the United States would have sided with Britain and interfered with the ability of German U-boat captains to torpedo ships at will. Japan's move was fortunate, he now explained, because a declaration of war by Germany on the United States without having a friendly counterweight in the Asian conflict might have been difficult for Germans to accept.

His goal for the next year was to "finish off" the Soviet Union "at least up to the Urals." Thereafter Europe could exist in a "half-peaceful situation" and no longer be vulnerable to attack.

The talk also touched on how winning booty would help finance the recovery and how the new lebensraum would one day be turned into Germany's "future India," a reference to Britain's imperial reign. In three or four generations the lands conquered in the east would become the kernel of the new Reich. As Hitler saw things, if the Germans were ready to spill their blood for the New Order in Europe, then other nations should contribute their laborers.

He was feeling strong, in fighting spirit, convinced of his ability to conquer the east and daring to anticipate the fulfillment of his dream to dictate the future direction of a new Europe. He then turned to the "Jewish question." The following day Goebbels recorded his impressions of Hitler's message:

> With regard to the Jewish question, the führer has made up his mind [*ist entschlossen*] to make a clean sweep. He prophesied to the Jews that if they once more brought about another world war, they would experience their extermination. That is no mere talk. The World War is here, the extermination of the Jews must be the necessary consequence. This question is to be regarded without any sentimentality. We are not here to pity the Jews, but to have pity for our German people. If the German people in the eastern campaign had lost close to 160,000 dead, so the originators of this bloody conflict will have to pay with their lives.[26]

Hitler also blamed the Jews for the anti-German attitude of the U.S. government and for engineering a situation in which the two countries found themselves at war. Himmler noted cryptically in his desk calendar after a meeting with Hitler on December 18: "Jewish question: to be exterminated as partisans."[27]

Early in the New Year, Hitler signaled his wishes yet again when talking to Himmler and other guests at his headquarters: "If I remove the Jew, then our bourgeoisie will be happy." He likened the coming operation to extracting a bad tooth: better to do the job quickly than to try to pull it out a little bit over several months. "When it is removed, the pain is over. The Jew must be removed from Europe," he said, otherwise there would be no peace. Soviet prisoners of war were dying in Nazi camps, but he claimed it was the Jews who had brought about the situation. He asked rhetorically why he should regard the Jews any differently than Soviet prisoners: "I see only one thing: the absolute eradication, if they do not go freely." Of course by then he and Himmler knew full well that the Jews were forbidden to leave the Third Reich. Even so, he ruminated two days later that it would be best if the Jews went off to Russia.[28] However we interpret this kind of talk, Hitler was no longer offering a serious proposal for a "territorial solution," and it was a cruel jest to suggest that the Jews, who were being rounded up and murdered, were free to leave Europe.

Throughout 1942, Hitler repeated his prophecy on three major occasions and several minor ones.[29] The threats were invariably phrased in terms of future events. On January 30, he stated that "the war can only end when either the Aryan peoples are exterminated or the Jews disappear from Europe."[30] Official surveys of popular reaction to the speech showed there was more concern about other issues raised in it. Nevertheless, the opinion survey said candidly that the people apparently interpreted the threat "to mean that the führer's battle against the Jews would be followed through to the end with merciless consistency, and that very soon the last Jew would be driven from European soil."[31] "The Jew will be exterminated [*ausgerottet*]," ran the headline story in a newspaper account of another "prophecy" speech written by Hitler and read by Gauleiter Wagner on February 26, on the anniversary of the founding of the Nazi Party. The paper reported Hitler's threat would be fulfilled "at the end of this war."[32]

Germans who might be alarmed by this harsh assessment could look the other way and comfort themselves by pointing to more ambiguous press reports, even denials of wrongdoing. In March, a paper alleged that Jews, in an effort to win public sympathy in Germany, "were threatened by the worst of fates in being sent to a secretive swamp area," which sounded like Auschwitz. This rumor was denied. "Such a danger does not threaten the Jews," the story said, adding the misinformation that "they would [merely] have to work."[33] Some pictures were occasionally published of Jews "as leaders of the partisans" and of alleged "Jewish criminal types" who were said to be the "instigators of a war of shooting people in the back" behind the lines.[34]

But news of the genocide was filtering back to Germany. Victor Klemperer learned about Auschwitz and its reputation in March 1942.[35] He had heard rumors of a mass murder near Kiev by April 1942, although the massacre of the Jews at Babi Yar took place at the end of September the year before.[36] In the summer and early autumn of 1942, the White Rose resistance students in Munich made mention of the fate of the Jews in one of their leaflets. They guessed that as many as 300,000 Jews had been murdered in Poland, when the figure was far higher.[37] Knowledge of what was happening, therefore, got through in bits and pieces.

The Holocaust, under way since the beginning of Operation Barbarossa, was a genocide that was compressed into a remarkably short period. Notwithstanding the killings carried out by the Einsatzgruppen and others, as well as the beginning of the use of gas facilities and gas vans, in March 1942 75 to 80 percent of the victims of the Holocaust were still alive. The greatest period of killing was in the year from March 1942 to March 1943, by the end of which only 20 to 25 percent of those who were to be murdered in the Holocaust were still living.[38]

The genocide proceeded along two tracks. The first was the continuation of execution by shooting, carried out not only by groups associated with the SS but by reserve police battalions and occasionally also the Wehrmacht. In addition, by mid-1942 thirty gas vans were operating. The other method of killing was by the use of gas inside specific camps.

DEATH CAMP TRAGEDY

In the Soviet Union, under Lenin's and Stalin's orders, there was mass murder greater in quantitative terms than in Nazi Germany. However, the Holocaust was a social and a human catastrophe the likes of which had never been seen before. While Lenin and Stalin created more concentration camps, the Communists did not create killing centers. The Soviets sometimes used a gas van (*dushegubka*), as in Moscow during the 1930s, but how extensive that was needs further investigation.[39] They used crematoriums to dispose of thousands of bodies, but had no gas chambers.

The Nazi death camps were designed for mass murder that required little hands-on effort. In the words of Omer Bartov: "What was—and remains—unprecedented about the Holocaust [was] ... the industrial killing of millions of human beings in factories of death, ordered by a modern state, organized by a conscientious bureaucracy, and supported by a law-abiding, patriotic, 'civilized' society."[40]

There were six main sites for the systematic murder; all of them used gas, sometimes carbon monoxide, but at Auschwitz people were murdered with Zyklon B. In addition to the Jews, other groups were killed in large numbers as well, including Soviet prisoners of war and the Sinti and Roma, or Gypsies.

These death camps were Belzec, Treblinka, Sobibor, Chelmno,

Auschwitz-Birkenau, and Majdanek. Each of these, and other sites that were used as well, has its unique story to tell, all of them horrific. They originated from a combination of regional initiatives, with support or orders from Berlin. Tracing how each camp was created, and who was responsible, has been complicated because much of the documentation was destroyed.

An example of how events unfolded can be seen with Gauleiter Arthur Greiser in the Warthegau. He asked Himmler's permission to remove 100,000 and make his district "free from Jews." This request was granted at some point in October 1941, and execution by shooting was stepped up. In addition, Special Commando Herbert Lange was put to work. Lange had already used a gas van in 1939–40 to kill thousands of chronically ill patients in the parts of Poland to be incorporated into the Reich. He now sought out a fixed place to use these vans and opted for the village of Chelmno, northwest of Lodz. The site was quickly readied, and the killing began on December 8. Estimates of the victims are usually set at around 150,000.[41]

To the east of the Warthegau in the former Poland was the new district the Nazis called the General Government, under the leadership of Hans Frank. It was regarded as a holding ground for Jews and Poles. According to Frank, the area contained 3.5 million Jews, but other German estimates were lower. Jews in small towns and villages who were not shot immediately were forced to the cities, where large ghettos were established. People tried to carry on a normal life and hoped for the best. The letters and diaries that survive, particularly those of young people, tell the heartrending stories of what happened.[42]

Once more the turning point was the autumn of 1941. In October, Odilo Globocnik was given the task of creating a camp at Belzec, and work began in early November. The limited capacity of the camp and its unhurried construction might be interpreted to mean Globocnik had not yet been ordered to kill all the Jews in the General Government. However, it was not long before that became his assignment, and along with it came the decision to build other camps with greater killing capacities.[43]

Some of the men who established Belzec had been involved in the German euthanasia program and had expertise with gassing facilities. The installation was ready by the end of February, and experimental killings began by means of bottled carbon monoxide, soon replaced by an internal combustion engine that piped deadly fumes into the chamber.[44]

SS officers sought another place in the General Government and selected Sobibor, where construction only began in March 1942; it was also under Globocnik, as the SS and police leader in Lublin. Franz Stangl, who was given oversight of the construction, traveled to Belzec to see how that camp functioned. He increased the scale of the operation. Sobibor used an internal combustion engine, with fumes piped into hermetically sealed rooms, each with a capacity to hold two hundred people. Experimental killings began in April 1942.[45]

The third camp in Globocnik's jurisdiction was Treblinka, located in the far north of the General Government, and its ten gas chambers were eventually able to take up to thirty-eight hundred people, beginning on July 23. The camp became a killing machine. No attempt was even made to exploit Jewish labor, apart from the people in a "special commando" selected to bury the dead.[46]

Belzec, Sobibor, and Treblinka were given the mission to kill all the Jews in the General Government. The Nazis later called the campaign— in "honor" of Reinhard Heydrich, who was assassinated and died on June 4, 1942—Operation Reinhard.

These camps lasted only a short time. Belzec ceased operations in December 1942. Transports continued to Treblinka until April 1943, after which the pace slowed. In August 1943 the Jewish "special commando" there decided they had nothing to lose and killed as many camp guards as they could before they were overwhelmed. The camp was closed, and the Nazis finished their efforts to cover up their crimes.

In October 1943 a similar uprising took place in Sobibor, after which it, too, was dismantled. There were few survivors from any of these camps, which is one of the reasons they remain less known than other such places. Nearly all the victims were Jews. The death toll is astounding: Belzec murdered at least 550,000; Sobibor 200,000–250,000; and Treblinka, 750,000–900,000.[47]

Rudolf Reder was one of only two survivors of Belzec, but no women lived through the experience at all.[48] Dov Freiberg, a survivor from Sobibor, remembered the sight, sound, and hopelessness of the victims transported there:

> The people who arrived from the last ghettos and labor camps of Poland had already passed through the seven circles of hell before they reached Sobibor. They were in despair; they already knew what awaited them;

and there was no need to tell them stories. The Germans did not even address them. They shouted at them to take off their clothes quickly, maltreated and struck them until the last moment. The deportees asked whether it would take much time until the gas chambers. There were among them people who had escaped from the Aktionen, who had jumped from the trains, who had been in the forests, who had gone into hiding, but did not manage to find refuge and had returned to the ghettos knowing exactly what awaited them.[49]

One of the most horrific of all the camps was Majdanek. Himmler ordered Globocnik on July 20, 1941, to construct a "regular" concentration camp there during a visit.[50] The work began in October, and the camp was used initially for Soviet prisoners of war. The plan was to have 25,000 prisoners in the camp, but that was doubled almost immediately, and by year's end it had reached 150,000, an expression of the "gigantomania" of those heady times when the Nazis were winning the war.

Majdanek and Auschwitz were under the jurisdiction of the SS Economic and Administrative Main Office (WVHA); that is, they were part of the regular concentration camp system, initially intended as a money-making operation, with profits financing the SS empire.

At some point, likely in mid-1942, Majdanek got another task, namely to kill Jews, and soon it had gas chambers that went into high gear in the autumn. Some 500,000 people, from fifty-four different countries, passed through this camp. An estimated 50,000 Jews died there, and as many as 250,000 non-Jews. The last mass execution is usually dated to November 3, 1943.[51]

In the beginning the victims in the camps, as well as those of Einsatzgruppen, were buried in mass graves. In early 1942, Himmler decided it would be prudent to cover the traces, and in March he instructed that the bodies be exhumed and cremated. The task was delayed when Heydrich was killed, and eventually Special Action 1005, led by Paul Blobel, was formed for this job.

Himmler also informed Globocnik in August 1942 that in his district bodies would henceforth have to be cremated and that, in addition, all those buried would have to be exhumed and cremated. According to one witness, Globocnik did not want to do this, because he thought the German people should be proud of what they had done. One witness quoted Globocnik as boasting among a group of SS men at Belzec, particularly when someone suggested it might be wise to cover up the crime: "Gentlemen, if there were ever, after us, a generation so cowardly and soft that they could not understand our work which is so good, so necessary, then, gentlemen, all of National Socialism will have been in vain. We ought, on the contrary, to bury bronze tablets stating that it was we who had the courage to carry out this gigantic task."[52]

AUSCHWITZ

Auschwitz was separate from the Operation Reinhard camps, located in an area overrun by German troops in 1939 and incorporated into the Reich as the Reichsgau Wartheland, a new district created out of pieces of Poland in January 1940 and put under Gauleiter Arthur Greiser. Auschwitz was thus part of Germany; it was not some distant camp in the vast stretches of the east.

In October 1939, Hitler had appointed Himmler the Reichskommissar for the strengthening of Germandom. His task was to "cleanse" areas in the east of undesired racial groups, bring in "racially valuable Germans," and make the lands productive. There were so many Jews and Poles in eastern Upper Silesia, and so few Germans, that plans had to be delayed, and the province, including the small town of Auschwitz, became a kind of holding ground where Jews were sent. Himmler decided to create a concentration camp at Auschwitz on or around April 27, 1940, after several inspection trips. On May 4, Rudolf Höss was appointed the first commandant.[53]

Auschwitz opened on June 14 and was initially intended to terrorize the region. The first prisoners were mostly Polish. The camp's large capacity, at ten thousand, set it apart from others, but it was not originally conceived for the mass murder of Jews. Another feature was that the cheap labor of prisoners and location of the camp made it attractive to private industry.

In early 1941 the I. G. Farben chemical concern began the construction of a factory at the camp, the so-called Buna works, designed to create synthetic rubber. The company eventually invested around 600 million marks there, and I. G. Auschwitz became the largest investment project by private industry in the Third Reich. Himmler paid a visit to accelerate matters on March 1 and ordered ten thousand prisoners put at the firm's disposal. Their wages were as good as nothing.[54] This arrangement, whereby factories would be created inside concentration camps, was exactly the kind of relationship Himmler wanted with industry. Virtually every leading German firm and many minor ones came to such arrangements with the SS.[55]

Himmler gave orders on September 26 for the construction of a new and larger camp a short distance down the road at Birkenau. Modeled along the same lines as Majdanek, which was created at the same time, the camp was massive. The SS kept expanding the planned capacity of Birkenau, which by August 1942 could hold 200,000. The entire complex would occupy an area of 432 acres, with three hundred barracks buildings, factories, and other structures.[56]

From autumn 1941 onward more than a thousand deaths at Auschwitz were reported every month. These statistics come from the standard chronicle of the camp, which is incomplete.[57]

The first major gassing in Auschwitz with Zyklon B was most likely in early September 1941, after a commission of the Gestapo sorted through Soviet prisoners of war in search of "fanatical Communists" and selected six hundred, along with several hundred sick prisoners. By December a crematorium had been converted into a gas chamber and began operating.[58]

Although there were some Jews in Auschwitz almost from the beginning, the first transport of them arrived on February 15, 1942, sent by the Gestapo from Beuthen. They were gassed at once. Inside the camp the SS barred off the area and made noises to conceal what was happening. Perhaps for that reason the prisoners, like Józef Garliński, member of the Polish underground, may have been misled. He swore that "the first time a transport reached the camp and was sent straight from the railway station to the gas chamber in Bunker No 1" was on May 12. He said that was the turning point in the minds of the prisoners. Until then Auschwitz was pure hell, but after that "the name *Vernichtungslager* (death camp) hung like an ominous cloud over the fenced-in marshes where a colony of human ants sought vainly for help."[59]

According to the *Auschwitz Chronicle*, on March 20 the gas chamber in a farmhouse located in Birkenau was put into operation, and a transport of Polish Jews from Upper Silesia went "without undergoing a selection" straight to their deaths. From mid-1942 onward, more transports from all over Europe began arriving. For example, 1,000 Jews arrived from Compiègne in France on June 7, and though they were not killed immediately, within ten weeks only 217 were still alive. A shipment of 1,004 Jewish men and 34 Jewish women arrived (the fifth transport) from Beaune-la-Rolande camp in France on June 30, with more to follow.[60]

Trains from France originated in Pithiviers, Angers St.-Laud, or Le Bourget–Drancy. On July 8, 1,170 non-Jewish and Jewish prisoners from Paris arrived, many of them French Communists, so that Auschwitz was also a camp for "serious" political prisoners. The seventy-fifth train from France arrived on June 2, 1944, only days before the Allied landings in Normandy.[61]

On July 17, 1942, 2,000 Jews came from Westerbork and Amersfoort camps in Holland. The transport of October 18 had 1,710 Jewish men, women, and children. Only 116 women were admitted to the camp, and the remaining people were gassed. There were "horrible scenes" when some women beseeched the SS to let them live.[62]

More than twenty trains came from the Malines camp in Belgium, beginning in August 1942. The same month Jews from Yugoslavia started to arrive. The first Jews from Czechoslovakia reached the camp in October 1942, and a train from Norway arrived in December. On March 20, 1943, a group of 2,800 Jewish men, women, and children came from the ghetto in Salonika, Greece; 2,191 were gassed immediately and the rest sent to work.[63]

The first "selection" among the Jews in the camp took place on July 4, 1942, in which those who arrived from Slovakia were combed through for able-bodied men. The less fit were killed, but 264 men were allowed to live. However, just over a month later only 69 of them were still alive. By this time, life expectancy for Jews in this camp, even for those not murdered immediately, could be measured in days and weeks.

Himmler paid a second visit to the camp on July 18, 1942, and witnessed a mass execution at Birkenau. He also inspected the Buna works. He had big plans for other industries at Auschwitz. Satisfied with what he saw, he gave Commandant Höss a promotion and ordered him to accelerate construction of Birkenau and to do away with any Jewish prisoners unfit for work.[64]

Mussolini's Fascist regime fell on July 25, 1943, when he was deposed and arrested. The new head of government, Marshal Pietro Badoglio, initially said he would stay in the war on Germany's side but secretly negotiated and signed an armistice with the Allies on September 8. The Germans rescued Mussolini, and when Hitler heard this, he was pleased. However, he held it against the Fascist leader for not taking energetic steps against the Jews, perhaps also for wishing to make peace with the Soviet Union. According to Goebbels, Hitler now saw that Mussolini "was no revolutionary in the sense of the führer or Stalin."[65]

Field Marshal Albert Kesselring declared Italy to be under military control on September 11. The Germans interned around 700,000 Italian troops, many of whom were sent to Germany, where they were treated as slave laborers. They suffered dreadfully, a story of heartbreak that has rarely been told.[66] The end of Fascism, initially welcomed by the Italian Jewish community of 44,500, soon brought them darker days. On September 12 orders were issued from Berlin to Herbert Kappler, commander of the security police and SD in Rome, to deport all of the Jews.

Kappler decided to extort money from the Jewish community by demanding a large quantity of gold—which the Jews raised with the help of the Vatican. Pressure from Berlin persisted, however, because it was not just the money but deaths of the Jews that Hitler and Himmler wanted. Word leaked out about the impending roundup, and the Vatican saved the lives of nearly five thousand, even as the pope kept his silence. On October 16, German forces apprehended 1,030 Jewish men, women, and children and sent them to Auschwitz; only 17 ever returned. Romans either offered passive resistance or were revolted by what they saw.[67] This raid was followed in other cities, including Florence, Venice, Milan, and Genoa. Four-fifths of the Jews in Italy survived, and did so because they got help from people of all classes. It was also the case that the SS was assisted in their work by Italian collaborators, so the record is a mixed one.[68]

Auschwitz-Birkenau became not only the largest concentration camp but the biggest death camp. Even excluding Birkenau, Auschwitz established a network of fifty sub-camps, and prisoners worked far afield for industry, agriculture, and at clearing up after bombing attacks. The I. G. Farben camp at Monowitz failed in every sense of the word. In trying to construct a plant, prisoners were badly mistreated and even murdered. Life expectancy in some of Farben's mines was four to six weeks.[69]

In a meeting with Hitler in April 1943, Admiral Horthy of Hungary said he had broken the economic power of the Jews, but Hitler wanted more. In answer to his question about what he should now do with the Jews, Horthy was told (by Ribbentrop, who was also at the meeting) either to put them in concentration camps or to exterminate them. Hitler said the problem had been faced and solved in Poland: "If the Jews did not want to work, they were shot. If they could not work, they had to be taken care of." He said it was not cruel to kill them, because they are "all parasites" and should be treated as though they were "tubercular bacilli." He asked Horthy point-blank: "Why should we spare these beasts any longer, those who wanted to bring us Bolshevism? Races who cannot defend themselves against the Jews go to ruin."[70]

The great tragedy for the Jews in Hungary began in March 1944, when, in response to Horthy's attempts to negotiate with the Allies, Hitler invaded the country. Just before the invasion there were around 700,000 Jews in Hungary, which was the largest remaining intact such community in Europe.

The *Daily Mail* reported on May 9 that Hungarian Jews had been concentrated into fifty-six camps in preparation for their deportation. "The elimination of Hungarian Jewry is proceeding faster than was ever dreamed of even in Germany," it said. Their destination was given as the death camps. Between May 15 and July 9, around 440,000 Jews, in 147 trains, were deported.[71]

This deportation of the Hungarian Jews to Auschwitz was compressed within seven weeks and became the single greatest massacre of the Second World War. Auschwitz was revamped to receive and kill the large contingents, and beginning in May the schedule was for three or four trains a day, each carrying 3,000 to 3,500. In total 438,000 were sent to Auschwitz between May 15 and July 9, 1944.[72]

Raul Hilberg estimates that in Auschwitz, around 1 million Jews and 250,000 non-Jews were murdered.[73] The non-Jews confined and killed in Auschwitz included 140,000 to 150,000 Poles; 23,000 Sinti and Roma, or Gypsies; 15,000 Soviet prisoners of war; and 25,000 drawn from every nationality in Europe.[74]

PART NINE

HITLER'S DEFEAT AND STALIN'S AGENDA

31

GREATEST CRISIS IN STALIN'S CAREER

I n the early morning hours of June 22, the German invasion broke
through Soviet defenses all along the western border. When Moscow
got word of these collapses, no one dared to phone Stalin at his
dacha. Zhukov finally drew the unhappy chore. Stalin was caught
unawares and raced to the Kremlin, where Commissar of Defense Timoshenko gave him irrefutable evidence. Despite all the warnings, Stalin
was shocked at Hitler's treacherous violation of their nonaggression
treaty.

FIRST RESPONSES

Stalin held on desperately to the bizarre idea that perhaps renegade
German generals were trying to provoke war. He had Molotov call the
German ambassador to find out what was going on. The tight-lipped
Friedrich Werner Graf von der Schulenburg arrived with a note saying
that in dealing with the Soviet Union, Germany had put aside the "grave
objections arising out of the contradiction between National Socialism

and Bolshevism." The Soviets were accused of breaking the nonaggression treaty and "about to fall on Germany's back while Germany is in a struggle for her life." In response Hitler had ordered the Wehrmacht "to oppose this threat with all the means at its disposal."[1]

There was no declaration of war, and Stalin persisted in the illusion that all this was some sort of elaborate ploy. The Soviets had fulfilled their treaty obligations to the letter and, in the eighteen months prior to the attack, had shipped two million tons of petroleum products and key war materials to Germany. The last deliveries crossed the border only hours before the invasion.

Stalin had made a disastrous mistake, and he now rattled off a stream of commands. The Politburo was called to his Kremlin office at 5:45 a.m. Even the directive they now issued to the border military districts, signed by Commissar of Defense Timoshenko, was timid, ordering troops not to cross the border without special authorization.[2] None of the Soviet leaders guessed how bad the situation was at the front.

Georgi Dimitrov, head of the Communist International, was summoned to the Kremlin at 7:00 a.m. Stalin blurted out when he arrived: "They attacked us without declaring any grievances, without demanding negotiations; they attacked us viciously, like gangsters." He still sounded convinced of one thing: "Only the Communists can defeat the Fascists."[3]

He set the new Party line at once. In August 1939, at the time of the nonaggression treaty with Germany, he told Communists around the world to drop their anti-Nazi stance. In countries like the United States their followers were told to come out against all involvement in Europe's conflict. The Moscow-oriented movements in countries like France were instructed to put their guns away.

Once the Nazis attacked the Soviet Union, however, all bets were off, and Communists were now instructed that "the issue of socialist revolution" was being put on hold. The primary focus was to mount a defense of the Soviet people, who were "waging a patriotic war against fascist Germany. It is a matter of routing fascism, which has enslaved a number of peoples and is bent on enslaving still more." This Stalinist portrayal of the war as a battle of rival ideologies was precisely how Hitler saw it as well. Stalin drove himself from the time he arrived back in the Kremlin, staying at his desk almost nonstop. He kept complaining that he had destroyed Lenin's heritage, the worst sin he could think of.[4]

He gave the chore of breaking the news to the country to Molotov,

whose speech he "edited" with other Politburo members. It was delivered on nationwide radio. Molotov spoke of the treacherous invasion
that was totally unjustified.[5] Stalin then vanished from public view, with
stories and pictures of him practically disappearing from newspapers.[6]

The military was put on a wartime footing early on June 23, when the
Politburo established Stavka, the Headquarters of the High Command
of the Armed Forces. Stalin was reluctant to take charge himself, so the
job was given to Timoshenko. Stavka was a stopgap measure that went
through several changes, but initially included Stalin, Molotov, the marshals of the Soviet Union Voroshilov and Semyon Budenny, and Admiral Nikolai Kuznetsov. Stalin also issued orders for the evacuation of
millions of people and even factories to keep them out of the hands of
the enemy.

Casualties reported from the front were staggering. Stalin was even
more infuriated that hundreds of thousands of Red Army troops were
being encircled and entire divisions were giving up without a fight. By
June 28, Minsk had been enveloped and cut off, with the Germans taking nearly a half million prisoners. The way was opened to Smolensk and
Moscow.

The first week brought the greatest crisis Stalin faced in his political
career. The Soviet Union, notwithstanding five-year plans and great sacrifices, seemed to be falling apart. The thought crossed Stalin's mind that
he might be deposed or arrested. After all, it was on his watch that the
country was left vulnerable to attack, and it was he who had brushed off
the warnings. By July 4 he had the commander of the western front,
General Dmitri G. Pavlov, and three of his top generals arrested.
Charged with "anti-Soviet military conspiracy," they were subjected to a
perfunctory trial and shot on July 22. Stalin told his trusted secretary
Aleksandr Poskrebyshev to inform the fronts that "defeatists will be
punished without mercy."[7] If there was no such thing as an unexpected
development or surprise, should the same rule not apply to Stalin?
Surely such a thought crossed his mind.

Stalin had chosen to ignore or downplay ominous signs. For example,
in a war game held after the Winter War with Finland of 1940, General
Zhukov, who favored the offensive approach, was able to defeat the
Soviet forces led by General Pavlov—the latter misnamed the "Soviet
Guderian" after the famous Wehrmacht tank commander. The lesson to
be drawn should have been to put more emphasis on defense. Stalin was

furious but nonetheless put Pavlov in charge of the western front, dismissed the chief of the General Staff, General Kirill A. Meretskov, and replaced him with Zhukov.[8]

With the knowledge of the unfolding disaster on the western front pressing down on him from all sides, Stalin left the Kremlin for his dacha in the early hours of June 29. It was as if the captain left the bridge, because a full twenty-four hours passed before anyone could figure out where he was, and even then callers were told he was not taking visitors.

Was this some kind of test to see who wanted to succeed him? Was he having a nervous breakdown? Was he trying to replicate the strategy of Tsar Ivan the Terrible in the sixteenth century? Ivan had withdrawn to a monastery to show his rivals how they needed him, and eventually they came on bended knee to plead with him to return to the Kremlin.[9]

Stalin left the yes-men to their own devices, but no one dared take the helm. Lavrenti Beria, leader of the terror and the only one who did not fear arrest, came up with the idea of the new State Committee of Defense (GKO), which would streamline the bureaucracy. He, Molotov, and several other Politburo members decided to seek Stalin's approval and in the night of June 30 drove out to his dacha. Stalin was depressed and half expected they would force him out. He said letters from citizens had rebuked him, and "maybe some among you wouldn't mind putting the blame on me." But his entourage was still far too cowed to think such things.[10]

Some who were there remembered Stalin suggesting they had let Lenin down. Beria's son recalled hearing his father talk about the scene at the dacha. Beria focused on Stalin's face so as "not to miss any of his expressions or gestures. It was obvious that he expected that anything could happen, even the worst. When Molotov told him that Malenkov and I proposed to form the GKO and make him its chairman, the tension left his eyes." Beria's son recalled: "When he referred to those memorable hours my father always said to his colleagues: 'We were witnesses to Stalin's moments of weakness and he will never forgive us for that. Don't forget it.' "[11]

The GKO had five members. With the exception of Voroshilov, whose failures in the Finnish Winter War had led Stalin to fire him as defense commissar, the others were politicians—Beria, Molotov, and Malenkov. Stalin's confidence was at an all-time low, and he had to be persuaded to lead the GKO.

ABOVE: Soviet prisoners of war surrendered in the millions in autumn 1941.
BELOW: Soviet POWs captured near Wisznice in autumn 1941 and later executed.

ABOVE: Jews rounded up in the Warsaw ghetto awaiting deportation. (July–September 1942)
RIGHT: The suppression of the Warsaw ghetto uprising. (April–May 1943) Here SS Major General Jürgen Stroop (*center*) surveys the scene.
BELOW: Preparing for the liquidation of the Cracow Ghetto (1943). The Jews march down the main street with the little they can carry.

ABOVE: Arrival and selection of Jews from Hungary
(May 1944) at Auschwitz-Birkenau.
BELOW LEFT: Young Jewish children and others from the same transport
who were selected for death await the inevitable.
BELOW RIGHT: Jewish women from the same transport who were selected to work.

Wehrmacht prisoners on the bank of the Volga River, captured in the
northern area of Stalingrad in February 1942.

ABOVE: British Prime Minister Winston Churchill, U.S. President
Franklin D. Roosevelt, and Soviet Premier Joseph Stalin
pose during the Yalta Conference in February 1945.
BELOW: American and Soviet soldiers in front of a portrait
of Stalin in bomb-damaged Berlin in 1945.

ABOVE: The victorious leaders meet. Field Marshal Bernard L. Montgomery, General Dwight D. Eisenhower, and Marshal Gregory K. Zhukov visit Eisenhower's headquarters at Frankfurt am Main. (June 10, 1945)

LEFT: The great victory parade in Moscow's Red Square. Here the standards of the fallen German armies are presented in front of the Lenin mausoleum and then symbolically cast in the dust. (June 24, 1945)

ABOVE: Lt. William Robertson of the U.S. and Lt. Alexander Sylasko
of the USSR celebrate the meeting of the American and
Soviet armies near Torgau in April 1945.
BELOW: Soviet civilians crowded onto a repatriation
convoy for return to the USSR at war's end.

Funeral procession in Poland for the victims
of the Kielce pogrom of July 1946.

STALIN'S CALL TO HIS SOVIET "BROTHERS AND SISTERS"

On July 1, Stalin appeared again in the Kremlin and on July 19 took over as commissar of defense. On August 8 he allowed himself to be "appointed" by the Supreme Soviet as the *verkhovnyi glavnokomanduyushchii*—supreme commander of the armed forces, or Supremo. At the same time Stavka was changed into the Headquarters of the Supreme High Command, shortened to the Supreme Command Headquarters.

All these ad hoc measures showed how the country was ill prepared for the war. The career officer General Dmitri Volkogonov concedes that in the first eighteen months the Germans took around three million prisoners, or an astounding 65 percent of the Soviet armed forces.[12] In the first week of the war "virtually all of the Soviet mechanized corps lost 90 percent of their strength."[13] As whole divisions disappeared, the Kremlin was left trying to figure out what happened. Nevertheless, in the end, the Soviets proved able to mobilize far more men (and many women) than the Germans and easily gained numerical superiority.

The Soviets had the T-34 and KV-1 tanks with a 76 mm gun whose range was greater than anything the Germans had, and were so heavily armored that they were all but impenetrable by enemy tanks. The Germans' initial success was due not to their technical superiority but to surprise and their ability to make good use of what they had, combined with Soviet disorganization. The Red Army failed to fashion its heavy tanks into compact "fists" to break through German lines, but they got a baptism of fire and eventually beat the Germans at their own game.[14]

Once he recovered from his loss of confidence, Stalin's immediate priority was not just to stop the bleeding but to pull the country together. On July 3 he addressed the nation on the radio for more than half an hour. The speech began with words never heard before from the haughty "leader." Many were struck by the opening phrase: "Comrades! Citizens! Brothers and sisters! Men of our army and navy! I am addressing you, my friends!" He underlined the gravity of the situation but admitted no mistakes. He explained away the Germans' advance by saying they had been fully mobilized and the Red Army was not. Was it wrong to have the nonaggression pact with Germany? he asked rhetorically. Certainly not, he said; any peace-loving country should do the same thing, even if the people on the other side happen to be scoundrels. He also saw prudence in the pact because it won the Soviet Union a year and a half to prepare. He maintained that Germany did not really have the advantage: what they gained militarily they lost in showing themselves as treacherous Fascists. Any "short-lived military gain is only an episode."

Stalin declared that the nation was engaged in an ideological war against "German Fascism." The people had to support the troops and recognize "the immensity of the danger that threatens our country. They should abandon all complacency, all thoughtlessness, all those moods associated with peaceful constructive work which before the war were so natural, but which are fatal today when war has fundamentally changed everything."

He ended by calling on the people "to rally round the Party of Lenin and Stalin, and round the Soviet government for the selfless support of the Red Army and Navy, demolish the enemy, and secure victory. All the strength of the people must be used to smash the enemy. Onward to victory!"[15]

Erskine Caldwell, an American writing for the *New York Times*, heard the speech in a plaza near Red Square. Men and women held their breath. The "silence was so profound" that twice during the speech when Stalin paused for a drink, it was possible to hear the sound of water poured into a glass. One woman said: "He works so hard I wonder when he finds time to sleep. I am worried about his health." Caldwell said nothing about any cheering, but there was a grim realization of the road ahead, together with a feeling of assurance about Stalin's iron will.[16]

TRYING TO AVERT COMPLETE DISASTER

Stalin's speech demanded a scorched-earth policy, reminiscent of what the Russians did against Napoleon's invasion, whereby everything that could not be taken away with the retreating forces was to be destroyed. Stalin had already ordered that factories and some twenty million people be moved away from the front to areas beyond the Ural Mountains. In fact, as early as 1928, the Soviets had been locating armaments factories east of the Urals out of fear of an attack from the west.

Alexander Werth's classic account suggests the "transplantation of industry in the second half of 1941 and the beginning of 1942 and its 'rehousing' in the east, must rank among the most stupendous organizational and human achievements of the Soviet Union during the war." In early July it was decided which industries to move and which to convert from peace to war use. By November 1,523 enterprises, including large armaments factories, were disassembled piece by piece, shipped on the shaky Soviet transportation system, and reassembled under adverse conditions. It was impossible to get everything up and running again, but by and large the operation was a great success.[17]

The Soviets were able to produce more tanks, artillery pieces, aircraft, and other weapons in the second half of 1941 than they did in the first half of the year. In 1942 they increased production of the feared T-34 and KV-1 tanks almost fourfold and nearly doubled the number of aircraft. There was not only a quantitative increase, but the factories turned out the latest models.[18]

This massive effort was the key to survival, and it was accomplished despite acute labor shortages. On June 26, 1941, a seven-day workweek, and a longer working day, were introduced, and by year's end everyone in the armaments industry had been declared a "mobilized person" — making it almost impossible to change jobs. On February 23, 1942, the entire urban population capable of work (men from ages sixteen to fifty-five, women from sixteen to forty) was essentially conscripted, and in the early spring the measure was applied to rural areas.

The Red Army was still retreating, but it was fighting, and Stalin wanted to encourage bravery. On July 5 he introduced special awards, including the Hero of the Soviet Union. He told the Propaganda Department to remember Lenin's call about "the Socialist Fatherland in danger."[19] But he was also vehement about punishing cowardice and mere incompetence.

TERROR IN THE RANKS

Soviet practice tolerated no such thing as a mistake, the big exception being Stalin himself. When something went wrong in the military, someone had to be punished. It has been estimated that nearly one hundred officers above the rank of colonel, including three marshals of the Soviet Union, were "repressed," that is, arrested, imprisoned, and shot, in 1939–53. There were times, such as on October 28, 1941, when Stalin dropped even the appearance of a court-martial and ordered twenty-five senior officers shot.[20]

Terror was used as well against someone like General Pavlov, who was blamed for the early setbacks. He was forced into "confessing" his part in a plot to "open the front to the enemy." He repudiated this confession at his "trial" and said defiantly: "We are here in the dock not because we committed crimes in time of war, but because we prepared for this war inadequately in peacetime."[21]

On July 15, Stalin and Lev Mekhlis (head of the army's Political Department) decreed that all units be purged of what were called "unreliable elements." Numerous such orders followed, all focusing on the officers and men who were captured or thought to have run away. If there was no such thing as a mistake, there were also no miracles whereby troops encircled by the Wehrmacht managed to escape and return to the Soviet lines without losing their honor. That scenario was declared to be a fable, and these escapees and the formerly "encircled" were to be "welcomed back with an execution order . . . by way of settling accounts with the traitors who had opened the front to the enemy." Such "unreliable elements" were shot in the tens of thousands.[22]

Mistrust, suspicion, and doubts about the staying power of troops deepened the more the front lines buckled against the German assault. On August 16, the Supreme Command Headquarters issued the notorious order No. 00270 against generals and other officials, including NKVD detachments, on the western and southern fronts for becoming encircled and taken prisoner. This behavior was branded "despicable cowardice" and a crime. Stalin dictated the order, which concludes as follows:

I order that:
1) anyone who removes his insignia during battle and surrenders should be regarded as a malicious deserter, whose family is to be arrested as the family of the breaker of the oath and betrayer of the Motherland. Such deserters are to be shot on the spot;
2) those falling into encirclement are to fight to the last and try to reach their own lines. And those who prefer to surrender are to be destroyed

by any available means, while their families are to be deprived of all
state allowances and assistance;

3) bold and brave people should be promoted more actively.

This order is to be read to all companies, squadrons, batteries.[23]

By the time order No. 00270 was issued, an estimated 1.5 million men
had been taken prisoner. Despite the dire threats, by mid-October the
number that had surrendered doubled to over 3 million, and by the end
of the year the figure had reached an astonishing 3.8 million.[24]

There has been some conjecture about the extent of the enforcement
of the stringent new rules against deserters or others who broke rank.
Alexander N. Yakovlev, among other things the president of the Commission for the Rehabilitation of the Victims of Political Repression in
Moscow, concluded that during the war at least 994,000 Soviet servicemen and women were convicted by military tribunals alone. Of that
number, 157,000 were to be shot, the equivalent of fifteen full divisions.
He concludes that "more than half the sentences were handed down in
1941 and 1942."[25] The main "crime" was that they had broken out of
encirclement or escaped a prisoner-of-war camp. Around 400,000 of all
those subjected to military "justice" were sent to "punitive battalions"
and told that if wounded their "debt had been paid in blood."[26] As of
December 27, 1941, any escapees or suspect enlisted persons were held
in special NKVD camps. The families of this wide array of people were
subjected to various deprivations, punishments, and incarceration.

Above and beyond the official statistics, however, many were shot out
of hand for suspected desertion, straggling, or showing up (even
wounded) at a hospital without their weapons. Officers had the right to
shoot for suspected insubordination, cowardice, or anything they considered "criminal." There is no way of knowing how many were killed, their
individual fates consumed in the fires of war. Special "blocking units,"
two hundred strong, followed closely behind advancing troops to stop
anyone trying to run away from the fighting.[27] There is anecdotal evidence that many infantrymen and others were shot in the back, but
there is no way even to estimate the fatalities.[28]

The figures for 1941 and 1942 mentioned of those caught up in the
wheels of justice likely include those sentenced under order No. 00227,
also known as the "Not one step backward" order. Dictated by Stalin, it

was issued on July 28, 1942, and designed to terrorize troops into fighting on. The measure was dropped in October, but it sent a shiver through the military as it threatened draconian punishments for retreating.

Some officers and men were sentenced to serve in *strafnyi,* or penal battalions. In addition, deserters and stragglers or released Gulag prisoners were allowed to serve in them. The units were sent to the most dangerous parts of the front and were usually destroyed by enemy fire immediately. Estimates of the number of men who were convicted and sentenced to serve in these units—called by one writer a "delayed death sentence"—have been put as high as 1.5 million, but there are no statistics on the numbers killed.[29]

As the Germans retreated in 1944, the Red Army liberated some Soviet prisoners of war. They were under suspicion and often charged with desertion or some other offense. The officers among them were assigned to special "assault battalions." Whatever their previous rank, they had to serve as privates. They could atone for their guilt by serving until decorated, wounded, or killed. An estimated twenty-five thousand officers died in this way.[30]

The Main Political Directorate of the Red Army was kept fully informed on the enforcement of these measures. After the war such orders were swept under the rug so as not to damage Stalin's image or that of the heroic Red Army. But at the time Stalin was constantly on the phone to frontline commanders demanding to know why, if there was any retreat, they were not enforcing the dreaded orders.

Daily reports had to be submitted to Moscow from every political administration at all levels of the army. Typical was the following one from mid-1942: "Between August 1 and 10, 2,099 men were seized by blocking units, of whom 378 were trying to run from the field of battle, 713 had escaped encirclement, 94 were cases of self-mutilation, and the remaining 914 were absent from their units. Of those seized, 517 have been sent to penal companies, 111 to special camps, 82 to dispatch points, 104 were arrested, and 83 have been shot in front of the ranks for cowardice, panic-mongering and self-mutilation."[31]

Despite the harsh punishments, desertion was and remained a chronic problem for the Red Army. It was pronounced at the beginning of the war, and even in 1944–45. It was necessary for the Germans to capture 4,692 American, British, or French soldiers before they found a single deserter. In that period one in every sixteen Soviet prisoners was a deserter. In other words, "there were 330 Soviet deserters to every one deserter from the armies of the Western powers."[32]

After some battles, especially in the early going, Soviet troops were totally routed and disorganized. Timoshenko told Khrushchev that this was also the case in the civil war. The only option was to set up mobile kitchens "and hope the soldiers would return when they got hungry." They would slowly straggle back, and the officers would then try to reorganize them.[33]

The interviewees for the Harvard Project on the Soviet Social System after the war said that what changed most people's minds to fight the Germans, rather than to surrender, was not love of Communism, much less loyalty to Stalin, but the barbaric treatment meted out by the Germans. One of the veterans said he had defended, but was dispirited to see, that at the first appearance of the Germans, the political commissars ran off. He let himself be captured, along with his entire regiment: "I thought that the Germans would free the people of Communism. In time, I came to reject this idea because the Germans killed the Jews and the Commissars. . . . They treated nationalities as though we were like Communists, despite the fact that we surrendered voluntarily. After three months I was freed and went back to the village where I was born. There I began to hate the Germans. If I had to do it over, I would have fought to the last cartridge I got."[34]

A classic study of German policy strongly suggests that a "skillful effort to win over the population, civilian and military alike, to oppose the Soviet regime could have yielded substantial, and during the first months of the war perhaps decisive, results."[35] The problem was that Hitler wanted not only to eliminate "Jewish Bolshevism" but to divide and conquer the Soviet Union as a whole. This was a view that was widely shared by a great many of those involved in Operation Barbarossa. They took it as almost self-evident that they should not extend a hand to the conquered peoples, not encourage their sympathies in any way.[36]

32

BETWEEN SURRENDER AND DEFIANCE

T he attack on the Soviet Union made such immediate and rapid progress that victory looked only days away. Winston Churchill was concerned that Stalin might be "compelled to sue for peace," as he told his War Cabinet on August 16.[1]

PEACE FEELERS

Stalin's despair in the first weeks was hinted at in several ways, most controversially by his efforts to come to an agreement with Hitler. After the war, there was no admission that such an offer had been contemplated, and to some extent the story is still shrouded in mystery. There is evidence from several sources, however, that on or around the end of July 1941 Stalin and Molotov decided to make an approach to Hitler by way of the Bulgarian ambassador, Ivan Stamenov. Although Bulgaria was a German ally, it had not declared war on the USSR, and in keeping with diplomatic practice, it represented what remained of German interests.

Beria delegated Pavel Sudoplatov, a trusted spy, to find out what it would take for Hitler to end the war.[2]

According to other testimony, namely of Marshal Kirill S. Moskalenko in July 1957 at secret hearings, Stalin, Molotov, and Beria not only discussed surrendering but agreed "to hand over to Hitler the Soviet Baltic Republics, Moldavia, a large part of the Ukraine and Belorussia. They tried to make contact with Hitler through the Bulgarian ambassador. No Russian Tsar had ever done such a thing. It is interesting that the Bulgarian ambassador was of higher caliber than these leaders and told them that Hitler would never beat the Russians and that Stalin shouldn't worry about it."[3]

The message delivered by Sudoplatov to Ambassador Stamenov (who happened also to be an agent of the NKVD) was that the Soviet Union might be prepared to accept a peace treaty. It would undoubtedly be like the one at Brest Litovsk in 1918, when Lenin had given away most of European Russia. As he had predicted, the USSR eventually clawed back everything they had been forced to give imperial Germany. The Leninist precedent, always important to Stalin, for concluding even an unfavorable peace had its attractions.[4]

After the war and Stalin's death, when Beria fell out of favor and was put on trial, he was charged with numerous crimes, including trying to make peace with Hitler. Beria said in his defense that he "received from Stalin an order to create through Stamenov conditions that could allow the Soviet government to maneuver and win time for collecting forces."[5] The alleged motive seems improbable, as does the aim to impede the German offensive by spreading "disinformation." Beria's story sounds more like an attempt to cover up efforts that could be held against him after the fact.

Stalin's shattered morale in the early weeks of the war might well have been enough for him to test the waters. When Khrushchev returned from the front at the end of July, he visited Stalin at his underground headquarters in Moscow's Kirov subway station: "The man sat there devastated and couldn't say anything, not even any words of encouragement which I needed. . . . What I saw before me was a leader who was morally crushed. He was sitting on a couch. His face was empty . . . he was at a complete loss and didn't know what to do."[6]

Hitler seemed to sense the very moment Stalin wanted to make a deal. He suggested to those at his headquarters at the time that the Communists' hope for a negotiated surrender was the reason their propaganda had not really attacked him. He thought Stalin—that "devious man from the Caucasus"—was prepared to give up European Russia out of fear that he might lose the entire Soviet Union. Whatever Stalin might have calculated, Hitler thought it would be impossible for the Red Army to carry on the war from the other side of the Urals.[7]

Most Soviet leaders said nothing about this business in their memoirs. Zhukov notes only that he was summoned to Moscow on October 7, and because Stalin was recovering from the flu, he was taken to the leader's home. Zhukov was then sent to the western front and told to pull out all the stops to save Moscow.[8]

Later Zhukov told a different story for the edition of his autobiography published after his death.[9] There, as in conversation with the historian Viktor Anfilov, Zhukov said he overheard Stalin and Beria when he entered the room: "Ignoring me, or perhaps unaware of my arrival, he was telling Beria to use his agencies to sound out the possibilities for making a separate peace with Germany, given the critical situation. That gives you an idea of just how disoriented our head of state was at the time! Finally he noticed me and, after greeting me, said with irritation that he had no idea what was happening on the Western and Reserve fronts."[10] Beria again tried to use the Bulgarian ambassador, and with no more success. Hitler would hardly have settled for even a very large part of the cake when at that moment he thought he could have it all.

Stalin almost certainly made other attempts to find peace with Hitler besides those in July and October 1941. Churchill warned FDR in September that the British officials negotiating with the Soviets thought it possible they "might be thinking of separate terms" with Hitler and advised against giving the Communists any assistance. Indeed, there were persistent rumors in Allied circles of similar efforts in November.[11]

Nikita Khrushchev heard whispers from Beria and Malenkov that Stalin was hoping for a deal with Hitler, but was unsure of the date. He recalled that it was "probably 1942." He had a sharp memory, and except for the date his account, including the involvement of the Bulgarians as intermediaries and all the rest, supports the others. He may not have been wrong about the date, and if so, Stalin's doubts persisted into 1942.

It was only in 1943, Khrushchev recalled, that Stalin began to show more confidence, and only after the first big victories did he begin to strut about "like a rooster, his chest puffed out and his nose sticking up to the sky." Before 1943 Stalin "walked around like a wet hen."[12]

FDR AND AMERICAN INTERESTS

For the Soviets the only glimmer of hope anywhere in the world was with the capitalist United States. The American lend-lease agreement signed with Britain on March 11, 1941, was drawn up to avoid the criticism of isolationists in Congress and in the country generally. It was designed to help Britain but with all possible steps taken to ensure America would not get dragged into the war. Congress insisted the navy not escort goods to Europe lest its ships get in harm's way. The United States became the "arsenal of democracy," but it was still far from entering the war. Americans were divided about whether to aid the Soviet Union after it was attacked, because of the long conflict between Soviet Communism and Western-style democracy.

When Churchill warned in September that Stalin might be leaning toward peace negotiations, his was not the only skeptical voice raised about offering aid. The *Chicago Tribune,* for example, said it was ridiculous for "sane men" to have the slightest faith in the "supreme monster . . . Bloody Joe"—that is, Stalin—"who brought on the war by selling out the democracies" and might well "sell them out again and make a deal with Hitler."[13]

Roosevelt had his own qualms and had made no bones earlier in saying the Soviet Union was run "by a dictatorship as absolute as any other dictatorship in the world." But he was willing to engage with the Soviets to ensure Germany's defeat and eager to have the United States play a role in that event and thus emerge as a major player in the postwar world. He did not want to pay in American lives, but was willing to spend treasure. His cabinet and chief advisers were not so sure. Secretary of War Henry L. Stimson and U.S. Army Chief of Staff George C. Marshall despised the Soviet system and loathed the Soviet ambassador, Constantine Oumansky, of whom Marshall said "that he will take everything we own," with Stimson adding that the man was "nothing but a crook" and "a slick and clever little beast."[14]

Roosevelt was right to feel the Soviets had to stay in the war. If the unthinkable happened and Hitler and Stalin reached an agreement, as they had in August 1939, the world would have been faced by unpredictable and growing disaster. Hitler aimed at global conquest, and his scientists were working on an atomic bomb, while others developed long-range missile systems. Does anyone doubt he would have used these weapons?

Here was one of the great turning points in history, easy to overlook when so much else was happening. FDR's thought was that with the Soviets doing the fighting and the dying, it might be possible to keep the United States out, or to come in at a later date, as happened in the First World War.

On July 9, 1941, FDR issued instructions that a plan be drawn up covering various contingencies, including American entry into the war. What emerged was the Victory Program, which gave precise details of future strategic goals and how they would be attained. The priority was to defeat Germany, but it acknowledged that the United States could not possibly mobilize, train, and equip the armed forces until July 1, 1943. The Program forecast fielding 215 divisions (or 8.7 million men) at a cost of $150 billion. The assumption was that the Soviet Union would not be in the war at that time.

FDR preferred to pay for victory in money, not lives, a policy that Stalin fully recognized and resented. But the Soviet ruler needed American aid. Perhaps more important to victory were the resolve and sacrifice of the Soviet peoples who contributed so much. For all that, knowledge that the United States now was backing the USSR was a comforting thought to the embattled men in the Kremlin. By late 1942 the United States had revised plans for the troops it would need: instead of 215 divisions as originally thought in the Victory Program, perhaps 90 would suffice. FDR's "arsenal of democracy" not only saved American lives but helped the United States, of all the combatants, emerge with a booming economy.

It was a wise Roosevelt, therefore, who rejected the advice of those around him. The otherwise sagacious Stimson was proven wrong when he said to Marshall that "this Russian munitions business thus far has shown the President at his worst."[15] Time revealed it might have been one of the president's finest hours, a fact that cannot be underlined enough. Roosevelt had the lend-lease agreement extended to the Soviet Union on October 1, 1941, granting it credits to pay for American goods.

Averell Harriman of the United States went with Lord Beaverbrook in late September to negotiate the terms, and found Moscow under siege. At the very least, the agreement was a badly needed morale booster.[16]

On October 3, Stalin wrote the president to express his "heartfelt gratitude" for the interest-free loan and promise of essential war materials. He was sure that the deal he had just made with Harriman would be acceptable to FDR. It most certainly was, and aid in the amount of $1 billion was extended to the USSR on November 2 under the lend-lease program. Stalin underlined his determination: "Like you, I am confident of final victory over Hitler for the countries now joining their efforts to accelerate the elimination of bloody Hitlerism, a goal for which the Soviet Union is now making such big and heavy sacrifices."[17]

PANIC IN MOSCOW

When Moscow was on the verge of being overrun, Stalin recalled Zhukov from Leningrad and sent him to assess the situation to the west. Zhukov concluded that the Germans were moving forward "on all important routes leading to Moscow." He asked for immediate reserve troops to prevent the worst. Not only Stalin but others concluded that Zhukov had to be put in charge in the hope that he could stop the advance. On October 10 he was appointed commander of the combined western and reserve fronts, but German air raids intensified and warnings sounded almost every night.[18]

Zhukov set up a new line of defense that ran southward from Kalinin, to Volokolamsk, Mozhaisk to Kaluga. If we look at that line today, we can see the Wehrmacht was closing in for the kill. Kaluga was captured in the south almost immediately, and the Germans broke into Kalinin in the north, shrinking the line and threatening to go around it. The Red Army was in danger of being encircled yet again, with Moscow less than fifty miles away. Making matters worse, the Germans had complete air supremacy and could operate at will.[19]

On October 13, Zhukov issued order No. 0345, which appealed to the Red Army to stand and fight while threatening all "cowards and panic-mongers," namely those leaving their positions without authorization, with being shot on the spot. In his memoirs Zhukov serenely called these "strict measures to prevent breach of discipline," and he had used similar methods earlier in Leningrad.[20]

Stalin was against any retreats or even tactical withdrawals and wanted battles to continue to the last man. The Germans would be made to pay for every inch, so as one line of defense crumbled, the Soviets threw together another.

Hitler was adamant that Moscow was not to be taken, but, like Leningrad, surrounded and destroyed from the outside. He wanted to trap thousands of troops, perhaps with their Communist leaders, inside the city and level it.[21]

Stalin ordered evacuation of the entire state and Communist Party apparatus on October 12 and 13. Moscow's armaments industries were disassembled and shipped out. Those that could not be moved were wired with heavy explosives and readied for demolition, as were the bridges in and near Moscow. The major commissariats (such as those of defense, foreign affairs, and internal affairs) were sent to Kuibyshev on the Volga—just over a thousand kilometers away—but others went to a dozen different cities, some in Siberia. Scientific and cultural institutions, like Moscow University, the Academy of Sciences, and major theaters (like the Bolshoi Ballet), were also dispatched, making it seem that Stalin thought the city was lost and not likely to be liberated anytime soon. People streamed out any way they could.

Preparations were drawn up for a line of defense hundreds of miles to the east along the distant Volga River. The official U.S. military history of the war states: "If Stavka contemplated having to defend that line, the future must have appeared dark indeed." If Germany had ever invaded up to that line, the Soviet Union would have lost 75 percent of its industrial capacity and would have been reduced to a third-rate power.[22]

The GKO, which was now in effect the government, as well as Stavka, remained in Moscow for the time being. Should Stalin do so as well and risk being taken hostage? A train was readied and a mansion in Kuibyshev prepared for his arrival.

The Germans were on the verge of surrounding Moscow and grew so near that the roar of the battle could be heard and wild rumors circulated. An alarming message was published in the press: "During the night of October 14–15 the position on the Western Front became worse. The German-Fascist troops hurled against our troops large quantities of tanks and motorized infantry, and in one sector broke through our defenses."[23]

Panic spread and looting grew on October 16. Stalin must have been shocked to witness what was happening as he drove to the Kremlin early in the morning. The city was under siege, and word was the government was leaving. Some citizens showed their loyalty to Stalin and Communism, but as many and more vented their hatred and resentment. A widely expressed view—impossible to quantify in an exact way—was that many thought they had little to fear, as the Nazis only wanted to eliminate the Communist system and the Jews.

According to an eyewitness, the scene on one of the roads out of town unfolded like this:

> People here and there stop cars, drag out their occupants, beat them up, and throw things into the street. You hear cries such as "Beat the Jews." People are starting to remember the insults, the oppression, the injustice, the bureaucratic humiliation by officials, the boasting and smugness of the Party people, the draconian ukases (decrees), the systematic deceit of the masses, the nonsense spread by the newspapers, the sweet talkers. . . . I never would have believed such a story if I had not seen it myself. We had Jews at school, and I don't remember any open, clear example of anti-Semitism. There were some quips, not malicious, more jokes than anything, nothing more. That's why these wild reprisals against the Jews, and not only against them, on October 16, 1941, at the Il'ych Gates shook me up so much.[24]

A report by the NKVD gave details of similar outbreaks of anti-Semitic and anti-Communist behavior in Moscow. For example, some workers at a motorcycle factory got drunk and the next day carried out "counterrevolutionary agitation of a pogrom character, calling on the workers to destroy the Jews." Elsewhere workers milling about in a crowd called on comrades to "beat the Communists and others." Some people put out white flags. One NKVD report mentioned the panic, hoarding, and belief that the Germans had superior forces and could not be stopped.

The report continued: "Although patriotic feelings flourished among the majority of the population of the capital at the same time many citizens had an openly anti-Soviet attitude . . . a hatred of Communism, including the families of Communists, and anti-Semitism." One man remembered his neighbor saying: "Come on, Hitler; come on, pal!"[25]

Peasants in the provinces were said to be sanguine about the German advance on Moscow: "What's it to us? It'll be bad for the Jews and Communists. There might even be a bit more order."[26] Knowledge of these attitudes was reflected in Soviet propaganda, which shifted away from an emphasis on Communism and the Stalin cult in favor of themes like traditional patriotism and the need to protect kith and kin against the invader.[27]

A refugee who ultimately made it out of the Soviet Union had been in Moscow during October 1941 and vividly remembered what happened:

> Such a panic was never seen. Everyone was going in all directions. Nobody was punished for any crime. They broke open store windows in broad daylight. Jewish pogroms started. The arrival of the Germans was expected from hour to hour. German planes were flying overhead from street to street and no one even shot at them; the Germans weren't afraid but they waved their hats and greeted the public from the planes. They could have taken Moscow easily. There was no one in command of anything.[28]

The broad sentiment at the time was that Moscow was within reach. That opinion was echoed by numerous other witnesses.[29] Discontent existed not just in Moscow and Leningrad but in other parts of the country.[30]

TRAGEDY OF LENINGRAD

Hitler's idea was to destroy Leningrad, and the encirclement was all but complete by September 1941. The siege of three million began, and unrest grew when it looked as though the city was going to fall. Even the NKVD fled, commandeering planes and every means available to make a break. Officers burned their files, Party lists, and documents lest these got into the hands of the Nazis, and they all be executed.

On November 7, instead of a parade in celebration of the anniversary of the Russian Revolution, there was a demonstration of several hundred who distributed a rebellious leaflet: "Dear fathers and brothers, your children, wives, and mothers are dying from hunger. The authorities decided to destroy us by a most terrible death. You twenty-four years ago were able to destroy Tsarist power; you are able as well to destroy the hated Kremlin and Smolny executioners as long as you have guns."[31] This demonstration was ineffectual but suggests the regime's hold on some hearts was tenuous. The siege would last nine hundred horrible days, and it turned into an epic struggle. The police recovered their nerve and used on-the-spot executions to keep order, even for such "crimes" as stealing a loaf of bread. By November most of the bombardment and shelling had stopped, and by mid-winter the city had become eerily quiet. "The Hitlerites are confident," wrote Yelizaveta Sharypina, "that hunger will break the resistance of the Leningraders. Why waste bombs and shells?"[32]

Social chaos descended on the city. Party Secretary Andrei Zhdanov used thirty-five hundred Young Communists to watch food stores and guard against thieves. When culprits—sometimes working in gangs—were caught, they were summarily shot. There was some traditional patriotism, and, despite everything, there were still those who believed in Communism and did their duty as defined for them by the Party.[33]

People experienced a degree of freedom they had not known before as the regime lost control. The historian Mikhail Gefter, who lived through the time, said the Soviet system fell apart under the pressure of the invasion, but by 1943 it had reasserted itself. "Strange as it may sound," he said, "1941 was more of a liberation than 1945."[34] Another man recalled how military defeats in 1941–42 led to questioning Stalin and how that "threw us back onto our own resources. So for many of us, those first two years of the war coincided with a spontaneous de-Stalinization, a true emancipation. We felt that everything depended on us personally, and that gave us an extraordinary feeling of freedom."[35]

Civilians in Leningrad—never mind the armed forces—paid a heavy price. At least ten thousand had died by November, and the number rose astronomically after that.[36] The total number of civilians who died during the siege will never be determined but is likely in the range of 1 million. By war's end the Red Army in the Leningrad region had over 1 million killed and 2.4 million sick or wounded.[37]

Some supplies made it to the city by crossing Lake Lagoda, but the rations were at starvation levels. Hunger drove people to desperation, and cannibalism became "normal." Vera Sergeevna Kostrovitskaia's diary recorded how in April 1942 she noticed a lamppost one day because a man, with his back to it,

> sits on the snow, tall, wrapped in rags, over his shoulders a knapsack. He is all huddled up against the post. Apparently he was on his way to the Finland Station, got tired, and sat down. For two weeks while I was going back and forth to the hospital, he "sat"
> 1. without his knapsack
> 2. without his rags
> 3. in his underwear
> 4. naked
> 5. a skeleton with ripped out entrails
> They took him away in May.[38]

In March 1942 the artist Anna Petrovna Ostroumova-Lebedeva listened to Churchill's talk on the radio, and when she heard him admit that 673,000 English soldiers had surrendered to Japan, she was amazed by his honesty. She wrote in her diary how he conveyed an image of the world gone mad. "What an immense panorama of fire has engulfed the whole world! The whole world! No, it seems there is no country whose peoples would not writhe and die in the flame of this fire. Some kind of mad desire for mutual extermination has seized everyone. And our Leningrad, its siege and we its inhabitants, perishing from hunger (20–25,000 per day), and from shells and bombs—we are only a tiny detail in this entire, horrible, nightmarish, but grandiose and amazing war."[39]

Such reflections fill the letters and diaries of those who lived and died in the siege. As it was, the struggle for Leningrad was not decisive to the outcome of the war, but for all that it would be correct to "accord the battle for Leningrad and its associated winter blockade the dubious distinction of being the most terrible and costly siege in recorded history."[40]

HOLDING MOSCOW: THE TURNING POINT IN THE WAR

At a meeting with Malenkov, Molotov, Shaposhnikov, Nikolai Voznesensky, and Dimitrov on October 15, Stalin admitted Moscow could not be defended. He said they had to leave before the day was out. According to Dimitrov, he muttered the words as casually as if he were saying, "Time for lunch!"[41] The next day Stalin informed them they were going to Kuibyshev and that he would leave himself in twenty-four hours. But he dithered for two days.

On October 17, the head of the Communist Party in Moscow, Aleksandr Shcherbakov, explained on the radio that their leader was in the city. He spoke of the "complexity" of the situation, which in wartime always meant "gravity." He said rumors of imminent surrender were false and that the capital would be defended at all costs. In fact the situation was deteriorating by the minute.[42]

It would seem Stalin decided late on October 18 that he was going to stay in Moscow after all. Several different leaders later claimed they had convinced him it was vital to remain. They no doubt echoed his view—when he finally chose to tell them what it was—that if he left Moscow, it would be lost, and perhaps so would the war. Stalin contacted Zhukov to see if the front could be held, but there was nothing good to report. He called a meeting of the GKO and the military commander and NKVD leader of Moscow for the morning of October 19. Many top Communists had left the city, with Dimitrov and others already in Kuibyshev. Stalin asked the circle gathered at the Kremlin: "What is the situation in Moscow?" He was told that it was still "alarming." He asked each whether they should defend the city or not, but he tipped his hand about the answer he expected. They agreed to fight on, but the immediate problem was that social order had broken down, there was looting, and steps had to be taken. "What do you suggest?" Stalin asked. The reply came: "The military council requests that a state of siege be declared in the city." "Correct!" Stalin answered after a few seconds. He requested a draft order to be prepared, but found it unsatisfactory and finally dictated it himself.[43] Like other measures to hold up morale, this one dripped with blood: "All those who break the law will be immediately brought to justice by a court-of-war tribunal, and all provocateurs, spies and other enemy agents calling for the breaking of the law will be shot on the spot."[44]

How far was this measure enforced? In October and November, 6,678, mostly servicemen or those of military age, were arrested. Another 32,599 were sent to "reinforcement companies," which could have meant being sent to the front in particularly dangerous engagements. A total of 357 were tried by tribunals and executed, and 15 were shot on the spot.[45]

Home guard divisions had to be raised, and thousands of men and especially women were put to work digging lines of defense and anti-tank trenches around the city. Zhukov managed to hold back the German onslaught throughout October. That task would have been impossible if the officers and men at key points on the approaches to the capital had not held their ground.

Already on October 12, Stalin ordered nearly half a million fresh troops from the Far East, together with a thousand tanks and as many planes. These buttressed the sagging western front, where the Germans were beginning to run out of steam. By the end of the month the Soviets had stabilized the situation.

Stalin called Zhukov back to Moscow and told him of his intention to hold a military review and ceremonial on November 6 for the anniversary of the Russian Revolution. He asked Zhukov: "Do you think the situation at the front will allow us to go ahead with our plans?" Zhukov thought it would indeed be possible as the enemy had suffered great losses recently, but advised calling in additional air cover.[46]

The audacious celebration was Stalin's imaginative idea. It was designed to raise morale and to show that the USSR was anything but finished. In his speech, he was upbeat, but admitted the enemy was steadily advancing. He reminded citizens of German predictions that the Soviet Union would be defeated in two months or less. He said Hitler had based his strategy on forming an international crusade by alarming the world with the specter of a Communist revolution. Stalin claimed (and firmly believed) that Hitler had sent Rudolf Hess (deputy Party leader) to Britain on May 10 to negotiate such a deal with Churchill.

There is no evidence that Hitler ordered Hess to make the foolhardy trip, only weeks before the opening of Operation Barbarossa. Hitler disavowed the whole thing, which was also a public relations disaster at home, for the deputy leader of the Party was in the land of the enemy. Stalin's great fear was that the Germans would succeed in creating an Anglo-German assault on the USSR, and he held to that view throughout the war. He made only scant mention of this worry in his speech this day, when he wanted to play up the newfound unity with Britain and the United States.

Stalin said the invaders had reckoned that the "instability" of the Soviet system would give rise to feuds among its many peoples. But far from collapsing, the system was bolstered by the attack, and the people felt greater solidarity than ever. Why had Soviet troops retreated at all? Stalin asked. Part of the reason was that the military was still young and relatively inexperienced, having fought only four months. But the mettle of the Red Army was being "forged in the fire of the patriotic war and tomorrow will be the terror of the German army." He added that another reason for the initial setback was the absence of a second front. Hitler could throw everything he had at the east because he felt secure in the west. Stalin (falsely) promised that a second front would open "in the nearest future" and relieve the pressure on the Soviet armies.

He used one telling phrase from Hitler. The Nazi leader was quoted as saying: "We must use any means possible to have the world conquered by Germans. To create our great German empire, we must first and foremost force out and exterminate the Slav peoples, the Russians, Poles, Czechs, Slovaks, Bulgarians, Ukrainians, and Byelorussians." Stalin made no mention of anything Hitler had said about the Jews. But he gave plenty of evidence of the murderous orders issued to the Wehrmacht. These said no mercy was to be shown to men, women, or children. The implications were obvious: "The German invaders are looking for a war of extermination against the peoples of the USSR. Well, if the Germans want a war of extermination, they will get it. Henceforth our job, the job of the peoples of the USSR and of the men, commanders, and political workers of our army and navy, will be to annihilate to the last man all those Germans who desecrated the territory of our country. No mercy to the German occupiers! Death to the German occupiers!"

Stalin used an interesting metaphor to characterize the war, saying it was "a war of motors. He who will have the overwhelming superiority in the production of motors will win the war." He concluded that with Great Britain and the United States linked by way of the lend-lease agreement, Hitler's defeat was inevitable. He called for a war of liberation from the Nazi yoke.[47] The next day the military parade took place, with Stalin and other notables reviewing it from the Lenin mausoleum in Red Square. This was no mock display of military might, but a march past with the soldiers heading straight off to battle raging only forty miles away.

SCORCHED EARTH

Stalin's speech entered folklore as a major turning point in the battle for Moscow. When he reviewed the troops from atop the mausoleum, Lenin's embalmed corpse was no longer inside it. Stalin had sent the body for safekeeping to distant Tyumen in Siberia. In the meantime, without even an embalmed Lenin, Stalin himself came to embody the spirit of a Communism fighting against its fiercest enemy.

He still had self-doubts. That was revealed when Zhukov came to headquarters on November 10, accompanied by General P. A. Belov. The latter recalled that "Stalin's eyes did not have their former steadfastness, and his voice lacked conviction. But what amazed me even more was Zhukov's behavior. He spoke sharply, in a peremptory tone. The impression was created that the senior commander here was Zhukov. And Stalin seemed to accept it as normal."[48]

Nevertheless, Zhukov gave Stalin his due. When later asked what event impressed him most in the war, he mentioned the battle for Moscow and said Stalin deserved credit for staying on and organizing the technical and military resources, and thus "achieving the virtually impossible."[49]

Dmitri Volkogonov's biography of Stalin never fails to point out the dictator's uncaring attitudes toward his own people. Volkogonov mentions a "scorched earth" order (No. 0428) signed by Stalin on November 17, 1941: "All inhabited locations up to a distance of 40–60 kilometers in the rear of German troops and up to 20–30 kilometers on either side of the roads, are to be destroyed and burnt to ashes. . . . Each regiment is to have a team of volunteers of 20–30 men to blow up and burn down inhabited locations. Those who excel themselves in the job of destroying settled locations are to be put forward for government awards."

Volkogonov felt the military effectiveness of the policy was questionable, was callous, even if it likely created problems for the Nazi invaders. There was no doubt, however, that the order destroyed the last shelter over many people's heads. General N. G. Lyashchenko told Volkogonov about an experience he had at the time:

> At the end of 1941 I was commanding a regiment in a defensive position. There were two villages ahead of us, Bannovskoe and Prishib, as I

recall. We got an order from division to burn down all villages within reach. We were in the dug-out where I was explaining how we were to carry out this order, when suddenly, breaking all regulations, the radio operator, a middle-aged sergeant, butted in.

"Comrade Major. That's my village! My wife and children and my sister and her children are all there. How can we burn them down? They'll all die!"

"You mind your own business, it's for me to sort out," I told him.

Lyashchenko found a way of capturing the villages without following the "stupid" order and admitted he was lucky to have been saved from the security police, because the order had come directly from Stalin.[50]

In traditional notions of warfare, the idea of a scorched-earth policy meant the people fled the invader and, before they left, burned anything of use. Stalin's version was different, as he did not blink an eye about ordering the obliteration of villages and towns without regard to his own people.

Typical of his lack of concern was order No. 170 007, from January 11, 1942. It was sent to the commander on the Kalinin front and called for the immediate capture of the city of Rzhev, with a population of fifty-four thousand. "All available artillery, mortars and aircraft" were to be used "to smash the entire city." The commander was told that he "should not be deterred from destroying it." Such orders led to the deaths of completely innocent bystanders—notably women, children, and older people who were not warned and evacuated.[51]

This kind of cruel determination ultimately led to victory, but at a terrible price.

33

SOVIETS HOLD ON, HITLER GROWS VICIOUS

Stalin stated the case for a follow-up to stopping the Germans at the gates of Moscow. On January 5, 1942, he put it this way: "The Germans are in disarray after their defeat near Moscow. They have prepared badly for the winter. Now is just the time to launch the general offensive." He wanted to strike along the entire front from north to south, with the main blow aimed at Army Group Center. Zhukov cautioned that Soviet forces, especially the tank divisions, needed replenishing, and others concurred.[1]

Stalin listened to various options until he stopped the discussion, pointing with his pipe at a page: "Write this: 'Our task is not to allow the Germans a breathing space, to pursue them westwards without pause, to force them to use up their reserves before the spring, when we will have large new reserves and they will have no reserves left, and this way to secure the complete rout of the Nazi forces in 1942.' "[2]

The attack he wanted required a level of troops and firepower that he simply did not have, but no one dared object. The Soviets had some initial success fighting on twelve fronts, but by early March the Germans had held the line. The Red Army took dreadful casualties, estimated by

General Volkogonov at a half million on the western front alone in these few months. The Wehrmacht also suffered badly, but far less.[3]

Hitler thought he saw hope and told military leaders (what they already knew) on March 28 that the "war will be decided in the east." A new assault would begin as soon as the land dried out.[4] Hitler's war directive of April 5 for Operation Blue stated that action against Moscow would wait, and emphasis would be on the south toward the Caucasus and its oil fields. The aim was to destroy "the entire defense potential remaining to the Soviets and to cut them off, as far as possible, from their most important centers of war industry." Army Group South was divided into Army Group A and Army Group B. Another war directive on July 23 following the fall of Rostov-on-Don changed the order of priorities. Whereas the first plan was to plunge into the vast and inhospitable Caucasus region only after victory against the major Soviet forces gathering near Stalingrad, now the two goals were pursued at the same time. Hitler's confidence was boosted because of what he said "was the unexpectedly rapid and favorable operations" near the Don River. Army Group A, the more powerful of the two, was sent off to the Caucasus to lay hold of the oil fields in Maykop, and beyond that in Grozny and Baku. Army Group B was to take Stalingrad, which, Hitler said in what turned out to be a classic understatement, "the enemy will probably defend tenaciously."[5]

According to Marshal Aleksandr M. Vasilevsky, Stalin stuck to the erroneous view well into July that the main German target would be Moscow, and so inadvertently made things easier than they needed to be for the attackers.[6] Hitler had the initial advantage when he launched Operation Blue on June 28. Wehrmacht leaders wanted an offensive but were skeptical about extending it hundreds of miles to the south. Initially, however, Hitler looked like he had found the magic touch again: the Wehrmacht surprised the Red Army and began chalking up more victories, encircling and capturing tens of thousands. Some cities and towns put up stiff resistance, and Hitler still did not want to get dragged into such battles.

Nevertheless, on July 23 he issued a revised plan that called for the capture of Stalingrad. Hitler gave Army Group B the "modest" mission of taking the city. Victory there would destroy essential industries and communications systems. Army Group B would then head down the

Volga toward Astrakhan. He was supremely confident of a quick victory in the south—with one wing heading off toward Stalingrad, the other driving due south into the Caucasus. Soon it would be possible, he thought, to release troops, who would then be rushed north to Leningrad and finish it off.[7]

STALIN MEETS CHURCHILL AND HARRIMAN

At this juncture Winston Churchill, ever worried about the Soviet ally, felt it was important to reassure Stalin as best he could that the West was not preparing to join Hitler in an anti-Soviet crusade. Churchill flew to Moscow in August 1942 to break bad news, however, that there would be no invasion of Europe anytime soon. Traveling with him was Averell Harriman, FDR's personal emissary to Churchill.

The visit came as the German blitzkrieg was in full swing again. Churchill was glum at their meeting and Stalin occasionally quite offensive about the continued absence of a second front. Harriman supported Churchill and tried to keep out of harm's way.

Churchill tried to explain the hopelessness of trying an invasion in the west and held out the prospect of one the following year. In the meantime, he said, the British would concentrate on bombing Germany. He described German civilian morale as "a military target. We sought no mercy and we would show no mercy." The Royal Air Force was trying to obliterate twenty German cities. "If need be, as the war went on," he said in his memoirs, "we hoped to shatter almost every dwelling in almost every German city." Stalin smiled and said "that would not be bad."[8]

Harriman concluded of the Soviets: "They were really desperate. Stalin's roughness was an expression of their need for help. It was his way of trying to put all the heat he possibly could on Churchill. So he pressed as hard as he could until he realized that no amount of additional pressure would produce a second front in 1942. He had the wisdom to know that he could not let Churchill go back to London feeling there had been a breakdown."[9]

At a late dinner on his last night Churchill mentioned the topic of collectivization. He asked Stalin whether "the stresses" of the war had been "as bad to you personally as carrying through the policy of Collective

Farms?" "Oh no," Stalin replied, "the Collective Farm policy was a terrible struggle." Wishing to sound sympathetic, Churchill said he guessed it must have been difficult for him "because you were not dealing with a few score thousands of aristocrats or big landowners, but with millions of small men." "Ten millions" was how Stalin replied, holding up both hands.

"It was fearful. Four years it lasted. It was absolutely necessary for Russia, if we were to avoid periodic famines, to plough the land with tractors. We must mechanize our agriculture. When we gave tractors to the peasants they were all spoiled in a few months. Only Collective Farms with workshops could handle tractors." There were some peasants who did not want these farms, and Churchill asked rhetorically: "These were what you call Kulaks?"

Stalin replied in the affirmative but would not mention the dreaded people by name. "Some of them were given land of their own to cultivate in the province of Tomsk or the province of Irkutsk or farther north, but the great bulk were very unpopular and were wiped out by their laborers." He added after a long pause: "It was all very bad and difficult — but necessary."

Churchill was struck by the thought "of millions of men and women being blotted out or displaced for ever." In his memoirs he recalled a dictum of Edmund Burke: "If I cannot have reform without injustice, I will not have reform." Churchill added, perhaps ashamed of his silence: "With World War going on all round us it seemed vain to moralize aloud."[10]

He came away thinking Stalin was his friend, but that benign view was not shared by the entire British delegation, one of whom thought that Stalin was a bit like a python. Another had asked what happened to the thousands of Polish officers taken prisoner in 1939 and was not impressed with the answer that they must have all run away.[11]

At their final meeting Churchill mentioned that a "serious attack" was scheduled. It went ahead on August 19 at Dieppe but was doomed to failure. Of the six thousand or so Allied soldiers involved (most of them Canadians), nearly half were killed, wounded, or captured in what turned out to be a fiasco and waste of lives. But the raid demonstrated that a landing in Western Europe would be years away. The French collaborationist leader Pétain was so pleased by the result that he offered troops "to join the Germans in fighting off any future landing attempts."[12]

FALL OF ROSTOV AS THE ANTI-MODEL

In the meantime, the Germans pressed their advantage. Army Group B moved relentlessly toward Stalingrad, and in July Army Group A fought for the key city of Rostov-on-Don. It was not the walk in the park Hitler seemed to think it would be. The Soviets turned it into a "death trap, the streets tangled with spectacular barricades, houses sealed up into firing-points." John Erickson's masterful account notes: "For fifty hours German assault troops fought ferocious battles in each sector of Rostov, and none more fierce than against the NKVD machine-gunners sited on the Taganrog road leading to the bridge."[13]

General Halder grew critical of Hitler, at least in his diary, blaming him when Rostov became "crammed with useless armor." He (rightly) noted Hitler's "chronic tendency to underestimate the enemy capabilities" and his growing propensity to explode in "a fit of rage" when things did not go well.[14]

The Wehrmacht finally broke through on July 23 and opened the gateway to the south. That was the same day Hitler shifted some forces to drive on Stalingrad, but even with greater strength, taking the mountainous and forbidding Caucasus was a very tall order. It may have been crucial for Germany to gain control of the region because it needed the petroleum resources, but the way the operation was conceived made success impossible. Army Group A managed to cover 350 miles and took the small oil fields at Maykop. However, the Soviets' standard operating procedure was to destroy anything the enemy might consider valuable, so the Germans could hardly have been surprised to find the production facilities demolished. The next stop for oil fields was Grozny, 200 miles away, and from there, the Germans would have to travel nearly 300 miles, to Baku—across the Caucasus. Army Group A forged on.

At first glance the June–July offensive looked as though the blitzkrieg was working again, as it swept aside everything in its path. The distances, however, were just too great, the oil fields far beyond reach. The Wehrmacht failed to capture masses of Soviet prisoners, as it had done with ease before and needed to do again in order to win. But this time Stalin authorized retreats, and his troops escaped to fight another day.[15]

Halder recorded how the Red Army often fought bravely, and even ferociously. However, in the Soviet newspapers of the day there were hints that the troops lost their nerve and ran away. Press slogans shouted: "Pull yourselves together!" The soldiers in Rostov had supposedly become "panic-stricken creatures."[16]

The story of the cowardice of the Red Army at Rostov appears to have been concocted and spread by the regime to absolve Stalin and top leaders of blame for how the war was going. The alleged slack behavior of troops also provided a justification for introducing broad changes, beginning with a new emphais on discipline in the armed forces.

The newspapers published veiled threats like one from a *Pravda* editorial on July 30: "It is necessary that every soldier should be ready to die the death of a hero rather than neglect his duty to his country. That is the pledge of victory." The editorial did not neglect to invoke first Lenin, then Stalin: "During the Civil War, Lenin used to say: 'He who does not help the Red Army wholeheartedly, and does not observe its order and iron discipline, is a traitor. . . .' At the Eighth Congress of the Party, Stalin said: 'Either we shall have a strictly disciplined army, or we shall perish.' Today the officer's order is an iron law."[17] The *Red Star* also quoted Lenin, ending with one of his typically bloodcurdling slogans: "He who does not observe order and discipline is a traitor, and *must be mercilessly destroyed.*"[18]

After Rostov, propaganda changed and so did the national mood. Whereas until then the emphasis had been on anti-Nazism and pity for the suffering victims, the new tone was of a country in imminent danger of losing the war. The morale of the armed forces had to be restored, such as by invoking the theme of the personal honor of officers and men. Henceforth, even if they were ordered to retreat, taking a step backward would be a blot on their reputation. The new line was that "the Army itself was largely to blame for what had been happening—and *not* the government—or Stalin."[19]

Alexander Werth noted in his diary on July 30 that Rostov represented a psychological turning point. Even with the Red Army in retreat, the regime took the unusual step of announcing three new distinctions, named after the legendary military figures Suvorov, Kutuzov, and Nevsky, to be awarded for officers' bravery under fire.[20] Not long afterward, at the battle of Stalingrad, officers' epaulets were restored to their uniforms, the very symbols of authority that had been torn away by revolutionary troops in 1917 as a sign of the equality of the officers and men. Gold braid was soon added to the officers' uniforms, supposedly reflecting the fires of Stalingrad.[21]

Another way Stalin signaled that the army needed to be criticized and changed was his response to a play, *The Front,* making the rounds in 1942. The General Staff wanted to repress it for criticizing the Red Army. According to General S. M. Shtemenko, for a time Stalin's staff officer, the Supremo's view was for more self-criticism and said the play correctly indicated the "shortcomings of the Red Army." They had to be acknowledged and eliminated. "This is the only way of improving and perfecting the Red Army."[22]

Political commissars were ubiquitous in the Red Army, and some-times it was unclear whether the "real" commander was the military man or the commissar. For most of the two decades preceding 1942, the two had shared power. The commissars may have kept up morale, but they detracted from the authority of the officer. This dual command was modified on October 9, in favor of *edinonachalie* (unified management command) in the hands of the military officer.

The political commissars were now demoted to the officers' deputies in the political field. While restricted to matters like political education and welfare issues, they were still capable of dressing down anyone for a hint of disloyalty, and their tasks remained important. As an article in the *Red Star* put it, the standard of political education would not be diminished. The officers' job would be to forge men of iron who were "capable of the greatest fearlessness, of the greatest spirit of self-sacrifice in this battle with the hated Hitlerites."[23]

Issues with the commissars persisted, however, and they continued searching out officers and soldiers with faulty pasts and even encour-aged attacks on German positions against impossible odds. When these failed, they were perfectly capable of blaming the military men for poor planning and even treason. The reforms suggested that commissars who were up to it should transfer to a military post.[24]

The regime remained convinced that "good Communists" made the best and most loyal soldiers. In order to infuse the army with ideology, the Central Committee sought out soldiers to join the Party and facili-tated their membership. Party members in the armed forces were encouraged to extend their ideological and political work there, and all commanders were asked to "carry out propaganda work among the soldiers."[25]

In the wake of the Rostov disaster Stalin also issued order No. 00227, mentioned earlier. This was the "not one step backward" decree. One soldier recalled that it was not just the threat of punishment but the situation Stalin conjured up as a prelude to the order that was so striking:

> The people of our country, who love and respect the Red Army, are becoming disappointed in the Red Army, are losing faith, and many of them curse the Red Army for sentencing our people to the yoke of the German oppressors and even retreating into the east. What are we lacking? We are lacking order and discipline in every company, battalion, regiment, division, tank unit, and air squadron. We must introduce the strictest order, initiate an iron discipline in our army, if we wish to save the situation and defend our Fatherland. . . . We must immediately end all talk of forever being able to retreat, of having a great deal of territory, of our country being big and rich, of having a large population, and of always having grain available. Such talk is not true and is dangerous; it weakens us and strengthens the enemy, because if we do not halt the retreat, then we will lose grain, fuel, metal, raw materials, factories and railways.[26]

For many who had negative experiences with the Stalinist regime, such threats only reinforced their disenchantment. But another soldier recorded more positive impressions: "All my life I will remember what Stalin's Order meant. . . . Not the letter, but the spirit and the content of this document made possible the moral and psychological breakthrough in the hearts and minds of all to whom it was read . . . the chief thing was the courage to tell people the whole and bitter truth about the abyss to whose edge we were then sliding."[27]

The Nazi occupation and murderous treatment of prisoners of war contributed to stiffening the backbone of the Red Army. Alexander Werth's diary entry for August 12, of his conversation with X, likely a high official in the army or defense establishment, went as follows:

> "All things considered," said X, "the morale in the Red Army still continues to be extraordinarily good. They retreat, not with a sense of defeat, but with terrible bitterness, and a touch of shame in their hearts. But there is much less pessimism, not only in the army, but in the country as a whole, than there was in October 1941. And in spite of the terribly

hard conditions in which the people are living, particularly in the evacuation areas, where both food and housing conditions are dreadful."[28]

Werth remembered how much changed after Rostov, in the week before the battle for Stalingrad really got going:

One can only marvel at the relative calm with which people awaited the Stalingrad battle. For some strange instinct suggested to them that here the supreme test would come; and somehow, during that month of August they had ceased to be panicky—as so many were in July, especially on the day Rostov fell. In the interval something had happened; and that "something" was a combination (a) of far-reaching decisions by Government and High Command; (b) of propaganda; and (c) of the spontaneous realization which was perhaps stronger even than all the propaganda—that this was the "last ditch" and that it was really "Now or Never."[29]

STALINGRAD

For the Soviets, the fall of Rostov magnified the importance of holding Stalingrad. If the Germans could take that strategic city, they would be able to separate the southern from the central part of the country. Because the Red Army had already forfeited the Don River to German Army Group A, if Army Group B took Stalingrad, the Soviets would lose the Volga, their most important river, one that was used to carry essential materials like oil from the Caucasus. Stalingrad's very name gave it obvious and perhaps even additional significance.

Zhukov was appointed deputy supreme commander on August 26. He was still on the western front, but the next day he was in Moscow, where he spoke with Stalin, who was fearful that Stalingrad and the Caucasus were on the verge of defeat. Zhukov was promptly sent off with a promise that reinforcements would follow.[30]

At Stalingrad, the Red Army faced the weaker Army Group B. On July 23, Hitler had decided to shift more troops there and take the city, but Halder noted that they were meeting "a bitterly resisting enemy."[31]

Over the next month or so, Army Group B managed to take only 150 miles; this was no "lightning war" but a sign of things to come.[32]

German forces were hopelessly strung out from Leningrad in the north, Moscow in the center, and the Caucasus in the far south. Stalingrad was the fourth major undertaking in the USSR alone. Halder recorded that since the opening of hostilities in the east, the Wehrmacht had suffered 1.6 million casualties, including 336,349 killed. He knew full well that such losses could not be sustained.[33]

Nevertheless, by September 3 the Wehrmacht was within striking distance of Stalingrad, and it looked as if the city would fall unless immediate steps were taken. Stalin was ready to throw troops into the fray, even though, as Zhukov told him, they were almost without ammunition, and had few tanks and little artillery support. The Soviet leader was persuaded to wait until early September, when reinforcements and supplies would be on hand. Zhukov won the gamble because in the meantime the Wehrmacht did not press its advantage.[34]

By September 8, Hitler had begun to see what he called World War I conditions. His soldiers were becoming mired in the hand-to-hand combat that the blitzkrieg strategy was designed to avoid.[35]

Stalin called Zhukov back to Moscow on September 12, where he was joined by General (later Marshal) Vasilevsky, chief of the General Staff and member of Stavka. These were the two military leaders upon whom Stalin now came to rely. He demanded something bold, and they developed a plan with two components. The first was to continue an "active defense" by engaging the Germans in battles that cost them men and machines.

The second component was Operation Uranus, a massive counteroffensive that was going to take forty-five days to prepare. The German troops were already short of vital materials, above all tanks and artillery, and their best forces were being sucked into Stalingrad and getting "stuck in the mud" there. Uranus would attack their flanks, in effect surrounding the outstretched enemy's arm from three sides and then cutting it off. They had learned much from their enemy.[36]

The Soviets used every trick in the book, including heavy use of snipers, one of whom was credited with 224 kills. It was precisely because of the high casualties—such as he had seen in taking Kiev in 1941—that Hitler had sworn to avoid entering cities.[37]

THE TIDE CHANGES FOR GERMANY
AND THE "JEWISH QUESTION"

The führer's anger boiled over, and on September 24 he had had enough of Halder and replaced him as chief of the army's General Staff with a young and passionate general, Kurt Zeitzler, a "true believer" in Hitler and the Nazi cause.[38] Halder had been confident up to the summer of 1942, but began to regard the odds as growing against victory, and was troubled to see how the Red Army was preparing at Stalingrad. He could not agree with Hitler's burst of optimism, and in fact concluded that "the war as a whole could no longer be won by Germany."[39] Hitler also replaced Field Marshal Wilhelm List, in charge of Army Group A, which was trying to take the Caucasus. The führer had broken his own rules by ordering Army Group B to seize Stalingrad.

The inescapable problem was far greater than laying hold of that city. Even if by some miracle the Wehrmacht won there, where would it go next? It would have to cross the Volga, the greatest river in the Soviet Union. The Red Army would be sitting on the opposite bank. How would the Germans get across? And even if that were accomplished, and assuming the best possible scenario, how could they move forward with another winter approaching?

On September 30, Hitler briefly returned to Berlin from his field headquarters. In public he remained steadfast and determined and told his military men that the city named for Stalin had to be taken. Its population, as he said of Moscow's and Leningrad's, would be destroyed.

Hitler was traveling to Munich on November 7 to give his annual speech to the Party faithful on the anniversary of the Beer Hall Putsch when word reached him that American forces were gathering at Gibraltar and would soon be in North Africa. During the night of November 7–8, in Operation Torch, 106,000 American and British troops landed at three major points along the coast and were soon taking cities from Casablanca to Algiers. Hitler was astounded. It was beyond his imagination that the United States, the sleeping giant, could have been mobilized, battling and beating German troops in Africa.

Ribbentrop joined the führer's train on the way to Munich. When he heard about the American landing and the scale of their supplies, he proposed that Hitler allow him to put out peace feelers to Stalin. In a remarkable turn of events, the foreign minister went so far as to suggest giving up the gains made in the east.

The situation faced by the two dictators had changed almost 180 degrees in just one year. In October and November 1941, Stalin had contemplated seeking a peace with Hitler and was even preparing to hand over the better part of the western USSR. Now Ribbentrop proposed to relinquish Germany's eastern conquests in return for peace with Stalin. Hitler was infuriated by the suggestion and forbade Ribbentrop to speak of it again. In fact the idea came at a time when the Germans still had room to negotiate. Just over a week later, when the massive Soviet counteroffensive began, the situation deteriorated drastically.[40]

Hitler's speech on November 8 dashed any hope of seeking peace. He expressly ruled out such negotiations. The Americans were chalking up successes, and the British were pursuing Field Marshal Erwin Rommel, "the Desert Fox." Rommel was finally being run to ground. His famed Afrika Corps was headed for defeat despite everything he could do. By May 12, 1943, the Allies had resoundingly defeated the Axis powers in North Africa, taking 238,243 prisoners, half of whom were German. It was every bit as disastrous as Stalingrad would soon turn out to be.[41]

When he returned to his East Prussian headquarters, Hitler seemed upbeat. The Germans had taken over unoccupied France, and German-Italian forces for the moment were hanging on in Africa. General Walter Warlimont noted in his memoirs that a "deceptive atmosphere of confidence" returned. "There was no realization that this time the tide of the war had really turned, and we went back to the dance of tactical expedients with Hitler as the master of ceremonies."[42]

The issue was sealed with the massive Soviet counteroffensive at Stalingrad on November 19, 1942. They initially thought they had encircled 85,000–90,000 enemy troops, but found they had bottled up more than a quarter of a million.[43] By the time Field Marshal Friedrich Paulus surrendered on January 31, in the New Year the Germans had lost 100,000 men, and another 113,000 German and Romanian troops had been taken prisoner.

Hitler was shaken, and there are many reports of the depressed situation at his headquarters. Nevertheless, he soon rebounded, perhaps believing as he did that, above all, leaders had to show confidence. One of his secretaries recalled him as saying: "We will win this war, because we fight for an idea and not for Jewish capitalism, which drives the soldiers of our enemies. Only Russia is dangerous, because Russia fights with the same fanaticism as we do for its worldview. But the good will be the victor, there is nothing else for it."[44]

34

ETHNIC CLEANSING IN WARTIME SOVIET UNION

T he Soviet Union had more than a hundred nationalities and countless ethnic groups. From 1917 onward official policy, called "indigenization," fostered multiple cultures but demanded loyalty to Moscow. By the 1930s doubts about some ethnic groups or nations had led to waves of repression. In the war years, as the USSR took over countries like parts of former Poland, the Baltic States, Finland, and other areas, native elites were "cleansed" and sometimes murdered, and hundreds of thousands more were deported.

FEAR OF ETHNIC GERMANS

The outbreak of hostilities with Hitler in June 1941 increased exponentially the determination of the Soviets to deal with all actual or potential "enemy" groups inside the country. Highest on the list were the 1.4 million or so ethnic Germans, some of whom could trace their origins back to the age of Tsarina Catherine the Great in the eighteenth century.

In response to the invasion, all German passport holders were interned, and by August 15 fifty thousand had been deported from the Crimea. Just over a week later the same treatment was given to Soviet citizens of German ethnicity living in the Volga, Saratov, Stalingrad, and other regions. The Supreme Soviet explained these actions in a special decree of August 28 as follows: "According to reliable information received by the military authorities, there are in Volga province among its German population thousands and tens of thousands of diversionists and spies who, upon a signal from Germany, are to commit acts of sabotage in the areas occupied by the Volga Germans." In order to avoid blood that would surely flow if such acts took place, the government "has found it necessary to resettle the entire German population to other areas." In a follow-up order, the NKVD—which devoted at least fifteen thousand men to the operation—was told to separate the heads of households from their families at the last minute and to deport them separately.[1]

This was no "surgical operation" but one conducted with great cruelty. Many of those in charge had gained experience in deporting tens of thousands from the recently "reclaimed" areas to the west. Now they went to work inside the Soviet Union itself. Entire populations were to be sent to distant places in Siberia. People were told to take what little they could gather and were deported in the worst conditions imaginable in voyages of despair that lasted as long as two months.

A Volga German soldier heard what happened back home, where his wife and child were deported. He came upon settlers on their way "to occupy our homes—homes completely furnished, farmlands, with domestic animals and machinery, potatoes to dig and cabbages to harvest—in fact everything to start life anew."[2]

On Stalin's orders, the Soviet Germans were driven from Leningrad, Moscow, and other cities beginning on September 15. His aim was to use them as forced laborers alongside Gulag prisoners. In total, 9,640 Germans were deported from Moscow; 3,162 from Gorky; 38,288 from Rostov; 31,320 from Zaporizhzhya; 38,136 from Krasnodar; and so on. More Germans were deported in 1942, bringing the final tally to 1,209,430.[3]

A hint of German blood or association with the enemy nationality was enough. Thousands caught up in the dragnets were completely innocent. Even potential victims of the Nazis, like Jews, were considered guilty if they had once had contact with the Germans. Gabriel Temkin, for example, was a Jewish refugee from German-occupied Poland. He joined the Red Army and was being trained until the taint of his distant link to Germans was discovered. Dismissed from the army, he was sent to a camp where he found many people like himself and became part of a labor battalion. Temkin remembered:

> I was in shock and so were many others. I recall the reaction of a Soviet cadre officer, a lieutenant; Miller was his name, of German ancestry, born in Russia in the city of Engels on the Volga. He knew almost no German. He was now bitterly cursing in pure, juicy Russian. Though he had already been engaged in front-line battles and wanted to continue fighting the German Fascists, he was removed from his regular military unit and assigned to become a company commander in a labor battalion.[4]

The deportations of the Germans stretched into the winter. The reception areas were completely unprepared for so many people. The total number of Germans who died as a result of the operation has been estimated at 175,000. The vibrant culture and rich social life of the Russian Germans in regions like the lower Volga and elsewhere was all but extinguished.[5]

MORE QUESTIONS ABOUT LOYALTY

Ethnic groups with historic grievances against the Russians also came under scrutiny, particularly in the Caucasus. During the 1920s and 1930s the Soviet regime had carried on a veritable crusade in that region, and that picked up again during the war.[6] Suspect groups included the Kalmyks, a Mongol Buddhist people from the lower Volga region; and the Karachays, a Turkic Islamic group living between the Black and the Caspian seas. Both areas were occupied by German forces, and in varying degrees the people there fought against the Reds. The Wehrmacht created limited "Eastern Legions" out of these and others from Georgia, Armenia, and Dagestan and Tartars from the Volga.

The combination of traditional resistance to Moscow and collaboration with the Germans moved these people to the top of Stalin's hate list. In October 1943 the regime sought its revenge, dissolving whatever independence the Kalmyks once had. By the end of the year this entire people had been deported. As usual the operation was cruel, with transport on disease-ridden trains to nowhere. Isolated records show that hundreds died en route. The NKVD ensured that the hundred thousand or so people involved were put in "special settlements." More than one-fifth died in captivity, but material hardships were such that by war's end, less than half those alive were capable of working.[7]

At the same time the NKVD exiled seventy thousand Karachays, virtually the entire population they could find. Stalin expressly ordered their deportation to punish them for collaborating with the enemy. Ultimately even those in the Red Army were released from service to be deported. In February 1944, Beria informed Stalin of the "treason" of the Balkars (also a Muslim people with Turkic language from the Caucasus), who were accused of having "joined German organized armed detachments." The decision was made to deport this entire people (around forty thousand) for "betrayal of the motherland." The charge was that after the retreat of the Wehrmacht, the Balkars had "joined German organized bands to fight against Soviet power." It did not matter that some had been loyal to Moscow. The group as a whole had to pay. There is little information on their fate, but it could hardly have been a happy one.[8]

The Chechens and Ingush were converts to Islam and had even declared a jihad against the Russian government back in 1827. Their popular image was of a group of bandits impossible to control. Chechen insurgency continued in the 1930s, when Stalin's terror was in full swing, and these spirited people, not even a half million strong in 1941, were fighting the Red Army even before the Wehrmacht arrived.[9]

Soviet authorities drew up plans for revenge as soon as the Germans were driven from the Caucasus. Beria was in charge but took his cue from Stalin. Red Army and NKVD troops occupied the area, supposedly to rest from the war raging in the west. Stalin authorized an NKVD plan on January 31, 1944, and the secret police prepared to deport the entire Chechen and Ingush people, a total of 496,460, whether they lived in the immediate region or not.[10]

The surprise attack came on the night of February 23–24. The sweep descended on the victims like a whirlwind, and in a matter of just six days nearly half a million were deported, a feat that was possible because the Soviets had honed their "cleansing" methods through practice. An estimated three thousand were killed during the roundup, and up to ten thousand more did not survive the transit to the east. Perhaps as many as a hundred thousand died during the first three years of their exile. As invariably had happened, the localities where the deportees were sent were unprepared and completely overwhelmed when so many arrived out of the blue.[11]

A decree of the Supreme Soviet on March 7 validated the operation after the fact in the following terms:

> In connection with this subject, in the period of the Fatherland war, especially in the time of the operations of the German-Fascist military in the Caucasus, many Chechens and Ingush betrayed the Motherland, gave over the country to Fascist occupation, joined the ranks of diversionists and intelligence agents, infiltrated Germans into the rear of the Red Army, created on orders from the German armed bands to fight against Soviet power and in the course of this prolonged time, did not occupy themselves with honest labor, carrying out bandit raids on collective farms in neighboring districts and killing Soviet people.[12]

This was the same rationalization given for most ethnic cleansing during the war. In 1944 the authorities singled out other groups in the Crimea and Caucasus. These included the Tartars, Greeks, Turks, Kurds, and Khemshils. Although some of these groups were small, the operations, taken together, involved hundreds of thousands. In the case of the Turks, Kurds, and Khemshils, who lived in Georgia along the border with Turkey, every man, woman, and child was rounded up, making a total of 92,307. As usual, this was done on Stalin's orders, conveyed through Beria. It was considered irrelevant that some in these groups were in the Communist Party or that others fought against the Germans. What counted was that they were Muslims with potential ties to "foreigners." They were driven out in eleven days in a typically brutal operation and sent off to distant lands in the east.[13]

According to a note from Beria to Stalin on May 29, 1944, there were "anti-Soviet elements" in the Crimea, and he counted among them 14,300 Greeks, 9,919 Armenians, and 12,075 Bulgarians. Some were said to have shown "passivity" during the German occupation, and others were accused of having ties to foreign states. Stalin authorized Beria to deport them all. The NKVD descended on the Crimean Greeks, sending a total of 15,040 east as if they were animals going to slaughter. Even Greeks serving in the Red Army were dismissed and deported, or put in labor battalions. If they survived the war, they were sent to the east as well. The closest anyone has come to explaining this campaign has been to cite a statement from Beria that the "German authorities received assistance from the Greeks in trade, transportation of goods, etc."[14]

The Crimean Tartars, a Turkic people and Sunni Muslims, had settled in Russia in the thirteenth century. In the 1930s Stalin turned against them when they (like most Muslims) resisted collectivization. The so-called kulaks among them were deported at once. In 1942 the Tartars in areas under German threat were moved out. The Germans tried to exploit the conflicts with the Soviet regime and mobilized some to fight, but as soon as the Crimea was recovered, the regime took its revenge. On May 11, 1944, Stalin sought the deportation of the entire Crimean Tartar population of around 200,000. Non-Tartar spouses could choose to stay behind.

In just two days, May 17–18, Red Army and NKVD troops surrounded Tartar villages. Although Beria said the operation went off without "excesses," more than twenty thousand died in transit.[15]

Ayshe Seytmuratova survived to tell the tale that applies to many of the other deportations. He said: "We Tartars call these Soviet railcars 'crematoria on wheels.' So we were transported for weeks without proper food or medical attention. There was not even any fresh air, for the doors and the windows were bolted shut. For days on end, corpses lay alongside the living. And only out in the sands of Kazakhstan did the transport guards open the doors, so as to toss out the corpses alongside the railway. They did not give us time to bury the dead. Many people went insane."[16]

Tartar historians believe that losses during the deportation and in the early settlements wiped out as much as 45 percent of their people. Human-rights activists have claimed there was an attempted genocide. The Soviets tried to erase the Tartars from memory by burning their books, manuscripts, and other documents. Unlike other groups, even the despised Chechens, they were not allowed to return to their former homes until long after Stalin's death.

UNCOVERING REAL ENEMIES AND "CLEANSING" THEM

At his famous speech in 1956 signaling the thaw from Stalinism, Khrushchev mentioned all these deportations and blamed them on Stalin. Khrushchev admitted that the "monstrous acts" did not even spare members of the Party and Communist Youth (Komsomol). As the Ukrainian "expert," he claimed to know that the Ukrainians had been arguably the most disloyal of all nationalities in the Soviet Union. He said that their limitless hatred of the Communists sometimes led them to collaborate with the Nazis.

There is evidence that on June 22, 1942, Zhukov and Beria, presumably under Stalin's instructions, signed order No. 0078/42 for the deportations of all Ukrainians.[17] Khrushchev said in his memorable speech that they avoided the fate of the others not because Stalin did not want to deport them but "only because there were too many of them and there was no place to which to deport them. Otherwise, he would have deported them also." Estimates of the Ukrainian population in 1945 were just under thirty-five million people. When Khrushchev said Stalin would like to have deported the entire Ukrainian nation, as the minutes of the meeting recorded, there was "laughter and animation in the hall."[18]

Ethnic cleansing as proposed on this scale was deeply shaming after the fact. The cruelties were unspeakable, and the scale of the calamity proposed defies the imagination.

At the time the operations went ahead, NKVD units were celebrated for their cruelty. One trying to drive 730 Chechens through the mountains became bogged down and completed its mission by locking them all in a barn and setting it aflame.[19] Others suffered the same fate when they were shut inside mosques and burned alive. Hospital patients were killed as a matter of course when they could not be moved, and children and others considered too sick to travel were shot out of hand.[20]

Murad Nashkoyev, a Chechen journalist, described his family's experience of being rounded up by the NKVD in February 1944. After he and his mother boarded the truck, the NKVD simply threw his baby brother in alongside them for the transport to the east: "In my cattle-truck, half of us died during the journey. There was no toilet — we just had to cut a hole in the floor, and that was also how we got rid of the corpses. I suppose we could have escaped that way, but the men did not want to leave their families. When we arrived in Kazakhstan, the ground was frozen hard, and we thought we would all die. It was the German exiles who helped us to survive—they had already been there for several years."[21]

Stalin wrote to congratulate the NKVD for the "successful fulfillment of state tasks in the North Caucasus."[22] When told there had been "abuses," he agreed but did nothing, because he preferred more rather than less zealotry and it was far better to exceed quotas than to fall short.

For Stalin and the Soviet system, the ethnic groups involved had shown themselves for what they really were, and that was much more than collaborators; they were "eternal enemies whom the war and occupation helped to uncover. They were the embodiment of the evil other, not accidental tourists trapped in a cataclysmic event. Their destruction was therefore not merely an act of defense but the execution of the will of history."[23]

These groups were singled out "on the basis of *blood*," as one justly famous Russian account puts it, so no bother was taken to fill out questionnaires, and it counted for nothing if someone was a proven Party member, a hero of labor, or an ardent Soviet patriot.[24]

The overriding factors that led to the "repression" were questions of loyalty or political reliability. The distrust of certain ethnic minorities, particularly the Germans and the Crimean Tartars, as well as the Chechens and Ingush, was magnified by the war. The concern was all the greater when Islam was the religion of a suspect group.

Geography played a role in the case of the Caucasian and Crimean minorities, because they lived in a strategically important area and their religious beliefs and/or foreign ties made them untrustworthy. That they might reach across the border to link up with their brethren put them under suspicion of having divided loyalties.[25]

Notwithstanding the Soviets' brutal and often murderous practices, the regime held that victims of Communist ethnic cleansing could redeem themselves through work or service in the war. In fact, the deportations in wartime, as well as in the postwar period, involved mass death in many cases and deep suffering for the survivors. As well, the culture and way of life of many of these minorities were destroyed.

Some were eventually allowed to return from exile, but only when the "thaw" set in after 1956. The scars inflicted on a number of these groups, like the Chechens, endure to this day.

THE GULAG AT WAR

The brutality of the regime toward its own people during the war spilled over into the Gulag concentration camp system. To avoid being overrun by the Wehrmacht in 1941, prisoners in the westernmost camps were sent to the east. An estimated 750,000 from 27 camps, 210 labor colonies, and 272 prisons were evacuated, and, as a recent account concludes sadly, "a significant proportion of them—though we still do not know the real numbers—never arrived."[26]

Many in the Gulag preferred to fight the Germans than to rot inside these camps and volunteered to serve in the Red Army. They were often refused, especially the "politicals," but "ordinary convicts" were permitted to join up shortly after the outbreak of the war. Decrees on July 12 and November 24 freed more than 600,000 from the camps, 175,000 of whom were mobilized. According to a recent Russian account, which gives an optimistic spin to the harsh choices, they were "true champions of the USSR. They coped with their new military tasks, since the liberation of their homeland was their personal concern."[27] It adds that "after the fighting the people would have to be put back in this place."

Aleksandr Solzhenitsyn, a survivor of the Gulag, gives a sobering picture of what was meant by being "put back in this place." Many volunteers not only had to return to the Gulag but had their sentences extended.[28]

It is next to impossible to study the turnover in the camps from the data now available, but simply focusing on the annual census of the corrective labor camps and colonies, one observes a slow decline from the high of 1.9 million in 1941, to 1.7 million the following year, to 1.4 million in 1943, and to 1.1 million in 1944. The numbers began going back up in 1945, to 1.4 million, and almost every year thereafter until 1952, the year before Stalin's death, when they reached an all-time high of 2.5 million.[29] Information on the gender of prisoners is available for 1943–45. The number of women in the camps and colonies stood at 17.3

percent in 1943, 24.9 percent in 1944, and 28.4 percent in 1945. The figures were higher than usual because of the large number of men who volunteered and were accepted for military service.[30]

The plight of women in the Gulag camps is vividly described by Solzhenitsyn in what must rank as one of the most horrifying chapters in modern literature:

> Attractiveness was a curse. Such a woman had a constant stream of visitors on her bunk and was constantly surrounded. They propositioned her and threatened her with beatings and knives—and she had no hope of being able to stand up against it but only to be smart about whom she gave it to—to pick the kind of man to defend her with his name and his knife from all the rest, from the next in line, from the whole greedy queue, from those crazy juveniles gone berserk, aroused by everything they could see and breathe in there. . . .
>
> And what about the women in the Kolyma? After all, women were extremely rare there and in desperate demand. It was better for a woman not to get caught on the work sites there—by a convoy guard, a free employee, or a prisoner. The Kolyma was where the expression *streetcar* for a gang rape arose. K.O. tells how a truck driver lost at cards a whole truckload of women, including K.O. herself, being transported to Elgen. And, turning off the road, he delivered them for the night to a gang of unconvoyed construction workers.[31]

Some women resisted and even managed to kill the guards who tried to rape them, but mostly they either submitted or were beaten until they did. Sexually transmitted disease became endemic in the Gulag, particularly among ordinary convicts who were notorious rapists.[32]

Stories of survivors like Solzhenitsyn are shocking. Sometimes in just a few lines, he conveys a horrific vision impossible to forget, like the "two unconvoyed girls who were caught running to see friends in the men's column. The guard tied them behind his horse and, mounting his horse, *dragged them across the steppe.*" Solzhenitsyn says that not even the worst serf-owners in tsarist Russia would have killed in such a brutal way, but the Gulag guards "used to do it at Solovki." In a footnote to the story he wonders about the guard: "Who today will seek out his name? And him? Yes, and if one were even to speak to him about it, he would be astonished: What's he guilty of? He was ordered to do it! So why did they have to go to the men anyway, the bitches?"[33]

Conditions deteriorated in the vast Gulag during the war. As Solzhenitsyn writes, if food was short everywhere, the prisoners were on starvation rations. At the same time they were pushed to work harder and longer. The mortality rate went up. In just five years, from 1941 to 1945, official records show that 621,637 died in Gulag camps. It would seem that these statistics do not include the deaths in the labor colonies. In any case, it would be prudent to regard these numbers as the minimal ones.[34]

Regular inflows of new prisoners made up the numbers, particularly from the ethnic-cleansing operations. There was a steady influx of those charged with breaking article 58 of the criminal code, the notorious paragraph that could be stretched to catch almost anyone suspected of having anti-Soviet attitudes. Another source of new prisoners was directive 221, issued on June 22, 1941, with the aim of arresting "threats" to state security. Such crimes could include anything from "anti-Soviet agitation," to being regarded as a "socially harmful element." In the first ten months that this directive was on the books, 84,034 were arrested.[35] The Gulag was also populated by some German prisoners of war who were declared "war criminals." From 1943 onward many "suspect persons" from the areas liberated by the Red Army were picked up and consigned to the Gulag.

The Soviets had no extermination camps but killed hundreds of thousands and worked as many to death. There were rumors of a gas wagon in Moscow in the 1930s already mentioned, but there were also persistent stories in the 1970s that "gas chambers were operating in one Soviet camp from 1938 onwards." This point is played down by the highly skeptical Gábor Tamás Rittersporn. However, dismissing the allegation because it did not fit the official theory of punishment and redemption rather overlooks the incredible number of people who were murdered by quota after not even having their file read. We will never know the full story of the Gulag, not least because not a single post-Soviet trial of the perpetrators has been conducted.[36]

It is true that the Communists had nothing of the nature of Auschwitz or Treblinka. Soviet camps more closely resembled the Nazi camps inside wartime Germany, where prisoners were forced to work and were killed or died in the hundreds of thousands from maltreatment, under-nourishment, or disease.

The Gulag was uneconomical and wasteful. Most historians have concluded that the labor would have been more productive if it had been free, so that, quite apart from the cruelties and deaths it inflicted, the Gulag was "more of a financial burden than a generator of income."[37]

Stalin remained a firm believer in harsh punishments and also favored grandiose projects that could be built with massive forced labor. As long as he lived, the Gulag in all its horror could not be changed. Only after his death did it become possible to begin dismantling the utterly wasteful and morally disastrous system.

PART TEN

FINAL STRUGGLE

35

FROM STALINGRAD TO BERLIN

The front page of the *New York Times* on February 1, 1943, carried the story of the defeat of the Wehrmacht at Stalingrad and the capture of Field Marshal Friedrich Paulus. Elsewhere in the east, the newspaper reported, the German forces were under severe pressure or in retreat. The USSR, aided by the Western Allies, was growing stronger by the hour.

As we have seen, for Hitler and the German war effort, the devastating news from the eastern front was reinforced by near-simultaneous U.S. and British success in North Africa. The Battle of the Atlantic also reached a turning point in May 1943, with so many U-boats sunk that Admiral Karl Dönitz opted to give them new missions, away from the convoy routes, where they were being destroyed faster than they could be replaced.[1] These disasters showed that the inexorable decline of the Third Reich was well under way.

The Battle of Stalingrad had a particularly magical ring to it, because the city bore the name of the Red dictator himself. The climax there marked the beginning of the German retreat from Russia, and it would become infinitely worse than anything Napoleon and his grand army ever suffered. On the Soviet home front there was elation, and the doubts gave way to relief and hope. Soviet troops who survived Stalingrad became heroes and were sprinkled among Red Army units to spur them on.

The change in Hitler's fortunes was reflected in the attitudes of the millions of foreign workers in Germany. The police picked up one man for saying, "In the last while we've had to run around in rags, but soon you'll have to run around in rags and we'll put on the nice clothes." French workers in the country could hardly conceal their glee that Germany was losing.[2] The Nazi faithful needed a pep talk from their führer, and he summoned Reich leaders and Party gauleiters to his headquarters on February 7, 1943. Hitler's adjutant, Nicolaus von Below, remembered his astonishment at how easily Hitler succeeded in leaving his paladins "obviously relieved" and believing the war was still winnable.[3]

Hitler mentioned the conference held on January 14–24 at Casablanca between Roosevelt and Churchill, where the Allies first demanded unconditional surrender. He said that "liberated him" from all efforts to make a separate peace. As usual he claimed that "international Jews" were the driving force in all the enemy states. For Hitler— as well as for Goebbels, who recorded the remarks—it followed that they had to "eliminate the Jews not only from the Reich but from all of Europe."[4]

He painted the alternatives facing Germany in typically apocalyptic terms: "Either we will be the master of Europe, or we will experience a complete liquidation and extermination."[5] Now was the time to mobilize the nation for the struggle ahead. Goebbels and Albert Speer, minister of armaments and war production, were pleased that Hitler was finally ready to go all out. Goebbels announced the declaration of "total war" in a fire-eating speech to a packed house that was broadcast nationwide. Some citizens said it was a little late, but their general attitude was still supportive.[6]

Hitler addressed the nation in a radio broadcast on January 30, 1943, the anniversary of the seizure of power. He blamed everything on the "conspiracy of international capitalism and Bolshevism," behind which stood as always "international Jews."[7] In February he broke with the custom of an annual visit to Munich for the celebration of the Party's founding and instead had a faithful Party comrade read a proclamation reeking of anti-Semitism. Hitler said his aim was the "destruction of the power of the Jewish world coalition." He said the Jews in New York, London, and Moscow had made their designs clear: "We are determined to give them a no less clear answer. This struggle also will not be ended, as they think, with the extermination of Aryan humanity, but will find its end with the eradication of the Jews in Europe." Their destruction had become his real war aim.[8]

Goebbels wanted Hitler to get more involved on the home front and do walkabouts after bombings as Churchill did. Instead, the führer grew more reclusive and had to be coaxed back to Berlin to speak on the Heroes' Memorial Day on March 21. In conversation with Goebbels the day before, he said that only brutal methods would make it possible to win in the east. He harped on his favorite themes, particularly his hatred of Bolshevism. He told Goebbels he felt like an old propagandist with their tried-and-true definition of earlier times: "Propaganda means repetition."[9]

The talk was supposed to transmit the message "the danger is broken," but his words carried little conviction. He touched on his wartime obsessions, the Bolsheviks and the Jews, repeating his "prophecy" about the Jews—which was already well known everywhere in the country. The twist was that he now said the war would not end with the fall of Germany and its allies to Bolshevism—as the Jews allegedly hoped. Instead, those nations dominated by the Jews would be poisoned by Bolshevism and would ultimately find their end. The bombastic assertion was that the future belonged neither to the "Jewish-Bolshevik" nor to the "Jewish-capitalist" peoples, but to the "true community of the people" that was Germany and National Socialism.[10]

Opinion researchers noted that citizens were left wondering whether the "last crisis" really had been overcome in the east, as Hitler claimed. They worried about whether the nation would be able to finish off the Soviet Union in the coming summer, but remained behind him.[11] Their dream of the great eastern conquest was fading. However, that fantasy, so integral to Nazi ideology, was still intact for some people. The novelist Heinrich Böll, for example, who was anything but a hard-bitten Nazi, wrote his family from a field hospital in the USSR at the end of 1943. He yearned to return home, but added, "I still think often about the possibility of a colonial existence here in the east after a war that is won." Evidently he shared Hitler's dreams at least on that score.[12]

Although several operations against Stalin were being planned for the future, the military situation after Stalingrad was, all factors considered, hopeless.[13]

STALIN TAKES THE OFFENSIVE

Stalin immersed himself in the details of military operations and had to be informed up to the minute. He gave tongue lashings to anyone who crossed him and brought the most fearsome warriors to tears, as he did with Zhukov. If he suspected a leader was not pushing hard enough or lacked courage, he was dismissed. That fate awaited General Ivan Konev, the commander of the western front, at the end of February 1943. He got a chance to redeem himself, however, and was fortunate he was not executed.[14]

Stalin as military leader was not the genius he was painted during his lifetime, though Zhukov thought "he had a good grasp of the broad strategic issues." Russian military historians have been harsher lately and claim that Stalin "came to strategic wisdom only through blood-spattered trial and error." He was "utterly insensitive to the countless tragedies caused by the war," and in his desire to inflict "the greatest possible damage on the enemy," he gave no thought to the costs of his own troops. "The thousands and millions of human lives became for him cold, official statistics."[15]

He promoted Zhukov to a marshal of the Soviet Union on January 18, 1943, the day after the Red Army broke through the German defenses at Stalingrad. Not to be outdone, Stalin assumed the same title in February, when the scent of victory was in the air. The new title embellished his aura as the supreme commander. For the first time, military operations began to be publicly called part of a "Stalinist strategy." The early defeats were retroactively labeled "planned withdrawals." The changing tides of war, therefore, were the occasion for refurbishing his image and personality cult, which had been tarnished by the German attack.[16]

The military was transformed still more into a professional corps, complete with formal ranks. The political commissars, who had shared command with the military, had been demoted, as we saw earlier. However, even with victory on the horizon, Stalin's suspicious mind did not relent. On April 16, 1943, the NKVD was reorganized yet again, likely because it had become too big. With Stalin's eye on "cleansing" the liberated area to the west, it would have to grow larger still. So it was divided into two branches, the People's Commissariat for State Security (NKGB) and the Main Directorate of State Security (GUGB). Military counterintelligence was taken away from the NKVD and given a new name, SMERSH—the acronym for "Death of Spies." There was an intensified search for "enemies within," even with the Germans in retreat. Stalin intended to "cleanse" the areas he liberated, so the Red Army's advance was closely followed by secret police operations against ethnic groups and whole nationalities that had collaborated with the Nazis or were suspected of being disloyal.[17]

The armed forces were subjected to constant surveillance. There were three levels of repression, from the bottom up they were: SMERSH; the military prosecutor; and the military courts-martial.[18]

Stalin sounded confident in his radio broadcast on February 23, 1943, the twenty-fifth anniversary of the Red Army. He said the country stood at a decisive point and that the army's victories were its own since the Western Allies had not opened a second front in Europe. He thought Germany was already exhausted and bound to lose.

As usual he cited Lenin as the infallible guide to what needed to be done: "First, do not be carried away by victory, and do not become conceited; second, consolidate the victory; third, finish off the enemy." Stalin wanted the enemy hunted down, and he fanned guerrilla warfare behind the lines. His address ended with reminders that the conflict was about patriotism, Communism, and death to the invaders.[19]

Roosevelt sent his congratulations: "The Red Army and the Russian people have surely started the Hitler forces on the road to ultimate defeat and have earned the lasting admiration of the people of the United States."[20]

As the Soviets drove out the Germans, they began to find signs of German atrocities. A small concentration camp was discovered toward the end of 1942 near the river Don. Pictures of this and other camps circulated in the Soviet press and fostered anti-German feelings. The Soviets came upon more evidence of barbarities, including the use of a gas van at Krasnodar.[21]

The extermination of the Jews, which had been an open secret within Western intelligence and military circles, was now publicized. As early as

December 19, 1942, the Allied governments had issued a statement saying the Germans had used gas in places like Belzec and Chelm—the latter may have referred to a town by that name or to the death camp at Chelmno. The *New York Times* issue carrying the statement also published a shortened version of blunter remarks from the Soviet government. These said that the "extermination" of millions of Jews had already taken place. The Soviets pledged that "neither the ruling Hitlerite clique nor the base executioners of its bloody orders will escape the vengeance of liberated nations."[22]

OPERATION CITADEL AND THE BEGINNING OF THE END

The Germans were not giving up and counterattacked the Red Army with success at several points. By March 13, 1943, Hitler had issued orders for Operation Citadel, focused on Kursk. There was a bulge in the lines there, and the aim was to smash it. He preferred to wait on a Soviet attack, which he thought would give the Wehrmacht advantages. Stalin accepted the advice of his military and did not follow his instincts to charge ahead.[23] From the German perspective, this time the front was to be "only" along a line of 100 miles (150 kilometers) instead of the more than 1,200 miles (2,000 kilometers) of Operation Barbarossa. After numerous postponements their attack finally went ahead on July 5. Hitler was still hoping, only days before the Allied landing in Sicily, that a victory at Kursk would be "a beacon to the world" of Germany's continuing prowess.[24]

The Soviets were informed by their intelligence service in advance and, just as the Germans were about to attack, opened fire with heavy artillery. The battle for Kursk became the last great offensive Hitler ever ordered in the Soviet Union.[25]

Germany's vaunted new tanks, the Panther and the Porsche-powered Tiger, failed to live up to expectations. Soviet tanks remained superior, and Soviet generals, who learned their tactics the hard way from the Germans, proved equal to the task. The Red Army General Staff prepared heavily fortified bridgeheads "to bleed the attacking German groupings dry, and then shift to a general offensive."[26]

Kursk was one of the greatest tank battles in history. When the German ranks started to thin and the offensive bogged down, the Soviets opened an all-out attack. In despair Hitler called off the operation after little more than a week. Allied landings in Sicily on July 10, followed by a collapse of Mussolini's regime soon after, meant that the Germans had to send divisions to Italy to hold the line. The full implications of a multifront war had become only too evident.

For years the Soviets tried to cover up the extent of their losses, but newly opened archives—which still leave room for debate—reveal the staggering figures. At Kursk they suffered 177,847 casualties; at Orel, 429,890; and in the last great chapter of this confrontation, 255,566. What the Soviets call "irrevocable" (as opposed to "medical") losses may be taken to mean deaths—not mentioned at all as such in the figures. Accordingly, in the three areas of the battle for Kursk the Red Army suffered a total of 254,447 deaths. Although the German numbers were horrific as well, usually given at around one-third of the Soviet losses in men and equipment, the great difference was that the Red Army had significant and growing reserves.[27]

German generals would grudgingly agree with General Warlimont, who was in Hitler's headquarters. Looking back he said: "Citadel was more than a lost battle; it handed the Russians the initiative we never recovered right up to the end of the war."[28]

HITLER'S APOCALYPTIC VISIONS AND ACCELERATION OF THE WAR ON THE JEWS

Hitler met with the leaders of the countries allied with him in April 1943. All felt the imminence of defeat. In the early part of the month, Mussolini proposed he try for peace with the USSR, in the belief that an agreement would free up troops needed against the Americans and the British. Whereas Mussolini was more interested in surviving, Hitler was adamant that the greater enemy was in the east. As defeat appeared on the horizon, he grew more obsessed than ever with stamping out "Jewish Bolshevism."

Hitler visited with Mussolini for four days at a castle hideaway near

Salzburg. He told Goebbels later he convinced the Italian dictator that he could not be rescued by concluding peace with Stalin; there were only two possibilities, to have "victory with us or to die."[29]

During the other April meetings Hitler held either near Salzburg or in the Berghof in Bavaria, he came down hard on those, like Marshal Antonescu of Romania, who had put out peace feelers to the Allies. He took to task those leaders he held uncooperative in delivering "their" Jews to the Nazi death machine. Notable on that count was King Boris of Bulgaria and Admiral Horthy of Hungary. In March 1944, in response to attempts to negotiate with the Allies, Hitler finally invaded Hungary. As we have seen, the tragedy of the Hungarian Jews swiftly followed. In Bulgaria, King Boris agreed to everything, but no sooner had he left Hitler's immediate presence than he changed his mind. By and large the Bulgarian Jewish community survived the war, largely because the people and especially the metropolitans of the Orthodox Church would not consent to Nazi plans.

In March and April 1943, as victory was slipping away, Hitler renewed his call to Europe for a struggle against "Jewish Bolshevism." It so happened that the burial ground of Polish officers murdered by the Soviets in 1939 was discovered at Katyn at this time. Goebbels thought twelve thousand bodies were found in the forest near Smolensk. Hitler ordered him to shift the "Jewish question" to the forefront of the propaganda agenda, to expose the "Jews in the Kremlin," and to "sharpen" anti-Semitic propaganda. Goebbels told Hitler on May 10 that anti-Semitism was already taking up 70 to 80 percent of the Nazis' foreign radio broadcasts. They hoped that transmitting such messages to England would cause a split between the people and the government, but that was pure fantasy.[30]

THE BATTLE OF "IDEAS"

Hitler talked with the Reich leaders and gauleiters on May 7, when he returned to Berlin for the funeral of the Party veteran Viktor Lutze, the head of the SA who was killed in an automobile crash. His address at noon to the leadership of the Party, including the SA, SS, and Hitler Youth, focused on the sacrifices of the Nazi movement in the war.

He underlined the great difference between Nazi Germany and the West. He said it would have been easy to beat them because the Third Reich was based on an ideology (*Weltanschauung*) and their states were not. That gave the Germans an enormous "spiritual" advantage, which they took east with them. The problem was the Soviets also had an ideology—if a "false" one.

Stalin had other advantages, Hitler said, that they had overlooked. The purges of the Red Army in the 1930s did not weaken it, but had eliminated all defeatists, a result Hitler envied. He admired Stalin for putting political commissars next to the officers in the army, thereby making sure that the armed forces were constantly reminded of the ideals they were fighting for. That was why, he thought, the Red Army fought with such bitter determination. Although he said there was no opposition in Germany, he believed there was too much grumbling: "Bolshevism had recognized this danger and got rid of it, so that it can direct its complete strength at the enemy."

He also spoke of the "spiritual basis of the struggle against the Soviet Union." Just as anti-Semitism was used in the Nazi rise to power, it now had to become "the central element" in the war against Stalin. He wanted a unified Europe, which Germany alone could build, notwithstanding problems he saw with his allies—particularly Horthy in Hungary, who did not take anti-Semitism seriously enough.

Hitler wondered "whether the white man really could maintain his superiority in the long run against the massive reservoirs of people in the East," by which he meant also the Far East and Japan. But even in Europe the eastern part would inevitably try to conquer the rest, and Germany had to introduce the "necessary security measures." The "present anti-Semitic propaganda," he said, had to hammer home the message that "Eastern Bolshevism" as well as "Western plutocracy" was led and dominated by Jews. "The Jews must be banished from Europe. That is the *ceterum censeo* [unquestioned certainty] that we in the political conflict have above all to repeat over and over in this war."

As he saw it, there was no possibility for a compromise peace. He extrapolated from earlier experiences: just as the Nazis had to beat the Communists in Germany to attain power, now the Soviet Communists would have to be crushed. Goebbels quoted him as saying he had no fear of a revolution in Germany, because the "Jewish leaders for such a thing were absent."[31]

Hitler still refused to say the unutterable: that he had ordered Himmler to carry out the mass murder of the Jews. He spoke of their fate in the future tense. Everyone in his entourage knew they were never to mention this delicate matter, but the reason for this great silence remains to be explained. When, in late June 1943, Baldur von Schirach—then gauleiter of Vienna—and his wife, Henriette, visited Hitler at the Berghof, she decided to tell him about what she had witnessed recently in Amsterdam. Jewish women were brutally handled by the SS as a prelude to their deportation. The SS even offered her some valuables taken from the Jews. Hitler was infuriated when Frau Schirach brought up the matter, and the couple left in disgrace.[32]

He was hardly going to show sympathy for the Jews. His anti-Semitic convictions were by then an integral part of his being. He and Goebbels had long been convinced by *The Protocols of the Elders of Zion* and now spent fruitless hours trying to figure out how their knowledge of the supposed international conspiracy could be turned to political advantage. Hitler regarded it as his "historical mission" to cast out the Jews, and even losing the war would not save them. He told Goebbels the Jews "believe they are on the verge of a world victory," but that would be denied them, and instead they would experience "world downfall."[33]

It was in keeping with the dual military and ideological mission that he spent so much time talking about the Jews in April and May 1943, when the battlefront situation was in crisis. By that time, Allied bombing of German cities had become a nightly event. The world was coming down around the heads of those living in the embattled Third Reich.[34] Hitler was concerned about Mussolini's increasingly untenable situation in Italy. The problem there, as he said to military leaders, was that Mussolini "has Jews everywhere. He can't get rid of them, because the clerics are suddenly protecting the Jews . . . just as it was during the revolution of 1918 in our country."[35]

He kept rerunning his warped narrative of the traumatic year 1918 and highlighting the alleged role of the Jews whenever the war took a turn against Germany. When Mussolini fell from power on July 25, for Hitler the culprits were obvious: "No one is behind the new regime except the Jews and the rabble who draw attention to themselves in Rome."[36]

WARSAW GHETTO UPRISING

Given that Hitler and other Nazi leaders identified the destruction of the Jews as a vital war aim, the pursuit of the "final solution" continued with as much determination as the war on the battlefield. Although millions had been murdered already, the Nazi killing machine moved toward destroying all the Jews still alive.

In the General Government, the administrative district created as a holding ground for Jews and other groups despised by the Nazis, thousands were still in ghettos in the districts of Warsaw, Lublin, and Galicia. The official aim at this point was not to murder all Jews, but those not essential to war production. Thirty percent of the Galician Jews were still alive, but with the Red Army driving ethnic Germans from eastern Ukraine, Himmler's problem was how to make space for them. The answer was to begin killing off the Jews in the ghettos.[37]

In January 1943, Himmler traveled to Warsaw, the largest ghetto of all, to press the deportations. The capital of former Poland, with a population of over one million, had been the largest center of Jewish life in Europe. There were 375,000 Jews in Warsaw in 1939, but that number grew when more were forced off the land and into the larger cities, where by December they had to wear the yellow star. On November 16, 1940, the Warsaw ghetto was sealed, and behind its walls close to a half million were slowly starved to death.[38]

Despite all the self-help measures they could organize, some forty-three thousand died inside the ghetto in 1941. Rumors of impending doom circulated from April of the next year, when Jews heard about the deportations of other ghettos. The worst fears were realized, and on July 22, 1942, Adam Czerniakow, chairman of the Jewish Council, was informed by the Germans that "all the Jews irrespective of sex and age, with certain exceptions, will be deported to the East." He was told there would be a daily quota of six thousand.[39]

Czerniakow was warned that for the moment his wife was free, but if deportations were impeded in any way, she would be arrested. The next day the Jewish Council in fact was ordered to assemble 9,000. The psychological burden was too much for Czerniakow, who committed suicide. His death did not slow the deportations in the least. The leaders of the community felt that perhaps 60,000 would be transported, not the entire remaining 380,000, and so thought that resistance might make things worse.[40]

The voices of reason were proven to be wrong. Chaim Kaplan, the head of a Hebrew school in Warsaw, described in detail the daily agonies the Jews had to endure. He admitted that what he was witnessing was beyond his powers to convey. His diary recorded for August 2, 1942:

> Jewish Warsaw is in its death throes. A whole community is going to its death! The appalling events follow one another so abundantly that it is beyond the power of a writer of impressions to collect, arrange, and classify them; particularly when he himself is caught in their vise—fearful of his own fate for the next hour, scheduled for deportation, tormented by hunger, his whole being filled with the fear and dread which accompanies the expulsion.
>
> And let this be known: From the beginning of the world, since the time when man first had dominion over another man to do him harm, there has never been so cruel and barbaric an expulsion as this one. From hour to hour, even from minute to minute, Jewish Warsaw is being demolished and destroyed, reduced and decreased. Since the day the exile was decreed, ruin and destruction, exile and wandering, bereavement and widowhood have befallen us in all their fury. . . .
>
> We have no information about the fate of those who have been expelled. When one falls into the hands of the Nazis he falls into the abyss. The very fact that the deportees make no contact with their families bodes evil. Nothing that is related—and many things are related—is based on exact information.[41]

Between July and September 1942, hundreds of thousands were sent to Treblinka. By early October the Warsaw ghetto had been reduced to at most sixty thousand. The weak, sick, and elderly were among the first to go, so the majority remaining were in their twenties and thirties. Jewish resistance began to organize. Most political factions, from the Communists to the Zionists, merged and prepared to fight.[42]

When Himmler visited Warsaw in early January 1943, he was displeased to hear that as many as 40,000 remained in the ghetto (the number was even higher) and ordered the immediate deportation of 8,000.

Another 16,000 involved in war industry were to be sent to Lublin. For the rest, it was irrelevant whether they did useful work or not: all were to be destroyed. The shock attack caught the would-be resisters off guard, but they fought back. Something on the order of 6,500 were sent to their deaths, another 1,171 were shot in Warsaw, all at the cost of wounding one German police captain. That was enough of an excuse for Himmler to order the complete destruction of the ghetto in early February.[43]

The last remaining Jews went into hiding, and within days their armed resistance began. They were given modest but important help by non-Jewish Polish resistance groups. The Jews knew their fate was sealed but were determined to fight back. Yitzhak Zuckerman, one of the leaders, put it this way: "We saw ourselves as a Jewish underground whose fate was a tragic one . . . a pioneer force not only from the Jewish standpoint but also from the standpoint of the entire embattled world—the first to fight. *For our hour had come without any sign of hope or rescue.*"[44]

The resistance in Warsaw reinforced Himmler's determination to complete the "final solution" in the General Government as quickly as possible. In the meantime, a Jewish fighting organization took shape. Their resistance was remarkable because they had no illusions about the desperate situation and realized there was no chance of success as that word is usually understood.

On April 19, the eve of Passover, Himmler put SS General Jürgen Stroop in charge of the "action." Stroop had a reputation for ruthlessness and wanted to snuff out resistance as quickly as possible. He had just over two thousand heavily armed men, including units from the German order police, the SS, and the Wehrmacht.[45] Far from crumbling, the Jews beat the Germans back, on that day and on subsequent days as well. The fighting turned into a struggle for city blocks and then individual houses. On April 27, Zegota, the Council for Aid to Jews Among the Poles, announced: "The opposition of the Jewish Fighting Organization now continues for nine days, which at first was fought from defensive positions and has now adopted partisan tactics, and has made a tremendous impression among the Polish population of Warsaw. The Poles now call the ghetto Ghettograd."[46] The reference here was to the siege at Stalingrad. With their backs to the wall, the Jews fought bravely and gave the German forces all they could handle.

The last letter from Mordecai Anielewicz on April 23 conveyed a sense of the dire situation the resistance faced, but also gave a hint of his own sense of fulfillment: "I cannot describe the conditions in which the Jews of the ghetto now live. Only an unusually determined person could hold out. The remainder will die sooner or later. Their fate has been decided. In almost all the bunkers in which thousands are hiding it is impossible to light a candle because of the lack of air."[47]

On May 16, nearly a month later, Stroop boasted, "The Jewish quarter in Warsaw is no more!" He reported that his forces caught 56,065, of whom 7,000 were shot on the spot and the same number sent to Treblinka. In addition, 15,000 were shipped to the killing center at Lublin (Majdanek), while the rest went (for the moment) to labor camps.[48] The Nazi attack wrote a whole new chapter in the annals of horror. What remained of the ghetto was systematically leveled. The ferocity of the assault was, however, soon matched elsewhere. On June 19, Himmler reported to Hitler and came away from the meeting with a decision that "the evacuation of the Jews, despite the unrest that would thereby still arise in the next three to four months, had to be radically carried out and seen through."[49]

In the shadow of the events in Warsaw, the decision to liquidate all the ghettos was reinforced. The acceleration of what was euphemistically called "ghetto clearing" as well as the destruction of Jews in work camps—including those producing war-related materials—involved the murder of untold thousands.

The Lvov (Lemberg) ghetto, for example, counted twenty-four thousand in early January 1943, but in reality there were more. In one "action" after the next, most inhabitants were shot. As district SS and police leaders complained about "their" Jews, surveys were taken, death squads sent in, and tens of thousands more executed. In terms of the numbers of victims, these killings—though carried out over a somewhat longer period—were almost as great as those committed by the SS Einsatzgruppen at the beginning of the war against the Soviet Union.[50]

The Warsaw ghetto uprising led to a consensus among Nazi leaders that the remaining Jews in the General Government should—as Goebbels put it—be "removed as quickly as possible."[51] Himmler and Hitler had apparently backed away from their earlier decision to use Jews as forced labor, and on May 10 Himmler said that the approximately 300,000 who remained in this district were to be "resettled," which is to say, murdered.[52]

Blood flowed in the streets, as can be imagined when the executioners were given, as they were in places, a quota of 1,000 to kill in a day.[53] A sense of the scale of the killing can be gathered from a report of Friedrich Katzmann, the SS and police leader in Galicia. In what must rank as one of the most chilling accounts of the "final solution" ever written, he noted on June 30 that since early 1942, at least 434,329 Jews had been "resettled," that is, killed, on his orders. If some of the reports on which this total was based were too high, other murders went unreported, so that Katzmann's figures were fairly accurate. When the Germans arrived, there were more than a half million Jews in Galicia. At the end of Katzmann's posting there, only 21,156 survived, confined to twenty-one work camps. That number, he reported, was "being steadily reduced."[54]

Katzmann complained about the Jews' lack of cooperation and their armed resistance. He said it was only through the energetic work of the SS and police that they could "overcome this plague as quickly as possible."[55] There were additional uprisings throughout 1943 in Treblinka (August), Sobibor (October), and elsewhere. Until 1943 there was little resistance, mostly because Jews had been clinging to the hope they would "merely" be exploited.

As the last illusions faded, their will to resist increased. Himmler set up a surprise attack in the Lublin camps. In late October the Jews were put to work digging trenches outside the camps at Majdanek, Trawniki, and Poniatowa. Operation Harvest Festival was sprung early in the morning of November 3, and the killing continued all day and into the next. Most of those shot were so-called work Jews employed in various activities, all of them profitable.

None of the wanton destruction of life made economic sense but was consistent with Nazi ideology as understood and implemented by Himmler and the SS. Himmler had his mission to kill and had been "plagued with complaints from industrial and military authorities" who began losing essential Jewish workers as the killing picked up after 1942. Now he was acting on Hitler's "wishes" and killed off the Jews en masse. The executioners were the SS, but also groups like the reserve police battalions. The activities of Reserve Police Battalion 101, a group of about five hundred older men, show how it and other units carried out "Jew hunts" to find anyone who had escaped the "festival."[56]

An estimated forty-two thousand were shot in two days or so of Operation Harvest Festival, which stood out even in the context of the serial mass murders of that time.[57]

"GLORIFYING" THE MURDER OF THE JEWS

At Posen on October 6, Himmler addressed a meeting of Party and Reich leaders, which included not only upper-level SS officers, as is often supposed, but many other influential persons, like Albert Speer—who later steadfastly denied he knew anything about the mass murder of the Jews.[58] Fifty typewritten pages, the speech was more than three hours long.

Himmler began by mentioning the Soviet Union. Echoing Hitler's words earlier that year, he claimed the Germans had been wrong to suppose that Stalin's purges in 1937 and 1938 had weakened the Red Army. Like the führer, he believed they had replaced the equivocal old tsarist generals and the doubters with politically committed Bolsheviks.

Himmler thought the German advance was stopped at Moscow partly because of the political commissars, whose "fanatical, brutal will" turned the raw Slavic and Mongolian people into a force.

He spoke also about the Soviet system and the NKVD. "The Russians," he said, "know themselves very well and had invented a very practical system," whether it was the tsars and their Okhrana "or Mr. Lenin and Mr. Stalin with the GPU or the NKVD." That system provided "absolute security" and was impervious to conspiracy, backed up by the pistol or deportation, "and that's the way these people are governed."

Germans had to operate that way, and he thought their "idealism" was completely out of place. The basic principle for the SS man was "honor, honesty, trust, and comradely feelings for members of our own blood and otherwise to no one else. What happens to the Russian, how the Czech gets along is totally irrelevant to me." The "good blood" of other peoples, insofar as there was any, would be taken as needed by "robbing their children and raising them as Germans." But if the rest lived in prosperity or perished, it was of interest to him "only insofar as we need them as slaves for our culture."

These "human animals" (*Menschentieren*) would be treated appropriately, Himmler said, but added it was "a crime against our own blood" to become overly humane, because the Germans who came after would pay. "If someone comes to me and says, 'I cannot build antitank ditches with children and women. That's inhumane, because they will die in the process,' then I have to say, 'You are a murderer of your own blood, because, if the ditches are not built, then German soldiers will die and they are the sons of German mothers. That's our blood.' " The duty was to "our people and our blood."

He surveyed the war fronts. He was not worried about the coming winter offensive by the Communists, which he saw as "the last blow of a desperate beast." As for the home front in Germany, he said he would go after the defeatists with as many executions as needed. Expressing satisfaction that Communists in Germany were locked up, he cheerfully pointed to fifty to sixty thousand "political and criminal" prisoners in concentration camps who, along with a "small number" of Jews and many more Poles and Russians, were "working" for Party comrade Speer.

After a review of SS activities, Himmler turned to what he called "the evacuation of the Jews." He spoke of their "extermination" as a people.

He began with the ominous phrase "I also want to speak to you quite frankly about a very grave matter. We can talk about it completely openly among ourselves, and yet we will never speak of it publicly. I mean here the evacuation of the Jews, the extermination of the Jewish people. It is one of those things that are easy to talk about. 'The Jewish people will be exterminated,' says every Party comrade. 'It's clear, it's in our program. Elimination of the Jews, extermination and we'll do it.' "

Himmler congratulated SS officers and other leaders for what he viewed as the professional way they had gone about fulfilling Hitler's promise. In a particularly chilling passage he uttered the following: "Not one of those who talk like that has watched it happening, not one of them has been through it. Most of you will know what it means when a hundred corpses are lying side by side, or five hundred or a thousand are lying there. To have stuck it out and—apart from a few exceptions due to human weakness—to have remained decent, that is what has made us tough. This is a glorious page in our history and one that has never been written and can never be written."

He proceeded to reassure any wavering listener by reciting the Hitlerian and robotlike rationale for exterminating the Jewish people: "For we know how difficult we would have made it for ourselves if, on top of the bombing raids, the burdens and deprivations of war, we still had Jews today in every town as secret saboteurs, agitators, and troublemakers. We would probably have reached the 1916–17 stage when the Jews were still part of the German body politic."[59] This last point tied into Hitler's longtime insistence that German soldiers had been stabbed in the back by the home front in the First World War.

Himmler mentioned that they had taken everything the Jews owned for the German state. This was one of the few times any major Nazi leader ever made that point. Material gain was never the real issue, however. It was easy enough to steal Jewish property, and it could have been done with less wastage. The Jews might have been allowed to work longer and produce more. The obsessive desire to kill all the Jews became foundational to Hitler's thinking from at least January 30, 1939. In the war years, certainly after the attack on the Soviet Union, their complete annihilation became one of Germany's war aims.

It was Himmler's hope that "the Jewish question in the countries occupied by us will be finished off by the end of the year." He concluded the long speech on a note of cautious optimism, pointing out that the coming winter was going to be the real test. His vision of the future, when peace came, was of an empire stretching to the Urals. After another century the empire would reach beyond the Urals to challenge Asia.[60]

36

STALIN TAKES THE UPPER HAND

Stalin's brief visit to the front in August 1943 gave him a psychological advantage over Franklin Roosevelt and Winston Churchill. He was in the thick of war, and the Red Army was carrying the fight to the Germans. He told Roosevelt and Churchill he was unable to meet with them because he had to be at the front. He never let them forget that his country had done the bleeding and should be given its due.[1]

Stalin managed to project himself as larger than life in international affairs. But he had not been outside the USSR since before 1914 and never flown in an aircraft. No one was sure what he was really like. Churchill had met him briefly in Moscow in 1942, but otherwise he was known mostly by reputation. Churchill and the Americans—represented by Averell Harriman—faithfully promised that the Allies intended a major offensive in Western Europe in 1943.[2]

Stalin was difficult to read or predict. At close quarters he impressed many clever people, including Churchill. Harriman had contact with him at wartime meetings and said he was more than just a tin-pot dictator:

I saw the other side as well—his high intelligence, that fantastic grasp of detail, his shrewdness and the surprising human sensitivity that he was capable of showing, at least in the war years. I found him better informed than Roosevelt, more realistic than Churchill, in some ways the most effective of the war leaders. At the same time he was, of course, a murderous tyrant. I must confess that for me Stalin remains the most inscrutable and contradictory character I have known—and leave the final judgment to history.[3]

The Battle of Stalingrad elevated him in the eyes of the Western Allies and put to rest the widely held belief that Russia could not survive. As we have seen, the Americans scaled back the Victory Program of 1941, reducing the amount of troops they thought they needed to mobilize.[4]

Stalin was grateful to receive goods under the lend-lease program, and Roosevelt's decision to provide such aid helped to keep the Soviet Union in the war. But what Stalin desperately needed was another battlefront in Western Europe that would draw German troops out of the Soviet Union and give the Red Army some relief.

TEHRAN CONFERENCE

From November 28 to December 3, 1943, he pressed his case at the first Big Three meeting. The event took place in Tehran, a convenient location on neutral turf. Never missing an opportunity to proselytize, Stalin paid the young shah a visit and tried to foster Soviet influence by offering arms. These were declined.[5]

His main prey was Roosevelt, and he wanted to separate the president from Churchill, who was known as a died-in-the-wool anti-Communist. FDR was considered likely more sympathetic. He also wanted to impress the Soviet dictator and embraced the opportunity to act independently of Churchill and to show there was no basis for suspecting American intentions.

Stalin invited FDR to stay in the Soviet embassy for security reasons. He manipulated Roosevelt with care, striking various poses during the meetings. He favored the facade of a contemplative and heavily burdened leader of the nation bearing the brunt of the war.

Just after 3:00 p.m. on November 28 the two met (with their translators), and Roosevelt asked the perfect first question: How were things going on the Soviet battlefront? That opened the door for Stalin to underline the Germans' resistance. Within five minutes FDR was apologizing for not being able to do more. He shifted to global concerns, including the fate of the British Empire, a matter of great interest to Stalin, who never lost sight of his ultimate aim of spreading Communism.[6]

Roosevelt said later that Stalin was not like the men he was used to dealing with: he was "correct, stiff, solemn, no smiling, nothing human to get a hold of. . . . I had come there to accommodate Stalin. I felt pretty discouraged because I was making no personal headway." Even before the conference began, Stalin established his advantage. During the meetings Roosevelt would go to great lengths to agree with him, often at Churchill's expense, so as to cut through Stalin's "icy surface."[7]

American officials and experts on the USSR were still not sure the Soviets would stay in the war; they thought Stalin might try for a separate peace with Hitler. Churchill continued to share these misgivings, reinforced when Stalin frankly admitted the Red Army was "war weary" and might not carry on if there was still no new front in the west to take off the pressure.[8] An alternative scenario among American officials was that the Soviets might not want Anglo-American troops in Europe, even if Stalin said that was what he needed. Perhaps he hoped to defeat Germany on his own and have Europe to absorb as he saw fit. In either case, Roosevelt and his advisers favored an Allied invasion of Western Europe and decided with Churchill to call it Operation Overlord.[9]

Roosevelt's opening remarks to the first main gathering paid due respect to the great sacrifice of the Soviets. The Big Three got down to talking about Overlord, which Stalin seemed genuinely to support. Roosevelt and Churchill had agreed about the invasion the previous August at their meeting in Quebec. They favored attacking directly across the English Channel. Thirty-five divisions (sixteen British and nineteen American) would land initially, but before the summer of 1944 the goal was to have a million soldiers in Europe. Stalin wanted to know the timetable for Overlord and who would be the military commander. He was kept waiting on both counts.[10]

An important aspect of the conference was how to deal with the postwar era. Stalin had harsh things to say about France. At the evening meal on November 28, along with dismembering Germany, he said "the French nation, and particularly its leaders and ruling classes, were rotten and deserved to be punished for their criminal collaboration with Nazi Germany."[11]

He was keen to make Germany pay and came out in favor of a draconian approach. Official American notes mentioned how he

> appeared to regard all measures proposed by either the President or Churchill for the subjugation and for the control of Germany as inadequate. He on various occasions sought to induce the President or the Prime Minister to go further in expressing their views as to the stringency of the measures which should be applied to Germany. He appeared to have no faith in the possibility of the reform of the German people and spoke bitterly of the attitude of the German workers in the war against the Soviet Union.[12]

Stalin ventured few of his own opinions, but kept trying to figure out FDR's and Churchill's in order to make countermoves. Typical of his style was when Churchill asked about the territorial ambitions of the USSR. Stalin dodged by answering: "There is no need to speak at the present time about any Soviet desires, but when the time comes, we will speak."[13]

Churchill made a fuss about presenting Stalin with a sword of honor between sessions. It was inscribed with the words "To the steel-hearted citizens of Stalingrad, a gift from King George VI as a token of the homage of the British people." Stalin was touched and even shed a tear, but he kept his eye on the prize. That meant winning the war, getting his allies to do their share, and expanding Soviet control of the postwar world as much as possible.

He was particularly pleased with Churchill's view on Poland. The prime minister suggested that after the war Poland "might move westward," which is to say, give up its eastern border region to the USSR. It would be given a slice of eastern Germany in compensation. Certainly Churchill wanted "an independent and strong Poland," as he stated in an evening meeting with FDR and Stalin on November 28, but he could accept shifting the borders of the country westward.[14] Churchill noted in his memoirs: "This pleased Stalin, and on this note our group parted for the moment."[15]

Roosevelt agreed with this drastic step but, in a private meeting with Stalin in the early afternoon of December 1, asked him to understand that as a politician who would be seeking reelection, he did not wish to have his stance published, lest he lose the Polish-American vote. FDR noted that the Baltic republics of Estonia, Latvia, and Lithuania "had in history and again more recently been a part of Russia and added jokingly that when the Soviet armies re-occupied their areas, he did not intend to go to war with the Soviet Union on this point." He hoped for a referendum in those states, but Stalin was past master at getting people to express their "free will" to join the USSR. Roosevelt gave him the green light.[16]

Back home later FDR confided to New York's archbishop, Francis Spellman, that besides Poland and the Baltic States, Finland and Bessarabia were already lost to the Soviet Union. "So better give them up gracefully," because there was nothing the United States could do about it. He asked the disappointed Polish ambassador in Washington: "Do you expect us and Great Britain to declare war on Joe Stalin if they cross your previous frontier? Even if we wanted to, Russia can still field an army twice our combined strength, and we would just have no say in the matter at all."[17]

KEEPING GERMANY DOWN PERMANENTLY

Dinner on November 29 was hosted by Stalin, and amid many toasts and a vast show of food that ordinary Soviet citizens had not seen in their lifetime, Stalin brought up the issue of how to deal with the Germans. The concept of postwar trials had been suggested by Molotov as far back as October 1942 when he wrote several Eastern European exile governments in London about Moscow's inclination to try the most prominent leaders of "the criminal Hitlerite government" before a "special international tribunal."[18]

Moscow was upset that Britain was unwilling to try Rudolf Hess, Hitler's deputy, who had flown to Scotland in 1941. Still, on November 1,

1943, all three Allies issued the Moscow Declaration. It stated that those who had committed crimes would be returned to the localities where these had taken place and be "judged on the spot." Trial and punishment would follow the laws of each locality, but different treatment would be accorded the major war figures. It was left up in the air precisely what ought to happen to these men and whether they would be tried or summarily executed.[19]

Churchill suggested at a cabinet meeting that they might draw up a short list of specific war criminals. The named individuals would become isolated figures in their own country, and dealing with them summarily instead of getting caught up in messy legal entanglements might well shorten the war. He favored a list of fifty to a hundred or so. Once reviewed by a committee of jurists, these men would be declared "outlaws" and considered fair game for anyone who wished to kill them. For Churchill, if there was to be anything like a trial, its job would be to verify the identity of these "outlaws."[20]

There was a remarkable exchange on this topic over dinner on November 29. Stalin worried that "in fifteen or twenty years" Germany could plunge the world into another war. As a preventive step he suggested that "at least 50,000 and perhaps 100,000" of their commanding staff be "physically liquidated." In addition, "the victorious Allies must retain possession of the important strategic points in the world so that if Germany moved a muscle she could be rapidly stopped." The same should happen to Japan.[21]

Stalin was absolutely serious.[22] Churchill took strong exception to "cold-blooded executions of soldiers who had fought for their country." War criminals should be held responsible for their acts according to the Moscow Declaration of November 1. He "objected vigorously, however, to executions for political purposes."[23] He also said the British parliament and public would never accept such a thing. Roosevelt responded more warmly to Stalin, and when Churchill became upset (or so Churchill recalled), FDR said the Allies should execute not 50,000 but "only 49,000." Elliott Roosevelt, the president's son, who happened to be present, chimed in to say he was sure the United States Army "would support it."[24]

The conversation bothered Churchill so much he walked out, but he was chased down by Stalin, who said he was only joking. Churchill allowed himself to be persuaded to return to dinner, but was not "fully convinced that all was chaff and there was no serious intent lurking behind."[25]

Stalin's point about dividing Germany, which he repeated afterward in a completely different context, was based on his belief that the German national character was such that the country would quickly recover. They "were like sheep," followed orders faithfully, and were too disciplined. They had to be run into the ground.[26]

The issue of whether to execute selected Nazi war criminals or to put them on trial remained unresolved. In the meantime, the Soviets began settling scores their own way.

One of the points mentioned by Stalin on that memorable evening in Tehran was the need for the Allies to control strategic areas around the globe. He claimed to want to keep an eye on Germany, but he was also thinking in terms of the postwar world, where the Soviets could exercise influence. The other two leaders showed little resolve to oppose Stalin's ambitions.

As the Soviets liberated their land in the summer of 1943, they began carrying out trials, including of their own citizens, for participation in Nazi war crimes. In the first such trial, on July 14–17, 1943, at Krasnodar, the Soviets made public the mass murder of the Jews. There were eight death sentences of Russian and Ukrainian auxiliaries, carried out in the city square in front of tens of thousands.[27] More trials followed, including of German captives such as Gestapo officers.

The Western Allies worried such events might lead to the execution of American and British prisoners of war in German captivity. There was reason for concern. Hitler, incensed at the Soviet proceedings, ordered trials of what he called "English-American war criminals" and especially "Anglo-Saxon terror bombers."[28] Hitler's orders ultimately came to nothing, given his weakened position to wreak havoc. The U.S. government, urged on by Secretary of War Stimson, decided that judicial proceedings were preferable to summary executions.

The Big Three, led by America, initially agreed to split Germany into five self-governing units, under international control. Stalin wanted the divisions made permanent, and he coveted (and got) the northern part of East Prussia.[29] He said the land would give the USSR an ice-free port, "a small piece of German territory which he felt was deserved."

Churchill thought that "with a generation of self-sacrificing, toil and education, something might be done with the German people," but Stalin dissented and "did not appear satisfied as to the efficacy of any of the measures proposed by Mr. Churchill."[30]

Agreement was reached on the Allied invasion of Western Europe. Stalin said he would join the war against Japan as soon as Germany was defeated. The Big Three also decided to form an international organization, and Roosevelt sketched in rudimentary outline what was to become the United Nations. Stalin thought it could work, but said the United States might have to commit ground troops to Europe or other trouble spots in the future. FDR was not so sure Americans would agree and added that if the United States had not been attacked, "he doubted very much if it would have been possible to send American forces to Europe."

Stalin took this sincere admission to mean that he could throw his weight around in Europe without much worry about the United States.[31] Sergo Beria remembered hearing Stalin say at Tehran: "Now the fate of Europe is settled. We shall do as we like, with the Allies' consent."[32] The young Beria, the son of the notorious spy chief and personally instructed by Stalin to bug the conversations between Roosevelt and Churchill, was puzzled by FDR's stance. Churchill tried to warn the president that Stalin was engineering "a Communist replacement for the Polish government." To Sergo Beria's surprise, Roosevelt countered by accusing Churchill of trying to prepare an anti-Communist government. Beria recalled thinking at the time: "Why, then, get excited? It was all quite fair. Roosevelt put Churchill and Stalin on the same plane and presented himself as arbiter between them." That, at any rate, was how he remembered the conversations.[33] He also recalled that both Allied leaders knew Stalin's appetite was not going to stop with Poland.

Despite his personal brilliance, Churchill was unable to control the flow of events at Tehran. World power had shifted away from Britain to the United States and the USSR. Churchill asked prophetically about Stalin: "Will he become a menace to the free world, another Hitler?"[34]

Tehran was a great political victory for Stalin, who got almost everything he wanted. He returned by way of a quick visit to Stalingrad, the city that had changed the course of the war. His destructive urges were hardly sated by Tehran, and no sooner was he back in Moscow, as we have seen, than he urged Beria to get on with the ethnic-cleansing operations already under way.

WARSAW UPRISING

The summer and early autumn of 1944 brought another turning point in the war. D-day finally came on June 6, and the long-awaited second front opened in Western Europe. Operation Overlord was the largest amphibious invasion in history. It took another two months to push the Germans back, but their reversal was inevitable. In early July the Soviets launched an attack to coincide with the Normandy invasion. On July 24 they liberated Majdanek, the first extermination camp, and stories about it filled the news around the world.

Four days before, there was an unsuccessful attempt to assassinate Hitler at his headquarters in Rastenburg. Colonel Count Stauffenberg, part of a conspiracy, brought a time bomb into the briefing room just past noon, placed it under the map table, and made his way out. Hitler was magically protected from the blast as he leaned over the heavy table. The conspirators, assuming Hitler's demise, proceeded with their plan to take over the army, but everything had come to a halt by 6:30 p.m., when a radio broadcast said he was alive and would speak presently. The plot was foiled.[35] Hitler told the nation he had been saved by fate to continue the struggle.

By this point in the war, support for the regime was beginning to dissipate. Nonetheless, people remained surprisingly steadfast behind Hitler. Although they were fed up, they were resilient, and despite Normandy and one defeat after the next, the surveyors of public opinion at the time found that morale was not collapsing.

Hitler's narrow escape on July 20 drew the public to him, and there was outrage that anyone would even try to assassinate him. In addition, the use of V-1 flying bombs and V-2 rockets—retaliatory "miracle weapons"—helped renew the public's faith in a favorable outcome to the war. Opinion reports stated that "almost everywhere the bonding to the führer is deepened and the trust in the leadership strengthened."[36]

Marshal Konstantin K. Rokossovsky, the leader of the Red Army from Byelorussia across Poland, reached the Vistula near Warsaw at the end of July. At least one company of T-34 tanks actually broke through into one of the eastern suburbs on July 31. From an observation post not far away, Rokossovsky could see the city.[37]

On July 29, Radio Moscow appealed for help in freeing the city from the Germans: "Warsaw already hears the guns of the battle which will soon bring her liberation. . . . For Warsaw which did not yield, but fought on, the hour of action has already arrived."[38] On August 1, an attack, encouraged by Allied radio, was launched by the Polish Home Army on German forces inside Warsaw. Contrary to expectations, however, the Red Army did not try to link up with the insurgents in Warsaw. Who was responsible for the tragedy that ensued remains shrouded in controversy, although it was true that Soviet troops were exhausted and could barely hold the bridgeheads they had gained. Rokossovsky decided to wait, even though by August 2 he could see the battle raging.

The delay left the Polish Home Army to face the German forces alone. The "Red Army steamroller of two million men," went a report in the *New York Times,* had fought for 440 miles and had only 300 left to Berlin. Yet it suddenly stopped outside Warsaw.[39]

Stalin spoke bluntly about the future of Poland at Tehran, when Churchill and Roosevelt tried to interest him in linking up with the Polish government in exile in Britain. Stalin's reply was that the latter was "connected with the Germans and their agents in Poland were killing partisans." He coveted eastern Poland, but with no Poles left there. To his great satisfaction, FDR had even suggested some "population transfers."[40]

Churchill wrote Stalin on August 4 to say the British were dropping sixty tons of supplies to help Warsaw. He pleaded for the Red Army to offer aid. Stalin responded coldly the next day and played down the significance of the Home Army's attack. On August 15, Anglo-American aircraft flying in supplies were denied permission to land for refueling on Soviet airfields.[41] Churchill kept pressuring the Soviets into helping the Poles, as did the Americans, until August 16, when the Soviet government formally dissociated itself from the "Warsaw adventure." Stalin was intent on supporting the Polish Communist Committee of National Liberation in Lublin, his puppet government.[42]

In Churchill's words, Stalin aimed "to have the non-Communist Poles destroyed to the full" while keeping alive the myth the Red Army was coming to the rescue. Churchill concluded this sorry chapter of his memoirs with the remark that the Russians ended up ruling Poland, but added bitterly: "This cannot be the end of the story." It was not, but the

Polish people were going to have to wait more than half a century for their liberation from the Communists.[43]

On the ground the situation in Warsaw was a dreadful mess. The war correspondent Alexander Werth, who was sympathetic to the Soviet side, interviewed Rokossovsky on August 26. Werth wondered why the Red Army had stopped, especially as Radio Moscow had called for an uprising. Rokossovsky's off-the-record answers to Werth's questions were elusive, but he blamed the Home Army for acting precipitously. He ended the interview with a rhetorical question to Werth: "And do you think that we would not have taken Warsaw if we had been able to?"[44] Precisely that conclusion has lingered about the tragic events to this day.

The Red Army waited, and by August 22 Stalin was calling the uprising an attempt by a "handful of power-seeking criminals." His decision was to let the Germans do his dirty work for him.[45] On August 20 Churchill and FDR said something had to be done to save the anti-Nazis fighting for their lives in Warsaw. Stalin refused to lift a finger and let the uprising perish.[46]

Zhukov's memoirs note how, on October 1, he agreed with Rokossovsky to wait outside Warsaw, but by then the uprising had been defeated. Stalin called both men to Moscow for consultations. To Stalin's question about whether the Red Army should press on through Warsaw, Zhukov replied: "My view is that this offensive will bring nothing but casualties." The Red Army stayed on the east bank of the Vistula until early January 1945.[47]

Stalin was surprised at the outcry in the West, where sympathy for the hopelessly outgunned Poles was matched by condemnation of the Soviets who waited in the distance as the Germans annihilated the Home Army. The survivors surrendered on October 2,[48] and just over a week later, Hitler ordered the complete destruction of the city.[49]

Himmler's remarks on September 21 to regional commanders show his genocidal thinking toward the Poles:

I said: "Mein Führer, the time is disagreeable. Seen historically, however, it is a blessing that the Poles are doing it. We'll get through the five, six weeks. But by then Warsaw, the capital, the head, the intelligence of this former 16–17 million Polish people will be extinguished—this people that has blocked the east for us for seven hundred years and has always stood in our way. . . . The Polish problem will historically no longer be a big problem for our children and for all who come after us, nor indeed for us."[50]

Churchill was pained to record the casualty figures, which counted 15,000 out of the 40,000 men and women in the Polish Home Army. The city's population of 1 million lost another 200,000. German losses were significant, with around 10,000 killed, 7,000 missing in action, and another 9,000 wounded.[51] The conclusion to this tragic tale came on April 21, 1945, when Stalin took time away from the battle for Berlin to sign a "treaty of friendship" with the Communist government in Poland. It was publicized the next day, on Lenin's birthday, and so achieved the Leninist dream that had been stopped before the gates of Warsaw in the early 1920s.[52]

DIVIDING THE SPOILS

The Red Army waited outside for the sixty-six days of the Warsaw uprising, but everywhere else the Allies moved ahead. The Americans and British swept through France and Belgium and were heading for the Rhine. The Soviets took Romania and Bulgaria, and threatened Germany on a long front from north to south. The United States drove back the Japanese and landed on Okinawa in preparation for the final assault on Japan itself.

Some American insiders were convinced Stalin intended Communism for all of Germany and much more. For Churchill, the behavior of the Red Army at Warsaw rekindled his long-standing phobias, and he became alarmed about the danger of the "Red Army spreading like a cancer from one country to another."[53] It was in this context that Churchill flew to Moscow on October 9. He went alone, as Roosevelt was not up to such a trip.

Churchill had been a staunch anti-Communist all his life, but the war had forced him to put aside his moral scruples. He now thought the moment auspicious to settle some major issues of what postwar Europe would look like, and, no doubt hoping to rescue the best he could under the circumstances, he scribbled on a scrap of paper the following allocation of postwar spheres of influence:

Romania
> Russia 90%
> The others 10%

Greece
> Great Britain 90%
> > (in accord with U.S.A.)
> Russia 10%

Yugoslavia 50–50%

Hungary 50–50%

Bulgaria
> Russia 75%
> The others 25%

Stalin looked quickly at the numbers and took out his famous blue pencil to mark agreement. Churchill recalled: "It was all settled in no more time than it takes to set down."[54] In fact there was no real chance he could make even those figures stick. What was Britain to do about its share of influence in Yugoslavia or Hungary, Romania or Bulgaria? The numbers were tossed back and forth in the days that followed, but without reaching agreement. Harriman, who was present for the United States, suggested the figures were meant only as a rough guide.[55] It finally occured to Churchill he might be helping to consign millions to Communist rule. Becoming concerned about what he had done, he suggested the ungodly piece of statesmanship might be considered cynical and proposed they burn the paper. Stalin was not about to agree.

He had long since made up his mind that territory liberated by the Red Army would be dominated by the USSR in the name of Communism. Not only were the Western Allies disinclined to challenge this vision of the future; militarily they were not in a position to do much. Therefore, whether Churchill or FDR agreed, Stalin knew perfectly well he had a free hand in the east and told Churchill he had plans for the complete reshuffling of Europe.

Somewhat unexpectedly at the meeting, "Uncle Joe," or just U.J., as Churchill called him in letters to FDR, came out in favor of war crimes trials for the major Nazi leaders. His view now was that "there must be no executions without trial; otherwise the world would say we were afraid to try them." He also said that if there were no trials, there could be no executions. Thus, the way was finally cleared for what would become the trials of the major war criminals at Nuremberg.[56]

At the meeting with Churchill and thereafter, Stalin grew more arrogant, even among his own cronies. The coarse side of his character got the upper hand. He conducted business not in the bureaucratic style for which he was known but in late-night drinking parties where he gratuitously humiliated even loyal followers. Behind the drunken joviality was the bloody dictator, who was as prepared to have someone shot as to order another round of toasts. His jokes became crude. When the Yugoslavian Milovan Djilas, a visitor awestruck in the presence of the great man, said soberly that the resistance in his country did not take prisoners, in retaliation for the actions of the Germans who had routinely killed all Yugoslav prisoners, Stalin laughed and told a tasteless joke.[57]

Djilas was still entranced on the morning after the all-night fest, as he left for home. Stalin and Molotov gave him a send-off, and Djilas remembered his thoughts at that moment, which suggest the persistent fantasy of Communist world conquest:

> The car bore me away into the morning and to a not yet awakened Moscow, bathed in the blue haze of June and the dew. There came back to me the feeling I had had when I set foot on Russian soil: The world is not so big after all when viewed from this land. And perhaps not unconquerable—with Stalin, with the ideas that were supposed finally to have revealed to man the truth about society and about himself.
>
> It was a beautiful dream—in the reality of war. It never even occurred to me to determine which of these was the more real, just as I would not be able today to determine which, the dream or the reality, failed more in living up to its promises. Men live in dreams and realities.[58]

YALTA AND THE OPPORTUNITY TO EXPAND COMMUNISM

The Big Three held another conference at Yalta, in the Soviet Crimea, to iron out difficulties and plan the postwar settlement. Although Roosevelt's health was deteriorating, he made the long trip. He had delivered his fourth inaugural address as president on January 20, 1945, in what was the shortest such speech in American history. His main point: "We can gain no lasting peace if we approach it with suspicion and mistrust—or with fear."[59] But his own diplomats and advisers were talking of their worries that the USSR might become a bully. Harriman wrote in September 1944 of his concerns that the Soviets were interpreting America's "generous attitude toward them as a sign of weakness and acceptance of their policies."[60]

The Yalta Conference met from February 4 to 11 and confirmed what the Big Three had more or less already agreed upon. Of greatest immediate importance was the treatment to be accorded Germany and what was to happen to Eastern Europe, especially Poland. Stalin was given latitude in the discussions because the Soviets had sacrificed so much and because his allies wanted his help in the war against Japan. A decision was also made to form the United Nations, and a conference was called to open in San Francisco on April 25, 1945.[61]

The Allies agreed to divide Germany into three zones, with France possibly given a fourth zone. Stalin was at the height of his powers and said at the first plenary session that the Red Army was twenty miles or so into Germany. Besides liberating Ukraine and the Baltic States, the Soviets had already swept through Romania, Bulgaria, Hungary, Poland, and East Prussia.

The Allies in the west had not yet done so well. They had to fend off a German counterattack in the Ardennes at the Battle of the Bulge in December and had still not crossed the Rhine into Germany. Hitler put great stock in this surprise counterstroke but had to keep delaying it because of supply shortages. The Americans brought up reinforcements, and the outcome, which was never in doubt, was sealed within a few weeks.[62] Despite that impressive victory and the heavy losses the Allies sustained, FDR and Churchill could hardly emphasize their sacrifices in comparison to the Soviets', and they kept trying to ingratiate themselves to the assertive Stalin. The Soviet leader had the additional advantage of numerical superiority in troops on the ground, more than double those of the Allies and more than triple the forces the Germans had.[63]

Stalin said the three powers that liberated Europe would play the dominant role in the future. He talked about preserving the peace, but he had no intention of having his actions "submitted to the judgment of the small powers." Churchill waxed poetic on the topic: "The eagle should permit the small birds to sing and care not wherefore they sang."

This point was completely lost on Stalin, who saw a golden opportunity to continue the Leninist legacy of spreading Communism: how far west he might go remained to be seen.[64]

Stalin was even more hard-hearted about Poland. At the February 6 plenary meeting, he said it was to be made a kind of buffer zone for the USSR. Having been liberated by the Red Army, the country was not going to be permitted to have opposition forces. A Communist government was going to be in place, and there was nothing further to be said. Stalin's method was to be ostentatiously generous on issues that did not matter to him but unyielding when it counted. FDR said lamely that the Lublin Communists represented at best "a small portion of the Polish people."[65]

Churchill was prepared for compromises in return for an independent Poland. Stalin pretended but he told Beria later he had "not moved one inch."[66] The notion of forcing early elections in Poland, put forward by FDR, was a dead letter without backing from Western armies. What was at stake at Yalta for Stalin, as throughout the latter part of the war, was to achieve Communist ideological aims and improved national security.[67]

FDR got Stalin to agree to go to war with Japan by offering concessions in the Far East. Stalin wanted the territory lost to Japan in 1904, which included part of Sakhalin and adjacent islands; Port Arthur and Dairen; and the rights to operate major railroads in Manchuria. Although Chinese sovereignty would supposedly be untouched, obviously these concessions infringed on it. Finally, the Kurile Islands were to be handed over to the USSR. The deal would make it possible for the USSR to spread its ideas and influence eastward.[68] Churchill was right that the Soviets "undoubtedly had great ambitions in the East," but FDR decided the priority was to get Soviet help against Japan.[69]

The Soviets would demand reparations from Germany, both in kind—that is, factories, rolling stock, and so on—and monetary compensation (the figure of ten billion dollars was mentioned). These measures were to be spread over a period of ten years or so. German heavy industry would be cut by 80 percent, but all military-oriented industry would be confiscated. Churchill recalled what happened when the Allies tried to collect reparations after the First World War and worried about the specter of eighty million starving Germans. FDR said they should not try "to kill the people." These reservations left Stalin unimpressed.[70] He was more inclined toward solutions like that proposed by U.S. Secretary of the Treasury Henry Morgenthau at the Quebec Conference in September 1944.

Morgenthau had presented a plan for what was in effect the pastoralization of Germany. The country would be stripped of its war-making abilities and reduced to a land of shepherds. Churchill was initially outraged at the idea: "I am all for disarming Germany but we ought not to prevent her living decently. . . . You cannot indict a whole nation. . . . Kill the criminals, but don't carry on the business for years."[71]

At the Quebec conference, Churchill and FDR agreed "to consider" the Morgenthau plan.[72] Once the U.S. president returned to Washington, the prudent secretaries Cordell Hull and Henry Stimson (who were not at Quebec) prevailed, and FDR backed away from such a draconian approach. Stalin brought a similar proposal at Yalta, and it was only with difficulty that FDR and Churchill managed to avoid making such a commitment.

FDR told Stalin the American people would not let him keep forces in Europe much longer—a fateful revelation as far as Stalin was concerned. Beria's son said that thenceforth Stalin "took account of what Roosevelt had said in all his subsequent plans."[73]

President Roosevelt kept one major piece of news to himself. The Americans were developing the atomic bomb. Although the Germans had knowledge of how the bomb could be made, Albert Speer had canceled its development in the autumn of 1942 because Germany could not spare the enormous resources required and could not afford to wait for the lengthy development process to be completed. Hitler would certainly have used such a weapon against Britain, but in Speer's view the führer could not quite imagine an atomic bomb.[74]

The American Manhattan Project was a monumental undertaking that included establishing a vast industrial complex and new infrastructure of roads, bridges, and dams. All of this was needed to produce, sometimes one spec at a time, the material to make the U-235 radioactive pellets. The project had manufactured enough material to make one bomb by mid-1945.[75] FDR and Churchill spoke about it in September 1944 at Quebec and agreed under all circumstances to keep the Soviets in the dark.[76]

37

END OF THE THIRD REICH

itler spoke to his commanders on December 11 and 12, 1944, and tried to fire them up for the counterattack into the Ardennes region against the Americans. He said a war to stop the complete unification of Germany had been in the cards since the middle of the nineteenth century. It had been carried on again in the First World War, and was still under way. The country was being "fought so fiercely," he said, because there was an "ideological possibility of unifying all the German tribes." That was why the war was on and why the enemies were "supported by international Jewry."[1]

The Americans could not be allowed to think they would ever surrender. There could be no defeatism—which he saw as fatal in the First World War. He underlined the contradictions in the Allied camp, with an "ultra-Marxist" state (the USSR), a "dying empire" (Britain), and a "colony [the United States] waiting to claim its inheritance." Believing it only a matter of time before the coalition dissolved, he planned a surprise counterattack on the Americans. After delays caused by various shortages, the assault was finally launched on December 16, but despite initial successes, it ground to a halt in ten days when the Americans brought up large-scale reserves.

Sensing this was his last chance—and a faint one at that—Hitler wanted to restart the counterattack. On December 28 he again addressed the commanders and surveyed the situation with an optimistic tone. He thought the German people "breathed more freely" once they saw the Wehrmacht on the offensive. That mood could not be "allowed to turn into lethargy again." He said, "There are no better people than our Germans." All they needed was a victory and they would come forward and "make every sacrifice which is humanly possible."

The other side of the coin was that the nation had to win this battle or it would be annihilated. "A victory for our enemies must undoubtedly lead to Bolshevism in Europe. Everyone must and will understand what this Bolshevization would mean for Germany. This is not a question of a change in the state, as in the past. . . . But this concerns the existence of the essence itself. Essences are either preserved or eliminated. Preservation is our aim. The elimination would destroy a race like this, possibly forever." Here was another all-or-nothing alternative: "Germany will either save itself or—if it loses this war—perish."[2]

The attackers had the advantage of surprise, committed heavily against the Americans, but found the going tough. The Germans suffered between eighty and a hundred thousand casualties, losing as well most of their tanks and much of what was left of the air force. In the two phases of the battle, running from December 16 to January 2 and again from January 3 to 28, the Americans had around eighty thousand killed, wounded, and missing. That made the Battle of the Bulge the deadliest they fought in northwest Europe. The Allies, however, rushed in new troops from hundreds of thousands gathering in the west. They had overwhelming superiority in supplies and munitions and above all in the air. The route to Germany now stretched out before them.[3]

Field Marshal Sir Bernard Montgomery, never one to offer praise lightly, pointed to the main reason for the Allied victory: "The Battle of the Ardennes was won primarily by the staunch fighting qualities of the American soldier." It was an Anglo-American effort, Churchill said in a speech to Parliament, but "the United States troops have done almost all the fighting, and have suffered almost all the losses."[4]

The Battle of the Bulge helped the Soviets, because Hitler had to draw away divisions from the east. The door was opened to the Red Army, which was preparing for a great offensive and already talking about taking Berlin.

Despite the German military setback, from which there was no possible recovery, Hitler mustered the energy for a New Year's Day broadcast. He conveyed anything but a defeatist attitude. He swore there would be no repeat of November 9, 1918. As long as he was leader, there would be no letting down the troops. He gave the impression that superhuman effort from the people could still succeed, but their backs were against the wall.

There would be no "miracle weapons" to come to the rescue. There had been rumors and whispers for years about such weapons, but Hitler did not even mention them. He would not raise false hopes, and he bet that humans, not machines, were the key to victory.

In his New Year's address he once again pointed the accusing finger at the Jews, whom he charged with bringing about the war. They were his obsession, and he blamed the supposed "Jewish-international world enemy" for everything that went wrong. He swore "the Jew" would "not only fail in this effort to destroy Europe and exterminate its people, but would bring about his own destruction." This renewed threat to take vengeance on them, as in all the others he made in public or in private for years on end, was still phrased in the future tense. Yet he was making the threat when the mass murder of the Jews had already resulted in the deaths of millions. Why would he not take responsibility? The simple answer is more apt here. Hitler was shifting the responsibility for the Nazi extermination of the Jewish people onto the Jews themselves; he was making the case, utterly groundless and cowardly though it was, that the victims were themselves to blame for their own destruction. Hitler cut a pathetic figure, thrashing helplessly away in anguish, bitterness, and narcissistic despair, as the Third Reich was going up in smoke.

There was more to Hitler's New Year's speech than his anti-Semitic tirade, such as his hopes about the military situation, but these were of little consequence. It was the anti-Semitism and his rant about the international conspiracy of the Jews that was impossible to ignore.[5]

Hitler decided to move his headquarters from the Wolf's Lair back to Berlin on November 20, just before the Ardennes offensive was launched. One evening when he was driven into his bunker by a bombing raid, Nicolaus von Below, his faithful adjutant, found him depressed unlike anything he had seen before. Hitler had finally recognized that the war was lost and said precisely that in this unguarded moment. He blamed the generals he had "spoiled" with decorations and honors. It was always someone else's fault. Below recalled Hitler using words he would never forget: "We will not capitulate, never. We can go down. But we will take a world with us."[6]

Although Hitler had not responded well during the latter part of the war when Goebbels tried to persuade him to speak to the people, Goebbels was surprised to learn the führer was going to do just that on January 30, 1945, the anniversary of his appointment as chancellor.

Hitler's message was consistent with what he had expressed for decades. This time, with the Soviet army beating at the gates, he again made the comparison with 1918. It was in 1919–20, he said, that National Socialism arose to fight for "defenseless Germany" against the "Jewish-international world conspiracy." Lenin would have overrun Europe at the time. But then "Jewish-Asiatic Bolshevism" was too weak. They were stopped in Poland and failed in Hungary. "Bolshevik power" could not succeed in Germany, either, "but the Jews began immediately on the systematic internal destruction of our people." Germany was supposedly saved by his National Socialist movement. Europe, he said, was suffering from a disease, namely the spread of Bolshevism. The Western Allies would not be able to stop it. The "Kremlin Jews" used different tactics here and there, "but the end is always the same."

He wanted to make German hearts stronger against the "plutocratic-Bolshevik conspiracy of the victors." There would be no surrender. His appeal was for "total fanaticism," not just of soldiers but even of women and youth. His plea was that Europe had to win against "Inner-Asia," which presumably meant "Jewish Bolshevism." In this moment of grave national danger, he clung to the ideas that had been integral to his life since the early 1920s.[7]

Although he could hardly expect Germans to arise and wipe out the millions of heavily armed troops about to enter their country, his entreaty suggests the continuity in his thinking: 1945 was a replay of 1919–20. The threat was the same, namely mythical "Jewish Bolshevism." It had to be stopped again, even in the last minute, just as in the 1920s.

By 1945 Germans were beginning to accept the inevitable. At the same time, the sources on public opinion revealed that many people were prepared to fight on. What was surprising was the "astonishingly positive reception" to Hitler's New Year's proclamation for 1945 and his confidence in victory.[8] Many people, and not just the dyed-in-the-wool Nazis, were still anxious to interpret events in the most optimistic way possible.

On February 24, Hitler issued a proclamation on the occasion of the annual celebration of the foundation day of the Nazi Party. There was little to praise now, and far more to curse and ridicule. He repeated the supposed vow he took in 1920 to fight "exploitative capitalism and human-destroying Bolshevism." As always, he portrayed "international Jews" as those who took advantage of both systems. It was in Munich in 1920 with the foundation of the Nazi Party, he said, that he saw this danger clearly, and now Germans were experiencing in the east what the "Jewish plague," what "Jewish Bolshevism," was all about. The intention was to destroy the German people with the help of "West European and American pimps," but the "devilish pact of democratic capitalism and Jewish Bolshevism" could still be beaten. If the will to victory remained steadfast in the entire German nation, there was still hope. He was sure, as he had been twenty-five years earlier, that in the end the German Reich would be victorious.[9]

As anyone could see, however, Hitler's world was disintegrating even as he spoke. His hatred of the Jews and other enemies like the Americans, British, and Soviets grew beyond bounds. He even began to show a disdain for the German people for letting him down.

Hundreds of thousands of completely innocent people would die before the end. Quite apart from noncombatant civilians, there were hundreds of thousands in German concentration camps and prisons. The end may have been approaching, but for these people the nightmare was going to get worse.

FINDING MORE CONCENTRATION CAMPS

As the Battle of the Bulge was being fought in the west, the Red Army was preparing a massive assault in the east. The attack would be launched simultaneously along a front of 560 miles (900 kilometers) from Lithuania far to the south. The threat ran from East Prussia, all the way through Poland, and on to Czechoslovakia and Hungary.[10]

Soviet bombardment began on January 12, and over the next several days the attack picked up. The Wehrmacht could have used the fire-power Hitler had withdrawn from the east and sent to the Ardennes, but even that would only have delayed the inevitable.

The rapid advance of the Soviet forces was startling. By the end of January, Konev and Zhukov were stretched along the river Oder—at one point only forty-eight miles from Berlin. The Soviets began making shocking discoveries. On January 27, a Russian soldier appeared on the grounds of the camp at Monowitz, one of the larger camps in the Auschwitz complex. A division of Soviets arrived an hour later. By the afternoon, the Red Army had found the Auschwitz main camp, as well as Birkenau. Fighting broke out with German units still there after every-one who could travel had already left, and 231 Red Army soldiers died in liberating the camp. At the time the Red Army arrived, there were only around seventy-six hundred mostly sick and infirm prisoners alive there.[11]

Yulia Pozdnyakova, a member of the Red Army, was among those assigned to help the doctors ministering to the prisoners. She recalled the stench of death and the physical evidence of how many people were murdered. She was struck by the thousands of shoes she came across in one building. She looked through the remains and papers trying to fig-ure out what had happened: "I felt somehow guilty that I was touching all these things. The ghosts of the dead were all around us. It was hard to sleep at night." When they returned to their camp late in the day, they washed and scrubbed themselves, as if they had been in hell itself.[12]

Konev himself did not bother to visit the camp, as the Americans would do of the camps they liberated. The Soviets did not publicize what they found at Auschwitz until much later. There was nothing about the camp in American newspapers until after the war.

A census of the Nazi concentration camp empire on January 14, 1945, showed 511,537 men and 202,674 women still alive.[13] There were rudi-mentary plans already worked out to evacuate all who could travel, but these "evacuations" were rightly named by anyone who survived them as "death marches." All prisoners were weak even before they began. There was little food and poor clothing, and to make matters worse, the marches took place during the depths of the winter in 1944–45.

We have no written record of when Himmler ordered the evacua-tions. There must have been centrally directed instructions because all the main concentration camps, most of their sub-camps, and even many prisons were evacuated at about the same time. The guards did not simply try to escape and leave their prisoners behind.

At Auschwitz-Birkenau they accelerated the killing until November 1944, when the "special commando" of prisoners who serviced the gas chambers and crematoriums were murdered. The camp began to be evacuated in August 1944, and through mid-January 1945 the Nazis moved out approximately sixty-five thousand, including nearly all the remaining Poles, Russians, and Czechs.

We can only partially reconstruct the reasoning behind the decision to move thousands of already weak people. A December 21, 1944, document signed by Fritz Bracht, the gauleiter and commissar of defense of the Reich in Upper Silesia, stated that all civilians, especially the "working population," had to be moved to the west in five "treks." The Bracht order suggests the aim was not to kill all prisoners but to preserve them within the German sphere of influence.[14]

The last roll call held at Auschwitz (including Birkenau) was on January 17, 1945, and almost immediately afterward fifty-eight thousand left, most of them on foot.[15] Survivors of these marches later testified that conditions were, if anything, worse than they had been in the camps. The treatment of the Jews remained terrible, but all were not shot out of hand. At Auschwitz, Jews and other prisoners unable to travel were left behind and, contrary to their own expectations, not killed.[16]

If Hitler's wishes or orders had been followed, none of these "enemies" would have survived. Himmler's views vacillated between wanting to kill them all and keeping some alive, particularly the Jews. He entertained the possibility that they and certain other nationalities might be used in negotiations for money or for essential war goods.[17]

Buchenwald's camp commandant decided on evacuation when he heard how close the Americans were. On April 8 he demanded that the camp be cleared within the hour. Well-led prisoner resistance subverted this order, which would have cost thousands of lives. On April 10 guards rounded up Russian, Polish, and Czech prisoners who had just arrived and led them away. The next day the SS took flight, and the camp's 21,400 prisoners were liberated.[18]

Hitler was enraged to learn that Buchenwald prisoners had supposedly pillaged the nearby town of Weimar. On or about April 15, he ordered yet again that no concentration camp be surrendered before it was evacuated or all prisoners liquidated.[19] A written Hitler order to this effect has not been found, but something akin to one, addressed also to Dachau and Flossenbürg, ran as follows: "Surrender is out of the question. The camp must be evacuated immediately. No prisoner may fall into enemy hands alive. The prisoners behaved brutally against the civil population of Buchenwald."[20]

These death marches were one of the most horrific aspects of the Third Reich. Some scholars have suggested that "at least" one-third of the 700,000 or so prisoners in the camps at the beginning of 1945 died as a direct result or perished later.[21] These almost certainly do not include additional tens of thousands of concentration camp prisoners, many of them Jews, who were working as forced laborers. We have no accurate statistics on the number of survivors found in the camps.

STALIN'S DETERMINATION TO BE FIRST IN BERLIN

Who would fill the void left by the Third Reich in Europe? At Yalta the Allies had agreed on the division of Germany into zones, but the more territory any of them liberated, the greater political clout they would have in the postwar world. However, the Anglo-Americans, especially General Dwight D. Eisenhower, as supreme commander, were concerned about sparing as many of their troops as possible. Such a reservation never crossed Stalin's mind.

At Yalta he acted as the conquering generalissimo and staked his claims to nearly all of Eastern Europe. Getting his hands on the spoils was another matter and, he believed, involved beating the Anglo-American forces to Berlin. By early 1945 the Americans and British were making strides, and Stalin's suspicions of the intentions of the West, which never went away, were inflamed. Would the Anglo-Americans try to take Berlin, or even worse, link up with Germans in an anti-Soviet campaign? Stalin had spoken to the troops only rarely during the war, but tried to inspire them on February 23, 1945, the anniversary of the founding of the Red Army—credited to the great Lenin. He outlined the tremendous scope of their victories, urged them on to finish the task, and claimed that since the beginning of the year, 350,000 Germans had been taken prisoner and 800,000 killed.[22]

The Western Allies had had considerable success themselves since the beginning of 1945. From the end of February to the end of March, they took 300,000 prisoners.[23] On March 23–24 the Allies crossed the Rhine in strength, and thereafter German efforts to hold the line were spotty, strenuous in some places but hardly worthy of note elsewhere.[24] The Rhine-Ruhr region had been encircled by April 1 in a pincer movement that trapped twenty-one divisions, or 320,000 troops. That was a greater loss than the Russians inflicted at Stalingrad. Attempts to break out of the "Ruhr pocket" were fruitless.[25]

To keep up morale and defend against the mythical stab in the back of 1918, the Gestapo began shooting Germans for any signs of defeatism. They hanged people in the street for a mere hint of resistance. Hitler did not need to be terrorizing his own people. Rather, at this point in the war, he required many more soldiers than he could possibly muster to fend off the Allied advance on all fronts.[26]

The Soviets engaged in shadowboxing about Berlin. General Eisenhower wanted it, but not if it was going to cost a lot of casualties. To calm Stalin's suspicions and coordinate operations, he sent him a telegram on March 28 outlining his plans. He said that after the great Anglo-American success in the Ruhr, he would aim in the direction of Erfurt-Leipzig-Dresden, south of Berlin, and also swing to the south toward Regensburg-Linz, cutting off what he felt would be the area where Hitler might make a last stand. His forces would stop at the Elbe River, forty miles short of Berlin, as agreed already with the Soviets.[27]

Eisenhower's subordinate officers—particularly Montgomery—desperately wanted to push on and craved the prize of Berlin. Churchill was furious, as he was worried that, having cleared Europe of the Nazis' tyranny, the Communists would now take their place. Eisenhower awaited Stalin's answer. The Soviet leader was pleased with the news about Berlin, not that he took it at face value.

On April 1 he disingenuously informed Eisenhower that "Berlin has lost its former strategic importance," so the Soviet Union would forsake its conquest and commit only secondary forces there. That was a lie: he was actively preparing to attack Berlin with everything he had. He falsely said the main Soviet blow was likely to come in the second half of May (when it was to come in mid-April) and that the Red Army would drive to meet up with the Western forces at Erfurt-Leipzig-Dresden, and not head toward Berlin to the north.

Stalin had grave doubts about the West and knew from his spies that the Americans were conducting negotiations with high Nazi officials in Bern, Switzerland. Indeed, in February, the SS general Karl Wolff contacted Allen Dulles of the U.S. Office of Strategic Services about the possibility of a German surrender in Italy. Wolff met Dulles on March 8 and again on March 19. Churchill saw immediately that if the Soviets got wind of these meetings—as indeed they already had—they would assume the worst. The British ambassador in Moscow, under instructions from Churchill, informed the Soviet government on March 21, but that only made things worse.[28]

FDR sent a personal note to Stalin on March 25 saying there was no thought of reaching a separate peace with Germany or ending the war short of unconditional surrender. He said the Bern talks simply opened contact with "competent German military officers for a conference to discuss details of a surrender" of Italy, but thus far no success could be reported.[29]

Stalin, already well into planning the final assault on Berlin himself, replied on March 29 and again on April 3. He said he was well informed that the Allies had concluded an agreement with the Germans whereby in return for easing the terms of an armistice, the Wehrmacht would open the front and let the Allies move forward. The accusatory tone—which was also used in exchanges with the British on the Bern negotiations—astonished Roosevelt, who could not have seen the irony of the following passage, an uncanny reflection of Stalin's own state of mind: "Finally I would say this, it would be one of the great tragedies of history if at the very moment of the victory, now within our grasp, such distrust, such lack of faith should prejudice the entire undertaking after the colossal losses of life, material and treasure involved."[30]

Stalin said the negotiations were designed to make it possible for the Allies "to advance into the heart of Germany almost without resistance." Churchill wrote to FDR on April 5 that Stalin's accusations made it imperative for Anglo-American forces to move as far to the east as possible. He ended his letter by stating they could not allow themselves to seem afraid of the Soviets and look like they could be "bullied into submission." He wanted to stand up to the insults. "I believe this is the best chance of saving the future."[31]

Stalin certainly had his eye on the future as well. On April 1 he had gathered his most senior military leaders, including Zhukov and Konev, at the Kremlin. An intelligence report, which was read to them, said the

Anglo-Americans in Bern were trying to negotiate a separate peace. Although the Allies supposedly rejected a deal with General Wolff, the Soviets still thought it possible the Germans would let the Western Allies through to Berlin. Not only Stalin but his military leaders were convinced the Anglo-Americans were capable of such duplicity.[32]

Stalin asked the Kremlin gathering provocatively: "Well, who is going to take Berlin, we or the Allies?"[33] He presented them with a strategic plan. No matter what the condition of their armies, they had to be ready to strike to reach the Elbe River, west of Berlin, within twelve to fourteen days. Zhukov and Konev were aware the Germans would fight as bitterly as the Red Army had done when its back was against the wall at Moscow. Moreover, the Soviet route to Berlin was obvious. Leaders of the Red Army knew it was being heavily fortified. Word about Soviet atrocities was already well known, and Wehrmacht soldiers would fight to the death to keep the Red Army at bay.

The Soviets would have liked to have had more time to prepare, but political, not military, considerations dictated taking the capital as quickly as possible. A three-pronged attack across an arc of 235 miles would converge on Berlin. Who would go down in history as the victor, Zhukov or Konev? At the Kremlin, Stalin dangled the plum: "Whoever breaks in first let him take Berlin." Both hungered for victory so much that they would drive on their troops, to the point of taking unnecessarily high casualties.[34]

Not only Stalin but the Red Army desired revenge and wanted to finish off the Hitlerites. They had reason enough for their passions, because when the Wehrmacht went east it took on the Nazi ethos and became in that sense Hitler's army. It "not only tolerated mass murder of a totally new quality, but also to a large extent supported it."[35] The treatment of Soviet prisoners was abominable, breaking every convention of war with apparent ease because the "Russians" were seen almost as "subhumans." An estimated 3.3 million Soviet prisoners died in captivity; many thousands were shot out of hand to avoid having to take prisoners; and still more had been brought back to Germany to be worked to death or executed by the Gestapo.[36]

Roosevelt died on April 12. In his last message to Stalin, which arrived the next day, he hoped there would be no more distrust: "I feel sure that when our armies make contact in Germany and join in a fully coordinated offensive the Nazi armies will disintegrate."[37]

The Soviet fight for Berlin, which they continued to play down, opened in full force on April 16. They threw at least 2.5 million men into the battle, with over six thousand tanks and massive artillery. Stalin called Zhukov and Konev to stoke the competition between them. The aim was to defeat the enemy by April 22, Lenin's birthday. The Soviets wanted to surround Berlin to warn off the Western Allies and to claim the mighty prize. Zhukov's forces linked up with Konev's on April 25 northwest of Potsdam, thus cutting off the city completely. Konev deferred to Zhukov, whose men took the Reichstag on April 30. When Army Commander V. I. Kuznetsov called Zhukov to report that the Red flag was atop the building Zhukov asked about the situation and was told that German troops were still fighting in the upper floors and in the cellars. They surrendered only late on May 1.[38]

It would be difficult to calculate how many Soviet soldiers had to die needlessly because of Stalin's determination and also the Red Army's ambitions. There were wasteful charges against heavily defended German positions and attacks on major hills with tanks that bogged down. The battle as a whole cost the Red Army 78,291 killed and 274,184 wounded. The exact German casualties are unknown.[39] According to the standard work on the battle for Berlin, the most conservative estimate would be that both sides lost a total of a half million lives, including perhaps 100,000 civilians.[40]

Stalin was delighted and, in his annual address on the international workers' day, heralded the victories. He was still suspicious of the West and mentioned how the Hitlerites, in their desperation, "made overtures to the Allies in order to create dissension." He denied Nazi propaganda that the Soviets would try to destroy the German people. The war criminals would be punished, reparations would have to be paid, but the war was not against the people as a whole. He promised the invading forces would not "molest" the peaceful population, but such a statement was belied by events on the ground.[41]

Soviet posters sounded the note of the horror to come at the beginning of 1945: "Red Army Soldier: You are now on German soil; the hour of revenge has struck!"[42] A January order from Zhukov went as follows: "Woe to the land of the murderers. We will get our terrible revenge for everything." A directive to the Red Army on the eve of crossing into East Prussia said that "on German soil there is only one master—the Soviet soldier, that he is both the judge and the punisher for the tor-

ments of his fathers and mothers, for the destroyed cities and villages. . . . Remember your friends are not there, there is the next of kin
of the killers and oppressors."[43]

Guidelines and orders were conveyed in many ways. More junior officers said they had to give an incentive for the soldier to "climb out of the
trench and face that machine gun once again. So now, with this order,
everything is clear: he'll get to Germany, and there everything is his—
goods, women, do what you want! Hammer away! So their grandchildren and great-grandchildren will remember and be afraid!" That did
not sound very Communistic to Lev Kopelev, one of the few Red Army
idealists to question how women and children were being treated. His
officer's answer was simple: "First let's send Germany up in smoke then
we'll go back to writing good, theoretically correct books on humanism
and internationalism. But now we must see to it that the soldier will
want to go on fighting. That's the main thing."[44]

When rape was not encouraged, it was tolerated, and at least in the
beginning of the invasion it was not punished.[45] Not only did the Red
Army conduct a campaign of rape unlike anything seen in modern
European history, but soldiers humiliated their victims in despicable
ways. Nor did they spare the women of their own allies. Stalin's reply to
a visiting delegation of Yugoslav Communists who complained of the
Red Army's rapes in their country was memorable: Could they not
understand, he asked, "if a soldier who has crossed thousands of kilometers through blood and fire and death has fun with a woman or takes
some trifle"?[46]

Women, from the youngest girls to grandmothers, were subjected to
the campaign of rape, and some were raped to death. Others were not
just raped but sexually mutilated and killed. Villages of women roped
themselves together and jumped into rivers to commit suicide to avoid
the marauding troops. Eventually Stalin tried to rein in the troops, but
their sullied reputation was already fixed. They were a poor advertise-
ment for the "radiant future" promised by Communism. According to
Alexander Werth, to the extent there was an "alarm" that made its way
to the top, the concern was more about the wanton destruction of "German property" than about the "atrocities." There was a candid admission
that the troops were burning down factories and a lot more that the Soviets wanted to take as reparations or the spoils of war. Sometimes this
booty was referred to euphemistically as "trophies," but that word con-

cealed massive suffering, humiliation, and death deliberately inflicted on the vanquished.[47]

A sense of the mentality of the Soviet forces was conveyed by Vasily Grossman, the novelist, who kept notes on the campaign with one of Zhukov's armies. He recorded his impressions on entering Berlin, but said little about the atrocities. He was struck most of all by the evident wealth of the country compared with the USSR. It was particularly in Berlin, he said, "that our soldiers really started to ask themselves why did the Germans attack us so suddenly? Why did the Germans need this terrible and unfair war? Millions of our men have now seen the rich farms in East Prussia, the highly organized agriculture, the concrete sheds for livestock, spacious rooms, carpets, wardrobes full of clothes." They saw all the paved roads and what was by comparison boundless plenty and luxury and asked themselves plaintively: "But why did they come to us? What did they want?"[48]

The answer of course was that the Germans had accepted in whole or in part Hitler's version of the need to rid the world of "Jewish Bolshevism" and to secure lebensraum in the east. He gave them his own vision of a "radiant future," a return to the Garden of Eden, racially pure and cleansed of all enemies. They followed that dream when it led down the path to hell.

HITLER'S WILL TO DESTRUCTION

Just after the opening of the attack on the Soviet Union in 1941, when Hitler was expecting a victory, he told a foreign dignitary that when or if a crisis ever arose, he would annihilate all "deadbeats." His favorite story ran like this: "If on the one hand the valuable people put their lives on the line at the front, it is criminal to spare the scoundrels. They have to be destroyed or, if not dangerous to society, barred in concentration camps from which they will never again be permitted to leave." This was the same conversation in which Hitler talked about getting rid of all the Jews.[49]

As the battlefront grew closer, Hitler inspired the use of terror. On February 15, 1945, new drumhead courts were established on his orders. These tribunals with a judge, a Nazi Party functionary, and an officer from the Wehrmacht, the Waffen-SS, or the police could try anyone thought to endanger Germany's ability or determination to fight on. The military had similar courts from January 20, 1943, and by 1945 all of them were operating inside Germany. The mentality of judges and other perpetrators became infused with viciousness, compounded by revenge seeking, bitterness, disappointment, and fear. Local dignitaries who dared issue calls to surrender were not immune. Men or women who raised the white flag or tried to resist the Wehrmacht's decision to make a last stand in one place or another were trampled into the dust. Nazi terror, hitherto reserved for the Jews and for non-Germans in the east, was turned on the German people in the last months of the war.[50]

Albert Speer recalled how Hitler often said German soldiers would have nothing to fear from the home front, because no mercy would be shown to "back-stabbers." During the last months Hitler kept emphasizing, as he had for years, that the concentration camps and all their prisoners should be blown up.[51] However, in 1945 his wishes were not immediately put into effect as they once might have been. Speer remembered an exchange he had with Hitler in mid-March about the destruction of German infrastructure in the face of the advancing enemy forces. Speer stated in a note to Hitler for a meeting on March 18: "It cannot possibly be the purpose of warfare at home to destroy so many bridges that, given the straitened means of the post-war period, it will take years to rebuild this transportation network.... Their destruction means eliminating all further possibility for the German people to survive."[52]

After the meeting broke up early the next day, Hitler met privately with Speer and reiterated: "If the war is lost, the people will be lost also. It is not necessary to worry about what the German people will need for elemental survival. On the contrary, it is best for us to destroy even these things. For the nation has proved to be the weaker, and the future belongs solely to the stronger eastern nation. In any case only those who are inferior will remain after this struggle, for the good have already been killed."[53]

Hitler then issued an order for the destruction of "all military, transport, communication, industrial, and supply installations, as well as anything else of value inside the Reich area."[54] He threatened to kill all prisoners of war. Before being forced out of France, he wanted its factories destroyed, but nothing came of that order.[55] Similarly, his wishes for the Netherlands went unheeded. He wanted to flood that country by destroying the dikes.[56] He was still capable of wreaking vengeance on sworn enemies, and many of the prominent individuals suspected of being part of the July 1944 plot were now executed. Some survived by pure luck.[57]

Across Germany in the last months of war the Nazi terror system was used against "enemies" as never before. Foreign workers were particularly vulnerable, and hundreds were shot in one locality after the next. The slightest sign of resistance was obliterated.

HITLER'S POLITICAL TESTAMENT

Hitler's final proclamation was made known on April 17 and addressed to soldiers in the east. He appealed to them to save Germany's women and children. He began: "For the last time the Jewish-Bolshevik deadly enemy, with its masses, is preparing for an attack. They attempt to destroy Germany and to eradicate our people." He said that after the old men and children were murdered, "the women and young girls will be forced to become camp whores. The remainder will be marched to Siberia." If every soldier on the eastern front did his duty in the coming weeks, "the last attack from Asia will collapse, exactly as, in spite of everything, will finally happen with the breakthrough of our enemy in the west." He struck a note of hopeless bravado: "Berlin remains German. Vienna will be German again, and Europe will never be Russian." He still wanted a "bloodbath" of the Bolsheviks and weakly hoped for a turnaround in the war.[58]

The last conversations recorded by stenographers in the bunker were between Goebbels—who had moved in with his family—and Hitler. They kept hoping the Allies would break up after all. Hitler wondered what Molotov would be looking for now, when as Soviet foreign minister he had tried to get so much earlier. The macabre dialogue was an exaggerated example of "after us, the deluge," from a script written amid an inferno.

On April 25 at his daily conference to discuss the situation, Goebbels mentioned how good it would if the battle for Berlin went well. But if it did not, he speculated, "and the führer were to find an honorable death in Berlin and Europe were to become Bolshevik, in five years at the latest the führer would be a legendary personality and National Socialism a myth. He would be hallowed by his last great action, and everything human that they criticize in him today would be swept away in one stroke." Hitler responded: "That's the decision: to save everything here and only here, and to put the last man into action—that's our duty."[59]

During the night of April 24–25 the chancellery came under heavy fire. The next day Hitler desperately grasped onto news that relief was on the way—concluding that word would spread "like wildfire" among Berliners. It was not to be. Worse still, there was news that the Americans and the Red Army had met at Torgau on the river Elbe, and instead of shooting at each other, as Hitler predicted, or at least hoped, they celebrated.[60] On April 28, Hitler and his military advisers in the bunker realized their prospects were bleak, and by midnight the next day, when the last possible chance of rescue was definitively snuffed out, Hitler had reached the end. He lived only another sixteen hours.[61]

On April 29 at around 10:30 p.m. word reached the bunker that Mussolini and his mistress, Clara Petacci, had been killed by partisans and their bodies desecrated in public. That reinforced Hitler's resolve to commit suicide so that his remains could be burned before the Soviets captured him. Around midnight Hitler married Eva Braun, his mistress of many years. Their relationship had been quietly accepted by those around him but rarely acknowledged as sexual in nature. Hitler had presented himself as standing apart from ordinary men, of being married to "Germany," as he proudly said at the height of his political success. Now, with his marriage to Eva, he was in retreat from his former life, relinquishing the fantasy of being savior of Germany, yielding to his mortality, and preparing for his own death and that of his new wife.

At 11:30 p.m. on April 29, just before his marriage, Hitler took aside Traudl Junge, his faithful and sympathetic secretary, to dictate his personal and political testaments—in effect the last documents of the "thousand-year Reich."[62] As on so many earlier occasions, his message to those who came after him was that the Jews were to blame for everything that had gone wrong. He repeated, one last time, his "prophecy," first issued on January 30, 1939, of what would happen to the Jews should "they" bring about another world war. He said, at least indirectly, that the Jews had been made "to pay for their sins," and that he had brought their punishment about, albeit, he said, "through more humane means" than the methods used against the German population. But what was still missing in his last written statement was a clear and unequivocal admission that he had started the war to realize his ambitions and had ordered millions of Jews to be killed. He ended his testament by demanding that even after his death the "leaders of the nation" observe the "laws of race" and continue the "merciless opposition" against the Jews.[63]

By 4:00 a.m. on April 30 the witnesses had signed these last documents, and Hitler had gone off to bed. He had lunch with Frau Hitler and the secretaries at 1:00 p.m. and retired to his room. After a short pause, the denizens of the bunker who were close to Hitler, including Bormann, Goebbels and his wife, Magda, and the secretaries, were led in for a final farewell. Magda Goebbels begged him to leave Berlin, but he refused and went to his rooms, where he and Eva committed suicide. Not long afterward Frau Goebbels poisoned her six children, and then she and the increasingly desperate propaganda minister took their own lives.

The entire Nazi enterprise was reduced to rubble, enveloped in chaos and human misery. Hitler and his followers had together created a catastrophe of unprecedented proportions for Germany and much of Europe. Now they reaped what they had sown. Even after Hitler's death, the tragedies continued to unfold. A calamity of monumental proportions and fierce energy had swept over the continent from the west to the far reaches of Russia, a "horrible and violent whirlwind" that was far too fierce to be stopped and would not blow itself out for a time. The victorious Soviet armies were now in Berlin and beyond, and Stalin was intent that they should put their stamp on all they could claim.

EPILOGUE

I n the course of completing this book, I spoke with a number of people along the way. Quite a few were disconcerted, sometimes also
intrigued, by my naming Lenin, along with Stalin and Hitler, as one of
the three truly vile despots of the first half of the twentieth century.
Social scientists I met, at home but especially in Europe, castigated me
for not giving Lenin enough credit for his "good intentions." A colleague
in the United States pleaded, "Of course, Lenin made a few mistakes."
Not everyone reacted so defensively to my portrayal of Lenin, however.
Some confided that all along they had regretted the tendency of many
scholars to place Lenin above history and shield him from the criticism
he deserves. I submit that we have to avoid slipping into the role of apol-
ogist for Soviet leaders, including, and in some respects above all, Lenin,
a heartless and ambitious individual who was self-righteous in claiming
to know what was good for "humanity," brutal in his attempt to subject
his own people to radical social transformation, and convinced he held
the key to the eventual overthrow of global capitalism and the establishment of world Communism.

This book is an attempt to record the evils perpetrated by both Soviet
Communism and German Nazism and to figure out how it came about

that, separately and together, the two systems brought such misery and destruction to the world.

As I have explained, the ideological battle lines between Soviet Communism and German Nazism had their origins in the First World War. We can trace them to the collapse of the old regime in Russia, when it became possible for a fringe group of radicals to get control of the state apparatus. Lenin's prescience was to recognize more than anyone that the new provisional government of early 1917 had made a mistake in continuing the war and it would inevitably fall. He saw that the reins of power would soon be there for the taking, and by October he had convinced his more timid comrades that they should grasp them. Maxim Gorky, that shrewd observer of his time, was aghast at the sheer recklessness of the Bolshevik seizure of power. He wrote, barely two weeks into the revolution, that the Leninists imagined themselves to be the "Napoleons of socialism." He sincerely believed they would destroy what was left of Russia, and called forth a chilling image: "The Russian people will pay for this with lakes of blood."[1]

Lenin introduced Soviet Communism, complete with new secret police and concentration camps. He was responsible for suppressing all liberal freedoms and for ridding the country of a Constituent Assembly that might have led toward democracy. In January 1918 it was he who demanded the assembly be shut, and when there were protests, he ordered demonstrators shot down. The seals put on the doors of the Duma were not broken until the 1990s, when long-suffering citizens finally had a chance to determine their own fate again.

Once in power, Lenin enthusiastically hunted down anyone who did not fit in or who opposed the new regime, and he introduced the Communist Party purges that periodically called forth nationwide witch hunts. Whole classes came to be deemed superfluous, be they nobles, members of the bourgeoisie, or "rich" peasants. Holding up the terrorists of earlier European revolutions as their models, Lenin and his followers shed blood with such complete abandon that they made their heroes look restrained and hesitant by comparison. Stalin took his cue from his mentor and was later only too delighted by the thought that he walked in the footsteps of Ivan the Terrible, by reputation the most ruthless of the tsars.

The Soviet Union adopted the ideological mask of collective leadership, all in the name of the proletariat and peasants, but the political structure put in place by Lenin was especially susceptible to being manipulated by shrewd operators like himself and his successor. Lenin did not become dictator simply by taking on the mantle of chairman of Sovnarkom (in effect the premier). Rather, he made his will prevail by his control of the great Marxist texts and perhaps above all by his ferocity. These qualities and his brilliance added up to a certain kind of charisma that gave him a hold on his comrades and on large sections of the country.

After Lenin's death, Stalin emerged triumphant. A fanatical Leninist before any of his rivals, he had been elevated from obscurity by the great man himself, who saw to it that the "wonderful Georgian" would belong to the uppermost ranks of the Bolshevik Party and Soviet state. Later on, Lenin had a falling-out with Stalin but grudgingly admitted that, on balance, his protégé had fewer marks against him than the others.

Stalin was too cunning to claim he was Lenin's successor, even as he insinuated himself into that very spot. For example, he avoided taking over Lenin's place as chairman of Sovnarkom, but he ensured it went to a relative nobody, Aleksei Rykov, and in 1930 he passed it on to Molotov. Stalin decided the situation was threatening enough in May 1941 that he took the job himself. He, like Lenin, was never the head of state—the chairman of the Central Executive Committee, or what might be called the president.

By the mid-1920s Stalin was dictator in everything but name, and Trotsky and other rivals were removed from the Politburo and soon dumped from the Party. But it would have been out of keeping with the myths of Communist ideology to proclaim that he had won. By custom he did not sit at the head of the table, and it was in keeping with the image of "collegial" leadership that he would continue to argue his points, to make "suggestions," and like Lenin also to be formally challenged by the members of the ruling circle. These rituals, like the constitution, merely veiled his dictatorship. On Stalin's fiftieth birthday in 1929 he was widely applauded and praised, but he still craved the one thing he lacked, namely the adoration and respect showered on Lenin, not just by members of the Party, but by many others as well. He had secured his position as dictator by making himself into the keeper of Lenin's memory, by becoming the most devoted Leninist of all. It took some time before he could present himself as sufficiently distinct from Lenin and thus also as one to be held in awe on his own account.

Lenin and Stalin successively headed a vanguard Party and presided over a similarly inclined dictatorship. They made decisions from on high, brushed obstacles aside, and all but ignored public opinion. Those who deviated from the Party line were defined as enemies or wreckers. While many people, above all in the countryside, hated everything Communism stood for, there were plenty of idealists whose deepest wish was to follow Lenin and Stalin.

The contrasts with Hitler's dictatorship, in style and substance, were considerable. The führer of the Nazi Party, with his explicit mission to launch a simultaneous assault on Jews and Bolsheviks, made it clear from the early 1920s that his plan was to establish a dictatorship. He was appointed head of government in 1933, and after President Hindenburg's death the next year was acclaimed also head of state. It was not just these positions that elevated Hitler, but the charismatic bond that quickly emerged with the German people. He ostentatiously put his apparently undisputed power and leadership on display for all to see and loved public reviews, fanfare, parades, spectacle, and speeches before the multitudes. He soaked up the adulation and scorned Stalin as a mere secretary and pencil pusher.

Hitler sought an authoritarian regime backed by the "German" people, what I have referred to as a consensus dictatorship. He flattered Germans with the idea of establishing their own "community of the people" and aimed terror primarily against social outsiders, individuals who belonged to specified groups, the Jews, Communists, criminals, Gypsies, or homosexuals. Many good citizens embraced or at least accepted such persecutions as part of the bargain for the "accomplishments" of the new system.[2]

The two regimes were distinguished by their ideologies. As the founder of Communism, Lenin developed plans for the conquest of power based on his vanguard interpretation of Marxist teachings. Stalin in his turn became the chief proponent of Leninism, the "provisional dictatorship of the proletariat and the peasantry," which in fact was the forced communization of Soviet society. It was Stalin who determined the Party "line," that is, the interpretation of what needed to be done and what was constituted by Leninism-Marxism at any given moment. The ideas had enormous appeal among the Party faithful because of the promises they made and the vistas of hope they offered. That hundreds of thousands of people, and ultimately millions, would have to be sacrificed was quietly and conveniently ignored by the idealists and the utopians.

Hitler blended an ideology out of nationalism, anti-Semitism, and anti-Bolshevism, with a desire for lebensraum in the east. Whereas Lenin wanted to bring the Soviet "paradise" to the world, the Nazi utopia was designed for Germans only. In the future, certain select Western Europeans might be allowed—like the Norwegians, Danes, Dutch, and a few others—but most would be excluded.

Together with many others in Germany, Hitler developed a particularly radical phobia about the Jews in the shadow of the First World War. In 1919 and the years that followed, he raged against what he called "Jewish Bolshevism" and insisted that the Jews had taken over Russia and threatened Germany and the West.

Although revolutions on the Soviet model failed in postwar Germany, the repeated efforts to bring them about spread anxiety. Here was a nation of property owners, and for the Reds to threaten them in 1919 or again in 1923 was to drive the great majority to the right and into the arms of newly emerging parties like the Nazis.

Hitler became the first in a long line of twentieth-century dictators who sought popularity by going after the Communists or other revolutionaries and crusading in the name of law and order. These campaigns, plus the obvious success at beating unemployment and the first great victories in foreign affairs, turned the down-and-out straggler into a beloved führer.

Both dictatorships used terror, but in somewhat contrasting ways. The Communist variety was inflicted overwhelmingly against patently innocent people. Anyone in the Soviet Union could run afoul of the terror, and in that sense it was completely arbitrary. The means corrupted and destroyed the ends. How can we sum up all the suffering or even the fatalities resulting from the continuous Communist terror from 1917 to Stalin's death? We would have to count all the deliberate murders in the civil war, the famines, and collectivization. Then we would have to add those killed in the Great Terror and during the wartime ethnic cleansing, the Red Army soldiers executed by their own on various grounds, and all those who died or were killed in the Gulag.

Aleksandr Solzhenitsyn suggested that Soviet authorities used "internal repression" from the October Revolution up to 1959 to kill an estimated sixty-six million. He admits the figure is tentative and will need adjusting by future research.[3] He had been a "true believer" himself and for a time held on to his faith in Communism even in the Gulag. His book points an accusing finger at anyone today, in his own country or anywhere else, who might suggest there were "productive" aspects to Soviet terror.

More recent estimations of the Soviet-on-Soviet killing have been more "modest" and range between ten and twenty million. In the penal system alone, according to one scholar, 2,749,163 died between 1929 and 1953. These numbers are still incomplete, not only because they do not cover every year since 1917 but also because they exclude labor colonies completely.[4] The total makes no mention of the deaths in transit or the hundreds of thousands executed by quota during the Great Terror or done to death during the wartime ethnic cleansings and in countless other ways.

Anne Applebaum is right to insist that the statistics "can never fully describe what happened."[5] They do suggest, however, the massive scope of the repression and the killing.

A haunting sense of what happened is conveyed in remarkably few words by David Remnick, in the late 1980s a reporter for the *Washington Post*. He accompanied Aleksandr Milchakov of Memorial—a group trying to rescue the murdered victims from oblivion—to see the mass graves around Moscow. He heard from witnesses how at the Donskoi Monastery in the 1930s, the furnaces of the crematoriums worked all night to get rid of the executed bodies delivered there. Fine ash went up the chimneys and covered the domes of nearby churches, the roofs of houses, and the fresh snow. Great ditches were filled with the remnants scraped from the cooling incinerators. Everyone in the area knew what was going on and adjusted to it. No one knows how many such sites there were across the great land.[6]

The murderousness of Hitler's regime came in its final years. Nazi terror was used mainly during the war and then outside the borders of the "old" Reich. In Hitler's first six years in power, state-sponsored killing was highest in 1933, when in camps like Dachau there were fifty or fewer deaths and in most others there were fewer than ten. A maximum of "several hundred" were killed in all the early camps.[7]

The terror of these early years was real enough, but it was primarily aimed against Jews, specific social outsiders like criminals, and certain political opponents, above all the Communists. As a recent study puts it, apart from those groups "the average German's chances of avoiding secret-police harassment were high."[8] Soviet terror was an entirely other matter. In Germany it is true that thousands suffered dreadfully in the first camps, most of them Communists, but they were usually released after a short and nightmarish stay. The aim was not to terrorize the population as a whole. Even the left-wing Socialists were not particularly unhappy at the fate of the Communists. Most people wanted an end to the violence and uproar in the streets, and to have middle-class values restored. In that respect the silent majority was in tune with the regime from the outset. Indeed, as Ian Kershaw has rightly concluded, because the first waves of Nazi terror were aimed primarily at Bolshevism, "the violence and repression were widely popular. The 'emergency decree' that took away all personal liberties and established the platform for dictatorship was warmly welcomed."[9]

Hitler was a strong advocate of the death penalty and talked about it often. However, until 1939, there was only one year in which the regular courts sentenced more than 100 to capital punishment, and not all of these were carried out. The People's Court used the death penalty even less in the same period. Between 1934 and 1939 an average of 18 per year were sentenced to die, but many of these were commuted. Over the course of the Third Reich all civil courts sentenced around 16,500 people to death, and mainly during the war. Most of the defendants were non-Germans, and as many as one-quarter of the sentences were commuted. This is by no means the full story of "legalized" terror, for during the war—particularly in its last phase—many people were killed without trial.[10]

The war changed everything, starting in Poland in 1939, when the terror went wild. Operation Barbarossa, the attack on the Soviet Union in June 1941, spread the horror and began the bloodiest chapter in the age of social catastrophe. This war became the greatest killer of all time and so unprecedented in its many appalling faces that it raised questions about the very meaning and future of Western civilization.

The Soviet people endured by far the greatest number of casualties. In 1990, after years of repressing the truth, General Mikhail A. Moiseyev, chief of the Soviet General Staff, said that 8,668,148 men and women were lost in the war. The figure includes those killed, missing in action, prisoners who did not return, accidental deaths, suicides, and so on. General G. F. Krivosheyev, who also studied this matter, agreed on the fatalities and also on the "medical casualties," which he put at 18,344,148. The latter number meant that some wounded were counted more than once. These figures for the USSR alone are roughly equal to the entire military losses in the First World War.[11]

The experts also agree that as in Europe as a whole, civilian deaths in the Second World War were even greater than the military losses. One of the lowest estimates for the USSR is that 16.9 million were killed. That would bring the total losses in that country to a staggering 25.5 million, well over 10 percent of the population in 1939.

Germany's losses were far worse than those it suffered in the First World War. Combined with Austria, which was incorporated into the Reich in 1938, the total deaths by 1945 had reached 7.2 million, of which 3.2 million were civilians. These fatalities represented close to 10 percent of the 1939 population.[12]

European Russia was laid to waste either during the invasion or while the Nazis were in retreat, when the Wehrmacht exercised its own scorched-earth policy. Metropolitan areas like Leningrad, Stalingrad, Kiev, and many other cities were reduced to ruins. Countless villages and towns were destroyed along with factories, bridges, and tens of thousands of miles of railway. The efforts of whole generations were wiped out without a second thought.

Across Europe an estimated 36.5 million were killed.[13] We will never know the exact number. Hitler and his regime have to bear the burden of responsibility for this turn of events.[14]

It is chilling to be reminded of the inhumanity surfacing in the argument that the terror unleashed by Lenin and Stalin, through forced collectivization and industrialization, was vindicated by the survival of the USSR in the Second World War. Yet many made that argument and were apparently even cheered by the view that the Soviets had ultimately prepared the country well for the supposed inevitable clash with the West. Surely a more wasteful, immoral, and inhumane approach cannot possibly be imagined than the one adopted by Soviet leaders. No rulers could be more profligate with the lives of their own citizens. On a whim Stalin and his cronies had their own people enslaved and built miles of railroad that were unneeded and went unused; had canals hacked out of granite that proved to be too shallow and were practically useless; and ordered glamour projects to reflect their own glory that would have made the pharaohs blush. And on top of all that Soviet leaders left their country hopelessly vulnerable to war and ignored the best evidence provided by their own spies. When the attack came, all kinds of improvisations had to be made with the enemy already at the gates.

The crime that sets the Third Reich apart was the mass murder of the Jews. The Holocaust stands alone. The Soviet Union never had factories designed to produce nothing but mass death, even if they managed to kill millions just the same.

The mass murder in the Nazi camps constructed expressly to kill the Jews was without precedent. Around 2 million were gassed with carbon monoxide in Chelmo, Belzec, Sobibor, and Treblinka. Zyklon B gas killed more than a million in Auschwitz-Birkenau and tens of thousands in Majdanek. If we include those shot outside camps or persecuted to death in the ghettos and elsewhere, then the number rises to at least 5.3 million. The great majority of the Jewish victims came from Poland, the USSR, Romania, and Hungary. Practically everywhere Jews lived was affected, whether in distant Norway and Greece or the Netherlands, Belgium, and France.[15]

The "regular" camps spread like a cancer during the war, when most of the Germans in them, as we saw, were made up of Communists and groups like the "antisocial elements." The percentage of Germans began to fall throughout the war until 1945, when they made up between 5 and 10 percent of the total. The camp population itself rose steadily during this period, despite shockingly high mortality rates, but it was internationalized and drew victims from across Europe. Between 795,889 and 955,215 prisoners died in these hellholes—figures that do not include the Jews who were gassed or murdered in other ways. Every nation in Europe was represented among those who died, most coming from Eastern Europe. As dreadful as this death toll is, it is likely an underestimation. The number includes around 100,000 who perished during the "evacuations" of all the camps at the end of the war. Other scholars put the number twice as high.[16]

Hitler's ideology, along with his geopolitical plans, dictated that most of those killed by the Nazis were targeted in the name of stamping out "Jewish Bolshevism." When they launched their full-scale genocide in 1941–42, it was enough merely to have been born a Jew, in accordance with Nazi definitions of Jewishness, for someone to be sentenced to die in the most wretched way possible. The Nazis were also merciless with

Red Army prisoners, allowing millions to die in captivity. No one will ever know how many Red Army soldiers were shot out of hand rather than made captive.

T he Nazis were stopped and Berlin was in flames, but at the price of a reinvigorated Soviet Union. Like Lenin before him, Stalin wanted to capitalize on the situation brought on by war. In April 1945 he was candid with a visiting delegation led by Marshal Tito, the head of the Communist resistance in Yugoslavia: "This war is not as in the past; whoever occupies a territory also imposes on it his own social system. Everyone imposes his own system as far as his army can reach. It cannot be otherwise."

He was already thinking ahead: "We shall recover in fifteen or twenty years, and then we'll have another go at it." That presumably meant an attempt to conquer the rest of Europe. Stalin admitted he had taken half and coveted the rest. These aims foreshadowed the Cold War that was to last almost a half century.[17]

Milovan Djilas, who accompanied Tito on a visit with Stalin and saw him alone as well, noted how the "cult of personality" grew exponentially and turned him into a deity. Djilas identified the mercilessly buoyant Stalin and the mood of the time at war's end:

His country was in ruins, hungry, exhausted. But his armies and marshals, heavy with fat and medals and drunk with vodka and victory, had already trampled half of Europe under foot, and he was convinced they would trample over the other half in the next round. He knew he was one of the cruelest, most despotic personalities in human history. But this did not worry him one bit, for he was convinced that he was executing the judgment of history. His conscience was troubled by nothing, despite the millions who had been destroyed in his name and by his order, despite the thousands of his closest collaborators whom he had murdered as traitors because they doubted that he was leading the country and people into happiness, equality, and liberty. . . .

Now he was the victor in the greatest war of his nation and in history. His power, absolute over a sixth of the globe, was spreading farther without surcease. This convinced him that his society contained no contradictions and that it exhibited superiority to other societies in every way.[18]

Stalin was infuriated to learn on May 7 that the Germans had just agreed to unconditional surrender, not in Berlin in the conspicuous presence of the Soviets, but rather in the small French city of Rheims. He called Zhukov and ordered him to Berlin for the ceremony the next day to represent the Supreme Command of the Soviet forces, along with the appointed leaders of the Supreme Command of the Allied forces. The documents were finally signed early in the morning on May 9, 1945. It would be that day the USSR celebrated, not May 8—considered V-E day in much of the rest of the world.[19]

Stalin's announcement of victory from Moscow was not the kind that touched the hearts of the people, though they were relieved and enraptured to hear it. Many hoped they would be rewarded with greater freedoms, but Stalin made no such promises. Instead, he spoke about how the independence of the country had been secured.[20]

The agony persisted for millions, particularly the Soviet POWs and those men, women, and children who had been picked up and deported (often against their will) to work as slaves in the Third Reich. Between nine and ten million endured that fate at the hands of the Nazis, and barely half of them were alive at the end of the war. At the Yalta Conference in February 1945, the Americans and British agreed to repatriate "liberated prisoners of war and civilians." In making this decision, the Western Allies were concerned about the safe return of their own nationals found in camps by the Red Army, but their agreement had fateful consequences for Soviet citizens then in the West.

From Stalin's point of view all who survived Nazi captivity were under suspicion. Special NKVD filtration camps went over the cases of 1.8 million military personnel and the 3.6 million civilians who returned to the Soviet Union. The investigations took years. Some people were shot straightaway, while others were given long prison terms. One former POW recalled how they were gathered for meetings on their return where a political officer "told us that we had committed a grave offense before the motherland and our people, and proposed that we sign on voluntarily for five years' construction work in the Urals as the only way to atone for our guilt."[21] Soviet citizens who had fought for Hitler and ended up in the distant United States had to be returned. They took all kinds of desperate measures to resist, but it was to no avail.

All returnees were given a "temporary certificate," which was a black mark on their record they could never erase. Soviet leaders harbored doubts and suspicions about their own partisans who had fought courageously behind the German lines on Stalin's explicit instructions. Questions were even raised about members of the Red Army who had seen what life was like abroad. Konstantin Simonov wrote how "the contrast between living standards in Europe and among us, which millions of fighting people encountered, was a moral and psychological blow that was not so easy for our people to bear despite the fact they were the victors in the war."[22] Had the soldiers seen too much? Could they ever be trusted again?

On June 24 an emotional victory parade took place in Moscow. Stalin decided he was physically unable to mount horseback for the salute and so delegated the task to Marshal Zhukov. On the appointed day at 10:00 a.m. the war hero rode into Red Square on a white horse, where he met Marshal Rokossovsky and they reviewed the troops. After Zhukov's brief speech, the music picked up, and then, to the accompaniment of a long drumroll, two hundred veterans carrying the banners of two hundred defeated German armies stepped forward and flung these tokens of victory in the dust before Lenin's mausoleum. Looking at the newsreels, one gets an idea of the surging emotions, the grief, the elation, and the hopes for the future. The ceremony should have been enough to satisfy Stalin's pride as he stood atop Lenin's tomb, for he was held in such esteem at that moment that he might have been assured a place in the hearts of the people forever. It was not to be.

On the eve of the Potsdam Conference in the summer of 1945, Stalin let himself be made a generalissimo to be set above mere marshals. Within a year, Zhukov's power was whittled down, and he was sent off to Odessa and obscurity. Stalin felt threatened by the war hero and by the adulation heaped on the armed forces. In 1947, Victory Day was turned into a regular working day (to be reinstated later); veterans' associations were barred (until 1956); and the generals were strongly discouraged from writing their memoirs.

These decisions might have been related to Stalin's concerns about sharing the limelight, but the causes of the neglect of the war wounded need a different explanation. Many such people were reduced to begging in the streets until a campaign in 1947, reminiscent of the 1930s, sent them off to "special colonies." One writer concludes that "having won a great war, the nomenklatura ruling class was digging in and constructing new pyramids of patron-client dependency. The habit of classifying, labeling, commanding, threatening, punishing, and granting or withholding benefits helped them to consolidate their dominance."[23] A sign that "normalcy" was going to return was that women, who had played an important role in the war and not merely on the home front but in uniform, were not permitted to march in the victory parade.

Although tired and aging, Stalin reasserted his power inside the ruling elite and stripped colleagues of any independence they might have acquired during the war. In effect he restored the "leadership system that he had created in the wake of the Great Terror."[24] He would brook no rivals, and, like Lenin before him, he tried to stave off any thoughts of a successor—hence the need to demote Zhukov, who was sometimes mentioned as a possible heir. He had other candidates humiliated and sometimes pushed aside.

The mills of the Gulag kept on grinding. The number of prisoners in labor camps and colonies rose almost continuously from 1941 until Stalin's death in 1953, when there were 2.4 million people in the system.[25]

At the same time Stalin was zealous enough to impose Soviet-style Communism in every country of Europe liberated by the Red Army. If Soviet military and economic power in 1945 was about what it had been in 1939, the great difference was that for the first time in Russian history, there were no major enemies on the borders. Stalin had made his intentions perfectly clear to Churchill and Roosevelt, and he set up regimes like his own when the Red Army toppled collaborationist governments or crushed resistance movements as it marched west. The one exception was Yugoslavia, where Tito and his Party not only liberated their country mostly by themselves but wanted to impose their own brand of Communism. They were expelled from the new Communist International in 1948. There were civil wars involving Communists and their opponents in other parts of Europe, most notably in Greece and Ukraine, which represented further ripple effects of the war.

Spreading Communism to the West had been an integral part of the Bolsheviks' ideology, and Stalin intended to make good on it. A ring of suitably "cleansed" states was established around the western Soviet border. They endured, complete with secret police and terror, for almost a half century. Communism undoubtedly held back the development of these nations for two full generations. They are still trying to recover.

At Yalta, FDR and Churchill were willing to accept that the Germans living in the east would be pushed out as Stalin desired. Churchill admitted that people in England were shocked at the idea that so many would be moved against their will.[26] It turned out that something on the order of nine million Germans were hounded out of the USSR, Poland, Romania, Hungary, Czechoslovakia, and elsewhere in the east. FDR did not live to see victory and what happened, for he passed away on April 12. President Harry Truman was instinctively distrustful of Stalin, and when he met him at the Potsdam Conference (July 17 to August 2, 1945) expressed concerns about "population transfers." Stalin disingenuously said he could do nothing about them and that anyway the Germans had already left.

Truman wanted the USSR to enter the war against Japan, and he told Stalin offhandedly at the end of another contentious session at Potsdam that he "had a new weapon of unusual destructive force." He recalled that all Stalin said was that "he was glad to hear it and hoped we would make 'good use of it against the Japanese.' " At the time many in the room focused on Stalin's expression to see if they could read his mind. He was inscrutable, but he was every bit as informed about the atomic bomb as Truman, thanks to Klaus Fuchs, a Soviet spy at Los Alamos. Stalin's view of the sudden announcement, echoed by Zhukov, who was there, though not an official member of the delegation, was that the U.S. president was trying to intimidate the USSR and assert himself "from a position of strength." The ideological clash between the two new superpowers was on, and it would rage across the globe for the next half century, a creature born during the age of catastrophe.[27]

Truman confided to his diary that he was troubled about the discovery of "the most terrible bomb in the history of the world." He wondered whether it might be "the fire of destruction" mentioned in the Bible. He told himself it would be used only against the Japanese military and not against civilians, but he knew better. His consolation was that "it is certainly a good thing for the world that Hitler's crowd or Stalin's did not discover this atomic bomb."[28]

As the meetings went ahead at Potsdam, what happened on the ground was another atrocious chapter in the history of ethnic cleansing. This time mainly the Germans would suffer. They were pillaged, plundered, and the women raped, and ethnic Germans were terrorized into leaving for the West. Tens of thousands were butchered in the former Sudetenland along the western Czech border. In Poland it was worse, and a recent account concludes that as many as a half million were killed in the "cleansing" there.[29]

One of the saddest developments in the immediate postwar period was the rise of yet another series of anti-Semitic attacks. In Poland, 90 percent of the prewar Jewish population had been murdered during the Holocaust. The survivors who returned to their homes after the war found not sympathy but hostility. Some Poles had gained materially at the expense of the Jews, and they feared claims by survivors. The new authorities in Poland, taking their anti-Semitic cues from Stalin, were intent on breaking the Nazi myths about the links between the Jews and Communism.[30]

Stalin's turn to anti-Semitism was out of character with his early life and career and a complete contradiction of what Marxists had said about the Jewish question for almost a century. Jews had always been welcomed into the Bolshevik Party, and, as we have seen, many leaders of the Soviet regime were from Jewish backgrounds, even if they themselves rejected all religion. Stalin's attitude grew hostile to the Jews during the war in lockstep with the growth of his new Russian nationalism, which became more pronounced after the end of hostilities. Although he was the first to recognize Israel in 1948, he did so because he thought it could be turned into a Soviet outpost. When that failed and the new country looked instead to America, the ideological enemy, he became a staunch anti-Zionist.

Recently revealed documents show that just before his death, Stalin seemed to be preparing a major action against the Jews in the Soviet Union. This development began in 1948, when one of his colleagues in the Politburo, Andrei Zhdanov, suffered a heart attack and other problems in June and was hospitalized. In July Zhdanov had what was likely another heart attack, and Stalin had his own physician investigate. The patient held on, but, perhaps because he had been misdiagnosed, suffered another attack and died on August 31. A year later Georgi Dimitrov, an old colleague, a former head of the Communist International, and then premier of Bulgaria, died suddenly as well. He was being treated by the same doctor.

Thus began the *dyelo vrachey* (case of the doctors). What we had here was not a Jewish "doctors' plot" against the Soviet Union, as was propagated by the regime, but the leader's attempt to root out the Jews in the medical profession. In addition, thousands lost their jobs in the government, poets were put on trial, and it is not hard to conclude that Stalin intended to cut a wide swath through the Jewish population in the country.[31]

On January 13, 1953, *Pravda* published an account of the "vast Jewish conspiracy," after which rumors abounded that on a particular day soon, all would be "voluntarily" deported. Eleanor Roosevelt appealed to President Eisenhower to do something to help the Jews in the USSR, and that was enough for Stalin the same day to break off all relations with Israel.

The net was thrown wider still when German, Austrian, and other foreign "criminals" were arrested in Soviet zones in the West and returned to the USSR for trial and punishment. Instructions were issued for the creation of four new concentration camps in the east where prisoners would be separated from the rest of the Gulag. Rumor had it that these camps were for Jews, and construction began only three weeks before Stalin died. Then the matter was shelved, and we are left to speculate what might have happened, had he lived longer.[32]

The age of social catastrophe contained forces of such destructive power that even Stalin's death on March 5, 1953, could not bring the era to a close. The shock waves and eruptions, almost like gigantic earthquakes, could be felt as far away as South and Central America and eventually all over Asia, particularly in China, Korea, Vietnam, and Cambodia. Centuries of Asian civilization were threatened or rooted out, and new Communist regimes were formed at the cost of immeasurable suffering. As in many parts of Eastern Europe, the scars left on the land and on the people can be seen to this day.

NOTES

ABBREVIATIONS IN NOTES

AHR	*American Historical Review*
BAB	Bundesarchiv Berlin
DGFP	*Documents on German Foreign Policy, 1918–1945, Series D* (Washington, D.C.)
DRZW	*Das Deutsche Reich und der Zweite Weltkrieg* (Stuttgart, 1979ff.)
EAS	*Europe-Asia Studies*
Hitler Aufzeichnungen	*Hitler: Sämtliche Aufzeichnungen, 1905–1924,* ed. Eberhard Jäckel, with Axel Kuhn (Stuttgart, 1980), collected writings
Hitler: Reden, Schriften	*Hitler: Reden, Schriften, Anordnungen, 1925–1933* (Munich, 1992ff.); collected speeches, writings, and directives
Hitler: Reden und Proklamationen	*Hitler: Reden und Proklamationen, 1932–1945,* ed. Max Domarus (Leonberg, 1973); collected speeches and proclamations
HP	Harvard Project on the Soviet Social System, in Harvard's Russian Research Center
IMT	*Trials of the Major War Criminals Before the International Military Tribunal* (German ed.)
KP	*Komsomol'skaya pravda;* Communist Youth newspaper
KTB	*Kriegstagebuch des Oberkommandos der*

	Wehrmacht (Frankfurt am Main, 1965ff.); war diary, High Command of the German Armed Forces
Lenin, *Polnoe sobranie sochinenii*	V. I. Lenin, *Polnoe sobranie sochineniia* (Moscow, 1959ff.); the complete collected works in Russian
McNeal, *Stalin sochineniia*	Robert H. McNeal, ed., *Stalin sochineniia* (Stanford, 1967ff.); these volumes continue the series of Stalin's works (vols. 1–13) with 3 additional vols. They are in Russian and part of Stalin's complete collected works
Meldungen aus dem Reich	Regular SD reports on public opinion from across Germany
1941 god	*1941 god: Dokument,* ed., A. N. Yakovlev (Moscow, 1998)
Noakes and Pridham	Jeremy Noakes and Geoffrey Pridham, eds., *Documents on Nazism* (Exeter, 1974ff.)
NYT	*New York Times*
RGBL	*Reichsgesetzblatt;* official German gazette
SDFP	*Soviet Documents on Foreign Policy,* ed. Jane Degras (New York 1978)
Stalin, *Sochineniia*	J. V. Stalin, *Sochineniia* (Moscow, 1952ff.); the complete collected works in Russian
VB	*Völkischer Beobachter;* main Nazi newspaper

INTRODUCTION

1. See Raymond Aron, *The Century of Total War* (Boston, 1954), 13–14.
2. Paul Kennedy, *The Rise and Fall of the Great Powers: Economic Change and Military Conflict from 1500 to 2000* (New York, 1987), 278.
3. Robert Wohl, *The Generation of 1914* (Cambridge, Mass., 1979), 217.
4. Anna Petrovna Ostroumova-Lebedeva, March 8, 1942, diary entry, reprinted in Cynthia Simmons and Nina Perlina, eds., *Writing the Siege of Leningrad: Women's Diaries, Memoirs, and Documentary Prose* (Pittsburgh, 2002), 31.
5. See Tony Judt, *Postwar: A History of Europe Since 1945* (New York, 2005), 35.
6. See Alan Bullock, *Hitler and Stalin: Parallel Lives* (Toronto, 1991); and

Richard Overy, *The Dictators: Hitler's Germany and Stalin's Russia* (New York, 2004).

7. See, for example, his remarks at the third congress of the RSDLP in London (April 1905), in Lenin, *Polnoe sobranie sochinenii*, vol. 10, 126–29.

8. Stalin, *Sochineniia*, vol. 1, 193–95, articles of Nov. 20, 1905; 206–13, March 8, 1906.

9. *Novaya zhizn*, Nov. 10, 1917, reprinted in Maxim Gorky, *Untimely Thoughts: Essays on Revolution, Culture, and the Bolsheviks, 1917–1918* (New Haven, Conn., 1995), 89.

10. Lenin, *Polnoe sobranie sochinenii*, vol. 45, 343–48, his "last testament."

11. Speech reprinted in Strobe Talbott, ed., *Khrushchev Remembers* (Boston, 1970), 571.

12. See Richard Pipes, ed., *The Unknown Lenin: From the Secret Archive* (New Haven, Conn., 1996).

13. Eric J. Hobsbawm, a prominent historian, frankly said that if the Communists had produced the promised "radiant tomorrow," then the violent deaths of fifteen or twenty million people in the Soviet Union would have been "justified." See Michael Ignatieff's famous interview with him in the *Times Literary Supplement*, Oct. 28, 1994, 16.

14. Adolf Hitler, "Warum sind wir Antisemiten?" in *Hitler Aufzeichnungen*, 184–204.

15. See his "Positiver Antisemitismus der Bayerischen Volkspartei," Nov. 2, 1922, in *Hitler Aufzeichnungen*, 717–21.

16. For important aspects of the controversy, see esp. François Furet and Ernst Nolte, *Fascism and Communism* (Lincoln, Neb., 2001). Original material from the bitter exchanges in the 1980s can be found in *"Historikerstreit." Die Dokumentation der Kontroverse um die Einzigartigkeit der nationalsozialistischen Judenvernichtung* (Munich, 1987). For a recent perspective see the remarks by four historians in *German History* (2006), 587–607.

17. See the interesting essays, which all but exclude Lenin, in the collections of Henry Rousso, ed., *Stalinism and Nazism: History and Memory Compared* (Lincoln, Neb., 2004); and Ian Kershaw and Moshe Lewin, eds., *Stalinism and Nazism: Dictatorships in Comparison* (Cambridge, U.K., 1997).

18. Charles S. Maier, *The Unmasterable Past: History, Holocaust, and German National Identity* (Cambridge, Mass., 1988), 71–84.

19. Richard Overy, foreword to Henrik Eberle and Matthias Uhl, eds., *The Hitler Book: The Secret Dossier Prepared for Stalin from the Interrogations of Hitler's Personal Aides* (New York, 2005), xi.

20. See Hitler's comments to Himmler in Werner Jochmann, ed., *Monologe im Führerhauptquartier, 1941–1944* (Hamburg, 1980), 82.

21. See the highly instructive contrasts drawn by Stefan Plaggenborg, "Stalinismus als Gewaltgeschichte," in Stefan Plaggenborg, ed., *Stalinismus: Neue Forschungen und Komplexe* (Berlin, 1998), 71–112.

22. Robert Gellately, *Backing Hitler: Consent and Coercion in Nazi Germany*

(Oxford, 2001). For a useful review, see Volker Ulrich, "Die Konsensdik-tatur," *Die Zeit*, March 2002; also Hans-Ulrich Wehler, *Deutsche Gesellschaftsgeschichte*, vol. 4, *1914–1949* (Munich, 2004), 675–83.

23. Ian Kershaw, *The "Hitler Myth": Image and Reality in the Third Reich* (Oxford, 1987), 147.

24. Lev Kopelev, *To Be Preserved Forever* (New York, 1977), 92–93.

25. See Frank Bajohr, *Parvenüs und Profiteure: Korruption in der NS-Zeit* (Frankfurt am Main, 2001).

26. See Michael Voslensky, *Nomenklatura: The Soviet Ruling Class* (Garden City, N.Y., 1984); and Alena V. Ledeneva, *Russia's Economy of Favors: Blat, Networking, and Informal Exchange* (New York, 1998).

27. For a return to a materialist explanation that ignores the roles of idealism and ideology in the mass murder of the Jews, see Götz Aly, *Hitlers Volksstaat: Raub, Rassenkrieg, und nationaler Sozialismus* (Frankfurt am Main, 2005). For a review, see Michael Wildt, "Alys Volksstaat: Hubris und Simplizität einer Wissenschaft," in *Mittelweg* 36 (June–July 2005), 69–80.

CHAPTER I: THE FIRST WORLD WAR AND THE RUSSIAN REVOLUTION

1. Quoted in Mark D. Steinberg and Vladimir M. Khrustalëv, eds., *The Fall of the Romanovs: Political Dreams and Personal Struggles in a Time of Revolution* (New Haven, Conn., 1997), 46.

2. Reports of U.S. ambassador in U.S. Department of State, *Papers Relating to the Foreign Relations of the United States, 1918. Russia* (Washington, D.C., 1918), vol. 1, 1–14.

3. Doc. 25, March 2, 1917, in Steinberg and Khrustalëv, *Fall of the Romanovs*, 96–97.

4. Doc. 29, March 3, 1917, in ibid., 105.

5. Mark D. Steinberg, *Voices of Revolution, 1917: Documents* (New Haven, Conn., 2001), 57.

6. U.S. Department of State, *Russia* (1918), vol. 1, 5–6.

7. Orlando Figes, *A People's Tragedy: The Russian Revolution, 1891–1924* (New York, 1996), 321.

8. See the classic account by Franco Venturi, *Roots of Revolution: A History of the Populist and Socialist Movements in Nineteenth Century Russia* (London, 1960).

9. Anastas Mikoyan, *Memoirs* (Madison, Conn., 1988), vol. 1, 31–32.

10. Nadezhda K. Krupskaya, *Memories of Lenin* (New York, 1930–32), vol. 1, 8–48.

11. Lenin, *Polnoe sobranie sochinenii*, vol. 6, 6–191.

12. Stalin, *Sochineniia*, vol. 1, 56–61 (Sept.–Oct. 1904), letters.

13. Nicolai Valentinov, *Vstrechi s Leninysm* (New York, 1953), 71–119.

14. Lenin, *Polnoe sobranie sochinenii*, vol. 10, 21–31.

15. Ibid., vol. 11, 93–104.
16. See Andrzej Walicki, *Marxism and the Leap to the Kingdom of Freedom: The Rise and Fall of the Communist Utopia* (Stanford, Calif., 1995), 324.
17. Lenin, *Polnoe sobranie sochinenii,* vol. 12, 224–28.
18. See, for example, his critique of the Socialists' agrarian program in ibid., vol. 16, 193ff.
19. Ibid., vol. 30, 327–28.
20. Ibid., vol. 31, 131–44.
21. Krupskaya, *Memories of Lenin,* vol. 2, 208–10.
22. Robert Service, *Lenin: A Biography* (Cambridge, Mass., 2000), 294.
23. *Pravda,* April 7, 1917.
24. Richard Pipes, *The Russian Revolution* (New York, 1990), 394; Robert C. Tucker, *Stalin as Revolutionary: A Study in History and Personality, 1879–1929* (New York, 1973), 165–66.
25. See Manfred Hildermeier, *Geschichte der Sowjetunion, 1917–1991* (Munich, 1998), 72–80.
26. Pipes, *Russian Revolution,* 399–405.
27. Steinberg, *Voices of Revolution,* 78.
28. Ibid., 149–50.
29. Figes, *People's Tragedy,* 427–29.
30. Tucker, *Stalin as Revolutionary,* 170, 173.
31. Stalin, *Sochineniia,* vol. 3, 130–33 (July 23, 1917), article.
32. Figes, *People's Tragedy,* 436–38; Pipes, *Russian Revolution,* 436–37.
33. Steinberg, *Voices of Revolution,* 156–57.
34. Lenin, *Polnoe sobranie sochinenii,* vol. 33, 123–307.
35. Boris Souvarine, *Staline: Aperçu historique du bolchévisme,* new ed. (Paris, 1985), 157.
36. Figes, *People's Tragedy,* 442–51.
37. Ibid., 454.
38. See, for example, Stalin, *Sochineniia,* vol. 3, 206–9 (Aug. 13, 1917); 286–88 (Sept. 12, 1917).
39. Lenin, *Polnoe sobranie sochinenii,* vol. 34, 239–47.
40. See the discussion in Leon Trotsky, *History of the Russian Revolution* (1932; New York, 2001), 936–41.
41. Lenin, *Polnoe sobranie sochinenii,* vol. 34, 391–93.
42. Trotsky, *History of the Russian Revolution,* 1003.
43. Lenin, *Polnoe sobranie sochinenii,* vol. 34, 419–22, 435–36.
44. Trotsky, *History of the Russian Revolution,* 1011.
45. Service, *Lenin,* 305–7.
46. Cited in Isaac Deutscher, *The Prophet Armed: Trotsky, 1879–1921* (Oxford, 1954), 304.
47. Leonard Schapiro, *1917: The Russian Revolutions and the Origins of Communism* (Harmondsworth, U.K., 1984), 129–30.
48. Trotsky, *History of the Russian Revolution,* 1030–31.

49. Stalin, *Sochineniia,* vol. 3, 387–90.
50. Hildermeier, *Geschichte der Sowjetunion,* 111–12.
51. Pipes, *Russian Revolution,* 491.
52. Figes, *People's Tragedy,* 493.
53. Hildermeier, *Geschichte der Sowjetunion,* 112.
54. Deutscher, *Prophet Armed,* 312.
55. Lenin, *Polnoe sobranie sochinenii,* vol. 35, 1.
56. Estimate is by Sir Alfred Knox, cited in Deutscher, *Prophet Armed,* 310 n. 3.
57. Figes, *People's Tragedy,* 489; Pipes, *Russian Revolution,* 498.
58. Marc Ferro, *The Bolshevik Revolution: A Social History* (London, 1980), 255.
59. John Reed, *Ten Days That Shook the World* (1919; Harmondsworth, U.K., 1982), 104.
60. See the table in Pipes, *Russian Revolution,* 542.
61. Pamphlet of July 1905, in Lenin, *Polnoe sobranie sochinenii,* vol. 11, 102–4.
62. Ibid., vol. 35, 191–94.

CHAPTER 2: ON THE WAY TO COMMUNIST DICTATORSHIP

1. Lenin, *Polnoe sobranie sochinenii,* vol. 35, 13–18.
2. Dmitri Volkogonov, *Lenin: politichesky portret* (Moscow, 1987), vol. 1, 250–51.
3. See the examples given in Lenin's October 26 speech on land. See also docs. 123–32, in Mark D. Steinberg, *Voices of Revolution, 1917: Documents* (New Haven, Conn., 2001), 293–308.
4. Lenin, *Polnoe sobranie sochinenii,* vol. 35, 23–24.
5. See the memoir of Eduard M. Dune, *Notes of a Red Guard* (Urbana, Ill., 1993), 87.
6. Lenin, *Polnoe sobranie sochinenii,* vol. 35, 28–29.
7. Ibid., 53–56.
8. John Reed, *Ten Days That Shook the World* (1919; Harmondsworth, U.K., 1982), 239–40.
9. Ibid., 239.
10. Orlando Figes, *A People's Tragedy: The Russian Revolution, 1891–1924* (New York, 1996), 510–11.
11. Richard Pipes, *The Russian Revolution* (New York, 1990), 534–36.
12. Ibid., 502–3.
13. Ibid., 526–31.
14. Figes, *People's Tragedy,* 509; Pipes, *Russian Revolution,* 544. At the time some estimated the crowd at 200,000.
15. Lenin, *Polnoe sobranie sochinenii,* vol. 35, 162–66.
16. Ibid., 156–57.
17. Cited in George Leggett, *The Cheka: Lenin's Political Police* (Oxford, 1981), 17.

18. Ibid., 19.

19. Jan. 9, 1918, republished in Maxim Gorky, *Untimely Thoughts, Essays on Revolution, Culture, and the Bolsheviks, 1917–1918* (New Haven, Conn., 1995), 126.

20. "Plekhanov o terrorye," in Lenin, *Polnoe sobranie sochinenii,* vol. 35, 184–86.

21. Lenin, *Polnoe sobranie sochinenii,* vol. 35, 238–42.

22. It became the Union of Soviet Socialist Republics (USSR) in another constitution adopted in January 1924. For the above, see Pipes, *Russian Revolution,* 550–55; Figes, *People's Tragedy,* 513–15.

23. See Elise Kimerling, "Civil Rights and Social Policy in Soviet Russia, 1918–1936," *Russian Review* (1982), 30.

24. Lenin, *Polnoe sobranie sochinenii,* vol. 35, 357–58.

25. Isaac N. Steinberg, *In the Workshop of the Revolution* (New York, 1953), 145.

26. Ibid., 146.

27. Leggett, *Cheka,* 58–61.

28. Pipes, *Russian Revolution,* 594–95; Figes, *People's Tragedy,* 547–51.

29. Lenin, *Polnoe sobranie sochinenii,* vol. 36, 210–11.

30. Ibid., 503.

31. See Aleksandr Solzhenitsyn, *The Gulag Archipelago, 1918–1956* (New York, 1973), vol. 2, 432–55.

32. Lenin, *Polnoe sobranie sochinenii,* vol. 50, 106.

33. Cited in Leggett, *Cheka,* 114 (emphasis mine).

34. Cited in Pipes, *Russian Revolution,* 802.

35. Leggett, *Cheka,* 100, 233.

36. Lenin, *Polnoe sobranie sochinenii,* vol. 50, 142–43.

37. See doc. 24, in Richard Pipes, ed., *The Unknown Lenin: From the Secret Archive* (New Haven, Conn., 1996), 50.

38. See Leon Trotsky, *Terrorism and Communism* (1920) cited in Robert Service, *Lenin: A Political Life,* vol. 3, *The Iron Ring* (London, 1995), 37.

39. Michael Jakobson, *Origins of the Gulag: The Soviet Prison Camp System, 1917–1934* (Lexington, Ky., 1993), 152 n. 7; Solzhenitsyn, *Gulag Archipelago,* vol. 2, 142–47.

40. Peter H. Solomon, *Soviet Criminal Justice Under Stalin* (Cambridge, U.K., 1996), 17–48.

41. David J. Dallin and Boris I. Nicolaevsky, *Forced Labor in Soviet Russia* (New Haven, Conn., 1947), 150–51.

42. Lenin, *Polnoe sobranie sochinenii,* vol. 45, 190–91.

43. Andrzej J. Kaminski, *Konzentrationslager 1896 bis Heute* (Munich, 1990), 34–35.

44. See Jan M. Meijer, ed., *The Trotsky Papers, 1917–1922* (London, 1964), vol. I, 109 n. 4; Kaminski, *Konzentrationslager,* 72–73; for a slightly different dating, see Anne Applebaum, *Gulag: A History* (New York, 2003), 8.

45. Cited in Pipes, *Russian Revolution,* 808–9.

46. Doc. 28, n.d., likely Sept. 3 or 4, 1918, in Pipes, *Unknown Lenin,* 56.

47. Cited in Leggett, *Cheka,* 108.

48. Ibid., 111.

49. Jörg Baberowski, *Der rote Terror: Die Geschichte des Stalinismus* (Munich, 2003), 40.

50. Cited in Leggett, *Cheka,* 109–10.

51. Kaminski, *Konzentrationslager,* 73.

52. Cited in Pipes, *Russian Revolution,* 834.

53. Applebaum, *Gulag,* 9.

54. Leggett, *Cheka,* 178–81; Galina Mikhailovna Ivanova, *Labor Camp Socialism: The Gulag in the Soviet Totalitarian System* (London, 2000), 14.

55. See Nicolas Werth, "A State Against Its People: Violence, Repression, and Terror in the Soviet Union," in Stéphane Courtois et al., *The Black Book of Communism* (Cambridge, Mass., 1999), 114.

56. Volkogonov, *Lenin: politichesky portret,* vol. 1, 413–15; Dallin and Nicolaevsky, *Forced Labor in Soviet Russia,* 157.

57. Dallin and Nicolaevsky, *Forced Labor in Soviet Russia,* 173.

58. This organization is devoted to recovering the memory of those who suffered and died under Communism.

59. See Joël Kotek and Pierre Rigoulot, *Das Jahrhundert der Lager: Gefangenschaft, Zwangsarbeit, Vernichtung* (Berlin, 2001), 139–40.

60. See the account of Solovki and Kem in Dallin and Nicolaevsky, *Forced Labor in Soviet Russia,* 181–88.

61. Leon Trotsky, *History of the Russian Revolution* (1932; New York, 2001), 295–96.

62. Mark von Hagen, *Soldiers in the Proletarian Dictatorship: The Red Army and the Soviet Socialist State, 1917–1930* (Ithaca, N.Y. 1990), 40.

63. Ibid., 126. For the desertion figures, see Figes, *People's Tragedy,* 599.

64. Lenin, *Polnoe sobranie sochinenii,* vol. 35, 195–205.

CHAPTER 3: CIVIL WARS IN THE SOVIET UNION

1. Dmitri Volkogonov, *Lenin: politichesky portret* (Moscow, 1987), vol. 1, 349.

2. Stalin, "The Foundations of Leninism," in his *Sochineniia,* vol. 6, 112 (April 26–30 and May 9–18, 1924).

3. Robert Service, *Lenin: A Biography* (Cambridge, Mass., 2000), 330–31.

4. Doc. 9.9, in Ronald Kowalski, ed., *The Russian Revolution, 1917–1921* (New York, 1997), 143–44; Alec Nove, *An Economic History of the USSR* (Harmondsworth, U.K., 1990), 50–51; George Leggett, *The Cheka: Lenin's Political Police* (Oxford, 1981), 64.

5. Donald J. Raleigh, *Experiencing Russia's Civil War: Politics, Society, and Revolutionary Culture in Saratov, 1917–1922* (Princeton, N.J., 2002), 337–41.

6. Stalin, *Sochineniia,* vol. 4, 128 (Aug. 31, 1918); 130 (Sept. 19, 1918).

7. Cited in Boris Souvarine, *Staline: Aperçu historique du bolchévisme,* new ed. (Paris, 1985), 205.

8. Trotsky to Lenin, in Jan M. Meijer, ed., *The Trotsky Papers, 1917–1922* (London, 1964), vol. 1, 72–74; see also Roy Medvedev, *Let History Judge: The Origins and Consequences of Stalinism* (New York, 1989), 56–59; Robert C. Tucker, *Stalin as Revolutionary: A Study in History and Personality, 1879–1929* (New York, 1973), 192–96.

9. Volkogonov, *Lenin: politichesky portret,* vol. 1, 374.

10. Jörg Baberowski, *Der rote Terror: Die Geschichte des Stalinismus* (Munich, 2003), 41.

11. Hiroaki Kuromiya, *Freedom and Terror in the Donbas: A Ukrainian-Russian Borderland, 1870s–1990s* (Cambridge, U.K., 1998), 103–8.

12. Instructive here is George F. Kennan, *Russia and the West Under Lenin and Stalin* (New York, 1960), 70–115.

13. Serge Schmemann, *Echoes of a Native Land: Two Centuries of a Russian Village* (New York, 1997), 208.

14. *Krasnyi mech* (Red Sword), Aug. 18, 1919, cited in Leggett, *Cheka,* 203.

15. Stalin, *Sochineniia,* vol. 2, 332–47; useful here is Jacob Miller, "Soviet Theory on the Jews," in Lionel Kochan, ed., *The Jews in Soviet Russia Since 1917* (Oxford, 1970), 46–63.

16. Strobe Talbott, ed., *Khrushchev Remembers* (Boston, 1970), 266–67; Yuri Slezkine, *The Jewish Century* (Princeton, N.J., 2004), 106–16.

17. Slezkine, *Jewish Century,* 175.

18. Orlando Figes, *A People's Tragedy: The Russian Revolution, 1891–1924* (New York, 1996), 676–77; Slezkine, *Jewish Century,* 178–79.

19. See Norman Cohn, *Warrant for Genocide: The Myth of the Jewish World-Conspiracy and the Protocols of the Elders of Zion* (London, 1967), 114, 119–20.

20. See Peter Kenez, "Pogroms and White Ideology in the Russian Civil War," in John D. Klier and Shlomo Lambroza, eds., *Pogroms: Anti-Jewish Violence in Modern Russian History* (New York, 1992), 300.

21. Kuromiya, *Freedom and Terror in the Donbas,* 111.

22. Peter Holquist, "To Count, to Extract, and to Exterminate: Population Politics in Late Imperial and Soviet Russia," in Ronald Grigor Suny and Terry Martin, eds., *A State of Nations: Empire and Nation-Making in the Age of Lenin and Stalin* (New York, 2001), 111–44.

23. See Richard Pipes, *Russia Under the Bolshevik Regime* (New York, 1995), 109.

24. Eduard M. Dune, *Notes of a Red Guard* (Urbana, Ill., 1993), 168–69.

25. See the memoir of a captured Red Army soldier and his evidence in ibid., 163–64.

26. Volkogonov, *Lenin: politichesky portret,* vol. 1, 360–61.

27. Cited in Peter Holquist, *Making War, Forging Revolution: Russia's Continuum of Crisis, 1914–1921* (Cambridge, Mass., 2002), 180.

28. Nicolas Werth, "A State Against Its People: Violence, Repression, and Terror in the Soviet Union," in Stéphane Courtois et al., *The Black Book of Communism* (Cambridge, Mass., 1999), 99.

29. Ibid., 101–3.

30. Holquist, *Making War,* 187. The human face of the tragedy can be seen in the novel *And Quiet Flows the Don* by the Nobel Prize winner Mikhail Sholokhov.

31. Cited in Robert Service, *Lenin: A Political Life,* vol. 3, *The Iron Ring* (London, 1995), 39.

32. Sergey Petrovich Melgounov, *The Red Terror in Russia* (London, 1926).

33. Leggett, *Cheka,* 200; Werth, "A State Against Its People," 106–7.

34. Cited in Pipes, *Russia Under the Bolshevik Regime,* 135.

35. Stalin, *Sochineniia,* vol. 4, 27 (Jan. 11, 1918).

36. Trotsky to Zinoviev, in Meijer, *Trotsky Papers,* vol. 2, 443.

37. See the vivid correspondence in ibid., 153–255.

38. Josef Korbel, *Poland Between East and West: Soviet and German Diplomacy Toward Poland, 1919–1933* (Princeton, N.J., 1963), 16–67.

39. Cited in Stephen F. Cohen, *Bukharin and the Bolshevik Revolution: A Political Biography, 1888–1938* (New York, 1974), 101.

40. Raleigh, *Experiencing Russia's Civil War,* 391–94; Figes, *People's Tragedy,* 753.

41. Pipes, *Russia Under the Bolshevik Regime,* 377; Orlando Figes, *Peasant Russia, Civil War: The Volga Countryside in Revolution, 1917–1921* (London, 1991), 321–23, 342; Raleigh, *Experiencing Russia's Civil War,* 337–41.

42. Pipes, *Russia Under the Bolshevik Regime,* 386–87.

43. Figes, *People's Tragedy,* 768.

44. Table in Nove, *Economic History,* 58. The index of one hundred in 1913 reached twenty-one in 1921.

45. Ibid., 76.

46. For a full study, see Bertrand M. Patenaude, *The Big Show in Bololand: The American Relief Expedition to Soviet Russia in the Famine of 1921* (Stanford, Calif., 2000).

47. Figes, *People's Tragedy,* 779.

48. Volkogonov, *Lenin: politichesky portret,* vol. 2, 159–160.

CHAPTER 4: NAZISM AND THE THREAT OF BOLSHEVISM

1. Adolf Hitler, *Mein Kampf* (Munich, 1943), 139, 171.

2. See Brigitte Hamann, *Hitler's Vienna: A Dictator's Apprenticeship* (New York, 1999), 348; Anton Joachimsthaler, *Hitlers Weg begann in München, 1913–1923* (Munich, 2000), 45.

3. Joachimsthaler, *Hitlers Weg,* 102–22.

4. Ibid., 174–76.

5. Hans-Ulrich Wehler, *Deutsche Gesellschaftsgeschichte,* vol. 4, *1914–1949* (Munich, 2003), 232.

6. Cited in Heinrich August Winkler, *Weimar, 1918–1933: Die Geschichte der ersten deutschen Demokratie* (Munich, 1998), 29.

7. Ibid., 41.

8. Detlev J. K. Peukert, *Die Weimarer Republik: Krisenjahre der klassischen Moderne* (Frankfurt am Main, 1987), 44.

9. Wehler, *Deutsche Gesellschaftsgeschichte,* 207.

10. Winkler, *Weimar,* 64, 69.

11. Albert S. Lindemann, *The "Red Years": European Socialism vs. Bolshevism, 1919–1921* (Berkeley, Calif., 1974), 190.

12. Allan Mitchell, *Revolution in Bavaria: The Eisner Regime and the Soviet Republic* (Princeton, N.J., 1965), 217, 271–72.

13. Cited in Peter Nettl, *Rosa Luxemburg,* abr. ed. (Oxford, 1969), 455.

14. Ibid., 477–81; Winkler, *Weimar,* 56–57.

15. See the complete list of demands, Dec. 14, 1918, in Wolfgang Treue, ed., *Deutsche Parteiprogramme, 1861–1961* (Berlin, 1961), 91.

16. Eberhard Kolb, *The Weimar Republic* (London, 1988), 8–10.

17. Nov. 20, 1918, article, cited in Eric Waldman, *The Spartacist Uprising* (Milwaukee, 1958), 111.

18. Cited in Winkler, *Weimar,* 58.

19. Ibid., 60.

20. Mitchell, *Revolution in Bavaria,* 299–300.

21. Cited in ibid., 319.

22. Winkler, *Weimar,* 80; Mitchell, *Revolution in Bavaria,* 320.

23. Lenin, *Polnoe sobranie sochinenii,* vol. 38, 321–22.

24. Cited in David Clay Large, *Where Ghosts Walked: Munich's Road to the Third Reich* (New York, 1997), 116.

25. Winkler, *Weimar,* 81.

26. See Yuri Slezkine, *The Jewish Century* (Princeton, N.J., 2004), 85.

27. Cited in Large, *Where Ghosts Walked,* 120.

28. Ruth Fischer, *Stalin and German Communism: A Study in the Origins of the State Party* (Cambridge, Mass., 1949), 108. For a critique of her feigned anti-Bolshevism, see Klaus-Michael Mallmann, *Kommunisten in der Weimarer Republik: Sozialgeschichte einer revolutionären Bewegung* (Darmstadt, 1996), 71.

29. See Uwe Lohalm, *Völkischer Radikalismus: Die Geschichte des Deutschvölkischen Schutz- und Trutz-Bundes, 1919–1923* (Hamburg, 1970), 181–83.

30. Joachimsthaler, *Hitlers Weg,* 221–24.

31. Esser cited in Georg Franz-Willing, *Ursprung der Hitlerbewegung, 1919–1922* (Oldendorf, 1974), 52–55. See also Hitler, *Mein Kampf,* 232.

32. See Joachimsthaler, *Hitlers Weg,* 209–12; also Ian Kershaw, *Hitler, 1889–1936: Hubris* (London, 1998), 118–20.

33. Letter in *Hitler Aufzeichnungen,* 88–90.
34. Card in Joachimsthaler, *Hitlers Weg,* opp. 259; for Hitler's account, see Hitler, *Mein Kampf,* 236–44.
35. Winkler, *Weimar,* 89–95; Kolb, *Weimar Republic,* 21–33.
36. Treue *Deutsche Parteiprogramme,* 146–49.
37. Hitler, *Mein Kampf,* 556.
38. Sebastian Haffner, *Geschichte eines Deutschen: Die Erinnerungen, 1914–1933* (Munich, 2000), 48.
39. Joachimsthaler, *Hitlers Weg,* 272, 274.
40. Kershaw, *Hitler, 1889–1936,* 156–57.
41. Hitler, *Mein Kampf,* 658.
42. Joachimsthaler, *Hitlers Weg,* 292.
43. Hitler, *Mein Kampf,* 650–51.
44. For a recent account, see Michael Kellogg, *The Russian Roots of Nazism: White Émigrés and the Making of National Socialism, 1917–1945* (Cambridge, U.K., 2005), 30–47.
45. Speeches in *Hitler Aufzeichnungen,* 451–57, 458–59.
46. Kai-Uwe Merz, *Das Schreckbild: Deutschland und der Bolschewismus, 1917 bis 1921* (Berlin, 1995), 452.
47. *Hitler Aufzeichnungen,* 108–9.
48. Ibid., 127–29.
49. June 6, 1920, in ibid., 140.
50. *Hitler Aufzeichnungen,* 165–66.
51. Aug. 6, 1920, in ibid., 172.
52. Dec. 8, 1920, in ibid., 276.
53. July 21, 1920, in ibid., 163.
54. Aug. 7, 1920, in ibid., 175.
55. Ibid., 279.
56. Citations in Dmitri Volkogonov, *Lenin: politichesky portret* (Moscow, 1987), vol. 2, 265–66.
57. Eric D. Weitz, *Creating German Communism, 1890–1990: From Popular Protests to Socialist State* (Princeton, N.J. 1997), 103–5.
58. *Hitler Aufzeichnungen,* 298–302.
59. Ibid., 317–20.

CHAPTER 5: FIRST NAZI ATTEMPT TO SEIZE POWER

1. Sven Reichardt, *Faschistische Kampfbünde: Gewalt und Gemeinschaft im italienischen Squadrismus und in der deutschen SA* (Cologne, 2002), 256.
2. Denis Mack Smith, *Mussolini* (New York, 1982), 171.
3. Robert O. Paxton, *The Anatomy of Fascism* (New York, 2004), 89, 275 n. 1.
4. Mack Smith, *Mussolini,* 52–56.
5. Adolf Hitler, *Mein Kampf* (Munich, 1943), 774.

6. *Hitler Aufzeichnungen,* 721–22.

7. Heinrich August Winkler, *Weimar, 1918–1933: Die Geschichte der ersten deutschen Demokratie* (Munich, 1998), 190.

8. Georg Franz-Willing, *Ursprung der Hitlerbewegung, 1919–1922* (Oldendorf, 1974), 355.

9. Cited in Anton Joachimsthaler, *Hitlers Weg begann in München, 1913–1923* (Munich, 2000), 304.

10. Winkler, *Weimar,* 186–88; Eberhard Kolb, *The Weimar Republic* (London, 1988), 45–46.

11. See newspapers, Jan. 12, 1923, in *Hitler Aufzeichnungen,* 785–86.

12. Winkler, *Weimar,* 188–89.

13. Gerald D. Feldman, *The Great Disorder: Politics, Economics, and Society in the German Inflation, 1914–1924* (New York, 1993), 5.

14. For the impressions of a young man in Berlin, see Sebastian Haffner, *Geschichte eines Deutschen: Die Erinnerungen, 1914–1933* (Munich, 2000), 54–68. Also Winkler, *Weimar,* 207.

15. See Rosa Leviné-Meyer, *Inside German Communism: Memoirs of Party Life in the Weimar Republic* (London, 1977), 46–55.

16. Winkler, *Weimar,* 200, 210–16.

17. For an account based on an interview with Brandler, see Isaac Deutscher, *The Prophet Unarmed: Trotsky, 1921–1929* (New York, 1959), 142–45.

18. See Richard A. Comfort, *Revolutionary Hamburg: Labor Politics in the Early Weimar Republic* (Stanford, Calif., 1966), 125–26.

19. Isaac Deutscher, *Stalin: A Political Biography* (Harmondsworth, U.K., 1966), 390–91.

20. *Hitler Aufzeichnungen,* 794–97.

21. Ibid., 811.

22. Feb. 26, 1923, speech, in ibid., 840.

23. March 25, 1923, speech, in ibid., 848–49.

24. See, for example, March 27, 1923, speech, in ibid., 853.

25. June 17, 1923, speech, in ibid., 937.

26. April 10, 1923, speech, in ibid., 876, 881.

27. May 1 police report, in ibid., 918–19.

28. See, for example, Aug. 5, 1923, speech, in ibid., 965.

29. May 17, 1923, speech, in ibid., 929.

30 *Hitler Aufzeichnungen,* 955–62; see also 920.

31. Ibid., 1023–26.

32. Ibid., 1027.

33. Peter Longerich, *Die braunen Bataillone: Geschichte der SA* (Munich, 1989), 33–36.

34. *Hitler Aufzeichnungen,* 990.

35. Ibid., 991–92.

36. Cited in Harold J. Gordon, *Hitler and the Beer Hall Putsch* (Princeton, N.J., 1972), 213.

37. *Hitler Aufzeichnungen,* 1022.
38. Feldman, *Great Disorder,* 736.
39. Gordon, *Hitler and the Beer Hall Putsch,* 221–24; Feldman, *Great Disorder,* 778–79.
40. Gordon, *Hitler and the Beer Hall Putsch,* 238–56; Ian Kershaw, *Hitler, 1889–1936: Hubris* (London, 1998), 204.
41. Gordon, *Hitler and the Beer Hall Putsch,* 259–60.
42. Ibid., 260.
43. Ibid., 264–67.
44. Ernst Hanfstaengl, *Hitler: The Missing Years* (1957; New York, 1994), 91–109.
45. Cited in Gordon, *Hitler and the Beer Hall Putsch,* 287–88.
46. Hanfstaengl, *Hitler,* 100.
47. Gordon, *Hitler and the Beer Hall Putsch,* 290–312, 342–43.
48. Cited in ibid., 351.
49. See Kershaw, *Hitler, 1889–1936,* 211; Gordon, *Hitler and the Beer Hall Putsch,* 356–65.
50. *Hitler Aufzeichnungen,* 1210.
51. Cited in Winkler, *Weimar,* 252.
52. Feldman, *Great Disorder,* 780–802; Winkler, *Weimar,* 237.

CHAPTER 6: HITLER STARTS OVER

1. *Hitler Aufzeichnungen,* 1226.
2. Hitler to Adolf Gemlich, Sept. 16, 1919, in ibid., 88–90.
3. Cited in Noakes and Pridham, vol. 1, 37.
4. Ian Kershaw, *Hitler, 1889–1936: Hubris* (London, 1998), 242–43.
5. For an overview, see Eberhard Jäckel, *Hitler's World View: A Blueprint for Power* (Cambridge, Mass., 1981).
6. Adolf Hitler, *Mein Kampf* (Munich, 1943), 751.
7. Ibid., 318.
8. The modern concept of "Aryan" is usually attributed to linguistic writings in the late eighteenth and nineteenth centuries. See George L. Mosse, *Toward the Final Solution: A History of European Racism* (New York, 1978), 39–44.
9. Hitler, *Mein Kampf,* 420–21.
10. The problems of tracing Hitler's racist ideas are shown well by Richard Weikart, *From Darwin to Hitler: Evolutionary Ethics, Eugenics, and Racism in Germany* (New York, 2004).
11. Hitler, *Mein Kampf,* 579–80.
12. Ibid., 585–86.
13. Ibid., 739, 742.
14. Ibid., 743.
15. Ibid.

16. Ibid., 751–52.
17. See the authoritative Gerhard L. Weinberg, ed., *Hitler's Second Book: The Unpublished Sequel to "Mein Kampf"* (New York, 2003).
18. This statement is in Theodore Abel, *Why Hitler Came to Power* (repr., Cambridge, Mass., 1986), 240.
19. Ernst Hanfstaengl, *Hitler: The Missing Years* (1957; New York, 1994), 128.
20. Ibid., 131–32.
21. *VB*, Feb. 26, 1925, in *Hitler: Reden, Schriften*, vol. 1, 4–9.
22. See *VB*, Feb. 27, 1925, in *Hitler: Reden, Schriften*, vol. 1, 14–32.
23. *Hitler: Reden, Schriften*, vol. 1, 14 n. 5, 36.
24. Ibid., 35–37.
25. Heinrich August Winkler, *Weimar, 1918–1933: Die Geschichte der ersten deutschen Demokratie* (Munich, 1998), 281.
26. *VB*, Feb. 25, 1926, in *Hitler: Reden, Schriften*, vol. 1, 294–96.
27. Feb. 15, 1926, in Elke Fröhlich et al., eds., *Die Tagebücher von Joseph Goebbels* (Munich, 2005ff.), part 1, vol. 1–2, 55–56.
28. Ibid., 73.
29. Kershaw, *Hitler, 1889–1936*, 270–77.

CHAPTER 7: BATTLE FOR COMMUNIST UTOPIA

1. On Stalin's family background and early years in the Caucasus, see Robert Service, *Stalin: A Biography* (Cambridge, Mass., 2004), 3–55.
2. Lenin, *Polnoe sobranie sochinenii*, vol. 6, 29–30.
3. Stalin, *Sochineniia*, vol. 1, 59–61 (Sept.–Oct. 1904), 74–80 (Jan. 1905), articles.
4. Lenin, *Polnoe sobranie sochinenii*, vol. 6, 78–80, 134–37.
5. Anna Geifman, *Thou Shalt Kill: Revolutionary Terrorism in Russia, 1894–1917* (Princeton, N.J., 1993), 21–22.
6. Service, *Stalin*, 70; Robert C. Tucker, *Stalin as Revolutionary: A Study in History and Personality, 1879–1929* (New York, 1973), 107–8; Edvard Radzinsky, *Stalin* (New York, 1996), 63–65.
7. Stalin, *Sochineniia*, vol. 1, 84–88 (Feb. 15, 1905), pamphlet.
8. Lenin, *Polnoe sobranie sochinenii*, vol. 13, 369–77, article.
9. Cited in Isaac Deutscher, *Stalin: A Political Biography* (Harmondsworth, U.K., 1966), 90.
10. Stalin, *Sochineniia*, vol. 1, 193–95 (Nov. 20, 1905), pamphlet; 206–13 (March 8, 1906), article.
11. Ibid., 206–38 (March 8, 1906).
12. Service, *Stalin*, 74–75; Deutscher, *Stalin*, 102–3.
13. Geifman, *Thou Shalt Kill*, 112–22; for more, see Dmitri Volkogonov, *Lenin: politichesky portret* (Moscow, 1987), vol. 1. 101–4. Some funds were also donated to the cause by wealthy people.
14. Tucker, *Stalin as Revolutionary*, 144–50; Service, *Lenin*, 204–5.

15. Stalin, *Sochineniia,* vol. 2, 359–67 (Jan. 1913), pamphlet.
16. See Terry Martin, *The Affirmative Action Empire: Nations and Nationalism in the Soviet Union, 1923–1939* (Ithaca, N.Y., 2001).
17. See Robert M. Slusser, *Stalin in October: The Man Who Missed the Revolution* (London, 1987), 244–55.
18. For the refutations, see Service, *Stalin,* 140–47.

CHAPTER 8: LENIN'S PASSING, STALIN'S VICTORY

 1. Lenin, *Polnoe sobranie sochinenii,* vol. 45, 69–88 (March 27, 1922, speech).
 2. March 15, 1921, speech, in ibid., vol. 43, 68–69.
 3. Dec. 23, 1921, speech, in ibid., vol. 44, 291–329.
 4. July 5, 1922, speech, in ibid., 53–54.
 5. Feliks Ivanovich Chuev and Vyacheslav Molotov, *Sto sorok besed s Molotovym: iz dnevnika F. Chueva* (Moscow, 1991), 200.
 6. Lenin, *Polnoe sobranie sochinenii,* vol. 44, 298–99.
 7. George Leggett, *The Cheka: Lenin's Political Police* (Oxford, 1981), 346–48.
 8. Lenin, *Polnoe sobranie sochinenii,* vol. 44, 396–97.
 9. Robert Service, *Lenin: A Biography* (Cambridge, Mass., 2000), 444–46.
10. March 27, 1922, speech, in Lenin, *Polnoe sobranie sochinenii,* vol. 45, 89–114.
11. Stalin, *Sochineniia,* vol. 6, 172.
12. See John Löwenhardt, James R. Ozinga, and Erik van Lee, *The Rise and Fall of the Soviet Politburo* (London, 1992), 11.
13. Robert C. Tucker, *Stalin as Revolutionary: A Study in History and Personality, 1879–1929* (New York, 1973), 212.
14. Dmitri Volkogonov, *Lenin: politichesky portret* (Moscow, 1987), vol. 2, 106–7.
15. See ibid., vol. 1, 300. There is a serious error in the English translation on this point in the book.
16. Chuev and Molotov, *Sto sorok besed,* 179–80; Roy Medvedev, *Let History Judge: The Origins and Consequences of Stalinism* (New York, 1989), 68.
17. Service, *Lenin,* 445.
18. Volkogonov, *Lenin: politichesky portret,* vol. 2, 40; Richard Pipes, *Russia Under the Bolshevik Regime* (New York, 1995), 464–65.
19. Tucker, *Stalin as Revolutionary,* 250–53.
20. Service, *Lenin,* 452. For an alternative view, long held, see Moshe Lewin, *The Soviet Century* (New York, 2005), 24–26.
21. Pipes, *Russia Under the Bolshevik Regime,* 474.
22. Cited in Volkogonov, *Lenin: politichesky portret,* vol. 1, 350–51; vol. 2, 185–86.
23. Lenin, *Polnoe sobranie sochinenii,* vol. 45, 343–48.
24. Chuev and Molotov, *Sto sorok besed,* 239; Medvedev, *Let History Judge,* 75, 80–81.
25. Letters reprinted in Medvedev, *Let History Judge,* 72–73.

26. Tucker, *Stalin as Revolutionary*, 289–90.

27. Dmitri Volkogonov, *Triumf i tragediya. Politichesky portret J. V. Stalina* (Moscow, 1989), vol. 1, part 1, 251.

28. Chuev and Molotov, *Sto sorok besed*, 184–85.

29. Cited in Medvedev, *Let History Judge*, 118–19.

30. Ibid., 112.

31. Opening speech, March 8, 1921, in Lenin, *Polnoe sobranie sochinenii*, vol. 43, 5–6.

32. For the letters, see Pipes, *Russia Under the Bolshevik Regime*, 483–85.

33. Stalin, *Sochineniia*, vol. 6, 220–33 (May 27, 1924), speech.

34. Stephen F. Cohen, *Bukharin and the Bolshevik Revolution: A Political Biography, 1888–1938* (New York, 1974), 325–26; Tucker, *Stalin as Revolutionary*, 220–22.

35. See Nina Tumarkin, *Lenin Lives! The Lenin Cult in Soviet Russia* (Cambridge, Mass., 1997), 208.

36. Robert H. McNeal, *Stalin: Man and Ruler* (New York, 1988), 89, doubts Stalin had anything to do with creating the cult.

37. Leonard Schapiro, *The Communist Party of the Soviet Union*, 2nd ed. (New York, 1971), 231–41.

38. See Sheila Fitzpatrick, *The Cultural Front: Power and Culture in Revolutionary Russia* (Ithaca, N.Y., 1992), 49.

39. See I. A. Sats, cited in Roy Medvedev, *On Stalin and Stalinism* (Oxford, 1979), 46.

40. See Mikhail Heller and Aleksandr M. Nekrich, *Utopia in Power: The History of the Soviet Union from 1917 to the Present* (New York, 1986), 184–85.

41. Stalin, *Sochineniia*, vol. 6, 324–57.

42. See Isaac Deutscher, *The Prophet Unarmed: Trotsky, 1921–1929* (New York, 1959), 158–60.

43. Cited in Medvedev, *Let History Judge*, 154.

44. See his discussion of his critics in Stalin, *Sochineniia*, vol. 7, 353–91 (Dec. 23, 1925).

45. Medvedev, *Let History Judge*, 155.

46. Tucker, *Stalin as Revolutionary*, 393.

47. Cited in Cohen, *Bukharin and the Bolshevik Revolution*, 240.

48. Stalin, *Sochineniia*, vol. 10, 172–205.

49. Medvedev, *Let History Judge*, 169–73; Schapiro, *Communist Party of the Soviet Union*, 303–8; Tucker, *Stalin as Revolutionary*, 404.

50. See Stalin, *Sochineniia*, vol. 10, 354–71.

CHAPTER 9: STALIN'S NEW INITIATIVES

1. Stalin, *Sochineniia*, vol. 10, 305.

2. Ibid., 371.

3. Ibid., vol. 9, 322–61 (July 28, 1927), article.

4. Hiroaki Kuromiya, *Freedom and Terror in the Donbas: A Ukrainian-Russian Borderland, 1870s–1990s* (Cambridge, U.K., 1998), 143–45, 151.

5. Stephen F. Cohen, *Bukharin and the Bolshevik Revolution: A Political Biography, 1888–1938* (New York, 1974), 281.

6. For an overview, see William Chase, "Stalin as Producer: The Moscow Show Trials and the Production of Mortal Threats," in Sarah Davies and James R. Harris, eds., *Stalin: A New History* (Cambridge, U.K., 2005), 226–48.

7. See Arkady Vaksberg, *Stalin's Prosecutor: The Life of Andrei Vyshinsky* (New York, 1990), 42–45.

8. Hiroaki Kuromiya, *Stalin's Industrial Revolution* (Cambridge, U.K., 1988), 27.

9. Stalin, *Sochineniia*, vol. 11, 172 (July 9, 1928).

10. Stalin to Molotov, Sept. 30, 1930, in Lars T. Lih, Oleg V. Naumov, and Oleg V. Khlevniuk, eds., *Stalin's Letters to Molotov, 1925–1936* (London, 1995), 200–1.

11. See Paul R. Gregory, *The Political Economy of Stalinism: Evidence from the Soviet Secret Archives* (New York, 2004), 34–48.

12. Stalin to Molotov, Aug. 29, 1929, in Lih, Naumov, and Khlevniuk, *Stalin's Letters,* 175.

13. See Stephen Kotkin, *Magnetic Mountain: Stalinism as a Civilization* (Berkeley, Calif., 1995), 31–32.

14. Stalin, *Sochineniia*, vol. 11, 248 (Nov. 19, 1928), speech.

15. See Richard Cartwright Austin, *Building Utopia: Erecting Russia's First Modern City, 1930* (London, 2004), 18, 51–56.

16. Robert Lewis, "Foreign Economic Relations," in R. W. Davies, Mark Harrison, and Stephen G. Wheatcroft, eds., *The Economic Transformation of the Soviet Union, 1913–1945* (New York, 1994), 198–215.

17. Cited in Austin, *Building Utopia,* 13.

18. For the above, see Kotkin, *Magnetic Mountain,* 50, 86, 108–23.

19. Stalin, *Sochineniia*, vol. 12, 118, 135.

20. Sheila Fitzpatrick, *Everyday Stalinism: Ordinary Life in Extraordinary Times: Soviet Russia in the 1930s* (New York, 1999), 70.

21. See ibid., 6, 18; Robert C. Tucker, *Stalin in Power: The Revolution from Above, 1928–1941* (New York, 1990), 101–2.

22. Ante Ciliga from Yugoslavia, cited in Mikhail Heller and Aleksandr M. Nekrich, *Utopia in Power: The History of the Soviet Union from 1917 to the Present* (New York, 1986), 205.

23. OGPU report, Dec. 1927–Jan. 1928, in Lynne Viola et al., eds., *The War Against the Peasantry, 1927–1930: The Tragedy of the Soviet Countryside* (New Haven, Conn., 2005), 34–44.

24. For Stalin's reports, see Viola et al., *War Against the Peasantry,* 69–75; Cohen, *Bukharin and the Bolshevik Revolution,* 278.

25. Moshe Lewin, *Russian Peasants and Soviet Power: A Study of Collectivization* (New York, 1968), 241.

26. See two OGPU statistical reports, Nov. 4, 1929, in Viola et al., *War Against the Peasantry,* 150–51.

27. For these stories and more, see Elena Osokina, *Our Daily Bread: Socialist Distribution and the Art of Survival in Stalin's Russia, 1927–1941* (New York, 2001), 21–27.

28. Stalin to Molotov, Aug. 10, 1929, in Lih, Navmov, and Khlevniuk, *Stalin's Letters,* 165–66.

29. Stalin, *Sochineniia,* vol. 11, 1–9 (Jan. 6, 1928), speech.

30. Osokina, *Our Daily Bread,* 36, 41.

31. Tucker, *Stalin in Power,* 138.

32. Stalin, *Sochineniia,* vol. 12, 166–67.

33. Ibid., 170.

34. See Lynne Viola, "The Other Archipelago: Kulak Deportation to the North in 1930," *Slavic Review* (2001), 734.

35. Politburo decree, Jan. 30, 1930, reprinted in Viola et al., *War Against the Peasantry,* 228–34.

36. Yagoda memorandum, Jan. 23, 1930, in Viola et al., *War Against the Peasantry,* 237–38.

37. Simon Sebag Montefiore, *Stalin: The Court of the Red Tsar* (New York, 2004), 46–47.

38. Gorky, Nov. 15, 1930, in Heller and Nekrich, *Utopia in Power,* 236.

39. See James R. Harris, *The Great Urals: Regionalism and the Evolution of the Soviet System* (Ithaca, N.Y. 1999), 116–18.

40. Sebag Montefiore, *Stalin,* 46.

41. See Lev Kopelev, *The Education of a True Believer* (New York, 1980), 186–87.

42. Sheila Fitzpatrick, *Stalin's Peasants: Resistance and Survival in the Russian Village After Collectivization* (New York, 1994), 48–62.

43. Lewin, *Russian Peasants and Soviet Power,* 502.

44. Nicolas Werth, "A State Against Its People: Violence, Repression, and Terror in the Soviet Union," in Stéphane Courtois et al., *The Black Book of Communism* (Cambridge, Mass., 1999), 147–48.

CHAPTER 10: STALIN SOLIDIFIES HIS GRIP

1. OGPU report, July 31, 1931, for 1930, in Lynne Viola et al., eds., *The War Against the Peasantry, 1927–1930: The Tragedy of the Soviet Countryside* (New Haven, Conn., 2005), 339–40. See also Stephen G. Wheatcroft, "Towards Explaining the Changing Levels of Stalinist Repression in the

1930s: Mass Killings," in Stephen G. Wheatcroft, ed., *Challenging Traditional Views of Russian History* (London, 2002), 112–46.

2. See the report (not before July 1, 1930) compiled for the Sixteenth Party Congress, in Viola et al., *War Against the Peasantry,* 328.

3. Stalin, *Sochineniia,* vol. 12, 191–99.

4. See the documents in Viola et al., *War Against the Peasantry,* 362–66.

5. See Lynne Viola, *Peasant Rebels Under Stalin: Collectivization and the Culture of Peasant Resistance* (New York, 1996), 234–40.

6. George Leggett, *The Cheka: Lenin's Political Police* (Oxford, 1981), 352; the constitution was finally ratified on January 31, 1924.

7. Anne Applebaum, *Gulag: A History* (New York, 2003), 48–50; Edwin Bacon, *The Gulag at War: Stalin's Forced Labor System in the Light of the Archives* (New York, 1995), 46–47.

8. See the series, with many editors, *Istoria stalinskogo Gulaga: konets 1920-kh-pervaia polovina 1950-kh godov: sobranie dokumentov v semi tomakh* (Moscow, 2004), here doc. 3 in N. V. Petrov (ed.), *Istoria stalinskogo Gulaga* (Moscow, 2004), vol. 2, 58–59; also Oleg V. Khlevniuk, *The History of the Gulag: From Collectivization to the Great Terror* (New Haven, Conn., 2004), 9–12.

9. See his note, April 12, 1930, in Petrov (ed.), *Istoria stalinskovo Gylaga,* vol. 2, 80–81.

10. Michael Jakobson, *Origins of the Gulag: The Soviet Prison Camp System, 1917–1934* (Lexington, Ky., 1993), 125–26.

11. Oleg W. Chlewnjuk (a.k.a. Oleg V. Khlevniuk), *Das Politbüro: Mechanismen der Macht in der Sowjetunion der dreißiger Jahre* (Hamburg, 1998), 52–54.

12. Stalin to Molotov, Sept. 7, 1930, in Lars T. Lih, Oleg V. Naumov, and Oleg V. Khlevniuk, eds., *Stalin's Letters to Molotov, 1925–1936* (London, 1995), 212–13.

13. See doc. 32, in A. B. Bezborodov and V. M. Khrustalëv, eds., *Istoria stalinskogo Gulaga* (Moscow, 2004), vol. 4, 110. For further analysis, see J. Arch Getty, Gábor Tamás Rittersporn, and Viktor N. Zemskov, "Victims of the Soviet Penal System in the Pre-war Years: A First Approach on the Basis of Archival Evidence," *AHR* (1993), 1017–49. For 1930, see Stephen G. Wheatcroft, "Victims of Stalinism and the Soviet Secret Police: The Comparability and Reliability of the Archival Data—Not the Last Word," *EAS* (1999), 315–45.

14. See doc. 5 (1935), in Bezborodov and Khrustalëv, *Istoria stalinskogo Gulaga,* vol. 4, 68–69.

15. Stalin to Molotov, n.d., not before March 1931, in Lih, Naumov, and Khlevniuk, *Stalin's Letters,* 228.

16. See James R. Harris, *The Great Urals: Regionalism and the Evolution of the Soviet System* (Ithaca, N.Y., 1999), 118–22.

17. See Nicolas Werth, "A State Against Its People: Violence, Repression, and

Terror in the Soviet Union," in Stéphane Courtois et al., *The Black Book of Communism* (Cambridge, Mass., 1999), 153–55.

18. Ibid., 155; for the northern camps in 1930, see Lynne Viola, "The Other Archipelago: Kulak Deportation to the North in 1930," *Slavic Review* (2001), 752, which shows many prisoners had run away.
19. Stalin, *Sochineiia*, vol. 13, 38–39.
20. Ibid., 41–42.
21. James Lee Heizer, "The Cult of Stalin, 1929–1939" (Ph.D. diss., University of Kentucky, 1977), 59–68.
22. The phrase is from R. W. Davies et al., eds., *The Stalin-Kaganovich Correspondence, 1931–36* (New Haven, Conn., 2003), 16.
23. Simon Sebag Montefiore, *Stalin: The Court of the Red Tsar* (New York, 2004), 182.

CHAPTER 11: NAZI PARTY AS SOCIAL MOVEMENT

1. See, for example, the autobiographies reprinted in Theodore Abel, *Why Hitler Came to Power* (repr., Cambridge, Mass., 1986), 282.
2. May 22, 1926, article, in *Hitler: Reden, Schriften,* vol. 1, 445.
3. Ibid., 443, 446.
4. William Sheridan Allen, *The Nazi Seizure of Power: The Experience of a Single German Town, 1922–1945* (New York, 1984), 144; Henry Ashby Turner Jr., *German Big Business and the Rise of Hitler* (New York, 1985), 112–15.
5. *Hitler: Reden, Schriften,* vol. 1, 443.
6. Brigitte Hamann, *Winifred Wagner oder Hitlers Bayreuth* (Munich, 2002), 164–66.
7. Nov. 15, 1936, entry, in Elke Fröhlich et al., eds., *Die Tagebücher von Joseph Goebbels* (Munich, 2005ff.), part 1, vol. 3, part 2, 252.
8. *Hitler: Reden, Schriften,* vol. 1, 432 n. 7.
9. May 22, 1926, speech, in ibid., 451–52.
10. *Hitler: Reden, Schriften,* vol. 1, 15–16; Peter Longerich, *Die braunen Bataillone: Geschichte der SA* (Munich, 1989), 45–59.
11. Michael H. Kater, *The Nazi Party: A Social Profile of Members and Leaders, 1919–1945* (Cambridge, Mass., 1983), 169–72.
12. Noakes and Pridham, vol. 1, 52.
13. See, for example, the Jan. 26, 1927, police report from Oldenburg of a gathering of twenty thousand, in ibid., 59–61.
14. See, for example, the Aug. 21, 1927, speech to a Party rally in Nuremberg, in *Hitler: Reden, Schriften,* vol. 2, part 2, 497.
15. *Hitler: Reden, Schriften,* vol. 2, part 2, 593.

16. Ibid., 771–72.
17. Dietrich Orlow, *The History of the Nazi Party, 1919–1933* (Pittsburgh, 1969), 119.
18. See Conan Fischer, *The German Communists and the Rise of Nazism* (New York, 1991), 102.
19. Himmler carried on the complete correspondence of the propaganda leadership from 1926 up to and including the "breakthrough" elections of September 1930. See Udo Kissenkoetter, *Gregor Strasser und die NSDAP* (Stuttgart, 1978), 59.
20. Ibid., 58.
21. Ibid.; Gerhard Paul, *Aufstand der Bilder: Die NS-Propaganda vor 1933* (Bonn, 1992), 67.
22. Orlow, *History of the Nazi Party,* 158–61.
23. *Hitler: Reden, Schriften,* vol. 3, part 1, 35 n. 1, 36 n. 7. See Paul, *Aufstand der Bilder,* 69; Kater, *Nazi Party,* 263.
24. *Hitler: Reden, Schriften,* vol. 3, part 1, 56–62.
25. *Tagebücher von Goebbels,* part 1, vol. 1, part 3, 124–25.
26. *Hitler: Reden, Schriften,* vol. 3, part 1, 236–40.
27. Ibid., 245–53.
28. See Orlow, *History of the Nazi Party,* 161–62. For the insistence that this was Himmler's original idea, see Longerich, *Die braunen Bataillone,* 76–77; Kissenkoetter, *Strasser,* 56–57. On the speakers and their fees, see Turner, *German Big Business,* 119.
29. See the table in Orlow, *History of the Nazi Party,* 153.
30. Oct. 20, 1929, entry in *Tagebücher von Goebbels,* part 1, vol. 1, part 3, 353; on cooperation, see the Nov. 22, 1929, entry, 377.
31. Statistics in *Hitler: Reden, Schriften,* vol. 3, part 2, 478 n. 9.
32. April 18, 1929, entry, in *Tagebücher von Goebbels,* part 1, vol. 1, part 3, 229–30; also Sept. 7, 1929, entry, 338–39.
33. *Hitler: Reden, Schriften,* vol. 3, part 2, 335.
34. Jill Stephenson, *The Nazi Organization of Women* (London, 1981), 36, 50.
35. *Hitler: Reden, Schriften,* vol. 3, part 2, 354–55 n. 3.
36. See ibid., 318–35; for Hitler's speech of August 4, 345–54.
37. Ibid., 469 n. 1; Eric G. Reiche, *The Development of the SA in Nürnberg, 1922–1934* (Cambridge, U.K., 1986), 90; Oct. 28, 1929, entry in *Tagebücher von Goebbels,* part 1, vol. 1, part 3, 358–59; on Berlin, see Nov. 18, 1929, entry, in *Tagebücher von Goebbels,* 374–75.
38. *Hitler: Reden, Schriften,* vol. 3, part 2, 538–41.

CHAPTER 12: NAZISM EXPLOITS ECONOMIC DISTRESS

1. Gustavo Corni and Horst Gies, eds., *Blut und Boden: Rassenideologie und Agrarpolitik im Staat Hitlers* (Idstein, 1994), 180.

2. J. E. Farquharson, *The Plough and the Swastika: The NSDAP and Agriculture in Germany, 1928–1945* (London, 1976), 25–31.

3. *Hitler: Reden, Schriften,* vol. 3, part 3, 115–20. See also Jeremy Noakes, *The Nazi Party in Lower Saxony, 1921–1933* (Oxford, 1971), 124–25.

4. Henry Ashby Turner Jr., *German Big Business and the Rise of Hitler* (New York, 1985), 118.

5. Gustavo Corni and Horst Gies, *Brot, Butter, Kanonen: Die Ernährungswirtschaft in Deutschland unter der Diktatur Hitlers* (Berlin, 1997), 22.

6. Jan. 3, 1933, speech, in *Hitler: Reden, Schriften,* vol. 5, part 2, 317–19.

7. March 7, 1930, speech, in ibid., vol. 3, part 3, 120.

8. Heinrich August Winkler, *Weimar, 1918–1933: Die Geschichte der ersten deutschen Demokratie* (Munich, 1998), 372.

9. Sebastian Haffner, *Geschichte eines Deutschen: Die Erinnerungen, 1914–1933* (Munich, 2000), 86.

10. Winkler, *Weimar,* 374–81.

11. Dietmar Petzina, Werner Abelshauser, and Anselm Faust, eds., *Sozialgeschichtliches Arbeitsbuch III: Materialien zur Statistik des Deutschen Reiches, 1914–1945* (Munich, 1978), 119.

12. Jürgen W. Falter, *Hitler's Wähler* (Munich, 1991), 292.

13. Table 7 in M. Rainer Lepsius, "From Fragmented Party Democracy to Government by Emergency Decree and National Socialist Takeover," in Juan J. Linz and Alfred Stephan, eds., *The Breakdown of Democratic Regimes: Europe* (Baltimore, 1978), 56.

14. See *Statistisches Jahrbuch für das Deutsche Reich* (1933), 291; (1941–42), 426.

15. David F. Crew, *Germans on Welfare: From Weimar to Hitler* (New York, 1998), 70–71.

16. Detlev J. K. Peukert, *Die Weimarer Republik: Krisenjahre der klassischen Moderne* (Frankfurt am Main, 1987), 246, 271.

17. See Paul Weindling, *Health, Race, and German Politics Between National Unification and Nazism, 1870–1945* (Cambridge, U.K., 1989), 457–62; Atina Grossmann, *Reforming Sex: The German Movement for Birth Control and Abortion Reform, 1920–1950* (New York, 1995), 79–135.

18. Turner, *German Big Business,* 118.

19. Aug. 18, 1930, speech, in *Hitler: Reden, Schriften,* vol. 3, part 3, 356, 357.

20. Ibid., 420 n. 4.

21. Sept. 16, 1930, speech, in ibid., 420–30.

22. According to table 6 in Lepsius, "Fragmented Party Democracy," 52.

23. See Heinrich Brüning, *Memoiren, 1918–1934* (Munich, 1970), 633.

24. June 4, 1932, entry, in Harry Kessler, *In the Twenties: The Diaries of Harry Kessler* (New York, 1971), 419.

25. Winkler, *Weimar,* 481.

26. Julia Sneeringer, *Winning Women's Votes: Propaganda and Politics in Weimar Germany* (Chapel Hill, N.C., 2002), 266.

27. Falter, *Hitler's Wähler*, 364–75.

28. Oct. 13, 1932, speech, in *Hitler: Reden, Schriften*, vol. 5, part 2, 22 n. 8.

29. Table 4 in Lepsius, "Fragmented Party Democracy," 49.

30. Detlef Schmiechen-Ackermann, *Nationalsozialismus und Arbeitermilieus: Der nationalsozialistische Angriff auf die proletarischen Wohnquartiere und die Reaktion in den sozialistischen Vereinen* (Bonn, 1998), 386, 394, 399.

31. Sven Reichardt, *Faschistische Kampfbünde: Gewalt und Gemeinschaft im italienischen Squadrismus und in der deutschen SA* (Cologne, 2002), 258–60.

32. Turner, *German Big Business*, 116–17.

33. See Sept. 1, 1930, police report, in *Hitler: Reden, Schriften*, vol. 3, part 3, 378–79.

34. Peter Longerich, *Die braunen Bataillone: Geschichte der SA* (Munich, 1989), 110–11.

35. Feb. 22, 1932, entry, in Elke Fröhlich et al., eds., *Die Tagebücher von Joseph Goebbels* (Munich, 2005ff.), part 1, vol. 2, part 2, 224–25.

36. *Hitler: Reden, Schriften*, vol. 4, part 3, 161, 202.

37. Ian Kershaw, *Hitler, 1889–1936: Hubris* (London, 1998), 363.

38. *Hitler: Reden, Schriften*, vol. 5, part 1, 52–53.

39. Ibid., 57–98.

40. Longerich, *Die braunen Bataillone*, 122.

41. Winkler, *Weimar*, 489–90; James M. Diehl, *Paramilitary Politics in Weimar Germany* (Bloomington, Ind., 1977), 286–88.

42. See Anthony McElligott, *Contested City: Municipal Politics and the Rise of Nazism in Altona, 1917–1937* (Ann Arbor, Mich., 1998), 194.

43. See Geoffrey J. Giles, *Students and National Socialism in Germany* (Princeton, N.J., 1985), 81.

44. See Johnpeter Horst Grill, *The Nazi Movement in Baden, 1920–1945* (Chapel Hill, N.C., 1983), 212–14.

45. See Franz von Papen, *Memoirs* (London, 1952), 200; *Hitler: Reden, Schriften*, vol. 5, part 1, 317–20; Kershaw, *Hitler, 1889–1936*, 381–83.

CHAPTER 13: "ALL POWER" FOR HITLER

1. Elke Fröhlich et al., eds., *Die Tagebücher von Joseph Goebbels* (Munich, 2005ff.), part 1, vol. 2, part 2, 333.

2. Heinrich August Winkler, *Weimar, 1918–1933: Die Geschichte der ersten deutschen Demokratie* (Munich, 1998), 508–9.

3. Aug. 7, 1932, entry, in *Tagebücher von Goebbels*, part 1, vol. 2, part 2, 334–35.

4. Winkler, *Weimar*, 509.

5. See Franz von Papen, *Memoirs* (London, 1952), 195–98.

6. Winkler, *Weimar*, 511–12; Papen, *Memoirs*, 210–11.

7. See Papen, *Memoirs*, 208–9.

8. Sept. 7, 1932, speech, in *Hitler: Reden, Schriften,* vol. 5, part 1, 341; also Oct. 16, speech, in vol. 5, part 2, 58.

9. Hans Mommsen, *Die verspielte Freiheit: Der Weg der Republik von Weimar in den Untergang, 1918 bis 1933* (Frankfurt am Main, 1989), 308–9.

10. See Oded Heilbronner, *Catholicism, Political Culture, and the Countryside: A Social History of the Nazi Party in South Germany* (Ann Arbor, Mich., 1998), 236, 127; for remarks on anti-Semitism, see 135–38. His quantitative analysis of words used by Nazi speakers in the Reichstag elections of 1930 (table 8, p. 126) shows that the word "Jews" was mentioned only six times. But far from indicating the lack of importance of anti-Semitism, this minute approach reveals that practically half the words used were synonyms or code words for Jews.

11. See Anthony Kauders, *German Politics and the Jews: Düsseldorf and Nuremberg, 1910–1933* (Oxford, 1996), 182–91.

12. Theodore Abel, *Why Hitler Came to Power* (repr., Cambridge, Mass., 1986), 164.

13. This latter poster is not included among the eighty-seven in Gerhard Paul, *Aufstand der Bilder: Die NS-Propaganda vor 1933* (Bonn, 1992).

14. Ulrich Herbert, *Best: Biographische Studien über Radikalismus, Weltanschauung, und Vernunft, 1903–1989* (Bonn, 1996), 108–9.

15. Richard Bessel, *Political Violence and the Rise of Nazism: The Storm Troopers in Eastern Germany, 1925–1934* (New Haven, Conn., 1984), 89.

16. Sven Reichardt, *Faschistische Kampfbünde: Gewalt und Gemeinschaft im italienischen Squadrismus und in der deutschen SA* (Cologne, 2002), 631–43.

17. See Dirk Walter, *Antisemitische Kriminalität und Gewalt: Judenfeindschaft in der Weimarer Republik* (Bonn, 1999), 200–56.

18. *Hitler: Reden, Schriften,* vol. 5, part 2, 130–31.

19. Nov. 3, 1932, speech, in ibid., 170.

20. Nov. 5, 1932, speech, in ibid., 181–82.

21. *Hitler: Reden, Schriften,* vol. 3, part 3, 445.

22. Ibid., 448–49.

23. See Klaus-Michael Mallmann, *Kommunisten in der Weimarer Republik: Sozialgeschichte einer revolutionären Bewegung* (Darmstadt, 1996), 87.

24. *Hitler: Reden, Schriften,* vol. 5, part 2, 297–311.

25. Nov. 6, 1932, entry, in Elke Fröhlich et al., eds., *Die Tagebücher von Joseph Goebbels* (Munich, 1987), vol. 2, 272.

26. Udo Kissenkoetter, *Gregor Strasser und die NSDAP* (Stuttgart, 1978), 162–71.

27. Ernst Hanfstaengl, *Hitler: The Missing Years* (1957; New York, 1994), 181.

28. Nov. 22–25, 1932, entries, in *Tagebücher von Goebbels,* vol. 2, 283–85.

29. Kissenkoetter, *Strasser,* 171–73; Hanfstaengl, *Hitler,* 190; Papen, *Memoirs,* 216–17.

30. Cited in his brother's account: Otto Strasser, *In My Time* (London, 1941), 243.

31. Papen, *Memoirs,* 225–31; Ian Kershaw, *Hitler, 1889–1936: Hubris* (London, 1998), 392–93, 414; Henry Ashby Turner Jr., *German Big Business and the Rise of Hitler* (New York, 1985), 314–17; Winkler, *Weimar,* 567–69.

32. *Hitler: Reden, Schriften,* vol. 4, part 3, 74–110.

33. Winkler, *Weimar,* 573–74; Turner, *German Big Business,* 318–19; Kershaw, *Hitler, 1889–1936,* 416–17.

34. For the detailed negotiations, see Papen, *Memoirs,* 236–40; Winkler, *Weimar,* 575–94; Kershaw, *Hitler, 1889–1936,* 417–23.

35. Cited in Winkler, *Weimar,* 592–93; see also Papen, *Memoirs,* 241–44.

36. *Hitler: Reden, Schriften,* vol. 5, part 2, 391–93.

37. Cited in Karl Dietrich Bracher, *Die deutsche Diktatur: Entstehung, Struktur, Folgen des Nationalsozialismus,* 2nd ed. (Cologne, 1969), 213.

38. Richard Overy, *Goering: The "Iron Man"* (London, 1984), 22.

39. Jan. 30, 1933, entry, in *Tagebücher von Goebbels,* vol. 2, 357–61.

40. Papen, *Memoirs,* 264.

41. Karl Dietrich Bracher, *The German Dictatorship: The Origins, Structure, and Effects of National Socialism* (Harmondsworth, U.K., 1970), 243–52.

CHAPTER 14: FIGHT AGAINST THE COUNTRYSIDE

1. Nicolas Werth, "A State Against Its People: Violence, Repression, and Terror in the Soviet Union," in Stéphane Courtois et al., *The Black Book of Communism* (Cambridge, Mass., 1999), 155.

2. R. W. Davies et al., eds., *The Stalin-Kaganovich Correspondence, 1931–36* (New Haven, Conn., 2003), 6; for the total, see Sheila Fitzpatrick, *Stalin's Peasants: Resistance and Survival in the Russian Village After Collectivization* (New York, 1994), 82.

3. See table in Alec Nove, *An Economic History of the USSR* (Harmondsworth, U.K., 1990), 161.

4. Elena Osokina, *Our Daily Bread: Socialist Distribution and the Art of Survival in Stalin's Russia, 1927–1941* (New York, 2001), 61.

5. See table in Nove, *Economic History,* 163.

6. Davies et al., *Stalin-Kaganovich Correspondence,* 137 n. 5.

7. Stalin letter, June 18, 1932, in ibid., 138–39.

8. Letters of July 25 and Aug. 5, 1932, in ibid., 167–68, 177–78.

9. Stalin to Kaganovich, July 20, 1932, in ibid., 164–65.

10. Peter H. Solomon, *Soviet Criminal Justice Under Stalin* (Cambridge, U.K., 1996), 126.

11. Letter in Davies et al., *Stalin-Kaganovich Correspondence,* 179–81.

12. Werth, "State Against Its People," 162–63.

13. Cited in Nove, *Economic History,* 169.

14. Lev Kopelev, *The Education of a True Believer* (New York, 1980), 226.

15. Ibid., 235.

16. Ibid., 250–51.

17. Victor A. Kravchenko, *I Chose Freedom* (1946; New Brunswick, N.J., 2002), 111.

18. Stephen G. Wheatcroft, "More Light on the Scale of Repression and Excess Mortality in the Soviet Union in the 1930s," in J. Arch Getty and Roberta T. Manning, eds., *Stalinist Terror: New Perspectives* (New York, 1993), 282–86.

19. See Gijs Kessler, "The Passport System and State Control over Population Flows in the Soviet Union, 1932–1940," *Cahiers du monde russe* (April–Dec. 2001), 483–84.

20. Werth, "State Against Its People," 164.

21. Miron Dolot, *Execution by Hunger: The Hidden Holocaust* (New York, 1985), 180.

22. Ibid., 229.

23. Vasily Grossman, *Forever Flowing* (New York, 1972), 164–65, as cited in Robert Conquest, *Harvest of Sorrow: Soviet Collectivization and the Terror-Famine* (New York, 1986), 256–57.

24. See, for example, in Kravchenko, *I Chose Freedom,* 128.

25. Conquest, *Harvest of Sorrow,* 257–58.

26. Stalin to Kaganovich, June 7, 1932, in Davies et al., *Stalin-Kaganovich Correspondence,* 124.

27. Cited in Werth, "State Against Its People," 165–67.

28. R. W. Davies and Stephen G. Wheatcroft, "The Soviet Famine of 1932–33 and the Crisis in Agriculture," in Stephen G. Wheatcroft, ed., *Challenging Traditional Views of Russian History* (London, 2002), 84, 86.

29. Table 48 in R. W. Davies, Mark Harrison, and Stephen G. Wheatcroft, eds., *The Economic Transformation of the Soviet Union, 1913–1945* (Cambridge, U.K., 1994), 316.

30. Alec Nove, "Victims of Stalinism: How Many?" in Getty and Manning, *Stalinist Terror,* 262.

31. Wheatcroft, "More Light on the Scale of Repression," 275–90.

32. Werth, "State Against Its People," 167.

33. Conquest, *Harvest of Sorrow,* 306.

34. Stephen G. Wheatcroft and R. W. Davies, "Population," in Davies, Harrison, and Wheatcroft, *Economic Transformation,* 57–80; for a summary, see Manfred Hildermeier, *Geschichte der Sowjetunion, 1917–1991* (Munich, 1998), 398–401.

35. See Stalin to Kaganovich, Aug. 5, 1932, in Davies et al., *Stalin-Kaganovich Correspondence,* 175–77.

36. Merle Fainsod, *Smolensk Under Soviet Rule* (New York, 1963), 280–93; for the production, see Paul R. Gregory, *The Political Economy of Stalinism: Evidence from the Soviet Secret Archives* (New York, 2004), 39.

37. In the 1990s the peasants even resisted "de-collectivization." Lynne Viola, *Peasant Rebels Under Stalin: Collectivization and the Culture of Peasant Resistance* (New York, 1996), 239–40.

38. Fitzpatrick, *Stalin's Peasants,* 291–96.
39. Andrea Graziosi, *The Great Soviet Peasant War: Bolsheviks and Peasants, 1917–1933* (Cambridge, Mass., 1996), 70.
40. Doc. 23, in J. Arch Getty and Oleg V. Naumov, eds., *The Road to Terror: Stalin and the Self-Destruction of the Bolsheviks, 1932–1939* (New Haven, Conn., 1999), 121.
41. See Kravchenko, *I Chose Freedom,* 170.
42. The decree was publicized in Khrushchev's secret 1956 speech. See Strobe Talbott, ed., *Khrushchev Remembers* (Boston, 1970), app. 4, 574.
43. For Yezhov's rise, see Marc Jansen and Nikita Petrov, *Stalin's Loyal Executioner: People's Commissar Nikolai Ezhov* (Stanford, Calif., 2002), 21–51; for his appointment, see Davies et al., *Stalin-Kaganovich Correspondence,* 359–60.
44. See, for example, Kopelev, *Education of a True Believer,* 299–300.

CHAPTER 15: TERROR AS POLITICAL PRACTICE

1. Lev Kopelev, *The Education of a True Believer* (New York, 1980), 258.
2. David R. Shearer, "Social Disorder, Mass Repression, and the NKVD During the 1930s," *Cahiers du monde russe* (2001), 519.
3. Gijs Kessler, "The Passport System and State Control over Population Flows in the Soviet Union, 1932–1940," *Cahiers du monde russe* (April–Dec. 2001), 484.
4. Golfo Alexopoulos, *Stalin's Outcasts: Aliens, Citizens, and the Soviet State, 1926–1936* (Ithaca, N.Y., 2003), 58.
5. Cited in ibid., 76.
6. Stalin, *Sochineniia,* vol. 13, 207, 210 (Jan. 7, 1933), report.
7. Kessler, "Passport System and State Control," 485–95.
8. S. V. Mironenko and N. Werth, eds., *Istoria stalinskogo Gulaga* (Moscow, 2004) vol. 1, 156–57; Shearer, "Social Disorder," 520–21.
9. Paul M. Hagenloh, " 'Socially Harmful Elements' and the Great Terror," in Sheila Fitzpatrick, ed., *Stalinism: New Directions* (New York, 2000), 288–90.
10. Ibid., 287.
11. See the diary of Stepan Podlubny in Jochen Hellbeck, ed., *Tagebuch aus Moskau, 1931–1939* (Munich, 1996), 237–57.
12. Shearer, "Social Disorder," 524, 526.
13. Nicolas Werth, "A State Against Its People: Violence, Repression, and Terror in the Soviet Union," in Stéphane Courtois et al., *The Black Book of Communism* (Cambridge, Mass., 1999), 177–78.
14. Doc. 58, in Mironenko and Werth, *Istoria stalinskogo Gulaga,* vol. 1, 268–75.
15. Oleg V. Khlevniuk, *The History of the Gulag: From Collectivization to the Great Terror* (New Haven, Conn., 2004), 170.

16. Marc Jansen and Nikita Petrov, *Stalin's Loyal Executioner: People's Commissar Nikolai Ezhov* (Stanford, Calif., 2002), 92–93.

17. Cited in ibid., 89.

18. Nicolas Werth, "The Mechanism of a Mass Crime: The Great Terror in the Soviet Union, 1937–1938," in Robert Gellately and Ben Kiernan, eds., *The Specter of Genocide: Mass Murder in Historical Perspective* (Cambridge, U.K., 2003), 229.

19. Doc. 182, in J. Arch Getty and Oleg V. Naumov, eds., *The Road to Terror: Stalin and the Self-Destruction of the Bolsheviks, 1932–1939* (New Haven, Conn., 1999), 519.

20. Barry McLoughlin, "Mass Operations of the NKVD, 1937–8: A Survey," in Barry McLoughlin and Kevin McDermott, eds., *Stalin's Terror: High Politics and Mass Repression in the Soviet Union* (New York, 2003), 129.

21. Cited in Khlevniuk, *History of the Gulag,* 171.

22. David Nordlander, "Magadan and the Economic History of Dalstroi in the 1930s," in Paul R. Gregory and Valery Lazarev, eds., *The Economics of Forced Labor: The Soviet Gulag* (Stanford, Calif., 2003), 105–25.

23. McLoughlin, "Mass Operations," 129–30.

24. Werth, "Mechanism of a Mass Crime," 231. The town was Ulan-Ude.

25. Khlevniuk, *History of the Gulag,* 170; figures in Jansen and Petrov, *Ezhov,* 91.

26. Werth, "Mechanism of a Mass Crime," 231.

27. Doc. 83, in Lewis Siegelbaum and Andrei Sokolov, *Stalinism as a Way of Life: A Narrative in Documents* (New Haven, Conn., 2000), 237–38.

28. McLoughlin, "Mass Operations," 136.

29. See Gábor Tamás Rittersporn, *Stalinist Simplifications and Soviet Complications: Social Tensions and Political Conflicts in the USSR, 1933–1953* (Chur, Switzerland, 1991), 244–55.

30. Sarah Davies, *Popular Opinion in Stalin's Russia: Terror, Propaganda, and Dissent* (New York, 1997), 121, 123.

31. William B. Husband, *"Godless Communists": Atheism and Society in Soviet Russia, 1917–1932* (DeKalb, Ill., 2000), 47–49.

32. See Steven Merritt Minor, *Stalin's Holy War: Religion, Nationalism, and Alliance Politics, 1941–1945* (Chapel Hill, N.C., 2003), 20–22.

33. Lenin in Richard Pipes, ed., *The Unknown Lenin: From the Secret Archive* (New Haven, Conn., 1996), 152–55.

34. Donald Rayfield, *Stalin and His Hangmen: The Tyrant and Those Who Killed for Him* (New York, 2004), 126–28.

35. Timothy J. Colton, *Moscow: Governing the Socialist Metropolis* (Cambridge, Mass., 1995), 228.

36. David J. Dallin and Boris I. Nicolaevsky, *Forced Labor in Soviet Russia* (New Haven, Conn., 1947), 182–83.

37. Husband, *"Godless Communists,"* 37.

38. Sheila Fitzpatrick, *Stalin's Peasants: Resistance and Survival in the Russian Village After Collectivization* (New York, 1994), 204.
39. Cited in Werth, "State Against Its People," 200.
40. Aleksandr Solzhenitsyn, *The Gulag Archipelago, 1918–1956* (New York, 1973), vol. 1, 42–43.
41. Feliks Ivanovich Chuev and Vyacheslav Molotov, *Sto sorok besed s Molotovym: iz dnevnika F. Chueva* (Moscow, 1991), 321, 416, 428.

CHAPTER 16: "MASS OPERATIONS"

1. Doc. 57, in S. V. Mironenko and N. Werth, eds., *Istoria stalinskogo Gulaga* (Moscow, 2004), vol. 1, 267–68.
2. Case in Lewis Siegelbaum and Andrei Sokolov, *Stalinism as a Way of Life: A Narrative in Documents* (New Haven, Conn., 2000), 234.
3. Nicolas Werth, "The Mechanism of a Mass Crime: The Great Terror in the Soviet Union, 1937–1938," in Robert Gellately and Ben Kiernan, eds., *The Specter of Genocide: Mass Murder in Historical Perspective* (Cambridge, U.K., 2003), 232, also 235.
4. Cited in Marc Jansen and Nikita Petrov, *Stalin's Loyal Executioner: People's Commissar Nikolai Ezhov* (Stanford, Calif., 2002), 98.
5. Doc. 59, in Mironenko and Werth, *Istoria stalinskogo Gulaga,* vol. 1, 275–77.
6. Barry McLoughlin, "Mass Operations of the NKVD, 1937–8: A Survey," in Barry McLoughlin and Kevin McDermott, eds., *Stalin's Terror: High Politics and Mass Repression in the Soviet Union* (New York, 2003), 134.
7. Doc. 60, in Mironenko and Werth, *Istoria stalinskogo Gulaga,* vol. 1, 277–81; Jansen and Petrov, *Ezhov,* 96–97.
8. Nikita Petrov and Arsenii Roginskii, "The 'Polish Operation' of the NKVD, 1937–8," in McLoughlin and McDermott, *Stalin's Terror,* 168–69; Jansen and Petrov, *Ezhov,* 99; Werth, "Mechanism of a Mass Crime,"237.
9. Werth, "Mechanism of a Mass Crime," 235–36.
10. Figures in Jansen and Petrov, *Ezhov,* 99.
11. See the case of Alexander Tivoli, and his wife and son, mentioned in J. Arch Getty and Oleg V. Naumov, eds., *The Road to Terror: Stalin and the Self-Destruction of the Bolsheviks, 1932–1939* (New Haven, Conn., 1999), 2–5.
12. See doc. 32, in A. B. Bezborodov and V. M. Khrustalëv, eds., *Istoria stalinskogo Gulaga* (Moscow, 2004), vol. 4, 110.
13. Anne Applebaum, *Gulag: A History* (New York, 2003), 62.
14. Oleg V. Khlevniuk, *The History of the Gulag: From Collectivization to the Great Terror* (New Haven, Conn., 2004), 36; Timothy J. Colton, *Moscow: Governing the Socialist Metropolis* (Cambridge, Mass., 1995), 258.
15. Cited in Aleksandr Solzhenitsyn, *The Gulag Archipelago, 1918–1956* (New York, 1973), vol. 2, 105.

16. Cited in David J. Dallin and Boris I. Nicolaevsky, *Forced Labor in Soviet Russia* (New Haven, Conn., 1947), 223.

17. Oleg V. Khlevniuk, "The Economy of the Gulag," in Paul R. Gregory, ed., *Behind the Façade of Stalin's Command Economy* (Stanford, Calif., 2001), 126–28.

18. Cited in Vladimir Paperny, *Architecture in the Age of Stalin: Culture Two* (Cambridge, U.K., 2002), 97.

19. Kathleen Berton, *Moscow: An Architectural History* (New York, 1990), 202.

20. Colton, *Moscow*, 331–32.

21. Ibid., 263.

22. Ibid., 333.

23. Solzhenitsyn, *Gulag Archipelago*, vol. 2, 98.

24. Cited in Applebaum, *Gulag*, 44; see also Solzhenitsyn, *Gulag Archipelago*, vol. 2, 60–62.

25. Dallin and Nicolaevsky, *Forced Labor*, 189.

26. Cited in Solzhenitsyn, *Gulag Archipelago*, vol. 2, 85–86.

27. On these Western apologists, see François Furet, *The Passing of an Illusion: The Idea of Communism in the Twentieth Century* (Chicago, 1999), 153–54.

28. Applebaum, *Gulag*, 76–77.

29. Khlevniuk, "Economy of the Gulag," 118.

30. Khlevniuk, *History of the Gulag*, 336.

31. Doc. 30, in Bezborodov and Khrustalëv, *Istoria stalinskogo Gulaga*, vol. 4, 109.

32. Based on three years, 1934, 1937, 1940, in J. Arch Getty, Gábor Tamás Rittersporn, and Viktor N. Zemskov, "Victims of the Soviet Penal System in the Pre-war Years: A First Approach on the Basis of Archival Evidence," *AHR* (1993), 1025, table 2.

33. Anton Antonov-Ovseyenko, *The Time of Stalin: Portrait of a Tyranny* (New York, 1981), 125.

34. Victor A. Kravchenko, *I Chose Freedom* (1946; New Brunswick, N.J., 2002), 284.

35. Ibid., 296.

36. Ibid., 296–97.

37. John Scott, *Behind the Urals: An American Worker in Russia's City of Steel*, enl. ed. prepared by Stephen Kotkin (Bloomington, Ind., 1989), 282–83.

38. Pohl, *Stalinist Penal System*, 59.

39. Stephen Kotkin, *Magnetic Mountain: Stalinism as a Civilization* (Berkeley, Calif., 1995), 133.

40. Pohl, *Stalinist Penal System*, 61, table 31; for slightly lower "minimum" numbers, see Stephen G. Wheatcroft, "The Scale and Nature of German and Soviet Repression and Mass Killings," *EAS* (1996), 1340, table 7.

41. See Kotkin, *Magnetic Mountain*, 459 n. 131, for the four different kinds of ITK.

42. Scott, *Behind the Urals*, 86.

43. Ibid., 285.

44. Kotkin, *Magnetic Mountain,* 134.

45. Getty, Rittersporn, and Zemskov, "Victims of the Soviet Penal System," 1019–20.

46. Cited in Khlevniuk, "Economy of the Gulag," 128.

47. Colton, *Moscow,* 334, 851 n. 168.

48. Khlevniuk, *History of the Gulag,* 328.

49. Ibid., 329.

50. See, for example, Nicolas Werth and Gaël Moullec, eds., *Rapports secrets soviétiques, 1921–1991* (Paris, 1994), 224–28.

51. Hiroaki Kuromiya, *Freedom and Terror in the Donbas: A Ukrainian-Russian Borderland, 1870s–1990s* (Cambridge, U.K., 1998), 251–53; Nicolas Werth, "A State Against Its People: Violence, Repression, and Terror in the Soviet Union," in Stéphane Courtois et al., *The Black Book of Communism* (Cambridge, Mass., 1999), 214.

52. Kuromiya, *Freedom and Terror in the Donbas,* 253.

53. Ibid., 255–56.

54. Werth, "State Against Its People," 214.

55. Wolfgang Leonhard, *Child of the Revolution* (Chicago, 1958), 92–94.

56. See Werth and Moullec, *Rapports secrets soviétiques,* 229.

57. Dmitri Volkogonov, *Triumf i tragediya. Politichesky portret J. V. Stalina* (Moscow, 1989), vol. 2, part 2, 77.

CHAPTER 17: "CLEANSING" THE SOVIET ELITE

1. Lenin, *Polnoe sobranie sochinenii,* vol. 44, 124.

2. For convenient tables on Party membership, with social and ethnic composition, see Merle Fainsod, *How Russia Is Ruled* (Cambridge, Mass., 1965), 212–39.

3. Cited in J. Arch Getty, *The Origins of the Great Purges: The Soviet Communist Party Reconsidered, 1933–1938* (Cambridge, U.K., 1985), 67–68.

4. J. Arch Getty and Oleg V. Naumov, eds., *The Road to Terror: Stalin and the Self-Destruction of the Bolsheviks, 1932–1939* (New Haven, Conn., 1999), 198. See also doc. 54, table 2, 202.

5. See doc. 73, in ibid., 250–55.

6. See, for example, ibid., 261–63.

7. R. W. Davies et al., eds., *The Stalin-Kaganovich Correspondence, 1931–1936* (New Haven, Conn., 2003), 324.

8. See Arkady Vaksberg, *Stalin's Prosecutor: The Life of Andrei Vyshinsky* (New York, 1990), 80–81.

9. See Vadim Z. Rogovin, *1937: Stalin's Year of Terror* (Oak Park, Mich., 1998), 103.

10. Cited in Igal Halfin, *Terror in My Soul: Communist Autobiographies on Trial* (Cambridge, Mass., 2003), 277.

11. Davies et al., *Stalin-Kaganovich Correspondence,* 322–38.

12. Cited in Simon Sebag Montefiore, *Stalin: The Court of the Red Tsar* (New York, 2004), 192.

13. Lev Kopelev, *The Education of a True Believer* (New York, 1980), 308–14.

14. Lev Kopelev, *To Be Preserved Forever* (New York, 1977), 19.

15. Doc. 94, in Getty and Naumov, *Road to Terror,* 304–8; for other speeches, see docs. 95–101, in ibid., 309–22.

16. Sheila Fitzpatrick, *Everyday Stalinism: Ordinary Life in Extraordinary Times: Soviet Russia in the 1930s* (New York, 1999), 192.

17. All cited in Elena Osokina, *Our Daily Bread: Socialist Distribution and the Art of Survival in Stalin's Russia, 1927–1941* (New York, 2001), 157.

18. Vaksberg, *Vyshinsky,* 95.

19. Ibid., 96–97.

20. Cited in Sebag Montefiore, *Stalin,* 210–11.

21. Cited in Stephen F. Cohen, *Bukharin and the Bolshevik Revolution: A Political Biography, 1888–1938* (New York, 1974), 370.

22. Sebag Montefiore, *Stalin,* 215.

23. Cohen, *Bukharin and the Bolshevik Revolution,* 372.

24. Cited in Vaksberg, *Vyshinsky,* 108.

25. Cited in Cohen, *Bukharin and the Bolshevik Revolution,* 380.

26. Kopelev, *To Be Preserved Forever,* 92.

27. Victor A. Kravchenko, *I Chose Freedom* (1946; New Brunswick, N.J., 2002), 282.

28. Rogovin, *1937,* 425–47.

29. Dmitri Volkogonov, *Triumf i tragediya. Politichesky portret J. V. Stalina* (Moscow, 1989), vol. 1, part 2, 276–77.

30. Marc Jansen and Nikita Petrov, *Stalin's Loyal Executioner: People's Commissar Nikolai Ezhov* (Stanford, Calif., 2002), 70; Sebag Montefiore, *Stalin,* 225–27.

31. Cited in Amy Knight, *Beria: Stalin's First Lieutenant* (Princeton, N.J., 1993), 78.

32. Cited in ibid., 84.

33. For the *raion* show trials, see Sheila Fitzpatrick, *Stalin's Peasants: Resistance and Survival in the Russian Village After Collectivization* (New York, 1994), 310.

34. March 3 speech, reprinted in McNeal, *Stalin sochineniia,* vol. 1 (vol. 14), 197, 213–14.

35. See Gábor Tamás Rittersporn, "Extra-judicial Repression and the Courts: Their Relationship in the 1930s," in Peter H. Solomon Jr., ed., *Reforming Justice in Russia, 1864–1996* (New York, 1997), 214.

36. Oleg V. Khlevniuk, *Das Politbüro: Mechanismen der Macht in der Sowjetunion der dreißiger Jahre* (Hamburg, 1998), 294–95.

37. Sebag Montefiore, *Stalin,* 246–49.
38. Cited in William Taubman, *Khrushchev: The Man and His Era* (New York, 2003), 99–100.
39. See Oleg V. Khlevniuk, "The Objectives of the Great Terror, 1937–1938," in David L. Hoffmann, ed., *Stalinism: The Essential Readings* (Oxford, 2003), 87–104.
40. Fitzpatrick, *Everyday Stalinism,* 202–5.
41. Nicolas Werth, "A State Against Its People: Violence, Repression, and Terror in the Soviet Union," in Stéphane Courtois et al., *The Black Book of Communism* (Cambridge, Mass., 1999), 189.
42. Evan Mawdsley and Stephen White, *The Soviet Elite from Lenin to Gorbachev: The Central Committee and Its Members, 1917–1991* (Oxford, 2000), 74–76.
43. Robert C. Tucker, *Stalin in Power: The Revolution from Above, 1928–1941* (New York, 1990), 528.
44. Getty, *Origins of the Great Purges,* 176–77.
45. Getty and Naumov, *Road to Terror,* 588, table 5.
46. Ibid., 592.

CHAPTER 18: WINNING OVER THE NATION

1. Cabinet minutes are reprinted in Noakes and Pridham, vol. 1, 127–29; see also Ian Kershaw, *Hitler, 1889–1936; Hubris* (London, 1998), 438–39.
2. See Karl Dietrich Bracher, Wolfgang Sauer, and Gerhard Schulz, *Die nationalsozialistische Machtergreifung: Studien zur Errichtung des totalitären Herrschaftsystems in Deutschland, 1933–34* (Cologne, 1969), 50–51; Martin Broszat, *Hitler and the Collapse of Weimar Germany* (New York, 1987), 149.
3. *Hitler: Reden und Proklamationen,* vol. 1, 191–94.
4. Ibid., 194–95.
5. Konrad Heiden, *Der Fuehrer: Hitler's Rise to Power* (1944; Boston, 1969), 542.
6. See Samuel W. Mitcham Jr., "Generalfeldmarschall Werner von Blomberg," in Gerd R. Ueberschär, ed., *Hitlers militärische Elite* (Darmstadt, 1998), vol. 1, 28–36; and Bernd Boll, "Generalfeldmarschall Walter von Reichenau," in ibid., 195–202.
7. See Hans-Erich Volkmann, "Von Blomberg zu Keitel—Die Wehrmachtführung und die Demontage des Rechtsstaates," in Rolf-Dieter Müller and Hans-Erich Volkmann, eds., *Die Wehrmacht: Mythos und Realität* (Munich, 1999), 51.
8. Richard R. Muller, "Werner von Blomberg: Hitlers 'idealistischer' Kriegsminister," in Ronald Smelser and Enrico Syring, eds., *Die Militärelite des Dritten Reiches* (Berlin, 1995), 53.

9. Volkmann, "Von Blomberg zu Keitel," 49.

10. Cited in *IMT,* vol. 14, 29–30.

11. Cited in F. L. Carsten, *The Reichswehr and Politics, 1918–1933* (Berkeley, Calif., 1973), 396.

12. See Peter Hoffmann, *Stauffenberg: A Family History, 1905–1944* (Cambridge, Mass., 1995), 69.

13. Klaus-Jürgen Müller, *Das Heer und Hitler: Armee und nationalsozialistisches Regime, 1933–1940* (Stuttgart, 1969), 37–46, 63.

14. Cited in Carsten, *Reichswehr and Politics,* 394. Full document in Noakes and Pridham, vol. 3, 627–28.

15. There is a slight variation in the published text of this presentation, recorded in the notes of General Curt Liebmann and the originals, which omits the notion of "continental great power." The originals are cited in Volkmann, "Von Blomberg zu Keitel," 52.

16. Document reprinted in Noakes and Pridham, vol. 3, 628–29. See also Gerhard L. Weinberg, *The Foreign Policy of Hitler's Germany: Diplomatic Revolution in Europe, 1933–36* (Chicago, 1970), 25–27.

17. The Hitler speech is reprinted as doc. 203-D, in *IMT,* vol. 35, 42–48; Krupp's response is doc. 204-D, in ibid., 48.

18. Henry Ashby Turner Jr., *German Big Business and the Rise of Hitler* (New York, 1985), 332.

19. See Richard Overy, *War and Economy in the Third Reich* (Oxford, 1994), 132–33.

20. See Jonathan Petropoulos, *Royals and the Reich: The Princes of Hessen in Nazi Germany* (New York, 2006), 106; for the list, see 380–89.

21. Hans Mommsen, *Die verspielte Freiheit: Der Weg der Republik von Weimar in den Untergang, 1918 bis 1933* (Frankfurt am Main, 1989), 534.

22. Michael H. Kater, *Doctors Under Hitler* (Chapel Hill, N. C., 1989), 12–15, 59.

23. *Hitler: Reden und Proklamationen,* vol. 1, 208–9.

24. Kershaw, *Hitler, 1889–1936,* 452.

25. Cited in Bernard P. Bellon, *Mercedes in Peace and War: German Automobile Workers, 1903–1945* (New York, 1990), 219.

26. Overy, *War and Economy,* 68–89.

27. Noakes and Pridham, vol. 2, 316–17.

28. Elke Fröhlich et al., eds., *Die Tagebücher von Joseph Goebbels* (Munich, 1987), vol. 2, 362.

29. Ibid., 368.

30. Martin Broszat, *Der Staat Hitlers: Grundlegung und Entwicklung seiner inneren Verfassung* (Munich, 1969), 91.

31. *RGBL,* vol. 1, Feb. 6, 1933, 35–41.

32. See Robert Gellately, *Backing Hitler: Consent and Coercion in Nazi Germany* (Oxford, 2001), 12.

33. Michael Schneider, *Unterm Hakenkreuz: Arbeiter und Arbeiterbewegung, 1933 bis 1939* (Bonn, 1999), 49, conveys the impression that the "murder" of

Socialists and Communists was on the agenda from the outset of the regime but mentions only two instances as of February 5. See Richard Bessel, *Political Violence and the Rise of Nazism: The Storm Troopers in Eastern Germany, 1925–1934* (New Haven, Conn., 1984), 98, for a case from Breslau on January 31, where the police killed a demonstrator.

34. Schneider, *Unterm Hakenkreuz,* 40, 44; Heinrich August Winkler, *Weimar, 1918–1933: Die Geschichte der ersten deutschen Demokratie* (Munich, 1998), 593–94.

35. Cited in Mommsen, *Verspielte Freiheit,* 543.

36. See, for example, Sebastian Haffner, *Geschichte eines Deutschen: Die Erinnerungen, 1914–1933* (Munich, 2000), 105–6.

37. Feb. 10, 1933, speech, Berlin, in *Hitler: Reden und Proklamationen,* vol. 1, 204–7.

CHAPTER 19: DICTATORSHIP BY CONSENT

1. Rudolf Diels, *Lucifer ante Portas: . . . es spricht der erste Chef der Gestapo . . .* (Stuttgart, 1950), 193–94.

2. *RGBL,* vol. 1, Feb. 28, 1933, 83.

3. Martin Broszat, *Der Staat Hitlers: Grundlegung und Entwicklung seiner inneren Verfassung* (Munich, 1969), 105. See also Peter Fritzsche, *Germans into Nazis* (Cambridge, Mass., 1998), 204–8.

4. March 6 and 7, 1933, entries, in Elke Fröhlich et al., eds., *Die Tagebücher von Joseph Goebbels* (Munich, 1987), vol. 2, 387–88.

5. Cited in Broszat, *Staat Hitlers,* 112.

6. Cabinet minutes in Noakes and Pridham, vol. 1, 155–56; Franz von Papen, *Memoirs* (London, 1952), 272–73.

7. March 20, 1933, entry, in *Tagebücher von Goebbels,* vol. 2, 395.

8. *Hitler: Reden und Proklamationen,* vol. 1, 229–37.

9. Ludwig Kaas, cited in Ian Kershaw, *Hitler, 1889–1936: Hubris* (London, 1998), 467; law reprinted in Noakes and Pridham, vol. 1, 161–62.

10. Michael Schneider, *Unterm Hakenkreuz: Arbeiter und Arbeiterbewegung, 1933 bis 1939* (Bonn, 1999), 72; Papen, *Memoirs,* 274.

11. March 24 and April 22, 1933, entries, in *Tagebücher von Goebbels,* vol. 2, 397, 410.

12. April 17, 1933, entry, in ibid., 408; see also Schneider, *Unterm Hakenkreuz,* 74–102.

13. Noakes and Pridham, vol. 1, 163.

14. These laws are in *RGBL,* vol. 1, 479ff.

15. Hans-Ulrich Wehler, *Deutsche Gesellschaftsgeschichte, 1914–1949* vol. 4, (Munich, 2004), 737.

16. See table 12 in Klaus Drobisch and Günther Wieland, *System der NS-Konzentrationslager, 1933–1939* (Berlin, 1993), 73–75.

17. Martin Broszat, "Nationalsozialistische Konzentrationslager," in *Anatomie des SS-Staates*, 5th ed. (Munich, 1989), vol. 2, 20. See also Johannes Tuchel, *Konzentrationslager: Organizationsgeschichte und Funktion der "Inspektion der Konzentrationslager," 1934–1938* (Boppard, 1991), 96–103.

18. See Drobisch and Wieland, *System der NS-Konzentrationslager*, 71, 100. See also Monika Herzog and Bernhard Strebel, "Das Frauenkonzentrationslager Ravensbrück," in Claus Füllberg-Stolberg et al., eds., *Frauen in Konzentrationslagern: Bergen-Belsen Ravensbrück* (Bremen, 1994), 13.

19. Karin Orth, *Das System der nationalsozialistischen Konzentrationslager* (Hamburg, 1999), 25.

20. *Hitler: Reden und Proklamationen*, vol. 1, 364–65.

21. Tuchel, *Konzentrationslager*, 308.

22. Kershaw, *Hitler 1889–1936*, 460.

23. Sebastian Haffner, *Geschichte eines Deutschen: Die Erinnerungen, 1914–1933* (Munich, 2000), 132–33.

24. See Michael H. Kater, *The Nazi Party: A Social Profile of Members and Leaders, 1919–1945* (Cambridge, Mass., 1983), 263.

25. Mathilde Jamin, *Zwischen den Klassen: Zur Sozialstruktur der SA-Führerschaft* (Wuppertal, 1984), 1–5.

26. Jill Stephenson, *The Nazi Organization of Women* (London, 1981), 139, 148.

27. Adelheid von Saldern, "Victims or Perpetrators? Controversies About the Role of Women in the Nazi State," in David F. Crew, ed., *Nazism and German Society, 1933–1945* (London, 1994), 151. See also Gisela Bock, "Ordinary Women in Nazi Germany: Perpetrators, Victims, Followers, and Bystanders," in Dalia Ofer and Lenore J. Weitzman, eds., *Women in the Holocaust* (New Haven, Conn., 1999), 85–100.

28. Tim Mason, *Nazism, Fascism, and the Working Class*, ed. Jane Caplan (Cambridge, U.K., 1995), 150.

29. Wehler, *Deutsche Gesellschaftsgeschichte*, vol. 4, 738.

30. *Statistisches Jahrbuch für das Deutsche Reich* (1941–42), 426.

31. Richard Overy, *War and Economy in the Third Reich* (Oxford, 1994), 37–67.

32. See Shelley Baranowski, *Strength Through Joy: Consumerism and Mass Tourism in the Third Reich* (New York, 2004), 197.

33. Gabriele Czarnowski, "The Value of Marriage for the 'Volksgemeinschaft': Policies Towards Women and Marriage Under National Socialism," in Richard Bessel, ed., *Fascist Italy and Nazi Germany: Comparisons and Contrasts* (Cambridge, U.K., 1996), 94–112.

34. Alison Owings, *Frauen: German Women Recall the Third Reich* (New Brunswick, N.J., 1993), 119. For the other examples, see 36, 59, 73, 187.

35. Richard Overy, *The Nazi Economic Recovery, 1932–1938*, 2nd ed. (Cambridge, U.K., 1996), 60.

36. See Robert Gellately, *The Gestapo and German Society* (Oxford, 1990), 38–39.

37. Hartmut Mehringer, *Widerstand und Emigration: Das NS-Regime und seine Gegner* (Munich, 1997), 129–30.

38. Detlef Schmiechen-Ackermann, *Nationalsozialismus und Arbeitermilieus: Der nationalsozialistische Angriff auf die proletarischen Wohnquartiere und die Reaktion in den sozialistischen Vereinen* (Bonn, 1998), 712. Wehler, *Deutsche Gesellschaftsgeschichte,* vol. 4, 737.

39. Victor Klemperer, *Ich will Zeugnis ablegen bis zum letzten: Tagebücher, 1933–1941* (Berlin, 1995), 69.

40. Ute Frevert, *Women in German Society: From Bourgeois Emancipation to Sexual Liberation* (New York, 1989), 168–216.

41. See Anton Kaes et al., eds., *The Weimar Republic Sourcebook* (Berkeley, Calif., 1994), 721–41.

42. Hans Mommsen, *Beamtentum im Dritten Reich* (Stuttgart, 1966), 14.

43. Lothan Gruchmann, *Justiz im Dritten Reich, 1933–1940: Anpassung und Unterwerfung in der Ära Gürtner* (Munich, 1988), 166.

44. Ralph Angermund, *Deutsche Richterschaft, 1919–1945* (Frankfurt am Main, 1990), 52.

45. *RGBL,* vol. 1, 995–99. Karl-Leo Terhorst, *Polizeiliche planmäßige Überwachung und polizeiliche Vorbeugungshaft im Dritten Reich* (Heidelberg, 1985), 75ff.

46. Gruchmann, *Justiz im Dritten Reich,* 719–21.

47. *RGBL,* vol. 1, 995–99.

48. They fell to 1,464, in 1935; 946, in 1936; and 765, in 1937; thereafter there was an increase, to 964, in 1938; 1,827, in 1939; 1,916, in 1940; and 1,651, in 1941. See Christian Müller, *Das Gewohnheitsverbrechergesetz vom 24. November 1933: Kriminalpolitik als Rassenpolitik* (Baden-Baden, 1997), 54.

49. Between 1934 and 1939, the courts sent 5,142 people to state hospitals; 885 alcoholics to rehabilitation institutes; 7,503 individuals to workhouses; and 1,808 people to be sterilized. Ibid., 53.

50. Heinz Boberach, ed., *Richterbriefe: Dokumente zur Beeinflussung der deutschen Rechtsprechung, 1942–1944* (Boppard, 1975), xi; Hans Peter Bleuel, *Sex and Society in Nazi Germany* (Philadelphia, 1973), 211.

51. Hans-Jürgen Eitner, *Hitlers Deutsche: Das Ende eines Tabus* (Gernsback, 1990), 179.

52. *Hitler: Reden und Proklamationen,* vol. 1, 286–87.

53. Kershaw, *Hitler, 1889–1936,* 504.

54. Papen, *Memoirs,* 309.

55. For the above, see Peter Longerich, *Die braunen Bataillone: Geschichte der SA* (Munich, 1989), 206–19; Kershaw, *Hitler, 1889–1936,* 505–17.

56. July 14, 1934, entry, in Klemperer, *Ich will Zeugnis ablegen bis zum letzten,* 121.

57. Richard Bessel, *Political Violence and the Rise of Nazism: The Storm Troopers in Eastern Germany, 1925–1934* (New Haven, Conn., 1984), 139–40; Longerich, *Die braunen Bataillone,* 227–30; Hans-Ulrich Thamer, *Verführung und Gewalt: Deutschland, 1933–1945,* 2nd ed. (Berlin, 1986), 333.

58. *Sopade* (1934), 197.

59. *Sopade* (1934), 249–50. For official reports of July, Aug. 2, and Aug. 10, 1934, see Gerd Steinwascher, ed., *Gestapo Osnabrück meldet . . .* (Osnabrück, 1995), 77, 80. See, for example, Aug. 8, 1934, in Klaus Mlynek, ed., *Gestapo Hannover meldet . . .* (Hildesheim, 1986), 198.

60. An excellent introduction is Klaus Hildebrand, *The Foreign Policy of the Third Reich* (Berkeley, Calif., 1973), 1–23.

61. Cited in Wolfgang Sauer, "Die Mobilmachung der Gewalt," in Karl Dietrich Bracher, Wolfgang Sauer, and Gerhard Schulz, *Die nationalsozialistische Machtergreifung: Studien zur Errichtung des totalitären Herrschaftsystems in Deutschland, 1933–34* (Cologne, 1969), 871.

62. Bernd Stöver, *Volksgemeinschaft im Dritten Reich: Die Konsensbereitschaft der Deutschen aus der Sicht sozialistischer Exilberichte* (Düsseldorf, 1993), 178.

63. Cited in Norbert Frei, "People's Community and War: Hitler's Popular Support," in Hans Mommsen, ed., *The Third Reich Between Vision and Reality: New Perspectives on German History, 1918–1945* (Oxford, 2001), 63.

64. See Gerhard Paul, *"Deutsche Mutter—heim zu Dir!" Der Saarkampf, 1933 bis 1935* (Cologne, 1984), 361, for the testimony of the man released from the concentration camp to vote.

65. Stöver, *Volksgemeinschaft im Dritten Reich,* 181.

66. *Sopade* (1935), 279.

67. Stöver, *Volksgemeinschaft im Dritten Reich,* 183.

68. *Hitler: Reden und Proklamationen,* vol. 2, 638.

69. Sept. 12, 1936, speech, in ibid., 643.

70. *Sopade* (1938), 248.

71. Ibid., 246.

72. Heinrich August Winkler, *Der lange Weg nach Westen: Deutsche Geschichte vom "Dritten Reich" bis zur Wiedervereinigung* (Munich, 2000), vol. 2, 55.

73. *Sopade* (1938), 940, 1062.

74. Marlis G. Steinert, *Hitler's War and the Germans: Public Mood and Attitude During the Second World War* (Athens, Ohio 1977), 40.

CHAPTER 20: PERSECUTION OF THE JEWS IN THE PREWAR YEARS

1. Peter Longerich, *Politik der Vernichtung: Eine Gesamtdarstellung der nationalsozialistischen Judenverfolgung* (Munich, 1998), 25–30.

2. Elke Fröhlich et al., eds., *Die Tagebücher von Joseph Goebbels* (Munich, 1987), vol. 2, 398.

3. *Hitler: Reden und Proklamationen,* vol. 1, 252–53.

4. Sebastian Haffner, *Geschichte eines Deutschen: Die Erinnerungen, 1914–1933* (Munich, 2000), 146–49.

5. See Simone Ladwig-Winters, "The Attack on Berlin Department Stores (Warenhüser) After 1933," in David Bankier, ed., *Probing the Depths of German Anti-Semitism: German Society and the Persecution of the Jews, 1933–1941* (New York, 2000), 256.

6. Michael Burleigh and Wolfgang Wippermann, *The Racial State: Germany, 1933–1945* (Cambridge, U.K., 1991), 77–78; Ian Kershaw, *Popular Opinion and Political Dissent in the Third Reich: Bavaria, 1933–1945* (Oxford, 1983), 232.

7. April 4, 1933, entry, in *Tagebücher von Goebbels,* vol. 2, 402.

8. Raul Hilberg, *The Destruction of the European Jews,* rev. ed. (New York, 1985), vol. 1, 87–88.

9. *NS-Stimmungungsberichte, 1933–1945,* 75.

10. See, for example, Kershaw, *Popular Opinion and Political Dissent in the Third Reich,* 239.

11. Marion A. Kaplan, *Between Dignity and Despair: Jewish Life in Nazi Germany* (New York, 1998), 63.

12. *NS-Stimmungungsberichte,* 134.

13. Ibid., 140–42, 144, 146–48, 152.

14. For an analysis of the social background to these laws, see Robert Gellately, *The Gestapo and German Society* (Oxford, 1990), 102–10.

15. See Saul Friedländer, *Nazi Germany and the Jews: The Years of Persecution, 1933–1939* (New York, 1997), 148.

16. *NS-Stimmungungsberichte,* 158–70.

17. Reinhard Rürup, ed., *1936: Die Olympischen Spiele und der Nationalsozialismus* (Berlin, 1996), 53.

18. Axel Eggebrecht, "In Berlin There Were People Who Were Willing to Help," in Jörg Wollenberg, ed., *The German Public and the Persecution of the Jews, 1933–1945* (Atlantic Highlands, N.J., 1996), 43.

19. Jan. 1937, speech, in *Hitler: Reden und Proklamationen,* vol. 2, 665–77.

20. Regensburg, in *NS-Stimmungungsberichte,* 220.

21. *Hitler: Reden und Proklamationen,* vol. 2, 727–31.

22. See Dan Diner, *America in the Eyes of the Germans: An Essay on Anti-Americanism,* trans. A. Brown (Princeton, N.J., 1996), 79–103.

23. Philipp Gassert, *Amerika im Dritten Reich: Ideologie, Propaganda, und Volksmeinung, 1933–1945* (Stuttgart, 1997), 183ff.

24. Many examples, including the Vatican, can be seen in Beth A. Griech-Polelle, *Bishop von Galen, German Catholicism, and National Socialism* (New Haven, Conn., 2002), 143–44.

25. SD *Hauptamt,* Jan.–March 1938, in *NS-Stimmungsberichte,* 266.

26. Friedländer, *Nazi Germany and the Jews,* 241–42.

27. See Avraham Barkai, "*Volksgemeinschaft,* 'Aryanization,' and the Holocaust," in David Cesarani, ed., *The Final Solution: Origins and Implementation* (London, 1994), 41.

28. See Frank Bajohr, *"Arisierung" in Hamburg: Die Verdrängung der jüdischen Unternehmer, 1933–1945* (Hamburg, 1997), 137, 141.

29. David Cesarani, *Becoming Eichmann: Rethinking the Life, Crimes, and Trial of a "Desk Murderer"* (Cambridge, Mass., 2004), 62.

30. Friedländer, *Nazi Germany and the Jews,* 243–44.

31. *VB,* July 17, 1938.

32. *NS-Stimmungungsberichte,* 268, 270–71, 273–74.

33. Helmut Genschel, *Die Verdrängung der Juden aus der Wirtschaft im Dritten Reich* (Berlin, 1966), 175.

34. July report, *Sopade* (1938), 732–71, esp. 750, 758.

35. *Hitler: Reden und Proklamationen,* vol. 2, 899.

36. *NS-Stimmungungsberichte,* 293–94, 297–98.

37. See BAB R58/276; also Trude Maurer, "Abschiebung und Attentat: Die Ausweisung der polnischen Juden und der Vorward für die 'Kristallnacht,' " in Walter H. Pehle, ed., *Der Judenpogrom 1938: Von der "Reichskristallnacht" zum Völkermord* (Frankfurt am Main, 1988), 52–73.

38. *NS-Stimmungungsberichte,* 298; Friedländler, *Nazi Germany and the Jews,* 266–68.

39. *NS-Stimmungungsberichte,* 356–57.

40. Nov. report, *Sopade* (1938), 1177.

41. Nov. 9, 1938, entry, in *Tagebücher von Goebbels,* part 1, vol. 6, 178.

42. Nov. 10, 1938, entry, in ibid., part 1, vol. 6, 180.

43. See Gellately, *Gestapo and German Society,* 112ff.

44. Doc. 3058-PS, in *IMT,* vol. 32, 1–2. The Nazi Party high court later estimated ninety-one Jews were killed, and this must be taken as a minimum figure.

45. See Konrad Kwiet and Helmut Eschwege, *Selbstbehauptung und Widerstand: Deutsche Juden im Kampf um Existenz und Menschenwürde, 1933–1945* (Hamburg, 1984), 199, 202. By 1944 an estimated three to four thousand German Jews had committed suicide.

46. Heinz Lauber, *Judenpogrom "Reichskristallnacht" November 1938 in Grossdeutschland* (Gerlingen, 1981), 124.

47. *IMT,* vol. 28, 499–540, 1816-PS, 534.

48. *NS-Stimmungungsberichte,* 304–9.

49. Ibid., 339, 341.

50. Ibid., 315–16.

51. Borgentreich, in ibid., 322.

52. Ibid., 318–19, 326, 332.

53. Ibid., 319, 328, 338.

54. Ibid., 357, 361.

55. Ibid., 365.

56. Ibid., 375–76.
57. See Daniel Jonah Goldhagen, *Hitler's Willing Executioners: Ordinary Germans and the Holocaust* (New York, 1996), 103.
58. Ruth Andreas-Friedrich, *Der Schattenmann: Tagebuchaufzeichnungen, 1938–1945* (Frankfurt, 1983), 25–35; Herbert Obenaus and Sibylle Obenaus, eds., *"Schreiben wie es wirklich war!" Aufzeichnungen Karl Dürkefäldens aus den Jahren, 1933–1945* (Hanover, 1985), 85–102.
59. Feb. report, *Sopade* (1939), 201–2; *Sopade* (April 1940), 256–68.
60. David Bankier, *The Germans and the Final Solution: Public Opinion Under Nazism* (Oxford, 1992), 86–87.
61. Feb. report, *Sopade* (1939), 201–2; *Sopade* (April 1940), 256–68.
62. *Hitler: Reden und Proklamationen,* vol. 3, 1047–67.

CHAPTER 21: "CLEANSING" THE GERMAN BODY POLITIC

1. Stefan Kühl, *The Nazi Connection: Eugenics, American Racism, and German National Socialism* (New York, 1994), 24.
2. See Mark B. Adams, "Eugenics in Russia, 1900–1940," in Mark B. Adams, ed., *The Wellborn Science: Eugenics in Germany, France, Brazil, and Russia* (Oxford, 1990), 153–216, also for what follows. Muller was awarded the Nobel Prize in 1946 for his work in genetics.
3. Ibid., 197.
4. The best introduction remains George L. Mosse, *Toward the Final Solution: A History of European Racism* (New York, 1978), 72–75. See also Robert N. Proctor, *Racial Hygiene: Medicine Under the Nazis* (Cambridge, Mass., 1988), 14–38.
5. Adolf Hitler, *Mein Kampf* (Munich, 1943), 279–80.
6. Aug. 4, 1929, speech, in *Hitler: Reden, Schriften,* vol. 3, part 2, 348–49.
7. Henry Friedlander, *The Origins of Nazi Genocide: From Euthanasia to the Final Solution* (Chapel Hill, N.C., 1995), 23.
8. Kühl, *Nazi Connection,* 39, 88.
9. Gisela Bock, *Zwangssterilisation im Nationalsozialismus: Studien zur Rassenpolitik und Frauenpolitik* (Opladen, 1986), 230–38.
10. Richard F. Wetzell, *Inventing the Criminal: A History of German Criminology, 1880–1945* (Chapel Hill, N.C., 2000), 262–63.
11. Ibid., 269–70.
12. Proctor, *Racial Hygiene,* 203.
13. Cited in Kühl, *Nazi Connection,* 46.
14. See Gabriele Czarnowski, "The Value of Marriage for the 'Volksgemeinschaft': Policies Towards Women and Marriage Under National Socialism," in Richard Bessel, ed., *Fascist Italy and Nazi Germany: Comparisons and Contrasts* (Cambridge, U.K., 1996), 94–112.

15. Cited in Tim Mason, *Nazism, Fascism, and the Working Class,* ed. Jane Caplan (Cambridge, U.K., 1995), 162, 172–73.

16. The professional criminal (*Berufsverbrecher*) was defined as someone who made crime his business and who lived in part or whole from the gains of his crimes; the professional criminal was sentenced at least three times for a minimum of three months. The repeat offender (*Gewohnheitsverbrecher*) was not a professional but, urged on by a criminal drive and predisposition (*Treiben oder Neigungen*), had a similar record.

17. Wolfgang Ayaß, *"Asoziale" im Nationalsozialismus* (Stuttgart, 1995), 143.

18. See Michael Wildt, ed., *Die Judenpolitik des SD, 1935 bis 1938: Eine Dokumentation* (Munich, 1995), 56.

19. RKPA VE: RKPA an Kripostellen, Sept. 1, 1938.

20. See Jan Erik Schulte, *Zwangsarbeit und Vernichtung: Das Wirstschaftsimperium der SS: Oswald Pohl und das SS-Wirtschafts-Verwaltungshauptamt, 1933–1945* (Paderborn, 2001), 103–19.

21. See Michael Thad Allen, *The SS, Slave Labor, and the Concentration Camps* (Chapel Hill, N.C., 2002), 58–59.

22. Hitler, *Mein Kampf,* 269–78.

23. David F. Crew, *Germans on Welfare: From Weimar to Hitler* (New York, 1998), 150–51.

24. Brigitte Hamann, *Hitler's Vienna: A Dictator's Apprenticeship* (New York, 1999), 362.

25. See the 1937 speech of Dr. Josef Meisinger in Noakes and Pridham, vol. 4, 391; also Claudia Schoppmann, "National Socialist Policies Towards Female Homosexuality," in Lynn Abrams and Elizabeth Harvey, eds., *Gender Relations in German History: Power, Agency, and Experience from the Sixteenth to the Twentieth Century* (Durham, N.C., 1997), 177–87.

26. Günter Grau, ed., *Homosexualität in der NS-Zeit: Dokumente einer Diskriminierung und Verfolgung* (Frankfurt am Main, 1993), 197.

27. Sybil Milton, "Vorstufe der Vernichtung: Die Zigeunerlager nach 1933," *Vierteljahrshefte für Zeitgeschichte* (1995), 115–30.

28. Michael Zimmermann, *Rassenutopie und Genozid: Die nationalsozialistische "Lösung der Zigeunerfrage"* (Hamburg, 1996), 127.

29. See Friedlander, *Origins of Nazi Genocide,* 260–61.

30. Ritter cited in Ludwig Eiber, *"Ich wußte, es wird schlimm": Die Verfolgung der Sinti und Roma in München, 1933–1945* (Munich, 1993), 41.

31. BAB R18/5644, 229, RMI to Sipo, RKPA, Jan. 24, 1940.

32. *Hitler: Reden und Proklamationen,* vol. 2, 525–26.

33. See Ulrich Herbert, *Best: Biographische Studien über Radikalismus, Weltanschauung, und Vernunft, 1930–1989* (Bonn, 1996), 168–70; Johannes Tuchel, *Konzentrationslager: Organisationsgeschichte und Funktion der "Inspektion der Konzentrationslager," 1934–1938* (Boppard, 1991), 312–13.

34. Tuchel, *Konzentrationslager,* 361. These figures, from October 28, were before the mass arrests of the Jews that followed *Kristallnacht.*

35. Zimmermann, *Rassenutopie und Genozid,* 120.
36. See Karl-Leo Terhorst, *Polizeiliche planmäßige Überwachung und polizeiliche Vorbeugungshaft im Dritten Reich* (Heidelberg, 1985), 153.
37. Toni Siegert, *30,000 Tote mahnen! Die Geschichte des Konzentrationslagers Flossenbürg und seiner 100 Außenlager von 1938 bis 1945* (Weiden, 1984), 9.
38. See Ayaß, *"Asoziale" im Nationalsozialismus,* 162.
39. Toni Siegert, "Das Konzentrationslager Flossenbürg: Gegründet für sogenannte Asoziale und Kriminelle," in Martin Broszat et al., eds., *Bayern in der NS-Zeit* (Munich, 1979), vol. 2, 446.
40. Ibid., 452.
41. See ibid., 446, 461, 469.
42. Ibid., 450.
43. Ibid., 470.
44. Siegert, *30,000 Tote mahnen!* 6; Siegert, "Das Konzentrationslagen Flossenbürg," 477.
45. For the exact figures, see Siegert, "Das Konzentrationslager Flossenbürg," 490–92.
46. Common estimates of those killed in the French Revolution range between eleven and eighteen thousand. This is the number cited by John Merriman, *A History of Modern Europe* (New York, 1996), vol. 2, 536.
47. Tuchel, *Konzentrationslager,* 315–17.
48. Klaus Drobisch and Günther Wieland, *System der NS-Konzentrationslager, 1933–1939* (Berlin, 1993), 339.
49. Pohl to Himmler, April 30, 1942, doc. 129-R, in *IMT,* vol. 38, 362–65.
50. See Albert Speer, *Infiltration: How Heinrich Himmler Schemed to Build an SS Industrial Empire* (New York, 1981), 22–24.
51. See ibid., 22–25, and app. 1, 307–10, for more details on the impact of those meetings.

CHAPTER 22: RIVAL VISIONS OF WORLD CONQUEST

1. See the "Appeal for the Formation of the Communist International," *SDFP,* vol. 1, 136–37.
2. George F. Kennan, *Russia and the West Under Lenin and Stalin* (New York, 1960), 239.
3. Stalin, *Sochineniia,* vol. 7, 14. See also Andreas Hillgruber, *Deutschlands Rolle in der Vorgeschichte der beiden Weltkriege,* 2nd ed. (Göttingen, 1979), 97.
4. Stalin, *Sochineniia* (May 9, 1925), vol. 7, 109–21, report.
5. Ibid., vol. 13, 333–79.
6. McNeal, *Stalin sochineniia,* vol. 1 (vol. 14), 197.
7. Ibid., 338–39.

8. Georgi Dimitrov, *Tagebücher, 1933–1943* (Berlin, 2000), vol. 1, 115.

9. For a summary of the debate and a study that emphasizes power-political over ideological considerations in Soviet foreign policy, see Gabriel Gorodetsky, *Grand Delusion: Stalin and the German Invasion of Russia* (New Haven, Conn., 1999).

10. Hans Mommsen, *Beamtentum im Dritten Reich* (Stuttgart, 1966), 98. He qualified this exaggeration by saying that Hitler was a weak dictator when it came to "all questions which needed the adoption of a fundamental and definitive position," but that point does not hold, either.

11. *DRZW*, vol. 1, 538.

12. Cited in Klaus Hildebrand, *Das vergangene Reich: Deutsche Außenpolitik von Bismarck bis Hitler* (Berlin, 1999), 666.

13. See Klaus Hildebrand, *The Foreign Policy of the Third Reich* (Berkeley, Calif., 1973), 79; Gerhard L. Weinberg, ed., *Hitler's Second Book: The Unpublished Sequel to "Mein Kampf"* (New York, 2003), esp. 134–52.

14. Hildebrand, *Foreign Policy of the Third Reich,* 22.

15. See Gerhard L. Weinberg, *The Foreign Policy of Hitler's Germany: Diplomatic Revolution in Europe 1933–36* (Chicago, 1970), 21–22.

16. *IMT,* vol. 25, 402–13; Gerhard L. Weinberg, *Foreign Policy of Hitler's Germany: Starting World War II, 1937–1939* (Chicago, 1980), 34–43.

17. Cited in Hillgruber, *Deutschlands Rolle,* 76–77.

18. Nevile Henderson, *Failure of a Mission: Berlin, 1937–1939* (New York, 1940), 181.

19. Noakes and Pridham, vol. 3, 718–19.

20. Ibid., 724; William Carr, *Arms, Autarky, and Aggression: A Study in German Foreign Policy, 1933–1939* (London, 1972), 102.

21. Doc. 100-R, in *IMT,* vol. 38, 274–76.

22. Henderson, *Failure of a Mission,* 225, 227.

23. *Hitler: Reden und Proklamationen,* vol. 3, 1131–33.

24. Doc. 079-L, in *IMT,* vol. 37, 546–56.

25. See Michael Wildt, *Generation des Unbedingten: Das Führungskorps des Reichssicherheitshauptamtes* (Hamburg, 2002), 421–22; Alexander B. Rossino, *Hitler Strikes Poland: Blitzkrieg, Ideology, and Atrocity* (Lawrence, Kans., 2005), 12, 21.

26. Wildt, *Generation des Unbedingten,* 426–28.

27. Rossino, *Hitler Strikes Poland,* 14–16, 244 n. 83.

28. See Wolfram Wette, *Die Wehrmacht: Feindbilder, Vernichtungskrieg, Legenden* (Frankfurt am Main, 2002), 90–94.

29. No. 192, in *DGFP,* vol. 7, 200–4; also Nuremberg doc. 798-PS.

30. No. 193, in ibid., 205–6; also Nuremberg doc. 1015-PS.

31. Nicolaus von Below, *Als Hitlers Adjutant, 1937–45* (Mainz, 1980), 181.

32. See Wolfgang Jacobmeyer, "Der Überfall auf Polen und der neue Charakter des Krieges," in Christoph Kleßmann, ed., *September 1939: Krieg, Besatzung, Widerstand in Polen* (Göttingen, 1989), 16–17. He cites part of

Nuremberg 1014-PS apparently omitted from the document submitted at the trials, and thus not translated in *DGFP.*

33. McNeal, *Stalin sochineniia,* vol. 14, 340–41.

34. No. 1, in *DGFP,* vol. 6, 1–3.

35. Litvinov note, March 18, 1939, in *SDFP,* vol. 3, 322–23. See also Dmitri Volkogonov, *Triumf i tragediya. Politichesky portret J. V. Stalina* (Moscow, 1989), vol. 2, part 1, 12.

36. Cited in Derek Watson, *Molotov: A Biography* (London, 2005), 155.

37. Volkogonov, *Triumf i tragediya. Politichesky portret J. V. Stalina,* vol. 2, part 1, 19.

38. No. 105, in *DGFP,* vol. 7, 114–16; no. 113, 123.

39. Feliks Ivanovich Chuev and Vyacheslav Molotov, *Sto sorok besed s Molotovym: iz dnevnika F. Chueva* (Moscow, 1991), 45, 46, also Volkogonov, *Triumf i tragediya. Politichesky portret J. V. Stalina,* vol. 2, part 1, 24–28.

40. Geoffrey Roberts, *The Soviet Union and the Origins of the Second World War: Russo-German Relations and the Road to War, 1933–1941* (London, 1995), 62–91; Joachim von Ribbentrop, *Zwischen London und Moskau: Erinnerungen und letzte Aufzeichnungen* (Leoni am Starnberger See, 1953), 178–85.

41. See nos. 228 and 229, in *DGFP,* vol. 7, 245–47.

42. Cited in Hildebrand, *Das vergangene Reich,* 805.

43. Dimitrov, *Tagebücher,* vol. 1, 273–74, also for what follows.

44. Jung Chang and Jon Halliday, *Mao: The Unknown Story* (New York, 2005), 228–30.

45. No date is given for this march or marches in Stanley G. Payne, *The Spanish Civil War, the Soviet Union, and Communism* (New Haven, Conn., 2004), 312.

CHAPTER 23: GERMAN RACIAL PERSECUTION BEGINS IN POLAND

1. Hitler remark to Alfred Rosenberg on September 28, 1939, cited in Martin Broszat, *Zweihundert Jahre deutsche Polenpolitik* (Frankfurt am Main, 1972), 277.

2. Aug. 28, 1939, entry, in Hans-Adolf Jacobson, ed., *Generaloberst Halder, Kriegstagebuch; tägliche Aufzeichnungen des Chefs des Generalstabes des Heeres, 1939–1942* (Stuttgart, 1962–64), vol. 1, 38; see also Klaus Hildebrand, *Das vergangene Reich: Deutsche Außenpolitik von Bismarck bis Hitler* (Berlin, 1999), 804.

3. Nevile Henderson, *Failure of a Mission: Berlin, 1937–1939* (New York, 1940), 280–91.

4. No. 493, in *DGFP,* vol. 7, 477–79. His vacillation is reconstructed in detail by Ian Kershaw, *Hitler, 1936–45: Nemesis* (New York, 2000), 211–23; and Gerhard L. Weinberg, *The Foreign Policy of Hitler's Germany: Starting World War II, 1937–1939* (Chicago, 1980), 628–55.

5. No. 576, in *DGFP*, vol. 7, 548–49.

6. Jacobson, ed., *Halder, Kriegstagebuch*, vol. 1, 61.

7. Martin Moll, ed., *Führer-Erlasse, 1939–1945* (Stuttgart, 1997), 100.

8. *DRZW*, vol. 2, 133.

9. Alexander B. Rossino, *Hitler Strikes Poland: Blitzkrieg, Ideology, and Atrocity* (Lawrence, Kans., 2005), 183–85.

10. Czeslaw Madajczyk, *Die Okkupationspolitik Nazideutschlands in Polen, 1939–1945* (Berlin, 1988), 12.

11. Helmut Krausnick and Hans-Heinrich Wilhelm, *Die Truppe des Weltanschauungskrieges: Die Einsatzgruppen der Sicherheitspolizei und des SD, 1938–1942* (Stuttgart, 1981), 63–64.

12. Rossino, *Hitler Strikes Poland*, 171, 173.

13. Jacobson, ed., *Halder, Kriegstagebuch*, vol. 1, 67.

14. Rossino, *Hitler Strikes Poland*, 66.

15. BAB R58/285, 1ff.; Michael Wildt, *Generation des Unbedingten: Das Führungskorps des Reichssicherheitshauptamtes* (Hamburg, 2002), 449.

16. Wildt, *Generation des Unbedingten*, 449.

17. Rossino, *Hitler Strikes Poland*, 68, 73.

18. Jan T. Gross, *Revolution from Abroad: The Soviet Conquest of Poland's Western Ukraine and Western Belorussia* (Princeton, N.J., 2002), 228–29.

19. See Michael Burleigh, *Death and Deliverance: "Euthanasia" in Germany, 1900–1945* (Cambridge, U.K., 1994), 97.

20. Morell told Hitler of a 1920 survey by Ewald Meltzer (an opponent of euthanasia) of two hundred parents of whom only twenty answered no to all four questions put to them. See Götz Aly, "Medicine Against the Useless," in Götz Aly et al., *Cleansing the Fatherland: Nazi Medicine and Racial Hygiene* (Baltimore, 1994), 29–31.

21. The circular is reprinted in Noakes and Pridham, vol. 3, 1006–7.

22. Kershaw, *Hitler, 1936–45*, 259.

23. *Hitler: Reden und Proklamationen*, vol. 3, 1354–66.

24. Volker Rieß, *Die Anfänge der Vernichtung "lebensunwerten Lebens" in den Reichsgauen Danzig-Westpreußen und Wartheland, 1939–40* (Frankfurt am Main, 1995), 24–25.

25. Figures in ibid., 171.

26. Israel Gutman et al. (eds.), *Enzyklopädie des Holocaust: Die Verfolgung und Ermordung der europäischen Juden* (Munich, 1995), vol. 3, 1559.

27. Rieß, *Anfänge*, 273–80, 306.

28. Christopher R. Browning, *The Origins of the Final Solution: The Evolution of Nazi Jewish Policy, September 1939–March 1942* (Lincoln, Neb., 2004), 188–89.

29. For the refutation, see Peter Longerich, *Politik der Vernichtung: Eine Gesamtdarstellung der nationalsozialistischen Judenverfolgung* (Munich, 1998), 648 n. 36.

30. For minutes of the meeting (with a misprint in the target figure, which is seventy thousand, not seventy-five thousand), see Noakes and Pridham, vol. 3, 1010–11.

31. Correspondence is reprinted in *IMT,* vol. 35, 689.

32. See the internal T-4 statistics, dated Sept. 1, 1941, in Ernst Klee, ed., *Dokumente zur "Euthanasie"* (Frankfurt am Main, 1985), 232.

33. For letters of concern from local officials, see ibid., 221–32.

34. See Burleigh, *Death and Deliverance,* 180.

35. See the extensive postwar trial in Adelheid L. Rüter-Ehlermann and C. F. Rüter (eds.), *Justiz und NS-Verbrechen: Sammlung deutscher Strafurteile wegen nationalsozialistischer Tötungsverbrechen 1945–1966* (Amsterdam, 1966 ff.), vol. 1, 304–79.

36. Ernst Klee, *"Euthanasie" im NS-Staat: Die "Vernichtung lebensunwerten Lebens"* (Frankfurt am Main, 1983), 345.

37. See Hans-Walter Schmuhl, *Rassenhygiene, Nationalsozialismus, Euthanasie: Von der Verhütung zur Vernichtung "lebensunwertes Lebens," 1890–1945* (Göttingen, 1987), 218.

38. See Burleigh, *Death and Deliverance,* 221.

39. See ibid., 220–29; Schmuhl, *Rassenhygiene, Nationalsozialismus, Euthanasie,* 218; and Henry Friedlander, *The Origins of Nazi Genocide: From Euthanasia to the Final Solution* (Chapel Hill, N.C., 1995), 142–50.

40. Notes of the April 23, 1941, meeting are reprinted in Klee, *Dokumente zur "Euthanasie,"* 219–20.

41. Doc. 2852-PS, in *IMT,* vol. 31, 231–33.

42. See Wildt, *Generation des Unbedingten,* 452; Browning, *Origins of the Final Solution,* 18.

43. Sept. 20, 1939, entry, in Jacobson, ed., *Halder, Kriegstagebuch,* vol. 1, 82.

44. BAB R58/825, 26–30, in Wildt, *Generation des Unbedingten,* 458.

45. BAB R58/276, 232–35.

46. Sept. 30, 1939, entry, in Elke Fröhlich et al., eds., *Die Tagebücher von Joseph Goebbels* (Munich, 2005ff.), part 1, vol. 7, 130; see also Longerich, *Politik der Vernichtung,* 254–55.

47. *Hitler: Reden und Proklamationen,* vol. 3, 1377–93.

48. *Tagebücher von Goebbels,* part 1, vol. 7, 141, 147, 157, 176.

49. Ibid., 177, 180.

50. Dec. 5, 1939, entry, in ibid., 220–21.

51. Doc. 864-PS, in *IMT,* vol. 26, 378–83.

52. Longerich, *Politik der Vernichtung,* 262; Browning, *Origins of Nazi Genocide,* 39–41.

53. Longerich, *Politik der Vernichtung,* 264–65.

54. Browning, *Origins of Nazi Genocide,* 52; Longerich, *Politik der Vernichtung,* 264–65.

55. Longerich, *Politik der Vernichtung,* 267–69.

CHAPTER 24: HITLER AND WESTERN EUROPE

1. Sept. 27, 1939, entry, in Hans-Adolf Jacobson, ed., *Generaloberst Halder, Kriegstagebuch; tägliche Aufzeichnungen des Chefs des Generalstabes des Heeres, 1939–1942* (Stuttgart, 1962–64), vol. 1, 86, 90. 61–66.
2. Oct. 17, 1939, entry, in ibid., vol. 1, 107.
3. Klaus-Jürgen Müller, *Das Heer und Hitler: Armee und nationalsozialistisches Regime, 1933–1940* (Stuttgart, 1969), 520–23.
4. Alan Bullock, *Hitler and Stalin: Parallel Lives* (Toronto, 1991), 642.
5. See *VB*, Nov. 11, 1939.
6. Ian Kershaw, *Hitler, 1936–45: Nemesis* (New York, 2000), 271–72.
7. Nov. 13, 1939, *Meldungen aus dem Reich*, vol. 3, 449.
8. *Sopade* 6 (Dec. 2, 1939), 1024–25.
9. See Peter Hoffmann, *The History of the German Resistance* (Cambridge, Mass., 1977), 152.
10. *Hitler: Reden und Proklamationen*, vol. 3, 1421–27.
11. Kershaw, *Hitler, 1936–45*, 278.
12. Walter Warlimont, *Im Hauptquartier der deutschen Wehrmacht, 1939–1945* (Frankfurt am Main, 1962), 74.
13. See Ernest R. May, *Strange Victory: Hitler's Conquest of France* (New York, 2000), 229–39.
14. Gerhard L. Weinberg, *A World at Arms: A Global History of World War II* (Cambridge, U.K., 1994), 129.
15. May 24 1940, entry, in Jacobson, ed., *Halder, Kriegstagebuch*, vol. 1, 318.
16. See Kershaw, *Hitler, 1936–45*, 294–96; Weinberg, *World at Arms*, 130; Geoffrey P. Megargee, *Inside Hitler's High Command* (Lawrence, Kans., 2000), 85.
17. Nicolaus von Below, *Als Hitlers Adjutant, 1937–45* (Mainz, 1980), 217.
18. Cited in Derek Watson, *Molotov: A Biography* (London, 2005), 181.
19. Albert Speer, *Inside the Third Reich* (New York, 1970), 172–73.
20. July 24 and 26, 1940, entries, in Victor Klemperer, *Ich will Zeugnis ablegen bis zum letzten: Tagebücher, 1933–1941* (Berlin, 1995), vol. 1, 542, 544.
21. July 11, 1940, *Meldungen aus dem Reich*, vol. 5, 1363.
22. Jacobson, ed, *Halder, Kriegstagebuch*, vol. 2, 49.

CHAPTER 25: THE SOVIET RESPONSE

1. *Khrushchev Remembers: The Glasnost Tapes* (Boston, 1990), 48.
2. *SDFP*, vol. 3, 374.
3. Ibid., 393–94.
4. Molotov speech to the Supreme Soviet, Oct. 31, 1939, in ibid, 393.

5. Jan T. Gross, *Revolution from Abroad: The Soviet Conquest of Poland's Western Ukraine and Western Belorussia* (Princeton, N.J., 2002), 3, 44.

6. Richard Overy, *Russia's War* (Harmondsworth, U.K., 1998), 52, mentions the figure of 230,000 Polish soldiers in captivity, but excludes the officers.

7. Michael Parrish, *The Lesser Terror: Soviet State Security, 1939–1953* (Westport, Conn., 1996), 54–55.

8. Ibid., 56–57; for the behind the scenes, see Simon Sebag Montefiore, *Stalin: The Court of the Red Tsar* (New York, 2004), 333–34.

9. Norman Davies, *God's Playground: A History of Poland, 1795 to the Present* (Oxford, 1981), vol. 2, 448.

10. The lower number (and three deportations) is given by Józef Garliński, *Poland in the Second World War* (London, 1985), 36–37. Gross, *Revolution from Abroad,* 194, adds the deportation of June 1941 and gives the higher figures.

11. See the literature and argumentation in Gross, *Revolution from Abroad,* 229.

12. Davies, *God's Playground,* vol. 2, 451.

13. For these figures, and what follows, see Dieter Pohl, *Nationalsozialistische Judenverfolgung in Ostgalizien, 1941–1944* (Munich, 1996), 30.

14. Cited in Gross, *Revolution from Abroad,* 222.

15. Cited in ibid., 50.

16. William Taubman, *Khrushchev: The Man and His Era* (New York, 2003), 135–36.

17. Ibid., 139.

18. Strobe Talbott, ed., *Khrushchev Remembers* (Boston, 1970), 146.

19. Ibid., 141.

20. Martin Dean, *Collaboration in the Holocaust: Crimes of the Local Police in Belorussia and Ukraine, 1941–44* (New York, 2000), 6.

21. Witness cited in Nicholas P. Vakar, *Belorussia: The Making of a Nation* (Cambridge, Mass., 1956), 166.

22. Cited in ibid., 169.

23. Cited in Gross, *Revolution from Abroad,* 223.

24. Karel C. Berkhoff, *Harvest of Despair: Life and Death in Ukraine Under Nazi Rule* (Cambridge, Mass., 2004), 15. The estimate is by Gross, *Revolution from Abroad,* 229.

25. Berkhoff, *Harvest of Despair,* 17.

26. *SDFP,* vol. 3, 393–94; Izidors Vizulis, *The Molotov-Ribbentrop Pact of 1939: The Baltic Case* (New York, 1990), 26–30.

27. *SDFP,* vol. 3, 382–86.

28. Figures cited from March 27, 1940 meeting in Georgi Dimitrov, *Tagebücher, 1933–1943* (Berlin, 2000), vol. 1, 127.

29. *Khrushchev Remembers,* 155. The figure of 127,000 is mentioned in Robert Service, *Stalin: A Biography* (Cambridge, Mass., 2004), 403.

30. *Khrushchev Remembers,* 153, 157.

31. R. W. Davies, *Soviet Economic Development from Lenin to Khrushchev* (Cambridge, U.K., 1998), 42.

32. Mark Harrison, *Soviet Planning in Peace and War, 1938–1945* (Cambridge, U.K., 1985), 8.

33. This rapid growth built up an unwieldy force. Roger R. Reese, *The Soviet Military Experience* (New York, 2000), 93.

34. *Khrushchev Remembers,* 154–56.

35. *SDFP,* vol. 3, 453–58.

36. Ibid., 461–69.

37. Nicolas Werth, "A State Against Its People: Violence, Repression, and Terror in the Soviet Union," in Stéphane Courtois et al., *The Black Book of Communism* (Cambridge, Mass., 1999), 212.

38. Cited in Sigrid Rausing, *History, Memory, and Identity in Post-Soviet Estonia: The End of the Collective Farm* (Oxford, 2004), 120.

39. Timothy Snyder, *The Reconstruction of Nations: Poland, Ukraine, Lithuania, Belarus, 1569–1999* (New Haven, Conn., 2003), 157.

40. Ibid., 82–84.

41. Quoted in Sebag Montefiore, *Stalin,* 334.

42. See Geoffrey Swain, *Between Stalin and Hitler: Class War and Race War on the Dvina, 1940–46* (London, 2004), 39.

43. Werth, "State Against Its People," 212–13.

44. See John Hiden and Patrick Salmon, *The Baltic Nations and Europe: Estonia, Latvia, and Lithuania in the Twentieth Century* (London, 1994), 115; Swain, *Between Stalin and Hitler,* 39–41.

45. Rausing, *History, Memory, and Identity in Post-Soviet Estonia,* 123.

CHAPTER 26: THE WAR SPREADS

1. Hans-Adolf Jacobson, ed., *Generaloberst Halder, Kriegstagebuch; tägliche Aufzeichnungen des Chefs des Generalstabes des Heeres, 1939–1942* (Stuttgart, 1962–64), vol. 2, 210, 330.

2. *DRZW,* vol. 4, 423.

3. Misha Glenny, *The Balkans: Nationalism, War, and the Great Powers, 1804–1999* (New York, 1999), 486.

4. For a participant's story, see Milovan Djilas, *Wartime* (New York, 1977).

5. On Serbia, see Christopher R. Browning, *Fateful Months: Essays on the Emergence of the Final Solution* (New York, 1985), 39–85; also Walter Manoschek, "Partisanenkrieg und Genozid: Die Wehrmacht in Serbien, 1941," in Walter Manoschek, ed., *Die Wehrmacht in Rassenkrieg: Der Vernichtungskrieg hinter der Front* (Vienna, 1996), 142–67; Raul Hilberg, *The Destruction of the European Jews,* rev. ed. (New York, 1985), vol. 3, 1048.

6. See Mark Mazower, *Salonica, City of Ghosts* (New York, 2005), 392–417.

7. See Mark Mazower, *Inside Hitler's Greece: The Experience of Occupation* (New Haven, Conn., 1993), 235–61.

8. *DRZW,* vol. 4, 197.

9. Strobe Talbott, ed., *Khrushchev Remembers* (Boston, 1970), 134–35.

10. Georgi Dimitrov, *Tagebücher, 1933–1943* (Berlin, 2000), vol. 1, 315–17.

11. Dmitri Volkogonov, *Triumf i tragediya. Politichesky portret J. V. Stalina* (Moscow, 1989), vol. 2, 47.

12. David E. Murphy, *What Stalin Knew: The Enigma of Barbarossa* (New Haven, Conn., 2005), 162–72.

13. See the memoirs of the chief of staff of the Odessa military district, Matvei V. Zakharov, *Generalny shatb v predvoennye gody* (Moscow, 1989).

14. Figures in Roger R. Reese, *The Soviet Military Experience* (New York, 2000), 95–96.

15. Roger R. Reese, *Stalin's Reluctant Soldiers: A Social History of the Red Army, 1925–1941* (Lawrence, Kans., 1996), 172–75.

16. Cited in Dimitrov, *Tagebücher,* vol. 1, 380–82.

17. There is an enormous literature on the controversy, begun by Viktor Suvorov (a former Soviet military intelligence officer), who, in exile in Great Britain since 1983, published numerous works, beginning with *Ledokol* (Moscow, 1993)—in English, *Icebreaker: Who Started the Second World War?* (London, 1990). His books have sold in the millions in Russia. The best summary of the debate, critique of the documents—some of them fabrications—as well as citation of all the relevant publications in Russian, German, and English, and refutation of the "preventive war" argument is Bernt Bonwetsch, "Die Forschungskontroverse über die Kriegsvorbereitung der Roten Armee 1941," in Bianka Pietrow-Ennker, ed., *Präventivkrieg? Der deutsche Angriff auf die Sowjetunion* (Frankfurt am Main, 2000), 170–89.

18. See Juri Gorkov, "22. Juli 1941: Verteidigung oder Angriff? Recherchen in russischen Zentralarchiven," in Pietrow-Ennker, *Präventivkrieg?* 190–207.

19. Robert Service, *Stalin: A Biography* (Cambridge, Mass., 2004), 408.

20. Valentin Berezhkov, *History in the Making: Memoirs of World War II Diplomacy* (Moscow, 1983), 71.

21. Mikoyan as cited in Simon Sebag Montefiore, *Stalin: The Court of the Red Tsar* (New York, 2004), 341.

22. Bradley F. Smith, *Sharing Secrets with Stalin: How the Allies Traded Intelligence, 1941–1945* (Lawrence, Kans., 1996), 12.

23. Cited in Gabriel Gorodetsky, *Grand Delusion: Stalin and the German Invasion of Russia* (New Haven, Conn., 1999), 155–78, esp. 176, 178.

24. See Volkogonov, *Triumf i tragediya. Politichesky portret J. V. Stalina,* vol. 2, part 1, 145–48.

25. Cited in Sebag Montefiore, *Stalin,* 355.

26. Murphy, *What Stalin Knew,* 208.

27. Feliks Ivanovich Chuev and Vyacheslav Molotov, *Sto sorok besed s Molotovym: iz dnevnika F. Chueva* (Moscow, 1991), 32–33, 39–40.
28. *DRZW*, vol. 4, 714.
29. Sebag Montefiore, *Stalin*, 358.
30. *1941 god*, vol. 2, 422.

CHAPTER 27: WAR OF EXTERMINATION AS NAZI CRUSADE

1. *Hitler: Reden und Proklamationen*, vol. 3, 1565; Hans-Adolf Jacobson, ed., *Generaloberst Halder, Kriegstagebuch; tägliche Aufzeichnungen des Chefs des Generalstabes des Heeres, 1939–1942* (Stuttgart, 1962–64), vol. 2, 50, 241–46.
2. Nov. 15, 1940, entry, in Hildegard von Kotze, ed., *Heeresadjutant bei Hitler, 1938–1943: Aufzeichnungen des Majors Engel* (Stuttgart, 1974), 91.
3. Dec. 5 and 18, 1940, and Jan. 9, 1941, entries, in *KTB*, vol. 1, 203–9, 237, 257–58; Dec. 5, 1940, entry, in Jacobson, ed., *Halder, Kriegstagebuch*, vol. 2, 211–14.
4. *Hitler: Reden und Proklamationen*, vol. 4, 1726–29.
5. *DRZW*, vol. 4, 911.
6. John Erickson, *The Road to Stalingrad: Stalin's War with Germany* (New Haven, Conn., 1975), 237–38.
7. No. 614, in *DGFP*, vol. 12, 996–1006; also Andreas Hillgruber, ed., *Staatsmänner und Diplomaten bei Hitler: Vertrauliche Aufzeichnungen über Unterredungen mit Vertretern des Auslandes, 1939–1941* (Frankfurt am Main, 1967), vol. 1, 581–94.
8. Jean Ancel, "Antonescu and the Jews," in Michael Berenbaum and Abraham J. Peck, eds., *The Holocaust and History: The Known, the Unknown, the Disputed, and the Reexamined* (Bloomington, Ind., 1998), 466.
9. *DRZW*, vol. 4, 346–47.
10. Mihail Sebastian, *Journal, 1935–1944* (Chicago, 2000), 369–70.
11. July 12, 1941, entry, in ibid., 378.
12. For a graphic account, see Michael Burleigh, *The Third Reich: A New History* (London, 2000), 620–29.
13. Ancel, "Antonescu and the Jews," 470.
14. Ilya Ehrenburg and Vasily Grossman, eds., *The Complete Black Book of Russian Jewry* (London, 2002), 59.
15. No. 167, in *DGFP*, vol. 13, 266–67.
16. No. 661, in ibid., vol. 12, 1071.
17. No. 667, in ibid., vol. 13, 1077–78.
18. Cited in *DRZW*, vol. 4, 360.
19. Hillgruber, *Staatsmänner und Diplomaten bei Hitler*, vol. 1, 614–15.

20. The compelling story is told well by Michael Bar-Zohar, *Beyond Hitler's Grasp: The Heroic Rescue of Bulgaria's Jews* (Holbrook, Mass., 1998).

21. See Robert O. Paxton, *Vichy France: Old Guard and New Order, 1940–1944* (New York, 1972), 95, 118.

22. No. 78, in *DGFP,* vol. 13, 94–95.

23. No. 114, in ibid., 149–50.

24. Paxton, *Vichy France,* 314, 320.

25. Barry Leach, *German Strategy Against Russia, 1939–1941* (Oxford, 1973), 176–91.

26. See Michael R. Marrus and Robert O. Paxton, *Vichy France and the Jews* (New York, 1981), 368, 372.

27. No. 532, in *DGFP,* vol. 11, 899–902.

28. Jan. 9, 1941, entry, in *KTB,* vol. 1, 258.

29. March 3, 1941, entry, in ibid., 341.

30. Ibid.

31. Doc. 1, in Hans-Adolf Jacobson, "Kommissarbefehl und Massenexekutioen sowjetischer Kreigsgefangener," in Hans Buchheim et al., *Anatomie des SS-Staates* (Frankfurt am Main, 1967) vol. 2, 167.

32. Doc. 2, in ibid., 170–71.

33. Jacobson, ed., *Halder, Kriegstagebuch,* vol. 2, 320.

34. Cited in *DRZW,* vol. 4, 416–17.

35. March 30, 1941, entry, in Jacobson, ed., *Halder, Kriegstagebuch,* vol. 2, 336–37.

36. *DRZW,* vol. 4, 428.

37. Doc. 2718-PS, in *IMT,* vol. 31, 84.

38. For an overview, see Robert Gellately, "The Third Reich, the Holocaust, and Visions of Serial Genocide," in Robert Gellately and Ben Kiernan, eds., *The Specter of Genocide: Mass Murder in Historical Perspective* (Cambridge, U.K., 2003), 241–63.

39. The plan and its implications are discussed by the excellent Christian Gerlach, *Kaluklierte Morde: Die deutsche Wirtschafts- und Vernichtungspolitik in Weißrußland, 1941 bis 1944* (Hamburg, 1999), 44–58.

40. See Czeslaw Madajczyk et al., eds., *Vom Generalplan Ost zum Generalsiedlungsplan* (Munich, 1994).

41. See the examples in Mechtild Rössler and Sabine Schleiermacher, eds., *Der "Generalplan Ost": Hauptlinien der nationalsozialistischen Planungs- und Vernichtungspolitik* (Berlin, 1993).

42. Doc. 5a, in Jacobson, "Kommissarbefehl," 176; *DRZW,* vol. 4, 429.

43. Doc. 8, in Jacobson, "Kommissarbefehl," 182–83.

44. *DRZW,* vol. 4, 433–34.

45. Fedor von Bock, *The War Diary, 1939–1945* (Atglen, Pa., 1996), 217–18.

46. Doc. 11, in Jacobsen, "Kommissarbefehl," 187.

47. Doc. 12, in ibid., 189.

48. *DRZW,* vol. 4, 437.

49. May 6, 1941, entry, in Jacobson, ed., *Halder, Kriegstagebuch,* vol. 2, 399.
50. *DRZW,* vol. 4, 445–46.
51. Cited in ibid., 446.

CHAPTER 28: WAR AGAINST THE COMMUNISTS: OPERATION BARBAROSSA

1. Barry Leach, *German Strategy Against Russia, 1939–1941* (Oxford, 1973), 192.
2. June 22, 1941, entry, in *KTB,* vol. 1, 417; June 24, 1941, entry, in Hans-Adolf Jacobson, ed., *Generaloberst Halder, Kriegstagebuch; tägliche Aufzeichnungen des Chefs des Generalstabes des Heeres, 1939–1942* (Stuttgart, 1962–64), vol. 3, 11.
3. June 26 and July 7, 1941; *Meldungen aus dem Reich,* vol. 7, 2443, 2470.
4. David M. Glantz, *Colossus Reborn: The Red Army at War, 1941–1943* (Lawrence, Kans., 2005), 5–24.
5. Geoffrey P. Megargee, *Inside Hitler's High Command* (Lawrence, Kans., 2000), 143.
6. *DRZW,* vol. 4, 183.
7. Jacobson, ed., *Halder, Kriegstagebuch,* vol. 3, 38, also for what follows.
8. Elke Fröhlich et al., eds., *Die Tagebücher von Joseph Goebbels* (Munich, 2005ff.), part 2, vol. 1, 30–32.
9. Doc. 221-L, in *IMT,* vol. 38, 86–94.
10. See Leach, *German Strategy Against Russia,* 213.
11. Ibid., 219.
12. For the background and enforcement of stringent regulations, see Robert Gellately, *Backing Hitler: Consent and Coercion in Nazi Germany* (Oxford, 2001), 151–82.
13. No. 265, in *DGFP,* vol. 13, 431.
14. *KTB,* vol. 1, 1061–68; Aug. 22, 1941, entry, in Jacobson, ed., *Halder, Kriegstagebuch,* vol. 3, 192–93.
15. Aug. 21, 1941, entry, in *KTB,* vol. 1, 1061–68; *DRZW,* vol. 4, 552.
16. Cited in David M. Glantz, *The Battle for Leningrad, 1941–1944* (Lawrence, Kans., 2002), 81.
17. No. 327, in *DGFP,* vol. 13, 518–20.
18. Cited in Glantz, *Battle for Leningrad,* 86.
19. *DRZW,* vol. 4, 553.
20. *Hitler: Reden und Proklamationen,* vol. 4, 1756–57.
21. For example, it was finally published in Romania more than a week later. See Oct. 10, 1941, entry, in Mihail Sebastian, *Journal, 1935–1944* (Chicago, 2000), 415.
22. No. 388, in *DGFP,* vol. 13, 623–24.
23. Ian Kershaw, *Hitler, 1936–45: Nemesis* (New York, 2000), 465.
24. Cited in Megargee, *Inside Hitler's High Command,* 135.

25. Oct. 10 and 19, 1941, entries, in Fedor von Bock, *The War Diary, 1939–1945* (Atglen, Pa., 1996), 329, 336.

26. Oct. 20, 1941, entry, in ibid., 337.

27. Oct. 12, 1941, entry, in ibid., 331.

28. See Nov. 7, 1941, entry, in Jacobsen, ed., *Halder, Kriegstagebuch,* vol. 3, 282–83.

29. *DRZW,* vol. 4, 589.

30. Bock, *War Diary,* 366.

31. Ibid., 373.

32. Jacobson, ed., *Halder, Kriegstagebuch,* vol. 3, 321–22. On the distance and dates, see I. C. B. Dear and M. R. D. Foot, eds., *The Oxford Companion to World War II* (Oxford, 1995), 112–13.

33. See Klaus Latzel, *Deutsche Soldaten—nationalsozialistischer Krieg? Kriegserlebnis—Kriegserfahrung, 1939–1945* (Paderborn, 1998), 52.

34. *Tagebücher von Goebbels,* Nov. 30, 1941, entry, in part 2, vol. 1, 398–99.

35. *Hitler: Reden und Proklamationen,* vol. 4, 1793–1811.

36. *Tagebücher von Goebbels,* Dec. 10, 1941, entry, in part 2, vol. 1, 459–69; on the Dec. 12, 1941, letters, see ibid., 483.

37. Gerd R. Ueberschär, in Dear and Foot, *Oxford Companion to World War II,* 113.

CHAPTER 29: WAR AGAINST THE JEWS: DEATH SQUADS IN THE EAST

1. "Der Bolschewismus enthüllt sein jüdisches Gesicht," in *VB,* July 10, 1941.

2. See, for example, Helmut Krausnick and Hans-Heinrich Wilhelm, *Die Truppe des Weltanschauungskrieges: Die Einsatzgruppen der Sicherheitspolizei und des SD, 1938–1942* (Stuttgart, 1981), 637–46.

3. The document, also for what follows, is cited in Peter Longerich, *Politik der Vernichtung: Eine Gesamtdarstellung der nationalsozialistischen Judenverfolgung* (Munich, 1998), 315–16.

4. See Christopher R. Browning, *The Origins of the Final Solution: The Evolution of Nazi Jewish Policy, September 1939–March 1942* (Lincoln, Neb., 2004), 274.

5. See Christopher R. Browning, *Ordinary Men: Reserve Police Battalion 101 and the Final Solution in Poland* (New York, 1992).

6. Jan T. Gross, *Neighbors: The Destruction of the Jewish Community in Jedwabne, Poland* (Princeton, N. J., 2001), 155.

7. Ibid., 46.

8. Ibid., 78.

9. Doc. 180-L, in *IMT,* vol. 37, 670–717.

10. See Peter Klein, ed., *Die Einsatzgruppen in der besetzten Sowjetunion,*

1941–42: Die Tätigkeits- und Lageberichte des Chefs der Sicherheitspolizei und des SD (Berlin, 1997).

11. Krausnick and Wilhelm, *Truppe des Weltanschauungskrieges,* 540–41.

12. Longerich, *Politik der Vernichtung,* 336.

13. Martin Dean, *Collaboration in the Holocaust: Crimes of the Local Police in Belorussia and Ukraine, 1941–1944* (New York, 2000), 43.

14. See table 1 in Christian Gerlach, "Die Einsatzgruppe B 1941–42," in Klein, *Einsatzgruppen in der besetzten Sowjetunion,* 62.

15. Cited in Ian Kershaw, *Hitler, 1936–45: Nemesis* (New York, 2000), 465.

16. Cited in Omer Bartov, *Hitler's Army: Soldiers, Nazis, and War in the Third Reich* (Oxford, 1992), 129–30; see also Wolfram Wette, *Die Wehrmacht: Feindbilder, Vernichtungskrieg, Legenden* (Frankfurt am Main, 2002), 100–2; Longerich, *Politik der Vernichtung,* 405–6.

17. Bartov, *Hitler's Army,* 130–31.

18. Christian Gerlach, "Verbrechen deutscher Fronttruppen in *Weißrußland, 1941–1944: Eine Annäherung,*" in Karl Heinrich Pohl, ed., *Wehrmacht und Vernichtungspolitik: Militär im nationalsozialistischen System* (Göttingen, 1999), 101.

19. Ben Shepherd, *War in the Wild East: The German Army and Soviet Partisans* (Cambridge, Mass., 2004), 63.

20. Cited in ibid., 65.

21. Letter 352 from a corporal, July 22, 1942, in Ortwin Buchbender and Reinhold Sterz, eds., *Das andere Gesicht des Krieges: Deutsche Feldpostbriefe, 1939–1945* (Munich, 1982), 172.

22. Letter 351 from a noncommissioned officer, July 18, 1942, in ibid., 171.

23. Cited in Bartov, *Hitler's Army,* 163.

24. Walter Manoschek, ed., *"Es gibt nur eines für das Judentum: Vernichtung": Das Judenbild in deutschen Soldentenbriefen, 1939–1944* (Hamburg, 1995), 51.

25. Ibid., 59.

26. Bartov, *Hitler's Army,* 153–55.

27. See letters from the front cited in Stephen G. Fritz, *Frontsoldaten: The German Soldier in World War II* (Lexington, Ky., 1995), 195–206.

28. Cited in Shepherd, *War in the Wild East,* 71.

29. Bartov, *Hitler's Army,* 83–84.

30. *DRZW,* vol. 4, 1040–41.

31. Ibid., 1040, 1044.

32. Wette, *Wehrmacht,* 118, also for what follows.

33. Dieter Pohl, *Nationalsozialistische Judenverfolgung in Ostgalizien, 1941–1944* (Munich, 1996), 61; Longerich, *Politik der Vernichtung,* 337, cites a report of seven thousand killed in Lvov.

34. Pohl, *Nationalsozialistische Judenverfolgung in Ostgalizien,* 62–63.

35. Wette, *Wehrmacht,* 119.

36. Karel C. Berkhoff, *Harvest of Despair: Life and Death in Ukraine Under Nazi Rule* (Cambridge, Mass., 2004), 32–33.
37. Kate Brown, *A Biography of No Place: From Ethnic Borderland to Soviet Heartland* (Cambridge, Mass., 2004), 213, 218.
38. Wendy Lower, *Nazi Empire-Building and the Holocaust in Ukraine* (Chapel Hill, N.C., 2005), 70.
39. Peter Witte et al., eds., *Der Dienstkalender Heinrich Himmlers, 1941–42* (Hamburg, 1999), 201–49, 195.

CHAPTER 30: THE "FINAL SOLUTION" AND DEATH CAMPS

1. Henrik Eberle and Matthias Uhl, eds., *The Hitler Book: The Secret Dossier Prepared for Stalin from the Interrogations of Hitler's Personal Aides* (New York, 2005), 105.
2. For an excellent account of the scholarly literature and convincing analysis, see Ian Kershaw, "Hitler's Role in the 'Final Solution,'" *Yad Vashem Studies* (2006), 7–43.
3. Werner Jochmann, ed., *Monologue im Führerhauptquartier, 1941–1944* (Hamburg, 1980), 82.
4. *Hitler: Reden und Proklamationen*, vol. 3, 1058.
5. Ibid., vol. 4, 1663–64.
6. David Bankier, *The Germans and the Final Solution: Public Opinion Under Nazism* (Oxford, 1992), 139–40.
7. For an examination, see Robert Gellately, *Backing Hitler: Consent and Coercion in Nazi Germany* (Oxford, 2001), 121–50.
8. Cited in Richard Breitman, *The Architect of Genocide: Himmler and the Final Solution* (London, 1991), 192–93.
9. Christopher R. Browning, *The Origins of the Final Solution: The Evolution of Nazi Jewish Policy, September 1939–March 1942* (Lincoln, Neb., 2004), 371.
10. Christian Gerlach, *Kaluklierte Morde: Die deutsche Wirtschafts- und Vernichtungspolitik in Weißrußland, 1941 bis 1944* (Hamburg, 1999), 628–46; for a similar argument about the importance of decisions on the periphery, but also holding open the possibility that Berlin might have been involved, see Dieter Pohl, *Nationalsozialistische Judenverfolgung in Ostgalizien, 1941–1944* (Munich, 1996), 139–43; for an August date, see also Ralf Orgorreck, *Die Einsatzgruppen und die "Genesis der Endlösung"* (Berlin, 1996), 210; for a seamless transition to a "drastic sharpening" of measures against the Jews in Galicia, without a recognizable order from Himmler, see Thomas Sandkühler, *"Endlösung" in Galizien: Der Judenmord in Ostpolen und die Rettungsinitiativen von Berthold Beitz, 1941–1944* (Bonn, 1996), 137.

11. Peter Witte et al., eds., *Der Dienstkalender Heinrich Himmlers, 1941–42* (Hamburg, 1999), 201–49.

12. See Gerald Fleming, *Hitler and the Final Solution* (Berkeley, Calif., 1984), 50ff., esp. 51–52.

13. Reichsführer-SS to Gottlob Berger, July 28, 1942, Berlin Document Center, cited in Kershaw, "Hitler's Role," 37.

14. Elke Fröhlich et al., eds., *Die Tagebücher von Joseph Goebbels* (Munich, 2005ff.), part 2, vol. 1, 476–87.

15. Jochmann, *Monologue im Führerhauptquartier,* 90.

16. Ibid., 99.

17. Oct. 24, 1941, entry, in Witte et al., *Dienstkalender Himmlers,* 246.

18. Jochmann, *Monologue im Führerhauptquartier,* 106.

19. Peter Longerich, *Politik der Vernichtung: Eine Gesamtdarstellung der nationalsozialistischen Judenverfolgung* (Munich, 1998), 440, nevertheless insists there were still no specific plans to kill all the Jews.

20. *Hitler: Reden und Proklamationen,* vol. 4, 1771–81.

21. *VB,* Nov. 12, 1941.

22. "Die Juden sind Schuld!" *Das Reich,* Nov. 16, 1941, 1–2. For public reaction, see Nov. 20, 1941, *Meldungen aus dem Reich,* vol. 8, 3007.

23. *VB,* Dec. 3, 1941.

24. Browning, *Origins of the Final Solution,* 372.

25. Longerich, *Politik der Vernichtung,* 456–57.

26. Dec. 13, 1941, entry, for the previous day, in *Tagebücher von Goebbels,* part 2, vol. 1, 498–99.

27. Witte et al., *Dienstkalender Himmlers,* 294.

28. Jan. 25 and 27, 1942, in Jochmann, *Monologe im Führerhauptquartier,* 228–29, 241.

29. In 1942 the prophecy was mentioned in speeches he gave on January 30, September 30, and November 8. All were published in the press and are reprinted in *Hitler: Reden und Proklamationen,* vol. 4. For an analysis, see Ian Kershaw, *The "Hitler Myth": Image and Reality in the Third Reich* (Oxford, 1987), 241ff.

30. *Hitler: Reden und Proklamationen,* vol. 4, 1828–29.

31. See Feb. 2, 1942, *Meldungen aus dem Reich,* vol. 9, 3235.

32. *VB,* Feb. 27, 1942.

33. *VB,* March 27 and July 13, 1942.

34. *VB,* Oct. 9, 1941.

35. March 16, 1942, entry, in Victor Klemperer, *Ich will Zeugnis ablegen bis zum letzten: Tagebücher, 1942–1945* (Berlin, 1995), 47.

36. April 19, 1942, entry, in ibid., 68.

37. Inge Scholl, *Die weisse Rose* (Frankfurt am Main, 1955), 102.

38. Christopher R. Browning, *Ordinary Men: Reserve Police Battalion 101 and the Final Solution in Poland* (New York, 1992), xv.

39. See *KP*, Oct. 28, 1992, 2.

40. Omer Bartov, "Ordinary Monsters," *New Republic*, April 29, 1996, 38.

41. Raul Hilberg, *The Destruction of the European Jews*, rev. ed. (New York, 1985), vol. 3, 893; Browning, *Origins of the Final Solution*, 365–66, 418; Yitzhak Arad, *Belzec, Sobibor, Treblinka: The Operation Reinhard Death Camps* (Bloomington, Ind., 1987), 11; Henry Friedlander, *The Origins of Nazi Genocide: From Euthanasia to the Final Solution* (Chapel Hill, N.C., 1995), 287.

42. See Alan Adelson, ed., *The Diary of Dawid Sierakowiak: Five Notebooks from the Łódź Ghetto* (New York, 1998); Abraham I. Katsh, ed., *Scroll of Agony: The Warsaw Diary of Chaim A. Kaplan* (Bloomington, Ind., 1973).

43. This is the sensible conclusion of Longerich, *Politik der Vernichtung*, 455.

44. Arad, *Belzec, Sobibor, Treblinka*, 23–29.

45. Ibid., 30–33.

46. Ibid., 43.

47. Hilberg, *Destruction of the European Jews*, vol. 3, 893; Karin Orth, *Das System der nationalsozialistischen Konzentrationslager* (Hamburg, 1999), 343.

48. Cited in Arad, *Belzec, Sobibor, Treblinka*, 117–18.

49. Cited in ibid., 128.

50. Witte et al., *Dienstkalander Himmlers*, 186.

51. Hilberg, *Destruction of the European Jews*, vol. 3, 893, puts it at 50,000; Franciszek Piper, "Auschwitz Concentration Camp," in Michael Berenbaum and Abraham J. Peck, eds., *The Holocaust and History: The Known, the Unknown, the Disputed, and the Reexamined* (Bloomington, Ind., 1998), 374; Thomas Kranz, "Das KL Lublin—zwischen Planung und Realisierung," in Ulrich Herbert et al., eds., *Die nationalsozialistischen Konzentrationslager—Entwicklung und Struktur* (Göttingen, 1998), vol. 1, 362–89.

52. Cited in Arad, *Belzec, Sobibor, Treblinka*, 101; for the orders, 170.

53. Sybille Steinbacher, *Auschwitz: Geschichte und Nachgeschichte* (Munich, 2004), 9–27.

54. Ibid., 37–42.

55. Gellately, *Backing Hitler*, 214–15.

56. Steinbacher, *Auschwitz*, 71–72; Danuta Czech, *Auschwitz Chronicle, 1939–1945* (New York, 1990), 218.

57. Czech, *Auschwitz Chronicle*, 112, 120, 139.

58. Steinbacher, *Auschwitz*, 70; Longerich, *Politik der Vernichtung*, 444, gives the date in December.

59. Józef Garlinski, *Fighting Auschwitz: The Resistance Movement in the Concentration Camp* (London, 1975), 85–86; for the earlier date, see Czech, *Auschwitz Chronicle*, 135.

60. Czech, *Auschwitz Chronicle*, 146, 176, 189.

61. Ibid., 194, 638.

62. Ibid., 198, 255.

63. Ibid., 356, 399.

64. Ibid., 199; also Witte et al., *Dienstkalender Himmlers,* 493–94.
65. Sept. 23, 1943, entry, in *Tagebücher von Goebbels,* part 2, vol. 9, 567.
66. For an introduction, see Gellately, *Backing Hitler,* 239–40.
67. Meir Michaelis, *Mussolini and the Jews* (Oxford, 1978), 354–68; also Meir Michaelis, "The Holocaust in Italy," in Berenbaum and Peck, *Holocaust and History,* 439–62.
68. Michaelis, *Mussolini and the Jews,* 389.
69. See Peter Hayes, *Industry and Ideology: IG Farben in the Nazi Era* (Cambridge, U.K., 1987), 350–61.
70. Andreas Hillgruber, ed., *Staatsmänner und Diplomaten bei Hitler: Vertrauliche Aufzeichnungen über Unterredungen mit Vertretern des Auslandes, 1939–1941* (Frankfurt am Main, 1967), vol. 2, 256–59.
71. See Christian Gerlach and Götz Aly, *Das letzte Kapitel: Der Mord an den ungarishen Juden* (Munich, 2002), 258.
72. See Rudolph L. Braham, "Hungarian Jews," in Yisrael Gutman and Michael Berenbaum, eds., *Anatomy of the Auschwitz Death Camp* (Bloomington, Ind., 1994), 456–68.
73. Hilberg, *Destruction of the European Jews,* vol. 3, 894; Steinbacher, *Auschwitz,* 105.
74. Franciszek Piper, "The Number of Victims," in Gutman and Berenbaum, *Anatomy of the Auschwitz Death Camp,* 61–76.

CHAPTER 31: GREATEST CRISIS IN STALIN'S CAREER

1. No. 659, in *DGFP,* vol. 12, 1063–65.
2. John Erickson, *The Road to Stalingrad: Stalin's War with Germany* (New Haven, Conn., 1975), 124.
3. Georgi Dimitrov, *Tagebücher, 1933–1943* (Berlin, 2000), vol. 2, 392–93, also for what follows.
4. Robert Service, *Stalin: A Biography* (Cambridge, Mass., 2004), 412–13.
5. *SDFP,* 490–91; Feliks Ivanovich Chuev and Vyacheslav Molotov, *Sto sorok besed s Molotovym: iz dnevnika F. Chueva* (Moscow, 1991), 44–45.
6. Did Stalin admit he lacked the courage to speak to the nation about the German attack, as some have suggested? See Constantine Pleshakov, *Stalin's Folly: The Tragic First Ten Days of WWII on the Eastern Front* (Boston, 2005), 114. The author gives no source for Stalin's "admission," which seems improbable.
7. Dmitri Volkogonov, *Triumf i tragediya. Politichesky portret J. V. Stalina* (Moscow, 1989), vol. 2, part 1, 192–93.
8. On the military conference of December 1940, and war game of January 1941, see Erickson, *Road to Stalingrad,* 8–9.
9. See Service, *Stalin,* 414.

10. See *1941 god,* vol. 2, 498.

11. Sergo Beria, *Beria, My Father: Inside Stalin's Kremlin* (London, 2001), 71.

12. Volkogonov, *Triumf i tragediya. Politichesky portret J. V. Stalina,* vol. 2, part 1, 246.

13. David M. Glantz and Jonathan House, *When Titans Clashed: How the Red Army Stopped Hitler* (Lawrence, Kans., 1995), 51.

14. Erickson, *Road to Stalingrad,* 163–64; Roger R. Reese, *Stalin's Reluctant Soldiers: A Social History of the Red Army, 1925–1941* (Lawrence, Kans., 1996), 196.

15. McNeal, *Stalin sochineniia,* vol. 2 (vol. 15), 1–10.

16. *NYT,* July 4, 1941.

17. Alexander Werth, *Russia at War, 1941–1945* (New York, 1964), 213–23.

18. *DRZW,* vol. 4, 734–35, also for what follows.

19. Volkogonov, *Triumf i tragediya. Politichesky portret J. V. Stalina,* vol. 2, part 1, 185.

20. Michael Parrish, *Sacrifice of the Generals: Soviet Senior Officer Losses, 1939–1953* (Oxford, 2004), xix–xxi.

21. Cited in Dmitri Volkogonov, *Autopsy for an Empire: The Seven Leaders Who Built the Soviet Regime* (New York, 1998), 115.

22. *DRZW,* vol. 4, 725.

23. Cited in Volkogonov, *Triumf i tragediya. Politichesky portret J. V. Stalina,* vol. 2, part 1, 205.

24. *DRZW,* vol. 4, 727.

25. Alexander N. Yakovlev, *A Century of Violence in Soviet Russia* (New Haven, Conn., 2002), 174.

26. Marius Broekmeyer, *Stalin, the Russians, and Their War, 1941–1945* (Madison, Wis., 2004), 168–69.

27. Ibid., 94–95.

28. Ibid., 169–70.

29. Roger R. Reese, *The Soviet Military Experience* (New York, 2000), 116.

30. Yakovlev, *Century of Violence in Soviet Russia,* 175.

31. Cited in Volkogonov, *Autopsy for an Empire,* 118.

32. *DRZW,* vol. 4, 727.

33. Strobe Talbott, ed., *Khrushchev Remembers* (Boston, 1970), 189.

34. HP 117, 34–35, 46–49, 51–52.

35. Alexander Dallin, *German Rule in Russia, 1941–1945: A Study in Occupation Policies* (Boulder, Colo., 1981), 65.

36. Ibid., 41–58.

CHAPTER 32: BETWEEN SURRENDER AND DEFIANCE

1. Cited in Martin Gilbert, *Finest Hour: Winston S. Churchill, 1939–1941* (London, 1983), 1168.

2. Pavel Sudoplatov and Anatoli Sudoplatov, *Special Tasks: The Memoirs of an Unwanted Witness—a Soviet Spymaster* (New York, 1994), 145.

3. Central Archives of the Soviet Defense Ministry, TsAMO, f. 32, op. 701 323 d. 38, 1. 53, cited in Dmitri Volkogonov, *Triumf i tragediya. Politichesky portret J. V. Stalina* (Moscow, 1989), vol. 2, part 1, 172–73, who insists that Stalin, Molotov, and Beria met with the ambassador.

4. Additional evidence can be found in Sudoplatov and Sudoplatov, *Special Tasks,* 146–47; Simon Sebag Montefiore, *Stalin: The Court of the Red Tsar* (New York, 2004), 380; Constantine Pleshakov, *Stalin's Folly: The Tragic First Ten Days of WWII on the Eastern Front* (Boston, 2005), 189–90; and *1941 god,* doc. 651.

5. Beria's testimony cited in Sudoplatov and Sudoplatov, *Special Tasks,* 377.

6. Cited in William Taubman, *Khrushchev: The Man and His Era* (New York, 2003), 162–63.

7. July 11/12, 1941, in Werner Jochmann, ed., *Monologe im Führerhauptquartier, 1941–1944* (Hamburg, 1980), 42.

8. G. K. Zhukov, *Vospominaniya i razmyshleniya* (Moscow, 1969), 334–35.

9. See Sebag Montefiore, *Stalin,* 392, 710 n. 21.

10. The personal exchange is recorded in Viktor Anfilov, "Georgy Konstantinovich Zhukov," in Harold Shukman, ed., *Stalin's Generals* (London, 1993), 350–51.

11. See Warren F. Kimball, *Forged in War: Roosevelt, Churchill, and the Second World War* (New York, 1997), 112.

12. *Khrushchev Remembers: The Glasnost Tapes* (Boston, 1990), 65–67.

13. Cited in David M. Kennedy, *Freedom from Fear: The American People in Depression and War, 1929–1945* (New York, 1999), 484.

14. Cited in ibid., 485, also for what follows.

15. Cited in ibid.

16. See W. Averell Harriman and Elie Abel, *Special Envoy to Churchill and Stalin, 1941–1946* (New York, 1975), 80–105.

17. Stalin to Roosevelt, in Commission for the Publication of Diplomatic Documents of the USSR, ed., *Correspondence Between Stalin, Roosevelt, Truman, Churchill, and Attlee During WWII* (Honolulu, 1957), 13, 15.

18. A. G. Rybin, *Stalin v Oktyabre 1941* (Moscow, n.d.), 3–16.

19. Zhukov, *Vospominaniya,* 346.

20. Ibid.

21. *KTB,* vol. 1, 1070.

22. See Earl F. Ziemke and Magna E. Bauer, *Moscow to Stalingrad: Decision in the East* (Washington, D.C., 1987), 42. For the dispersal order of November 5 and the location of various branches of government, see John Erickson, *The Road to Stalingrad: Stalin's War with Germany* (New Haven, Conn., 1975), 228–30.

23. Cited in Alexander Werth, *Russia at War, 1941–1945* (New York, 1964), 235.

24. M. M. Gorinov, "Budni osazhdennoi stolitsy: zhizn' i nastroenie Moskvt,"

OI (1996), 20–21. This is partially reprinted in his "Muscovites' Moods, 22 June 1941 to May 1942," in Robert W. Thurston and Bernd Bonwetsch, eds., *The People's War: Responses to World War II in the Soviet Union* (Urbana, Ill., 2000), 123.

25. NKVD report and others cited in Marius Broekmeyer, *Stalin, the Russians, and Their War, 1941–1945* (Madison, Wis., 2004), 60, 65, 67.

26. Cited in David Brandenberger, *National Bolshevism: Stalinist Mass Culture and the Formation of Modern Russian National Identity, 1931–1956* (Cambridge, Mass., 2002), 117.

27. Jeffrey Brooks, *"Thank You, Comrade Stalin!"; Soviet Public Culture from Revolution to Cold War* (Princeton, N.J., 1999), 159–94.

28. HP 587, 10, 21–23, 42–45, 80–81, 94–95, 97–99.

29. See, for example, Broekmeyer, *Stalin, the Russians, and Their War,* 68.

30. See, for example, Gennadi Bordiugov, "The Popular Mood in the Unoccupied Soviet Union: Continuity and Change During the War," in Thurston and Bonwetsch, *People's War,* 54–70.

31. Richard Bidlack, "Survival Strategies in Leningrad During the First Year of the Soviet-German War," in Thurston and Bonwetsch, *People's War,* 100.

32. Information on the police panic and quotation in Harrison E. Salisbury, *The 900 Days: The Siege of Leningrad* (New York, 1969), 447–59.

33. Andrei R. Dzeniskevich, "The Social and Political Situation in Leningrad in the First Months of the German Invasion: The Social Psychology of the Workers," in Thurston and Bonwetsch, *People's War,* 71–83.

34. Cited in Nina Tumarkin, *The Living and the Dead: The Rise and Fall of the Cult of World War II in Russia* (New York, 1994), 65.

35. Cited in ibid., 66.

36. David M. Glantz, *The Battle for Leningrad, 1941–1944* (Lawrence, Kans., 2002), 148.

37. Ibid., 468–69.

38. Reprinted with other valuable materials in Cynthia Simmons and Nina Perlia, eds., *Writing the Siege of Leningrad* (Pittsburgh, 2002), 51.

39. Excerpts of this diary and others are reprinted in ibid., 31.

40. Glantz, *Battle for Leningrad,* 148, 470.

41. Georgi Dimitrov, *Tagebücher, 1933–1943* (Berlin, 2000), vol. 1, 440–41.

42. Werth, *Russia at War,* 240–41.

43. See K. F. Telegin, *Voprosy istorii KPSS* (Moscow, 1966), 104–7. For background and slightly different timing, see Sebag Montefiore, *Stalin,* 394–401.

44. Cathy Porter and Mark Jones, *Moscow in World War II* (London, 1987), 117.

45. Dmitri Volkogonov, *Autopsy for an Empire: The Seven Leaders Who Built the Soviet Regime* (New York, 1998), 118.

46. Zhukov, *Vospominaniya,* 352.

47. McNeal, *Stalin sochineniia,* vol. 2 (vol. 15), 11–35.

48. Cited in Anfilov, "Zhukov," 352.

49. Zhukov, *Vospominaniya,* 378.

50. Volkogonov, *Triumf i tragediya. Politichesky portret J. V. Stalina,* vol. 2, part 1, 286–87.
51. Ibid., 286–88.

CHAPTER 33: SOVIETS HOLD ON, HITLER GROWS VICIOUS

1. G. K. Zhukov, *Vospominaniya i razmyshleniya* (Moscow, 1969), 368–70.
2. Cited in Dmitri Volkogonov, *Autopsy for an Empire: The Seven Leaders Who Built the Soviet Regime* (New York, 1998), 120.
3. Ibid., 121.
4. Hans-Adolf Jacobson, ed., *Generaloberst Halder, Kriegstagebuch; tägliche Aufzeichnungen des Chefs des Generalstabes des Heeres, 1939–1942* (Stuttgart, 1962–64), vol. 3, 420.
5. H. R. Trevor-Roper, ed., *Hitler's War Directives* (London, 1964), 116–21; *KTB,* vol. 2, 315–16.
6. Memoir printed in Seweryn Bialer, *Stalin and His Generals: Soviet Military Memoirs of World War II* (New York, 1969), 404.
7. Trevor-Roper, *Hitler's War Directives,* 129–31.
8. Cited in Martin Gilbert, *Churchill: A Life* (New York, 1991), 727. For a study of the catastrophic impact of the bombing, see Jörg Friedrich, *The Fire: The Bombing of Germany 1940–1945* (New York, 2006).
9. W. Averell Harriman and Elie Abel, *Special Envoy to Churchill and Stalin, 1941–1946* (New York, 1975), 159, also for what follows.
10. Winston Churchill, *The Hinge of Fate* (Boston, 1950), 498.
11. Cited in Martin Kitchen, *British Policy Towards the Soviet Union During the Second World War* (London, 1986), 140.
12. Gerhard L. Weinberg, *A World at Arms: A Global History of World War II* (Cambridge, U.K., 1994), 360.
13. John Erickson, *The Road to Stalingrad: Stalin's War with Germany* (New Haven, Conn., 1975), 370–71.
14. July 23, 1942, entry, in Jacobson, ed., *Halder, Kriegstagebuch,* vol. 3, 489.
15. David M. Glantz and Jonathan House, *When Titans Clashed: How the Red Army Stopped Hitler* (Lawrence, Kans., 1995), 120.
16. Alexander Werth, *Russia at War, 1941–1945* (New York, 1964), 407.
17. Cited in Alexander Werth, *The Year of Stalingrad* (1947; Safety Harbor, Fla., 2001), 162.
18. Werth, *Russia at War,* 418.
19. Werth, *Year of Stalingrad,* 160.
20. Ibid., 156.
21. Werth, *Russia at War,* 415–16.
22. S. M. Shtemenko, *Generalniya Shtab v gordi voiny: ot Stalingrada do Berlina* (Moscow, 2005), 120.
23. Cited in Werth, *Russia at War,* 427.

24. Roger R. Reese, *The Soviet Military Experience* (New York, 2000), 126–29.

25. Zhukov, *Vospominaniya,* 389–90.

26. Cited in Marius Broekmeyer, *Stalin, the Russians, and Their War, 1941–1945* (Madison, Wis., 2004), 95.

27. Cited in John Barber and Mark Harrison, *The Soviet Home Front, 1941–1945: A Social and Economic History of the USSR in World War II* (London, 1991), 72.

28. Werth, *Year of Stalingrad,* 181–82.

29. Ibid., 161.

30. Zhukov, *Vospominaniya,* 397–98.

31. July 25, 1942, entry in Jacobson, ed., *Halder, Kriegstagebuch,* vol. 3, 490.

32. Werth, *Year of Stalingrad,* 159.

33. Sept. 15, 1942, entry in Jacobson, ed., *Halder, Kriegstagebuch,* vol. 3, 522–23.

34. Zhukov, *Vospominaniya,* 398–401.

35. Sept. 1 and 8, 1942, entries in Jacobson, ed., *Halder, Kriegstagebuch,* vol. 3, 516.

36. Zhukov, *Vospominaniya,* 402–3.

37. See Antony Beevor, *Stalingrad: The Fateful Siege, 1942–1943* (New York, 1998), 203–7.

38. Nicolaus von Below, *Als Hitlers Adjutant, 1937–45* (Mainz, 1980), 315–17.

39. *DRZW,* vol. 6, 955–56.

40. Joachim von Ribbentrop, *Zwischen London und Moskau: Erinnerungen und letzte Aufzeichnungen* (Leoni am Starnberger See, 1953), 260–63.

41. Noakes and Pridham, vol. 3, 846–48.

42. Walter Warlimont, *Im Hauptquartier der deutschen Wehrmacht, 1939–1945* (Frankfurt am Main, 1962), 285.

43. Erickson, *Road to Stalingrad,* 47–49.

44. Traudl Junge, *Bis zur letzten Stunde: Hitlers Sectretärin erzählt ihr Leben* (Munich, 2002), 95.

CHAPTER 34: ETHNIC CLEANSING IN WARTIME SOVIET UNION

1. See S. V. Mironenko and N. Werth, eds., *Istoria stalinskogo Gulaga* (Moscow, 2004), vol. 1, 455–75; Fred C. Koch, *The Volga Germans in Russia and the Americas, from 1763 to the Present* (London, 1977), 284–85.

2. Cited in Koch, *Volga Germans,* 288.

3. Nicolas Werth, "A State Against Its People: Violence, Repression, and Terror in the Soviet Union," in Stéphane Courtois et al., *The Black Book of Communism* (Cambridge, Mass., 1999), 218.

4. Cited in Amir Weiner, *Making Sense of War: The Second World War and the Fate of the Bolshevik Revolution* (Princeton, N.J., 2001), 150–51.

5. J. Otto Pohl, *Ethnic Cleansing in the USSR, 1937–1949* (Westport, Conn., 1999), 54. For a general study, see Gerd Stricker, ed., *Deutsche Geschichte im Osten Europas: Rußland* (Berlin, 1997).

6. See the brilliant study of Jörg Baberowski, *Der Feind ist überall: Stalinismus im Kaukasus* (Munich, 2003), 553–632.

7. Pohl, *Ethnic Cleansing in the USSR,* 61–69; Mironenko and Werth, *Istoria stalinskogo Gulaga,* vol. 1, 477–80.

8. Pohl, *Ethnic Cleansing in the USSR,* 74–77, 87–92.

9. Norman M. Naimark, *Fires of Hatred: Ethnic Cleansing in Twentieth-Century Europe* (Cambridge, Mass., 2001), 94.

10. Pohl, *Ethnic Cleansing in the USSR,* 83; Naimark, *Fires of Hatred,* 97.

11. Naimark, *Fires of Hatred,* 97.

12. Cited in Pohl, *Ethnic Cleansing in the USSR,* 85.

13. Ibid., 132.

14. Cited in ibid., 121.

15. Ibid., 115.

16. Cited in Naimark, *Fires of Hatred,* 102.

17. Marius Broekmeyer, *Stalin, the Russians, and Their War, 1941–1945* (Madison, Wis., 2004), 178–79.

18. Strobe Talbott, ed., *Khrushchev Remembers* (Boston, 1970), 596.

19. See Weiner, *Making Sense of War,* 151.

20. See Yo'av Karny, *Highlanders: A Journey to the Caucasus in Quest of Memory* (New York, 2000), 227.

21. Cited in Anatol Lieven, *Chechnya: Tombstone of Russian Power* (New Haven, Conn., 1998), 320.

22. Cited in ibid., 319.

23. Weiner, *Making Sense of War,* 136–37.

24. Aleksandr Solzhenitsyn, *Gulag Archipelago, 1918–1956* (New York, 1973), vol. 1, 84.

25. For a view, difficult to sustain with regard to groups like the kulaks, that suggests the Soviets engaged in genocidal practices in the 1930s and during the war, see Eric D. Weitz, *A Century of Genocide: Utopias of Race and Nation* (Princeton, N. J., 2003), 53–101.

26. Anne Applebaum, *Gulag: A History* (New York, 2003), 419.

27. Gennadi Bordiugov, "The Popular Mood in the Unoccupied Soviet Union: Continuity and Change During the War," in Robert W. Thurston and Bernd Bonwetsch, eds., *The People's War: Responses to World War II in the Soviet Union* (Urbana, Ill., 2000), 61.

28. Solzhenitsyn, *Gulag Archipelago,* vol. 2, 134–35.

29. A. B. Bezborodov and V. M. Khrustalëv, eds., *Istoria stalinskogo Gulaga* (Moscow, 2004), vol. 4, 109.

30. Edwin Bacon, *The Gulag at War: Stalin's Forced Labor System in the Light of the Archives* (New York, 1994), 151.

31. Solzhenitsyn, *Gulag Archipelago,* vol. 2, 233–34.

32. For a survivor's account, see Varlam Shalamov, *Kolyma Tales* (Harmondsworth, U.K., 1994), 415–31.

33. Solzhenitsyn, *Gulag Archipelago,* vol. 2, 241.

34. Computed from Bacon, *Gulag at War,* 167.

35. Ibid., 109.

36. Gábor Tamás Rittersporn, *Stalinist Simplifications and Soviet Complications: Social Tensions and Political Conflicts in the USSR, 1933–1953* (Chur, Switzerland, 1991), 295.

37. Oleg V. Khlevniuk, *The History of the Gulag: From Collectivization to the Great Terror* (New Haven, Conn., 2004), 337.

CHAPTER 35: FROM STALINGRAD TO BERLIN

1. See the tables in Noakes and Pridham, vol. 3, 851–53.

2. For further investigation and sources, see Robert Gellately, *The Gestapo and German Society* (Oxford, 1990), 244–45.

3. Nicolaus von Below, *Als Hitlers Adjutant, 1937–45* (Mainz, 1980), 330.

4. Elke Fröhlich et al., eds., *Die Tagebücher von Joseph Goebbels* (Munich, 2005ff.), part 2, vol. 7, 295.

5. Ibid., 296.

6. Feb. 22, 1943, *Meldungen aus dem Reich,* vol. 13, 4831.

7. Jan. 30, 1943, in *Hitler: Reden und Proklamationen,* vol. 4, 1978.

8. Ibid., 1990–93.

9. *Tagebücher von Goebbels,* part 2, vol. 7, 609–10.

10. *Hitler: Reden und Proklamationen,* vol. 4, 2000–2.

11. March 22, 1943, *Meldungen aus dem Reich,* 4981–82.

12. Dec. 31, 1943, letter, in Heinrich Böll, *Briefe aus dem Krieg, 1939–1945* (Cologne, 2001), vol. 2, 972.

13. See Bernd Wegner, "Defensive ohne Strategie: Die Wehrmacht und das Jahr 1943," in Rolf-Dieter Müller and Hans-Erich Volkmann, eds., *Die Wehrmacht: Mythos und Realität* (Munich, 1999), 197–209.

14. Oleg Rzheshevsky, "Ivan Stepanovich Konev," in Harold Shukman, ed., *Stalin's Generals* (London, 1993), 90–107.

15. Dmitri Volkogonov, *Triumf i tragediya. Politichesky portret J. V. Stalina* (Moscow, 1989), vol. 2, part 1, 268–69; 285–86.

16. John Erickson, *The Road to Berlin: Stalin's War with Germany* (New Haven, Conn., 1983), 39.

17. Amy Knight, *Beria: Stalin's First Lieutenant* (Princeton, N.J., 1993), 124–25.

18. Cited in Catherine Merridale, *Ivan's War: Life and Death in the Red Army, 1939–1945* (New York, 2006), 157.

19. McNeal, *Stalin sochineniia,* vol. 2 (vol. 15), 86–94.

20. Cited in *NYT,* Feb. 23, 1943.

21. Alexander Werth, *The Year of Stalingrad* (1947; Safety Harbor, Fla., 2001), 370.

22. *NYT,* Dec. 20, 1942. Alas, the story was carried on page 23.

23. A. M. Vasilevsky, *Delo vsei zhizni* (Moscow, 1983), 288–313.

24. Walter Warlimont, *Im Hauptquartier der deutschen Wehrmacht, 1939–1945* (Frankfurt am Main, 1962), 347–48.

25. G. K. Zhukov, *Vospominaniya i razmyshleniya* (Moscow, 1969), 451–53.

26. Cited in David M. Glantz and Jonathan House, *The Battle of Kursk* (Lawrence, Kans., 1999), 266.

27. Calculations based on tables in ibid., 275–76.

28. Warlimont, *Hauptquartier*, 348. See also Walter S. Dunn Jr., *Kursk: Hitler's Gamble, 1943* (London, 1997), 188–90.

29. May 7, 1943, entry, in *Tagebücher von Goebbels*, part 2, vol. 8, 225.

30. April 14 and 17 and May 10, 1943, entries, in ibid., 104, 114–15, 261.

31. The May 8, 1943, speech is summarized in ibid., 233–40.

32. Ian Kershaw, *Hitler, 1936–45: Nemesis* (New York, 2000), 590.

33. May 13, 1943, entry, in *Tagebücher von Goebbels*, part 2, vol. 8, 287–90.

34. May 14, 1943, entry, in ibid., 293.

35. March 12 and 15, 1943, in Helmut Heiber and David M. Glantz, eds., *Hitler and His Generals: Military Conferences, 1942–1945* (New York, 2002), 104.

36. July 26, 1943, in ibid., 252.

37. Dieter Pohl, *Nationalsozialistische Judenverfolgung in Ostgalizien, 1941–1944* (Munich, 1996), 246–47.

38. Useful primary material is reprinted in Ber Mark, *Uprising in the Warsaw Ghetto* (New York, 1975).

39. Raul Hilberg et al., eds., *The Warsaw Diary of Adam Czerniakow* (New York, 1979), 384.

40. Raul Hilberg, *The Destruction of the European Jews*, rev. ed. (New York, 1985), vol. 2, 503.

41. Abraham I. Katsh, ed., *Scroll of Agony: The Warsaw Diary of Chaim A. Kaplan* (Bloomington, Ind., 1999), 396–97.

42. Hilberg, *Destruction of the European Jews*, vol. 2, 507–10.

43. See Nuremberg docs. NO-1882, NO-2514, NO-2494, as cited in ibid., 510.

44. Cited in Israel Gutman, *Resistance: The Warsaw Ghetto Uprising* (Boston, 1994), xix.

45. Ibid., 203.

46. Cited in ibid., 228–29.

47. Cited in ibid., 225.

48. See doc. 1061-PS, in *IMT*, vol. 26, 628–93, for the full report.

49. Cited in Peter Longerich, *Politik der Vernichtung: Eine Gesamtdarstellung der nationalsozialistischen Judenverfolgung* (Munich, 1998), 540.

50. Pohl, *Nationalsozialistische Judenverfolgung in Ostgalizien*, 248–56.

51. April 25, 1943, entry, in *Tagebücher von Goebbels*, part 2, vol. 8, 163.

52. Pohl, *Nationalsozialistische Judenverfolgung in Ostgalizien*, 256.

53. See Thomas Sandkühler, *"Endlösung" in Galizien: Der Judenmord in Ostpolen und die Rettungsinitiativen von Berthold Beitz, 1941–1944* (Bonn, 1996), 374–87.

54. See docs. 019-L and 018-L, in *IMT*, vol. 37, 391–431.

55. Doc. 019-L, in ibid., 410.
56. For a description, see Christopher R. Browning, *Ordinary Men: Reserve Police Battalion 101 and the Final Solution in Poland* (New York, 1992), 133–42.
57. Longerich, *Politik der Vernichtung,* 540.
58. Speer's alibis about not being at Posen were utterly destroyed by Gitta Sereny, *Albert Speer: His Battle with the Truth* (New York, 1995), 388–401.
59. The complete speech is in *IMT,* vol. 29, 1919-PS, 110–72.
60. Bradley F. Smith and Agnes F. Peterson, eds., *Heinrich Himmler: Geheimreden, 1933 bis 1945* (Frankfurt am Main, 1974), 170. This timetable, recorded in the Posen speech by someone else, was not mentioned in the longer version that survives. See also Longerich, *Politik der Vernichtung,* 540 n. 31.

CHAPTER 36: STALIN TAKES THE UPPER HAND

1. Aug. 8, 1943, letter, in Commission for the Publication of Diplomatic Documents of the USSR, ed., *Correspondence Between Stalin, Roosevelt, Truman, Churchill, and Attlee During WWII* (Honolulu, 1957), 78–79.
2. W. Averell Harriman and Elie Abel, *Special Envoy to Churchill and Stalin, 1941–1946* (New York, 1975), 157.
3. Ibid., 536.
4. David M. Kennedy, *Freedom from Fear: The American People in Depression and War, 1929–1945* (New York, 1999), 619, 631, 645.
5. Feliks Ivanovich Chuev and Vyacheslav Molotov, *Sto sorok besed s Molotovym: iz dnevnika F. Chueva* (Moscow, 1991), 73.
6. U.S. Department of State, *The Conferences at Cairo and Tehran, 1943* (Washington, D.C., 1961), 482–86.
7. Cited in Kennedy, *Freedom from Fear,* 677.
8. Winston Churchill, *Closing the Ring* (Boston, 1951), 379–80.
9. Kennedy, *Freedom from Fear,* 674–75.
10. U.S. Department of State, *Conferences at Cairo and Tehran,* 490.
11. Ibid., 514.
12. Ibid., 513.
13. Ibid., 555.
14. Ibid., 512.
15. Churchill, *Closing the Ring,* 362.
16. U.S. Department of State, *Conferences at Cairo and Tehran,* 594–95.
17. Cited in Kennedy, *Freedom from Fear,* 678.
18. Cited in Arieh J. Kochavi, *Prelude to Nuremberg: Allied War Crimes Policy and the Question of Punishment* (Chapel Hill, N.C., 1998), 36. See also Richard Overy, *Interrogations: The Nazi Elite in Allied Hands, 1945* (New York, 2001), 8–9.

19. Reprinted in Michael R. Marrus, ed., *The Nuremberg Trial, 1945–46: A Documentary History* (Boston, 1997), 20–22.
20. Kochavi, *Prelude to Nuremberg,* 73–74.
21. U.S. Department of State, *Conferences at Cairo and Tehran,* 554.
22. Churchill, *Closing the Ring,* 373–74.
23. U.S. Department of State, *Conferences at Cairo and Tehran,* 554.
24. According to Elliott Roosevelt, FDR had used the figure of 49,500 that evening, as cited in Michael Beschloss, *The Conquerors: Roosevelt, Truman, and the Destruction of Hitler's Germany, 1941–1945* (New York, 2002), 27.
25. Churchill, *Closing the Ring,* 374.
26. Cited in Milovan Djilas, *Conversations with Stalin* (Orlando, Fla., 1990), 79.
27. Kochavi, *Prelude to Nuremberg,* 65.
28. See Gerd R. Ueberschär, "Die sowjetischen Prozesse gegen deutsche Kriegsgefangene, 1943–1952," in Gerd R. Ueberschär, ed., *Der National-sozialismus vor Gericht: Die alliierten Prozesse gegen Kriegsverbrecher und Soldaten, 1943–1952* (Frankfurt am Main, 2000), 245.
29. U.S. Department of State, *Conferences at Cairo and Tehran,* 598–605.
30. Ibid., 511.
31. Ibid., 529–30.
32. Sergo Beria, *Beria, My Father: Inside Stalin's Kremlin* (London, 2001), 92.
33. Ibid., 94.
34. Cited in Kennedy, *Freedom from Fear,* 684.
35. See Peter Hoffmann, *Stauffenberg: A Family History, 1905–1944* (New York, 1995), 258–77.
36. July 28, 1944, *Meldungen aus dem Reich,* vol. 17, 6684.
37. Norman Davies, *Rising '44: The Battle for Warsaw* (New York, 2003), 165.
38. Cited in ibid., 164.
39. *NYT,* Aug. 1, 1944.
40. U.S. Department of State, *Conferences at Cairo and Tehran,* 600.
41. Vojtech Mastny, *Russia's Road to the Cold War: Diplomacy, Warfare, and the Politics of Communism, 1941–1945* (New York, 1979), 185.
42. Letters reprinted in Winston Churchill, *Triumph and Tragedy* (Boston, 1953), 130–31, 134.
43. Ibid., 144–45.
44. Alexander Werth, *Russia at War, 1941–1945* (New York, 1964), 876–78.
45. John Erickson, *The Road to Berlin: Stalin's War with Germany* (New Haven, Conn., 1983), 285.
46. Commission for the Publication of Diplomatic Documents of the USSR, *Correspondence,* 152–57.
47. G. K. Zhukov, *Vospominaniya i razmyshleniya* (Moscow, 1969), 585; Richard Wolff, "Rokossovsky," in Harold Shukman, ed., *Stalin's Generals* (London, 1993), 191.
48. Davies, *Rising '44,* 433–34.
49. 128-USSR, in *IMT,* vol. 39, 377–80.

50. Bradley F. Smith and Agnes F. Peterson, eds., *Heinrich Himmler: Geheimreden, 1933 bis 1945* (Frankfurt am Main, 1974), 242.
51. Churchill, *Triumph and Tragedy,* 145.
52. Treaty signed on April 21, published the next day in *Pravda;* see McNeal, *Stalin sochineniia,* vol. 2 (vol. 15), 184–87.
53. Cited in Kennedy, *Freedom from Fear,* 738 n. 42.
54. Churchill, *Triumph and Tragedy,* 227.
55. For the follow-up meeting and in general, see Mastny, *Russia's Road to the Cold War,* 207–12.
56. Churchill to Roosevelt, Oct. 22, 1944, in Churchill, *Triumph and Tragedy,* 241.
57. Djilas, *Conversations with Stalin,* 79.
58. Ibid., 83–84.
59. Cited in Kennedy, *Freedom from Fear,* 798.
60. Harriman to Hopkins, Sept. 10, 1944, in U.S. Department of State, *Europe, 1944,* vol. 4, (Washington D.C., 1966) 989.
61. U.S. Department of State, *The Conferences at Malta and Yalta, 1945* (Washington, D.C., 1955), 976.
62. Walter Warlimont, *Im Hauptquartier der deutschen Wehrmacht, 1939–1945* (Frankfurt am Main, 1962), 505–24.
63. U.S. Department of State, *Conferences at Malta and Yalta,* 578.
64. Ibid., 589, 590.
65. Ibid., 669–70, 677–78.
66. Beria, *Beria, My Father,* 106.
67. For a study that emphasizes security concerns over ideological expansionism, see R. Craig Nation, *Black Earth, Red Star: A History of Soviet Security Policy, 1917–1991* (Ithaca, N.Y., 1992), 145.
68. U.S. Department of State, *Conferences at Malta and Yalta,* 896.
69. Churchill, *Triumph and Tragedy,* 154.
70. U.S. Department of State, *Conferences at Malta and Yalta,* 620, 630–32.
71. Cited in Francis L. Loewenheim et al., eds., *Roosevelt and Churchill: Their Secret Wartime Correspondence* (New York, 1975), 575.
72. Churchill, *Triumph and Tragedy,* 156.
73. Beria, *Beria, My Father,* 105.
74. Albert Speer, *Inside the Third Reich* (New York, 1970), 227.
75. Kennedy, *Freedom from Fear,* 664–67.
76. U.S. Department of State, *The Conference at Quebec, 1944* (Washington, D.C., 1972), 492–93.

CHAPTER 37: END OF THE THIRD REICH

1. Also for what follows, see Walter Warlimont, *Im Hauptquartier der deutschen Wehrmacht, 1939–1945* (Frankfurt am Main, 1962), 518–21; for a longer version of the December 12 speech, see Helmut Heiber and David

M. Glantz, eds., *Hitler and His Generals: Military Conferences, 1942–1945* (New York, 2002), 535.

2. Text in Heiber and Glantz, *Hitler and His Generals,* 554–68; also Warlimont, *Hauptquartier,* 522–24.

3. Gerhard L. Weinberg, *A World at Arms: A Global History of World War II* (Cambridge, U.K., 1994), 765–71.

4. Both citations in Winston Churchill, *Triumph and Tragedy* (Boston, 1953), 281–82.

5. *Hitler: Reden und Proklamationen,* vol. 4, 2179–85.

6. Nicolaus von Below, *Als Hitlers Adjutant, 1937–45* (Mainz, 1980), 398.

7. *Hitler: Reden und Proklamationen,* vol. 4, 2195–98.

8. Marlis G. Steinert, *Hitler's War and the Germans: Public Mood and Attitude During the Second World War* (Athens, Ohio, 1977), 293.

9. *Hitler: Reden und Proklamationen,* vol. 4, 2203–6.

10. John Erickson, *The Road to Berlin: Stalin's War with Germany* (New Haven, Conn., 1983), 449.

11. Danuta Czech, *Auschwitz Chronicle, 1939–1945* (New York, 1990), 801–5.

12. Cited in Max Hastings, *Armageddon: The Battle for Germany, 1944–1945* (New York, 2004), 248.

13. See Johannes Tuchel, ed., *Die Inspektion der Konzentrationslager, 1938–1945* (Berlin, 1994), 212–13.

14. See Robert Gellately, *Backing Hitler: Consent and Coercion in Nazi Germany* (Oxford, 2001), 242–52; Sybille Steinbacher, *Auschwitz: Geschichte und Nachgeschichte* (Munich, 2004), 97–100; Andrzej Strzelecki, "Evacuation, Liquidation, and Liberation of the Camp," in Danuta Czech et al., *Auschwitz: Nazi Death Camp* (Oswiecim, 1996), 272ff.

15. Czech, *Auschwitz Chronicle,* 781–805.

16. See the classic account of Primo Levi, *Survival in Auschwitz: The Nazi Assault on Humanity,* trans. S. Woolf (London, 1959).

17. See Yehuda Bauer, *Jews for Sale: Nazi-Jewish Negotiations, 1933–1945* (New Haven, Conn., 1994), 239–51.

18. See David A. Hackett, ed., *The Buchenwald Report* (Boulder, Colo., 1995), 328–31.

19. Peter Black, *Ernst Kaltenbrunner: Ideological Soldier of the Third Reich* (Princeton, N.J., 1984), 250.

20. See Stanislav Zamecnik, "Kein Häftling darf lebend in die Hände des Feindes fallen: Zur Existenz des Himmler-Befehls vom 14.–18. April 1945," *Dachauer Hefte* (1985), 219.

21. Martin Broszat, "Nationalsozialistische Konzentrationslager," in *Anatomie des SS-Staates,* 5th ed. (Munich, 1989), vol. 2, 132.

22. McNeal, *Stalin sochineniia,* vol. 2 (vol. 15), 178–82.

23. See Klaus-Dietmar Henke, *Die amerikanische Besetzung Deutschlands* (Munich, 1995), 343–77.

24. Weinberg, *World at Arms,* 812–13.

25. Henke, *Die amerikanische Besetzung Deutschlands,* 400.
26. See Bernd-A. Rusinek, *Gesellschaft in der Katastrophe: Terror, Illegalität, Widerstand Köln, 1944–45* (Essen, 1989), 446.
27. Erickson, *Road to Berlin,* 528.
28. Churchill, *Triumph and Tragedy,* 440–46.
29. Commission for the Publication of Diplomatic Documents of the USSR, ed., *Correspondence Between Stalin, Roosevelt, Truman, Churchill, and Attlee During WWII* (Honolulu, 1957), 198–99.
30. Ibid., 208.
31. Francis L. Loewenheim et al., eds., *Roosevelt and Churchill: Their Secret Wartime Correspondence* (New York, 1975), 704–5.
32. G. K. Zhukov, *Vospominaniya i razmyshleniya* (Moscow, 1969), 620–24.
33. I. S. Konev, *Sorok piatyi* (Moscow, 1966), 87–89.
34. Cited in Erickson, *Road to Berlin,* 533.
35. Christian Streit, "The German Army and the Policies of Genocide," in Gerhard Hirschfeld, ed., *The Politics of Genocide: Jews and Soviet Prisoners of War in Nazi Germany* (London, 1986), 7.
36. Christian Streit, *Keine Kameraden: Die Wehrmacht und die sowjetischen Kriegsgefangenen, 1941–1945* (Stuttgart, 1978), 244, 247.
37. Commission for the Publication of Diplomatic Documents of the USSR, *Correspondence,* 214.
38. Zhukov, *Vospominaniya,* 655.
39. Antony Beevor, *The Fall of Berlin, 1945* (New York, 2002), 424.
40. Erickson, *Road to Berlin,* 622.
41. McNeal, *Stalin sochineniia,* vol. 2 (vol. 15), 189–94.
42. Alexander Werth, *Russia at War, 1941–1945* (New York, 1964), 964–65.
43. Norman M. Naimark, *The Russians in Germany: A History of the Soviet Zone of Occupation, 1945–1949* (Cambridge, Mass., 1995), 72.
44. Cited in Lev Kopelev, *To Be Preserved Forever* (New York, 1977), 52–53.
45. See Catherine Merridale, *Ivan's War: Life and Death in the Red Army, 1939–1945* (New York, 2006), 299–335.
46. Milovan Djilas, *Conversations with Stalin* (Orlando, Fla., 1990), 95.
47. Werth, *Russia at War,* 966.
48. Antony Beevor and Luba Vinogradova, eds., *A Writer at War: Vasily Grossman with the Red Army, 1941–1945* (New York, 2005), 341.
49. Marshal Sladko Kvaternik, in Andreas Hillgruber, ed., *Staatsmänner und Diplomaten bei Hitler: Vertrauliche Aufzeichnungen über Unterredungen mit Vertretern des Auslandes, 1939–1941* (Frankfurt am Main, 1967), vol. 1, 609–15.
50. For sources and literature, see Gellately, *Backing Hitler,* 230–36.
51. Albert Speer, *Infiltration: How Heinrich Himmler Schemed to Build an SS Industrial Empire* (New York, 1981), 238.
52. See Speer-23, March 15, 1945, in *IMT,* vol. 41, 420–25; also Albert Speer, *Inside the Third Reich* (New York, 1970), 583–84.

53. Cited in Albert Speer, *Inside the Third Reich,* 588.

54. See Speer-25, in *IMT,* vol. 41, 430–31.

55. See Speer, *Inside the Third Reich,* 579.

56. See Felix Kersten, *The Kersten Memoirs, 1940–1945,* trans. C. Fitzgibbon and J. Oliver (London, 1956), 264–70; and Speer, *Inside the Third Reich,* 610–11.

57. Peter Hoffmann, *The History of the German Resistance, 1933–1945* (Cambridge, Mass., 1977), 529–30.

58. *Hitler: Reden und Proklamationen,* vol. 4, 2223–24.

59. Reprinted in Heiber and Glantz, *Hitler and His Generals,* 724–25.

60. Joachim Fest, *Der Untergang: Hitler und das Ende des Dritten Reiches* (Berlin, 2002), 105.

61. Anton Joachimsthaler, *Hitlers Ende: Legenden und Dokumente* (Berlin, 2004), 185–200, also for what follows. He cites Traudl Junge from earlier evidence that Hitler dictated his will after the marriage, around 2:00 a.m.

62. For the timing, see Traudl Junge, *Bis zur letzten Stunde: Hitlers Sekretärin erzählt ihr Leben* (Munich, 2002), 203.

63. Reprinted in *Hitler: Reden und Proklamationen,* vol. 4, 2236–39.

EPILOGUE

1. Maxim Gorky, *Untimely Thoughts: Essays on Revolution, Culture, and the Bolsheviks, 1917–1918* (New Haven, Conn., 1995), 88.

2. For the widespread attractiveness of the *Volksgemeinschaft,* see Norbert Frei, *1945 und Wir: Das Dritte Reich im Bewusstein der Deutschen* (Munich, 2005), 107–28.

3. Aleksandr Solzhenitsyn, *The Gulag Archipelago, 1918–1956* (New York, 1973), vol. 2, 10, citing the statistician I. A. Kurganov.

4. J. Otto Pohl, *The Stalinist Penal System: A Statistical History of Soviet Repression and Terror, 1930–1953* (London, 1997), 131.

5. Anne Applebaum, *Gulag: A History* (New York, 2003), 585.

6. See the remarkable David Remnick, *Lenin's Tomb: The Last Days of the Soviet Empire* (New York, 1994), 138.

7. Karin Orth, *Das System der nationalsozialistischen Konzentrationslager* (Hamburg, 1999), 25; also Klaus Drobisch and Günther Wieland, *System der NS-Konzentrationslager, 1933–1939* (Berlin, 1993), 131.

8. Steven G. Marks, *How Russia Shaped the Modern World: From Art to Anti-Semitism, Ballet to Bolshevism* (Princeton, N. J., 2003), 300.

9. Ian Kershaw, *Hitler, 1889–1936: Hubris* (London, 1998), 460.

10. For the background, see Robert Gellately, *Backing Hitler: Consent and Coercion in Nazi Germany* (Oxford, 2001), 85–87.

11. The studies are cited in John Erickson, "Soviet War Losses: Calculations

and Controversies," in John Erickson and David Dilks, eds., *Barbarossa: The Axis and the Allies* (Edinburgh, 1994), 259–60.

12. Dietmar Petzina, Werner Abelshauser, and Anselm Faust, eds., *Sozialgeschichtliches Arbeitsbuch III: Materialien zur Statistik des Deutschen Reiches, 1914–1945* (Munich, 1978), vol. 3, 27.

13. Gerhard L. Weinberg, *A World at Arms: A Global History of World War II* (Cambridge, U.K., 1994), 894, puts the figure at sixty million worldwide and admits the total is tentative.

14. Tony Judt, *Postwar: A History of Europe Since 1945* (New York, 2005), 17.

15. Orth, *Konzentrationslager,* 343.

16. Ibid., 105.

17. Milovan Djilas, *Conversations with Stalin* (Orlando, Fla., 1990), 114.

18. Ibid., 106–7.

19. G. K. Zhukov, *Vospominaniya i razmyshleniya* (Moscow, 1969), 663–64.

20. McNeal, *Stalin sochineniia,* vol. 2 (vol. 15), 197–99.

21. Cited in Geoffrey Hosking, *Rulers and Victims: The Russians in the Soviet Union* (Cambridge, Mass., 2006), 217, also for what follows.

22. Cited in Jeffrey Brooks, *"Thank You, Comrade Stalin!" Soviet Public Culture from Revolution to Cold War* (Princeton, N.J., 1999), 196.

23. Hosking, *Rulers and Victims,* 239–40.

24. Yoram Gorlizki and Oleg V. Khlevniuk, *Cold Peace: Stalin and the Soviet Ruling Circle, 1945–1953* (Oxford, 2003), 43.

25. Applebaum, *Gulag,* 579–83.

26. U.S. Department of State, *Conferences at Malta and Yalta, 1945* (Washington, D.C., 1955), 720.

27. Zhukov, *Vospominaniya,* 675.

28. Cited in David McCullough, *Truman* (New York, 1992), 442–44.

29. Norman M. Naimark, *Fires of Hatred: Ethnic Cleansing in Twentieth-Century Europe* (Cambridge, Mass., 2001), 126.

30. See Jan T. Gross, *Fear: Anti-Semitism in Poland After Auschwitz* (New York, 2006), 245–61.

31. Simon Sebag Montefiore, *Stalin: The Court of the Red Tsar* (New York, 2004), 622. See also Yuri Slezkine, *The Jewish Century* (Princeton, N.J., 2004), 308–10.

32. The documents can be found in Jonathan Brent and Vladimir P. Naumov, *Stalin's Last Crime: The Plot Against the Jewish Doctors, 1948–1953* (New York, 2003), 254–55.

ACKNOWLEDGMENTS

Research for the book was fostered by various institutions. I am sincerely pleased to record my gratitude to the Alexander von Humboldt Foundation, which has facilitated my work since the beginning of my career. Florida State University has generously provided me with financial assistance and an extremely congenial research environment. I am thankful for the encouragement offered by Don Foss, Joe Travis, Joe McElrath, and Neil Jumonville.

I had a unique opportunity to present my ideas at Oxford University, where I was the Bertelsmann Visiting Professor of Twentieth-Century Jewish History and Politics. The exchanges with students and faculty opened my eyes to many important issues and challenged me to think through my conclusions.

Special thanks are owed to Karen Colvard of the Harry Frank Guggenheim Foundation, who helped put together a conference I co-organized with Ben Kiernan on comparative genocide. The gathering came at a crucial time, when this book was germinating, and I gained enormously from the experience.

I am most grateful to Professors Sheila Fitzpatrick, Michael Geyer, Terry Martin, Guenther Heydemann, and Steven Miner for inviting me to various conferences where we explored the comparative study of dictatorships.

Friends and colleagues have come to my aid in countless ways. Some have provided key pieces of information or documents, and others have answered questions, encouraged me, or written letters on my behalf. I want to make particular mention of Omer Bartov, Gerhard Bassler, Christopher Browning, Jeffrey Burds, Michael Burleigh, Timothy Colton, Susan Gardos, David Godwin, Paul Hagenloh, Jochen Hellbeck, Susannah Heschel, Norbert Juraschitz, Peter Krafft, Luba Ostashevsky, Janice Pilch, Sven Reichardt, Heike Schlatterer, Detlef Schmiechen-Ackermann, David Shearer, Peter Steinbach, Sybille Steinbacher, Gerhard Weinberg, and Eric Weitz.

I am particularly indebted to my publishers Ash Green and Will Sulkin, who read the manuscript with care and made useful suggestions to improve it. Above all, I want to thank Marie Fleming, to whom I dedicate the book. Her intellectual challenges and steadfast encouragement made writing it possible. Without her it would not have been half as much fun watching the inexhaustible store of fascinating Soviet and Russian films.

INDEX

Abel, Theodore, 213–14
Abetz, Otto, 434–35
Abraham Lincoln Brigade, 359
Abwehr (German Military Intelligence), 363
Afrika Corps, 509
Agriculture, Commissariat of, 229
Alexander II, Tsar, 24
Alexander III, Tsar, 24
All-Russian Congress of Soviets, 139, 144
All-Russian Extraordinary Commission for Combatting Counterrevolution, Speculation, Sabotage, and Misconduct in Office, *see* Cheka
All-Union Congress of Soviet Architects, 258
Amann, Max, 98, 113, 188
American Jewish Congress, 315
American Relief Administration (ARA), 76
Andreyev, A. A., 266
Anfilov, Viktor, 484
Anielewicz, Mordecai, 537–8
Animal Farm (Orwell), 17
anti-Semitism, 12–14, 18, 81, 94, 122, 126, 203, 317, 454, 534, 562; anti-Bolshevism and, 12, 84, 91–2, 98–101, 107–9, 111, 118, 119, 213, 266, 416–17, 489–90 (*see also* "Jewish

Bolshevism"); attitudes of German populace toward, 328–30, 453; in Austria, 322; eugenics and, 332; in German-occupied territories, 400, 418, 419; in Nazi Party political strategy, 95–98, 107, 108, 120, 124, 189, 193, 197, 200, 203, 213–16, 315, 318, 533; postwar, 593–4; in pre–World War I Germany, 196; Russian, 67, 69, 155, 249, 356
Antipov, V., 246–7
Antonescu, Marshal Ion, 416–17, 532
Antonov, Alexander, 74, 75
Antonov-Ovseyenko, Anton, 261
Antonov-Ovseyenko, Vladimir, 261
Applebaum, Anne, 584
Arco-Valley, Count Anton, 86
Armenians, 513, 515; Turkish slaughter of, 329
Aryans, Nazi designation of, 109, 120, 122, 195, 309, 318, 414, 459, 527
Aryanization, 322, 324, 399
Atlantic, Battle of the, 525
atomic bomb, 559, 592
Auer, Erhard, 86
Aurora (battleship), 38
Auschwitz-Birkenau concentration camp complex, 457, 459, 461, 464–8, 521, 565, 566, 587
Austin Company, 163–4

Australia, 323

Austria, 83, 96, 123, 381, 398; Communists in, 88–90; concentration camps in, 340; Jews deported from, 322–5, 370, 373, 374; Nazi annexation of, 313

Austria-Hungary, 11, 31, 81–2

Axelrod, Towia, 90

Babi Yar massacre, 450, 459

Backe, Herbert, 424

Badoglio, Marshal Pietro, 466–7

Balkans, 76, 382, 413, 416; Communist Party in, 76; *see also specific nations*

Balkars, 514

Baltic States, 357, 409, 423, 430, 435, 443; liberation of, 557; postwar, 547; resettlement of ethnic Germans from, 373; Soviet occupation of, 266, 392–6, 401, 483, 511; *see also* Estonia; Latvia; Lithuania

Bamlag, 260

Barbarossa, Operation, 407, 410, 415, 421, 424, 425, 429–40, 453, 481, 494, 530, 585; slaughter of Jews during, 441–51, 459–60

Bartov, Omer, 460

Bavarian Peasant Party, 88

Bavarian People's Party, 289, 300

Bavarian Reichswehr Gruppenkommando 4 (Gruko 4), 91

Bavarian Reserve Infantry Regiment 16, 82

Beaverbrook, Lord, 487

Bechstein, Edwin, 187

Beer Hall Putsch, 104, 108, 110–15, 124, 325, 508

Belgium, 378–80, 406, 415, 416, 483, 554; Communists in, 358; invasion of Ruhr by, 104–5; Jews deported from, 466, 587

Belov, General P. A., 496

Below, Nicolaus von, 355, 526, 562–3

Belzec death camp, 457, 460–2, 530, 587

Berchtold, Reichsführer SS Josef, 187

Berezhkov, Valentin, 406–7

Berger, Gottlob, 454

Beria, Lavrenti P., 276, 356, 386, 395–6, 401–3, 405, 408–9, 474, 483, 484, 514–17, 550, 558

Beria, Sergo, 550, 559

Berlin Olympics (1936), 319–20

Berlin University, 456

Bernburg killing center, 369

Bessarabia, 266, 357, 384, 393, 417, 547

Best, Werner, 215

Beutel, Lothar, 364

Bismarck, Otto von, 185, 313

Blacks (Russian anarchists), 66

Blackshirts, 102, 103, 110

Blank, Alexander, 24

Blessed Virgin, Church of (Moscow), 249

Blobel, Paul, 450, 463

Blomberg, General Werner von, 289, 291, 309

Bloody Sunday (Germany, 1932), 209

Bloody Sunday (Poland, 1939), 364

Bloody Sunday (Russia, 1905), 26, 48, 135

Blue, Operation, 499

Bock, General Fedor von, 379–80, 426, 434, 436–38, 455

Böckel, Otto, 196

Boers, 55

Böhme, General Franz, 399

Böll, Heinrich, 527

Bolsheviks, 7, 23, 26–33, 62, 132, 137, 141, 154, 166, 346, 581; allied intervention against, 66; army founded by, *see* Red Army; assassination attempts on, 56, 57; civil service and, 142; "Declaration of the Rights of the Toiling and Exploited Masses" of, 49; disunity among, 158; economic vision of, 180 (*see also* Five-Year Plan; New Economic Policy); efforts to export revolution by, 73, 85–6, 157, 591; eugenics and,

332; Goebbels and, 126; Hitler's hatred of, 12–14, 352, 361; Jewish, 67–8, 90, 248–9, 255, 593 (*see also* anti-semitism, anti-bolshevism and); Kronstadt mutiny against, 74–5; Nazi propaganda against, 193, 216, 217, 291, 295, 313 (*see also* "Jewish Bolshevism"); 1905 conference of, 136; non-Russian, 139; peasants and, 42, 63, 144 (*see also* dekulakization); and post–World War I German radicals, 83–5, 87; repressiveness of, 3, 9, 43–4, 46–8, 52, 54 (*see also* Cheka; GPU; NKVD; OGPU); resistance to, *see* Russian Civil War; seizure of power by, 4–5, 44–6, 111, 580 (*see also* October Revolution)

Bolshoi Ballet, 488

Bonhoeffer, Dietrich, 340

Boris III, King of Bulgaria, 418–19, 532

Bormann, Martin, 366, 445, 455, 577

Bouhler, Philipp, 366–9

Bracher, Karl Dietrich, 223

Bracht, Fritz, 566

Brack, Viktor, 366, 368

Brandler, Heinrich, 106, 112

Brandt, Karl, 365, 367

Brauchitsch, Field Marshal Walther von, 352, 363, 369–71, 376, 380, 422, 426, 438

Braude, Ilya, 272–3

Braun, Eva, 576, 577

Brest Litovsk, Treaty of, 51, 66, 483

Brezhnev, Leonid, 166

British Expeditionary Force, 380

Bromberg massacre, 364

Bruckmann, Hugo, 187

Brundage, Avery, 319

Brüning, Heinrich, 201–5, 209

Brusilov, Aleksei, 31

Bubnov, Andrei, 35

Buchenwald concentration camp, 355, 326, 338, 340, 341, 369, 566, 567

Buddhists, 513

Budenny, Marshal Semyon M., 65, 473

Bukharin, Nikolai I., 23, 74, 140, 147, 150–2, 158, 160, 168, 269, 271, 273–4, 277, 280

Bukovina, 266, 393, 417

Bulgaria, 418–19, 483–4, 515, 532, 554, 555, 557, 593

Bulge, Battle of the, 557, 560–2, 564, 565

Burke, Edmund, 501

Byelorussia, 69, 148, 358, 386, 389–90, 395, 422–4, 444, 448, 551

Caldwell, Erskine, 476

Cambodia, 594

Canada, 160, 363

Canaris, Admiral Wilhelm, 363

Case Yellow, 376, 379

Catherine the Great, Tsarina, 67, 511

Catholic Center Party, German, 85, 125, 201, 286, 299–301, 338

Catholic Party in Bavaria (BVP), 86, 118, 299

Catholics, 89, 205, 213, 255, 295, 300, 321, 327, 334, 365, 368

Central Committee (of the Bolshevik, later Communist, Party), 9, 50, 131, 138, 148, 162, 181, 346, 347, 392, 581; and Communist Party purges, 268–71, 273, 277, 280; and de-Cossackization, 70; expansion of, 151; Jews on, 68; and Lenin's illness and death, 150, 152; Politburo created by, 146–7; Red Army and, 504; requests for Gulag labor to, 264; Stalin elected to, 30, 137; terror practices authorized by, 243, 245, 246, 250; and October Revolution, 34–6, 139; Trotsky and, 153–4

Cesarani, David, 322

Chamberlain, Neville, 351, 352, 375

Chancellery of the Führer (KdF), 365–7

Chechens, 514–19

Cheka (Soviet secret police), 46–8,
  50–53, 56–9, 63–6, 68, 71–2, 141, 144,
  162; clergy members arrested by,
  248; de-Cossackization by, 70–1;
  peasant uprisings and, 74; replaced
  by GPU, 145
Chelmno death camp, 457, 460, 530,
  587
Chetniks, 398
Chicago Tribune, 485
China, 347, 558; Communist, 10, 157,
  594
Christ the Redeemer, Cathedral of
  (Moscow), 250, 258–9
Christianity, 455
Chuev, Felix, 252
Churchill, Winston, 103, 379, 382, 482,
  484, 485, 492, 494, 543–4, 561, 568–9;
  at Casablanca Conference, 526;
  Moscow missions of, 500–1, 554–6;
  Stalin warned of German invasion
  by, 407; at Tehran Conference,
  544–6, 548–50; walkabouts of, 527;
  and Warsaw uprising, 552–4; at Yalta
  Conference, 556–9, 591–2
Ciano, Galeazzo, 424
Citadel, Operation, 530–1
Class, Heinrich, 97
Cold War, 14, 588
collectivization, 168–75, 179, 227,
  235–7, 250, 266, 586
Columbia University, 213
Combat Technical Group, 137
Comintern, *see* Communist
  International
Commissar Order, 426–8
Commission for the Rehabilitation of
  the Victims of Political Repression,
  479
Committee for the Constituent
  Assembly, 64
Committee for the Struggle Against
  the Counterrevolution, 33
Communist International
  (Comintern), 85, 100, 104, 109, 111,

144, 190, 258, 345, 403, 442, 472, 591,
  593
Communist Manifesto, The (Marx and
  Engels), 330
Communist Party, 17, 29, 52, 61, 84,
  146, 161, 165, 180–1, 254, 262, 265,
  442, 582; and German invasion, 472,
  488–91, 493; and Lenin's testament,
  153; assassinations of leaders of, 238;
  Central Committee of, *see* Central
  Committee; Congresses of, 75, 141,
  143, 145, 146, 154, 157–60, 163, 276,
  346, 347, 355, 503; de-Cossackization
  and, 71; dekulakization offensive of,
  169–72; disunity in, 153–5; drafting
  of members of, 60; ethnic groups
  expelled from, 515, 517, 518; fellow
  travelers of, 263; French, 381, 466,
  472; German, *see* Communist Party
  of Germany (KPD); Greek, 400; in
  electoral politics, 136; Kazakh, 235;
  Lenin cult in, 156; Machine Tractor
  Station and, 236; organization of,
  135; paramilitary groups of, 110;
  peasants terrorized by members of,
  230–1; Polish, 255, 387–8, 536, 552–4;
  Political Bureau of, *see* Politburo;
  purges of, 16, 145, 156, 261, 267–81,
  580; radicals in, 167, 168; religion
  and, 247–50; Ukrainian, 228, 230;
  Yugoslav, 399, 588, 591
Communist Party of Germany
  (KPD), 86–90, 104, 107, 113, 185,
  212, 219, 296–7, 300, 585; banning of,
  286; concentration camps for members of, 302–3, 311, 587; dissolution
  of, 301, 357; in elections, 125, 189,
  190, 204–6, 217, 299; founding of, 86;
  general strike against reparations
  called by, 105; and Hitler's appointment as chancellor, 221, 288; Hitler's
  rhetoric against, 187, 193, 533;
  "hunger government" protested by,
  201; information service of, 191; Jews
  in, 89, 90; linked to assassination

attempt on Hitler, 376; Nazi violence against, 296; paramilitary group of, 207; peasant recruitment efforts of, 198; persecution of, 306; Reichstag fire blamed on, 298, 299, 306–7; street violence between Nazis and, 209–10, 295–6; uprising attempts of, 87, 100–1, 106, 112

Communist Youth, see Komsomol

concentration camps, 3, 55; German, see Nazi concentration camps; Soviet, 7, 46, 55–9, 72, 113, 170, 171, 235, 236, 243, 249–50, 255, 256, 259, 460 (see also Gulag)

Congress of Peasants' Deputies, 44

Congress of Soviets, 36, 39, 41, 43, 49, 257

Conquest, Robert, 235

Constituent Assembly, Russian, 34, 35, 37, 39, 42, 43, 46, 48–9, 580

Constitution, Soviet, 147, 175

Conradstein (Kocborowo), killing center, 366

Conti, Leonardo, 365, 366

Corrective Labor Camps and Labor Settlements, Main Administration of, 177

corrective labor colonies (ITK), 263–4

Cossacks, 57, 63, 64, 69–72, 230, 422

Council for Aid to Jews Among the Poles, 537

Council of People's Commissars, 38; see also Sovnarkom

Cripps, Stafford, 357

Croatia, 398, 416, 418

Cuba, colonial, 55

Cultural Revolution, Soviet, 250

Cuno, Wilhelm, 104, 105

Czechoslovakia, 73, 323, 381, 416, 564; Communist Party in, 76, 100; Jews deported from, 324, 325, 370, 466; Nazi occupation of, 313–14, 324, 351, 352, 355; postwar, 592; Soviet prisoners of war from, 55–6, 64

Czerniakow, Adam, 535–36

Dachau concentration camp, 326, 337, 341, 369, 567, 584

Dagestan, 513

Daimler-Benz, 294

Dalstroi, 245

Darlan, Admiral François, 419

Darré, Walther, 199

Darwin, Charles, 16, 331

Darwinism, social, 12, 16, 188, 219

Davies, Sarah, 247

Dawes, Charles, 116

D-day, 551

death camps, 452–68, 530, 587; see also names of specific camps

Defense Ministry, German, 291

Dekanozov, Vladimir, 394

dekulakization, 63, 167–74, 176–9, 227, 229–32, 235–6, 241, 242, 263

Democrats, German, 86

Deniken, General A. I., 69, 72

Denmark, 379, 406, 415

Diels, Rudolf, 298

Dimitrov, Georgi, 357, 403, 472, 492–3, 593

Djilas, Milovan, 556, 588

Dolot, Miron, 232–3

Domarus, Max, 288

Don, Revolutionary Committee of the, 70

Dönitz, Admiral Karl, 525

Drexler, Anton, 93, 95, 97

Dulles, Allen, 569

Duma, 21–3, 135

Düsseldorf Industrial Club, 219

Dzerzhinsky, Felix, 35, 46–8, 52, 59, 72, 150, 175

Dzhughashvili, Ekaterina, 131–2

Dzhughashvili, Vissarion, 131

Eberhard, General Kurt, 449, 450

Ebert, Friedrich, 83, 87, 124–5

Eckart, Dietrich, 97, 99

Eher Verlag, 118

Eichmann, Adolf, 322–4, 326, 370,
    373, 400
Eicke, Theodor, 353
Eimann, SS Major Kurt, 366, 367
Einsatzgruppen (EGr), 352–3, 363,
    364, 366, 370, 371, 417, 441–6,
    449–51, 460, 463, 538
Eisenhower, Dwight D., 567, 568, 594
Eisenstein, Sergei, 38
Eisner, Kurt, 84, 86, 88, 90
Elser, Georg, 376
Enabling Law (Germany, 1933),
    300–301, 316
Engels, Friedrich, 32, 99, 330
Erickson, John, 502
Esser, Hermann, 91, 104
Estonia, 357, 384, 392–6, 444, 547
ethnic cleansing, 5, 583, 592; Nazi,
    363–4, 367, 369–74, 459, 468 (see also
    Jews, extermination of); Soviet,
    254–5, 511–22, 550, 592–93
ethnic Germans, 364; deportations of,
    391; resettlement of, 372, 373, 374; in
    Soviet Union, 253–4, 511–13, 535,
    592–3
eugenics, 331–4
euthanasia, 365–9, 444, 461
Évian Conference (1938), 323

famines, 74–6, 141, 228–36, 248
Far Northern Construction Trust, 245
Farben, I. G., chemical concern,
    464–5, 467
Fascism, 108, 332, 358, 472, 476;
    Italian, 3, 102–4, 111, 117, 190,
    216–17, 306, 466–7
Feder, Gottfried, 91–3, 95
"final solution," 16, 274, 452–68,
    537
Finland, 135, 136, 149, 357, 384, 413,
    418, 422, 423, 511; postwar, 547; SS
    recruits from, 415; Winter War with,
    392–3, 401, 403, 405, 473, 474
Fischer, Ruth, 90
"five ears of corn, law on," 229

Five-Year Plan, 161–6, 169, 174, 175,
    181, 228–9, 231, 235, 242, 258, 263,
    268, 287
Flossenbürg concentration camp,
    339–41, 369, 567
Food Supply, Commissariat of, 63
forced-labor camps, see concentration
    camps, Soviet
Ford, Henry, 164
Ford Motor Company, 164
Forster, Albert, 366
Förster, Jürgen, 449
Fortune magazine, 334
Fotieva, Lydia, 151
Foundations of Leninism, The
    (Stalin), 156–7
Four-Year Plan, Nazi, 320
France, 107, 108, 321, 329, 349, 350,
    405, 526, 546, 557, 574; fall of, 266,
    380–2, 397, 413; and Hitler-Stalin
    pact, 357; appeasement of Hitler by,
    312–14, 351; Communists in, 358,
    466, 472; Gulag condemned in, 257;
    in Berlin Olympics, 320; German
    invasion of, 348, 375, 379–80, 393;
    intervention against Bolsheviks by,
    66; Jews deported from, 466, 587;
    liberation of, 554; maps of, 406;
    peace offers from Hitler to, 366;
    Poland and, 347, 352, 354, 361;
    POWs, 480; Ruhr invaded by, 104–5,
    112, 116; Soviet friction with, 161;
    Soviet negotiations for alliance with,
    356; Vichy, 419–20, 434–35, 501, 509;
    Wehrmacht volunteers from, 416
Franco, General Francisco, 313, 321,
    358
Franco-Prussian War, 111
Frank, Hans, 457, 461
Franz Ferdinand, Archduke of
    Austria, 82
Frederick the Great, King of Prussia,
    185
Free Corps, 87, 90
Freedom of Conscience, Decree on,
    248

Freemasonry, 109
Freiberg, Dov, 462–63
French Revolution, 26, 27, 301, 311, 340
Frick, Wilhelm, 186, 285
Frieschärler (guerrilla), 426
Front, The (play), 504
Fuchs, Klaus, 592

Galen, Clemens August von, 368
Galton, Francis, 331
Garliński, Józef, 465
gas chambers, 338, 452, 460–6, 521, 529–30, 566, 587; mobile, 367, 399, 457, 460, 461, 529
Gdynia (Gotenhafen) killing center, 366
Gefter, Mikhail, 491
Gemlich, Adolf, 92
General Congress of Workers' and Soldiers' Councils (Berlin, 1918), 84
General Government (General-gouvernement), 371, 373, 374, 457, 461, 462, 535, 537, 538
General Motors, 163
George VI, King of England, 546
German Combat League (Deutscher Kampfbund), 111–15
German Earth and Stone Works, 335, 340
Germanization, 291–2
German National People's Party (DNVP), 196, 206, 216, 217, 285, 294, 299, 301
German Women's Enterprise (Deutsches Frauenwerk), 305
German Workers' Party (DAP), 93–5
Gestapo, 3, 274, 303, 318, 363, 373, 456; asocials arrested by, 335, 338, 339; Einsatzgruppen and, 353, 445; gassing operations run by, 369, 465; Germans shot for defeatism by, 568; Soviet prisoners executed by, 570
Gibson, Archibald, 416
Globocnik, Odilo, 461–4

Goebbels, Joseph, 18, 126, 187, 192, 218, 295–6, 467, 532, 533, 563; boy-cott of Jewish businesses advocated by, 315; diaries of, 194, 211–12, 220–2, 301, 454; on deportation plans for Polish Jews, 371, 372; and elec-tions, 196, 197, 217, 299–300; in Hitler's bunker, 575–6; and invasion of Soviet Union, 431, 439, 440; on Kristallnacht, 325–6; and extermina-tion of Jews, 445, 454–56, 458, 526, 534, 538; propaganda machine of, 190, 194, 208; at Reichstag fire, 298; speeches at mass meetings by, 186; suicide of, 577; war plans described to press by, 350
Goebbels, Magda, 577
Goglidze, Sergei A., 276
Goldschmidt, Jakob, 213
Gorbach, Grigorii, 245–6
Göring, Hermann, 113, 218, 221, 222, 285, 292, 293, 296, 298, 326, 380, 424, 432, 453
Gorky, Maxim, 8, 48, 76, 138, 171, 259–60, 580
Gosplan, 145
Gosudarstvennoe Politicheskoe Upravlenie, see GPU
GPU, 145, 150, 162, 423, 540; see also OGPU
Graf, Ulrich, 113
Graziosi, Andrea, 237
Great Britain, 334, 348–50, 384, 405, 406, 413–14, 457, 531, 560, 561, 592; in advance on Germany, 554, 568; air battles over, 266; appeasement of Hitler by, 313–14, 351; in armistice negotiations with Ger-many, 568–70; in Berlin Olympics, 319–20; Communist Party in, 76, 358; and fall of France, 379–81, 393; and German invasion of Soviet Union, 407–8, 455, 484; Greece and, 397–8; Gulag condemned in, 257; Hess in, 494; Hitler's attitude toward, 126, 321, 329, 564;

Great Britain *(continued)*
Hitler's plans for invasion of, 382–3,
402, 413; House of Commons, 352;
and Hitler-Stalin pact, 357; Indian
Army, 433; intervention against
Bolsheviks by, 66; interviews with
Hitler published in, 109, 110; Japanese capture of soldiers of, 492; and
Jewish refugees, 323, 447; lend-lease
agreement with, 485; linked to
assassination attempt on Hitler, 376;
Nazi radio broadcasts to, 532; in
negotiations with US and USSR,
500–1, 544–50, 552–9, 589; in North
African campaign, 509, 525; peace
offers from Hitler to, 366, 375;
Poland and, 347, 352, 354, 361;
POWs, 480; reparations and, 104,
112; Soviet negotiations for alliance
with, 356; Soviet support for strikers
in, 161; suicide rate in, 202; unconditional surrender demanded by, 526,
589; unemployment in, 204; War
Cabinet, 482
Great Depression, 76, 194, 197, 200,
201, 293, 305
Great Terror (Soviet), 241, 244–6,
251–2, 264–5, 278, 347, 396, 540;
against national minorities, 253–6;
purges in, 281; religious persecution
of, 250, 255
Greece, 397–8, 400–1, 406, 414, 433,
441, 515; Jews deported from, 466,
587; postwar, 555, 591
Greens (Russian peasant armies), 66
Greiser, Gauleiter Arthur, 367, 461,
464
Gross, Jan, 364
Grossman, Vasily, 233–4, 273–4, 573
Gross-Rosen concentration camp,
340, 341
Grynszpan, Herschel, 325
Guchkov, Aleksandr I., 22–3
Guderian, General Heinz, 379, 433,
473

Gulag, 175–9, 230, 251, 259–65, 281,
480, 583, 584, 591, 594; "anti-Soviet
elements" in, 244–7; children in, 243,
261; creation and control of system
of, 175–6; dekulakization and, 176–9,
227, 263; slave labor provided by,
175, 177, 256–7, 259–60, 262–4, 512;
wartime, 519–22
Günther, Rolf, 400
Gütt, Arthur, 333
Gypsies, 16, 334, 335, 337, 370, 373,
374, 399, 460, 468

Haffner, Sebastian, 97, 201, 304, 316
Hague Convention, 426
Halder, General Franz, 354, 361, 363,
375–77, 380, 382, 398, 422, 429–32,
434, 437, 438, 502–3, 506–8
Hammerstein-Equord, General Kurt
von, 291
Hanfstaengl, Ernst "Putzi," 113, 123,
218
Harrer, Karl, 93
Harriman, Averell, 487, 543–4, 555, 557
Hartheim killing center, 369
Harvard Project on the Soviet Social
System, 481
Harvest Festival, Operation, 539–40
Heizer, James, 181
Helldorf, Wolf Heinrich Graf von, 298
Henderson, Nevile, 351, 352, 361
Hess, Rudolf, 113, 118, 123, 193, 494,
547
Hessen, Prince Philipp von, 293
Heydrich, Reinhard, 326, 352, 353,
363, 364, 367, 369–71, 373, 374, 421,
441–4, 453–5, 457, 462
Hierl, Konstantin, 198
Hilberg, Raul, 468
Hilfspolizei ("deputy police"), 296
Himmler, Heinrich, 189, 207, 337, 421,
442, 540–1, 553–4; concentration
camp system expanded by, 338–40,
464–6; deportations of Jews organ-

ized by, 323, 324, 424; and euthanasia program of, 366–9; evacuation of concentration camps ordered by, 565; extermination of Jews carried out by, 369, 399, 443–5, 451–8, 461, 463, 466, 467, 534–9, 541–42, 566; propaganda techniques of, 190, 193, 194; recruitment of Germanic SS volunteers by, 415; resettlement plans of, 373, 424–5, 464; shoot-to-kill order against Polish insurgents issued by, 363; Speer and, 336, 341
Hindenburg, Oskar von, 204, 220
Hindenburg, Paul von, 125–6, 200, 201, 204–5, 208, 217, 286, 289–90; death of, 310; elected president of Germany, 125; emergency decrees issued by, 206; Hitler appointed chancellor by, 126, 211–12, 218, 220–2; Jews and, 307, 317
Hitler, Adolf, 3, 6–7, 10–16, 253, 271, 444–5, 532–3, 582–7; agricultural program of, 198–200, 287; annihilation of Jews as essential aim of, 414, 447, 452–9, 526–7, 533–5, 538, 542, 562, 573, 576–7; anti-Semitism as obsession of, 12–14, 18, 81–2, 96–7, 98–101, 107, 213; appeasement of, 313–14, 351, 352; appointed chancellor, 126, 191, 201–2, 206, 211–12, 216–18, 220–3; Ardennes offensive of, 560–2; aristocratic support for, 293; "asocial" campaign of, 334–6, 338; assassination attempts on, 376–7, 551; autobiography of, *see* *Mein Kampf*; Balkan offensive of, 397–9, 406; birth of, 11, 81; cabinet of, 285–7; collaborators with, 416–19; concentration camp expansion approved by, 340, 341; conscription reintroduced by, 312; consensus dictatorship of, 15, 120–1, 223, 298–314, 582; consolidation of power of, 299–302, 304; economic policies of, 305–6; and elections, 193–4, 203,

205, 208, 220, 297; eugenics policies of, 331–3; euthanasia program of, 365–9; final days of, 575–7; first wave of terror under, 302–3; and founding and growth of Nazi Party, 95–8, 124, 188–90; and French invasion of Ruhr, 105; industrialists and, 186–7, 219–20, 292–3; interviewed by British and American reporters, 109–10, 196–7, 208; "Jewish Bolshevism" deplored by, 108–9, 121, 122, 217, 320–1, 329–30, 381, 442, 526–7, 532, 453, 564, 573, 575, 583; during last months of war, 562–4, 568, 573–5; law and order measures of, 307–8; leader cult of, 123; marriage of, 576; and "moderates" in Nazi Party, 126–7; during Munich uprising, 90; Mussolini and, 103, 467, 531–2, 534; nationalism of, 11–13, 94, 96–7, 196; nonaggression pact with Hitler, *see* Nazi-Soviet pact; and North African losses, 508, 509, 525; officer corps support for, 289–92, 427–8; Poland invaded and occupied by, 352–5, 361–4, 366, 369–72, 377; popular support for, 293–5, 304, 376–7; populist view of, 15; prewar persecution of Jews by, 315–20, 325–6; prison sentence of, 115, 117, 123; purges carried out by, 207–8, 219, 310, 308–10; putsch attempt of, 104, 108, 110–15, 124, 325, 508; radio speeches of, 287–8, 311, 526–7; rallies addressed by, 191–3, 194–6, 202–4, 209, 323, 338; and Reichstag fire, 298–9; right-wing politics of, 91–4, 124–5; show trials and accusations of conspiracy with, 275; Soviet campaign of, 382–3, 397, 401, 406–10, 413–16, 420–3, 429, 431–40, 471, 472, 481–4, 488, 490, 494, 495, 499–500, 502, 506–11, 527, 530–1, 540; suicide of, 577; Vichy France and, 419–20; violence sanctioned by, 210;

Hitler, Adolf *(continued)*
and war crimes trials, 549; and
Warsaw uprising, 553; as "weak
dictator," 348; Western Europe
attacked by, 375–82, 401, 406, 413;
and Winter War, 392; worldview and
foreign policy of, 348–50; in World
War I, 11, 82, 84; youth of, 81, 118
Hitler Youth, 532
Hoepner, General Erich, 427–8
Hoffmann, Heinrich, 406–7
Hoffmann, Johannes, 88, 89
Holland, *see* Netherlands
Holocaust, 4; *see also* Jews,
annihilation of
homosexuals, persecution of, 16, 336
Hoover, Herbert, 76
Horthy, Admiral Miklós, 418, 467–8,
532, 533
Höss, Commandant Rudolf, 464, 466
Hossbach, Colonel Friedrich, 350
Hugenberg, Alfred, 196, 217, 221,
285–6, 294
Hull, Cordell, 407, 559
Hungary, 73, 415, 418, 533, 557, 564;
Communist revolution in, 88, 89,
100, 149, 321; Jews deported from,
339, 467–8, 532, 587; postwar, 555,
592

Illustrierter Beobachter (magazine),
191
Independent Social Democratic Party
of Germany (USPD), 83–8
India, 414
Ingush, 514, 518
Interior, German Ministry of, 285,
333, 335, 337
Internal Affairs, Commissariat of,
57, 58
International Automobile and Motor-
cycle Exhibition (Berlin, 1933), 294
International Olympic Committee,
319

Iskra (newspaper), 132–3, 135
Israel, 593, 594
Italy, 123, 126, 219, 347, 354, 402, 424,
509, 531–2, 569; Communist Party in,
76, 100; fall of Fascist regime in,
466–7; Fascist rise to power in, 3,
102–4, 111, 117, 190, 216–17, 306;
Greece invaded and occupied by,
397, 400; Jews in, 534; Olympics
awarded to, 319; in Tripartite Pact
with Germany and Japan, 413, 419
Ivan the Terrible, Tsar, 474, 580
Izvestia, 49

Jacobins, 26
Japan, 347, 394, 402, 416, 548, 554, 557,
558, 592; China and, 359; Intelligence Service, 272; intervention
against Bolsheviks by, 66; surrender
of English soldiers to, 492; in Tripartite Pact with Germany and Italy,
413, 419; United States attacked by,
439–40, 457
Jehovah's Witnesses, 334
"Jewish Bolshevism," 12, 90, 126, 361,
441, 582, 587; Hitler's diatribes
against, 108–9, 121, 122, 217, 320–1,
329–30, 381, 414, 453, 526–7, 532,
564, 573, 575, 583; invasion of Soviet
Union to destroy, 350, 383, 397, 414,
415, 417, 421–3, 425–8, 435–6, 439,
441–50, 481; in Poland, 387
Jews, 15–17, 104, 167, 195, 209, 223,
304, 390, 512–13, 574; agriculture
and, 198; anti-Communist, 307;
Aryanization of businesses of, 322,
324; in Baltic states, 395; blamed for
World War I, 83, 560, 583; in Bolshevik leadership, 67–8, 90, 155, 248–9,
593; boycott of business of, 315–18; in
Bulgaria, 419; in Byelorussia, 390; in
concentration camps, 326, 335,
338–9, 369; curtailment of rights of,
16, 118, 216, 293–4, 318–19, 329, 338;

on death marches, 566, 567; deportations of, 322–5, 337, 369–71, 373–4, 387, 389, 400, 420, 535–6; escalation of Nazi radicalism against, 369–72; expropriation of property of, 189, 199; extermination of, 3–6, 11, 16, 363, 367, 368, 398–401, 417, 423, 433, 441–68, 481, 495, 529–30, 532–42, 549, 587, 593; in France, 420; and German invasion of Soviet Union, 433, 435; in ghettos, 369, 372, 424, 535–40; in Greece, 400–1; Hitler's vow to destroy, 414, 526–7, 533–5, 562, 573, 576–7; *Kristallnacht* attacks on, 325–9; in Lenin's ancestry, 24; linked to assassination attempt on Hitler, 376; pogroms against, 68–9; in Poland, 352, 353, 360, 363, 364, 387, 389; prewar Nazi persecution of, 307–9, 315–30, 584; in radical movements, 88–91; in Romania, 416–17; in Soviet ruling elite, 248–9, 356; street violence against, 209, 210, 215; in Ukraine, 167, 390; Wehrmacht propaganda on, 353–4; in Yugoslavia, 398–400; *see also* anti-Semitism
Jodl, General Alfred, 382, 421
Jogiches, Leo, 90
Judenältestenräte (Jewish councils), 371, 535
Junge, Traudl, 576
Justice, Commissariat of, 54–5, 57, 173, 249

Kadet (Constitutional Democratic) Party, 21, 46, 49
Kaganovich, Lazar M., 167, 171, 228–30, 234, 268–70, 278, 280
Kahr, Gustav von, 112–14
Kalinin, Mikhail I., 164
Kalmyks, 513, 514
Kamenev, Lev B., 35, 44, 90, 147, 150–2, 154, 155, 157–9, 238, 268, 269
Kaplan, Chaim, 536

Kaplan, Fanny, 56
Kappler, Herbert, 467
Karachays, 513, 514
Karsikov, Petr A., 249
Katyn Forest massacre, 386, 501, 532
Katzmann, Friedrich, 539
Kazakhstan, 235, 389, 516, 518
Kazan University, 24
Kazbegi, Alexander, 133
Keitel, Field Marshal Wilhelm, 363, 372, 382, 399, 425, 432, 445
Kemshils, 515
Kennan, George F., 346
Keppler, Wilhelm, 219
Kerensky, Alexander F., 23, 31–4, 37, 38, 45, 60, 70
Kershaw, Ian, 15, 304, 378, 585
Kesselring, Field Marshal Albert, 467
Khan, Genghis, 355
Kharkov's House of Corrective Labor, 17, 72
Kholmogory camp, 58
Khrushchev, Nikita S., 10, 273, 279, 384, 388–90, 392, 393, 401–2, 481, 483–5, 517
Kirdorf, Emil, 187
Kirov, Sergei M., 238, 239
Klemperer, Victor, 307, 459
Knilling, Eugen von, 112
Knyazev, I. A., 272–3
Kogan, Lazar, 251
Kolchak, Admiral A. V., 64
Komitety Bednoty (Committees of the Poor), 63
Komsomol (Communist Youth Organization), 172, 243, 261, 280, 449, 491, 517
Konev, General Ivan S., 528, 565, 569–71
Kopelev, Lev, 231, 240, 270, 274, 572
Korea, 594
Kornilov, General Lavr G., 32, 33, 35
Kostrovitskaia, Vera Sergeevna, 492
Krasnaja gaseta, 57
Kravchenko, Victor, 231, 261–2, 274

Kremp, Captain Hermann, 446–7
Krestinskii, Nikolai, 147
Kriebel, Hermann, 113
Kripo (German Criminal Police), 308,
    335, 337, 339, 353, 363, 373
Kristallnacht, 325–9, 370
Krivosheyev, General G. F., 586
Kronstadt mutiny, 74–5
Krupp von Bohlen und Halbach,
    Gustav, 292, 293
Krupskaya, Nadezhda
    Konstantinovna, 9, 152–3
kulaks, 62–3; offensive against, see
    dekulakization
Kulik, Marshal Grigory, 386
Kun, Béla, 88, 90, 100
Kurds, 515
Kursky, Dimitri I., 55, 57, 145
Kutuzov, Field Marshal Mikhail, 503
Kuznetsov, Admiral Nikolai, 473
Kuznetsov, Commander V. I., 571
Kvaternik, Sladko, 418
KV-1 tanks, 475, 477

Lammers, Hans, 432
Landauer, Gustav, 88–90
Lander, Karl, 70–1
Landtag (Bavarian state parliament),
    86, 88, 118
Lange, Herbert, 367, 461
Latsis, Martyn I., 71
Latvia, 357, 384, 392–4, 396, 547;
    pogroms in, 443–4
Laval, Pierre, 419–20
League of Militant Atheists, 249, 250
League of Nations, 311, 313
League of Struggle for German
    Culture, 195
Lehmann, Wilhelm, 408–9
Lenin, Vladimir I., 3, 6–8, 95, 405, 408,
    433, 477, 529, 567, 571, 579–83, 588;
    assassination attempts on, 54, 56;
    background of, 24; birth of, 7; and
    charter of USSR, 148–50; civil
    liberties suppressed by, 43–4, 46; civil

service and, 141–2; during civil war,
    62–4, 142–3, 503; consolidation of
    power of, 41–6, 49–50; cult of, 155–7,
    180, 388–9, 496; death of, 10, 131, 155,
    157, 180; destruction of monuments
    of, 448; economic policy of, 143–6;
    efforts to export revolution by, 72–4,
    83–5, 87, 89, 106, 345; factions
    banned by, 154; and famine relief, 76;
    "good," myth of, 9; illness of, 55, 77,
    145, 148, 150, 157; and October
    Revolution, 4–5, 29–41, 139, 142; and
    peace with Germany, 41–2, 50–1; on
    Politburo, 147; in prerevolutionary
    period, 7–8, 25–8, 132–3, 135–8;
    purges of, 267; religions suppressed
    by, 248–9; repressive measures
    implemented by, 46–58; show trials
    advocated by, 145, 161; Stalin as
    successor to, 9–10, 77, 140, 148,
    151–3, 155, 157–8, 180, 581; terror
    policies of, 5, 7, 16, 47–8, 50–7, 59,
    60–1, 72, 75, 140, 142, 144–5, 460, 586;
    testament of, 150–3; vanguardism of,
    15, 40; youth of, 24–5
Leningrad, Siege of, 490–2, 500
Leninism, 8, 10, 73, 77, 119, 133, 160,
    217, 277, 388–9, 558, 580–2; after
    Lenin, 155–9; necessity of terror to
    maintain, 252
Leonhard, Wolfgang, 265–6
Levi, Paul, 89, 90
Levien, Max, 88, 90
Leviné, Eugen, 89, 90
Liberation (film), 388
Lichtenstein, 415
Liebknecht, Karl, 83, 84, 86, 87
List, Field Marshal Wilhelm, 508
Lithuania, 357, 384, 392–6, 547, 564;
    Memel region of, 351, 355; pogroms
    in, 443, 444
Little Red Book (Mao), 157
Litvinov, Maxim, 356
Lodz ghetto, 372
London Daily Mail, 110, 468
London Times, 208

Lossow, General Otto Hermann von, 112–14
Lubbe, Marinus van der, 298
Ludendorff, General Erich, 111, 114, 115
Luftwaffe, 362, 403, 429
Lüttwitz, General Walther von, 87
Lutze, Viktor, 532
Luxembourg, 415
Luxembourg, Rosa, 84, 86, 87, 90
Lvov, Prince Georgii E., 23, 32
Lyashchenko, General N. G., 496–7
Lysenko, T. D., 332

Machiavelli, Niccolò, 248
Machine Tractor Station (MTS), 236
Magnitogorsk concentration camps, 263
Maier, Charles, 14
Main Directorate of State Security (GUGB), 529
Majdanek death camp, 461, 463, 465, 538, 551, 587
Majority Socialists, German (MSPD), 83–8, 94; see also Social Democratic Party of Germany (SPD)
Malenkov, Georgy M., 250, 474, 484, 492
Manhattan Project, 559
Mann, Thomas, 90
Manstein, General Erich von, 379, 380
Mao Tse-tung, 157, 359
Marshall, General George C., 485, 486
Martov, Yuli, 39
Marx, Karl, 25, 29, 30, 32, 54, 62, 99, 134, 330
Marx, Wilhelm, 125
Marxism, 15, 23, 32, 83, 92, 95–6, 111, 132, 140, 142, 169, 187, 188, 582; anti-Semitism and, 84; class struggle in, 223, 277; dictatorship justified by, 40; end point "beyond history" in, 11; eugenics and, 331–2; factionalism in, 126; Nazi rhetoric against, 81, 100, 107, 109, 115, 117–22, 192, 193, 203, 209, 210–12, 286–8, 291, 292, 295, 297, 214; internationalism of, 28; in Italy, 103; Jews and, 84, 90, 214, 593; of Mensheviks, 32, 136; in prerevolutionary period, 7, 25–7, 132–34; religion and, 247–8; SA actions against, 211; women opposed to, 195; see also specific parties
Marxism-Leninism, 388–89, 409
Maurice, Emil, 118
Mauthausen concentration camp, 340, 341, 369
Max, Prince of Baden, 83
Mayr, Captain Karl, 91, 97
McKee, Arthur, & Company, 164
Mein Kampf (Hitler), 118–23, 203, 293, 318, 333, 336
Mekhlis, Lev Z., 478
Melgounov, S. P., 72
Memorial (Russia organization), 59, 584
Mensheviks, 23, 26, 27, 29, 30, 32–3, 39, 132, 135–7, 154, 267
Menzhinsky, Vyacheslav R., 45, 175, 176, 238
Meretskov, General Kirill A., 474
Messerschmidt, Manfred, 348–9
Mikhail Alexandrovich, Grand Duke, 23
Mikoyan, Anastas I., 25, 167, 171, 280, 386, 409
Milchakov, Aleksandr, 584
Military Revolutionary Committee (MRC), 35–8, 46, 139
Miliukov, P. A. (Kadet Party leader), 22
Ministerial Defense Council, German, 369
Mittlebau-Dora concentration camp, 341
Mogilev death camp, 457
Möhl, General Arnold von, 91
Moiseyev, General Mikhail A., 585
Moldavia, 395, 483
Moldenhauer, Paul, 203

Molotov, Vyacheslav M., 144, 152, 153, 162, 229, 381, 401–2, 413, 556, 575; appointed commissar of foreign affairs, 356; dekulakization campaign of, 170, 171; and famines, 167, 228, 232, 248; and forced labor for canal projects, 177, 257; and German invasion, 407, 409, 471–4, 482, 483, 492; and invasion of Poland, 385; non-aggression pact negotiated by, 356–8; and occupation of Baltic States, 392–4; and purges, 273, 278; terror defended by, 251–2; war-crimes trials proposed by, 547

Mommsen, Hans, 213, 307

Montgomery, Field Marshal Bernard, 561, 568

Morell, Theo, 365

Morgenthau, Henry, 559

Moscow, battle for, 487–90, 492–6, 498

Moscow Club of the Nobility, 162

Moscow Committee of Public Safety, 45

Moscow Declaration, 548

Moscow University, 488

Moscow-Volga Canal (Dmitrovsky Canal), 256–7

Moskalenko, Marshal Kirill S., 483

Mühsam, Erich, 90

Müller, General Eugen, 425–6

Müller, Heinrich, 373, 445

Müller, Hermann, 200

Muller, Hermann J., 332

Müller, Joseph, 289

Müller, Karl Alexander von, 91, 114

Munich conference, 314, 324, 351

Muslims, 513–16

Mussolini, Benito, 104, 117, 123, 216, 354, 531–2, 534; death of, 576; fall of, 466–7; Franco supported by, 359; Greece invaded by, 397; at Munich conference, 351; rise to power of, 102–3, 110–13, 118, 212, 217

Napoleon, Emperor of France, 259, 290, 430, 476, 535–6

Nashkoyev, Murad, 517–18

National Socialist Doctors' Union, 195

National Socialist German University Student Group, 192

National Socialist German Workers' Party (NSDAP), see Nazi Party

National Socialist Women's Group (NS-Frauenschaft), 195, 304–5

Navy, Soviet, 476

Nazi concentration camps, 113, 319, 337–41, 353, 360, 521, 529, 574, 584, 589; asocials in, 335, 338–9, 587; evacuation of, 565–7; gassings in, 367–9, 399, 529; Jews in, 326, 335, 338, 339, 399, 587 (see also death camps); political prisoners in, 302–3, 311, 360, 541, 587; Poles in, 339, 364, 370; see also names of specific camps

Nazi Party, 104–10, 117, 118, 124–27, 185–97, 297, 309, 443, 527, 532, 540–1, 582, 585; "actions" against Jews by, 315–18, 324, 326; agricultural program of, 198–200; annual commemorations of, 325, 376, 459, 508, 526; anti-Semitism and anti-Bolshevism of, 98–101, 108, 118–19; aristocratic support for, 293; attempted putsch of, 110–15, 124; charities of, 327; doctors in, 293–4; drumhead courts of, 573–4; economic policy of, 293; in elections, 196, 201–6, 214, 217, 287, 295, 299–300; escalation of actions against Jews of, 269; financing of, 186–7; foundation of, 93–4; Führer cult in, 123; Himmler's speech on extermination of Jews to, 540–2; justice system purged by, 307–8; Ludendorff as candidate for, 125; Nuremberg rallies of, 192, 194–5, 313, 320, 333, 338; organizational structure of, 188–9, 191, 194; para-

military groups of, *see* SA; SS; platform of, 95–8; police and justice system of, 335; popular support for, 303–5, 308, 312; propaganda of, 189, 193–4; publishing house of, 118; and Reichstag fire, 298; purge of, 16; removal of ban on, 124; rise to power of, 118, 124, 211–12, 216–19, 285 (*see also* Hitler, Adolf, appointed chancellor); speakers' school of, 190–1; Strength through Joy program of, 305–6; suborganizations of, 195; text of, *see Mein Kampf*; torture cellars of, 303
Nazi-Soviet pact, 348, 354–9, 361, 384, 392, 415, 471
Nebe, Arthur, 373, 451
Netherlands, 378–80, 406, 574–5; Jews from, 466, 534, 587; SS recruits from, 415
Neuadel aus Blut und Boden (Darré), 199
Neuengamme concentration camp, 341, 369
Nevsky, Alexander, 503
New Economic Policy (NEP), 75, 76, 143–6, 154, 158, 160, 161, 165, 168
New York American, 196
New York Times, The, 111, 476, 525, 530, 552; *Magazine*, 164
Nicholas II, Tsar, 21–3, 99, 136, 271
Niekisch, Ernst, 88
"night of the long knives," 219, 310
Nikolaenko, Polia, 278–9
NKVD, 46–7, 238–9, 243, 266, 271, 274, 403, 450, 483, 502, 540; in Baltic states, 394–6; in Byelorussia, 391; camps administered by, 58, 59, 177, 262, 264, 479, 589; during German invasion, 478–9, 489, 490, 493; establishment of, 46; ethnic cleansing by, 512, 514, 516–18; in Great Terror, 245–7, 253–6, 261; OGPU incorporated into, 237–8; in Poland, 386, 388; purges and, 275, 276, 278; reorgani-

zation of, 529; in Ukraine, 245, 261, 391
Nolte, Ernst, 13
Normandy invasion, 551
North Africa campaign, 433, 438, 509, 525
North Caucasus, Revolutionary Committee of the, 71
Norway, 379, 415, 587
Noske, Gustav, 87
"November criminals," 83, 105, 202–3
Nuremberg Laws (1935), 318–19, 324, 419
Nuremberg trials, 354, 556

October (film), 38
October Manifesto (1905), 135
October Revolution, 7, 24, 29, 34–40, 49, 74, 180, 274, 441, 583; anniversary of, 59, 106, 112, 159, 165, 394–5, 402, 491, 494; consolidation of Bolshevik power in, 41–3; creation of Red Army following, 60; distribution of land to peasants during, 136; events leading to, 29–33; French Revolution as inspiration for, 301; resistance to, 44–6; Stalin during, 138
OGPU, 173–7, 227, 229, 234, 236–8, 242
Okhrana (Tsarist secret police), 24, 48, 540
OKW, *see* Wehrmacht, High Command of
Old Bolsheviks, 261, 280
Olyanov, Alexander, 24
Olympic Games, 319–20
Omsk troika, 245
"On the Protection of the Property of the State Enterprises, Collective Farms, and Cooperatives and the Strengthening of Public (Socialist) Ownership" (1932 law), 229

Operation Barbarossa, 407, 410, 415,
    421, 424, 425, 429–40, 453, 481, 494,
    530, 585; slaughter of Jews during,
    441–51, 459–60
Operation Blue, 499
Operation Citadel, 530–1
Operation Harvest Festival, 539–40
Operation Marita, 397–8
Operation Overlord, 545, 550
Operation Reinhard, 462
Operation Torch, 508
Operation Typhoon, 435
Operation Uranus, 507
Ordzhonikidze, Sergo, 71, 163, 270,
    273
Orgburo (Organization Bureau),
    146–8
Orth, Karin, 303
Orthodox Church, 16, 248, 249, 263,
    419, 532
Orwell, George, 17
Ossietzky, Carl von, 297
Oster, General Hans, 340
Ostroumova-Lebedeva, Anna
    Petrovna, 492
Oumansky, Constantine, 485

Palace of Soviets (Moscow), 258
Pale of Settlement, 67
Panther tanks, 530
Papen, Franz von, 205, 209, 210,
    212–13, 219–23, 286–8, 296, 298, 300,
    309
Paris Commune, 27, 28, 248
Pasternak, Boris, 273
Paul, Prince of Yugoslavia, 397–8
Paulus, Field Marshal Friedrich, 509,
    525
Pavlov, General Dmitri G., 473–4,
    478
People's Commissariat for Internal
    Affairs, see NKVD
People's Commissariat for State
    Security (NKGB), 529
People's Court, German, 340, 585

Perekovka (newspaper), 257
Petacci, Clara, 576
Pétain, Philippe, 419, 420, 501
Peter the Great, Tsar, 163
Peters, I. K., 56
Petrovsky, G. I., 57
Philippines, American concentration
    camps in, 55
Pilsudski, Marshal Józef, 73
Podlubny, Stepan, 243
pogroms, 6, 69; Nazi, 325–9, 398–9;
    postwar, 390
Pohl, Oswald, 340
Poincaré, Raymond, 104
Poland, 43, 337, 339, 355; efforts to
    export Bolshevism to, 73, 75, 100,
    149, 345; ethnic cleansing in, 363–4,
    367, 369–74, 459, 468, 585, 587;
    Frontier Defense Corps (KOP) of,
    385; German invasion and occupa-
    tion of, 348, 351–6, 360–3, 377, 381,
    384, 421, 430, 433, 441, 443, 444, 446,
    461, 465, 513, 551–4 (see also Gen-
    eral Government); liberation of, 557,
    558, 564; postwar, 546–7, 552–4, 558,
    592–3; Soviet zone of occupation in,
    357, 358, 364, 371, 373, 384–91, 394,
    395, 401, 450, 501, 511, 532
Poles: Nazi annihilation policies
    against, 339, 360, 363–4, 367, 369,
    373–4, 395, 553–4; Soviet terror
    against, 254–5, 364, 385–91
Polish Home Army, 552–4
Polish Military Organization (POV),
    254
Politburo, 9, 131, 146–50, 152, 157, 158,
    180, 182, 238, 581, 593; canal projects
    approved by, 256, 259; cleansing in
    occupied territories authorized by,
    386; Commission for Judicial Affairs
    of, 280; concentration and forced-
    labor camps created by, 59, 175–7;
    creation of, 146–7; in dekulakization
    campaign, 171; grain shortages and
    policies of, 167–9, 228, 234, 239; and
    German invasion, 410, 472–4; Jewish

members of, 68; juvenile delin-
quency policies of, 243; KPD and,
106; at Lenin's death, 155; national
minorities persecuted by, 253–6;
secret police and, 145, 239; purges
approved by, 275, 276; terror prac-
tices of, 245, 248, 279
Poniatowa death camp, 539
Popular Enlightenment and Propa-
ganda, German Ministry of, 300
Posen concentration camp, 367
Poskrebyshev, Aleksandr N., 473
Potsdam Conference, 590, 592
Pozdnyakova, Yulia, 565
Pravda, 28, 46, 49, 156, 165, 181, 190,
229, 503, 594
Prevention of Defective Offspring,
Law for (Germany, 1933), 302, 333
Prosveshchenie (journal), 138
Protection of German Blood and
German Honor, Law for, *see*
Nuremberg Laws
Protocols of the Elders of Zion, The,
68, 99, 534
Provisional All-Russian
Government, 64
Prussian Political Police, 298
Pyatakov, Georgy L., 151, 159, 270–3

Quebec Conference, 559

racial hygiene, 332–4
Radek, Karl, 84, 86, 106, 159, 270, 272
Radio Moscow, 552, 553
Raeder, Admiral Erich, 290, 379
Rasch, Otto, 449
Rath, Ernst vom, 325, 327
Ravensbrück concentration camp,
341, 369
Red Army, 60, 107–8, 155, 234, 272–3,
345, 405–6, 417, 583; advance on
Germany of, 557, 558, 561, 563–65,
568, 571, 577; anniversary of found-
ing of, 567; atrocities committed by,

570–3; in Baltic states, 395, 401;
casualties of, 432, 433, 435, 440, 491,
498–9; in civil war, 60, 64–6, 261;
commissars of, 504; concentration
camps liberated by, 565, 589; Cossacks and, 70; counteroffensive
against Germans of, 438–40, 498–9,
502–3, 543–45; dekulakization
carried out by, 172; deserters from,
60, 480–1; disciplinary measures
imposed on, 487–8, 505; establishment of, 46, 60; expulsion of members of ethnic groups from, 514–16;
Finland invaded by, 392–3, 401; and
German invasion, 409, 410, 420, 429,
430, 432–40, 442, 449–50, 484, 495;
Gulag prisoners as volunteers in,
519; at Kursk, 530–1; Main Political
Directorate of, 478, 480; Nazi propaganda against, 214; pogroms carried
out by, 68; Poland attacked by, 362,
385, 388, 401; prisoners of war from,
432–34, 436, 473, 480, 505, 588–90;
Propaganda Department of, 477;
purges of, 275–6, 349, 404, 533, 540;
rallying of support for, 476, 505;
reinforcements from Siberia for,
416, 437; at Stalingrad, 506–8, 526,
528; tanks of, 475, 477, 498, 530–1;
territories liberated from Nazis by,
521, 529, 535, 555, 591; and Warsaw
uprising, 551–4
Reder, Rudolf, 462
Red Guards, 37, 42, 65
Red Star, 503, 504
Red terror, 56–9, 65
Reed, John, 39, 43
Reich Committee for the Scientific
Registration of Serious Hereditarily
and Congenitally Based Illnesses,
365
Reichenau, Field Marshal Walther
von, 289, 291, 445
Reichsbank, 200
Reichsbanner Schwarz, Rot, Gold
(Reichflag Black, Red, Gold), 207

Reich Security Main Office, 408, 454
Reichslandbund (Reich Agrarian League), 294
Reichstag, 83, 186, 200, 201, 205, 212, 215, 219, 220; captured by Red Army, 571; decline of legislative power of, 206; elections of members of, 118, 189–90, 204, 214, 217, 312; enabling law in, 286, 287, 300–1; fire in, 298–300, 304, 306–7; Hitler's speeches to, 320, 371, 375; Versailles Treaty opposed by, 105
Reichswehr, 110, 289; Bavarian, 112, 114
Reinhardt, Fritz, 190–91
Remnick, David, 584
Reparations Commission, 104
Republicans, Spanish, 313
Restoration of a Professional Civil Service, Law for (Germany, 1933), 307
Revolutionary War Council of the Republic, 65
Revolutionary Workers' Council, 86
Riabtsev, K. I., 45
Ribbentrop, Joachim von, 356–7, 413, 445, 468, 508–9
Ritter, Robert, 334, 337
Ritter von Leeb, Field Marshal Wilhelm, 438
Rittersporn, Gábor Tamás, 521
Robespierre, Maximilien de, 159
Rodichev, F. I., (Kadet Party leader), 22
Rodzianko, Mikhail V., 23
Röhm, Captain Ernst, 97, 110, 111, 113, 187–8, 208, 309, 310
Rokossovsky, Marshal Konstantin K., 551–3, 590
Roma, see Gypsies
Romania, 73, 89, 100, 373, 393, 431, 587; mass killings of Jews in, 416–18, 441; postwar, 555, 592; Soviet counteroffensive against, 509, 532, 554
Romanovs, 22, 23, 27, 28, 65, 68, 99
Römeris, Mykolas, 395

Rommel, Field Marshal Erwin, 16, 438, 509
Roosevelt, Eleanor, 594
Roosevelt, Elliott, 548
Roosevelt, Franklin D., 439, 484–7, 526, 543–8, 550, 552–9, 569, 591; death of, 570, 592
Roosevelt, Theodore, 331
Rosenberg, Alfred, 99, 432
Rosenberg, Arthur, 84–5
Rotefrontkämpferbund (Red Veterans' League), 207
Royal Air Force, 500
Rüdin, Ernst, 333
Rudnev, V. V., 45
Rundstedt, General Gerd von, 379, 380, 438
Russian Civil War, 3, 60, 62–77, 140–2, 148, 171, 172, 261; de-Cossackization in, 70–2; famine during, 74–6; pogroms in, 6, 69
Russian Federation, 148, 149, 177, 241, 249
Russian General Staff, 36, 37
Russian Revolution, 3–5, 7, 85, 88, 99, 102, 120, 141, 148, 308, 311; export of, 68, 73; factionalism and, 126; necessity of repression to maintain, 252; of 1905, 26–7, 48, 135; of October, 1917, see October Revolution
Russian Social Democratic Labor Party (RSDLP), 23, 26, 29, 132, 137; All-Russian Conference of, 136; factions of, see Bolsheviks; Mensheviks; "Unity Congress" of, 27
Russo-Japanese War, 135
Rykov, Aleksei I., 269, 273, 274, 581

SA (Sturmabteilung; Brownshirts), 107, 110, 187–8, 193, 207, 216, 220, 291, 304; banned by Hindenburg, 209; in Beer Hall Putsch, 114; clashes between Communists and, 195, 209–11, 292, 295, 303; deputy police from ranks of, 296; founding of, 187;

funerals of leaders of, 295–6, 532; and Hitler's appointment as chancellor, 222; Jews attacked by, 215, 315, 316, 324, 326; purge of, 309–10; rebellion against Nazi Party by, 207–8

Saarland, return to Germany of, 311–12

Sachsenhausen concentration camp, 326, 338, 341

St. Petersburg University, 24, 25

Sapir, Boris, 59

Savior in the Wood, Church of (Moscow), 258

Schacht, Hjalmar, 200

Schaeffer, Fritz, 289

Scheidemann, Philipp, 83, 87, 94

Scheubner-Richter, Max Erwin von, 99, 111, 113, 115

Schirach, Baldur von, 192, 534

Schirach, Henriette von, 534

Schleicher, Kurt von, 204–5, 209, 211, 212, 219, 220, 310

Schröder, Kurt von, 219

Schröder, Ludwig von, 399

Schulenburg, Friedrich Werner Graf von der, 471

Schutzformationen (Schufos; Protective Formations), 207

Schwarz, Franz Xaver, 187

Schwede-Coburg, Franz, 366

Schwerin von Krosigk, Lutz Graf, 221

Scott, John, 263

SD (Sicherheitsdienst), 324, 326–8, 352, 353, 363, 369, 374, 398, 421–2, 467

Sebastian, Mihail, 416–17

secret police: Nazi, see Gestapo; Soviet, 161, 172, 175, 249 (see also Cheka; GPU; NKVD; OGPU)

Seeckt, General Hans von, 112

Seifert, Gustav, 188

Seisser, Hans Ritter von, 112–14

Semlin concentration camp, 399

Serbia, 398, 399, 415

Serebriakov, Leonid, 270, 272

Serebrovsky, A. S., 331–2

Seytmuratova, Ayshe, 516

Shaposhnikov, Marshal Boris, 401, 492

Sharypina, Yelizaveta, 491

Shaw, George Bernard, 260

Shchastny, Admiral A. M., 51

Shcherbakov, Aleksandr, 493

Sholokhov, Mikhail, 234, 273

show trials, 145, 161–2, 269–76, 279, 347

Shtemenko, General S. M., 504

Shulgin, Vasily, 22

Simonov, Konstantin, 590

Sinta, see Gypsies

Slovakia, 415, 466

SMERSH, 529

Smolensk City Party Committee, 268

Smolny Institute, 32, 36, 37, 41

Sobibor death camp, 457, 460, 462, 539, 587

Sobolev, Party Secretary, 254

Social Democratic Party of Germany (SPD), 104, 113, 124, 219, 296–7, 312; banning of, 301, 357; in elections, 125, 189, 190, 196, 204, 206, 217, 299; Enabling Law opposed by, 301; and Hitler's appointment as chancellor, 221; "hunger government" protested by, 201; information service of, 191; Nazi violence against, 296; Nazi propaganda against, 214; paramilitary groups of, 195, 207; persecution of, 306; Reichstag fire and, 298, 299; trade union allies of, 105, 187

Socialism in one country, 157–8

"Socialist Fatherland in Danger" decree, 50

Socialists, 5, 17, 26–30, 32, 40, 43, 49, 54, 61, 293, 301, 302, 585; agrarian, 25; anti-Bolshevik, 56; anti-Semitism and, 67, 328, 329; Communist opposition to, 190; fundamental tenets of, 142; Hitler's view of, 100, 109; Italian, 103; nationalism debated among, 138; paramilitary groups of, 110; peasantry and, 143; Polish, 255;

Socialists *(continued)*
in post–World War I Germany, 84–8,
90, 92; propaganda against, 91; in
resistance to October revolution, 46;
underground, in Nazi Germany,
310–14, 323, 325, 329, 376–7; *see also
specific parties*
Social Revolutionary Party, Russian,
33, 34, 39, 42, 44, 45, 72
Sokolnikov, Grigory, 35, 270, 272
Solovetski Monastery, 249
Solovki concentration camps, 59, 176,
259
Solzhenitsyn, Aleksandr, 251, 259,
519–21, 583–4
Sonnenstein killing center, 369
Sorge, Richard, 408
South Africa, 55
Soviet Academy of Sciences, 488
Soviet Writers' Congress, 258
Sovnarkom (SNK), 42–3, 47, 49, 62,
64, 147–8, 182, 581; capital punish-
ment approved by, 51; civil liberties
curtailed by, 43–4; concentration
camps created by, 56, 176; national-
ization of banks by, 45; OGPU and,
175; Stalin on, 152, 180; terror decree
of, 57; Trotsky and, 154
Spain, 416; civil war in, 313, 321, 359
Spanish-American War, 55
Spartacus group, 84, 86–7
Special Action 1005, 463
Speer, Albert, 336, 341, 381–82, 419,
526, 540, 541, 559, 574
Spellman, Francis, 547
Squadre d'Azioni, *see* Blackshirts
SS (Schutzstaffel), 207–8, 216, 220,
354, 362, 400, 532, 540, 566, 569; at
Auschwitz-Birkenau, 465, 466;
banned by Hindenburg, 209; brutality toward Jewish women of, 534;
Death's Head Units, 353, 355;
deputy police from ranks of, 296;
doctors in, 369; founding of, 187;
ghettos destroyed by, 537; Himmler
appointed leader of, 189; and

Hitler's appointment as chancellor,
222; hospital patients shot by, 366,
367; Jews massacred by, 363, 460,
537–9, 541; *Kristallnacht* carried out
by, 326; Main Administrative Office
of, 454, 463; in Poland, 352, 367, 446;
in Soviet Union, 421–2, 442–43, 449;
slave labor exploited by, 335–6, 339,
340; *see also* Waffen-SS
Stahlecker, Franz Walter, 443–4
Stahlhelm (Steel Helmet), 207, 222,
296
Stalin, Ekaterina, 134–5
Stalin, Joseph V., 3, 6–11, 95, 123, 264,
388, 433, 460, 579, 581–2; American
aid to, 544; antagonism between
Trotsky and, 44, 64, 139–40, 146,
151–5, 157–60; architectural interests
of, 258–9; army and, 289; background of, 131–2; Baltic nations
seized by, 384, 394, 395; at Big Three
conferences, 544–50, 552, 556–9;
birth of, 8, 131; and charter of USSR,
148–50; during civil war, 64–5, 142;
counter-offensive of, 528–9, 543; cult
of, 180–2, 588; and cult of Lenin,
155–7; death of, 10, 522, 583, 593,
594; dekulakization campaign of,
169–72, 178, 227, 229–31; destruction
of monuments of, 448; economic
policy of, 160–6, 169, 174, 179–80,
228–9, 242, 287; eugenics program
rejected by, 332; and exportation of
revolution, 72–3, 106, 107, 346; and
final assault on Berlin, 567–72;
forced labor construction projects
of, 177, 256, 258–9, 522, 586; grain
policies of, 162, 167–9, 228–32, 234,
236–7; and German invasion, 382,
402–10, 431, 471–80, 482–90,
492–507; and German surrender,
589; Great Terror of, 241, 244–6, 250,
251, 253, 278, 347, 540; and Kirov
assassination, 238–9; as Lenin's
successor, 9–10, 77, 140, 148, 151–3,
155, 157–8, 180, 581; and Lenin's

terror policies, 16, 52, 53, 58, 71, 150; military buildup by, 393, 401; nationality policies of, 42–3, 67; Nazi propaganda against, 417, 441; non-aggression pact with Hitler, *see* Nazi-Soviet pact; and October Revolution, 30, 32, 37, 138–40; Poland invaded and occupied by, 384–6; on Politburo, 147; populist view of, 15; in postwar years, 589–93; in prerevolutionary period, 132–9; purges carried out by, 161–2, 268, 278–81; show trials held by, 161–2, 269–76, 347; showdown theory of, 277–8; territorial ambitions of, 547, 555, 577; Tito and, 398; wartime ethnic cleansing by, 513–19; and Warsaw uprising, 552–3; Winter War debacle of, 392, 394, 401–3; and workforce discipline, 265–6; and World War I armistice, 50, 73, 483–4; youth of, 132

Stalin, Yakov, 135

Stalingrad, Battle of, 500, 506–8, 525–26, 528, 544, 568

Stamenov, Ivan, 482, 483

Stangl, Franz, 462

State Committee of Defense (GKO), Soviet, 474, 488, 493

State Planning Commission, Soviet, *see* Gosplan

Stauffenberg, Claus Schenk Graf von, 290, 551

Stavka (Headquarters of the Supreme Command of the Armed Forces), 473, 475, 478, 488, 507

Steinberg, Isaac N., 50

Steinhardt, Laurence, 407

Stennes, Walter, 208

sterilization, forced, 333–4, 337

Stimson, Henry L., 485, 486, 549, 559

Strasser, Gregor, 126, 127, 189, 195, 217–19

Streckenbach, Bruno, 454

Streicher, Julius, 186

Strength Through Joy, 305–6

Stresemann, Gustav, 112, 115–16

Stroop, Jürgen, 537, 538

Studzińska, Kazimiera, 391

Stülpnagel, Karl Heinrich von, 445, 448–9

Sudoplatov, Pavel, 483

Suez Canal, 257

Sunni Muslims, 516

Supreme Soviet, 475, 512, 515

Suvorov, Aleksandr, 503

Svanidze, Alexander, 134

Sverdlov, Yakov, 52, 147

swastika, 96–97, 99, 108, 124, 195, 309, 414

Sweden, 76, 415

Switzerland, 76, 415

Sztójay, Döme, 418

Tartars, 513, 515, 516, 518

Tehran Conference, 544–50, 552

Ter-Petrosyan, Simon , 137

T-4 gassing operation, 368–9

Thälmann, Ernst, 125, 297

"thousanders," 230–32, 234

Thyssen, Fritz, 219

Tietz group, 317

Tiger tanks, 530

Tikhon, Patriarch, 249

Times of London, 416

Timoshenko, Marshal Semyon K., 401, 406, 408, 409, 471–3, 481

Tito, Marshal Josip Broz, 398, 588, 591

Todt, Fritz, 294

Toller, Ernst, 90

Tolstoy, Alexei, 273

Tomsky, Mikhail, 269

Traibman, R. M., 254

Trans-Siberian Railway, 64

Transcaucasian Federation, 148–9

Trawniki camp, 539

Treblinka death camp, 460, 521, 536, 538, 539, 587

Tripartite Pact (1940), 413, 419

Trotsky, Leon, 9, 10, 23, 85, 106, 345, 581; antagonism between Stalin and, 44, 64, 139–40, 146, 151–5, 157–60; Central Committee condemnation of, 153–4; concentration camps created by, 55–6; curtailment of civil liberties supported by, 43–4; Jewish background of, 68, 90, 155; in Menshevik faction, 135–7, 154–5; New Economic Policy opposed by, 145, 146, 158, 160; in October Revolution, 35, 36, 38, 39, 113; in Politburo, 147; purges of former supporters of, 268–71, 274, 280; Red Army and, 60, 64, 68; "Socialist Fatherland in Danger" decree of, 50; terror methods advocated by, 52–4

Trotskyism or Leninism? (Stalin), 157

Trotskyists, 154, 239; show trials of so-called, 268, 273–5

Truman, Harry S., 592

T-34 tanks, 475, 477, 551

Tukhachevsky, Marshal Mikhail N., 75, 275

Turkey, 422

Turks, 515; slaughter of Armenians by, 329

Ukhta concentration camps, 59

Ukraine, 43, 358, 385, 388, 409, 422, 423, 483; civil war in, 591; deportations of anti-Soviet elements from, 395–6; ethnic cleansing in, 386–7; expulsion of ethnic Germans from, 535; famine in, 76, 228–30, 232–5; German invasion of, 430, 432, 434, 445; liberation of, 557; mass killings of Jews in, 448–51; NEP in, 161; NKVD of, 245, 261, 391; pogroms in, 69; purges in, 278–79; religious persecution in, 250; revolt against Bolsheviks in, 57, 66; in Russian Federal Republic, 148; shortages in, 167; in World War I, 63–4

ULTRA (code-breaking machine), 407

Ulyanov, Alexander, 24

Union for National Socialist Lawyers, 195

Union for the Defense of the Constituent Assembly, 45–6, 48

Union of National Socialist Teachers, 195

United Nations, 550, 557

United Press, 112

United States, 289, 329, 347, 349, 355, 455, 494, 531, 564, 568–70, 592; in advance on Germany, 554, 568; agricultural production in, 160; ambassador to Soviet Union of, 346; Army, 485, 548; atomic bomb developed by, 559; in Berlin Olympics, 319; in Battle of the Bulge, 560–61; Civil War, 350; Communist Party in, 76, 358, 359, 472; concentration camps liberated by, 565; Congress, 256, 485; entry into World War II of, 14, 382, 439–40, 486; eugenics in, 331–4; factories in Soviet Union built by firms from, 163–4; famine relief from, 76; German declaration of war on, 439, 457; and German invasion of Soviet Union, 402, 407, 529; Gulag condemned in, 257; immigration policies of, 197, 350; intervention against Bolsheviks by, 66; interviews with Hitler published in, 109–10, 196; isolationism of, 394, 485; Israel and, 593, 594; Japanese attack on, 416, 439; and Jewish refugees, 323, 447; Jews blamed for anti-German attitude of, 458; lend-lease program of, 485–7; loans to Germany from, 200; Nazi propaganda against, 321; in negotiations with Britain and USSR, 544–50, 552–9, 589; in North African campaign, 509, 525; Office of Strategic Services, 569; POWs from, 480; presidential powers in, 125; repara-

tions and, 116, 196; suicide rate in, 202; Supreme Court, 331; unconditional surrender of Germany to, 526, 589; unemployment in, 204; Victory Program of, 544; in World War I, 350, 386
Ustaše, 398

Vannikov, Boris, 265
Vasilevsky, Marshal Aleksandr M., 499, 507
Verkhovsky, Alexander, 36
Versailles Treaty, 11, 14, 94, 105, 109, 111, 202, 214, 291, 295, 306, 311–13, 349, 351, 405
Victor Emmanuel, King of Italy, 103
Viereck, George Sylvester, 109–10
Vietnam, 594
Vikzhel (railway union), 44
Virgin Soil Upturned (Sholokhov), 234
Völkischer Beobachter, 99, 124
Volkogonov, General Dmitri, 403, 475, 496, 499
Volkswagen, 294
Volodarsky-Goldstein, Moisei, 52
Volunteer Regiment Reinhard, 87
V-1 flying bombs, 551
Voroshilov, Marshal Kliment E., 64, 65, 268, 273, 278, 280, 386, 393, 401, 473, 474
Voznesensky, Nikolai A., 492
V-2 rockets, 551
Vyshinsky, Andrei Y., 162, 255, 269, 270, 272, 273, 394
Waffen-SS, 415, 574
Wagner, Gauleiter, 459
Wagner, Quartermaster General Eduard, 369, 371, 421, 436
Wagner, Richard, 187
Wagner, Winifred, 187
Wagner cult, 111
war crimes trials, 548–9, 555–6
Warlimont, General Walter, 509, 531
Warsaw ghetto uprising, 535–8
Warsaw uprising (1944), 551–4

Washington Post, 584
Warthegau, mass killings in, 367, 461, 464
Webb, Sidney and Beatrice, 260
Wehler, Hans-Ulrich, 305
Wehrmacht, 308, 401, 415–16, 460, 565, 569, 570, 574; in France, 380, 561; General Staff of, 422, 425; in Greece, 300, 398; High Command of (OKW), 353, 354, 362, 363, 372, 376, 379, 399, 421, 423, 425, 427, 445; officer corps, support for Hitler in, 289–92; in Poland, 362–5, 367, 371, 373, 537; in Soviet Union, 410, 421–27, 430–34, 436–42, 445–50, 472, 473, 478, 487, 498, 499, 502, 506–8, 513, 514, 519, 525, 530
Weigand, Karl Henry von, 196–7
Weimar Republic, 108, 112, 118, 185, 196, 200, 206, 213, 214, 218, 293, 307, 314
Wels, Otto, 301
Werth, Alexander, 477, 503, 505–6, 553, 572
Werth, Nicolas, 235
Weserübung (Weser Exercise), 379
Wessel, Colonel, 362
Weyler y Nicolau, General Valeriano, 55
What Is To Be Done? (Lenin), 26, 133
White Army, 65, 66, 72, 74, 142; German, 90; pogroms carried out by, 69
White Guards, 57, 241
White Rose resistance group, 459
White Sea-Baltic Canal (Belomorkanal), 177, 256, 257, 259–60
Wilhelm II, Kaiser, 83, 99
Wilson, Woodrow, 94, 331
Winter War, 392–3, 403, 405, 473, 474
Wisliceny, Dieter, 400
Wolff, General Karl, 569, 570
Working Community of Fatherland Fighting Groups (Arbeitsgemeinschaft der Vaterländischen Kampfverbände), 110–11

World War I, 3, 7, 62, 99, 192, 288, 313,
346, 360, 507, 542, 580; aftereffects
of, 4–5, 102, 110, 141, 196, 345, 558;
Armenians slaughtered by Turks
during, 329; Bolshevik armistice
with Germany in, 41–2, 50–1, 66;
casualties in, 4, 82–3, 586; concentration camps during, 339–41; conditions in Russia during, 21–2;
Hindenburg in, 208; Hitler in, 11,
81–2; Hitler-Stalin pact influenced
by, 348, 354; Jews blamed by Hitler
for, 453, 560, 583; Jewish veterans of,
317; Kerensky and, 31–4; Lenin's
ties with Germany during, 29;
Ludendorff in, 111; October Revolution and, 34–8; tsarist police
during, 240; United States in, 350,
486; "war Socialism" in Germany
during, 163
World War II, 3, 5, 12, 15, 266, 330;
advance on Berlin at end of, 528–9,
554, 567–73; allied victory in, 6;
American entry into, 14, 382,
439–40, 486; in Balkans, 397–401; in
Baltic states, 392–6; Big Three
conferences during, 544–50, 556–9;
collaborators with Germany in,
416–20; concentration camp system
in, 341, 360, 565–7 (see also
Auschwitz; death camps); ethnic
cleansing during, 363–5, 513–19;
events leading to, 6, 313–14, 349–59;
in Finland, see Winter War; German
defeat in, 560–77; German invasion
of Soviet Union in, 382–3, 397, 401,
406–10, 413–16, 420–40, 446–51,
471–511; Gulag during, 519–22; mass
murder of Jews during, see Jews,
extermination of; in North Africa,
508, 509; outbreak of, 360–2; Poland
invaded and occupied during,
361–74, 385–92; Warsaw uprising
during, 551–4; in Western Europe,
375, 378–82, 393, 550, 554
Wrangel, General Peter N., 72

Yagoda, Genrikh G., 171, 175–6, 238,
239, 242, 273, 274
Yakovlev, Alexander N., 479
Yalta Conference, 556–9, 567, 589,
591–2
Yezhov, Nikolai I., 238–9, 244, 245,
253, 254, 255, 268, 270–1, 277
Young Plan, 196
Yudenich, General N. N., 64
Yugoslavia, 397–401, 406, 414, 433,
441, 457, 591; postwar, 555; Red
Army atrocities in, 572; resistance
in, 556, 588

Zegota, 537
Zeitzler, General Kurt, 508
Zhdanov, Andrei A., 280, 358, 394, 491
Zhukov, Marshal Georgy K., 406, 471,
473–4, 484, 487–8, 496, 592; advance
on Berlin led by, 565, 569–71, 573;
appointed Chief of Staff, 401, 474;
ethnic cleansing ordered by, 517; at
Berlin surrender ceremony, 589; at
Leningrad, 434, 488; in Moscow
victory parade, 590; postwar demo-
tion of, 590, 591; at Stalingrad, 506,
507, 528; Stalin warned of German
invasion by, 408, 410; and Warsaw
uprising, 553; on western front, 487,
493, 494, 506
Zinoviev, Grigory, 35, 44, 52, 90, 106,
147, 151, 152, 154, 155, 157–9, 238,
268, 269
Zinovievists, 239, 268
Zionism, 214, 317, 536, 593
Zuckerman, Yitzhak, 537
Zyklon B, 460, 465, 587

PHOTOGRAPHIC CREDITS

All photos not listed here are from the ullstein bild/Granger Collection.

Granger Collection: Lenin and Stalin at Lenin's dacha in Gorky in 1922.

United States Holocaust Memorial Museum: Hitler and Goebbels with local Party officials in Hattingen; Hitler with members of his new government soon after his appointment; A crowd in front of a Jewish-owned store in Berlin; Visitors at the opening of the Great Anti-Bolshevism exhibition; Officials at the opening ceremonies of the 1938 Party rally in Nuremberg; Soviet Foreign Minister Molotov signs the German-USSR non-aggression pact; Soviet POWs captured near Wisznice; Jews rounded up in the Warsaw ghetto; The suppression of the Warsaw ghetto uprising; Preparing the liquidation of the Cracow Ghetto; Arrival of Hungarian Jews at Auschwitz-Birkenau; Hungarian Jewish women selected to work; Young Jewish children selected for death; Churchill, Roosevelt and Stalin at Yalta; American and Soviet soldiers in front of a portrait of Stalin; Lt. William Robertson and Lt. Alexander Sylasko; Soviet civilians on a repatriation convoy; Funeral procession in Poland for the victims of the Kielce pogrom.

A NOTE ABOUT THE AUTHOR

Robert Gellately is the Earl Ray Beck Professor of History at Florida State University and was the Bertelsmann Visiting Professor of Twentieth-Century Jewish History and Politics at Oxford University in 2004–5. His work has appeared in fifteen foreign languages. He is the author of *The Gestapo and German Society: Enforcing Racial Policy, 1933–1945* and *Backing Hitler: Consent and Coercion in Nazi Germany*. He lives in Tallahassee, Florida.

A NOTE ON THE TYPE

The text of this book was set in a typeface called Times New Roman, designed by Stanley Morison (1889–1967) for The Times (London) and first introduced by that newspaper in 1932.

Among typographers and designers of the twentieth century, Stanley Morison was a strong forming influence—as a typographical adviser to the Monotype Corporation, as a director of two distinguished publishing houses, and as a writer of sensibility, erudition, and keen practical sense.

COMPOSED BY
North Market Street Graphics
Lancaster, Pennsylvania

PRINTED AND BOUND BY
Berryville Graphics
Berryville, Virginia

MAPS DESIGNED BY
Peter Krafft

BASED ON A TEXT DESIGN BY
Peter A. Andersen